SOUTH DAKOTA LEADERS

SOUTH DAKOTA LEADERS

From Pierre Chouteau, Jr., to Oscar Howe

Edited by
Herbert T. Hoover and Larry J. Zimmerman

University of South Dakota Press
Vermillion, South Dakota

Copyright © 1989 by

University of South Dakota Press

University of South Dakota
Vermillion, SD 57069

All rights reserved

Printed in the United States of America

British Cataloging in Publication Information Available

Distributed by arrangement with
University Publishing Associates, Inc.

4720 Boston Way
Lanham, MD 20706

3 Henrietta Street
London WC2E 8LU England

Library of Congress Cataloging–in–Publication Data

South Dakota leaders : from Pierre Chouteau, Jr., to Oscar Howe /
edited by Herbert T. Hoover and Larry Zimmerman ; introduction
by Frederick Manfred.
        p.   cm.
Includes index.
1. South Dakota– –Biography. 2. South Dakota– –History, Local.
3. Leadership. I. Hoover, Herbert T. II. Zimmerman, Larry J.,
1947–   .
        CT260.S67   1988   88–31942 CIP
        978.3– –dc19
        ISBN 0–929925–00–9 (alk. paper)

All University of South Dakota Press books are produced on acid-free
paper which exceeds the minimum standards set by the National
Historical Publications and Records Commission.

Dedicated to the memory of

Larry Remele, author, editor of
North Dakota History, project
consultant for *South Dakota Leaders*

Robert A. Alex, author, State Archaeologist
of South Dakota, project consultant
for *South Dakota Leaders*

Contents

x   CONTENTS

Preface

As a boy, born and raised in Northwest Iowa in what I now call eastern Siouxland, I was very aware of South Dakota.

South Dakota was a place of magic life, where the true West began. Beyond the Big Sioux River lived Indians, and cowboys, and desperado gold miners. And somewhere out there, where the sun set every evening, flowed a wide majestic river with the romantic name of the Wild Missouri.

The Indians I knew about first-hand. We lived on a farm alongside the old King's Trail, now known as Highway 75, which ran from Winnipeg to New Orleans, and every so often a caravan of Indians would come down from Flandreau on their way to Sioux City, and from there cross the Missouri, to visit their relatives in Santee, Nebraska.

My mother often told me that, on my way home from country school, should I see Indians coming down the road, I was supposed to hop over the fence and hide in the cornfield. They were known, she said, to kidnap little boys and make Indians out of them. Of course, being mortally curious, I never did hop over the fence. I only stepped into the ditch and watched those fabulous dusky-faced people slowly roll by, the dark faces of the older Indians masklike, the brown eyes of the little children twinkling. It was much later that I learned my mother was in part right, that once, eons ago, young braves would make it their mission to capture a boy from an enemy tribe and bring him home to assuage a grieving mother who'd lost her son. Many was the time I envied those Indian boys who were riding in the caravan and who I imagined were playing hookey from having to do yard chores. Often I wished they would kidnap me. And always, of course, I would fantasize that I would pull off some kind of heroic act when I escaped.

I learned about cowboys from two sources: from dime novels at the local drugstore and from young male relatives who had gone west to work for ranches beyond the Missouri. I never was flush with dimes, so Saturday nights I'd pretend, while browsing through a rack of garish wild Westerns, that I was about to buy a magazine—but of course I actually was reading into a story as far as I could before the druggist would ask me to leave. And always I had to hope that that particular magazine would still be in the rack the following Saturday so I could finish the story.

At every family reunion I'd seek out those daring male relatives who'd gone west to ride the line and I'd pump them for their stories. Often their tales were more dramatic than the novels of Zane Grey and Max Brand. Sometimes I caught on they were telling me stretchers, but I overlooked that because I wanted to believe them; believe that the real life was lived where the sun set.

Every now and then the local weeklies would run a squib about some farm hand or store clerk who'd quit his job and had gone west for the money cure, that is, had gone to the Black Hills to pan gold—only to return after a year to admit that what little gold he'd found he'd lost to gamblers like Wild Bill Hickok and Calamity Jane.

Well, that was why, after I graduated from college in 1934 and before I took on a job teaching, I finally decided to go see the West myself. It was in August and the winds had mostly died down when I began thumbing rides out of Sioux Falls. What I saw was the devastation of the Dirty Thirties. Everywhere. The ditches along the highway were drifted level with brown dust. Tumbleweeds were piled high along the fences. Bones of dead cattle ringed dust-filled watertanks. Barn doors flapped in what little wind was there.

And yet, when one stopped in a small town along Highway 16, there was always a cheerful waitress, or a witty cafe owner, to serve you a hamburger, a malted milk, and a cup of coffee for two-bits; and if you wanted a glass of water to wash it all down, that was a dime extra. "We have to haul in our water from the Missouri, and then let it set a couple of days before we can use it." The cheer and the lively repartee of those waitresses and cafe owners reflected that what the local people were really thinking was: "Yes, times are tough. But wait until next year. Then we'll do'er."

Reading through the various essays in this remarkable book, I find abundant recorded evidence of that indomitable spirit of the South Dakotan. Over and over again the reader will find that no matter who is being depicted, statesman, politician, farmer, teacher, artist, writer, scientist, nun, ranch wife—all have that trait of great courage in the face of what appears to be imminent disaster. This was true of the first White Man to come up the Missouri, of the mountain man and explorers, of the first pioneer farmers and merchants. And it is still true of the modern farmer and merchant.

And that is not to forget either the Red Man who was here first. They too had their great heroes, men as well as women. They too exhibited an indomitable spirit, a high art, an extraordinary vision of what the better life should be as well as what the spirit world wanted of us. They gave us the names of most of our rivers and landscapes and mountains. They presented us with seed (corn, squash, beans, etc.) and with many herbs for healing. And if we will look, and listen, to them, they can help us root in all the better in what we can someday say, if we can't already, is our native land.

Out of this tough matrix have emerged powerful figures, men and women, who have not only achieved notable success in our state, but have also made their imprint on the national conscience. We have contributed our share of geniuses to the nation. And we keep on producing them.

Biographies given in this volume will turn out to be a gold mine of information for future generations. The index in back reads like an important who's who.

Here we have in one volume the essential and varied histories of the state of South Dakota. By emphasizing the leaders, various great men and women, we get the true story of our country.

Frederick Manfred

Introduction

Chapters in this volume are about leadership and people of accomplishment in South Dakota who often have been regarded as "heroes," "legends," or "celebrities" in the history of the state. Even a tourist crossing South Dakota on Interstate 90 between the Big Sioux River and the Black Hills is able to recognize the names of a few of these individuals who contributed to the making of the state. The image of Gutzon Borglum is displayed on billboards along the highway. Wild Bill Hickock and Calamity Jane are immortalized in Deadwood. Crazy Horse is the subject of a monument conceived by Korczak Ziolkowski. The names of Arne Larson and The Shrine to Music Museum, and of Ted Hustead and Wall Drug, are the instruments of state economy in tourism.

More careful students of South Dakota will recognize such names as that of Joe Robbie, owner of the Miami Dolphins; or Tom Brokaw, *NBC Nightly News* anchorperson. They might know that Vice President Hubert H. Humphrey and Nobel Prize winning physicist E. O. Lawrence had their origins in South Dakota. They might have learned that Allen Neuharth of the Gannett Corporation, and founder of *USA Today*, was educated in the state.

As Frederick Manfred notes in his preface, South Dakota has contributed its share of celebrated people to the nation and to the world. It is not only such notable individuals who have contributed to the development of South Dakota, however, but also a cadre of others, much less celebrated, who have helped to orchestrate the emergence of a state group and its culture. In many walks of life they have been leaders.

The process of selecting those commemorated in this volume was not easy. A special selection committee took into consideration a variety of issues regarding leadership, which readers should bear in mind as they digest the contents of the many chapters. Prominent historians, anthropologists, and other social scientists who have written for western democracies about the special roles of leaders have grappled with the issue of leadership. Thomas Carlyle has been cited most for the observation in *Heros and Hero Worship* that "the history of what man has accomplished in this world, is at bottom the History of the Great men who have worked here . . . ; the soul of the whole world's history, it may be justly considered, were the history of these." Somewhat more circumspectly, Allan Nevins wrote in his *Gateway to History*: "the most prominent of the fortuitous chances of history is the intermittent appearance of commanding personalities, the great men," and, he should have added, the great women. Introducing an education series entitled *World Leaders: Past and Present*, Arthur M. Schlesinger, Jr., remarked without hesitation that "leadership, it may be said, is really what makes the world go round."

Schlesinger went on to qualify his statement with an explanation. The central role of leaders has never been accepted by historical determinists who regard some process or other as the motivating force behind history. "Marxism is the determinism of class," for example, and "Nazism is the determinism of race." Schlesinger also warned against hero worship with the observation that "leaders have been responsible for the most extravagant follies and the most monstrous crimes that have beset suffering humanity," and suggested some tests for use when judging the quality or the importance of any leader in the past. Did the person "lead by force or by persuasion?" Has the "end for which power has been sought" been just? How beneficial to humanity have been the "results?" Moreover, Schlesinger cautioned his readers to notice that "even 'good' leaders must be regarded with a certain wariness. . . . Making a cult of a leader is always a mistake."

Nevertheless, he concluded that "individuals do make a difference" for providing "leadership in thought as well as in action," and believed that "leaders in thought may well make the greater difference to the world," for "leaders in action have to be effective in their own time." In any case, "leaders are useless without followers." For the "signal benefit the great leaders confer is to embolden the rest of us to live according to our best selves, to be active, insistent, and resolute in affirming our own sense of things." Quoting Ralph Waldo Emerson: "We feed on genius." Hence, leaders "exist that there may be greater men" and women to lead societies of greater resolution and imagination in the future.

Others have felt the matter to be far more complex than this. Most

writers who have considered the question of leadership have championed great men or women as instruments in social movements, or have
seen great men and women as phenomena explainable in terms of
social processes and historical trends. The anthropologist Alfred Kroe-
ber, in his *Configurations of Culture Growth*, concluded that "geniuses
are the indicators of the realization of coherent pattern growths of
cultural values. . . ." By this he meant that leaders are largely the
creations of the cultural contexts of the times in which they live.
Cultural conditions at any moment allow but a limited number of
responses if a culture is to adapt successfully to the demands of both
the natural and social environments in which the society exists. At the
risk of sounding trite, the adage "necessity is the mother of invention"
would apply. If a particular individual had not responded to the
demands of the environment, another person would have done so.

In support of this idea is the view that the "great" man or woman
identified as a leader is the creation of succeeding generations and
their historians. Although a leader is sometimes celebrated within his
or her lifetime, an assessment of importance or contribution ordinarily
rests with the historians. Thus, leaders become the creations of history. David Lowenthal amply documents this notion in his book *The
Past is a Foreign Country*; a society creates its past according to its
contemporary needs. An individual who was considered a leader,
perhaps even a hero, during his lifetime might well be vilified in the
future. For Great Plains history, the changing views about George
Armstrong Custer's roles between the time of the nation's centennial
and its bicentennial present a useful example. The same point is
evident in this volume in a chapter by Richmond Clow that explains
how historians have treated the "greatness" of Sitting Bull and Spotted
Tail.

The nagging question remains: why do some people become leaders
while others do not? Certainly more than one person is affected by the
cultural context that produces a leader. Can genius or leadership
simply be a matter of timing and luck? We editors agree that cultural
context and historical process have something to do with it, but we
also recognize that there are certain characteristics marking the quality
called "leadership." Perhaps we are in agreement with the anthropologist Leslie White, who in his article "Genius: Its Causes and Inci-
dences" recognizes that the incidence of genius is a product of the
interaction of cultural context with the innate abilities of the individual,
and that the context of an era enhances individual qualities.

So what qualities does a leader have? Naming them all, let alone understanding precisely how they evolve from historical conditions, would probably be impossible. It is better that a reader glean from chapters in this book certain qualities that appear with regularity. An important factor is timing, which might better be described as the ability to recognize a challenge or opportunity presented by cultural context. A related factor is "luck." Another is risk-taking, the willingness to put oneself or ideas forward when a situation demands. Certainly, almost all leaders have perseverance, in some cases stubbornness, to succeed or meet their goals. Imagination and creativity, the ability to see potential for the future and a way to meet it, are important leadership traits. Finally, in many leaders there seems to be little inclination to recognize that they are leaders at all. Along with this comes a lack of self-promotion and the willingness to sacrifice oneself for the good of the whole society. This point has been most obvious to the editors, for it marks the difference between what Joseph Campbell calls in his *The Power of Myth* the "hero" versus the "celebrity."

We invite every reader to consider the qualities of leadership in each chapter that follows. The planning committee that chose biographies instead of chapters on historical themes intended to say more about the times in culture history than about the lives of the individuals or families that appear in chapter headings. The chapters are arranged generally in the chronological order of the lives of the subjects, for the editors believe that persons of special significance during a particular era ought to appear in close proximity in the text. With this organization, the pages unfold as a history book that suggests how prominent women and men simultaneously responded to conditions and gave direction to their times.

Some readers may be surprised at the list of leaders selected for treatment in this volume. Indeed, the names of some who are better known to the reading public are absent, and the names of others much less recognizable are included. Attribute this feature to the planning committee of distinguished regional scholars invited to create the table of contents. Not so much to celebrate a centennial as to commemorate the accomplishments of South Dakotans in the past, the South Dakota Committee on the Humanities funded a special project during the fall of 1982. It charged a small group of humanities and social science professors representing all higher educational institutions in the state to provide direction. In deliberations through two planning sessions, interspersed between periods of investigation into subject areas assigned, the professors designed two publications of book length. One is the volume entitled *Planning for the South Dakota Centennial: A Bibliography* (Vermillion: University of South Dakota, 1984), a compilation of source citations for use by citizens across the state in preparation for South Dakota's centennial activities, and by scholars as a guide for research in the future. The other is this volume, *South Dakota Leaders*, an anthology of chapters about persons and families who have had a pronounced effect on the history of South Dakota down to the end of its first century of statehood.

A planning committee deliberated through a frigid winter day on the campus of Augustana College in Sioux Falls to reduce a list of nominated subjects from more than one hundred to approximately forty names of men and women or families. Some were eliminated because they originated in South Dakota but made their contributions elsewhere: U.S. Senator and Vice President Hubert H. Humphrey, for example; coaches George "Sparky" Anderson and Frank Leahy; Miami Dolphins owner Joe Robbie; cowboy Casey Tibbs; and physicist E. O. Lawrence. Some were dropped from the list because their roles in shaping the history of the region have been more controversial than well defined: U.S. Agents Valentine V. McGillicuddy and James McLaughlin, for instance, and Russell Means. Some were eliminated because memories about them have contained more legend than substance: Calamity Jane, Wild Bill Hickock, and Korczak Ziolkowski. Others were left out because they remained contemporaries whose careers perhaps have not yet reached their fullest dimensions: newsman Tom Brokaw, Governor William Janklow, artist James Pollock, beadworker Clarence Rockboy, Indian cultural specialist Kevin Locke, and several more.

After excluding persons such as these, the academicians still had in hand a list containing more than sixty names of men and women who made contributions worthy of recognition. Out of necessity, they went on to pare the number to a list that would be manageable in a single volume. With regret they eliminated the names of Governors William Bulow, M. Q. Sharpe, and Richard Kneip, for example; of U.S. Senator Chandler Gurney and Congressman E. Y. Berry; of Indian leaders such as Cato Valandra. They could not include business leaders Thomas Grier of Homestake Mining Company, Joe Kirby of Western Surety Company, or Ted Hustead of Wall Drug. There was not enough space to recognize such educators as I. D. Weeks of the University of South Dakota or Hilton Briggs of South Dakota State University, or persons in other walks of life who have made important contributions. Gradually the list was reduced to a number of people whose biographies could fit into a single volume, and which would bring recognition of a substantial variety of developments in South Dakota's past. In the end, the process of selection was one of education for the committee. None of the academicians who acceded to the selections had ever before fully grasped the amazing breadth of contributions made by so many South Dakotans down to the end of the first one hundred years of statehood. Each saw some of his or her "favorites" eliminated from the list for the lack of space.

As the list was pared, the committee began to consider who should write each chapter and how each author should be instructed. Authors were chosen largely on the basis if their familiarity with the subjects and their previous contributions to regional literature. At the same time, the committee recognized that the chapters, although based on the best scholarly research, should not become academic treatises laden with endnotes. Anyway, the inclusion of heavy documentation would require the elimination of numerous subjects in this volume. Accordingly, some chapters were cut and honed to reasonable lengths. All were stripped of any except the essential endnotes, and documentation for their contents collapsed into the remarkable bibliography that follows the texts. Out of a plan that evolved from deliberations by a committee grew this hefty volume, which is almost encyclopedic in its treatment of the history of the state.

Some readers may use it only for its encyclopedic value, but others may wish to read it from cover to cover as a history book. To the latter group we recommend a preliminary examination of the index as well as the table of contents, for they suggest several prominent themes that exist not by accident but by the design that evolved through the deliberations of the planning committee. Chapters authored by John Rau, William O. Farber, Kenneth E. Hendrickson, Jr., Larry Remele, Loren Carlson, Alan Clem, and John S. Painter draw years of investigation by the authors into a history of state politics. These original chapters are complete enough to stand by themselves as a separate monograph. Chapters written by Lesta Van Der Wert Turchen, Sister Ann Kessler, Susan Peterson, Jeannette Kinyon, Ruth Alexander, and William T. Anderson recognize some central roles played by women in the history of the state. Chapters prepared by Richmond Clow, Leonard Rufus Bruguier, John Milton, John Painter, and Ruth Alexander all portray eminent Indian leaders. Chapters contributed by Robert Stahl, Gerald W. Wolff, Sister Ann Kessler, Susan Peterson, Thomas J. Gasque, and Leonard Bruguier underscore the intentions and contributions of religious men and women. Chapters authored by Herbert T.

Hoover, Lesta Turchen, Thomas Gasque, David Miller, and Jami Huntsinger illustrate the motivations and roles of "boomers" seeking financial gain. Essays by John E. Miller and Elizabeth Evenson Williams explain important themes in the evolution of agriculture as South Dakota's foremost industry. Those written by Ruth Alexander, Arthur R. Huseboe, William Anderson, John Milton, Robert F. Karolevitz, Larry J. Zimmerman, and Mary Keepers Helgevold illustrate how richly this state has been endowed by persons with historical vision and artistic flair. Through the contributions of all these authors, other themes of history appear.

The intention has been to put aside the "glorification" of important men and women and concentrate upon some trends in our past. The result of this treatment of our leaders must be that we come to better understand ourselves. From the commemoration of contributions by these leaders, in other words, inevitably evolves both the assessment of failures and the celebration of achievements that distinguish South Dakotans from all other state groups in the nation.

Larry J. Zimmerman
Herbert T. Hoover

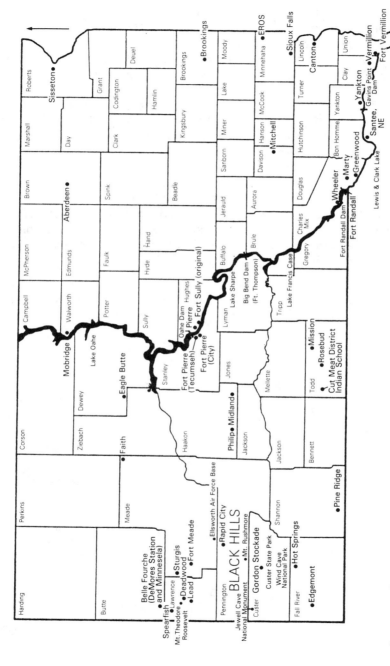

Important Locations in South Dakota History

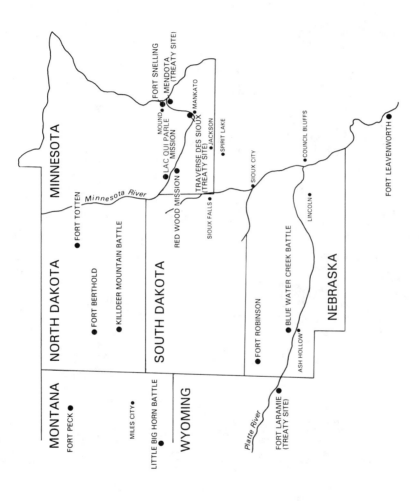

Locations of Events Important in Indian-White Relations

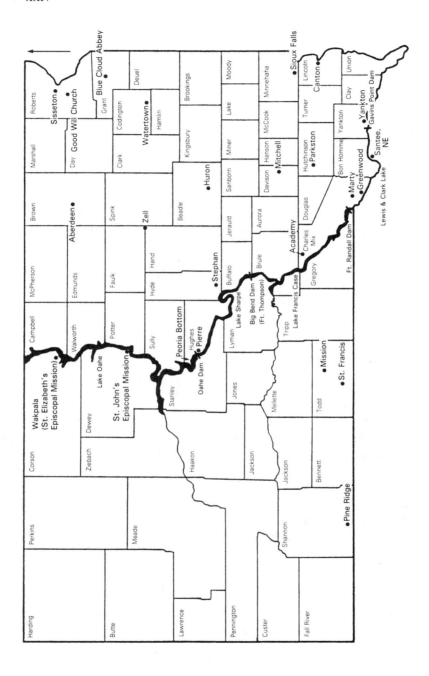

Places Important in the Religious History of South Dakota

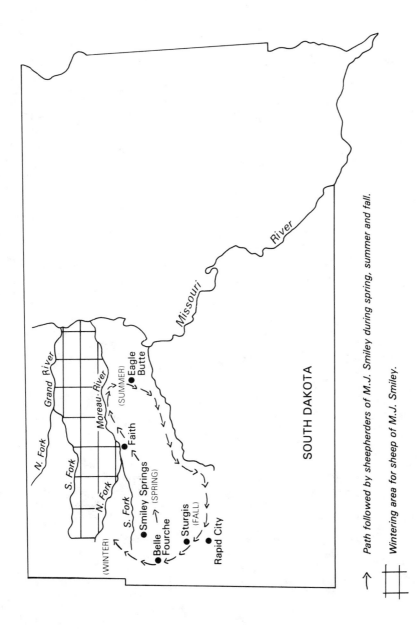

SOUTH DAKOTA

→ Path followed by sheepherders of M.J. Smiley during spring, summer and fall.

Wintering area for sheep of M.J. Smiley.

The Sheep Ranching Territory of M. J. Smiley

Pierre Chouteau, Jr.
Courtesy South Dakota State Historical
Society.

The Steamboat Yellowstone *from a painting by Karl Bodmer.*
Courtesy Richardson Archives, USD.

Early Fort Pierre from a painting by Karl Bodmer.
Courtesy Richardson Archives, USD.

Missouri valley steamboat landing, Yankton, D.T. (1878) photographed by Stanley J.
Morrow.
Courtesy W.H. Over State Museum.

The Arrival of Capitalism on the Northern Great Plains: Pierre Chouteau, Jr. and Company

Herbert T. Hoover

The personality of Pierre Chouteau, Jr., had little if any impact on the early recorded history of the area drained by the upper Missouri River and its tributaries, but the business ventures of Chouteau and his associates had greater influence upon economic change in the region than did any other force prior to the establishment of Dakota Territory in 1861. These pioneers recognized commercial promise in the activities of explorers, cartographers, tourists, and U.S. Indian Field Service personnel as well as fur traders and used them to the maximum benefit for personal gain. As the principal supplier of goods, commercial management, and transportation service, the younger Pierre Chouteau was the foremost business magnate in pre-territorial Dakota history.[1]

His family heritage was clouded by the issue of paternity. Rene Chouteau, who was born at the French village of L'Hermenault in 1723, migrated to North America and opened a lodging house and tavern at New Orleans in Lower Louisiana. Marie Terese Bourgois, who was born at New Orleans in 1733, married Rene and by him gave birth to Auguste in 1749. Evidently, Rene abandoned Marie and her son in 1752 and returned to France for approximately fifteen years. Legally, Marie remained the wife of Rene to his death in 1776, because neither civil statutes in New Orleans nor ecclesiastic laws of the Roman Church permitted divorce and remarriage. She began to live, however,

1

out of wedlock with Pierre Laclede soon after his arrival at New Orleans in 1755, and by him had four children: Jean Pierre, Marie Pelagie, Marie Louise, and Victoire. In one set of records, Marie named Chouteau as the father of all her children so she could raise them as legitimate offspring. In another set, she declared legal status as the widow of Chouteau (while he was still alive) so she could claim the right of a household head to raise her children and manage their inheritance. From appearances, Laclede and Marie lived happily together under the arrangement.

Laclede took the teen-aged Auguste Chouteau with him in 1763 to establish a trading post at the confluence of the Mississippi and Missouri Rivers. Marie remained in New Orleans until she gave birth to Victoire in March of 1764, then took the youngsters to join Laclede and Auguste at the new town of St. Louis. Laclede built a large house and developed a considerable estate doing business at the "Gateway to the West." Marie managed the properties of the household and passed them on to her children.

Thus, Auguste and (Jean) Pierre Chouteau, Sr., grew up as half-brothers in a household of considerable means at a major point of access to the Territory of Louisiana—an extension of New France established near the outset of the eighteenth century. For more than sixty years, exploration and trade had been sporadic across the Territory because it was regarded by Frenchmen mainly as a buffer in their contest with Spanish and English colonials for imperial advantage on North America. After the imperial forces of French and Spanish Bourbon monarchs were defeated by Englishmen in the Seven Years' War (called the French and Indian War in the North American theater), British diplomats claimed all territories east of the Mississippi River as their prize of war by the terms of the Treaty of Paris, 1763. Anticipating the British intention to expel them from North America, Frenchmen ceded Louisiana to Spaniards by secret agreement at San Ildefonso in 1762 with the understanding that a Bourbon Spanish king would return imperial claim to a Bourbon French king after the threat of British intervention had passed. By and large, Frenchmen remained in charge of affairs at the settlements, but the Bourbon flag of Spain flew over Louisiana.

Spanish colors remained aloft until Frenchmen had assassinated their Bourbon King, Louis XVI, and had transferred power over France and its empire to the revolutionary triumvirate of Napoleon Bonaparte. As part of a plan to declare himself the Emperor of France, Napoleon revitalized its languishing empire and demanded the return of Louisiana. The weak Spanish Bourbon, King Carlos IV, complied in the second Treaty of San Ildefonso, in 1800, through which Louisiana was ceded back to France. By 1803, however, it no longer seemed useful to Napoleon, so he sold it to the United States for $15,000,000 and Louisiana became part of President Thomas Jefferson's territorial system.

Federal officials proceeded to subdivide their acquisition into organized territories from which states could emerge to enter the union through procedures prescribed by the (Northwest) Ordinance of 1787. Present-day South Dakota was situated near the center of remote Upper Louisiana.[2]

For the purpose of trade, the region containing South Dakota became the principal meeting ground for Indians who held prior claim to Upper Louisiana and traders who represented two burgeoning commercial forces. Operatives from British Canada came as far west as Lake Traverse and the James River basin. They traveled by way of Green Bay, and the Wisconsin, Mississippi, and St. Peters (Minnesota) rivers, to exchange firearms, whiskey, and other trade goods for robes and furs. Men of French and Spanish extraction came up from St. Louis to barter along the upper Des Moines and the upper Missouri River basins.

(Jean) Pierre Chouteau, Sr., entered this competition shortly after the United States annexed Louisiana in 1803. First, he apprenticed as the chief trader for the family firm that worked among Osage Indians. When Manuel Lisa muscled into Osage Country and established a monopoly, Chouteau became the Indian Agent for the tribe. Thereafter, he invested as one of several partners in the St. Louis Missouri Fur Company and, with a dynamic group of merchants, participated in the extension of trade well into Sioux Country.

Pierre Chouteau, Jr., (1789–1865) followed in his father's footsteps. He apprenticed briefly as a worker in some lead mines along the upper Mississippi River. He entered a partnership with Bartholomew Berthold and the two men opened an independent trading enterprise along the upper Missouri. Evidently the younger Chouteau desired a career in the federal service, for at one point Pierre Chouteau, Sr., wrote the U.S. Superintendent at St. Louis, William Clark, requesting a job for his son. Because Clark never extended the offer of a federal appointment, however, the younger Chouteau enlarged his commitment to trade with investment in a second partnership called Bernard Pratt and Company (later re-named Pratt, Chouteau and Company).

In the 1820s conditions changed in two ways that offered young

Chouteau an almost ideal opportunity to further expand his interests. For one thing, the British pulled out. In 1821 they abandoned their outpost at Lake Traverse because their 1818 Convention with the United States required withdrawal from trade south of 49°. In 1822 they reorganized their frontier commercial operations by order of the Crown to emphasize trade farther west.

At the same time, Congress reorganized the fur trade dramatically. In 1822 its members withdrew support from a factory system that had purported to govern trading activities at remote rendezvous where merchants met trappers for commercial fairs on Indian turf at the pleasure of tribal leaders. In 1824 Congress legislated a requirement that all future trade take place at designated forts and posts to which traders and tribes would receive specific assignments under close supervision. By implication, the Act of 1824 required the confinement of tribes or their bands to particular areas. It offered incentive to fur trade leaders at forts and posts through monopolies under federal licenses, which were renewable every two years. While trading, they could also sell merchandise and transportation services to independent travelers, as well as to the United States as its agents made treaties, delivered annuities, and created bureaucracies among Indian peoples.

To take advantage of this, the veteran merchant Joseph Renville formed the Columbia Fur Company and employed traders who had lost their jobs and ready markets as the British pulled out. From a base of trade connections in southern Minnesota he moved west to take over the abandoned British station on Lake Traverse, then moved to the confluence of the Bad and Missouri Rivers and founded Fort Tecumseh. For a time it appeared that Renville and his associates would compete effectively with merchants from St. Louis, who by then had appeared in substantial numbers to barter as far up the Missouri as the eastern Montana plateau.

A consolidation of forces became inevitable, however, because representatives of the eastern firm of John Jacob Astor showed up. Drawing on the enormous resources of their sponsor, they took over the Columbia Fur Company, retained Renville's personnel, and merged his operation with others into the Upper Missouri Outfit for the Western Department of the American Fur Company. In 1827 they designated Fort Tecumseh their principal station for the northern Great Plains region. The same year they founded Fort Vermillion as a secondary trade center. With these two forts under federal license, and various outposts scattered along the upper Missouri River and its principal tributaries, the Company established a near monopoly across the entire Missouri River drainage system.

Pierre Chouteau, Jr., joined Astor's monopoly in 1827, when he hired on as manager of the Upper Missouri Outfit, but in the mid-1830s his own Pratt, Chouteau and Company purchased the entire Western Department of the American Fur Company. By 1838 the name of the partnership changed to Pierre Chouteau, Jr., and Company. Thereafter, Chouteau marketed robes and hides through American Fur Company buyers in New York, but with his own firm he controlled the lion's share of trade across the areas drained by the upper Mississippi as well as the Missouri River. With a near monopoly under his personal control, he dominated business activities throughout most of the region until his death in 1865.

Nearly all legendary merchants of the upper Mississippi and Missouri Rivers were at some time in his employ: Alexis Bailly, Henry Hastings Sibley, Honore Picotte, P. D. Papin, and Theophile Bruguier, to name a few. While Chouteau fashioned a business empire through federal licensure, he intimidated competitors, courted Indian leaders with lavish gifts, provided as many services and supplies as consumers demanded, and created a smooth connection between the great reservoir of robes and furs in Upper Louisiana and the ready markets of eastern states and Western Europe. At no time between his employment by the American Fur Company in 1827 and the decline of the fur trade in the 1850s was more than a handful of businessmen in the region entirely independent of his control.

Chouteau's commercial empire was flexible. While he worked for the American Fur Company, three regional operations received approximately equal amounts of attention. For the upper Mississippi, he established central Outfits at Prairie du Chien and Mendota, where rigorous operatives worked to establish sub-stations at remote places on principal tributaries. To serve an area farther down the Mississippi together with the lower Missouri basin, he supported special Outfits for the Ioways, Sacs, Kickapoos, Kanzas, Osages, and Otos. For the upper Missouri, he established the Sioux Outfit at Fort Tecumseh—which he re-named Fort Pierre (Chouteau, Jr.) for himself by 1832. From this central post, he developed special Outfits for the Yanktonais, Oglalas, Brules, Cherry Creek Tetons, Hunkpapas, and various tribes that traded along the White River. In addition, Chouteau drew into the network separate field units headed by pioneering operatives such as the Frenchman Henri Ange and the mixed-blood William Dickson, both of whom worked around Fort Vermillion.

After Chouteau established his own firm late in the 1830s, he curtailed operations where trade petered out and expanded his networks elsewhere to compensate. In the south the number of trading Outfits diminished to include small operations for the Miamis, Osages, Kickapoos, and Sac and Fox. To the northeast there was expansion through a Wisconsin Outfit headquartered at Prairie du Chien to include outposts at Little Rock, Turkey River, Iona River, Red Cedar, Chippewa River, Lake Pepin, Grand Rapids, and Point aux Paul plus a special Outfit run by George Culver. In Minnesota there was growth for the central St. Peters or Sioux Outfit at Mendota by the attachment of Kittson's Outfit at Pembina; Joseph R. Brown's station near Big Stone Lake; David Faribault's post; and trading stations at Lac qui Parle, the upper Des Moines, Traverse des Sioux, and Little Rapids.

Networks of stations in these three regions grew into a substantial enterprise by the early 1840s, but together they did not compare to Chouteau's operation on the upper Missouri. To Fort Pierre, Fort Vermillion, and surrounding Outfits he added trading stations at Forts Clark, Berthold, Union, John, Alexander, and Benton; and a Yancton Post. To nearly every one of these Chouteau's managers attached some seasonal trading stations.

Each major fort or post along the upper Missouri basin grew into a self-sustaining settlement. By 1844 Fort Pierre reported an inventory of livestock that included fifteen mules, thirty-eight oxen, thirty-five cows, seventeen yearlings, twenty-five calves, seven hogs, eleven pigs, two sheep, and a buffalo. In 1849 Vermillion Post had a livestock inventory comprising a yoke of oxen, three horses, four milk cows, two beeves, a bull, five calves, and six hogs. Vermillion managers reported a "Fort Farm and Crop" valued at $300 plus substantial inventories of traveling equipment, farming utensils, kitchen and household furniture, forty cords of wood, sixty pieces of dried meat, a quantity of tallow, and a store of iron.

People in the vicinity as well as passersby regarded the forts and posts as frontier urban centers, but Chouteau and his associates viewed them mainly as channels of commerce. Through them came tons of hides and furs every year that were pooled in warehouses at St. Charles or St. Louis for shipment by steamboat through Pittsburgh and New Orleans to New York or the major cities of Western Europe. Most important were the buffalo robes compressed into bundles, each of a dozen or so. More numerous were the skins of muskrats and their kittens, and the shaved or natural hides of grey and red deer. Adding variety were the hides of grizzly and black bears, and the furs of beaver, otter, mink, fisher, martin, raccoons, wild cats, wolves, foxes, pole cats, badgers, and lynx. Almost every shipment contained cargos of packaged buffalo tongue.

In return for the service of gathering these natural products among White traders and Indian hunters, Chouteau and his associates paid principal field operatives at major stations in cash and supplied their Outfits with a considerable array of comforts. Shipments came into upper Missouri valley trading stations that included barreled pork, corn, tea, salt, vinegar, sugar, tobacco, bread, spices, soap, whiskey, brandy, clothing, nails, hoop iron, candle sticks, pistols, rifles, spades, shovels, twine, cow bells, lanterns, ploughs, rasps, files, saws, axes, window glass, putty, oxen, horses, saddles, bridles, and horse collars.

In addition, there were enormous quantities of merchandise for use in the Indian trade. Demands varied from outfit to outfit and varieties changed over the years, but leading items of commerce were nearly always the same. Heading the list of every inventory each year were Hudson's Bay and French blankets in one to three point sizes of scarlet, blue, green, and white colors. Linen cloth goods in similar shades were popular, as were calico of several qualities, plaid cloth, and flannel. Ample supplies of buttons, lace, gartering, ribbon, thread, pins, and needles were included. Tribal members called for American and Chinese vermillion, chrome yellow, and verdigris pigments as well as scissors and awls. Trade goods included manufactured clothing for distribution among Indian leaders and their relations: scarlet and blue chiefs coats; hats and caps; and shawls, pants, shirts, leather belts, socks, and shoes. Traders distributed combs, sea shells, sleigh bells, hawk bells, medals, brass and silver gadgets, looking glasses, clay pipes, ear bobs, cock feathers, silver objects, and brass or copper finger rings. They bartered large amounts of wampum, and glass and colored beads in shades of white, black, blue, and red. Fancy beads appeared in the 1840s and glass cut beads were introduced by 1850. Traders exchanged household wares, including iron kettles, tin pots, pans, and cups. With every shipment they supplied goods useful for hunting and trapping: Northwest guns, Belgian fusils, gun worms, gun flints, gun powder, powder horns, block lead, shot, muskrat and beaver traps, and "scalping" or butcher knives. There was some alcohol in the orders, although the makings of spirituous beverages for use outside of licensed forts and posts became black market items imported covertly after the importation of whiskey became illegal by an act of Congress in 1830. Evidently, goods were chosen for the Missouri Outfits in large degree according to expressions of desire by tribal consumers who preferred items that added comfort, enhanced artistic or ceremonial expression, and improved efficiency in the gathering of robes and furs.

Traders imported enough manufactured articles to change the material culture of Indians appreciably, but they were not the only customers to whom Chouteau and his associates sold goods for distribution among the tribes. The Indian Department of the United States acquired a similar list for annual, springtime allocations as annuities due under treaties or as gifts to appease those tribes to whom few if any treaty benefits were due. As annuities and "presents," the St. Louis Superintendent bought and shipped blankets, cloth goods, beads, vermillion and verdigris pigments, needles and thread, looking glasses, guns and gun worms, flints and powder, bar lead, awls, nails, fish hooks and line, kettles, knives, sugar, large quantities of plug or twist tobacco, and a few trinkets. In other words, federal annuities and gifts included a lesser variety of embellishments, but they added fishing equipment and emphasized materials that brought efficiency to the hunt. Here and there across Sioux Country, U.S. Agents also distributed small quantities of corn hoes and axes to encourage the establishment of family farms.

As a part of its business Chouteau's firm established the first steamboat service on a regular schedule for the upper Missouri River. After the maiden voyage of the *Yellowstone* in 1831, the *Diana*, *Antelope*, *St. Peters*, *Burlington*, *Trader*, and possibly others appeared. These boats carried on the exchange of trade goods for robes and hides; transported Outfit and federal agency supplies; and carried officials, explorers, missionaries, artists, cartographers, and tourists.

A flourishing commercial empire supported by a steam powered transportation system inevitably attracted the new society known to the region as "Missouri Valley Culture" or "Steamboat Culture." It sprang up with demand for dock hands, warehouse workers, carpenters, cooks, couriers, interpreters, meat hunters, clerks, gardeners, wood cutters to supply fuel for steamers, and salvage workers to recover goods from boats that sank in turbulent waters. With them came gamblers, whiskey merchants, and ladies of the night.

There evolved, too, the separate society of mixed extraction labeled "Half Breed" in federal nomenclature. It originated with Pierre Dorion, the Frenchman who moved from the upper Des Moines to the Missouri Valley near the mouth of the James during the early 1780s. The first permanent non-Indian resident of present-day South Dakota, he took a Yankton wife who bore mixed-blood children. A few others settled in Sioux Country west of Minnesota before Pierre Chouteau, Jr., took over in 1827, but the greatest number arrived to serve as traders, interpreters, and business coordinators for his firm. To the older names of Dorion and Renville were added many others: in fewer than ten years William Dickson, the mixed-blood son of British Agent Robert Dickson and a Yanktonai mother; Colin Campbell; Charles DeGray; Joseph and Andre Lecompt; Francis Chardron; P. D. Papin; Honore Picotte; Constant Dauphin; Henri Ange; Pierre Menard; Velandry; Charles Primeaux; F[rancois] X[avier] Delorier; John and Charles Cabane; Joseph Robidoux; Alfred, Francois, and Auguste Traversie; John LeClaire; Michel, Denis, and Thomas Cournoyer; Theophile Bruguier; and various others came. These men and their mixed-blood progeny served prominently as bilingual, multi-cultural buffers in the merger of Indian with non-Indian society.

Chouteau and his associates made one other noteworthy contribution to regional development with the operation of a retail store in St. Louis. Among its hinterland patrons were leading fur trade coordinators such as Honore Picotte, federal employees such as William Clark, and missionaries such as the Jesuit Pierre Jean DeSmet. With steamboats plying the waters of the Missouri from early spring to midsummer, the store of Pierre Chouteau, Jr., and Company carried on a lucrative retail business. Among the hundreds who bought essential items for their expeditions was the explorer/cartographer Joseph N. Nicollet. For his journey onto the Dakota prairie in 1839, during which he drafted the map that guided travelers for a generation, Nicollet purchased empty boxes for specimens, barreled pork, corn flour, sugar, rice, tea, pepper, powder, shot, lead, hatchets, a sickle, some axes, netting, ticking, sheeting, linseed, and varnish, at a cost of $309.40.

Some major impacts of the business ventures sustained by Chouteau and his associates are obvious. With trading outfits linked to warehouses at St. Charles and St. Louis they fashioned a commercial system that marketed robes and furs at population centers in eastern states and Western Europe. At major trading forts they developed the first non-Indian urban communities in the region. On steamboats they carried personnel of the fur trade and the U.S. Indian Field Service, and transported explorers, missionaries, artists, cartographers, and tourists who described the peoples and resources of the upper Missouri River basin to an international audience for the first time. Among them were the artists George Catlin and Karl Bodmer, and the ornithologist John Audubon. By creating a demand for service personnel, Chouteau and his associates attracted the first wave of non-Indians with interest outside of the fur trade. They also sustained the growing body of multicultural mixed-bloods that remained to cushion the shocks of intercultural relationships.

Most of all, Chouteau and his associates supplied the packaged foods and manufactured articles that altered the culture of the Sioux. By purchasing traps, firearms, and accessories at trading stations on credit, tribal hunters acquired the best industrial equipment available for use in the pursuit of game. Through the acquisition of pots, pans, kettles, cups, knives, scissors, and other instruments, Sioux women experienced a revolution in domestic arts.

In the generous distribution of blankets, cloth goods, beads, pigments, ribbons, shawls, and other articles, Sioux people gained the wherewithal to transform artistic traditions and ceremonial paraphernalia into the refined expressions for which they have been so well known ever since. Traditional art forms and religious practices may not have been changed very much, but ease of expression and color of composition were greatly enhanced. Aesthetic value assigned to the high quality blankets introduced as trade goods, for example, remains on display in the use of ceremonial sashes at meetings of the Native American Church. Religious symbolism and artistic flair expressed through the use of cloth goods distributed in red, blue, green, white, and other colors is even more evident in brightly colored tobacco ties used during Peacepipe ceremonies and in magnificent star quilts. Shawls, feathers, and sleigh bells on trade lists have been replicated for use as paraphernalia of modern Sioux dance. Glass and colored beads similar to those distributed by hanks in exchange for robes and furs are still supplied by European manufacturers for use in the composition of modern Sioux beadwork.

In the environment created by Chouteau and his associates, Sioux social values and philosophical traditions were shaken severely for the first time by non-Indians. Traders and business leaders took Indian wives who raised children whose outlooks represented a blend of Indian and White traditions. Missionaries challenged social habits as well as basic beliefs and philosophies with the tenets of Christianity. Traveling artists, explorers, adventurers, and tourists aroused curiosities. Steamboat Culture exposed tribal members to the despicable aspects of Anglo-American society. Whiskey traders introduced chemical addiction. Prostitutes upset domestic life.

Undergirding the entire intercultural relationship was the lure of capitalism. Collectively, tribal groups tolerated the exchange of land by their diplomats for the promise of annuities. To be sure, particular leaders were threatened, cajoled, or enticed with spiritous beverages and gifts to surrender real estate. But they did so, more often than not, with approval by constituents in general councils on the promise that goods would be delivered each spring to band chiefs for allocation to family heads. Out of the desire for a better life style coupled with a subtle change in beliefs about the taking of animals, individual men and women of the tribes participated in the wanton slaughter of animals ranging in size from the buffalo bull to the muskrat kitten.

Inevitably, the destruction of game led to the further surrender of land by tribal groups that became increasingly reliant on trade and annuity goods, if not desperate for sustenance. The four Sioux tribes of Minnesota relinquished their heritage in real estate for a narrow reserve along the upper St. Peters in 1851. The Yankton tribe gave up more than 8,000,000 acres in present-day East River South Dakota in exchange for 430,000 acres on the Missouri Hills. Tetons and Yanktonais took up arms for a time to avoid a similar fate, but by 1889 they all had succumbed to the exchange of their aboriginal claims for tribal reservations.

Indirectly, the ranking trader of St. Louis was responsible for the subsequent plight of the tribes, but in his own time he was no more culpable than were the Sioux people themselves. They acted in concert with traders and service personnel to effect change and, from appearances, neither the Sioux nor the non-Indians who worked among them assigned collective blame to each other for the consequences. A young ethnologist named James W. Lynd reported that at mid-century the overall impression held by most Sioux people of non-Indians was, at its worst, one of guarded suspicion. Tetons and Yanktonais out west regarded the White man as "an enemy seeking to over run them." But Sissetons who lived around the headwaters of the St. Peters River considered a non-Indian as "a kind of superior genius" whom they "watched with jealousy." Wahpetons situated near Lac qui Parle viewed him as "a soi-disant friend, whose comforting luxuries are to be coveted." Mdewakantons along the Mississippi River thought the non-Indian to be "a convenient servant, whose labors and whose good will is to be coveted. . . . All this arises from the different degrees of intercourse they have had with the White," Lynd concluded; from the eastern Mdewakanton "the gradation is gentle" to the plainsman, "who, seldom seeing the White man, knows him but to hate him."[3]

Apparently, most non-Indians held similar impressions of Sioux people. Even after the Spirit Lake Massacre in northwestern Iowa,

Captain James Starkey, who led a unit of Minnesota volunteers on a punitive expedition against the Wahpekute leader Inkpaduta, complained about the lukewarm support he received from Whites.[4] "Such was the mixed character of the population at the time that a large proportion of citizens were either by ties of consanguinity, or trading interest, allied to the Indians and their interests," and refused to fight.[5]

Further corroboration for the assumption that an attitude of cooperation persisted to the end of the fur trade era lies in the perception by new arrivals that Sioux Country was a safe place to go. As many as 30,000 settlers rushed into southern Minnesota during the 1850s. Pioneers lined up to boom onto the eastern half of present-day South Dakota with confidence that it would be vacated by Yanktons without rancor, because the vast majority of members in the tribe had long been friendly, cooperative, and peaceable.

Armed conflict that began in Sioux Country during the mid-1850s lasted for more than three decades, but most of the causes arose from circumstances for which Pierre Chouteau, Jr., and his associates held little direct responsibility. For his many contributions to early development in South Dakota, it was fitting that the capital city would bear his name. There is some irony in its evolution. The hamlet of East Pierre may have originated as a whiskey station for Fort Pierre after the fur trade era had passed. The Fort went into sharp decline in the 1850s, after General William Harney rejected it as a site for a permanent military installation. It evolved rapidly as a river town in the 1870s, however, and as a commercial link to the gold fields of the Black Hills. Its leaders tolerated the presence of gambling establishments and even houses of ill-repute, but they could not permit the cache of spirituous beverages because this would be an obvious violation of federal statutes and policies that prohibited the sale of whiskey on the Great Sioux Reservation created by the 1868 Fort Laramie Treaty. Accordingly, illegal beverages were dispensed from East Pierre, even after a strip of land along the eastern shore of the Missouri River was attached to the Great Sioux Reservation with a Presidential Addition order issued by Ulysses S. Grant to curtail the whiskey trade. Thereafter, the hamlet evolved as the city of Pierre and the capital of the State of South Dakota. In its selection, South Dakotans honored the non-Indian who exerted the greatest influence upon the land within their state before it was organized as the Territory of Dakota in 1861.

Notes

1. The scope of this chapter confines discussion to the impact of Pierre Chouteau, Jr., on Dakota Territory and excludes his influence in other regions.

From the mid-1820s to the late 1850s he was the primary force behind economic development along the upper Mississippi River and its tributaries, and the Lower Missouri River and its tributaries, as well as the Upper Missouri River basin. This is clear in the contents of the Papers of Pierre Chouteau, Jr., and Company preserved by the Missouri Historical Society in St. Louis. Now available on microfilm, they provide most of the information contained in this chapter regarding the fur trade. Principal sources on the Chouteau family are William E. Foley's "The Laclede-Chouteau Puzzle: John Francis McDermott Supplies Some Missing Pieces," *Gateway Heritage: Quarterly Journal of the Missouri Historical Society,* IV, no. 2 (Fall 1983), pp. 19–25; and *The First Chouteaus: River Barons of Early St. Louis* (Urbana: University of Illinois Press, 1983).

2. For the purpose of political expansion, it was to be attached successively to Indiana, Michigan, Wisconsin, and Minnesota Territories before it became the most populous part of Dakota Territory in 1861.

3. "Migrations," James W. Lynd Papers, Minnesota Historical Society, St. Paul.

4. Strategic armed conflict between Sioux people and non-Indians began with the Grattan Affair along the Platte River in 1854 and ended at Wounded Knee on the Pine Ridge Reservation in 1890. In 1857 Inkpaduta led an assault in northwestern Iowa, called the Spirit Lake Massacre in non-Indian records, and attacked settlers near Jackson, Minnesota, before he fled into Dakota to escape capture. Faint evidence in records suggests that he continued to participate in the harassment of White people until he died a natural death near Fort Peck in the 1870s. His attack on Spirit Lake may be regarded as the opening of hostilities that evolved into the Minnesota Sioux War of 1862–1863.

5. *Reminiscences of Indian Depredations* (St. Paul: D. Famaley and Son, Printers, 1891), passim.

Newton Edmunds.
Courtesy Richardson Archives, USD.

Early Yankton photographed by Stanley J. Morrow.
Courtesy W.H. Over State Museum

Fort Berthold photographed by Stanley J. Morrow.
Courtesy W.H. Over State Museum

Political Leadership in Dakota Territory: Newton Edmunds as Governor, Peace Commissioner, and Elder Statesman

John E. Rau

With a few strokes of the pen on March 1, 1861, James Buchanan created the Territory of Dakota west of Minnesota. A handful of resident non-Indians had been clamoring for organized government since Minnesota's admission to the Union in 1858. At last, White pioneering settlers gained political respectability together with the prospect of statehood in years to come.

As the Northwest Ordinance of 1787 had prescribed, the organized Territory was served by a governor, a secretary, and three federal judges. Its citizens elected the one non-voting Delegate at large to the U.S. House of Representatives. The primary force in government was the Governor, who was in charge of all executive business including the conduct of Indian affairs. From 1863 to 1866 Newton Edmunds held the office and performed with distinction. He braved organizational confusion, Indian trouble, and political strife while most citizens elsewhere in the country were preoccupied by the Civil War. Of the ten territorial governors who served in Dakota, few created legacies or even remained in the Territory after leaving office. Edmunds, on the other hand, brought his family, served as Governor with considerable effect, and remained an active citizen in Dakota for the rest of his life.

Newton Edmunds was born in Hartland, New York, on May 31, 1819. His parents, both of English descent, settled there shortly before the War of 1812 and engaged in farming. When he was twelve years old, the family moved to Wastenaw County, Michigan, where he attended the public schools. After graduation, he joined his brothers in the operation of general merchandise and lumber businesses at Ypsilanti, Saginaw, and Vassar, Michigan. He married Margaret Heart of Troy, New York, in August of 1848. Born to their union were eight children, four of whom survived to adulthood in Dakota Territory.

When Abraham Lincoln entered the White House in 1861, Newton's brother James won appointment as U. S. Commissioner of Public Lands. With his brother's assistance Newton soon became Chief Clerk for the Surveyor General's office in Dakota Territory. He arrived at Yankton during July of 1861 and set up an office for his superior, George Hill. By then the first territorial Governor, William Jayne, had chosen Yankton as the capital. Edmunds and Jayne became close acquaintances, with Edmunds often joining the Governor on official junkets.

The new Territory was at great peril. Agitated by mistreatment in their confinement to a reservation along the upper Minnesota River Valley, many eastern Sioux people took up arms. The fighting spread to Dakota Territory in vigorous attacks; non-Indians were killed, wounded, or robbed in scattered attacks from Sioux Falls to the stage coach road near Chouteau Creek. At the urging of Governor Jayne, a company of militia was formed at Yankton and its members built a temporary stockade. Edmunds was a corporal in that force. Some residents of outlying communities took sanctuary here or in Sioux City, Iowa. Many never returned to the Territory.

The Minnesota Sioux War disturbed the territorial election of September 1, 1862. Anxious to save their own necks, election officials opened the polls early. They permitted irregularities throughout the Territory, some of which were not related to the Indian scare. Corruption was especially acute in the race for territorial Delegate, in which Governor Jayne ran against the incumbent John B. S. Todd. When Jayne was declared the winner, his bitter opponent sent a formal protest to Congress and a controversy erupted that would not be resolved for nearly two years.

Meanwhile, to fill the vacancy in the Governor's office, President Lincoln appointed John Fox Potter of Wisconsin, who declined to accept. Regular Republicans of the Territory preferred the hard-working and loyal Newton Edmunds over the Democratic Justice Philemon Bliss, whom they thought to be a Confederate supporter—a Copperhead. Accordingly, in October, 1863, the President sent Edmunds formal word of his appointment.

From the outset, Governor Edmunds was "less engrossed in politics than his predecessor," wrote historian Herbert S. Schell, and "directed his full energies toward putting the machinery of government in running order."[1] Of protracted interest to him was the management of Indian affairs, which seemed to be out of control. In November he asked U.S. Commissioner of Indian Affairs William P. Dole to issue instructions:

> The office of superintendent of Indian affairs having been virtually ignored by my predecessor, and Secretary and acting Governor Hutchinson having pursued the same policy, has led many of our local agents into habits of carelessness and negligence, from which I fear the Indians of this superintendency have greatly been the sufferers.[2]

Edmunds vowed to ensure the accountability of agents both to himself and to the Commissioner's office.

In December he delivered the first of three annual addresses to the Legislature. It opened with pointed remarks about the Civil War, referring to the Confederates as murdering, plundering traitors. The Territory, he claimed, was engaged in a border war of its own against wandering Indians. The Governor blamed military officers as well as Indian agents for their inability to pacify the tribes. Yet, he advocated swift and deliberate reprisals against any Indians who attacked Whites, adding that he hoped such action would soon become the official policy of the United States.

Edmunds courted friendly relations with legislators and became successful at the reform of electoral, fiscal, and educational conditions. He called for a law making it a crime to tamper with ballot boxes and proposed changing the date of territorial elections from September to October. The Governor also urged the creation of a territorial school superintendency, an immigration commission, and a congressional memorial for land and rail routes across Dakota. The Legislature responded with laws in every instance.

Despite his rapport with the legislators as well as the general White population, Edmunds took severe verbal abuse from the editors of the newly-formed *Dakota Weekly Union*. In an article entitled "Territorial Misfortunes", the Democratic tabloid said that Edmunds was better than Jayne but not as good as a governor should be. A newsman insisted that the two had "always joined their efforts in sustaining . . . shameless frauds upon the people," citing in particular Edmunds's support of Jayne in the corrupt election of 1862. They further charged that Edmunds had "always chosen to associate with young and imprudent converts to that faith."[3]

The Governor responded in a letter to the rival newspaper, *The Dakotian*. He had never been involved in any misrepresentation in this or any other territory. As for working with young, imprudent men, he said the youngest man with whom he associated was the senior editor of the critical *Union*, Moses K. Armstrong. Caustically, he declared that he knew Armstrong to be a "warm and earnest sympathizer with the Confederacy."[4] That must have been what his critic thought to be imprudent, for Edmunds's only direct affiliation with Democrats or contact with persons suspected of Confederate affiliations came through his association with the very persons who charged him with impropriety. Doubtless, they became antagonists because of Edmunds's support for the cause of President Lincoln and the northern states. He and his critics exchanged diatribes for several weeks until December, 1864, when the two newspapers merged under joint editorship and publicly exonerated Edmunds of any intentional wrongdoing. By that time Congress had made its decision regarding the 1862 election—unseating Jayne, and replacing him with Todd even though there was obvious fraud on both sides.

Having survived this challenge, Governor Edmunds shifted his emphasis at the opening of the next legislative session. Again, he called attention to the Civil War and expressed his hope that an end to bitter fighting was near. Again, he asked legislators to encourage immigration and commerce. In addition, he proposed a tax levy so the people of Dakota might share with federal officials the costs of territorial administration and development. This way, he hoped, officials in Washington, DC, would come to recognize that the Territory was maturing politically in preparation for statehood.

Edmunds also proposed a solution to the Indian problem with the suggestion that he visit President Lincoln and request the creation of a special commission to negotiate a peace with the Sioux. Costly military campaigns had failed. He would pacify tribal members with equitable treaties that would guarantee them food, shelter, and a sedentary occupation. In January, 1865, Edmunds left for Washington with this in mind. Lincoln was favorably disposed to the plan and sent a supportive note to Thaddius Stevens of the U.S. House of Representatives Committee on Indian Affairs. After some debate between congressmen and Interior Department officials, a special diplomatic mission was approved; Lincoln appointed Edmunds to lead a five-man delegation into Sioux Country.

Despite his eagerness to start, Edmunds's initial efforts at organization were thwarted by General John Pope, who refused to lend any military support. The General contended that Sioux people were in a state of war against the United States; therefore, it would not be judicious to permit negotiations within the territorial boundaries except those conducted by military leaders. Edmunds turned to Secretary of the Interior James Harlan for help, only to discover that a conflict over authority already existed between the War and Interior Departments. Dr. Walter A. Burleigh, the former U.S. Agent at Greenwood and recently-elected Delegate to Congress, had released the details of the disagreement between War and Interior Department officials to the press. As an overture to Pope, Secretary Harlan promised to prevent such leaks of information in the future, and reminded the General that Edmunds's treaty commission had been prescribed by Congress and had the force of law. Reluctantly, Pope agreed to support Edmunds, but the General made it clear that he opposed giving annuities to any Sioux at war with the United States.

During the course of subsequent negotiations the Governor exercised patience and compassion; he was firm yet friendly with tribal leaders. The treaties he completed by October of 1865 stated that Indians would permit the construction of roads across their land in return for annuities. Although Congress failed to ratify the documents until March 17, 1866, as soon as tribal leaders affixed their marks in the presence of the delegation Edmunds could announce there was peace in Dakota Territory.

Some historians have argued that the treaties were made with Indians already on friendly terms with Whites and had no impact on the behavior of troublesome groups among the Tetons and Yanktonais. There was some truth in this; compliant chiefs affixed their signatures nearby, while Sitting Bull and his followers continued to harass merchants above the Grand River. Nevertheless, Edmunds's treaties stabilized conditions in the southeastern part of the Territory to the extent of assuring safer transportation and offering relative security to newcomers filing homestead claims east of the Missouri River.

Besides creating a fairly peaceful environment, Edmunds took more direct steps to promote immigration. He corresponded about settlement in Dakota with the Free Homestead Association of Central New York. He supported a similar group from his home town, Ypsilanti, Michigan. In his third legislative address during December, 1865, he called for the establishment of a special commission to advertise the benefits of Dakota for potential immigrants.

All the while, Edmunds labored to persuade the people of Dakota to prove themselves worthy of statehood. His last address to lawmakers proclaimed a need to codify territorial statutes pertaining to such matters as ferry charters, townsite locations, and marriage dissolutions, all of which had been handled poorly through case-by-case legislation. Again, he asked for a tax levy and a resolution to encourage the construction of a rail line across Dakota. Once more, the territorial legislators responded favorably to all of his requests. Unfortunately, by the time they reconvened in 1866 Edmunds had been removed from office by President Andrew Johnson.

Doubtless, his removal came partly as a consequence of his loyalty to the Radical Republicans in Congress and consequent opposition to the political posture of Andrew Johnson, even though he publicly marshaled political support in Dakota Territory for the President. The Governor's removal resulted even more from his loss of accord with the U.S. Delegate to Congress. Walter Burleigh, who had befriended the hapless President, belatedly supported the Governor's agenda, especially in his work on the Indian peace commission. The Delegate's disposition changed, however, when he learned that Edmunds's control of treaty funds denied Burleigh either political or financial benefit from the use of the money. An even greater problem for Burleigh was a federal investigation, which Edmunds helped to facilitate, that alleged the Delegate had mishandled funds when he was the U.S. Agent at Greenwood.

While Governor Edmunds set out in the Summer of 1866 to negotiate a treaty with Indians in Sitting Bull country at Fort Berthold, Burleigh publicly assailed his work on the floor of the U. S. House of Representatives. The Delegate proclaimed that Edmunds's treaties were "not worth the paper they disgraced."[5] Because of such criticism, the Fort Berthold documents were not ratified. Burleigh did not stop there. Reconstruction politics ran rampant in Dakota and he had no trouble convincing President Johnson that Edmunds was an enemy of the administration who should be dismissed. Disregarding the Governor's prior overtures for cooperation, on August 4, 1866, Johnson fired Newton Edmunds and replaced him with Burleigh's father-in-law, Andrew J. Faulk. To make a clean sweep, Burleigh also persuaded Johnson to remove James Edmunds from the office of Commissioner of Public lands.

Unlike his predecessor, Newton Edmunds did not leave the Territory at the end of his tenure as Governor. He chose rather to nurture private interests as he worked on community development at Yankton. In the autumn of 1866, he began farming near the capital city and continued to do so until he entered the banking business eight years later. Edmunds remained active in the civic affairs of Yankton County, especially those pertaining to education. As a member of the district school board, he instigated an increase in the mill levy to support public schools and helped to create a set of regulations. A contemporary regarded him as a "perpetual foe to all those who would waste school lands."[6] Private education, too, took up a good deal of his time. In 1868 Edmunds became a trustee at the local Episcopal school for young children, called Dakota Hall. In 1872 the former Governor served as a founding trustee of Yankton Academy, an arm of the Congregational Church supported by all area denominations. Later, the Academy evolved into Yankton College, the first private institution of higher education in the Territory, and Edmunds presided over its organizational meeting in 1881.

Although dedicated mainly to private life, he could not stand aloof from politics. As a devoted Republican he participated in the Dakota [Ulysses S.] Grant Club and sustained his continuous involvement in party conventions. In 1869, when Yankton held its first election under a new city charter, Edmunds became an alderman. This new position drew him to the center of local politics in time for the bitter campaigns that preceded the general election of 1870.

The struggle in 1870 was over the office of Delegate to Congress. Incumbent Republican Solomon L. Spink opposed Democrat Moses Armstrong. A third candidate, the infamous Walter Burleigh, entered the race, claiming to be the rightful nominee of the Republican Party. Spink had fallen out of the favor with leaders of the old guard because he commanded no appointment privileges in Washington, and could do them no good. Edmunds's involvement began in August of 1870, when as a county party official he called for a "mass convention," which Spink did not want. This caused a pronounced split in party ranks. Ironically, Newton Edmunds supported the very man who had been responsible for his dismissal—Walter Burleigh. Whatever motivated Edmunds to do this, when in September National Republican Party leaders asked for his opinion about who was the bona fide candidate of the party, he declared:

I vote for Dr. Burleigh . . . in order that I place a seal of condemnation upon any man [Spink] who will attempt to disrupt and defeat the Republican party, when he fails to control it.[7]

Final balloting that year brought disappointing results for the Grand Old Party. In Yankton County the Democrats won nearly every contest. Across the Territory Moses Armstrong won the election by a plurality of ninety votes. Edmunds ran for county commissioner and lost. (Later he won appointment to the post when an incumbent resigned.)

The general election of 1872 broadened the schism in Republican ranks. Two jurists, Wilmont W. Brookings and Gideon C. Moody, faced each other for the Republican Party nomination in the congressional race. Newton Edmunds spoke out on behalf of his friend Moody but the electorate sent the Democrat Moses Armstrong back to Washington. Factionalism within their party had cost the Republicans two crucial elections in a row.

During the next several years the chagrined former Governor and his partisan colleagues turned their attention to business development. They worked on the opening of railroad service across the Territory. After the gold rush into the Black Hills started a new flow of immigration, they became involved in West River development. As early as 1864, Governor Edmunds spoke on the need for exploration into the Black Hills for timber and mineral resources he believed were necessary if Dakota Territory were to gain independence from eastern suppliers. He repeated his message for a decade thereafter. In the meantime, federal officials sponsored scientific expeditions into the area. The entry of non-Indians into the Black Hills was expressly forbidden by the 1868 Laramie Treaty, yet prospectors and explorers continued their encroachment in search of gold. Finally, officials in Washington, DC, dispatched a large-scale reconnaissance mission, commanded by the flamboyant Brevet General George A. Custer. His party of soldiers and scientists reported that reliable veins of gold were abundant throughout the area and enticed prospectors to enter in such numbers that it became impossible for federal troops to discourage their illegal entry. President Ulysses Grant implied that military leaders should look the other way while new negotiations were opened to acquire the land from the Sioux.

In 1875 a commission headed by William B. Allison of Iowa attempted to accomplish that goal, but its members met serious opposition from Sioux leaders when they attempted to secure the consent of three-fourths of the adult males of each signatory tribe as the 1868 Treaty required. Because they were unsuccessful in winning the cession of land, the commissioners recommended the federal government unilaterally set a fair price for the land and force the Indians to accept.

By then, Sitting Bull had a force of some 3,000 men under arms to resist. In June of 1876, General Custer attempted to round up the Sioux adversaries and his Seventh Cavalry unit was annihilated. Citizens of Dakota, like people across the nation, were incensed and frightened. With the memory of both Custer's discovery and Custer's defeat fresh in their minds, federal officials soon prepared to send another commission to negotiate for the cession of the Black Hills.

Included in this delegation were former Commissioner of Indian Affairs George Manypenny, Episcopal Bishop Henry Whipple, and ex-Governor Edmunds. According to official instructions given to Chairman Manypenny, they were to convince the Indians to forfeit their claim to lands lying between the 103rd and 104th Meridians and those lying between the north and south forks of the Cheyenne River. In return the federal government would furnish subsistence for western Sioux until they became self-supporting by the White man's standards. Annuities would come to them according to actual need, contingent upon the attendance of Indian children at school. The agreement addressed the possible removal of the Sioux to Indian Territory (Oklahoma), but the latter provision never came to fruition.

Edmunds's role in negotiations was fairly incidental, but he had some influence on proceedings about the possible removal of Sioux people to Oklahoma. On at least two occasions, the former Governor reminded Indian leaders they were not obligated to go; rather they were "simply agreeing to look at it."[8] The plan to move the Sioux out of Dakota failed, not because of Edmunds's words as much as the Indians' dislike for Oklahoma. In addition, congressional delegations from states close to Indian Territory feared trouble because of the reputation of Sioux people as fighters.

Manypenny's Commission succeeded in winning the Black Hills cession as proposed. Federal officials ignored Article Twelve of the Fort Laramie Treaty, which stated that future agreements must come at the consent of three-fourths of all adult males in signatory tribes. This condition, which had stifled the efforts of the Allison Commission, still stood in the way. Manypenny, Whipple, and Edmunds tried to circumvent it as an obstacle by accepting the marks of chiefs and headmen to secure the land, but eastern reformers forced Congress to reject their ruse.

Popular opinion among non-Indians still supported the Commission's effort. The economy of the Black Hills was progressing nicely. The gold rush brought new life to the entire Territory. A cry went out for a corridor of land to connect eastern Dakota with the Black Hills.

Responding in August, 1882, Congress approved yet another commission to negotiate, this time with Newton Edmunds as Chairman. His subordinate commissioners were Peter C. Shannon, one-time territorial justice; and James M. Teller, brother of the Secretary of the Interior. Edmunds took the Episcopal missionary Samuel D. Hinman along to serve as interpreter.

The Edmunds Commission presented Sioux leaders a prepared document that called for the extinguishment of their rights to approximately 11,000,000 acres. Their remaining land was to be divided into tribal reservations. Every family head would take an allotment in severalty containing 320 acres plus the right to select an additional eighty acres for each child under eighteen years of age. Federal authorities would provide a foundation herd of cattle for each tribe and see that educational benefits provided by the Fort Laramie Treaty would remain in force for at least twenty years.

As the negotiators had done in 1876, so did the Edmunds Commission ask that tribal leaders ignore Article Twelve of the 1868 Treaty. Interior Secretary Henry Teller agreed, at first, that the clause was no longer valid, inasmuch as it had been disregarded during previous negotiations. Under congressional pressure he later retracted the opinion and instructed the commissioners to return to the agencies with a request for approval from no less than three-fourths of the adult males.

When agreements from the several agencies were finished for submission to Congress, their approval was blocked by Senator Henry L. Dawes of Massachusetts, who believed they should have laid out a comprehensive plan for the development of farming on the reservations. At length, the U.S. Senate refused to ratify the documents and instead appointed a select committee, chaired by Dawes, to investigate the conditions of the Sioux and Crow tribes.

Dawes and the examiners chastised the Edmunds Commission for its non-compliance with Article Twelve and brought accusations against its members for their support of fraudulent and coercive maneuvers by Interpreter Hinman to obtain enough signatures to satisfy Article Twelve. In rebuttal, Edmunds stated that they had acted in good faith toward both the Indians and the United States Government. His Commission had not been provided enough funding to accomplish all that Dawes demanded. When asked whether the Indians had been told how much land they were giving up, Edmunds stated that tribal leaders did not think in terms of square miles; they were told only that they were surrendering the land between the White and Cheyenne Rivers. Chiefs Red Cloud and Spotted Tail accused the

Commission of deception but, in fairness to Edmunds and his colleagues, it must be said that both leaders were traditional chiefs. As such, they would not knowingly have supported the destruction of tribal rights to any portion of the Great Sioux Reservation. In the end, agreements negotiated by the Edmunds Commission were not ratified and no action was ever taken against Edmunds or the other members for their alleged devious tactics.

Proceedings by the Dawes Committee culminated in the passage of the Indian Allotment Act of 1887, a general law to provide allotments awarded in trust for twenty-five years, while the Native Americans were formally educated and in other ways schooled about the White man's way of life. Upon the completion of that goal, they would receive clear title to their allotted parcels of land together with citizenship in the United States. Two years later some Sioux people began to accept the general application of the Dawes Act. In 1889 they also affixed their marks to a general agreement in accord with Article Twelve of the 1868 Treaty and relinquished the land so coveted by non-Indians west of the Missouri River.

Edmunds devoted most of the eighties to private business, except for the time he gave to the statehood movement. He presided over several organizational meetings and served as a delegate to the 1883 and 1885 constitutional conventions. He was a member of the Territorial Legislature in 1879, but his direct involvement with politics ended there. The former Governor was satisfied with his accomplishments on behalf of southern Dakotans from early territorial times to the pursuit for statehood.

Serving as an elder statesman after statehood, in 1894 he cautioned the businessmen and politicians of South Dakota according to conventional conservativism. They should stay clear of the upstart Populist Movement, which he feared would "ruin the credit of the people of this state."[9] That appears to have been his last statement on public affairs. Although Edmunds lived in Yankton until his death in 1908, he remained quiet about issues; those he left to a younger generation.

The bank he founded in the seventies grew under his management into the Yankton National Bank, chartered in 1891. To house his expanding business, in 1892 he built a fine quartzite building, which remains in downtown Yankton as a lasting tribute to his many contributions.

Only a few men served as bona fide leaders in the fledgling Territory on its path to statehood. Most effective were those of older American stock from New York, New England, or the former Northwest Territory. Some nurtured business careers in southeastern Dakota and represented economic interests throughout territorial years. They were mainly Republican and Protestant. As experienced pioneers they retained control of political machinery and economic development with relative ease. Their prominence was sustained by geographic isolation in a society that grew mainly due to the arrival of new immigrants from abroad, who were as politically naive as they were socially compliant. Newton Edmunds was typical among the handful of leaders who supplied political and economic direction.

The image he projected was representative of the era. He was a beneficiary of nepotism who came to the Territory in an arrangement that was fairly common throughout the nineteenth century. Edmunds became embroiled in the kinds of factionalism and partisan politics that were characteristic to territorial life. In an effort to refine the society of Dakota and make it productive, he became involved in negotiations with Indian people. Although he was fair-minded in this endeavor, he was an apostle of late nineteenth century Indian policy, which required thoroughgoing acculturation and Christianization among Indians. Judged by the standards of his time, he was inordinately honest and unselfish. Edmunds dedicated himself to administration, legislation, extinguishment of Indian claim to land, encouragement of White immigration, promotion of business activity, educational growth, and statehood. No territorial resident contributed more to the transition of frontier life on the northern prairie and Great Plains than did Newton Edmunds.

Notes

1. Herbert S. Schell, *History of South Dakota* (3rd ed., rev.; Lincoln: University of Nebraska Press, 1975), pp. 105–106.
2. Newton Edmunds to William P. Dole, November 23, 1963, Letters of the Office of Indian Affairs (1824–1881), Dakota Superintendencey (1861–1867), Microfilm Reel No. 250.
3. *Dakota Weekly Union* (Yankton, D. T.), June 28, 1864.
4. *The Dakotian* (Yankton, D. T.), July 2, 1864.
5. *The Union and Dakotaian* (Yankton, D. T.), July 7, 1866.
6. Rev. Joseph Ward, "Governor Newton Edmunds," *The Monthly South Dakotan*, I (1898), p. 11.
7. *The Union and Dakotaian*, September 29, 1870.
8. 44 Cong., 2 Sess., *U.S. Senate Executive Documents*, No. 9 (Serial 1718),

"Message of the President on the Proceedings of the Commission Appointed to Obtain Certain Concessions from the Sioux Indians," December 26, 1876, pp. 68, 83.

9. *Yankton* (South Dakota) *Press and Dakotan,* October 24, 1894.

Spotted Tail.
Courtesy W.H. Over State Museum.

Spotted Tail, wife and daughter.
Courtesy W.H. Over State Museum.

Sitting Bull.
Courtesy W.H. Over State Museum.

Sitting Bull and wife.
Courtesy W.H. Over State Museum.

Slim Buttes captives.
Courtesy W.H. Over State Museum.

Sioux Response to Non-Indian Intrusion: Sitting Bull, Spotted Tail, and Crazy Horse

Richmond L. Clow

Sitting Bull (*Tatanka Iyotanka*, a Hunkpapa) and Spotted Tail (*Sinte Gleska*, an Upper Brule) were prominent among the leaders of western Sioux tribes responsible for relations with non-Indians during the crucial period following the American Civil War. Both resisted White intrusions into tribal land or infringements on Indian culture. Each had a unique tactic of resistance. Each had a different perception of leadership.

Sitting Bull attained the greater fame of the two, especially because of his involvement in the defeat of Brevet General George Armstrong Custer at the Little Big Horn in 1876. Some of the recognition was based more on myth than reality. After the demise of Custer, there were reports that Sitting Bull had been trained at West Point and that he had received formal education in Montreal. Only in this way could citizens of the United States accept the defeat of the legendary Custer by an Indian. None could have been more surprised by the rumor than Sitting Bull himself, for these and other reports in circulation bore no similarity whatever to the roles he played on behalf of his own society.

Spotted Tail was the victim of similar distortions. Because he was recognized often as the spokesman for western Sioux people most friendly to White people, many federal officials and other non-Indians dealt with him as though he represented all Teton people in their dealings with Whites. This image must have struck Spotted Tail as a grave distortion, for it bore little similarity to characteristics of leadership allowed by tribal ways.

To some degree both men were the victims of distorted images because of their success. Frank B. Fiske, a long time resident of Standing Rock Indian Reservation, wrote of Sitting Bull that "the higher" a Sioux man goes, "the more enemies he has—enemies among those who would dethrone" him and "usurp his glory."[1] Fiske might have said the same about Spotted Tail. The more prestige each man enjoyed the more envious were the adversaries they faced in their own communities, and both were eventually killed by members of their tribes.

Both Sitting Bull and Spotted Tail aspired to leadership as young men, but they followed very different avenues to power. Their options included the demonstration of special qualities in hunting and soldiering, or in spiritual leadership, plus open displays of generosity, including the gift of personal possessions to others during public events. "Each [of these actions] was a step on the way toward acquiring and maintaining status."[2] Ordinarily, hereditary leaders attained the highest rank. Because both men came from families of modest station, each had to rise almost exclusively through his own accomplishments.

Spotted Tail was the older of the two. Born in 1823 or 1824, he lived most of his early years in the area around the Platte River of western Nebraska. Sitting Bull was born approximately seven years later and spent nearly all of his life in the vicinity of the Grand River. The two never met but were ever aware of each other. Each respected the other because they had such similar experiences. As a young soldier, Sitting Bull fought to prevent infringement by the Crow on Hunkpapa land west of the Grand River. Spotted Tail battled the Pawnee along the southern edge of Sioux Country. For their military feats, both earned the highest honors. Spotted Tail became a warshirt-wearer and the head soldier of his camp; Sitting Bull became a sash-wearer and leader of the Strong Hearts military society in his tribe. Accordingly, as young men, both were honored as prominent soldiers.

Inevitably, the intrusion of White people into Sioux Country shaped the attitude of each man toward leadership. Eventually, Spotted Tail opted for diplomacy as the means of dealing with non-Indians. Sitting Bull assembled warriors and ridiculed any Indian who shrank from resistance with arms. Spotted Tail was at hand to encounter non-Indians who traveled up the Oregon and Mormon Trails of western Nebraska. Sitting Bull faced a similar challenge along the upper Missouri River where non-Indians appeared sporadically at first to engage in trade or to deliver the annuities due western Sioux people under treaty terms.

For Spotted Tail, the crisis in Indian-White relations began during the summer of 1854, when Brules destroyed U.S. Army Lieutenant John Gratten's command east of Fort Laramie. General William S. Harney commanded a punitive expedition during 1855 to make overland travel safer for non-Indians and to force western Sioux people to abide by peace terms they had accepted in the Fort Laramie Treaty of 1851. Harney's unit defeated Little Thunder's Brules on September 3 at Blue Water, a few miles north of Ash Hollow. White soldiers killed eighty-five Sioux and took seventy women and children prisoner. This was the first direct assault of a U.S. military force against any Sioux tribe. Harney threatened harsh retribution for subsequent resistance to the advance of the non-Indian frontier.

Following the Blue Water incident, Harney pursued the Brules and forced them to accept peace on his terms. They would surrender the ones who had killed several White men on a mail coach late in the fall of 1854. Spotted Tail was one of the three given up to Harney, and due to his involvement he suffered imprisonment at Fort Leavenworth for nearly a year. At the Fort, Spotted Tail obtained first-hand knowledge of U.S. military strength, which convinced him the Sioux could never win a general war against regular blue coats. As a result he changed his tactics to advocate non-violent resistance through diplomacy. Because of his subsequent demonstration of selflessness and his concern for the welfare and safety of Sioux people more than for his own image as a soldier, he gained stature and prestige. An increasing number of Indians who agreed with his belief that accommodation was preferable to war became his followers. Federal officials in charge of tribal relations along the upper Missouri River basin came to regard him as the head chief of all western Sioux. After his release from Fort Leavenworth, Spotted Tail began to use that recognition as a base of influence. For him it seemed best to deal with federal officials through oration and compromise, because these tactics would insure the survival of the Sioux. He continued to support military action wherever the lives of Indian people were threatened. For example, he participated in an inter-tribal alliance during December, 1864, when the Brules thought it necessary as a means of resisting White aggression. His usual stance, however, was insistence that diplomacy was better than war.

After the signing of the Fort Laramie Treaty of 1868, which was a diplomatic victory for western Sioux people, an ever increasing number of Brules came to accept Spotted Tail's strategy. There were critics, to be sure, who questioned his courage, but his active participation in a battle with Pawnees was ample evidence to the contrary. In 1873 some Brules and Oglalas hunting buffalo in southwestern Nebraska postponed the chase for an attack on a party of Pawnees engaged in a summer hunt, and Spotted Tail's men killed fifty-three men and women. Spotted Tail did not shrink from his responsibility as a military leader, yet he reaffirmed the reputation he held as a soldier who was prone to negotiate whenever possible. This was the hallmark of his public image to the end of his life.

Meanwhile, Sitting Bull was consistent in his reaction to intrusions by Whites. Without exception he wanted no change in Sioux culture and insisted that all non-Indians except those who entered to deliver trade or annuity goods remain outside of Sioux Country. Against all others he took up arms. His was a patriotic stand that "inevitably" led "to a clash and the subjugation of his people in the end."[3]

Sitting Bull went into action after the Minnesota Sioux War of 1862, when White volunteers pursued eastern Sioux refugees across Dakota Territory. Brigadier General Henry H. Sibley commanded a Dakota campaign that attacked a Hunkpapa hunting party which included Sitting Bull. Neither side hurt the other. In the summer of 1864 Brigadier General Alfred Sully came to the northern Great Plains and tried to track down eastern Sioux seeking refuge with Tetons. The General met a large group at Killdeer Mountain, where he forced the retreat of the Sioux and destroyed the provisions they left behind.

According to Stanley Vestal, Sitting Bull's biographer, neither Sibley nor Sully made much of an impression on Sitting Bull. He thought that White soldiers lacked humanity because they left their wounded on the battlefield, and they "do not know how to fight."[4] As these early confrontations ended and Red Cloud's War began on the Powder River, Sitting Bull remained steady in his determination to fight.

The difference between Sitting Bull and Spotted Tail became apparent in 1866 and 1867 and even more obvious during the signing of the Fort Laramie Treaty of 1868. Red Cloud, the Oglala, had directed Sioux military operations successfully to force the closure of the Bozeman Trail from Fort Laramie to central Montana and the abandonment of Forts Reno, F. C. Smith, and Phil Kearny. Because the warfare occurred in Oglala Country, Red Cloud's War had no direct effect on either Spotted Tail or Sitting Bull. Yet Spotted Tail advised Red Cloud that "quietness" was the best approach. Southern Brules wanted peace on their lands east of Fort Laramie and, as their representative,

Spotted Tail signed an unworkable treaty in 1866. When a new peace commission appeared at Fort Laramie during the spring of 1868, Spotted Tail signed again.

Sitting Bull refused to attend negotiations at Fort Laramie or any other place, even though his followers were not participants in Red Cloud's War and had experienced no catastrophe. Father Pierre Jean DeSmet traveled on behalf of the United States to the Hunkpapa's camp and asked him to declare his support of peace but Sitting Bull refused: "I use the tomahawk in hand, and I have done all the hurt to the Whites I could."[5] Only Gall and Bull Owl, of the Hunkpapa's northern camp, went to Fort Rice to sign the 1868 Treaty. Sitting Bull characterized their signing as an act of surrender and portrayed any Sioux leader who endorsed a treaty as a fool. This included his Hunkpapa contemporary Running Antelope, who commanded great respect in the tribe. While "modesty and reserve was the essence of fortitude" in some instances, he thought they had no virtue when a fight seemed in order.[6]

By refusing to sign the 1868 Treaty, Sitting Bull placed himself in a position of leadership for all western Sioux and some Yanktonais who favored military action against Whites. The dislike of non-Indians, coupled with Sitting Bull's natural leadership skills, made him a central figure in the combative war element that refused to enter the Indian agencies then under development. For this, many non-Indian contemporaries and authors grew to admire Sitting Bull. For example, Colonel Nelson A. Miles, the commander who later pursued him into Canada after the Battle of the Little Big Horn, described him as the perfect Indian because he represented the antithesis of "civilization." Miles even admired Sitting Bull for his shrewd and cunning attacks on White settlements.

Sitting Bull's popularity among western Sioux reached a high point during the months of turmoil prior to the Battle of the Little Big Horn. Gradually, his followers came to realize, however, that Sitting Bull's way could not prevail. Yet, after the victory of his army over Custer, when his followers began to fall away, the White man's fascination with Sitting Bull continued to grow. A newspaper reporter told him that "The white man admires your conduct in battle. You showed yourself to be a great chief in the Custer fight."[7] To outsiders like this, "wild" Indians evinced more admiration than did "tame" Indians. Later Sitting Bull responded by traveling with Buffalo Bill's Wild West Show to play the role of a "wild" Indian, and since that time he has retained an image in non-Indian literature as the most dedicated Sioux war leader of the nineteenth century.

From 1868 to 1877 Sitting Bull and Spotted Tail endured crucial years that required the most consummate leadership. Both wanted to preserve Sioux culture and protect tribal members. Each refined a separate strategy to accomplish these goals. In the role of a leader, Spotted Tail had the advantage over Sitting Bull. The Hunkpapa's unwavering commitment to resistance with arms left no room for compromise. The Brule pressed for a non-military solution with concessions. Spotted Tail's flexibility created options. Sitting Bull's rigidity forced confrontation.

In dialogue, Spotted Tail sparred with civil officials from Washington, DC, who came to his agency to carry out the federal policy on assimilation. The interlopers lacked a military force to back their orders and relied on their abilities of persuasion. This placed them at a disadvantage, for they could not match the diplomatic skills of Spotted Tail. Without the Brule leader's cooperation, nothing went as they planned, not even the geographic location of an agency site for Brule people. Spotted Tail refused to accept a permanent agency as he bought valuable time to allow a gradual transition to reservation life. He understood that the buffalo were depleted in Brule Country and that all Sioux people would soon become dependent on annuities for their survival. The influence of his strategy extended beyond the Brule and by that time blended well with the similar posture of Red Cloud.

Spotted Tail was by no means compliant. When, for example, he visited Richard Henry Pratt's Carlisle Indian School in Pennsylvania in 1880, he complained about living conditions and a school curriculum designed to teach manual labor. Spotted Tail removed seven children who were related to him and left no doubt about his rejection of off-reservation educational tactics.

At agency headquarters, he managed to control federal officials sent out to control him. Meanwhile, Sitting Bull turned his back on representatives of the United States almost entirely. In this he was successful as long as there were buffalo grazing and other game animals in numbers sufficient to support his following on the northern Great Plains. H. L. Clifford, a school principal at Fort Berthold Agency, wrote in 1871 that "Sitting Bull . . . declares that he will never give his hand in friendship to the whites."[8] Sitting Bull's posture led to a decade of war. As his followers resisted with arms, Spotted Tail attempted to make peace through negotiation. In these stressful years, each man experienced some success and some failure. Sitting Bull played a major role in the defeat of Custer's command at the Little Big Horn, then moved into Canada for safety. Spotted Tail emerged as a peaceable ambassador, helped to negotiate Crazy Horse's surrender, then agreed to cede lands in exchange for materials to assure Sioux survival. In the end the Brule leader's way prevailed as Sioux people moved onto the reservations. By doing so, they abandoned Sitting Bull's counsel. Even Sitting Bull came back from Canada to surrender and live near the Agency at Fort Yates.

Reservation life was cruel to both men. Uncertainty and confusion fostered factionalism and jealousy around them. Rivals grew bold as the two leaders came under federal control. In August, 1881, Crow Dog, a Brule traditionalist, murdered Spotted Tail. Nine years later at an isolated cabin near his birth place on the Grand River, tribal policemen assassinated Sitting Bull.

In retrospect, the image of each leader has remained highly controversial. Obviously, Spotted Tail gained ever increasing support from western Sioux people for his peaceable posture as Sitting Bull saw his following slip away. The Brule leader had the more realistic solution to the confrontation between White people and Indians on the northern Great Plains and tribal members demonstrated recognition for it by their acceptance of reservation life. Sitting Bull manifestly stood by a credo of segregation that could not work in the long run. The Hunkpapa leader saw a multitude dwindle to the few dozen who came back with him from Canada to surrender. He could do no more than encourage resistance to acculturation tactics and stop the further surrender of land following his return to the Grand River in 1881.

Over the past century the images of these two leaders have changed. Non-Indians have come to view Spotted Tail as an uncourageous and indecisive leader, while an increasing body of Sioux has grown to blame him for his capitulation without a fight. Conversely, White people have gained admiration for Sitting Bull as the prototypical Great Plains Indian leader and Sioux people have honored him for steady devotion to the cause of racial separation and cultural survival. Neither has deserved discredit. Both have merited respect for their divergent approaches to circumstances through which Sioux people were inevitably to suffer extreme loss and change.

The image of Crazy Horse, an Oglala, as a dedicated front line military leader, has never been a subject of much controversy among either Indians or Whites. Only the circumstances surrounding his death have caused dispute. After standing his ground through the Great Sioux War of the mid-1870s, he suffered death and left a legacy of sterling commitment and unbending courage. Few have ever blamed him for his behavior during his last days, which began in early May, 1877, when he gave Lieutenant William P. Clark his three Winchesters and "declared that he had made peace for all time" and relinquished the fight that had made him famous.[9] He Dog, Little Big Man, and Little Hawk followed Crazy Horse, and in their wake filed nine hundred men, women, and children. The war was over and the moment was not lost on federal troops, especially on those who commanded components of the U.S. Army that had seen Crazy Horse in action.

For many years both settlers and soldiers had been afraid of this quiet and unassuming man. Born in 1840, the year the Sioux "stole one hundred horses," he, like Sitting Bull, became a leader in the cause of keeping western Sioux Country free from White intrusion.[10] Newsmen of the time portrayed him as the leader of an unsurrendering, hostile faction of Sioux. They thought he created more trouble than Sitting Bull—and their view was understandable.

The 1860s offered ample opportunity to this young, ambitious Oglala soldier on the quest for position of military importance. Tribal culture encouraged men to fight for the preservation of traditional ways and rewarded a soldier for his willingness to die for the cause. Such honor in war was attractive to Crazy Horse. Through self-sacrifice in battle, a successful man could gain prestige and possibly preserve the Sioux Nation as it then existed. A man named Chips, also known as Encouraging Bear, was the contemporary of Crazy Horse who summed up his image most succinctly: Sioux people "expected [him] to make war; he was set apart in their minds to make war, and that was his business."[11] The Red Cloud Agency interpreter, William Garnett, on the other hand, characterized Crazy Horse as a man "good for nothing but to be a warrior or to be leading the strenuous life; stealing horses, or something of that kind." Garnett added: "He therefore would have nothing to do with affairs political or social or otherwise—like making treaties," or "moving camp."[12]

In his early twenties Crazy Horse received appointment by Oglala leaders as a *Wicasa*, or shirtwearer. Thereby, he became an official with responsibility for the welfare of the tribe. He was reckless enough to violate that oath of office by attempting to steal No Water's wife, named Black Buffalo Woman. For the moment, greed or love became priorities over honor, and he was censured by the Sioux community around him. No Water retaliated, committing an equally unacceptable act when he shot Crazy Horse in the face at close range. The bullet entered "the side of his nose low down on the right side and coming out at the base of the skull on the back side.''[13] He carried a facial scar as a reminder of his violation of Oglala tradition and that prohibited his rise to civil office. Military rank was the only avenue to recognition or power, and he made the most of it. Eventually, ''The older, more responsible men of the tribe conferred another kind of chieftainship on Crazy Horse. He was made war chief of the whole Oglala tribe.''[14]

The No Water Affair had consequences beyond the indignity of a facial scar. The bullet that tore through his upper jaw and throat also damaged his vocal cords. Contemporaries described his speech pattern as slow. He said little and was forced to rely upon his lieutenants to speak on his behalf. Too, Black Buffalo Woman was a niece of Red Cloud, who belonged to the politically active Bad Face band. Crazy Horse's involvement with No Water led to alienation and discord with Red Cloud, which erupted into political strife during the summer of 1877, shortly before Crazy Horse was killed.

Physically, he did not look like a dashing warrior, but he needed no coaxing to enter a fight. Crazy Horse understood that a Sioux soldier was expected to defeat an enemy in order to protect his community. For this purpose, he fought against the Omaha, Snake, and Crow. These engagements prepared him mentally and physically for the battle that followed against the United States Army.

Intertribal conflicts enabled Crazy Horse to gain prestige in his tribe before White people ever heard of him, but his reputation among Indians was greatly enhanced by the Powder River campaign. He played a subordinate but important role when he led decoys in the Fetterman Massacre. Even then, blue coats did not know him by either sight or name because other Sioux leaders remained in the spotlight. At the time, notoriety went mainly to Red Cloud, but gradually recognition shifted to Crazy Horse, as well as to Sitting Bull, for their open recalcitrance. From the 1868 Treaty negotiations onward Crazy Horse was identified as much a leader of Indian people who rejected negotiations from the southern part of Sioux Country west of the Missouri River as was Sitting Bull with those who rejected diplomacy as a solution to White intrusion farther north.

Thereafter, newsmen described Crazy Horse as a ''red devil'' and ''outlaw'' while he grew in prominence as a leader. He and his followers claimed buffalo hunting grounds along the Powder and Yellowstone Rivers. From there, they established contact with Sitting Bull's people and frequently joined forces with them. Early in the 1870s, as the Northern Pacific Railroad edged toward the Northern Great Plains, Sitting Bull threatened resistance by attacks on surveying parties. Crazy Horse joined him. Early in August, 1872, they enticed White soldiers into battle near Pryor Creek, Montana. That day Crazy Horse exhibited bravery to a point of recklessness, which made vivid impressions on Indians and blue coats.

Crazy Horse harassed Northern Pacific military escorts for another year; then, like Sitting Bull, he led no further resistance for nearly three years. In that time the United States Army entered the Black Hills region and ignited the Sioux War of 1876. Rumors of gold in the Black Hills had long existed and George Custer's summer survey of 1874 confirmed the stories. Miners swarmed to the new diggings in violation of the Fort Laramie Treaty of 1868. Their presence forced Sioux people either to side with diplomats such as Spotted Tail and Red Cloud or to join the forces of Sitting Bull and Crazy Horse in the Yellowstone River Country.

The stage was set for further hostilities when federal negotiators failed in their effort to purchase the Black Hills from the Sioux in 1875. Many Indians became disillusioned with the negotiators and fell in behind the war leaders during the early months of 1876. Commissioner of Indian Affairs John Q. Smith made a half-hearted gesture for peace when he summoned the followers of Sitting Bull and Crazy Horse to their agencies. When it became obvious that few would comply, the matter was turned over to the United States Army.

U.S. military leaders responded with the Big Horn and Yellowstone Expeditions. General George Crook, Commander of the Big Horn Expedition, attacked first from Fort Fetterman on the Bozeman Trail in Wyoming Territory. He headed northward on March 1, 1876, toward the Powder River in search of Crazy Horse. Sixteen days later his troops floundered in a springtime blizzard, ran low on rations, and came upon a Cheyenne village that they mistook for one under Crazy Horse. The only Sioux in camp were He Dog and his friends, who were visiting Old Bear and the Northern Cheyenne. Colonel Joseph P. Reynolds attacked but inflicted little damage. For his failure, Crook charged Reynolds with "misbehavior before the enemy."[15]

After the blunder at Powder River, federal troops under Crook regrouped for a summer campaign. Again, the General took command, trudging northward out of southern Wyoming into southern Montana, where he was to join General Alfred Terry and his forces on the Yellowstone Expedition out of Fort Abraham Lincoln. Blue coats on each expedition planned to drive their enemies toward the converging column of the other. Delay by either command could destroy the plan.

Crazy Horse reacted quickly in his first open appearance before a substantial non-Indian force. White soldiers may have been surprised to see that he was a slight man, weighing approximately 140 pounds, who did not look like a military leader at all. He demonstrated a deep perception of reality, however, and used it effectively as the blue coats entered the Powder River valley. Increased military activity in the region forewarned the Sioux that more federal troops were on the way. Experience suggested that U.S. troops preferred a campaign in the warm summer months. Crazy Horse was sure that more would appear and cautioned his Oglalas to keep watch.

Hunters returned to his camp along the Little Big Horn on June 16, and informed him that General Crook had entered the valley of the Rosebud to the west. Crazy Horse went on the offensive. Early the following day, Crook's column stopped. After the men unbridled their horses, the Sioux opened fire from the tops of the bluffs. Rough terrain on the slopes, plus the skill of Crow and Shoshone scouts with the U.S. Army, prevented a victory for either side. The men exchanged volleys of rifle fire for hours until the Sioux left the battlefield, but not in retreat. Crook's losses were slight, but the battle forced him to delay his rendezvous with Terry. That hesitation blemished Crook's reputation as an Indian fighter, because, in the delay, George Custer met his demise. By contrast, Crazy Horse emerged a victor, for he had retarded the progress of Crook's column. To Crazy Horse, the price of success was high. Nearly one hundred wounded Sioux returned to their relatives at the Red Cloud agency to recuperate, and eighty-six others died.

Crook's indecision gave time to the Sioux. They regrouped, knowing that there were White soldiers on Rosebud Creek to the west, and that Terry was coming from the east. Reno's charge against their camp at the Little Big Horn on June 25th caught them off guard. For instance, Red Horse, a Minneconjou, was off digging wild turnips with several women when the attack began. Fortunately for the Sioux, Reno's retreat enabled them to counterattack; at a crucial moment, Crazy Horse assumed control of Indians in disarray. He rode in front, commanding them to wait for the right moment to fire. Their unfortunate quarry comprised the remaining companies of Custer's command. When they moved into a vulnerable position, Crazy Horse ordered the attack and wiped them out. Sioux losses at the Little Big Horn were considerable, too. One estimate, based upon the numbers of mourning families at Red Cloud Agency, indicated that 280 Indians died in the fight.

The rest left quickly, with U.S. Army forces in pursuit. Eagle Shield described the tactics the Sioux employed to elude the blue coats for the next two months: "when the trail became too large," the Indians "would scatter to hide it [by burning the grass], and come together again at some previously appointed place."[16] The Sioux moved east that summer and, after scattering to conceal their location, the small groups converged at a new camp west of Slim Buttes.

In early September, Crazy Horse and Crook met again. Terry had disbanded his column, believing the Sioux had dispersed. Crook lost their trail but headed for the Black Hills. At Slim Buttes, a prominent rock formation three days' march north of Deadwood, his men attacked and captured American Horse's village group. After a day of heavy fire, during which reinforcements from Crazy Horse's camp joined the fray, U.S. troops repulsed a counterattack that inflicted heavy casualties.

Crook made up for his blunder on the Rosebud with success at Slim Buttes and pushed on with the search for Crazy Horse in the Black Hills. After his column passed Crazy Horse's hidden encampment, the Oglala retraced his trail west to the Powder River and during the next several months moved his village site from the Powder to the Yellowstone River. From there he moved to the valley of the Tongue and traveled southward until winter set in. As Crazy Horse changed positions, Northern Cheyennes joined his group.

Colonel Nelson Miles, Commander of the winter Powder River Expedition, ordered the continuation of war. It resumed on January 1, 1877, when Colonel Miles skirmished with Crazy Horse's men. Exchanges of fire continued on January 3. Five days later, Miles mounted an assault on Crazy Horse's encampment in the valley of the Tongue, slightly above Hanging Women's Creek. After a five hour engagement, Miles' troopers drove the Sioux through the Wolf Mountains toward the Little Big Horn Mountains. That battle, more than any other, broke the strength of Crazy Horse's military unit.

While Miles savored the victory, others tried to make peace with Crazy Horse. George Sword, an Oglala from Red Cloud Agency, went on behalf of federal officers at Fort Robinson to Crazy Horse's camp to open negotiations. Sword carried a bag of tobacco as a present. If Crazy Horse accepted his gift, he would acknowledge agreement to Sword's proposition. If he did not accept the present, he would not accede to the overture. Crazy Horse took the tobacco and his military career ended as the peace negotiations began.

The Oglala war leader now found himself in deliberations over the future of those who had followed him for many years. His prestige among Sioux people was unshaken. U.S. Army officers around him voiced great respect for his military skills. War honors brought him fame among Indians even though chaotic times brought internal division in Oglala and Brule communities.

His surrender in early May, 1877, at Fort Robinson, intensified discord at Red Cloud Agency. Four factions were identified by the names of the leaders they followed: Red Cloud, Little Wound, No Water, and Crazy Horse. Red Cloud and his Bad Faces were the most partisan and hence made up the most dangerous group. Crazy Horse had run afoul of both Red Cloud and No Water in the Black Buffalo Woman affair years before and now Crazy Horse was in his adversaries' encampments. Jealous detractors were determined to end his popularity and force his submission to agency life.

Crazy Horse had shunned diplomacy throughout his life, thinking a man skilled in diplomacy to be smooth in deception. Anyway, oration was a prerequisite for a diplomat and Crazy Horse had a speech impediment. Therefore, he conveyed through limited speech and forceful action what he intended, and seldom did anyone fail to get his message. A correspondent for the *New York Tribune* said Crazy Horse's "morals had so stiff an edge that he never permitted himself to gain any personal advantage from his power."[17] Indeed, even Crazy Horse's surrender bespoke his honor. From the day he met George Sword until his death, he never broke the vow to remain at peace and he compelled individuals with him to abide by that commitment.

Crazy Horse was in no way compliant. At the Agency, he called Indians to the first sun dance of the season in June of 1877 and, after a lodge was built, the Sioux participants began a mock war to "shoot both the image of the man and the image of the buffalo."[18] Crazy Horse's followers played the role of victors from the Little Big Horn, and the visiting Red Cloud and Spotted Tail followers impersonated the losers. In the frenzy the hosts landed such blows to their guests as to drive them from the dance grounds. For its symbolic intent the sun dance episode widened the rift between the Red Cloud and Crazy Horse people.

Red Cloud Agency and nearby Fort Robinson seemed almost serene to outsiders. In fact the Commander, Colonel Luther Bradley, said it was "as quiet as a Yankee village on Sunday."[19] Yet, there was evidence of impending crisis beneath the surface. Feasts followed the sun dance. Crazy Horse asked Lieutenant William Clark to attend the events. Clark assumed that Crazy Horse was only being social. That was true to a point but the central goal in these events was to gain political leverage over rivals with support from outsiders.

James Irwin, the new Agent for the Red Cloud Agency, scheduled a council in August of 1877. Such an official meeting was occasion for a large feast and honors went to Crazy Horse. Red Cloud people protested, claiming the young Oglala was a new resident who should defer the honor to Red Cloud.

In anger, Crazy Horse's adversaries spread false stories to destroy his influence with federal officers, resident Indians, and agency officials. At the approach of September, intrigue in the tribe entered a new phase. Innocently, Army officers began to enlist Oglalas to fight the Nez Perce. Frank Grouard, the interpreter, deliberately misconstrued Crazy Horse's refusal. The Oglala leader declined to attack Chief Joseph's people because the request contradicted his commitment to peace. Instead of telling the truth, Grouard informed his superiors that Crazy Horse wanted to continue his war against Whites. Grouard's comments charged the atmosphere at Fort Robinson and made the blue coats leery of Crazy Horse.

Deception continued. There was a plan for Crazy Horse to travel to Washington, DC, for a visit with the President. A rumor spread through the Indian camp that the trip was a diversion by federal officials who intended to confine Crazy Horse in an eastern prison. Indians protested, and General Crook returned to take charge. Women's Dress, a Red Cloud follower, informed Crook that Crazy Horse planned his assassination. The Commander ordered the arrest of Crazy Horse on September 2nd. Word of Crook's order leaked. Crazy Horse immediately left for the Spotted Tail Agency as though he were on the run. In truth, Crazy Horse left Fort Robinson for Spotted Tail's community because the camp of the Brule leader had the reputation of being peaceful.

Crook's decision to arrest Crazy Horse encouraged the Oglala leader's Indian adversaries. Lieutenant Jesse Lee, Acting Agent at the Spotted Tail Agency, and Louis Bordeaux, Agency Interpreter, brought Crazy Horse back to Fort Robinson and turned him over to the Officer of the Day, who took him to the guardhouse. Crazy Horse resisted. In a scuffle, a guard bayonetted him while Little Big Man, who was part of the maneuver, held Crazy Horse.

He died later that night. On his deathbed, he blamed the Oglalas, especially Little Big Man, not the blue coats, for the conspiracy that brought him down. Lakota historians depicted his slaying on their winter counts.

Because the legacy of Crazy Horse must be seen through oral tradition, sighting reports, and opinions scattered through military documents and popular reports, it is less distinct than that of most other prominent Sioux leaders of post-Civil War times. Obviously, he made a mark on history, like that of Sitting Bull, through resistance to White intrusion with arms. His presence as a military tactician was at times an impediment to the U.S. Army and always a threat. Like other leaders he died a violent death that resulted from the actions of his Indian opponents as much as through the behavior of federal officers.

The modern Sioux describe him as a man of stature in spiritual affairs. Many western Sioux have attributed the founding of the Yuwipi among Tetons to him and to Chips. His bequests in both spiritual and military leadership are distinct and abiding.

Notes

1. Frank Bennett Fiske, *Life and Death of Sitting Bull* (Fort Yates, ND: Pioneer-Arrow Print, 1933), p. 10.

2. Royal C. Hassrick, *The Sioux: Life and Customs of a Warrior Society* (Norman: University of Oklahoma Press, 1982), p. 15.

3. Usher L. Burdick, *The Last Days of Sitting Bull: Sioux Medicine Chief* (Baltimore: Wirth Brothers, 1941), p. 15.

4. Stanley Vestal, *Sitting Bull: Champion of the Sioux* (Norman: University of Oklahoma Press, 1957), p. 61.

5. Hiram Martin Chittenden and Alfred Talbot Richardson, eds., *Life, Letters and Travels of Father Pierre-Jean DeSmet, S. J. 1801–1873* (4 vols.; New York: Frances F. Harper, 1905), III, p. 912.

6. Hassrick, *The Sioux,* p. 36.

7. "A Talk with Sitting Bull," *New York Times,* August 7, 1881.

8. H. L. Clifford to E. S. Parker, March 10, 1871, George H. Bingenheimer Collection, State Historical Society of North Dakota, Bismark.

9. "The Trouble with the Indians," *New York Times,* September 7, 1877.

10. Personal interview with Chips (Encouraging Bear) by Eli S. Ricker, February 14, 1907, Tablet 18, Ricker Collection, Nebraska State Historical Society, Lincoln.

11. *Ibid.*

12. Personal interview with William Garnett by Eli S. Ricker, January 15, 1907, Tablet 1, Ricker Collection.

13. Personal interview with Chips by Eli S. Ricker, February 14, 1907, Tablet 18, Ricker Collection.

14. Personal interview with He Dog by Eleanor Hinman, published in

"Oglala Sources on the Life of Crazy Horse," *Nebraska History,* LVII (1976), p. 13.

15. Martin Schmitt, *General George Crook: His Autobiography* (Norman: University of Oklahoma Press, 1960), p. 192.

16. W. H. Wood to Assistant Adjutant General, Department of the Dakota, February 19, 1877, The Sioux War Papers, File 4163, Records of the Adjutant General, RG 94, National Archives.

17. "The Rebellious Sioux," *New York Daily Tribune,* September 7, 1877.

18. James K. Walker, *Lakota Belief and Ritual* (Raymond J. DeMallie and Elaine A. Jahner, eds.; Lincoln: University of Nebraska Press, 1980), p. 172.

19. Luther Bradley to George Crook, July 16, 1877, Letters Received, Division of the Missouri, Records of the Adjutant General, RG 94, National Archives.

Annie Tallent.
Courtesy South Dakota State Historical
Society.

Miners camp near Deadwood (1876)
photographed by Stanley J. Morrow.
Courtesy W.H. Over State Museum.

Army in camp on French Creek photographed by Stanley J. Morrow.
Courtesy W.H. Over State Museum.

*Deadwood (1876) photographed by
Stanley J. Morrow.
Courtesy W.H. Over State Museum.*

*Crook City (1876) photographed by Stanley J. Morrow.
Courtesy W.H. Over State Museum.*

Portrait of a Black Hills Boomer:
Annie D. Tallent

Lesta Van Der Wert Turchen

"Still chasing the illusive phantom," still reaching out after more than two decades for "that delusive 'will-o'-the-wisp'," Annie Tallent never regretted being among the "trespassers and outlaws" who entered the Great Sioux Reservation in 1874. "Ignoring the ethical side," she "turned over to the moralist and political economist" for discussion the issue: "should such treaties as tend to arrest the advance of civilization, and retard the development of the rich resources of our country, ever have been entered into?" Extolling the "spirit of adventure and aggression . . . abroad in the land," Annie helped extinguish "the campfires of the red man" and open the Black Hills to pioneers who would "advance the interests and add to the wealth of our whole country."[1]

Annie saw "no truer heroes" than the pioneers who developed the Black Hills. Those in 1874 "marched . . . through the entire length of the hostile Sioux domain into the wilderness, and planted the banner of civilization amid the mountain fastnesses." Those in 1875 blazed new routes "in the teeth of the most active military opposition, and built the first town." Those in 1876 "hewed their way through the most bloodthirsty and warlike of the Indian tribes, built towns, established newspapers, schools, stage lines, banking institutions, telegraph lines, mined gold-dust by the millions, discovered quartz ledges, imported mining machinery." Those in 1877 "ran the gauntlet of as villainous a lot of desperadoes and highway robbers as ever infested a new mining country, and helped to chisel out and lay the first blocks of our present grand superstructure on the foundation already built.'' They ''put their shoulders to the wheel of progress, by risking the investment of large capital, at a time when business enterprises were yet but an experiment; who helped to evolve order out of chaos.''

These Black Hills were far removed from Annie's childhood home on a 170 acre farm near York, New York. Born on April 12, 1827, to Scottish immigrants Donald G. and Margaret (Ferguson) Fraser, Anna Donna was the tenth of eleven children. Their father served as Deacon, Elder, and Trustee in the York Associate Reformed Church. As Scotch Covenanters they did not recognize civil government; refused to serve on juries, hold political office, or vote; kept the Sabbath free from labor; had no musical instruments; and sang only the Psalms. Yet they must have enjoyed life. Annie ''recalled with a thrill of amusement that, more than once did she, with a gay bevy of equally crude and unsophisticated village maidens, take a trip down through the locks of the Genesee Valley Canal, on a towboat, to the metropolis and trade center of Monroe County, to see the Falls, and the 'Elephant'.'' Educated in the Livingston County and Fort Edward schools, she trained as a teacher at Lima Female Seminary in Lima, New York, and taught school for several years. On July 5, 1854, in the Associate Reformed Church, Reverend John Van Eaton performed the marriage ceremony for Annie and David George Tallent, an attorney from Corning, New York. David had been born either in Canada or at sea. Apparently the newlyweds did not return to Corning, as they were not included in the 1855 census. Annie and David might have lived in Elgin, Illinois, where he was a pioneering settler.

Annie's and David's activities remain obscure over the ensuing two decades, but in 1874 their lives intertwined with Black Hills development because of the publicity generated by the Custer Expedition and the Black Hills Mining and Exploring Association of Sioux City, Iowa. Charles Collins, editor of the *Sioux City Times* and active member of the Fenian Movement, headed the Association. While Custer was in the Black Hills, Collins and Thomas Russell, a veteran prospector from the gold fields of Colorado and Montana, opened an office on Clark Street in Chicago. Through private circulars and letters Russell aroused enough interest to keep two clerks busy answering correspondence and personal inquiries. By August 13 they claimed to have enrolled 11,000 men anxious to invade the new Eldorado. An order from the United States Army forced them to close, but approximately 200 individuals received private correspondence. The letters assured success to those who made their intentions known at the *Times* office, and who carried a stake of $300 plus the ability to handle a rifle.

An August meeting in the quarters of the Irish Literary Society at the *Times* building produced a list of fifty men eager to enter the Hills. The newspaper reported a week later that two tents, holding fifty gold seekers each, were pitched on Prospect Hill. Others had hotel accommodations and all were told not to start until Collins and Russell gave the order. On September 10 Collins announced he would go to the Black Hills only with consent from federal officials. His statement camouflaged a gathering of twenty-six men, one woman, and a boy, among whom were experienced miners, lumberjacks, and a freighter. Some may have been with George Custer, who had notified his departmental headquarters on September 2 that "a party who accompanied the Black Hills expedition has started to one of the towns named to act as guide to a company which proposes to start to the Black Hills at an early day."[2]

Strangers for the most part, J. W. Brockett, J. Newton Warren, and M. R. Cordeiro were from Wichita, Kansas; R. H. Bishop from Flint, Michigan; Moses Aaron from San Francisco; Thomas McLaren, Charles Blackwell, and Henry Thomas from St. Louis; John J. Williams from Winfield, Kansas; Harry Cooper from Danville, Illinois; John F. Boyle and David Aken from Richland Center, Wisconsin; James Power, James Dempster, (Black) Dan W. McDonald, B. B. Logan, Angus McDonald, and Lyman Lamb from Eau Claire, Wisconsin; (Red) Dan McDonald from Chippewa Falls, Wisconsin; Thomas Quiner from Rome, Wisconsin; A. F. (Charles) Long from Adel, Iowa; and Thomas H. Russell, R. R. Whitney, Eph Witcher, John Gordon, David G. Tallent, Annie D. Tallent, and Robert Tallent (Annie's son) from Sioux City, Iowa. The party organized into five groups, and the Tallents formed a mess with Blackwell, McLaren, and Thomas.

On October 6, 1874, the expedition pulled out with "O'Neill's Colony" painted in large red letters on the canvas covers of the wagons. Few were misled as the caravan made its way through Nebraska, traveling fifteen to twenty miles a day. The Oakdale *Journal* reported an emigrant party bound not for O'Neill in Holt County but for "the Eldorado of the Northwest. . . . They were resolute, determined looking fellows, and one scarcely knows which to do first— admire their courage or condemn their judgment in this venturing into an Indian country in the present temper of the red men."

At O'Neill, members of the expedition discussed their plans freely with settlers who considered the undertaking foolhardy and "used all their native eloquence in trying to persuade" Annie to turn back. At that stage of the journey they could not tempt her; "but later on, when trouble and misfortune seemed to gather darkly over us, when the pitiless storms of winter overtook us, when sickness and death entered our midst," Annie would have returned to the comforts of home. Facing an uncertain future the party left O'Neill, reached the Niobrara River on October 31, and crossed onto "forbidden ground" on November 2. Henceforth, orders from their leader, John Gordon, were strictly obeyed. Annie later recalled how some men became arbitrary and domineering when vested with a little authority. She also described the entire party as "neither fillibusters, freebooters, nor pirates, but peaceable, law-abiding citizens of the United States . . . with keen eyes to the main chance'."

Annie's account of the journey emphasized events and conditions, especially the food. At the outset, she "protested strongly" against the "abominable stuff" and predicted death from starvation within a month. Soon, however, she developed "a voracious, almost insatiable appetite." Trudging behind the wagon, she would take from the grub box "a great slice of cold bacon and a huge flapjack as large around as the periphery of a man's hat—and a sombrero hat, at that—and devour them without ever flinching or exhibiting the slightest disgust." Although thankful that the men did most of the cooking, she never forgot the elk meat that aroused her "deep-seated, dyed-in-the-wool antipathy to smothered meats of all kinds."

A number in the party got sick, including Annie, who attributed it to "baked beans, hot biscuits, and alkali water." All recovered except Moses Aaron, who succumbed to dysentery. John Williams fashioned a coffin of hewn cottonwood, cribbed the grave like the shaft of a mine, and conducted the burial service from an Odd Fellows Ritual. A simple cross marked the grave on a hill overlooking the Bad River. Annie pondered why a young man "should be cut down . . . while a delicate woman, wholly unused to exposure, or any of the privations and hardships incident to such a journey, should be given strength to endure and overcome all the difficulties of that terrible march."

During a blizzard on December 9 their "feet first pressed Black Hills' soil, at a point about four miles below Sturgis" where a supply train accompanying the Custer expedition left the Hills. The discovery of horseshoes, kernels of corn, and other evidence of non-Indian presence made Annie so "utterly homesick" that she "sought the most convenient log, sat down upon it, and proceeded to shed a torrent of unavailing tears." Expecting Indians "galore," extra guards patrolled the train. Annie recalled magnifying "every bush and shrub along the top of the ridges, into the tufted heads of so many redskins." Following Custer's trail, the party marched in a southerly direction along the Box Elder Valley and across Little Rapid, Castle, Slate, and Spring Creeks through a vast wilderness that proved "one continuous poem."

Reaching a beautiful creek on December 14, the members established camp and began "washing, mending and baking." On December 23 they reached their destination at French Creek. When the train halted, some rushed to find where the miners with Custer had discovered gold. Two hours later Charley Cordero and Bob Tallent discovered a prospect hole about three feet wide, eight feet deep, and eight feet long. Two men lowered themselves down, shoveled out dirt, and washed fifteen cents worth of gold from the first pan. They took off their hats and cheered. Annie joined the celebration "frantically waving my much traveled and weather-beaten hood in genuine sympathy. Eureka! They had found particles of gold in the bottom of each gold pan."

Washing, mending, and making general repairs occupied everyone on Christmas Eve. Knowing "the children's patron saint" would not visit their camp, Annie vainly searched for something suitable to fill a stocking and found only the accustomed fare for Christmas dinner. A week long storm commenced the next day and dumped two feet of snow into the valley. When it ceased, weather as "warm and balmy as a June day" allowed the construction of a permanent shelter. While the men built the Gordon Stockade, Annie stood guard over the camp. She lost only one beautiful red, white, and blue striped tent to fire and one side of bacon to the donkey.

After settling into cabins inside the Stockade, the next step was to communicate with the outside world and stimulate immigration. The day the expedition began, Charlie Collins had exacted a promise from Annie and others to write letters for publication in the *Sioux City Times*. Bearing these and enough gold "to prove its existence in paying quantities, beyond dispute," John Gordon and Eph Witcher left on February 6, 1875, for Sioux City.[3]

In her correspondence, Annie described the journey, confirmed that "gold is here, and in paying quantities," and concluded that "it would give me much pleasure to receive some of the back numbers of your paper, so that we might learn what has been transpiring in the States since we left." David wrote:

We washed out several panfuls and found gold in every trail from the grass roots to the bottom of the prospect hole that had been dug about eight feet deep by the miners with Custer's party. . . . The country is one of the most beautiful I ever saw, although I have traveled from the Gulf of St. Lawrence to the Gulf of Mexico and from the Atlantic to the Pacific. I have never seen a country so full of romantic beauty and at the same time offering such inducements to labor and capital.

Independent of our rich silver mines, our inexhaustible iron deposits and hills of marble and gold quartz, with fertile valleys and rich prairies, the earth of which is mixed with gold at every step. We have inexhaustible forests of the finest pine timber known to the West, in quality rivalling the forests of Northern Wisconsin. We have also one of the finest stock countries west of the Mississippi.[4]

Headlines spread the excitement but alert military leaders overtook Gordon's second expedition near the Keya Paha River. "The party had been surprised at breakfast, the dry wood and boxes dumped against the side of a steep ravine and a fire started. The wagons, loaded with the goods, then were rolled to the edge of the ravine and backed into the fire. The men were made to march on foot back to Fort Randall."[5]

Unaware of Gordon's fate, those who waited in the stockade whiled away their time playing cards, hunting, or prospecting. Most located ranches along French Creek, and all participated in laying out Harney City. A committee of five, B. B. Logan, T. H. Russell, Lyman Lamb, R. R. Whitney, and D. G. Tallent, proposed laws to govern mining interests. On March 6 the group adopted the regulations, designated their site as the Custer Mining District, and elected Angus W. MacDonald recorder for one year. Using a "cheap, thin ledger, 8 x 12 inches, that apparently had earlier use," he recorded thirty-eight claims established between March 15 and April 7.[6]

Annie wandered the hills searching for gold she "expected to find scattered about quite plentifully," but did not. More than once she read Milton's *Paradise Lost* and a funny romance entitled *The English Orphans*. Yet her experience was gloomy. Soon, six men tired of the monotony and left for Fort Laramie. In April, Williams and Red Dan McDonald returned with a contingent of the Second United States Cavalry, commanded by Captain John Mix, to remove the remaining twenty prospectors. After hiding a trunk filled with her belongings, Annie climbed on the government mule provided for her transportation. The cheeky mule did not intimidate her but the masculine saddle on its back did. Although she was not "modeled after the pattern of the 'new woman','' the desire to ride rather than walk through twelve miles of snow overcame her conservative nature.

To Annie's gratification, an ambulance conveyed her from Captain Mix's camp to Fort Laramie but not without incident. At Red Cloud Agency, Indians excited by the "wanton breach of their treaty rights" vented "their entire displeasure" on Annie, who felt she was "the only innocent member of the party." She was in fact as guilty as the men and her presence meant the trespassers intended to remain in the Black Hills. To her great relief, they soon left the Agency. During the march to Fort Laramie, officers and men treated the party with consideration. Every day Captain Mix sent "a carefully prepared lunch" to the Tallent's tent, prompted most likely by Annie's "lean and hungry look."

Ten days of travel to Fort Laramie earned them three days of respite. On parole, they "demanded of Uncle Sam transportation to Cheyenne, as it was nearly 100 miles distant and the country very sparsely settled." Most could have walked there in three days, "but the incentive, the spur, was gone." They "simply sat down on the knee of Uncle Sam and told him his little job was not complete until" they reached Cheyenne. This "he forthwith proceeded to do." Charlie Collins met them enroute with money for their journey to Sioux City. "The help was very timely," as most "were dead broke and a long ways from home."[7] Those returning with Collins disembarked at the Sioux City depot amidst a throng of thousands, listened to the Mayor's welcome, and attended a banquet at Hubbard House.

The Tallents stayed in Cheyenne, ostensibly "awaiting developments in the Sioux problem." Instead, David and others tried to return to the Black Hills. On July 19, they "slipped quietly away at night and headed for the stockade. The soldiers overtook them, arrested them and carried them back. They started again, and were again arrested and carried back. This was repeated the third time; but before getting back to Cheyenne they escaped, and finally reached the Hills in October, 1875."[8]

While strolling along a main street in Cheyenne, Annie and a friend watched the approach of a tall, heavily built man whose sombrero covered shoulder length light brown hair. Except for a mustache curling at each corner of his mouth and a goatee, he might have passed for a Quaker minister. Drawing near, he doffed his sombrero and introduced himself. "My name is Hickoc [sic]. . . . I am called Wild Bill. . . . I suppose you have heard nothing good of me." Annie admitted knowledge of his reputation but added, "perhaps he is not as black as he is painted.'' Begging their pardon for his boldness, Wild Bill inquired about the Black Hills, and remarked that Annie "possessed a good deal of 'sand' to undertake so long and dangerous a journey.'' To their polite replies, he responded "with a gracious bow, that would have done credit to a Chesterfield, passed on down the street out of sight.'' Annie concluded that this "noted desperado . . . was not well up in street etiquette,'' yet "Wild Bill was by no means all bad.'' She neither saw nor heard of him again until a year later, "when the excited cry of 'Wild Bill is shot,' was carried along the main street of Deadwood.''

The years 1875 and 1876 proved eventful. Foreseeing the consequences of a gold discovery, officials in Washington, DC, dispatched a commission to renegotiate the Treaty of 1868 and authorized a scientific expedition led by Walter P. Jenney and Henry Newton to determine the value of the Black Hills. A. F. Long, who had been ejected from the Gordon Stockade, returned with the scientists, as did two newspaper reporters. Thomas C. MacMillan, of the Chicago *Inter-Ocean*, reported that "French Creek resembled more an active rural community in Illinois than a country as yet unopened.'' For despite military patrols, "hordes of gold seekers'' had slipped into the Hills in 1875. General George Crook removed many that August but failure of the commission to reach an agreement with the Sioux prompted their return. At a private conference with U.S. Army leaders in Washington, DC, President Ulysses Grant advised the withdrawal of military opposition. There was a rush of miners and businessmen during the spring of 1876, a year of chaos, disorder, crime, and danger.

In April the Tallents left Cheyenne for the Black Hills with a wagonload of household goods. "Deaf'' Thompson and Sam Gilbert drove two wagons full of merchandise and supplies. After they crossed the Platte River, their party expanded to about ninety members, including the Tallent's former mess partner Charles Blackwell, two women, and twenty-five or thirty wagons. Annie welcomed the added protection but objected to the advance guards shouldering their rifles in such a way as to put her directly in their line of fire. Relocating their wagon to the rear of the train caused her "vocabulary of adjectives in denunciation of the dangerous practice to become exhausted.''

Near the Black Hills, they encountered "outwardbound pilgrims'' whose "bright visions of suddenly acquired wealth had vanished. . . . Bitter maledictions'' did not deter the party from pressing on, "scarcely venturing to look back.'' Annie, "remembering the example of Lot's wife, was determined to take no chances on the possibility of being speedily converted into a 'pillar of salt'.'' After the train emerged from Red Canyon, guards rushed ahead and unleashed a fusillade of shots. Thinking the worst, Annie recanted her "shortcomings and fast-goings" only to find they had been shooting at a deer.

Upon reaching Custer, Annie found that French Creek had been diverted from its natural meanderings into ditches and sluice boxes. A city, where "no human habitation had existed," now boasted hotels, restaurants, stores, sawmills, and saloons. Returning to the Stockade, Annie felt kinship with Rob Roy, the Scottish outlaw, when he exclaimed, "My feet are on my native heath and my name is McGregor." Yet, she found her cabin in ruins and her trunk of belongings gone. According to one account, soon after federal troops escorted the Gordon party from the Hills, news of the abandoned stockade reached the Sioux Agency in Nebraska. White men who had Indian families entered the Hills, "gathered up the stock, wagons and everything that was of any value and took them to their wigwams as trophies."[9] Annie regarded everything taken as "legitimate booty" except the trunk of personal belongings, in which she had placed a cherished gold locket containing the picture of a young woman, "a much beloved classmate." Regret over the loss of her wardrobe ceased, "but the picture never; and woe betide the luckless maid, or fully-matured dame, red or white, who is ever found wearing that cherished locket."

After two weeks of waiting at Custer for something to "turn-up," the Tallents joined miners bound for the northern Hills in response to reports that claims on Deadwood Creek were paying from $100 to $2,000 per day. The exodus left Custer and Hill City nearly uninhabited. Annie arrived at Deadwood on May 22, 1876, and gazed at a conglomeration of log cabins and tents. Even the exodus of the disenchanted had not stopped the influx, and Annie understood why. "The belief in individual luck is so deeply implanted in the heart of every seeker after gold that each expects himself to succeed and every other fellow to fail."

Faced with the choice of living in the wagon, out in the open, or in an unfinished cabin attached to the saloon owned by Captain Jack Crawford, Annie accepted the latter. David transferred their belongings to the small section covered by a roof and joined a stampede to lay out the new townsite of Spearfish. During his absence a thunderstorm drenched Annie, Robert, and all their belongings. The next morning, amidst clouds of steam and wrapped in a bed quilt, Annie had unexpected visitors. Struggling into a half dry garment, she opened the door to Capt. C. V. Gardner and H. N. Gilbert. So delighted to see friendly faces, she "came dangerously near committing the grave indiscretion of falling upon their necks and embracing them then and there." After assessing the miserable scene, Gardner moved Annie and Robert into a small cabin on Williams street where the family lived during the summer of 1876.[10]

Having wasted two weeks in Custer, the Tallents discovered that the entire length of the gulch had been claimed. Other unfortunates like themselves fell prey to rumors of riches in various locations. Stampedes to False Bottom, Polo Creek, and the Wolf Mountains left most the "tattered and torn" victims of fraud. Upon reaching Polo Creek on July 30, Richard B. Hughes expressed astonishment at the sight of a tent surrounded by nearly 100 men. Inside, David "had been elected recorder and was prepared to record the ground for claimants at the rate of a dollar and a half per claim. He did not reap a great harvest, however, as the whole affair began to assume the appearance of . . . a 'frame-up;' and before recording, the majority of the stampeders decided to pan some gravel."[11]

Watching other miners in Deadwood extract pans of gold, Annie condemned herself for coveting her neighbor's goods and recalled, "Of all sad words of tongue or pen/The saddest are these, It might have been." During 1876–1877, three sawmills produced 32,000 board feet per day used by miners from "all parts of the land, Montana, Colorado, and . . . California" as they sluiced $3,000,000 to $4,000,000 in gold dust from the gulches. Every evening after supper, when the night shift went on duty, the cry "Oh, Joe" arose from the cabin farthest down the gulch. Repeated from one abode to the next, the cry rolled through the camps until it died out far up stream.[12]

Hydraulic placer mining contributed greater wealth but stability came to the mining industry with the development of quartz mines. Annie heard "the music of numberless of the tiny one-stamp mills . . . morning, noon, and night" from every quarter of Deadwood Gulch. The search for gold-bearing quartz left abandoned shafts, prospect holes, and rusting equipment scattered the length and breadth of the region. They told "a pathetic story of depleted purses, wasted energies, disappointed hopes, and days, months, yea, sometimes years, of unrewarded toil."

Despite the fate of the average miner, Annie found the Black Hills an exciting place. "A vast seething cauldron of restless humanity, composed of virtue and vice in about equal ratios," filled Deadwood's streets and businesses. Freight trains brought merchandise that commanded exorbitant prices; hotels and restaurants daily fed hundreds;

saloons and gambling houses grew rich; "human leeches" fed upon the weakness of men; and laughter, song, and music from "antiquated pianos and cracked violins" filled the night. News of Custer's defeat brought silence even to saloons, and denunciation of federal policy that exposed Black Hills settlers to Indian reprisals. Celebration of the nation's Centennial on July 4 began at midnight with artillery booming and anvil salutes. At dawn the flag unfurled and "floated none the less proudly in that the red portion of the emblem was composed of a patriotic lady's garment of 'mystical sublimity'." The day closed with the signing of a memorial to Congress to extinguish Sioux claims and open the Black Hills to non-Indians.

A short time later, Congress ratified and the President approved the Agreement of 1877. Annie concluded that the Indians "lost much, and gained but little." Yet, she thought rations and annuities provided Indians a fair living and exempted them from "the burdens and responsibilities of civilized existence. In view of the fact that there are thousands who are obliged to earn their bread and butter by the sweat of their brows, and that have hard work to keep the wolf from the door, they should be satisfied."

Thus opened a new era for the Black Hills. Territorial Governor John Pennington appointed three commissioners who organized Lawrence, Custer, and Pennington Counties. Federal officials established a court system and a postal service. Capital investment increased as non-Indians prospered and built permanent homes. Subsequently Meade, Fall River, and Butte Counties were carved out of Lawrence, Custer, and Mandan Counties. A local wit in Deadwood posted a notice: "County Seats Located, Removed and For Sale/Apply to Black Hills County Commissioners."[13]

Towns sprang up all across the Black Hills. Custer, platted on August 10, 1875, on a primary route, boomed briefly before its population fled for richer gold fields in the northern Hills. Hill City experienced a similar fate when the rush left only one man and a dog. These towns revived with subsequent discoveries of gold, mica, and tin, but others nearly disappeared—Sheridan, Rochford, Rockerville, Pactola, Harney, Hayward, Castleton, Sitting Bull, and Silver City.

On February 25, 1876, pioneers who preferred town founding to prospecting established Rapid City as a commercial depot to link mining centers with sources of agricultural produce and retail goods. On April 26, others founded Deadwood, and watched its population jump to 7,000 miners, businessmen, professionals, gamblers, and crooks. In the spring of 1877 the success of the Homestake Company prompted the growth of Lead City above Gold Run Gulch. Yet the destinies of Central City, Terraville, Crook City, Galena, and Terry faltered at the mercy of mining fortunes.

Settlers laid out Spearfish on May 29, 1876, along the banks of the stream for which it is named. Sturgis catered to the needs of military personnel at Fort Meade, and medical demands contributed to the founding of Hot Springs. News of the relief brought by baths in its warm waters led to the gradual growth of Hot Springs as a sanitarium center and resort. Hermosa, Edgemont, Oelrich, Minnesela, and Belle Fourche became ranching centers, while the railroad provided an economic base for Whitewood, Tilford, Piedmont, and Black Hawk.

Scores of early merchants stocked groceries, dry goods, clothing, shoes, jewelry, hardware, furniture, and pharmaceuticals. Bankers, attorneys, and physicians offered professional expertise while hotels, saloons, theatres, barber shops, and bath houses catered to patrons. Farmers and ranchers produced food, and industries provided employment. Tourists visited Sylvan Lake, Wind Cave, Hot Springs, and Bear Butte. The telegraph, postal service, and newspapers linked residents with the rest of the nation. Goods and passengers moved by stagecoach, freight line, and railroad. The advent of water systems, electrical plants, and fire departments made life easier. Amidst the push and shove, law officers and judges promoted order.

From her vantage point at the lower end of Deadwood's Main Street, Annie witnessed much of the excitement. On August 2, 1876, lower Main rang with "the hurried tramping of a multitude of human feet" and the cry "Wild Bill is shot!" Nearly a year later, a commotion interrupted Annie's leisurely walk down Sherman Street. "Skipping nimbly away out of the possible range of some stray bullet," she watched officers pursue one of the gang that had held up the Deadwood stage.

Politics further agitated the populace when the possible creation of Lincoln Territory led to criminal accusations. Captain C. V. Gardner denied destroying a letter supporting his opponent, Dr. C. W. Meyer, rather than publish it in the *Pioneer*. David Tallent responded with an affidavit claiming to have seen Gardner burn the letter in a stove. The Captain's response made front page news:

I have nothing further to say concerning my cheeky friend Walker, except that if his case is so hopeless as to call in the aid of such men as this man Tallent to bolster up his cause, he certainly is to be pitied. . . .
In regard to this man Tallent, I will defy any man to read his affidavit

BOOK REQUEST FORM

Your name: ___Lori Valenzuela___ Date: ___2/17/98___

Author: ___South Dakota Leaders: from Pierre Chouteau Sr,___
☑ ___to Oscar Howe___

Title: ___Herbert Hoover & Larry Zimmerman___

LOCATION	CALL#	STATUS
Book Stacks	CT260 .S47 M89	on the shelf

Phone Number(s):
Home (510) ___7542778___ Work (___) ___ OR ___

carefully, and note how indefinite it is as to time, place, and circumstances, and not come to the conclusion that 'perjury' is written all over it. And I do not hesitate to brand the author of that affidavit, as a cowardly perjurer. And as a man who, while he may cheat the gallows for a terrible crime, committed near Custer two years ago, can hardly escape wearing the mark of Cain, put upon him by the people of the Hills for the crime then there committed. A man that will commit as grave a crime as he is charged with, will not hesitate to stab a man in the back, or to utter perjury.[14]

Tallent replied, "In your issue of the 19th, I am assailed by one Gardner. Some of my witnesses being absent from the city, I am compelled to ask my friends and the public, to suspend judgment until I can procure my evidence."[15] Apparently cooler counsel prevailed, as the controversy disappeared from the newspaper.

Nature provided excitement the following spring, when melting snows flooded Deadwood and Whitewood Creeks and burst a dam. "Waves ten or more feet deep" swept through Deadwood. In the aftermath, a slightly built man struggled through waist deep water "towards a building near a Deadwood street bridge, in the door of which stood knee-deep in water, a stout woman of 200 pounds avoirdupois, calling lustily for help. Upon reaching the imperiled woman, he clasped his arms around her ample waist, and gallantly but pantingly bore her safely to higher ground." Annie stood "on the opposite side of the street in two feet of water laughing heartily at the ludicrous spectacle."

As if only extremes existed at Deadwood, in 1879 an upset coal lamp ignited a small fire in the Empire Bakery. When flames spread to the Jensen and Bliss hardware store, eight kegs of black powder exploded and the fire leaped to Main Street. By morning Deadwood's entire business district lay in smoking ruins. The fire had consumed 100 businesses and seventy-five homes. Within twenty-four hours, tents, borrowed from Fort Meade, rose from the ashes; and restaurants in Lead supplied meals for the hungry. Two days later businessmen laid new foundations for brick structures.

By June, 1880, the Tallents had moved to Rochford. Annie taught school and David became involved in unsuccessful efforts to carve Martin County from the western section of Pennington. Declining fortunes in Rochford prompted the Tallents to move to Rapid City in April of 1886. They rented a home in the Riverside addition from Mrs. Van Houten. While living in Rapid City, David practiced law, wrote insurance, and acted as a notary, when not prospecting. Also involved in efforts to make that community a manufacturing center, he handled the details for organizing a water right company to generate power and promoted the establishment of a foundry and machine shops.[16]

Annie too believed in development and mining fascinated her more than any other economic activity. Convinced that success awaited only capital and management, she recorded the number of stamp mills, earnings, and potential of numerous gold mines. Even the names, King Solomon, Hidden Treasure, and Cornucopia, promised wealth. Yet, the Deadbroke was reality for many including the Tallents, whose search left them "clear down to bed-rock, with not a dollar in sight." The Homestake, the best example of capital and management promoting success, received Annie's grudging respect. Its "900 ponderous stamps" caused the gold region "to throb from center to circumference" but left "small chance for small operations." Believing that the Black Hills natural resources offered prosperity, she enthusiastically recorded its mineral deposits and praised its forests, farms, ranches, and people.

Annie confessed admiration for the "dashing, festive cowboys," in spite of their faults. Although they occasionally fired shots in the streets and rode their broncos into the saloons, she found these "manly fellows" to be honest, generous, and kind. Also intrigued by the ethnic mix in Lead where they "make the most of life," she especially appreciated the musical abilities of the Cornish, Swedish, German, and Italian residents. A similar cosmopolitan air existed in Deadwood with its large Chinese population. While the men adopted American dress and manners, the women and girls adhered to native attire. "Dignified, demure little almond-eyed, olive-skinned maidens, in the very acme of Chinese fashions," decorously made their way to school. Annie's attitudes toward these groups contrasted sharply with her opinion of the Twenty-fifth Colored Infantry garrisoned at Fort Meade. Although admitting "the colored soldiers were not uniformly the guilty ones," she believed their replacement by the Third Infantry reduced to a minimum the lawlessness in Sturgis.

Besides commenting on types of people, Annie recorded their activities. A number of fraternal or secret orders sprang up throughout the Hills, including the Masons, Odd Fellows, Knights of Pythias, Eastern Star, and Daughters of Rebecca. Most communities also had commercial, athletic, and gun clubs for the men, literary clubs for the women, and social and musical clubs for both. The women's associations cultivated a taste for good literature and attempted to lift women of the late nineteenth century "to a higher intellectual plane." Annie felt their efforts would make the world "happier and better" despite "utter disregard" for the teachings and traditions of their grandmothers and greatgrandmothers. The Society of Black Hills Pioneers, formed on January 8, 1889, enlisted as members those men who arrived prior to December 31, 1876. Annie became an honorary member and Robert joined in 1892. The Society assisted with the funerals of members, held its annual meeting and banquet in January, and sponsored a picnic each June. Annie was introduced as the first White woman to "visit" the Black Hills when she related her early experiences to the picnic crowd at Custer in 1896.

A variety of other organizations and activities existed. Jack Langrishe, "the idol of the early Western mining camps," established the first legitimate theatre in Deadwood during July of 1876. At the maiden performance, rain penetrated a canvas roof in streams but failed to dampen the enthusiasm of audience or actors. Vaudeville performers such as "Banjo Dick" Brown and Kitty LeRoy entertained at the Bella Union and the Gem. In Lead the Phoebe A. Hearst Library sponsored monthly musicals for Homestake employees. In Rapid City numerous lectures, concerts, and dances took place at the Library Hall. Religious institutions flourished, and Annie was a faithful and active member of the Emmanuel Episcopal Parish in Rapid City. Her son Robert joined, too, but her husband David did not. Robert was baptized on August 18, 1887, at age 22, the same day that Bishop William O. Hare presided at his marriage to Jessie May Strohm. Their fathers, David and Cornelius, signed the marriage certificate as witnesses.

The following December Annie visited family in Elgin, Illinois, and during her absence David disappeared. He never returned. Many reasons seem probable but an unhappy marriage is most likely. David's drinking and desertion may have been the reasons why Annie barely mentioned him in her history of the Black Hills. Confusion surrounded his disappearance. Some newspapers reported that he left for the gold fields of British Columbia and perished there in a fire. Children of Annie's close friends never heard their parents talk about David, or thought he disappeared after leaving the Stockade for Cheyenne in 1875, or believed that Annie was a widow.

After David left, Annie continued her career in education. For each term as a teacher in Rochford, Tigerville, and Hill City, she received $50.00 per month including board. She taught reading, writing, spelling, arithmetic, geography, grammar, and history to classes ranging from seven to twenty-one students whose ages varied from four to eighteen. Students remembered Annie as refined, aristocratic, and well educated. She was tall, slim, patient, and a fine teacher:

> She required her pupils to demonstrate, on the blackboard, their lessons in arithmetic, geography and grammer. If a pupil could not do this, he must work until he could. To this day I can remember diagraming and parsing my grammar lesson, proving my arithmetic, and drawing different maps to illustrate geography lessons. She possessed the quality of teaching without anger or impatience. In appearance she was dignified and attractive. I never saw her punish a pupil altho [sic] she did make me stand in a corner of the room with my back toward the children and in my arms a stick of stove wood.[17]

Recognizing Annie's experience and ability, Pennington County voters twice elected her Superintendent of Schools. Richard B. Hughes placed her name before the Democratic convention in 1890. On November 7 she narrowly defeated her Republican opponent, J. C. Mears, a former Rochford teacher who had given Robert Tallent "98" in deportment—100 was perfect. As an Independent candidate in 1892, she easily won over the Republican, a Mr. Paxson. Her responsibilities as Superintendent included taking the school census, conducting teachers' institutes, and visiting county schools. During these trips she often had to open wire gates and earned a reputation for leaving them that way. In 1893 the State Superintendent of Schools, recognizing Annie's excellent work, selected her as one of twelve people to supervise South Dakota's educational exhibit at the Chicago World's Fair.

Following her terms as Pennington County Superintendent of Schools, Annie became a member of the Rapid City Board of Education for three years, two of which she served as President. Assessing her work in both positions, Richard Hughes commented that her terms as Superintendent were "marked by a notable advance in the cause of education throughout the county, and schools in the rural districts were much improved under her administration." She displayed the "same zeal and energy" during her second term. "Throughout her administration she gave evidence of fine executive ability. The same is true of her work as a member of the Rapid City school board."[18]

In June, 1897, Robert and Jessie, with sons Earl and Paul, moved to Sturgis and established residence in a substantial home at 1603 Main Street. Annie soon joined them and while living in Sturgis published her history of the Black Hills. Historian Doane Robinson commented,

"Of most events the author writes as an eye witness and it was her good, and sometimes bad fortune to be present when was enacted most of those stirring and frequently tragic events which made the Black Hills a household word throughout the world in the palmy days of the placer mine. Mrs. Tallent has performed for the state at large and for the Black Hills in particular a service of greatest present interest and which will constantly grow in value as time passes."[19]

After completing her book Annie's health began to fail. Her last illness, pneumonia, covered a period of two weeks. She died on February 13, 1901. Obituaries recounted her coming to the Black Hills and extolled her character. She was "a prominent figure . . . , one of the most remarkable women of the west . . . a lady of education and refinement," and a woman of "intelligence, energy and public spirit, withal a splendid example of Dakota womanhood."

Robert Tallent and his son Paul accompanied the casket to Elgin, Illinois, for burial among Annie's brothers and sisters. On Sunday, February 17, funeral services were held in the home of Mrs. Frank Heath, Annie's niece. Annie was buried near her sister Margaret in Lot 139, Section 4, of Bluff City Cemetery. The tombstone recorded her age at death as "73 years 10 months and 1 day."[20] Nearly twenty-four years later friends erected a monument in honor of her courage, leadership in education, and contributions to the advancement of women. Several commented that Annie was ahead of her time: "a lone woman, an extraordinary individual who in her own era must have been considered rather eccentric, and at least in advance, intellectually, of her generation."

Annie's own book revealed much about her character if not about her personal life. From her writing emerged the portrait of a woman who was religious, determined, outspoken, educated, sociable, and subject to the racial prejudices of her age. Despite homesickness, fear, and economic hardship, she retained a lively sense of humor. A difficult and unhappy marriage might have kept Annie silent about her husband. Yet, she wrote little about Robert, the son she loved very much. Her history of the first quarter century of White settlement in the Black Hills and testimonies by contemporaries marked her as a "boomer." Annie firmly believed in developing the region's wealth, respected the people who did, and numbered herself among those pioneers.

Notes

1. Annie D. Tallent, *The Black Hills: Or, the Last Hunting Ground of the Dakotahs* (Sioux Falls: Brevet Press, 1974), *passim*. All quotations that appear

without citations come from either the original or this reprint edition of Annie Tallent's autobiography.

2. *Sioux City Weekly Times,* September 10, 1874.

3. David Aken, *Pioneers of the Black Hills* (Fort Davis, TX: Frontier Book Company, n.d.), pp. 19–20.

4. *Sioux City Weekly Times,* March 6, 1875.

5. "Sioux City Inaugurates the Gold Rush to the Black Hills Country in 1874," *The Sioux City Sunday Journal,* August 22, 1926. For a discussion of Gordon's second expedition and the legal aftermath see Grant K. Anderson, "The Black Hills Exclusion Policy: Judicial Challenges," *Nebraska History,* LVIII, no. 1 (1977), pp. 1–24.

6. C. C. O'Harra, "The Earliest Mining Laws and Mining Organizations in the Black Hills," *The Black Hills Engineer,* XII, no. 4 (November 1924), pp. 240–241.

7. Aken, *Pioneers,* pp. 149–150.

8. Peter Rosen, *Pa-Ha-Sa-Pa, or the Black Hills of South Dakota* (St. Louis: Nixon-Jones Printing Co., 1895), p. 309.

9. Sidney Cornell, "The Opening of the Black Hills," *The Monthly South Dakotan,* I, no. 10 (February 1899), p. 161.

10. Nancy Niethammer Kovats, *Annie Tallent* (Hermosa, SD: Lame Johnny Press, 1893), p. 23.

11. Richard B. Hughes, *Pioneer Years in the Black Hills* (Glendale, CA: Arthur H. Clark Co., 1957), pp. 127–136.

12. *Ibid.,* p. 104.

13. *Ibid.,* p. 484.

14. "The Other Side," *The Black Hills Daily Times,* May 18, 1876.

15. *Ibid.,* May 21, 1876. See also Kovats, *Annie Tallent,* pp. 25–26.

16. "More About Manufacturing," *The Black Hills Weekly Journal,* April 9, 1886.

17. Teacher's Reports, Pennington County, Territory of Dakota, Archives, Pennington County Courthouse, Rapid City; Drusilla Troutman to Clay Curran, February 17, 1959, Willis Owen to Clay Curran, January 28, 1959, Mr. B. J. Gaetze to Clay Curran, January 28, 1959, Frank Thomson to Clay Curran, January 11, 1959, Interview with T. C. Martin by Clay Curran, February 7, 1959, Clay Curran Collection, Leland D. Case Library for Western Historical Studies, Black Hills State College, Spearfish, SD.

During the twenty-three years following his disappearance, David Tallent wandered through Old Mexico, California, Idaho, and Utah. He died July 3, 1911, and was buried on his copper claim near Arlington, Wyoming.

18. Mrs. C. B. Clark, "Annie D. Tallent, Pioneer Teacher," *The Black Hills Engineer,* XII, no. 4 (November 1924), p. 238.

19. "Mrs. Tallent's Book," *The Monthly South Dakotan,* II, no. 5 (September 1900), p. 171.

20. "The Life of Mrs. Tallent," *Daily Argus-Leader,* February 19, 1901;

"Mrs. Tallent Dead," *The Black Hills Mining Review,* February 18, 1901; "The First White Lady," *Daily Pioneer Times,* February 14, 1901; "Annie D. Tallent," *The Monthly South Dakotan,* no. 11 (March 1901), p. 382; *Elgin Daily Courier,* February 16, 1901; p. 382; *Elgin Daily Courier,* February 16, 1901; *Elgin Every Saturday,* May 19, 1894; Picture, Annie D. Tallent File, Rapid City Public Library, Rapid City.

Thomas S. Williamson.
Courtesy South Dakota State Historical
Society

John P. Williamson.
Courtesy South Dakota State Historical
Society

Thomas L. Riggs.
Courtesy Center for Western Studies.

Alfred L. Riggs.
Courtesy Center for Western Studies.

Stephen R. Riggs.
Courtesy Center for Western Studies.

Birds Nest Cottage, Normal Training
School, Santee Agency, photographed by
W.R. Cross.
Courtesy W.H. Over State Museum.

Oahe Industrial students.
Courtesy Center for Western Studies

Carrying the Word to the Sioux: The Williamson and Riggs Families

Robert Stahl

When Dr. Thomas Williamson and his wife Margaret first felt a calling to mission work among Indians, they hesitated to leave a comfortable home, young family, and thriving medical practice. Then tragedy struck. Their first child had died in infancy, and two more children died in January, 1833. Now they decided to heed a call in the belief that their children had been "gathered into the arms of the Almighty" to free their parents for entry into the mission field. A month after the children died, the Williamsons applied to the American Board of Commissioners for Foreign Missions (ABCFM) in Boston. Founded in 1810 by the Congregational Church and joined later by the Presbyterian Church, the ABCFM included American Indian missions in its scope of activities and its leaders were interested in expansion across the Old Northwest beyond the Mississippi River.

As the son of a Presbyterian minister, Williamson almost naturally thought to enter mission service through the ABCFM. From his home in Ripley, Ohio, he corresponded with the Board's Secretary, informing him of a plan to attend Lane Seminary in Cincinnati and requesting a position with an Indian mission. An exchange of letters over several months demonstrated Williamson's clarity of purpose and the Board's enthusiastic reception of his proposal. Rigors of life on the Indian frontier led most applicants to request foreign mission posts instead. Thomas and Margaret did not shrink from probable hardship, however, and in 1835 Williamson became the only ordained missionary to enter the "Indian field" under the aegis of the Board.

His placement was uncertain until he finished seminary training, when the Board sent him on reconnaissance into the Old Northwest. After his return he submitted a detailed report about opportunities for successful work among the four tribes of eastern Sioux. Quickly, the Board dispatched him to Fort Snelling.

Williamson wisely recruited the nucleus for a permanent mission station before leaving Ohio: Alexander Huggins as a mission farmer, and Sarah Poage, Margaret's sister, as a teacher. The small party arrived at Fort Snelling in mid-May, 1835, and so began the Dakota Mission. During the first few months it grew rapidly. Jedediah Stevens, a preacher licensed by the ABCFM, arrived with his wife and niece shortly after the Williamsons. Samuel and Gideon Pond, two unaffiliated volunteer missionaries who had worked for the U.S. Indian Agent as farming instructors near Fort Snelling, also gained Board approval to join the Mission.

Stevens and the Pond brothers remained near the lower St. Peters (Minnesota) River valley, but the heart of the Dakota Mission shifted immediately to Lac Qui Parle, situated on the St. Peters some 200 miles west of Fort Snelling. Joseph Renville, the most powerful and influential fur trader in the region, had operated a post there since 1826. When he chanced to meet Williamson at Fort Snelling, he invited the newcomer to build a mission near the Renville stockade. Leaving the Stevens family and Pond brothers behind, the Williamsons and the Hugginses embarked on a difficult journey to a place on the far end of Eastern Sioux Country near the northeast edge of a spacious prairie controlled by the Yankton Sioux. The move was fortuitous. Treaty negotiations later banished all Eastern Sioux from the Fort Snelling area. Joseph Renville offered the missionaries both his vital protection and a valuable introduction to Sioux people and their culture.

Renville was born near present-day St. Paul of mixed French and Eastern Sioux ancestry. He spent his entire childhood among White traders and Indians and married into an Eastern Sioux tribe. By the time of Williamson's arrival, Renville was fifty-six years old, the patriarch of a large family, and the forceful head of a strategically important outpost for the Upper Missouri Outfit of the Western Department of the American Fur Company under the administration of Pierre Chouteau, Jr. Surrounded by Indian relatives and Canadian interlopers, Renville took the missionaries into his care to serve as their sponsor in local Sioux villages. His motives were neither entirely altruistic nor strictly spiritual. Certainly he wanted missionaries at hand to aid the Indians with medicine and agricultural instruction, but he also expected them to educate his children and look after the health care needs of his family.

Renville was not stingy. He housed the missionaries at first within his fort and offered provisions when their supplies ran out or were lost in transit. He allowed his Canadian workers to assist with the construction of mission buildings. Most of all, he helped with Sioux language in eastern or Dakota dialect. The ABCFM had long instructed its missionaries to gain fluency in native languages with the belief that both acculturation and Christianization would thereby be better accepted. Hence, Williamson came with the charge to make the learning of Dakota language his first priority so he could preach the Gospel in Indian vernacular. He was also instructed to record and systematize the language so the Bible soon could be translated for use by Indians thus rendered literate in their own language.

Acquiring command of Dakota language was a difficult task complicated considerably by Renville's limited understanding of English. Williamson read passages from the Bible in French. Renville translated French into Dakota. Williamson wrote Dakota phonetically. Progress was slow but gradually Williamson gained proficiency. By 1838 the Gospel of Mark was translated in print and work was in progress on the development of a Dakota grammar and dictionary while Williamson envisioned the translation of the entire Holy Bible.

Vital assistance came with the arrival of Stephen Return Riggs and his wife, Mary, at Lac Qui Parle in 1837. Williamson and Riggs had met in Ripley as Dr. Williamson began his medical practice when Riggs was only sixteen years old. Although different in their ages, personalities, and backgrounds, the two formed a lasting friendship. After Riggs graduated from Western Theological Seminary, Williamson lost no time recruiting him for the Dakota Mission.

After the arrival of the Riggs family, Gideon Pond contributed knowledge of Dakota language he had picked up at his farm station on Lake Hariett. The Lac Qui Parle mission was alive with work on translation while Williamson introduced Sisseton and Wahpeton tribal members to the tenets of Christianity. There were enormous challenges and handicaps. It seemed to the missionaries that almost every aspect of Indian life would have to change if the Sioux were to become bona fide Christians. Funds were severely limited. With no real power over Indians, the missionaries could only try to lead them into a new way of life. First would have to come the replacement of seasonal villages with permanent settlements. Next would be the surrender of hunting, trapping, and gathering to be replaced by family farming.

This strategy had already been endorsed by the ABCFM. Its Secretary wrote Williamson at Ripley in 1834:

> Our present plan for the wandering tribes, like the Sioux, Ojibwas, Sacs & Foxes, etc. is to locate preachers, catechists, and schoolmasters among them and at each station, to hold out some inducement to the Indians to collect and settle and live by cultivating the soil, so as to bring themselves and their children within reach of religious instruction and of the schools. To do this some aid must be offered them in cultivating the land, and in obtaining tools.

Put another way in a letter addressed to Williamson through Fort Snelling in 1835:

> I hope you will spend as much time as possible with the Indians, without an interpreter, compelling yourself to learn to hold intercourse with them independently. . . . Can you not go out often and spend a day or two or sometimes two or three weeks in the lodges, learning their words and forms of expression, and attempting to communicate your thoughts to them? Could you in any other manner secure so well their confidence and affection; or prepare them to hear your message?[1]

ABCFM leaders expected courageous dedication from the missionaries. They got nothing less, not only from Williamson and Riggs, but also from their wives and children, who accepted geographic isolation and some danger to make Lac Qui Parle a thriving mission station.

Through the 1840s came additional mission workers and several new stations. Williamson and Riggs reported progress in the work of translation and publication. Their central goals of "civilization" and Christianization seemed frustrated. The Minnesota Sioux faced problems of their own and showed little interest. Returns from the fur trade plummeted and an extended drought forced the Indians to travel out of the area in search of food. Early contingents of Whites seeking land for agricultural use threatened their territory. Although missionaries were not seen as a threat but as a source of some assistance to the Sioux, their presence exacerbated an emerging struggle that pertained to the defense of Indian cultural autonomy.

Only a few Indians joined Dakota Mission. The first were relatives of Joseph Renville. Not until 1841 did the first full-blood Sioux man join and in 1848 Indian church membership rolls totaled a mere seventeen. The statistic is somewhat misleading, inasmuch as the missionaries refused to consider anyone eligible for church membership who had not received extensive religious instruction, been baptized, and evidenced sincerity of Christian commitment in daily life. Nevertheless, church service attendance was depressingly low and school matriculation was little better. It is hardly surprising that most personnel recruited to the Dakota Mission stayed only a few years. Discouraging results in the early years underscored the steadfast commitments of Thomas Williamson and Stephen Riggs.

The circumstances of the Minnesota Sioux continued to deteriorate. Following the establishment of Minnesota Territory in 1849, Euro-American immigration accelerated dramatically. The Treaties of Traverse des Sioux and Mendota two years later confined the Eastern Sioux to a narrow strip of land along the upper Minnesota River as they relinquished all other territory in return for the promise of annuity goods and payments. Responding, Williamson and Riggs built new mission stations near the center of the new reserve at Yellow Medicine (Pajutazee) and Hazelwood. The Indians around them struggled for survival on annuity issue rations because most of their hunting and trapping lands were gone. German and Norwegian settlers, especially, filed in and their presence alone brought social conflict. The revenge attack at Spirit Lake led by Inkpaduta in 1857, followed by his raids around Jackson, Minnesota, evoked suspicion on both sides.

The Minnesota Sioux War erupted in August, 1862, as an almost inevitable consequence of growing hostility over land loss and intercultural tension. A senseless killing of an isolated farm family near Acton, Minnesota, was only the catalyst for war. The economic condition of Indians had become so desperate and Indian-white relations so strained that the smallest incident might have caused the Eastern Sioux to take up arms.

Far more important than the killing near Acton was the late arrival of issue food because of pressure on national stores at the outset of the Civil War. Licensed traders helped little and some paid with their lives for the neglect.

Anticipating reprisals for the Acton killings, some Eastern Sioux felt they had little to lose by trying to drive homesteaders out of southern Minnesota. In a brief conflict several hundred Whites and many Indians were killed. Tribal members of Dakota Mission congregations led missionary families and many other non-Indians to safety as the stations were destroyed. Within six weeks the war ended, and 1,300 Sioux surrendered at Camp Release. Little Crow and most of the Indian combatants had already fled to the northwest.

Williamson and Riggs differed in their initial responses to post-war

needs and responsibilities. Riggs twice accompanied punitive campaigns led by General Henry Hastings Sibley, serving as interpreter
and chaplain for the expeditions. He stood by without making protest
at the summary trials of several hundred Indian prisoners that resulted
in the hanging of thirty-eight at Mankato. Swept along perhaps by the
emotions of non-Indians, he supported the idea of swift and severe
retribution. Williamson, on the other hand, did not excuse Indian
depredations but refused to be in any way identified with a general
clamor for retaliation against the Sioux. By then, most White Minnesotans had been frightened into a posture of racism, if not hatred.
Williamson's calm public voice contradicted the hysteria and for this
he endured vehement denunciation. In spite of it he refused to share
the common view that Indians had proven themselves to be less than
human. Because of his convictions he went to the prisoners held at
Mankato to preach the Gospel and followed those spared the gallows
into incarceration at Fort Davenport. It took Riggs two years to
recover his sense of equity and join Williamson again in their common
work.

Never did these two stalwart founders of the Dakota Mission demonstrate the same posture toward Indians. For example, Williamson
encouraged his children to associate with tribal playmates, while Riggs
was fearful of a demoralizing effect and kept his children apart from
Indians. Williamson was a no-nonsense proselytizer who was more
culturally accommodating in his interpretation of Christian doctrine
than were his fellow missionaries. His perception of polygamy was a
prime example. He thought that, in the absence of any clear biblical
injunction, it would be inconsistent with the spirit of Christ's teaching
to require an Indian man who was happily married to more than one
wife, before hearing the Gospel, to choose one wife and family in
preference to another in order to become a church member. Riggs did
not share this opinion. He was inclined toward a much more conventional, doctrinaire approach that on occasion led him into rash confrontations with Indians.

In spite of their fundamental differences, Williamson and Riggs made
an admirable team with remarkable courage and tenacity in the effort
to Christianize as they worked to acculturate the Sioux. Indisputably,
they were the driving force behind the Dakota Mission in the Minnesota phase of its history that lasted nearly thirty years.

Far too much has been made of the "prison conversions." Out of
322 Sioux prisoners-of-war held at Mankato, Thomas Williamson and
Gideon Pond baptized 274 during the first winter. Of an additional

1,600 non-combatants detained at Fort Snelling, the younger John P. Williamson baptized 140 during the same season. In addition, there were 328 Catholic and Episcopalian baptisms. Acquiescence to baptism by such an impressive number should not be misconstrued as evidence of a spiritual surrender to a victorious enemy's religion. Maltreatment and hardships experienced by Sioux prisoners and their families should have inspired bitter hatred of everything associated with the White man. But the missionaries, especially those connected with the ABCFM, had proven friendly and helpful to the beleaguered Sioux. By constancy and support, when every other hand was turned against the Indians, missionaries won the trust and attention of the Sioux. The Christian message of salvation and brotherhood must have seemed a welcome, if somewhat confusing, alternative to blanket condemnation or calls for extermination heard from most non-Indians. Sioux prisoners and their families, who for the most part were as innocent as they were vulnerable, doubtless accepted what was offered by their missionary friends in a spirit of religious pluralism that saw Christianity as another channel of communication with Wakan Tanka, "The Great Mystery." There is no way of knowing how many true "conversions" were made in the exclusive, conventional, Christian sense. Even Thomas Williamson had doubts about how many of those baptized were actually "born of the Spirit."

The prison conversions must be viewed in this light. Yet there can be no doubt about the substantial pre-war accomplishments of workers in the Dakota Mission. Williamson, Riggs, and their colleagues provided thirty years of instruction in farming and written Dakota dialect. They also gave medical assistance and served the Indians as interpreters and intercessors in their dealings with federal officials. By 1862 two dozen works or more had been produced in Dakota, including: primers, spellers, hymnals, sections of the Old and New Testaments, the Minnesota Constitution, and *The Grammar and Dictionary of Dakota* that was later published under the auspices of the Smithsonian Institution. In addition, twenty monthly issues of *The Dakota Friend*, one of the first Indian language periodicals, went into circulation. Church rosters listed only sixty-five members before the 1862 War but the missionaries trained a nucleus of teachers and ministers in the tribes. Out of this came John B. Renville, the son of Joe and the first officially authorized Sioux preacher, who was licensed at Mankato in 1865 despite an outcry from non-Indians that drove Dr. Williamson out of town.

Along with these legacies, Thomas Williamson and Stephen Riggs bequeathed to Dakota Mission, for its future, their sons John P. Williamson and Alfred L. Riggs. Both were born at Lac Qui Parle and reared in Dakota Mission communities. The elder by two years, John had completed his education and seminary training and opened a mission station at Red Wood in Minnesota by 1861, while Alfred remained at school in the East. John was absent when the fighting broke out, but he quickly returned and stood by Sioux noncombatants detained at Fort Snelling. Although the elder Williamson and Riggs remained active in the mission field for many more years, it was John who extended their work westward to the upper Missouri River basin, and, in close association with Alfred, carried it into the twentieth century.

The Minnesota Sioux War backfired for the Eastern Sioux, inasmuch as it led to their expulsion from their homeland in Minnesota. Wahpetons were barely involved, and Sissetons took little part in the fighting, but for fear of blanket retaliation they withdrew to the north and west. The Mdewakantons and Wahpekutes most directly involved in hostilities fled into Dakota Territory. Many crossed the Missouri River, and some took refuge in Canada. During the Spring of 1863 those convicted of wartime atrocities, but spared the gallows at Mankato, were moved to the military compound at Fort Davenport, Iowa. People thought wholly innocent of hostile action were moved by steamboat from Fort Snelling to a hastily constructed camp at Crow Creek in Dakota Territory.

Dr. Williamson stayed with the prisoners at Davenport and convinced Stephen Riggs to join him. While there, the two missionaries continued to preach the Gospel and give language lessons in written Dakota. Conditions may not have been as severe as those in other military prisons but the Sioux housed in seasonal barracks suffered gravely from cold and hunger. An estimated 120 died of tuberculosis. Although Williamson and Riggs made repeated pleas for their release, the prisoners remained at Davenport for three years, until they could be reunited with relatives at Santee, Nebraska.

John P. Williamson went with the noncombatants on their long and arduous journey by way of Dakota Territory to Santee. The 1,300 Sioux, mostly women, children, and elderly, along with 2,000 Winnebagos, who were mainly innocent people expelled from Minnesota because they were Indians, all suffered removal. While many Winnebagos moved overland, the Sioux refugees were loaded onto crowded steamers. Scores died in transit, and many more perished from complications because of exposure to the cold and from a critical shortage of rations during their stay at Crow Creek. Perhaps a total of more than 300 were lost. The suffering they endured has become legendary as the name of Crow Creek has been associated with the darkest period in the history of the Eastern Sioux. Confined at a strange place far from home, not knowing if they would ever see their imprisoned kinsmen again, grieving from the frequent deaths of their friends and relatives, and forced to rely upon an undependable government agency for food and shelter, the Sioux could scarcely have faced more tormenting times. What assistance John P. Williamson could offer must have seemed miraculous. In addition to holding religious services and teaching classes in Dakota, John translated, interceded, and labored for the Indians. He walked with them on a buffalo hunt to the Couteau des Prairie and in many other ways worked to ease their pain. The reputation he established among the Sioux during their three hard years at Crow Creek went with him for the rest of his life.

The two groups of Eastern Sioux were finally reunited in the Spring of 1866 near the Nebraska site of the confluence of the Niobrara and Missouri Rivers. Approximately 300 from Davenport joined at least 1,000 from Crow Creek, who were accompanied by John P. Williamson and Edward Pond. Thomas Williamson, Stephen Riggs, and John Renville soon followed. The next few years were busy for the missionaries as they labored to establish new missions. They were forced to move with the "Santees" (mainly Mdewakantons and Wahpekutes) again before they came to rest at a permanent agency. From temporary placement near the mouth of the Niobrara they went to a location five miles downriver on Bazile Creek, then to a site ten miles farther downstream to the U.S. Agency known since as Santee, Nebraska, across the river from Springfield, South Dakota. Within the first year and a half, the Pilgrim Presbyterian Church was organized, schools were opened, and the Dakota (Indian) Presbytery was established. Two native pastors, Titus Icaduze and Artemas Ehnamani, were ordained.

Once the Dakota Mission was on a solid footing at Santee, John P. Williamson grew restless. He was an evangelist to the core drawn by opportunity to work among the Yankton Sioux around their agency at Greenwood on the Dakota side of the Missouri River. Yanktons had experienced neither war and dislocation nor decades of ABCFM missionizing. It took Williamson several years to convince them to accept his presence as their resident missionary. On March 20, 1869, however, he crossed on the ice to place his family at Greenwood. By March of 1871 the Ihanktonwan Church was organized with eighteen charter members. Among them was Henry Tawa Selwyn, who later became the first regular Presbyterian minister of Yankton heritage.

During the summer of 1871 John P. Williamson built a church at Flandreau for 100 members belonging to families of recent emigres from Santee. Twenty-five families had moved two years earlier to take advantage of permission to homestead written into the 1868 Fort Laramie Treaty. They were soon joined by approximately thirty-five additional families. Williamson heartily approved of their initiative and intervened on their behalf with federal officials to secure titles to land and special assistance through their period of adjustment. As the Special U.S. Agent for several years, he brought in seed, draft animals, and farm equipment. Although he retained permanent residence at Greenwood, he spent much of his time from 1873 to 1879 lending assistance to the Flandreau colony. Despite hard work and planning, their early years in family farming were depressing. Repeated crop failures from drought and grasshopper invasions, coupled with national economic collapse, plagued all farmers in the region and forced Williamson to bring in gratuitous rations. Fearing the trap of dependence, he sought to minimize federal aid. When colony members urged him to add agency personnel, he refused and tried to meet the needs with his own labor.

Williamson was relieved to divest himself of responsibility for agency affairs in 1879. From the time of his move to Greenwood a decade earlier, he had operated an elementary school at his parsonage with little outside support and had labored vigorously on the development of higher grades at the mission in Santee to prepare more native pastors and teachers for work among the Sioux. This would require the full time commitment of someone with a scholarly mind, executive ability, and familiarity with the Dakota language. The right person was his childhood playmate and lifelong friend, Alfred L. Riggs.

After a brief visit to assess the situation, Riggs resigned a pastorate in Illinois and moved his family to Santee in May, 1870. Aided by Mr. and Mrs. Edward Pond and his wife, Mary, he began the construction of Santee Normal Training School, where he served as principal for the next forty-six years. The institution grew rapidly under his administration. Fifteen years later he boasted of eighteen buildings and a combined academic and industrial faculty of twenty-six with an average enrollment of 100 pupils.

Although living some distance from Santee and distracted by pressing matters on the opposite side of the Missouri, John P. Williamson found time to assist Alfred Riggs in many ways. Together in 1871 they founded *Iapi Oaye / The Word Carrier*, a bi-monthly Dakota Mission newspaper printed at Santee Normal. Riggs edited and wrote for the English language edition while Williamson translated and wrote for the Dakota edition. The paper carried news of national and local developments relevant to Indian missions as well as editorial sermons. Preceding the lead story in each issue was the following statement:

OUR PLATFORM
For Indians we want American Education! We want American Homes!
We want American Rights! The result of which is American Citizenship!
And the Gospel is the power of God for their Salvation!

On the surface it might have seemed that evangelical concerns were secondary, but such was not the case. Alfred Riggs and John P. Williamson believed, like their fathers, in a necessary connection between "civilization" and Christianization. *The Word Carrier* brought news and encouragement to an expanding network of Dakota Mission workers. The year the paper was founded the first annual camp meeting of the Conference of the Dakota Churches was also held, and five years later *Wotanin Washte*, or The Native Mission Society for Sioux missions, was established.

Content that younger missionaries had matters well in hand at Santee, Thomas Williamson and Stephen Riggs spent some years after 1866 traveling in Dakota to assess possible sites for additional missions. They visited the Sisseton and Wahpeton Reservation around Fort Wadsworth in 1870 and helped set up a mission for their former church members from Lac Qui Parle. Williamson and Riggs stayed briefly, leaving The Good Will Church in the care of Daniel Renville and turning over the satellite chapel named Ascension Church to John Renville. Eventually both Thomas Williamson and Stephen Riggs went to their homes and turned their attention to writing. Williamson was able to finish his translation of the Bible and Riggs to complete *Mary and I: Forty Years with the Sioux*.

Thirty-six years of partnership between the Congregational Church and the Presbyterian Church ended in 1871, when Presbyterians withdrew from the ABCFM and set up the Presbyterian Board of Foreign Missions (PBFM). The Williamsons and the Riggses were faced with a decision. In the end each family adhered to its original religious affiliation; the Williamsons went with the Presbyterians and the Riggses went with the Congregationalists. The official separation of the two families had little effect on their cooperative mission endeavors, however, or their deep friendship. Thomas Williamson died in 1879 and Stephen Riggs in 1883, leaving a legacy of cooperation in the Dakota Mission, which remained essentially intact despite the organizational division, and it continued to grow.

Thomas Riggs, Alfred's younger brother, had also been born at Lac Qui Parle. After completing his education and finishing seminary, he accepted the call in 1872 to establish an ABCFM mission for western Sioux across the Missouri from Fort Sully. Two years later he moved his mission to Peoria Bottom and built the Bogue Mission, which later became the Oahe Mission and Oahe Industrial School. He also served as Superintendent of Congregational Indian missions for the Cheyenne River and Standing Rock Reservations until his retirement in 1918.

The Dakota Mission expanded into Montana. John P. Williamson began visiting Sioux people on the Fort Peck Reservation in 1874, where he founded a mission and school in 1880. Thereafter he continued to make regular visits to assist the missionaries he placed in charge. After serving as interpreter for transactions of the western Sioux over two decades, Williamson also built a mission on the Pine Ridge Reservation in 1886 and spent a time in residence during 1891 and 1892.

All the while, Williamson and Alfred Riggs worked closely together. They continued to publish *The Word Carrier*, which reported news of all Presbyterian and Congregational missions to the Sioux. Their correspondence indicates that funds, educational supplies, and students freely made their way back-and-forth between the two at Greenwood and Santee despite the emergence of two Mission Boards.

The younger Williamson and Riggs were among the first to express concern that the Sioux would be changed by land allotments and the opening of "surplus" reservation acreages to non-Indian entry. They were anxious to ensure that the Indians be given every opportunity to succeed under the new system. In 1885 Alfred Riggs protested against the unrealistically small size of the allotments Santee people were to receive, and succeeded in having them enlarged. In the early 1890s Williamson helped the Yanktons through a similar, unsettling process.

Although Williamson and Riggs gave freely of their time and energy to help the Sioux through adjustments to the "civilization" plan imposed by federal officials, their first priority was always Christianization. John P. Williamson made the point forcefully in an article published in 1882:

To the friends of Indian progress these are propitious, perhaps critical days. The eyes of the country are turned towards the Indians as never before. Pressure, stronger and stronger, is brought to bear on the lawmakers to take up and discharge the nation's duty to this handful of aborigines.

At such a time the Church should see that her peculiar work is not neglected. Her work is not to give Indians an education, but the Gospel; not to teach them how to farm but how to be followers of Jesus. More or less of other work may be done by the Church, but if she neglects to preach Christ, the Son of God, she is no longer the Church of God, the pillar and ground of the truth.

So now, as we and others are wrestling with the educational and civilization problems, are we wrestling before God as we should with this still greater problem,—the Christianization of the Indian.[2]

In 1886 a directive from the Commissioner of Indian Affairs threatened the Dakota Mission's ability to both "civilize" and Christianize by forbidding the use of Indian languages in reservation schools. It was an old contest of wills that the missionaries had won before. This time, however, the Commissioner was adamant. Alfred and Thomas Riggs wrote letters to the Indian Office. John P. Williamson made a trip to Washington, DC, and in December, 1886, brought his plea directly to President Grover Cleveland, whose administration lifted the order.

At the time, Williamson was already exhausted from a two-year bout with recurring bronchial trouble, and from the accumulated stress of managing the Dakota Mission while helping the Sioux through initial procedures in their allotment transition. He suffered a physical and mental breakdown in January, 1887, and went to Florida on an extended retreat to recuperate.

The Indian language ban came again in 1889, and this time Alfred Riggs was compelled to comply because further objection could jeopardize the federal support extended to Santee Normal Institute. Despite forced acquiescence, the Training School achieved its zenith in the 1890s. It became a major educational center for all the Sioux, drawing students from Nebraska, North Dakota, and Montana as well as South Dakota. Its success was obvious later on in the number of students it trained who went on to work as teachers and ministers on the many Sioux reservations.

While Alfred Riggs focused his attention on the growth of Santee Normal Institute, John P. Williamson was busy elsewhere. For half a decade he wrote and translated articles for *Iapi Oaye / The Word Carrier*, helped with the development of new missions at Pine Ridge and Fort Peck, and assisted with allotment procedures and surplus land sale arrangements on the Yankton Reservation. Somehow in 1895 he also found time to enter a term in the South Dakota State Legislature.

The 1890s brought the culmination of work and planning for two generations of Williamsons and Riggses. As they entered the twentieth century, it became clear that times were changing, and that the Dakota Mission was in a state of flux. Following a period of continuous growth, Santee Normal Training School declined rapidly after federal funding ceased in 1901. The school remained open and continued to publish *Iapi Oaye / The Word Carrier* for some thirty additional years, but it never regained its former prominence. Oahe Mission and Industrial School experienced similar difficulties and closed in 1914 for the lack of funds.

Alfred Riggs died in 1916. John P. Williamson died in 1917. Thomas Riggs retired in 1918. John's son, Jesse P. Williamson, and Alfred's son, Frederick B. Riggs, continued the work at Santee Normal, which struggled until closure during depression times in 1936. The Dakota Mission and the Sioux tribes it served had entered a new phase in the history of their relationship with federal officials in particular, and with mainstream society in general. By 1920 the Dakota Mission had 57 churches, 20 ordained native ministers, and 3,500 communicants. Its schools had educated hundreds of Indian children. The Dakota language had been systematized in written form, and a small library of Dakota publications had been produced. The time had come for Sioux people to take charge.

With contemporary emphasis on respect for other cultures, some might judge the Williamson and Riggs families harshly, preferring to view them simply as agents of cultural imperialism. Consistent with nineteenth century values, they never questioned the propriety of "civilization" and Christianization for the Sioux. One should never overlook, however, that the Williamsons and Riggses respected Indians as people and valued their natural integrity and spiritual inclination. A sincere regard for the Sioux brought them at times into conflict with other non-Indians, especially with federal officials. They recognized very early that the westward expansion of the farmers' frontier would bring major change to Indian life and helped tribal members as best they could through the transition. Christianization was their first priority, even though they expended their greatest efforts in helping the Sioux prepare for economic and political adjustment. Their design was not to make imitation White Men but empowered, Christian, Indian citizens of the Sioux. The record of their words and actions bears witness to the vital assistance they gave. Their stomach for hard work and dedication to principle are laudable, whether or not their religious program seems valid by the standards of mainstream society late in the twentieth century.

Notes

1. David Greene, ABCFM Secretary, to Dr. Thomas Williamson at Ripley, March 19, 1834, August 18, 1835, ABCFM Papers, Houghton Library, Harvard University.

2. Winifred W. Barton, *John P.Williamson: A Brother to the Sioux* (New York: Fleming H. Revell, 1919), pp. 191–192.

Bishop William Hobart Hare.

Episcopal Choir at Yankton Agency photographed by W.R. Cross. Courtesy W.H. Over State Museum.

Holy Fellowship Church, Bishop's House and Emanuel House for girls at Santee Agency, Yankton Reservation ca. 1886.

Holy Fellowship Church and Bishop's House at Yankton Reservation ca. 1975.

Bishop's birthday at All Saints School, May 17, 1899.
Courtesy Center for Western Studies.

First Protestant Episcopal Bishop of South Dakota: William Hobart Hare

Gerald W. Wolff

Robert Frost once wrote,

> Two roads diverged in a wood, and I—
> I took the one less traveled by,
> And that has made all the difference.[1]

This thought generally symbolizes the career of William Hobart Hare, except, as a missionary in the northern Great Plains region, he seldom saw a woods or enjoyed the luxury of a road. Hare was a highly intelligent, emotionally sensitive, and physically delicate man who chose a very hard life-style when he did not have to do it. Why? He wanted to convert people to his creed, save souls, teach "civilization," and generally do good on a broader scale than most. It may be difficult to fathom why he persisted in this work or to measure exactly how much he accomplished, but it is certain that he was a figure of major influence among the people of Dakota from the early 1870s until his death on October 23, 1909.

Hare was born on May 17, 1838, in Princeton, New Jersey. Both sides of his family shared a rich, religious heritage within the Protestant Episcopal Church. His father, George, was a gifted biblical scholar. He was the rector of Trinity Church in Princeton when his son was born and would become an eminent professor and administrator at various educational institutions in the Philadelphia area. His mother, Elizabeth Catherine, was the daughter of John Henry Hobart, the Bishop of New York, whose ancestry boasted church leaders dating back to the colonial period.

From ages ten to seventeen, William studied at the Academy of the Protestant Episcopal Church in Philadelphia then moved on to the University of Pennsylvania in 1855. He was a superior scholar but dropped out after the second year because he lacked the money to continue. He suffered from a propensity for illness that would haunt him the rest of his life. Hare remained in the City of Brotherly Love and pursued the career so many of his ancestors had embraced. He taught school while preparing for the ministry and, when barely twenty-one years of age, entered the diaconate and became assistant minister at St. Luke's Church. In May, 1861, he was appointed rector of St. Paul's Church in Philadelphia and a year later was ordained as a priest.

Meanwhile, in October, 1861, he married Mary Amory Howe. In 1862 she gave birth to their son, Hobart Amory. Unfortunately, Mary had a serious, pulmonary disorder. In 1863 Hare resigned his rectorship and sojourned with his family to Minnesota and Michigan, hoping the change would improve his wife's health. While there, he met some American Indians for the first time. He was appalled by their life-style and by the way tribal members and White people treated each other. The visit kindled his belief that he could help and aroused his desire to change the relationship. Nonetheless, he returned to Philadelphia, took up parish work, and continued to function in that capacity until 1871, even after the crushing trauma of his wife's death in January, 1866.

Hare's professional life changed dramatically in 1871, when he was named Secretary and General Agent of the Foreign Committee of the Board of Missions. Using New York City as a base, he acted as liaison between Episcopal domestic and foreign operations, writing letters and making speeches to raise funds and morale. In this position, he broadened his vision, strengthened his convictions, increased his knowledge, and impressed his superiors. On November 1, 1872, Hare learned that the House of Bishops had appointed him Missionary Bishop of Niobrara in the northern Great Plains region, which was inhabited largely by the Sioux.

He was genuinely nonplussed by the offer and almost declined, in part because he enjoyed his job as Secretary. After carefully weighing the situation, however, he decided that the Indians needed and deserved special help and that Congress now offered such a unique opportunity in this field that it should not be ignored. At the same time, he also made clear his belief in his own ability. Hare claimed success in his position on the Board of Missions, and concluded that:

[T]he Indian work cannot afford to take one with the reputation of being an *un*successful man; that it is an easier thing to find a Secretary than a Bishop, because a Bishop (especially one for this new enterprise) needs all the qualities which a Secretary needs, and, besides those qualities, the qualities which fit a man to be Bishop.[2]

He was consecrated at St. Luke's Church in Philadelphia on January 9, 1873. He was the one hundredth Episcopal Bishop named in America and, at age thirty-four, was one of the youngest men his denomination had ever consecrated.

Protestant Episcopal leaders had been interested in promoting the welfare of American Indians for many years. Their work began in earnest during 1859, when Bishop Henry Whipple left his post in Chicago to serve among the Eastern Sioux. After their war in 1862 the Minnesota Sioux were moved to the upper Missouri River basin. In 1866 a majority was settled on land in northeastern Nebraska. During the period of conflict, missionaries continued to function almost unmolested, providing the Indians both spiritual and material succor. Episcopal Bishop R. H. Clarkson and Father Samuel D. Hinman helped Eastern Sioux people adjust to reservation life on semi-arid land. They built a mission house, chapel, and school near the U.S. Agency at Santee, and trained several Indian clergymen who began proselytizing among other tribes in the area. In 1869, under the leadership of merchant-philanthropist William Welsh, eastern Episcopal leaders began a successful drive to raise contributions to support this work. In the early 1870s Welsh convinced many eastern teachers and preachers to transfer their talents and services to the northern Great Plains. These combined efforts led to the creation of several durable missions, including those established near Santee for the Poncas and the Yankton Sioux.

Major incentives for missionary activity were President Ulysses S. Grant's so-called "Peace Policy" and related "Quaker Policy." Grant wanted to foster a peaceful, stable relationship between Indians and Whites of the West in the interest of national development. Political and military means had failed. The Society of Friends had urged Grant to appoint Quakers as U.S. Agents in order to restore morality to reservation administration. In 1869 the President initiated his Quaker Policy when he agreed to let personnel nominated by missionary societies take over several agencies. The same year Grant teamed with Congress to establish a Peace Policy to hasten the acculturation of Indians and prepare them for life in mainstream society as U.S.

citizens. Using congressional allocations, as well as support from private benefactors, religious organizations established churches and schools to teach Native Americans the ways of agriculture and civilization and to change their habits and beliefs through exposure to Christian attitudes and principles. In the summer of 1870 Congress made it mandatory that religious groups nominate all U.S. Indian Agents, who in turn were expected to select regular agency personnel of the highest quality.

In 1869 the President and Congress also created the U.S. Board of Indian Commissioners, a politically neutral group of distinguished advisers, to provide new perspective on the administration of Indian affairs. This nine-man, unsalaried body could visit agencies and investigate their records as well as those of the Indian Office, advise the U.S. Commissioner of Indian Affairs on all purchases made for the tribes, and officially express outrage or disgust over the inappropriate actions of any federal employee connected with Indian affairs. Board members lacked executive authority and were frequently at odds with the U.S. Secretary of the Interior and Commissioner of Indian Affairs, but they were not without influence. Two Episcopalians joined the first Board. One of them was William Welsh, the Board's first President.

Under this arrangement, church and federal officials gave Hare jurisdiction over a huge area that contained a goodly number of missions attached to agencies scattered throughout the Sioux and neighboring reservations. Over the years, missions were added to and dropped from his bailiwick, but for more than a decade certain elements remained constant. There were no railroads and only a few towns and military posts on the northern Plains, making missionary work a physically grueling, sometimes dangerous, experience. Missionaries also often found it difficult to convince Indians to accept Christianity and the White perception of civilization, since, in the past, both had provided them with only a smattering of tangible benefits and few fond memories.

Hare arrived at Yankton in April, 1873, on the heels of a killer blizzard. He decided to establish his See at Greenwood Agency on the Yankton Reservation. At Holy Fellowship Episcopal Church, he began his long career as Bishop by trekking to each of the missions in his charge, including those at Lower Brule, Crow Creek, and Spotted Tail's Camp. The closest one of these was nearly one hundred miles away; the farthest was three hundred miles away. Hare knew well that his trips were absolutely essential. He had to establish his authority as a leader as quickly as possible. Moreover, in order to select and delineate the best strategy for organizing and running such an extensive operation, Hare had to have accurate, first-hand information about mission personnel and the Indian communities they served. Among other things, what were their abilities, attitudes, accomplishments, needs, and living conditions?

After assessing the situation in his diocese, Hare developed a comprehensive administrative plan. Because of the great distances involved, he decided not to make frequent trips to the missions. Instead, he supervised and facilitated the efforts of resident pastors and lay leaders and endeavored to strengthen all existing missions before attempting to found new ones. Hare handled only the larger issues and those smaller, obnoxious problems that no one else would touch. He cut his territory into divisions, each of which was connected with an agency, and led by a presbyter. The presbyters, in turn, were responsible for the ministers and catechists who were in charge of satellite chapels surrounding central agency missions. Shrewdly, he increased the presbyters' influence by giving them direct responsibility for paying their workers. Substation ministers and catechists lived near their chapels, where they could count on monthly visits from their presbyters, who would observe and encourage them and try to improve their performance at all levels.

When Hare became Bishop he had only seven clergymen, five churches, two missionary houses, and no boarding schools. Over the years he considerably enlarged the number of institutions that served Indians. After the Black Hills gold rush in 1875 he added many non-Indian congregations to his flock. For a time the Bishop also supervised several U.S. Agents among the Sioux, who, thanks to the power of William Welsh, were nominated by the Protestant Episcopal Church. His primary need at first, however, was for buildings and staff and, to that end, he worked closely with Episcopal congregations in the East to raise money and recruit men and women for service at the missions.

Buildings were of little use without personnel to fill them. It was difficult to convince young men to become missionaries in the Niobrara Diocese because of low, unguaranteed pay; periodic Indian warfare; personal danger; the constant presence of itinerant, unsavory Whites; isolation; an unreliable natural environment; and an unstable rural economy. Near the end of his career, Hare maintained steadfastly that he was pleased with the missionaries who had chosen to join him. Yet, he always seemed to be short of workers and continued, to the end, to plead eloquently for more missionaries of the right type. In a way, he was trapped between his high standards and the increasing needs of the region he served.

Hare wanted men who were well-educated, who were of high spiritual quality, and who could think like lay people. They had to be tactful, sensitive, patient, and persistent individuals who could serve as wise counselors and moral examples. He required men with more than a single talent, who could adjust and improvise well; for they would be bereft of the kind of community support that was automatic in eastern parishes.

Hare freely admitted that being a missionary in Sioux Country meant enduring a rough life, but he also argued that this was a task that somebody had to do. "There are," he wrote, "human beings in it, good, careless, wicked, stricken, who must respectively be encouraged, awakened, converted, comforted."[3] The Bishop conceded that stable, eastern parishes were very important, but the comforts they provided might not bring young ministers the happiness and fulfillment that missionary work could furnish. Eventually they would become prisoners of the good life, ruined by softness and self-satisfaction. Sooner or later the results would be dire:

> Spiritual vigor, you will have none–enthusiasm, none–love of your work, none–accent of conviction when you preach, none–you will be a weariness to the laity and a mortification to your clerical brethren.[4]

To supplement this small band of trained personnel, Hare drew upon other human resources. Lay people supplied yeoman service, both as groups and as individuals. By 1898 women in some ninety societies or guilds were laboring and raising money for Episcopal churches in South Dakota. By then Indian men had formed the Brotherhood of Christian Unity and Whites the Brotherhood of St. Andrew, both of which furnished outstanding support. The wives of missionaries assisted willingly in a variety of unglamorous capacities. Women's auxiliaries in the East sent clothing and other items for the needy. These offerings sometimes included articles of little use to Indians, such as ball gowns and other formal attire, but the Indians appreciated the donors' desire to help. Boxes arrived in such quantity that Hare had to create a special storeroom in Yankton from which he systematically distributed items to meet each station's specific needs.

Dedicated Sisters also came to Dakota from the Bishop Potter Memorial House in Philadelphia to become nurses, teachers, and general helpers among the Sioux. Most importantly, Hare developed a crew of devoted Indian ministers and catechists who worked at remote satellite stations on the reservations. They were able to preach, teach, and counsel with great effectiveness, in part because they were bilingual and sensitive to the nuances of both Indian and White cultures.

Hare further improved his organization with the Convocation. The first of these met at Santee Mission in August, 1873, and attracted only about a hundred people. They discussed practical issues, such as how to get more rations and clothing from Washington, DC, or from the Bishop himself. No spiritual aura surrounded this meeting. By the end of Hare's career, however, annual convocations drew some three thousand Indians from at least a dozen reservations to participate in activities important to their religious and social lives. Participating Indian congregations reported offerings each year in the thousands of dollars. After 1883 Whites also gathered annually and, starting in 1885, every third year the two races mingled at general convocations. Hare had wisely nurtured an institution that continually reinvigorated his cause by both cheering and inspiring his workers and those they served.

Effective communication was crucial to the success of Hare's missionary enterprise. The Bishop never tried to master Sioux dialects, but he realized that using them would help gain and retain converts. He consistently advocated teaching Indians to read their own vernacular. In 1874 Hare created a committee to translate the *Book of Common Prayer* accurately into *Dakota*; it was published a year later. Over the next decade, he turned out a series of translated works, including the *Holy Bible*; catechisms; a hymnal; and the *Kings Highway*, a popular, four-hundred page interpretation of the Ten Commandments. Among the most useful publications was the *Dakota-English Service Book*, with pages printed on one side in Dakota and on the other in English equivalents. This book gave a new gloss to services, and gave Episcopalian Sioux the confidence to join their clergy in worship recitations. Hare's monthly newspaper, the *ANPAO*, appeared only in English, but it was widely read and much coveted. In 1883 the Missionary District began producing *Church News*, which carried all of Hare's official pronouncements, along with area news. This publication allowed the Bishop to assert his authority over his expanded See and to foster feelings in his flock that members were part of a calling beyond the boundaries of their stations and parishes.

Hare also communicated information and values through formal education, supported by congressional appropriations. Beginning in the 1870s, he developed a plan to found a group of Indian boarding

schools whose educated graduates would form the core of congregations at nearby chapels. More specifically, he determined to create a
central boarding school of very high quality at the Yankton Agency in
Greenwood where he would live and supervise operations. This
school, in turn, was to furnish the other educational institutions and
mission stations in the system with its best graduates as teachers,
catechists, and missionaries. The very best scholars would be sent to
eastern colleges, such as Hampton Institute, for advanced training. As
Hare intended, many graduates of these institutions of higher learning
returned to their tribes more self-confident and independent, ready to
provide service and leadership for their people.

Although Hare did not completely reject the value of day schools,
he preferred boarding schools, mainly because they allowed students
to learn non-Indian skills and values during long, uninterrupted periods
of time. So it was that, in December, 1873, Bishop Hare began St.
Paul's School for Indian Boys at the Yankton Agency, which was the
first reservation boarding school of any type in the northern Great
Plains region. A year later he added Emmanuel Hall for Girls on the
grounds near St. Paul's. Over the next fifteen years Hare founded half
a dozen other boarding schools and several day schools near his
Episcopal missions. Some of these were segregated by gender, while
others were co-educational.

What educational environment did Hare create for the average
students at his schools and what philosophy lay behind his choices?
His program involved teaching the three "Rs," trades, "civilized"
habits, and Christian values and dogma. All of his institutions were
designed to be self-sustaining, "plain and practical and not calculated
to engender fastidious tastes and habits, which would make the pupils
unhappy in, and unfitted for, the lowly life to which the people are
called."[5] He wanted to make their every day living easier by "teaching
them to do well the common acts of daily humble life."[6]

With these ends in mind, male students at Bishop Hare's schools
were divided into three squads, each assigned to a separate manual
work department for a week at a time. By 10:00 a.m. each day, all
mundane, manual tasks were completed. From that point each week
day, the boys attended class until noon, broke for lunch, did a few
chores from 2:00 to 3:00 in the afternoon, and returned to the classroom until 5:00.

Female students learned to read, write, and cipher, and the best
scholars among them were prepared to be teachers but, for most of the
girls, great emphasis was placed on training them to be "good" wives

and mothers. They learned the skills necessary for efficient homemaking, including cooking, sewing, weaving, milking, and churning. Hare believed that Indian girls should not be sent to eastern schools because they might absorb habits and develop desires that would make them balk at returning to domestic lives in their tribes.

In establishing an educational system, Hare was definitely condescending toward his students and their potential. In this he was a typical product of his times, as much a victim as a beneficiary. A paternal figure, he could be kind, thoughtful, and understanding as well as arrogant, autocratic, and demanding. He found it difficult to impose harsh discipline because it was not practiced in Sioux society. For example, Hare often punished the boys for their transgressions by making them cut firewood. In response, some refused to submit and simply left school, while others never returned from their vacations. Hare also established a system of rewards for those who agreed to stay and obey. They received scholarships, field trips, and farm animals they could raise at school and keep after graduation. The Bishop often treated pupils to rides in his traveling wagon and, on one occasion, walked miles to pick up and bring back gifts for the children in time for Christmas. He once wrote, "The Indians' old life was like a moccasin, soft and easy-fitting. The new life is like a tight, hard leather boot. It rubs him and makes him sore. Therefore, the more innocent fun we can have in our Indian Boarding Schools the better."[7]

One area of education that could not be fun was the continuous effort required to find money to support the schools. The expense of teaching, feeding, clothing, and obtaining equipment for pupils was enormous, and the cost of erecting and repairing buildings was often staggering. Virtually every Episcopal school encountered one or more natural disasters over the years, from tornadoes to prairie fires, and such catastrophes required expensive rebuilding. Hare had insurance to cover some losses, and his eastern benefactors were generous. Better still, beginning in 1869, the federal government provided money for sectarian Indian schools through a contract system. For years the Bishop refused to take advantage of the program, believing that it violated an American tradition of the separation of church and state and that it could lead to corruption and favoritism toward the Roman Catholic Church. From the outset, however, his educational system drew federal assistance by accepting rations and clothing due the scholars as annuity issues. By 1887 the Bishop ran so short of funds that he was forced to make contracts with federal officials.

By the early years of the twentieth century, all funding of this type vanished except tuition from tribal funds paid to ecclesiastical schools on behalf of the pupils at their parents' request. Because contract support ended, many mission schools were forced to close and others were sold to the U.S. Office of Indian Affairs, including St. Paul's at Greenwood. Educators on federal salaries simply occupied mission school buildings and adopted curricula and techniques the churches had used effectively for a generation.

Hare saw education as only one of several elements in a grand design for "civilizing" American Indians. In his view the practices and beliefs of Indians were merely temporary. He counseled outsiders to stop regarding them as a separate people. The false but pervasive idea that tribes were distinct entities had given rise to a pernicious reservation system. In his view, reservations confined Indians to insular ignorance, and prevented them from mastering and adopting the values and systems that made mainstream society prosperous and successful. The reservation arrangement, he declared, where anyone who wants:

> scratches a piece of land where he will, where beef, flour, sugar, coffee, etc. are doled out to vicious and virtuous, indolent and industrious alike is a monstrous evil which should be tolerated not a day longer than is absolutely necessary.[8]

Reservations also impeded the westward advance of bona fide White settlers. These were Caucasians who would obey the law and stay off tribal lands and yet they would serve as the finest role models for Indians. In their absence the first Whites Indians saw were usually reprobates and villains, who always seemed to linger long enough to do them damage. In Hare's opinion, federal officials had a duty to provide Indians with a constructive example and useful training, not a setup that created droves of paupers who did little more than hinder progress.

Hare recommended phasing out reservations as soon as possible and consolidating all the sundry tribes, which were, at that time, widely scattered, badly divided, and greatly outnumbered. If for no other reason than their own protection, tribes must ultimately agree to give up their separate identities. Barriers between Indians and Whites could then be eliminated and the culture of the majority in the United States could at first dominate and finally prevail.

For the short run Hare advocated a policy to promote Indian self-reliance with limited White assistance. As early as the 1870s he urged federal officials to survey and divide parts of reservations into individual farms and distribute them to Indians in severalty. At least for awhile officials should protect Indian titles to family farms from the machinations of unprincipled Whites and should provide food and tools to tribal farmers until they could support themselves. He suggested the reservation land that remained after allotment should be made available to respectable White farmers, who by intermingling with Indian neighbors could inspire and advise them. Hare garnered the seeds of these ideas by observing the Flandreau, Santee, and Sisseton Sioux, who had long associated with White farmers and by Caucasian standards had flourished in agriculture relative to other tribes. Such a close relationship with non-Indians, even if it led to intense competition, would teach tribal members such values as individualism and hard work. To Hare's delight, in 1887 Congress adopted a severalty plan of this type by passing Henry Dawes's Indian Allotment Act.

The Bishop supported other facets of federal policy for Indians. Yet, for him, their conversion to Christianity was the most crucial factor in the entire "civilizing" process. Many missionaries were insensitive to Indian culture, especially its religious components, and repeatedly tried to eradicate it with brash and boorish assaults. Hare was also ethnocentric but subtle. Hence, he was somewhat more successful than most. He used insight, tact, and friendly persuasion to convince Indians to relinquish elements of their religious heritage of their own free will. The Bishop realized that his approach required uncommon skill and great patience. He wrote in 1884:

A good deal of smoothing is sometimes necessary, for Indian life is a tangle of intrigue and diverse parties and clashing plans and interests through which the benevolent, however clever, may find it hard to make his way.[9]

Late in his career Hare summarized his experience and advised workers never to forget that Indians were, above all, human beings who appreciated fair play. Missionaries, to be effective, must identify with them and feel sympathy for their plight. At the same time they must free themselves of either prejudicial or sentimental illusions. He concluded sadly that, among Anglo-Saxons, there was often:

a haughty denial that any sentiment can be sacred unless it be our sentiment; . . . to turn a man from modes of thought and habits of action which are dear to him, must always be a delicate task. . . . And yet we are disposed to stand off as their critics from the people whom we are called to serve. . . . Even our petitions for them in intercessory prayer take on a condescending and patronizing air.[10]

Such pleas for toleration and understanding, however, were meant only to improve missionary methods and not to gain the acceptance of alternative values. Hare once wrote:

Our work is not that of building up a National Indian Church with a national liturgy in the Indian tongue. It is rather that of resolving the Indian structure and preparing its parts for being taken up into the great whole in Church and State.[11]

The Bishop never wavered in his conviction that, if Indians were ever to be truly happy, they must ultimately adopt Caucasian culture and Christian religion.

Some Sioux were enthusiastic about Christianity. Others were defiant. Most were apathetic. Disinterest was overcome, in part, because supplies came to areas containing chapels. Apathy gave way to gradual accommodation, too, because Indians were ecumenical in their approach to spiritual life, which was for them the guiding force behind their tribal existence. Hare once described the Indians as the most religious people he had ever seen, in the sense that they believed thoroughly in the supernatural, were alive with mysticism, and from an early age searched constantly in religion for meaning beyond themselves. In a fit of condescension, Hare once portrayed them as children more taken by the emotional side of Christianity than its moral dimension but he acknowledged their sincere devotion to the plan of God.

If the Sioux penchant for spirituality provided a useful foundation for Hare's work, it also proved a hindrance. In his opinion, worship by tribal members sometimes crossed the line into outright superstition and surfaced as some form of fear. When tragedy struck, traditional Sioux people tended to blame the intrusion of missionaries and claim that the event proved Christianity was meant only for Whites. At the same time, however, Sioux leaders also asked missionaries quite rational, if harsh, questions about Christianity. Why would a God of love, for example, allow his progeny to suffer? Why did Whites kill the Son of God?

Despite all this, Hare and his workers managed to influence the spiritual lives of the Indians and convert many of them. Sioux people were lured by the formal liturgy of the Episcopal Church, the Priests' resplendent vestments, the ornate chapels, and even the candle-lit altars. Realizing this, Hare carefully prepared the trappings of his services and urged others to do the same. He had a gift for creating clever analogies and meaningful imagery that made his sermons interesting. Hare advised his ministers not to read their sermons but rather to speak extemporaneously from their hearts, as much in the style of Indian oration as possible. He asked them to remember that the Indians' traditional religion had deep roots, so it was not easily altered. Religion was a stabilizing force in all aspects of their lives and the introduction of Christianity had upset that balance. Some were now confused and disoriented, enduring severe psychological pressures that might drive them to recklessness or break their spirits. He argued that missionaries had a duty to smooth this transition, remove the Indians' anxiety, and restore their serenity as quickly as possible.

Not everything went well for mission personnel; many problems arose and persisted, ranging from the mundane to the dramatic. The Dakota climate shunned moderation and embraced excesses of temperature, precipitation, wind, and drought. Weather was unpredictable, while dust storms, fires, and grasshoppers were abundant. All of these elements made it difficult to mold Indians into farmers and often stopped missionaries from visiting them for months at a time. When Hare was able to travel, he endured protracted, arduous, and monotonous movement over seemingly endless stretches of unbroken, treeless plains. In 1880, alone, he trekked more than two thousand miles in a springless, open-air wagon to bring solace to his followers. He also traveled by stage-coach and river-boat, neither of which represented a major improvement. During these trips, he frequently faced severe exposure, a variety of vermin, and a paucity of people, food, fuel, fresh water, and decent shelter. All this would have led most men to redefine their ideas about duty. Yet, Hare considered such adverse conditions as minor irritants, irrelevant when compared with the slow but steady progress he was making toward achieving his major goals.

Other problems were more annoying. During the 1870s, churches began competing vigorously for converts outside the agencies they had been assigned under the Quaker Policy. Episcopal, Presbyterian, and Congregational missionaries cooperated with each other on such matters as biblical translations, but rivalry was the rule. Hare resisted inter-denominational conflict for a long time. Eventually he acquiesced. By 1881 competition among denominations and bitterness on reservations escalated to a point where everyone agreed to abandon any pretence of respect for agency assignments. By 1883 the Quaker Policy had vanished forever and competition for federal funds, as well as Indian souls, became open and, occasionally, nasty.

Like other Protestant missionaries, Hare harbored and nurtured special antipathy for the Roman Catholic Church. He contended that Catholic missionaries had purposely moved beyond their rightful assignments under the Quaker Policy and were the recipients of several forms of government favoritism. As early as 1875 he was convinced the Catholics planned to invade Episcopal territory with malicious intent. As a result, he sent a letter to the heads of agencies where Episcopalians had government assignments requesting that Catholic employees be replaced with Protestants. The Bishop learned that one of his missionaries had offered the use of an Episcopal Cathedral to a Catholic priest to conduct a funeral service. Hare wrote his worker that he understood and appreciated his good intentions. Still, he was relieved that the cleric had declined the invitation, "the mere thought of a priest of Rome addressing the Virgin in prayer at the Cathedral altar being painful to me."[12]

Inter-denominational competition was aggravating but the danger of Indian war was terrifying. Major confrontations interspersed with smaller hostile encounters hindered the proselytizing process for years and frequently threatened missionaries' lives. On several occasions Hare barely escaped death at the hands of aroused bands of Sioux. Once a commission, backed only by a small cavalry force, met with Spotted Tail and several thousand of his followers. Deep into the discussion the Brule leader became angry and signaled his men to mount their horses and ready their weapons. Hare and the other Whites made no move to defend themselves. Respecting their courage, Spotted Tail ordered his warriors to ride away. Another time, Hare and several officials left the Lower Brule Agency against the Post Commander's advice to talk with some Sioux half a mile away. The Indians were incensed over the arrest of one of their own for trying to murder a post trader. Federal officials refused to free the culprit and hundreds of painted warriors prepared to attack. Then they suddenly left when a company of troops arrived with two cannons.

Some missionaries died. One of Hare's helpers, R. Archer B. Ffennell, was shot to death near the Cheyenne River Agency in September, 1876. From his mission, St. John's, Ffennell traversed the three miles to the agency to secure the release of a renegade Indian he had never met. He succeeded, but the freed Indian and a friend had promised themselves that they would kill the first White man they saw, who, ironically, happened to be Ffennell. Authorities never attempted to punish the murderers and Hare seriously contemplated closing the mission. He decided, in the end, to continue its operation, but the bloody incident produced severe and prolonged anxiety among his workers.

Because of these dangers and those created by White law-breakers who plagued the agencies, Hare concluded that something had to be done. He strongly advocated that federal officials combine moral suasion with military force to bring an end to this kind of nonsense. He was sensitive to the frequent charge that, by calling for such a policy, he was invoking violence and undermining the purity of his calling. Hare replied that he was as justified in requesting military protection from the few Indians who were hostile as he would be in asking urban police to guard him from the few Whites who occasionally formed mobs. Acknowledging that most tribal members obeyed the law, he wrote: "I have as a fact made it my habit to travel through the country and to appear in the most tumultuous scenes without any firearm or weapon whatever, and without any protection save such as was afforded by the presence of friendly Indians."[13]

For Hare the risk of assault was relatively rare, vanished rather quickly when it did occur, and may even have left him with a secret sense of exhilaration. It was the protracted and cumulative burdens of responsibility that strained his nerve, sapped his strength, and wearied his spirit. He was expected to handle the plethora of problems and shortcomings he found among his shepherds and flock. Whether Hare encountered general apathy, simple discouragement, alcohol abuse, or sexual indiscretion, it was up to him to deal with the situation and attempt to correct it. He was also left with the unenviable task of finding money and disbursing it fairly to support his various ventures. In meeting these and many other obligations, he was required to write a seemingly endless stream of letters. He was not always successful in his efforts and, when he was forced to watch a promising project atrophy or die, or to listen to opportunity banging loudly on a stuck door, he had no confidant to share his frustration and sorrow.

This type of pressure might have worn out a healthy man, and Hare was far from that. By the mid-1870s his health was so broken by the demands of his schedule that he and his doctors believed he must leave the field for kinder conditions or soon die. In fact, in October, 1875, he drafted a letter of resignation but the House of Bishops convinced him to take an extended vacation in Europe. During his stay he slowly recovered enough of his health to function, but he continued to feel guilty about neglecting Niobrara. In October, 1876, he returned to resume his activities among the Indians and did so against the advice of his physicians and many of his friends and relatives. He came back because he felt it was necessary to bolster his workers, his converts, his Church, and his sense of duty. The Bishop was a brave man of uncommon character who continued to risk his life by refusing to accept a number of legitimate opportunities to quit a strenuous station.

Hare needed all of the strength he could muster for a long and bitter battle with one of his presbyters, Samuel D. Hinman, the first Episcopal missionary to work closely with the Sioux. Hinman had served well as an interpreter for several government commissions, and had come within two votes of being named Bishop of Niobrara. In 1873 he had been exonerated after an investigation into charges of sexual misconduct and misappropriation of funds. The accusations resurfaced, however, and Hare, believing he had solid evidence, finally removed him from the Santee Mission in March, 1878. Hinman appealed the decision through appropriate Episcopal agencies but received no satisfaction. Taking another approach, he produced a lengthy and widely-circulated pamphlet stating his views of the whole matter in the bluntest terms. Hare responded with an eight-page account of the indictment against Hinman and sent it to key Episcopal leaders as well as to several of his friends.

In 1880 Hinman raised the level of controversy by suing Hare for libel and asking $25,000 in damages. The case, which was tried in New York, attracted a good deal of unsavory publicity. After much deliberation, a jury found in Hinman's favor but awarded him only $10,000. Hare appealed but the issue was not resolved until 1887. As a result, for nearly a decade the Bishop suffered grave torment and considerable humiliation. Except on Sundays, he was barred from entering New York and newspapers refused to let the story die. Hare also had to spend $12,000 beyond the contributions he received from wellwishers to meet his legal expenses. An appeals judge finally overturned the verdict and suggested the case be settled through arbitration. In a token reconciliation, Hinman and Hare both signed documents saying in essence that, if the charges against Hinman were invalid, the Bishop had sincerely believed them to be true when he discharged the missionary.

At the outset of this difficult ordeal, Hare's Episcopal superiors increased his official responsibilities. Rather than crushing his spirit, the new assignment actually seemed to improve his morale. In October, 1883, the House of Bishops appointed him Bishop of South

Dakota. He now had jurisdiction over both Indians and Whites in what would become, in 1889, the State of South Dakota, plus the Santee Reservation in Nebraska. Over the previous decade, White migrants had created many new towns. They needed schools and churches, and Hare wanted to help provide them. "We shall," he declared, "cease to be Missionaries to classes or races, and be Missionaries to men." [14]

The Bishop moved energetically to organize the new domain by dividing his diocese into Deaneries. The Western or Niobrara contained all of the Indian missions; the Eastern held the White congregations; and later, he added another for the Black Hills. He put rural Deans in charge of these segments of his Diocese and furnished them and their helpers with a full description of their general responsibilities and specific duties.

As Bishop of South Dakota, Hare had to select a new site for his headquarters. Regardless of his choice he planned to locate a school for girls there. Many towns wanted the school but Sioux Falls offered land along with ten thousand dollars if the Bishop could match the amount. He managed to find the funds, and All Saints School opened in September, 1885, primarily, but not exclusively, for the benefit of his missionaries' daughters. Hare elected to live there and, with the assistance of principal Helen Peabody, hired teachers and crafted the curriculum. For a good share of the previous decade he had endured a physically demanding life in a harsh environment. So the weary Bishop welcomed the peace and relative comfort of his new home and continued to enjoy it to the end of his life.

As the All Saints School and the Sioux Falls congregation grew, Hare found his original church building was too small. Thanks to generous donations from the benefactor John Jacob Astor, by the autumn of 1889 the Bishop was able to conduct services in a new, stone cathedral of considerable size.

Since 1875, when many White migrants began entering Dakota, Hare had been unofficially and sporadically ministering to their needs. After his 1883 appointment, he became much more thorough and systematic in the services he provided to non-Indians. He began at once visiting various towns, some of which were just establishing churches. Hare found that these citizens were hard-working and ambitious, and that they welcomed him with open enthusiasm. He was very astute in his assessment of the nature and derivations of their positive attitudes:

> A whole community, religious and profane alike, will unite in an effort to build a church, each expecting to reap from it the benefit which he most

desires; one the appreciation of the value of his town lots, another the gratification of his wife and children, a third the encouragement of morals and religion and all, the general improvement of their town.[15]

They were willing to make substantial economic sacrifices and devote a considerable portion of their time and scant resources to help secure the future of their towns.

By the time South Dakota became a state in 1889, Hare could report considerable progress. His Niobrara Deanery for Indians had eight parishes, nineteen missions, eleven unorganized stations, forty tribal congregations, more than twelve hundred converts, and over forty workers. Among his White followers he had thirty-three clergymen serving ninety parishes and missions, which together boasted more than two thousand members plus as many others on Sunday School rolls. Adult Episcopalians regularly contributed their time and money to support church activities. At the Indian missions there were no outstanding debts, except a loan on one building. Overall, Hare had developed a successful program.

Because he had done so well in the South Dakota Diocese, in February, 1891, the House of Bishops asked Hare to solve some problems within the Asian missions. As a result of his two trips abroad, in Japan, American missionaries went about their work with renewed commitment and appropriate respect for native leadership. A new Bishop was named, and the bickering between operatives representing the Church of England and the Protestant Episcopal Church of America all but ceased. In China, American Episcopal mission personnel found solutions to problems related to the recent death of their Bishop.

Hare's service in the orient underscored his political ability. He had long been involved with national political figures, agencies, and issues. Hare's relationship with federal officials was multifaceted, and was more frustrating and unproductive near the end of his career than it was at the start. In the 1870s he served on a variety of commissions established to help resolve problems with certain Indian leaders and to investigate the activities of the military and agents scattered about Sioux Country. He also provided advice to national political leaders, including presidents, on general Indian policy. More specifically, in 1874 he admonished federal leaders repeatedly that national honor required them to resist pressure from gold-hungry Whites and to guard Sioux rights to the Black Hills region under the terms of the Fort Laramie Treaty of 1868. A year later, however, Hare suggested to the Secretary of the Interior that he find out whether there was enough gold in the Hills to make mining profitable. If not, Indian claims must be protected. If gold was found to be abundant, however, federal officials were obligated to pay the Sioux a fair price for their land. He had concluded that nothing short of a miracle could prevent the forward rush of White gold-seekers. Throughout his career Hare had a consistent habit of mixing his principles with large doses of pragmatism and realism.

In 1890 the Bishop also recommended that federal officials allow the "Messiah Craze" to run its natural course. The movement, after all, was popular in only a few locations among relatively few Indians. Hare argued that Ghost Dancers were not much of a threat, because they were convinced that God, Himself, would shortly destroy White civilization. The Almighty's assault, of course, would not happen and the movement would collapse. Sadly, Hare's plea went unheeded. In December, 1890, came the infamous Wounded Knee Affair.

On a less elevated political plane, the Peace and Quaker policies allowed religious denominational leaders, such as Hare, to work with federal officials to promote Indian acculturation. From the start, Hare requested and received the right to supervise the process in the field. This arrangement worked well during most of the 1870s, and Hare's program derived many benefits. Congress allocated funds. U.S. Agents often provided housing for missionaries, turned over federal buildings for Indian education, helped obtain worship facilities, and sometimes excluded competing denominations. Agents were known to aid missionaries in personal ways, too, occasionally exceeding the bounds of propriety and raising ethical concerns.

Politicians, however, soon began to see opportunities for themselves and their political parties at agencies and conspired to curtail the power of religious denominations. Their aggression was so gradual and subtle that by the time clergymen recognized the change it was too late. The last Church-nominated U.S. Agent pulled out in 1879. Those who had not resigned voluntarily were charged with incompetence or dishonesty and removed. Three of Hare's nominees were fired under a cloud of suspicion in March, 1878. The Bishop protested. They were eventually exonerated, but they were never rehired. By 1879 every agency was controlled by either political appointees or "temporary," low-ranking military officers. From that year forward, the Quaker Policy faded rapidly until it was officially ended in 1883. Hare's relationship with federal employees at agencies now became much more difficult, requiring all the political acumen he could muster and ending in more defeats than victories.

He had greater success, however, dealing with certain social-political issues within the State of South Dakota. In 1890 the Legislature considered adopting a rigid prohibition law. It prescribed a heavy fine and imprisonment for those who sold, gave away, or shipped alcoholic beverages to adults or minors, except for scientific, medicinal, or mechanical purposes. This proposal would make it impossible for Episcopal clergy to carry out the sacrament of the Lord's Supper, because the House of Bishops had ruled in 1886 that real wine must be used. Hare, therefore, petitioned the Legislature to amend the bill to allow him and his workers to perform their duties without the threat of going to prison.

Many, including ministers from other denominations, chastised him for his position. One of his detractors argued that Hare, as a citizen, had the right to petition the Legislature but that he was wrong to follow his signature with the words "Missionary Bishop of South Dakota." This amused Hare, who pointed out that his critic had finished his letter with the title, "Presiding Elder of Aberdeen District Methodist Episcopal Church." The Bishop noted that this appellation was at least twice as long as his, that the author should probably narrow his definition of "Presiding," and that, although he was an "Elder," he ought not speak to other adults as if they were children. Hare concluded that many prohibitionists had become self-righteous, intolerant, and bigoted, holding that any deviation from teetotaling was equivalent to drunkenness.

The Bishop was as disgusted and dismayed with the individual abuse of wine and liquor as any prohibitionist and wanted it stopped. He did not believe, however, that prohibition was the solution. Rather, he wanted a licensing system. Legislation designed to eliminate virtually all alcohol would not prevent those who wanted beer, wine, and liquor from getting them. Drinkers would merely evade the law. Once again combining practicality and principle, he declared that, "Intended to make men sober, this law will tend to make them liars."[16]

It took some time, but Hare was eventually vindicated on this issue. After several years of controversy, in 1897 the Legislature sent a proposed constitutional amendment for prohibition to the voters, who rejected it. Soon, the Legislature adopted a licensing system to control the distribution and sale of alcoholic beverages.

Another political issue that occupied much of Hare's time was South Dakota's divorce law. The Bishop had an unusually deep respect for marriage and a strong belief that man and wife should live together permanently. He had long maintained that too many people treated the institution lightly and entered it without much reflection about consequences. Since the 1870s he had urged his clergy to probe and assess the motives of couples before agreeing to join them. Hare held that even well-written divorce laws did not deal adequately with the moral and religious aspects of the process. But South Dakota's divorce legislation disgusted him to the point of moral and physical nausea. In 1893 he started a movement to reform the law.

In January, 1893, the Bishop hand-carried to the Legislature a petition, bearing nine hundred signatures, requesting that the divorce regulations be changed. He was allowed to make a speech to the Legislature on its behalf, and also to testify before a joint session of the judiciary committees. There were many deficiencies in the law but to Hare perhaps the worst was that it required only a three month residence for those desiring to file for divorce. Knowledge about this aspect of the legislation had spread far. Transients flocked by the hundreds to South Dakota, stayed a short time, gained their divorces, and left. South Dakota citizens who supported the law included lawyers, hotel owners, jewelers, and florists, whose businesses thrived on the divorce traffic. Hare, on the other hand, contended that the reputation of South Dakota was being stained throughout America.

The Bishop's trip to Pierre was well worth the effort. In 1893 the Legislature increased the residency requirement to six months. Certain business interests were dismayed by the change. As their profits diminished, they mounted a campaign to have the original law reinstated. Hare responded with a public appeal opposing their purpose, using the newspapers and yet another petition to the Legislature. Once again, he prevailed. For years after this encounter, Hare preached sermon after sermon lauding the family unit and imploring his clergy to obey the letter of Church doctrine on divorce and remarriage.

In 1906 Governor Samuel Elrod asked Hare to join a Washington, DC, convention that worked to create a divorce code the entire nation could accept. Delegates sent the results of their deliberations to every state legislature. A few attorneys in South Dakota objected but the state bar association recommended the adoption of three proposals. In 1907 the legislature passed these measures into law and asked the people to consider them in a 1908 referendum.

For a third time, Hare entered the public arena on the issue of divorce. With the help of others, he asked the people to accept the new law in hundreds of newspapers around the state and meted out nearly one hundred thousand broadsides to all of the congregations he could locate. Voters approved the changes by a considerable margin.

As a result, the required time of residence before filing for divorce was extended to one year, and suits had to be brought within the county of residence. Divorces could no longer be rushed through any time it was convenient by some judge in private chambers but had to take place during a regular court term. Hare lived long enough to savor still another victory for yet another cause.

This last campaign was unusually arduous, draining most of the energy and health he had left. Since 1875, Hare knew he had mitral stenosis, a progressive narrowing of a crucial heart valve. From 1895 on, he was forced to take periodic vacations that sometimes lasted several months. His health deteriorated rapidly after 1903, when he acquired a malignant growth on his face. After repeated treatments and frequent operations, in April, 1907, Hare underwent radical surgery, which included the removal of his right eye-ball. Through years of excruciating pain, he seldom complained and was virtually free of selfpity or meanness toward others.

In 1904 he offered to resign but his letter was refused. He then requested that the range of his responsibilities be reduced, either by dividing his diocese or appointing an assistant. In October, 1904, the General Convention sent Rev. Fredrick Foote Johnson of Massachusetts to be his Assistant Bishop. Hare was pleased with his coadjutor, both professionally and personally. The burden of his official duties was cut in half. All this is not to suggest that, during these years, he was not working diligently. Between vacations and trips to various hospitals, he was active and productive, both in his Sioux Falls office and out at the mission stations. He told his Convocation in 1906, for example, that during that year:

> My visitations have not been a little interfered with and curtailed by the state of my health, but I have notwithstanding, preached and made addresses one hundred and twenty-five times, confirmed on twenty-five occasions, and celebrated the Holy Communion twenty-six times.[16]

Modern science and medical advances could help ease his pain and delay his decline but could not halt them. Bishop Hare died on October 23, 1909, at age seventy-one. He had asked to be buried in South Dakota and he was laid to rest on the grounds of Calvary Cathedral in Sioux Falls. Hundreds of dignitaries and ordinary citizens attended the funeral, during which government offices and businesses in the city closed. The following April, Sioux Falls held a massive memorial day in his honor. Again, all business ceased as speaker after speaker paid tribute to his life of service before a huge audience.

Bishop Hare had many admirable traits. He was intelligent, sensitive, methodical, energetic, courageous, and generally shrewd in his evaluation of character and motives. He had a special talent for organizing and communicating. His behavior also reflected many Christian virtues, including faith, kindness, forgiveness, sympathy, devotion to duty, and altruism. All of these attributes and others combined to help him perform well in his chosen career. For thirty-six years, he skillfully walked a tightrope between the cliffs of mammon and the spirit of God without toppling into the abyss of total failure and corruption. As the lives of many other clergy have long demonstrated, this, in itself, was not an easy accomplishment.

The crucial problem of a biographer, however, is to determine the extent to which he succeeded in reaching his goals. Among non-Indians, it would seem that Hare made substantial progress and left a lasting legacy. He built a cathedral, founded a school and, indirectly at least, helped many towns achieve permanency and respectability. Before the end of his career, the Bishop established nearly forty parishes and missions for Whites, scattered throughout the entire state. Shortly before his death, Hare reported that there were nearly 2,500 White Episcopalians in South Dakota, who, in 1907, donated some thirty-thousand dollars to the church. He was obviously satisfied with the results of his efforts.

It is more difficult to evaluate Hare's contributions to the Sioux. The Bishop strove mightily to save the Indians' souls and to replace their culture with his own set of assumptions and values. For him, assimilation was imperative, and the reservation system was anathema. He failed to achieve what he wanted in both areas. Nonetheless, Bishop Hare effected many changes. After he and his workers arrived, Sioux people seemed to be more peaceful, more educated, more Christian, and more acculturated.

For these changes, however, Indians paid a high price. Former tribal groups that had thrived on hunting, gathering, and gardening had to accept sedentary farming, dress like the intruders, speak their language, and relinquish many tribal traditions. Conversion cost some individuals even more. In May, 1879, for example, a young and well-known member of a Sioux warrior society named Truth Teller publicly renounced his heritage and promised to dedicate his life to the Episcopal Church and White civilization. After Truth Teller announced his intentions, he handed Hare his war eagle feather and the ceremonial drum of the Order of the Grass Dance. He went on to become a catechist, but his people no longer honored him or showed him respect; indeed, they persecuted him vigorously.

Hare and his helpers placed every Sioux they approached in a spiritual and cultural bind of great magnitude. The Bishop realized the friction and frustration they experienced. As a result he developed tolerance and patience and learned increasingly to compromise, but the value of Indian culture never occurred to Hare or his workers. They surrendered little of their own cultural and religious advantage and beliefs to accommodate its survival.

What was the depth, longevity, and meaning of Hare's influence on the Sioux? The Bishop tended to measure success by counting converts. Before his career ended, he claimed to have personally confirmed some seven thousand Indians. By 1907 he had ministered to nearly four thousand tribal communicants who had contributed some ten thousand dollars that year. Evidence of this type, however, was somewhat deceiving, especially where Indians with strong traditions of their own were involved. The existence of large congregations that made substantial donations was not necessarily an accurate measure of individual devotion to traditional Episcopal religion. The Bishop, for instance, failed to anticipate that Indian communicants, shortly after his death, would begin fashioning a version of Episcopal theology that he could never have endorsed.

The problem of analysis is even more difficult and complex. Were there significant differences in the level of commitment to Hare's cause among women as opposed to men, children as opposed to adults, fullbloods as opposed to mixed-bloods? What percentage made up the converted, or the unconverted, or those caught and held between two worlds? How much and how often did those numbers change over the years? Unfortunately, a paucity of evidence makes it impossible to answer those questions. With regard to the extent and depth of Hare's influence on the Sioux, it seems appropriate to say only that the impact and importance of Christianity and White civilization was different for each individual.

As for the Bishop, himself, he realized that he had caused many Indians considerable distress. On the other hand, he sincerely believed that everyone would benefit, in the long run, by adopting his values, and he tried to speed the process of cultural transition and reduce the pain it produced. Although he failed to achieve all he desired, there can be no doubt that he altered Indian attitudes and institutions in substantial and important ways.

Notes

1. Robert Frost, "The Road Not Taken," A Pocket Book of Robert Frost's Poems (New York: Washington Square Press, Inc., 1960), stanza 4, lines 3–5.
2. M. A. DeWolfe Howe, *The Life and Labors of Bishop Hare: Apostle to the Sioux* (New York: Sturgis & Walton Company, 1911), p. 36.
3. *ibid.*, pp. 346–47
4. *Ibid.*, p. 351.
5. William H. Hare, "Extracts From the Address of the Bishops, Delivered at the Missionary Conference, June 29, 1879." The Center for Western Studies, Augustana College, Sioux Falls, South Dakota. Episcopal Diocese of South Dakota Archives, William Hobart Hare Papers. Series 4: Subject Files, 1876–1909, Box 5.
6. *Ibid.*
7. Howe, *Life and Labors*, p. 214.
8. Hare, "Extracts from the Address of the Bishops, June 29, 1879." Hare Papers. Series 4: Subject Files, 1876–1909, Box 5.
9. Howe, *Life and Labors*, p. 204.
10. *Ibid.*, pp. 338–39.
11. *Ibid.*, p. 55.
12. William H. Hare to J. W. Cook, January 12, 1880. Hare Papers, Series 3: Outgoing Correspondence, 1873–1909, Box 4.
13. Howe, *Life and Labors*, p. 120.
14. *Ibid.*, p. 219.
15. William H. Hare, "Letter from Bishop Hare," April, 1885, *Domestic and Foreign Missionary Society: Domestic Missions*. Hare Papers, Series 4: Subject Files, 1876–1909, Box 5.
16. William H. Hare, *Church News*, February, 1890. Hare Papers. Series 5: Sermons and Speeches, 1870's–1908, Box 7.
17. Howe, *Life and Labors*, p. 395.

Bishop Martin Marty.

*Academy of Sacred Heart (ca. 1880).
Courtesy W.H. Over State Museum.*

First Catholic Bishop of Dakota: Martin Marty, The Blackrobe Lean Chief

Sr. Ann Kessler, OSB

Martin Marty was known to Indians as the Blackrobe Lean Chief, and to Dakota territorial citizens as their first Catholic Bishop who served not only the Native Americans, but also the German, Irish, Polish, Czech, and other immigrants that settled across the upper Missouri River basin. Born in Switzerland in 1834, the former Abbot of Benedictines at St. Meinrad, Indiana, came to Dakota in 1876 to fill the void in religious leadership left by Pierre Jean DeSmet, SJ, after he died in 1873. Marty lived out his own personal description of the *homo Americanus*: one who is "reasonable in his judgments," and "not intolerant." Further "he does not believe that he knows and understands everything; he willingly listens and accepts things from others," but, Marty maintained, he is also "an empirical man of experience, not of theory. He seeks effectiveness, results."[1]

Marty was forty-two years old when he arrived at the territorial capital in July of 1876, two weeks after the Battle of Little Big Horn. George Custer and his Seventh Cavalry were dead. Sitting Bull, Crazy Horse, and their followers had become fugitives in hiding from U.S. Army units out for revenge on behalf of the men killed on the Little Big Horn. The Benedictine Abbot was an unlikely candidate for an intercessory role. He was spare of frame, gray-eyed, and less than five feet, nine inches tall. He carried two physical scars, one on his square jaw from a childhood incident involving shoe polish made of acid and tallow and one on his forehead from a near fatal fall down a Swiss mountainside. His German accent was slight for one who had been in the United States a short time, but he had no experience whatsoever with the Sioux language.

The Abbot became a missionary at the request of Father J. B. A. Brouillet, Director of the Bureau of Catholic Indian Missions. Catholics had been awarded only Fort Yates and Fort Totten Agencies in Sioux Country under Ulysses S. Grant's Quaker Policy. Marty was en route to establish a mission on dangerous turf at Standing Rock Agency, the home of Sitting Bull and many of his followers. The Abbot had no experience with missions. He was only twenty-six years of age when he came from Einsiedeln, Switzerland, where he had taken the vows of a Benedictine monk and had been ordained to the Catholic priesthood. From his arrival in 1860 he demonstrated gifts of personality and administrative skill as he stabilized the financial condition of the monastery. For this reason, in 1865 he was named Prior Superior of a residence dependent on another Abbey and in 1870 he became the first Abbot (by election and papal appointment) of the monastery at St. Meinrad when it achieved its independence from the Swiss Alpine Abbey.

Marty had long aspired to mission work and drew inspiration from Father DeSmet during the Jesuit's lecture tour across Europe some years earlier. At St. Meinrad his ministry was among German and Irish Catholic immigrants. The emphasis changed, however, when he met Father Brouillet, who requested the assignment of two priests from the Abbey at St. Meinrad to staff a Catholic mission at Standing Rock. Father Chrysostom Foffa was first to volunteer, and the Abbot himself was second. Twenty-year-old Brother Giles Laugel was third. In 1876 their venture opened the first Catholic mission for Sioux people with resident priests in Dakota Territory.

Marty paused to familiarize himself with Yankton City as he transferred from a train to the Missouri River steamboat that carried him to Standing Rock. Once at his destination he began the study of Sioux language, made his first acquaintance with Indian people, and established a financial and ministerial base for the expansion of work among both Indians and White people. At first he dealt mainly with Hunkpapas, Blackfoot Sioux, and Yanktonais. Before long, however, his ministry extended to all of the western Sioux as well as the Yanktons and Yanktonais.

The Abbot's outlook on the dilemma of Indians was fairly common to missionaries:

Less than 20 years ago this territory was crossed by innumerable herds of buffalo which the Indians followed every summer with bow and arrow.

With them they roamed the immense prairies and gathered their winter supplies which they consumed in snug comfort and peace in the tree-lined shores of the streams during the cold part of the year. The tents and clothing fashioned from buffalo skins kept them warm. The trees protected them from the storms and provided fuel for their tent fires. Unfortunately all this has changed. The Dakota Indians are freezing and famine stricken. With powder and lead the Whites have destroyed the herds—only for the sake of the hides thousands were killed and there were not enough wolves and fox, hawks and eagles to consume the meat. Uselessly the brave Dakotas attempted to defend their source of supplies against the avaricious intruders. . . . Numerical superiority of the Whites and their use of deception made the original inhabitant prisoners who are not allowed to leave their Reservations without a pass from a military or civil functionary. . . . Forts have been erected where several companies of soldiers now guard the defenseless Dakotas.[2]

Sioux people generally were delighted to meet the Blackrobe successor of Father DeSmet. Marty took the characteristic posture of a Benedictine. Conversion and acculturation of those who did not know Christianity entailed the development of a community based on Gospel values. In letters to a friend, Prior Frowin Conrad, Marty disclosed a longtime hope of personal involvement with the establishment of such a Benedictine mission among the Indians:

> The education of several generations is unthinkable without stability, and the family life of a genuine Benedictine family, embracing the material as well as the spiritual life, upon which the welfare of the individual and of society rests. The *ora et labora* is today still the only remedy for healing the children of Adam and neither the one nor the other can be taught in words alone.[3]

To avoid any confrontation and provide some security for Native American families, Marty urged the Sioux to comply with demands by federal officials who were in control of the reservations to which they were assigned. He was effective in heading off trouble at Standing Rock. Helped by the positive recollections of DeSmet among western Sioux people, he and the other priests were able to approach tribal members in a way that was impossible for military or civil agents, whose roles were to tighten security and control the behavior of the Sioux.

Marty practiced but never mastered the Sioux language, even though he learned to carry on personal conversations. When he preached the

Gospel to large groups of Indians, he used interpreters. Later he commented that the Sioux language was very difficult to master for anyone over thirty years of age. Brother Giles learned more quickly than did the priests, all of whom learned very slowly. Their first teacher at the Catholic mission was a woman of mixed extraction. They had available the grammars and dictionaries published earlier by Protestant missionaries, plus a short Bible history and the rite of the Eucharistic liturgy (*Katolik Wocekiye*) published in Sioux language by Father Augustin Ravoux at Mendota.

Once the mission at Standing Rock was in operation, Marty wrote the Director of the Bureau of Catholic Indian Missions for authorization to visit Sitting Bull and Crazy Horse in the hope that he could entice them to lay down their arms and accept reservation life. Bureau personnel contacted federal officials, and on March 12, 1877, a U.S. War Department memorandum extended permission for Marty to travel at his own risk with the understanding that he went not as an emissary of the United States (as had Father DeSmet in 1867) but as an individual who would in no way alter, modify, or delay military operations in progress. The Commissioner of Indian Affairs spoke for the U.S. Department of the Interior in a similar notice addressed to the U.S. Agent at Standing Rock. Marty could go at his own expense and he could take as an escort a few of the Indians from the Agency suited to that purpose. The Indians could draw rations and arrange transportation at federal expense. Otherwise the expedition was in no way supported by federal officials, who supposed that conditions Marty would offer to fugitives might be the same as those accepted by all Indians as they returned to their reservations: capitulation as prisoners of war and the surrender of arms and ponies.

Marty set out to track Sitting Bull, who by then had placed a following of more than 2,000 in exile at points of high ground in western Canada. At Fort Peck the Abbot obtained a horse and secured the services of eight Indians as companions and scouts. William Halsey, a mixed-blood interpreter, also went along. After trekking across a wilderness in ignorance of the country, often beset by bad weather conditions, he approached the camp of Sitting Bull on May 26, 1877. According to some reports, 100 mounted warriors rode out with Sitting Bull. The Hunkpapa leader is said to have greeted the Abbot: "Though you have come from our enemies, since you are a *Sina Sapa* (Blackrobe), we will hear you." Then he led Marty to his lodge, where he entertained generously, remarking again that although Marty came from the society of the enemy he was welcome as a clergyman. "The priest does nobody any harm," he said, so "we will give you food and protection and will listen to your words."[4]

Abbot Martin reminded Sitting Bull and the leaders with him that they could not remain permanently in Canada. Their sources of food would diminish to a point of starvation. They were free to return in safety to the reservation assigned them. Sitting Bull responded that as long as hunting was good, and Canadian officials dealt with him favorably, he saw no reason to return. Only when livelihood became scarce would he follow the advice of the Blackrobe. Officers from Fort Walsh came out, and Sitting Bull said in their presence: "That is our good friend—a good man and a priest, who has come far to tell us what to do. We want to tell him if the English are willing for us to stay on their soil."[5] The officers gave their assurance that Sitting Bull's people could remain as long as they obeyed the law.

Two weeks later Marty was back in Fort Peck, convinced that in the aim of bringing Sitting Bull back to the United States he had been unsuccessful. Yet, the expedition had drawn attention to the presence of Catholic missionaries, especially the Abbot himself. Now his prestige and influence, together with that of other Catholic clergy, were on the increase. They were helped even by word that the trip so enfeebled Marty he was carried on a stretcher aboard a steamer from Fort Peck to Bismarck. So dedicated a man earned the admiration of White people and Indians alike.

Marty tried again in 1879, without success, to lure Sitting Bull back across the border and he was at hand to assist the Hunkpapa leader after his return in 1881. Marty visited Sitting Bull and his family while they were incarcerated at Fort Randall and labored to see them settled in areas of the Standing Rock Reservation they considered their own. Doubtless Marty played a role in the appointment of James McLaughlin, a devout Catholic, as U.S. Agent at Fort Yates. From Standing Rock he wrote that he and McLaughlin were in agreement that the only way to shorten Sitting Bull's captivity and "save him from Episcopalian hands" was to bring him back to the reservation where he belonged.[6]

The two men forwarded a petition to J. B. Hassett at White Swan near Fort Randall. After securing Sitting Bull's signature on the document, Hassett sent it to the U.S. Commissioner of Indian Affairs. War Department officials were anxious to free Sitting Bull's band, but they preferred the Hunkpapa leader be sent to the Rosebud or Pine Ridge, not to Standing Rock Reservation, where many recalcitrants lived. At length, with Marty's support, James McLaughlin convinced the U.S.

Commissioner of Indian Affairs to transfer Sitting Bull and a party of a few dozen to Standing Rock early enough for planting crops and gardens in the spring of 1883.

No doubt the recognition given Marty for his involvement with Sitting Bull affected his rapid rise to prominence as a religious leader in Dakota Territory. On his return in 1877, after a brief sojourn at the Abbey in Indiana, he had a meeting in Omaha with Bishop James O'Connor, who had nominal jurisdiction over the region where Marty was working. The Bishop had been unable to provide priests for the Territory. Aware of the Abbot's personal dedication and enthusiasm for missions, O'Connor named him Vicar General to fill the void, and offered a site for a Benedictine monastery adjacent to southern Dakota in Cedar County, Nebraska, where German Catholics were homesteading.

Marty proceeded incognito to Yankton on horseback with a coffee pot dangling around his neck and scant provisions in his saddle-bag. Shortly thereafter he trekked west about seventy miles to the old Ponca Agency. En route he visited the Yankton Reservation, where Episcopalians had won Quaker Policy assignment. Among Yanktons were people whom Fathers DeSmet and Ravoux had earlier baptized and given instruction in Catholic doctrine. For Yankton Catholics he ministered in secret, then pressed on, sleeping in the snow with only a woolen blanket for cover. Later he recounted the story of intense cold that at times pressed from his eyes tears which froze as they trickled down his cheeks. In 1877 and 1878 he also visited the peoples of Spotted Tail and Red Cloud. Episcopalians convinced agency personnel to order him out. When one of his priests came to serve the Catholic people, a small group of Catholic Indians took the Benedictine missionary sent by Marty to a spot away from an agency, where he camped through the summer and early fall. Indians came to his tent to receive sacraments and attend Eucharistic liturgy until cold weather forced him to retire. The scenario became common. Marty or one of his missionaries would appear. Episcopalians working under Bishop William Hobart Hare would get federal officials to run him out, but he would return in secret. Only after 1881, by which time the Quaker Policy was no longer enforced by federal officials, was the Benedictine free to go about his work without fear anywhere among Indians instead of being limited to the communities around Standing Rock and Fort Totten Agencies.

From the outset Marty had problems within his own clerical ranks. He lacked personnel to meet all demands for clergy and too often accepted on probation the priests who had been rejected by their own bishops or religious houses for their troublesome behavior. At one point he was compelled, through orders from Father Brouillet, to recall two young priests who had come to him from other dioceses to serve in the camps of Spotted Tail and Red Cloud. Such serious charges were leveled against Father A. H. Frederick that Marty recommended he should never again attempt to participate in clerical ministry. At the new Rosebud Agency the U.S. Agent declared that Father Francis Craft was persona non grata because of "imprudence," and Marty reassigned him to Standing Rock.

Personnel problems coupled with interdenominational competition brought delay to Indian mission work for several years. The elimination of the Quaker Policy in 1883 and corresponding freedom of competition among denominations was most advantageous to Catholics. It was the Presbyterian missionary-teacher Daniel Renville, however, who initiated the movement for change after he had received abusive treatment from a Catholic U.S. Agent at Fort Totten. As agents began to ignore official denominational assignments after 1881, the (Calvinist) American Board of Commissioners for Foreign Missions induced parishioners to send petitions to the U.S. Secretary of the Interior, Carl Schurz. By the time they arrived he had resigned from office but the new Secretary ruled in 1883 that any denomination would be free to engage in mission work on any reservation except where the presence of rival organizations would endanger peace and order.

To facilitate the work and give Marty authority and power, the Pope appointed him Vicar Apostolic of Dakota Territory and Titular Bishop of Tiberias, a long-vacated ancient Middle-Eastern See of the Church. The diocese extended from Sioux City to Canada, and from Yankton and Sioux Falls far westward across the Black Hills. Into the diocese filed White immigrants by the thousands, while Sioux people took residence on their reservations.

The new Bishop felt obligated to visit every reservation and each parish of Catholic immigrants under his jurisdiction as often as possible. This meant "circuit-riding" much of the time, mainly on horseback, or by ox team and lumber wagon, bobsled, or stagecoach.

Within three years after Marty's appointment, a region that had been bereft of Catholic churches and clergy could boast ninety-two priests, 154 churches, ten convents, thirty-six parochial schools, eight Indian missions, and teachers from nine different religious orders. This came about not only as a consequence of the freedom Marty now had to exercise his energy and leadership in evangelizing Indians and caring for White immigrants, but also because the new Bishop was little constrained by precedents. When he saw a need, little stood in his way.

From a visit to St. Meinrad in February, 1880, he returned with Father Henry Hug, and a short time later Father Felix Rumpf came out. By then Marty had in his diocese fourteen Benedictines. Because of a perennial shortage of missionaries, Marty sent two Indian boys, Fintan Mantochna and Giles Tapetola, to St. Meinrad's Abbey to prepare for the priesthood. Taking advantage of their presence, Father Luke Gruwe gained familiarity with Sioux language and composed a grammar, which he sent back to the Dakota missionaries.

This early effort to train Indian clergy never materialized. The two young men found lifestyle at the monastery and seminary too far removed from that to which they had been accustomed. When the improbability of such drastic adjustment by young Indian men became apparent, and it was obvious there would not be enough Benedictines or diocesan priests to staff all parishes and reservations in his jurisdiction, Marty appealed to the Superior of the German Jesuits in Buffalo, New York. Jesuits arrived on the first day of 1886 and Marty assigned them to the missions at Rosebud and Pine Ridge.

It was, however, the Benedictine priest from St. Meinrad, Father Pius Boehm, who came on January 21, 1887, to manage the newly organized Immaculate Conception Mission at Stephan on the Crow Creek Reservation. It was the Benedictine Father Sylvester Eisenman who took residence in 1920 to open a permanent mission on the Yankton Reservation, named Marty Mission after the first Dakota Bishop. The evolution of mission stations did not come so steadily and smoothly as it did for Episcopalians, Presbyterians, and Congregationalists. Struggling with shortages of personnel and inter-denominational prejudice, Marty pieced together a suitable system on a schedule dictated more by opportunity than request by Indians.

He believed that education for the young was the key to Christianization and acculturation and hastened to open mission boarding schools. One at St. Francis near Rosebud Agency admitted children in 1885. Stephan School opened on Crow Creek Reservation in 1886. Pine Ridge Agency Catholic School took students in 1887. The construction, financing, and maintenance of these schools, and the inducement of families to enroll their children, proved very difficult for the Bishop and his intrepid priests and sisters. Until about 1900 mission schools received financial assistance from federal sources under contract. Congress appropriated a fixed sum for each pupil to the religious organization that would then be responsible for organizing a staff and constructing a physical plant. After 1900, however, federal aid diminished sharply. For a short time even rations were withdrawn from Indian children at mission schools in order to force them into enrollment at federal boarding schools. Thereafter, the best religious schools could arrange was tuition support from tribal or Individual Indian Money Accounts for children enrolled at their parents' request. Under this arrangement, the three original Catholic schools—St. Francis near Rosebud, Stephan near Crow Creek, and Holy Rosary at Pine Ridge—continued to draw support from tribal funds held in trust by the United States as tuition paid on behalf of Indian students.

The search for priests and struggle for funds were hard enough. The attraction of Nuns in sufficient number to staff all Catholic institutions was even more difficult. Bishop Marty was in constant contact with convents in Europe, Canada, and the eastern United States in the effort to increase the number. His first recruits came from the feminine branch of his own Order; he arranged the transfer of four Benedictine Sisters from Ferdinand, Indiana, one from St. Joseph, Minnesota, and another from Chicago. Most of these would later become part of the largest group he brought almost en masse: the Swiss foundation of Benedictine Sisters at Maryville, Missouri.

Marty also attracted assistance from the Grey Nuns of Montreal, the Sisters of St. Agnes of Fond du Lac, Wisconsin, and the Mercy Sisters from Omaha, whom he brought to his See at Yankton City. Soon there were enough Benedictine Sisters from Minnesota to open an academy at Bismarck, and enough Franciscan Sisters to share the apostolate to Native Americans at Pine Ridge and Rosebud with Jesuit priests. In 1879 Marty also called at George's Hill, Dublin, where he secured the promise of missionaries from the Presentation Order of Sisters.

Sisters of several Orders, who came in response to the call, would meet a great challenge as they adapted to life either on reservations or in White communities. Pioneering Nuns have recalled that mice ran along the rafters of their crude homes and fell onto open stoves or into cooking vessels. They have told about dry, whitewash flakes floating down like snow from the ceilings in tiny churches and of snakes lapping breakfast milk set out at night in the rooms where Sisters slept. One related how she fell off a mule into a brook while Indian families awaited her arrival on the other side, and being hoisted unceremoniously to the shoulders of an Indian man, who toted her across the water and respectfully dropped her to the ground before an attentive, sober-faced audience. Most difficult of all was cultural adaptation, which meant adjustment to ministering among peoples unfamiliar with liturgical etiquette who, for example, might interrupt worship services by lighting their pipes from the flames of altar candles.

German, Swiss, and French-born women had to add the Indian language to their understanding when they had scarcely mastered the English language. Most prominent among such newcomers were Benedictines. As early as 1880, five Sisters arrived in Maryville, Missouri, from Maria Rickenbach Convent, in the Alps. By November, the former Superior and co-foundress of the Swiss convent, Mother Gertrude Leupi, arrived in Missouri with four Sisters and almost immediately invested four novices. When Marty met these Sisters during a conference at Maryville in early 1881, he outlined an opportunity: they could share in extending God's Kingdom among the Great Plains Indians of Dakota. When it seemed he had convinced the group, the Bishop selected three women he felt would be most valuable: Sisters Jodoka Villiger, Adela Eugster, and Gertrude McDermott. Soon they were escorted to Standing Rock by Marty's successor at St. Meinrad, Fintan Mundwiler, arriving in August from a ten-day journey between Missouri and central Dakota.

After some years of ministering to the Indians at Standing Rock in the Fort Yates and Kenel areas, the Swiss Sisters of St. Benedict built a school and motherhouse in the Dakotas at Zell, a small town west of Redfield. Their move to Yankton in 1887 at Marty's behest had mixed religious and economic motivation. Since 1878 the Mercy Sisters of Omaha had been in Yankton, sponsoring and staffing a girls' academy near the center of town, which they moved to a combination residence-school on the hill in 1880. Mercy Sisters had gone deeply into debt and paid high interest to creditors. Pledges from parishioners were not always redeemed. Revenues from the school were scarcely sufficient to make regular payments. There was a local scandal that prompted the Bishop to assume the debt of more than $25,000 and ask them to leave the city. The *Yankton Press and Dakotaian* carried the story on December 29, 1882:

> Yankton has been considerably interested today over the marriage of Dr. V. Sebiakin-Ross to Miss Nellie Kerns. Dr. Sebiakin-Ross is a popular young Russian physician here and Miss Kerns has been known to the community and generally beloved, as Sister Mary Paul of the Convent of the Sacred Heart.

The news spread rapidly. A local manufacturer named a popular cigar the "Mary Paul." The upshot was a decision by the Bishop to replace the Mercy Sisters with Benedictines.

The transfer of Benedictine Sisters from Zell came soon after the closing of the Indian Boys Normal and Industrial School, on the hill at Yankton. In 1885 Marty reported seventy-five boys from the Rosebud and Pine Ridge Agencies at the School. The Bishop dreamed of opening a seminary to educate candidates for the priesthood at the same facility. Indeed, at one point he had nine seminarians in residence under the tutelage of Father George Willard (the local parish priest) and himself. Approval for federal funding to open a boarding "Industrial and future Normal School" for fifty Sioux boys made the development of a large facility seem probable. At length, the withdrawal of federal funds forced Marty to abandon all hope for a seminary and prompted the closure of the Indian school. On July 15, 1885, the *Press and Dakotaian* reported that "Indian boys at the industrial school are picking up the rudiments of labor with surprising aptitude. They are in the hay field today and one of them finished and topped a stack with the skill of an old granger. They seem to like work and are ambitious to learn." Two years later the boys were moved to the new Immaculate Conception Mission at Crow Creek Reservation, which had a building valued at $20,000 constructed on 160 acres allotted the Catholic Church by the U.S. Secretary of the Interior. They would have more room there, and girls could be accommodated.

Greater responsibility came to the Bishop with burgeoning population during the Dakota Boom years. By early 1884 he could report nine students under seminary instruction, eighty-two churches in the vicariate, and forty-five priests to sustain them. He had scores of Sisters involved in parishes throughout his vicariate.

In the spring of 1885 Marty traveled to the Vatican to report on the progress of his diocese. His promotional message was published abroad: "For the last eight years the 8,000 Indians of Pine Ridge, the 7,000 of the Rosebud and the 2,000 of the Crow Creek reservations have been begging me for schools, and I have had to put them off with promises of the future. But if I'm not able soon to realize at least a few of their hopes, their confidence in the 'Blackrobe' will be lessened." He reminded his readers that the Dakotas would not then be Christianized, "not through their fault but ours."[7]

At the Vatican, Pope Leo XIII listened intently while Marty recapitulated his five years as Vicar Apostolic and expressed his needs. Much had been accomplished but there were even greater opportunities if more priests and more money were available. As a gift from his Indian converts, the Bishop presented the pontiff an enormous buffalo robe with the leather side adorned by a Sioux artist in depictions of Sioux history, including the triumph of Sitting Bull's people on Little Big Horn. Marty had a gold medallion of the Immaculate Conception blessed by the Pope for James McLaughlin, and recommended that the widespread Dakota vicariate be cut in half to assure that Indians and Whites alike be properly served.

After his return from Rome he faced a variety of distractions. Marty was named to a special committee for the promotion of Catholic University of America in Washington, DC. While there he spent time with Father Joseph Stephan, the new Director of the Bureau of Catholic Indian Missions. They went together to Philadelphia to call on Katherine Drexel, the twenty-seven year old heiress to the Drexel and Morgan banking fortune. Francis Drexel bequeathed to her and two other siblings $15,000,000. Through Marty's appeal, a considerable part of her inheritance was soon channeled into the Dakota Indian missions. In addition she founded and took vows in the new Order of the Sisters of the Blessed Sacrament for Indians and Colored People. Many of these served in Sioux Country, and later supported the establishment of the Oblate Order of the Blessed Sacrament for Indian women, founded at Marty Mission by the Benedictine Father Sylvester Eisenman.

Mother Katherine Drexel soon funded the establishment of several Catholic schools. An initial donation led to the opening of St. Francis, named in honor of her father's patron saint, in 1886, where Jesuits took over the management on a 160-acre land grant extended by the U.S. Government. A donation from Mother Katherine brought the establishment of Holy Rosary Mission school at Pine Ridge in 1887. A donation of $20,000 led to the construction of buildings at the Benedictines' Stephan school on Crow Creek Reservation a short time later.

The Bishop was a man of great vision and energy whose main weakness was his unwillingness to delegate responsibility to other missionaries. This meant his involvement in domestic details at Indian missions and White parishes that should have been wholly in the purview of local priests. In 1887, for example, Father Pius wrote Marty from Stephan Mission complaining about a cook who tried to dominate the place. "Concerning Katie," he wrote, "I have this to say: she is simply incorrigible. I can pacify my growling stomach, but I cannot control the disposition of this woman." Two friendly interviews led to her taking it out on her detractors by "splitting" the whole house and consequently setting two different tables—one for those she did not care for getting only black coffee and bread, the other getting meat "and a fair table in every respect." Besides that "she has no economy in her cookery.''[8] She was using twenty-five pounds of flour a day and three-quarters of the steer had been used up in less than two weeks. He begged the Bishop to take her away and send someone else. No one at the mission dared reprimand her because she maintained that only the Bishop could "command her." At length Marty replaced her under the threat that brothers and priests would leave if she did not go. Father Pius involved the Bishop even in concern over the death of a white-faced ox in a winter storm. Expenditure of time on trifling issues like these reflected a flaw in administrative acumen on Marty's part and a great waste of his time and energy.

Other distractions were unavoidable, of course, such as the memorable and disastrous blizzard of 1888. Beginning on January 12, it raged for more than twelve hours. Children were trapped in their rural schools and men were caught unaware in the fields. Livestock wandered aimlessly, became stranded in drifts, and froze to death. In southern Dakota gale winds gusted to more than sixty miles an hour while the temperature dropped to 20 degrees below zero Fahrenheit. More than one hundred people died in the storm, among them the twenty-five year old Sister Wilhelmina Kaufmann, one of the pioneer Benedictine Sisters stationed at Stephan Mission. She was in the laundry building some distance from the main house when the storm hit. It was noon when she was missed. A search party braved the weather to look for her. They fastened a long rope to the main building and conducted the search by following its length as a circle radius. It was almost mid-afternoon before they found her body in a kneeling position in a deep drift near a fencepost against which she had been crouched, helplessly lost in the driving snow.

Marty's responsibilities diminished somewhat after statehood in 1889, when two separate dioceses were formed: one centered at Jamestown, later transferred to Bismarck; and one at Sioux Falls. As South Dakota's Catholic Bishop, Marty watched while Indian missions and parish schools continued to grow. Constantly he carried on the search for more teachers. He brought in more Benedictines from two Swiss convents.

In 1889, he also accepted appointment from President Benjamin Harrison to a special commission with Henry M. Rice of St. Paul and Joseph B. Whiting of Wisconsin to negotiate with the Chippewa Indians of Minnesota for the cession of most of their reservation lands. Marty agreed to serve on the assumption that the cession was just. Later he championed the Chippewas, however, lodging a complaint that they were being cheated by the sale of timber from the reservation, which had not been ceded.

Marty's health deteriorated from overwork through such commitments. He was constantly in demand—confirming hundreds in small German, Irish, Bohemian, and mixed ethnic parishes; responding to all kinds of calls and correspondence; being the shepherd to a flock constituting Catholics settled across all of present-day South Dakota. The Bishop at Jamestown later commented: "Sod houses, buggy beds, no privies, long wagon rides of eighty and ninety miles. Day after day of that life, and weeks of it at a stretch. No wonder stomach, liver, kidney, nerves, brain and everything in the human machinery went to pieces."[9]

Internal problems in the diocese aggravated his fragile condition. One constant concern was leadership in the Presentation and the Benedictine Orders. He was not loath to appoint his own candidates to fill vacancies in administration, as he did in the case of the Benedictines when Mother Gertrude returned to Switzerland to open a convent, or to reprimand personnel if he felt compelled to do so. More distressing was his rift with Father Robert Haire, a colorful, pioneer priest known well for his adherence to socialism.

The volatile Irishman had come west with a colonizing party from Flint, Michigan, in 1880. Haire filed his claim to land near Columbia in Brown County and became instrumental in the creation of parishes in Groton, Redfield, Huron, Aberdeen, and other communities of the area. In 1887 he was entrusted by Marty with the editorship of the *Dakota Catholic American*, the first Catholic newspaper in Dakota. When the periodical began to reflect the editor's strong personal opinions on labor reform, temperance, women's suffrage, and other political issues, Marty remonstrated with him. Haire resigned and began to espouse his causes in the columns of the publication of the Knights of Labor, the new union of workingmen. He referred to the Bishop as "that old rascal in Sioux Falls." Eventually Haire became a founder of the South Dakota People's Party, championing the inclusion of the initiative and referendum rights in the state constitution. Because of his access to the public press—especially the *Aberdeen Star*—he remained a nagging thorn to Bishop Marty, who for several years suspended Father Haire's faculties to act as a priest. (They were not restored until 1901, five years after Marty's death.)

Another episode mushroomed into accusations of favoritism toward German over Irish parishes, and Indians over Whites. Newsmen in Minneapolis, Sioux Falls, and Aberdeen printed charges and countercharges of two dissident priests, who throughout 1893 used the media to accuse Marty with incompetence, financial mismanagement, favoritism to German-speaking priests, and injustice in the suspension of Haire and others. In synod during August of that year, an assembly of priests sided with Marty, giving him a vote of confidence. The Bishop was comforted but imprudently blundered into a political campaign, which led him into difficulties among Catholics who disagreed with his actions.

Marty, like Episcopal Bishop Hare, became a victim of some abuse by those engaged in controversies surrounding the use of South Dakota as the "divorce mill" of the nation. Through liberal court decisions and ninety day residence requirements, Sioux Falls became a center for women seeking divorce. Ursuline Sisters teaching in the parochial school were receiving as their guests such women from New York. Father William V. Nolon objected. When the Sisters maintained their right to harbor these women, he closed their school. Mother Stanislaus, who considered hospitality an appropriate work of charity, appealed to the Apostolic Delegate, Archbishop Satolli. Marty permitted the Sisters to attend to their religious duties in the chapel of his residence until they left the city because Father Nolan had forbidden them access to the parish church. The Sisters returned to New York in 1898 and the case was closed when the parish priest, under advice, made a public apology.

Late in his career Marty faced a series of crises. There was the Wounded Knee Affair of 1890, the Panic of 1893, and a searing drought in the summer of 1894. Farmers and businessmen alike went down in financial failure. Doubtless a combination of pressures brought the collapse of the Bishop's health. After five years in Sioux Falls he was transferred as a concession to physical deterioration to head the Diocese of St. Cloud and relinquished his office at Sioux Falls to Father Thomas O'Gorman.

On September 19, 1896, he died in his episcopal residence at St. Cloud and was buried in the Calvary Cemetery near that city. In the eulogy at Bishop Marty's funeral, Archbishop John Ireland recounted the Indian missionary's passionate love for Native Americans, and his sacrifice for all people in South Dakota. He maintained that the outstanding trait in Marty's life had always been an inflexible obedience to his conscience—for in that voice he had heard the voice of God. Whenever his conscience had bade him act, nothing could hold him back. When his conscience told him to terminate an act, it seemed that all the powers of earth could not move him. With these words ringing in their consciousness, all clergy and parishioners of the dioceses of St. Cloud and Sioux Falls who could attend paid their respects as he was interred. Those conspicuous by their absence were the thousands of Indians whose lives he had touched in his two decades of ministry in Dakota Territory and the Diocese of Sioux Falls.

The Bishop's abiding contributions to the region came mainly in the organization and development of Catholic Native American missions, and of German, Irish, Czech, and Polish Catholic parishes for the immigrants, plus the establishment of convents for religious women who would become prominent as teachers, nurses, and missionaries into the twentieth century. Marty spearheaded educational efforts at institutions for Indian children on the Crow Creek, Rosebud, and Pine Ridge Reservations, which recently have come under Indian administration. To him belongs credit for the founding of important institutions long after his death, including Mount Marty College, Sacred Heart Convent, and Blue Cloud Abbey. The Mission on the Yankton Reservation southwest of Wagner is named in his honor. These and numerous other Catholic institutions trace their origins to his efforts.

Bishop Marty was an idealist; yet, he was so often practical. He was sensitive to cultural differences; yet, at times he dealt with Indians in a condescending manner. He could be manipulative; yet, he was a generous man. He was a leader of principle, always a missionary, willing to make personal sacrifice for the Indians' sake to a point of promoting total abstinence from the use of alcoholic beverages. This revealed how deeply he cared for people around him. Bishop Marty had the most profound love for the Indian people, but he was Abbot, pastor, Bishop, and missionary to non-Indians, too.

Martin Marty would have been the first to admit that the role of a Bishop became him much less than did that of a monk or a missionary. Yet in the role of a Bishop he was of inestimable service to the Catholic Church of the United States, to the Bureau of Catholic Indian Missions, and to his own See in Dakota. If he sometimes lacked keen political perception, tact, or the administrative genius of a model Bishop, he compensated for his weaknesses with personal warmth, pastoral energy, and personal example of holiness.

In whatever role he found himself, the Bishop brought to his work both spirit and personality completely devoted to every task. He was, more often than not, controversial, but like the prophets of old he was not adverse to disturbing the comfortable while he comforted the disturbed. His high idealism and rigid religious values were often tempered by personal pragmatism in his dealings with people and events. Above all, he was unsparing in his willingness to give himself fully to whatever cause or personal needs called him. In this light, he epitomized one of his favorite passages of Scripture from the Gospel of Matthew (20:16–17): "Anyone among you who aspires to greatness must serve the rest, and whoever wants to rank first among you must serve the needs of all." Nor did he ignore the call of the Sermon on the Mount to do unto others as one would do unto the Lord Himself. So he fed the hungry, clothed the naked, housed the homeless, visited the sick and dying, educated the unschooled, and sought justice for those imprisoned by circumstances. Goodness as much as greatness made up the fabric of the life of Bishop Martin Marty.

Notes

1. Lecture by Marty in Munster, Germany to the *Katholikentag* in 1885, cited in Colman J. Barry, *The Catholic Church and German Americans* (Washington, DC: Catholic University of American Press, 1953), p. 39.

2. "Das Apostolische Vikariat Dakota," in the *Munchener Fremdenblatt* at Munich in 1885. A translation by Louis Pfaller, OSB, into English is available at Assumption Abbey Archives, Richardton, ND, File on "Martin Marty."

3. Marty to Abbot Basil and Prior Frowin in Albert Kleber, *History of St. Meinrad Archabbey, 1854–1954* (St. Meinrad, IN: The Grail Press, 1954), p. 267.

4. Kleber, *St. Meinrad*, p. 277; *Yankton Press and Dakotan*, March 22, 1939.

5. Kleber, *St. Meinrad*, p. 281.

6. Louis Pfaller, *James McLaughlin: The Man with an Indian Heart* (New York: Vantage Press, 1978), pp. 94–95.

7. "Das Apostolische Vikariat Dakota."

8. Stephan Mission File, Blue Cloud Abbey Archive, Marvin, South Dakota.

9. Robert F. Karolevitz, *Bishop Martin Marty: The Black Robe Lean Chief* (Yankton: Sacred Heart Covent, 1980), p. 109.

Mother Joseph Butler.
Courtesy Presentation Heights Archives.

Mother Raphael McCarthy.
Courtesy Presentation Heights Archives.

Mother Jerome Schmitt with parishioner.

Valiant Religious Women: Mothers Superior Joseph Butler, Raphael McCarthy, and Jerome Schmitt

Susan Peterson and Sr. Ann Kessler, OSB

Mother Joseph Butler, PBVM, Mother Raphael McCarthy, PBVM, and Mother Jerome Schmitt, OSB, stand out among women who have led religious communities in the establishment and development of important Catholic institutions on the Dakota frontier. The three Mothers Superior displayed unusual vision, flexibility, and strength as they led the Presentation and Benedictine Sisters who came to Dakota Territory at the request of Martin Marty, OSB. Initially the Sisters planned to teach Indian students at mission schools on Sioux reservations established by the federal government. Eventually the three Mothers Superior provided leadership as the two Orders of Nuns added educational institutions for Catholic immigrants and their descendants in the upper Missouri River region. They supplied administrative direction as the Sisters undertook the founding of hospitals and went on to develop health care ministry for all of the White ethnic groups that appeared on the northern prairie and Great Plains.

Immigrant Sisters of the Presentation of the Blessed Virgin Mary belonged to an Irish Order of Nuns founded in 1776 by Honoria "Nano" Nagle. Some of them were already at work in New York and California by the time the former Abbot Martin Marty (from Benedictine Abbey at St. Meinrad, Indiana) invited others to Dakota Territory in 1879. He needed them as staff for mission schools he hoped soon to establish among the Sioux, especially those assigned to Catholics by the federal Quaker Policy on the Standing Rock and Fort Totten Reservations. A small contingent arrived in 1880 to open the new apostolate at a school in Wheeler near the edge of the Yankton Reservation.

Benedictine Sisters came to Dakota Territory at about the same time by a more circuitous route. These Nuns left Switzerland for Missouri in the 1870s due to the persecution of Catholic Orders by officials. They established a convent near the Benedictine Monastery in Missouri and soon were in contact with Martin Marty. He left St. Meinrad in 1876 to succeed Pierre Jean DeSmet, SJ, as the primary force behind the spread of Catholicism across the upper Missouri River region and became the first Catholic Bishop of Dakota five years later. Marty asked the Benedictine Sisters to open a mission school on Standing Rock Reservation. After working in that apostolate, they began to staff White parish schools for Catholic immigrants who arrived on the prairie during the Great Dakota Boom. Eventually they moved their motherhouse from Missouri to Dakota Territory and chose the city of Yankton as a permanent site.

The two Orders of Nuns opened their health care centers almost simultaneously to meet an obvious need: the Benedictines in Yankton at Sacred Heart Hospital in 1897, and the Presentation Sisters in Aberdeen at St. Luke's Hospital in 1901. Subsequently each Order founded additional facilities in several states across the region while developing Sacred Heart and St. Luke's Hospitals as primary centers for health care delivery.

Principal differences between the two Orders stemmed from their early histories. Benedictine Sisters originated as members of a monastic movement founded by Benedict of Nursia early in the sixth century. His push for monasteries "combined a degree of withdrawal from the distracting interests of worldly life with a deep concern for and service to one's fellow men, [sic] especially care for the poor and sick."[1] Orders of Benedictine monasteries for Monks and Nuns sprang up across Western Europe, often in the same locations. Nuns tended to work in concert with Monks as brother-sister teams of apostles patterned after the team of Benedict and his sister Scholastica. Benedict saw the importance of a teaching ministry under "a communal 'rule' rather than simply a loosely organized community of like-minded pious individuals."[2]

Presentation Sisters were organized by Nano Nagle at Cork in Ireland in 1776, initially to provide education together with health care for the poor of Ireland who lived at a disadvantage under English Penal

Laws. The daughter of a wealthy landowning family, she used her inheritance to finance the teaching of poor Catholic children (in violation of a British prohibition against Catholic schools) by inviting Ursuline Sisters from France to staff a school under her supervision. Due to some difficulties related to providing education for children in slums by a community of Sisters that enclosed or cloistered its members in the walls of a convent, Nagle established a group of teachers outside the constraints of Papal restrictions. In addition she directed the Nuns of her Order to minister to the social needs of slum dwellers at Cork, nursing all of the ill and the infirm as she educated the youngsters.

Because of their divergent European beginnings, the two Orders differed in their approaches to service on the American frontier. Presentation Sisters did not have financial or administrative stability comparable to that demonstrated by Benedictine Sisters because the Presentation Nuns did not share the long tradition of community building that the Benedictines had inherited from their founder. At the outset, Presentation Sisters were more prone to brave the danger of frontier environment, moving at Martin Marty's request to isolated Wheeler, Deadwood, and Fargo before establishing a permanent convent in South Dakota at Aberdeen. Benedictine Nuns entered the region from established headquarters in nearby Missouri to found a convent at the center of White Dakota settlement, along the Missouri River near the mouth of the James. After a brief time in residence at Vermillion they settled in a comfortable center of operations at Yankton, and from there branched out into extended apostolates.

Following a party of three Presentation Sisters that came to Wheeler in 1880, many women have taken leadership roles in the Irish Order. Two have stood out for their unusual abilities: Mother Joseph Butler (Superior from 1894 to 1915), and Mother Raphael McCarthy (Superior from 1932 to 1946). Both women showed propensities similar to those of Nano Nagle: the ability to make opportunity out of adversity and the strength to lead communities through periods of crisis. Together their traits have enabled Presentation Sisters of South Dakota to survive the rigors of frontier life, progress as educators and health care providers, and meet the challenges of changing times in the twentieth century.

Doubtless it was Nano Nagle's example that influenced Mary Ellen Butler to journey in 1885 as a postulant from Bandon, Ireland, to Fargo, where she joined a small community of Sisters in the founding of Presentation Academy. She moved in 1886 from Fargo to Aberdeen, at the request of Father Robert Haire, and rose to leadership as Mother Superior by 1894, after the Fargo and Aberdeen motherhouses severed their administrative connections and separate statehood for North and South Dakota placed the two cities under different diocesan jurisdictions. By then she had received the religious habit and taken the name Mary Joseph Butler.

As a Sister, she was disappointed to learn she was not to be a teacher at the new Presentation Academy in Aberdeen but a mendicant traveling with Sister Martin O'Toole to beg for donations. "On periodic tours for several years, they approached railroad men, merchants, and farmers for money, however small the coins. Providence was preparing Sister Butler for the years to come when she needed these contacts to help'' in financing other projects.[3]

Sister Butler went on her last tour as a mendicant in 1894, when she traveled to finance and arrange the funeral of Mother Aloysious Chriswell. She was chosen soon thereafter to serve the remaining years of her Superior's term, was elected in 1898 in her own right, and was re-elected in 1910. Her tenure as Mother Superior came at a pivotal period in the history of the Presentation Sisters in South Dakota. These were difficult years of community-building in the city of Aberdeen, work on the establishment of nine parish schools in eastern South Dakota, and expansion of the apostolate to include health care as well as teaching. Inspired by the sacrifices in Nano Nagle's life, she moved about "in her horse-drawn buggy to beg the farmers for food for her Sisters," and made several recruiting visits to Ireland and Canada.[4] She also encouraged young women from South Dakota and other states in the region to join a growing Order.

Within four years Mother Butler agreed to staff a school for Holy Family Parish at Mitchell with assistance from Sister Gertrude McBride, whose previous experience in the American educational system was an obvious asset in a venture more than 100 miles south of Aberdeen. Their success at Mitchell led them to staff eight more parish schools in eastern South Dakota over the next twelve years. This in turn compelled Mother Butler to recruit many more women for her community. At parish schools, young Sisters bowed to the authority of local priests. On behalf of the Sisters, Mother Butler accepted a somewhat subservient role in order to operate parochial schools for Catholics as alternatives to worldly public schools.

There were dramatic changes in the 1890s. Bishop Martin Marty moved to the Diocese of St. Cloud in 1895, and in his place came Bishop Thomas O'Gorman. As the new leader in Sioux Falls, he authorized the deletion of specific provision for "enclosure" or cloister from the Presentation Sisters' constitution, thus enabling them to travel freely and take residence throughout eastern South Dakota. Quickly the Sisters could staff new parish schools as Catholic populations in farming settlements called for Christian education. The Bishop enlisted support for their effort from small town pastors, too, with a directive requiring Catholic parents to provide parochial schooling for their children. As the Sisters arrived to teach in these scattered parish schools, they also started Notre Dame Academy at Mitchell in 1898. They staffed nine schools some distance from their motherhouse by 1910 at Mitchell, Milbank, Jefferson, Bridgewater, Woonsocket, Dell Rapids, Elkton, Marion, and Bristol. During subsequent years they closed some of these and added others in response to change in the sizes and locations of immigrant Catholic populations.

Meanwhile Mother Butler and Bishop O'Gorman led Presentation Sisters into health care delivery because of a diphtheria epidemic at Aberdeen. After the crisis had passed, city leaders asked Mother Butler to staff a permanent hospital. A shortage of funds, the lack of training for nurses, and the absence of provision in the Order's constitution all stood in the way, but Mother and Bishop worked together on solutions because the need was so grave. Bishop O'Gorman could offer no financial assistance at the time, so Mother Butler sought a loan from a local banker. With funds in hand she directed the revision of the Presentation Sisters' constitution to include health care and encouraged her Sisters to accept the change with a reminder that Nano Nagle had nursed the sick in the slums of Cork. Next she created procedure for the training of nurses. Rather than face the expense of sending Sisters away to hospital schools of nursing in Minneapolis or Omaha, Mother Butler enlisted Sister Dominic Boyson, who had previously been trained as a nurse, to introduce a professional course for other members of the community. Construction began on a fifteen-bed hospital, which received patients in 1901 under the name of St. Luke's. The school of nursing opened at the new facility during the following year.

Over the next twelve years the Presentation Sisters founded three more hospitals: St. Joseph in Mitchell (1906); Holy Rosary in Miles City, Montana (1910); and McKennan in Sioux Falls (1913). Each operated a school for training nurses, several of whom became Presentation Sisters. It was in the field of health care that Mother Butler's followers experienced their broadest range of contact with non-Catholic South Dakotans, extending their ministry to all in need, despite their racial origins or religious preferences.

Mother Butler demonstrated unusual insight into needs and administrative procedures by articulating plans, encouraging prospective members of the Order to leave the comforts of family for the uncertainties of religious life on the northern prairie and Great Plains, and leading tours to acquire financial or material support. She demonstrated flexibility in her willingness to team with Bishop O'Gorman in the termination of enclosure for her community of Nuns. She revealed raw courage as she traveled through the settlements to raise funds and worked on the enrollment of Catholic students at parish schools.

Mother Raphael McCarthy, Mother Butler's successor, was a great deal like her predecessor in the vision, persistence, and flexibility she brought to the task. Born Margaret McCarthy in Bandon, Ireland, in 1888, she had such poor eyesight that her parents did not send her to college but provided for her education by tutors. She met Mother Butler when Mother made a recruiting trip to Ireland in 1907 and came to South Dakota as a postulant. Received into the congregation the next year, Margaret took the religious name of Sister Raphael. After practice teaching, she trained in the Order for nearly three years, pronounced her vows in 1910, and received assignment on her first mission at St. Peter's Church in Jefferson to work in education.

Soon she became too ill to teach, and Mother Butler sent her to Holy Rosary Hospital in Miles City for recuperation. After a time in convalescence, she entered nurses' training at St. Luke's Hospital in Aberdeen. "Whether this was by choice or assignment, the records do not reveal. Upon becoming a registered nurse, she no doubt mused 'Now this is it—I'll be a nurse instead of a teacher.' "[5]

Such was not to be the case. Soon her acumen in business matters and flair for public relations led to her assignment as Superior-Administrator at St. Joseph Hospital in Mitchell. There she developed new leadership skills and in 1927 she moved to McKennan Hospital in Sioux Falls to serve in a similar capacity. A year later Sister McCarthy was elected Assistant Superior General to Mother Aloysius Forrest. After the death of the Superior she finished out a term. By election in her own right in 1940, she assumed complete responsibility for the advancement of Presentation apostolates.

Mother McCarthy had scarcely unpacked at Aberdeen when Bishop Bernard J. Mahoney called upon Presentation Sisters to undertake the operation of a diocesan children's home. A fire had destroyed the building at Turton, South Dakota, southeast of Aberdeen. Sisters of

Charity from a community in St. Louis, who had worked there since 1924, were recalled to their motherhouse in Canada. The children lived in temporary quarters at Northern State Teachers College in Aberdeen. Mother McCarthy accepted the charge, kept a temporary home in operation at Woonsocket for a time, then enlisted federal Works Progress Administration support for the construction of the Presentation Children's Home that opened at Sioux Falls in 1940:

> The new children's home provided a haven for homeless children throughout the diocese. Since their arrival in South Dakota, the Presentation Sisters had cared for orphans in the parochial schools they staffed, boarding them with reliable families during summer vacations. Now that a large facility was available, the children were sent to live at the Presentation Children's Home. Numbers varied from sixty to ninety boys and girls between the ages of three and fifteen, several of whom were non-Catholic. The children studied grades one through eight at the home, then the boys went to Boy's Town in Nebraska, the girls either to Notre Dame in Mitchell or Mount Marty in Yankton. Funding for the orphanage came from private donations, diocesan aid programs, and the state department of welfare. Many of the children were not strictly orphans but came from broken homes or those judged unsuitable by the department of welfare.[6]

Sister McCarthy's elevation to the office of Mother Superior had come in the midst of depression, dust storms, drought, and social dislocations. Like Pope Pius XII she believed that religious should be as professionally competent as their lay counterparts and labored hard to upgrade teacher training and nursing education. "Her openness to the future affected the steady growth of the Order, and the continuing effort to keep the hospitals and schools up-to-date."[7]

Later in the 1930s she responded to a request from the Archbishop of St. Paul for Nuns to teach catechetical classes at Mound and Willmar, Minnesota. Three Presentation Sisters moved to the old rectory of Our Lady of the Lake Parish in Mound, where they lived on the second floor and held classes for more than 100 pupils downstairs. Their schedule followed an arrangement provided by the Superintendent of Schools in the district whereby students in public institutions took release-time each week for religious instruction. Children from rural schools attended classes on Saturdays. A new convent opened at Mound in 1941. A parish school for grades one through eight opened a short time later. Located in suburban Minneapolis, the school grew rapidly from an enrollment of 280 pupils to nearly 500 within ten years.

Presentation Sisters taught catechism at Willmar for fifteen years, too, before a parochial elementary school opened, serving nearly 700 students in release-time instruction each week.

Despite depression-era economic constraints, Mother McCarthy purchased an abandoned structure (Lincoln Hospital) located some ten blocks away from St. Luke's at Aberdeen, and, in spite of advice to the contrary, arranged its relocation as a hospital annex. She hired the Crowe Brothers Company from Chicago to conduct the move, which took five months due to foul weather, sharp street corners, and narrow curbs. "Finally in November, 1940 the five-thousand ton building was set on its foundation, having received scarcely a crack during the long move. Mother Raphael had been vindicated. 'A woman with vision who overcame obstacles and performed deeds that seemed impossible.' "[8]

While World War II raged overseas, Mother McCarthy and the Presentation Sisters faced many demands on the home front. A shortage of nursing personnel inspired federal officials to organize the Cadet Nurse Corps, a program that provided uniforms and small financial stipends for students who would serve domestic nursing needs, thus releasing nurses with more advanced training for service abroad. Mother McCarthy saw great advantage in this for Presentation Sisters. Her staff met federal enrollment requirements by the development of a general school of nursing that included rotations by students from all four Presentation hospital schools, thus increasing the total number of students at Presentation hospitals to meet federal guidelines. Students participated enthusiastically in the Cadet Nurse Corps out of patriotic fervor as well as desire for personal advancement. By the final months of the war, nurses trained by Presentation Sisters had made a large contribution to a reduction in the shortage of nurses across the region.

Throughout her term as Superior, Mother McCarthy worked also to gain recognition for the Presentation Sisters' community as a Pontifical Order and received willing assistance from Bishop William Brady after he took over the South Dakota diocese in 1940. She had begun her drive soon after assuming the role of Mother Superior in 1933, with assistance from Bishop Mahoney. With enthusiastic support from two bishops, she sent voluminous correspondence to other Orders asking for information on procedures as she consulted experts on constitutional revision. "Finally in 1946 she had the joy of seeing the document which granted the Pontifical status."[9]

That year Mother Viator Burns succeed her in the office of Mother Superior. In semi-retirement Mother McCarthy assisted with administration as the Order continued to grow. She was involved in the purchase of land on which to build a new motherhouse and in the designing and building of the new facility during the early 1950s. She participated in the transfer of Notre Dame Academy (which had grown into a junior college) from Mitchell to Aberdeen, where it could flourish as the new and larger facility. With keen business acumen, Mother McCarthy worked with architects, contractors, and benefactors:

> She held weekly luncheons at the convent for the businessmen of Aberdeen to acquaint them with the proposed plans, and to solicit their financial support. She was persistent in seeking help for the two million dollar complex which would become Presentation Convent and Junior College, the largest project to be completed in the city up to that time. The beautiful building became a reality and the Sisters moved there in 1954.[10]

The pleasure of life in her final years was enhanced by release from her personal malady. Lifelong affliction with poor eyesight grew steadily worse until she heard of an eye surgeon in California who could perform a corneal transplant. Mother spent six months at Los Angeles in periodic hospitalization. Between hospital visits she and her companion, Sister Evarista Reddy, RN, made trips to stay with the Presentation Sisters at San Francisco. After the eye surgery and some time for recuperation, Mother McCarthy began a new life of wonder as her vision dramatically improved. "For the first time she could distinguish the Sacred Host, a line of cars, the chapel roof . . . ever so many beautiful things awaited her."[11] After her operation, she served as administrator at Holy Rosary Hospital in Miles City, Montana, and at Mother Joseph Manor in Aberdeen. "The Manor" and Brady Memorial at Mitchell, which had been constructed by the Diocese of Sioux Falls, were administered by the Presentation Sisters.[12]

Mother McCarthy lived to age seventy-eight, and died in 1966. At the funeral, Sioux Falls Bishop Lambert Hoch summed up her importance in his homily when he said: "so valiant a woman, so singularly competent, so constantly involved in helping every deserving cause . . . so happily restless until she had given her all."[13] Mother McCarthy's life was a composite of heritage from Nano Nagle and Mother Butler, of her own drive inspired by both necessity and spirituality, and of her own persistence and flexibility.[14]

Mother Jerome Schmitt made similar contributions in her service to the Benedictine Sisters at Yankton. Under inauspicious circumstances, she was born on March 30, 1899, at Epiphany, South Dakota, to German-speaking immigrants of Rhenish, French, and Italian ancestry. Her parents baptized her Mary Catherine. The family was very religious; four of the children would dedicate themselves to the service of God in religious life: Monsignor William Schmitt, who gave long service in the Diocese of Sioux Falls; Sister Regula, who joined the Benedictine community at St. Joseph, Minnesota; Brother Oswald, who served as Superior General of the Xaverians for twelve years; and Mary Catherine, who took the name Jerome when she entered the novitiate of Sacred Heart Convent in Yankton.

Her parents were homesteaders on adjoining claims some thirty miles from Mitchell. Epiphany had not yet emerged as a town when they came from Germany late in the 1870s to escape Chancellor Bismarck's *Kulturkampf* and the mass conscription of young men into an expanded German army under Prussian control. German was the language spoken at home. Mary Catherine learned French from Nuns exiled by the Laic Laws of 1904, which had forbidden their engagement as teachers in France. She later learned English and written German from Benedictines who came from the Yankton convent to teach at the parochial school close to her home.

As World War I broke out in Europe in 1914, Mary Catherine joined the Benedictine Sisters' community at Yankton. She graduated from Yankton (public) High School in 1918, and was invested later that summer in the habit of the Benedictine Sister. After receiving some college credits at Creighton University during the summer, she matriculated at St. Theresa's College in Winona, Minnesota, as a full time student and went on to earn a baccalaureate degree in time to join the staff at the newly established Mount Marty Academy in 1922. She taught English, Latin, and French for a year, then became principal to release Sister Stanislaus Van Well, who was sent to Catholic University to study for a graduate degree.

Sister Jerome became Mother Jerome by election from the 291 Sisters of Sacred Heart Convent in the year 1932. She would lead them through a continuous term that lasted until 1961. By the end of her tenure in office the convent membership had risen to more than 500.

After she took over as Mother Superior, the Benedictine Sisters plunged deeply into debt with the construction of a new hospital in Pierre. They had purchased the abandoned Park Hotel in 1899, in which they operated a day school and boarding academy until 1903, when they constructed the academy facility with used lumber near the church on Euclid Avenue that they operated until 1943. They had also admitted the first patients at the old Park Hotel under the name St. Mary's Hospital in 1899, and developed an annual patient load in excess of 1,500 by the early 1920s. This fifty-bed hospital, which in 1922 became the first in the state to gain approval and accreditation by the American College of Surgeons, was replaced by a new 102-bed, brick structure in 1930.

Subsequently, the Benedictines added to their indebtedness by the acquisition of many more facilities: new wings on the two hospitals in existence at the time of Mother Jerome's initial election, the addition of Thomas More Hospital at Canon City, Colorado (1938), as well as three newly organized homes for the aged at Yankton (1948), Pierre (1953), and Lincoln, Nebraska (1959); a four-year college to award nursing, teaching, and other degrees; a home for nurses; and expanded housing for staff. Throughout Mother Superior's tenure, the Order carried an enormous burden of debt.

Stable administration despite this adversity was her greatest strength. Money was always at a premium. Sisters skimped and saved to staff and maintain their hospitals, the Academy at Yankton, and more than twenty satellite parochial schools. At the Zell School near Redfield, for example, boarders paid five dollars for room and board per month. A farm on the Zell School grounds was in dire straits. Government subsidies of surplus food stocks saved the Sisters and their students from constant hunger.

Special needs required attention. In 1934, for instance, the Benedictine Sisters agreed to buy and staff the Dr. Waldner Hospital in Parkston, which had been closed for several years. It opened in August as St. Benedict's. Due to a shortage of space, a new wing was added in 1944. Before the end of her administration, Mother Jerome supervised the erection of a whole new building at another site in Parkston.

With her reelection as Prioress in 1935, Mother Jerome felt she had a mandate to establish a two-year junior college adjacent to the Convent. There was only one Catholic institution of higher education in the state at the time—Columbus College in Sioux Falls. There was some ready cash available at the Convent because Marienheim, the Benedictine's recruiting center in Einsiedeln, Switzerland, had just been sold for $60,000. Through the penurious efforts of the Mother Superior and Sisters, the building fund of the Order had grown to a princely $30,000. Hence, Mother Jerome had $90,000 at hand and had confidence that the Sisters could somehow raise the balance of funding for construction. Bids were let and a contractor was engaged to start building. The facility was already under roof when the funds were exhausted. No more seemed to be in sight. Attempts to secure $200,000 to carry on were frustrated by word that Columbus College, the diocesan institution in Sioux Falls, had defaulted on its bonds.[15] Investors had become suspicious of all borrowers affiliated with the Diocese. The First National Bank of Yankton loaned to its limit of $20,000, however, and the Abbot of Conception monastery sent an interest-free loan of $4,000. Denver and Chicago banks would not consider Mother Jerome's pleas, but finally a St. Louis firm accepted the Yankton, Pierre, and Zell properties as collateral and approved a loan. Papal officials in Rome, who had earlier refused permission to build, were willing to accept the *fait-accompli*. Later Mother Jerome would recall that she was reminded of the words of Virgil, who had difficulty in an ancient foundation: *"Tantae molis erat Roman urbem condere,* or "Such a task it was to found the city of Rome."[16]

The two-year college opened in 1936, with the name Mount Marty in honor of the first Catholic Bishop of Dakota. The Sisters housed their academy (high school) in the same building. This model institution of higher learning offered practice teaching instruction for one and two-year certificate programs to train grade-school teachers. Fifteen years later, the College expanded to award a baccalaureate degree. Mother Jerome took over the College presidency at the same time she occupied the Prioress' office and served from the opening in 1936 to 1957, when she appointed as her successor Sister Evangeline Anderson.

As Mount Marty College grew, so did the other institutions around it. At Yankton there was expansion in the motherhouse, the Sisters' residence, the hospital, the nurses home, and a grade school in town. When the Franciscan Sisters of Greenfield Park-Milwaukee withdrew from their parochial school at Geddes in 1935, three Benedictine teachers and a housekeeper went to keep it open until 1942, when declining enrollment finally forced its closure.

Father Edwin Callahan visited Yankton to plead for a Catholic hospital in Gregory, South Dakota, in 1936. Mother Jerome had no nurses to spare. Because the Benedictine Sisters at Sturgis hoped to have personnel ready in a year and a half, however, she agreed to staff it until that time. When eighteen months later the Sturgis Benedictines announced their unreadiness to assume control, Benedictine Sisters from Yankton agreed to continue to staff the hospital, and remained until 1948, when it was finally turned over to Franciscan Nuns.

Much of Mother Jerome's energy went into the establishment of the nursing home in Lincoln, mentioned above, which was later fashioned into a complete health care center called Madonna Home. She also worked steadily on the operation of parochial schools in Nebraska and Colorado. In the 1950s she and her community took over the staffing of three Sioux Falls parish schools: St. Theresa's, Christ the King, and St. Lambert's. She provided the initial assignment of teachers to staff O'Gorman High School in Sioux Falls during 1961. Mother Jerome assumed responsibility for opening a school at Farmer, South Dakota, near her hometown of Epiphany, as well as a new school in Pierre that opened in 1958 to replace the old school on Euclid Avenue. As the number of Sisters available for the various apostolates began to wane in the 1960s, some of these educational endeavors were turned over to others, were only partially staffed by Sisters, and in some cases were closed completely. By then, the Benedictine Sisters corps of teachers was dispersed across a four-state area. Along with responsibility for the hospitals, a college, the parochial schools, and other facilities, Mother Jerome served as supervisor for many departments in the convent where the Sisters were at work: making altar-beads, sewing and embroidering vestments worn by the priests, and providing other services.

Somehow she found time for the humanities and the arts. Mother Jerome reveled in seeing Mount Marty College host a variety of groups with aesthetic interests. There were drama festivals, workshops by the dozens, and music festivals. Two of many national meetings she helped sponsor were especially important: The National Catholic Rural Life Conference at the College in 1956; and The National Catholic Art Association meeting at the Mount in 1957. Under her aegis, two scholars evolved at the Convent to earn international acclaim: the historian Sister Claudia Duratschek and the calligrapher Sister Leonarda Longen.

To her credit is the home for nurses adjacent to the hospital; a home , on the farm built originally for hired men and later converted into a mens' dormitory; a new College physical plant to provide ample classroom and dormitory space; and a new chapel to replace the structure built in 1919, which was far too small to accommodate growing numbers at the convent and the College. World War II was over no more than a month when she contracted to build all of these. Construction was halted for a time because of federal restrictions. The nurses' home was considered a facility of critical nature, but according to a federal order the chapel was not. Wrote a bureaucrat: ''one can, after all, worship under a tree.'' She responded in typical fashion that one could indeed do that in some times and places but not in January in South Dakota! Two years passed before federal permission to build came through.

In 1948, when the South Dakota Hospital Association was organized, Mother Jerome became its first president. Like her predecessors, she gave leadership in the enhancement of the liturgy of the church, monastic prayer, and Eucharistic services. Mother Jerome gave papers at three convocations of the National Liturgical Conference. When the Jesuit liturgist Father Gerald Ellard wrote his book on church rites, he asked that the convent's unique offertory procession during the Mass be photographed for incorporation into *The Mass of the Future*. Because the Prioress and the Sisters' Chaplain, Father Henry Huber of Conception Abbey, complied with the request, students of liturgy in colleges throughout the country since have seen in a text on liturgical worship the South Dakota Benedictine Sisters at liturgical worship pictured as paradigms for renewal of certain liturgical rites.

This inimitable and indefatigable Nun from South Dakota achieved international recognition for her prophetic stance in the liturgical movement of the Catholic Church. During 1956 she was one of only three American women honored with an invitation to participate in the International Liturgical Congress in Assisi, Italy. Her six weeks' stay ended in a memorable meeting at Rome with Pope Pius XII, who gave these women the privilege of a private audience.

Mother Jerome voiced her guiding principles as she shared in the changing commitment of the Catholic Church: "We are gospel people, but I feel that this must be more than just lip service."[18] Her commitment to social action necessitated the expansion of physical facilities if the religious community were to respond to the needs of the people both in and out of state. In 1953 she supervised construction on a new nurses' home and the Maryhouse Home for the aged adjacent to the hospital in Pierre. At the same time she helped with plans for a new wing at St. Thomas More Hospital in Canon City, Colorado. She supervised the arrangement of architects' drawings for the College facilities at Mount Marty in Yankton, including Whitby Hall Dormitory and Marian Auditorium.

When the number of Sisters at Sacred Heart Convent exceeded 500, Mother Jerome was advised by Benedictine leadership to consider the foundation of another community in the Order to preserve the family spirit and relieve the overcrowding at the motherhouse in Yankton. After the decision was made to establish a new community temporarily in Pierre, Mother Jerome began to designate which 140 Sisters would leave Yankton for the new home. Individuals were permitted to express their wishes, choosing to go or remain in Yankton, or to leave their choice to the Superior. Of 279 who expressed willingness to go to Pierre, Mother Jerome selected 140 whose names she submitted to her Council for approval. Some modification of the list resulted, but 140 were on the final list.

Preparations for their departure took at least a year. When land for the new motherhouse in Pierre was preempted by the city as a lagoon for sewage disposal, the new convent was planned between Maryhouse Home for the aged and the hospital. Inasmuch as no academy could be built there, the site would be temporary. Eventually, they moved to Watertown, on the site called Harmony Hill.

Now plans advanced for the building of a new motherhouse at Yankton. The original building had served as part of an Academy for Indians erected by Bishop Marty that closed in the mid-1880s. A wing of wood construction had been expanded in the years 1907 and 1908 with the use of salvaged lumber from a structure torn down in Vermillion when the Order moved from there. Because the Yankton City Fire Department had condemned the old wooden structure, architects and contractors were engaged. Sisters were in their new dining room by Christmas of 1960 and were able to move into new dormitory areas by the following summer.

Mother Jerome's final term of office expired in 1961. She rejoiced in the completion of the new priory and the official separation of the community into two independent units. Now the Prioress of twenty-nine years bequeathed leadership to another; her Subprioress, Sister Julia Hunhoff, was elected as her successor.

During the 1961–1962 school year, Mother Jerome, now age sixty-three, began work at Marquette University on a Master of Arts Degree in German. She fulfilled all requirements in time to teach at Mount Marty College the following fall. In 1969 she celebrated the golden anniversary of her religious profession of vows, and took a new position in the chaplaincy department at the Benedictines' St. Thomas More Hospital in Canon City. Later she took up similar duties at Sacred Heart Hospital in Yankton. In 1974, at age seventy-five, she was asked to head the Governing Board of Sacred Heart Hospital, and filled that position for three years. In 1979 she celebrated sixty years in religious profession. The following year she was honored as Citizen of the Year by the City of Yankton.

Steadily she had followed her charge in the tradition of Benedict and Scholastica, repeating often the exclamation: "We are gospel people, but I feel that this must be more than just lip service." At age eighty-four, on March 14, 1983, she asked to be taken to pay her last respects at the funeral home to a local resident to whom she had ministered in her pastoral care days at Sacred Heart Hospital. She returned to the Convent, alerted the infirmarian that she was tired, and would take a short rest. She retired to her room and died shortly thereafter. Her funeral was on the Feast of St. Patrick, March 17. Abbott Jerome Hanus of the Benedictine Abbey at Conception, Missouri, traveled to serve as the main celebrant of her final liturgy; Monsignor John McEneaney of Sioux Falls was the homilist.

Mother Jerome may have spoken for Mothers Butler and McCarthy of the Presentation Order as well as for herself as she addressed Mount Marty College faculty in the first annual Sister Jerome Schmitt address during 1976: "As we build on our heritage, we realize only too well that the high road to life in any capacity is not easy, and that people who have a message such as ours, must endure for that message, especially when it means communicating the Good News of the Gospel."[19] As Superiors for two leading Orders of Catholic religious in South Dakota history, they all had served with great distinction in fulfilling both social and Christian missions.

Notes

1. Elsie Thomas Culver, *Women in the World of Religion* (New York: Doubleday and Company, 1967), pp. 78–87.
2. *Ibid.*
3. Mother Butler biography, file 1, Presentation Archives, Aberdeen, SD, p. 2.
4. Mother Butler correspondence, file 2, Presentation Archives, p. 2.
5. Mother McCarthy biography, file 1, Presentation Archives, p. 1.
6. Susan Peterson, "The Presentation Sisters in South Dakota, 1880–1976," (Unpublished doctoral dissertation, Oklahoma State University, 1979), p. 38.
7. Mother McCarthy correspondence, file 2, Presentation Archives, p. 2.
8. Mother McCarthy biography, p. 3.
9. *Ibid.*, p. 5.
10. *Ibid.*, pp. 6–7.
11. *Ibid.*, p. 8.
12. The Presentation Sisters' roles in diocesan affairs included teaching at diocesan high schools in Sioux Falls and Aberdeen, administering homes for the elderly in Mitchell and Aberdeen, and working at diocesan headquarters in Sioux Falls.
13. Mother McCarthy biography, p. 9.

14. Present-day Presentation Sisters continue to take inspiration from models given them by Butler and McCarthy. Two examples are Sister Elizabeth Remily, missionary hospital administrator in Mexico, and Sister Bonaventure Hoffman, national service officer for a nursing association.

15. Named after the Catholic Knights of Columbus, a layman's club, this College opened at the abandoned federal Indian boarding school facility at Chamberlain in 1909. The Viatorian Fathers came from Illinois to staff it until the move to Sioux Falls in 1921, after which diocesan priests carried on until the College closed in 1940, at which time the facility was converted into the U.S. Veterans Hospital. Priests of the Sacred Heart from Hales Corner near Milwaukee accepted the vacant site at Chamberlain in 1927, where they have operated St. Joseph's boarding school for Indian children ever since.

16. Mother Jerome Schmitt File, Sacred Heart Convent Archives, Yankton, SD.

17. *Ibid.*

18. *Ibid.*

19. *Ibid.*

Rev. Joseph Ward (1897).
Courtesy South Dakota State Historical
Society.

Statue of Ward in the U.S. Capitol.
Courtesy U.S. Representative Tim
Johnson.

Church, School, and State Affairs in Dakota Territory: Joseph Ward, Congregational Church Leader

Thomas J. Gasque

On November 6, 1868, Joseph Ward, only thirty years old and newly married, arrived in Yankton to lead a handful of members in the recently organized Congregational Church. Because there was no meeting place, services were held at first in the two-story frame Territorial Capitol. A bell salvaged from a steamboat wreckage stood atop the building to summon worshipers as well as legislators. Later, after the capital moved to Bismarck and the building was torn down, the same bell rang for generations of students at Yankton High School, a fitting symbol for Ward. From the day of his arrival until the time of his death twenty-one years later, he summoned Dakotans with regularity to responsible performance in the development of government, education, and religion.

In government he held no elective office, but through personal influence, speaking, and writing Ward was one of Dakota's most articulate spokesmen for responsible leadership as territorials worked their way toward statehood. In education, especially as the founder of Yankton College, his influence was longlasting. In the ministry he had few peers. In 1963 the South Dakota Legislature voted to honor this versatile man with a seven-foot marble statue in the United States Capitol. Officiating at the dedication was Donald Ward, like his grandfather a president of Yankton College. More than two hundred people were in attendance, including nearly twenty descendants of Joseph

Ward, as well as U.S. Senator George McGovern, U.S. Representative Benjamin Reifel, and South Dakota Governor Archie Gubbrud. McGovern read a statement from President John F. Kennedy, who praised Ward as "an intrepid clergyman and educator. . . , an outstanding son of his state and a credit to his country."[1]

Joseph Ward was, in the words of his biographer, "a Pilgrim of the later day."[2] He was born on May 5, 1838, in Perry Centre, New York, a little town settled by New England Congregationalists who had trekked westward out of Massachusetts. Throughout his life Ward maintained a close New England connection, and it was in that tradition that he fashioned his contributions to the development of Dakota. New England Congregationalism had evolved to a great extent out of dissatisfaction with the structure and doctrines of the Church of England, and for this reason Puritan churches in America emphasized congregational self-government in creed as well as in governance. Yet church and state in New England were as inseparable as in old England, and Congregationalists were intensely involved in the management of political affairs. They were also devoted to the support of education under ecclesiastical guidance, and education, as seen in the number of institutions founded by this denomination, has been one of the enduring monuments to Congregationalism in the United States. Best known are Harvard (1636), Yale (1701), Dartmouth (1769), Bowdoin (1794), Amherst (1825), Oberlin (1846), Grinnell (1847), and Carleton (1866). Ward brought with him to Dakota a commitment to a social system based upon Congregational practices that might be compared to a tripod, a society standing on the three legs of church, state, and education. He believed in a system whereby church behavior under local governance encouraged a church-state partnership in guiding public behavior as well as parallel commitments to education for all citizens.

His philosophies flowed, too, from previous personal experience. Ward's father died of pneumonia when Joseph was only five. His mother, already in poor health, died nine years later. The care of Joseph and his brothers was left to an older sister, Sarah, who would later marry Stewart Sheldon, a Congregational minister. Ward received most of his early education at home or at small private schools in Perry Centre and Leroy, a short distance away. When he was about seventeen years old, he experienced spiritual conversion at a Presbyterian revival. Strong religious feelings that had come from family and community ties intensified. He had two false starts in careers other than the ministry. For a brief period he taught in a school that he organized himself, but it was not successful. Next, on land he and his brother had obtained in Illinois, Ward tried farming, but this was even less successful than his school, and he gave up after a year. By the time he was nineteen his decision to enter the ministry was firm, and to further his education he enrolled in Phillips Academy in Andover, Massachusetts. After graduation in 1861 he entered Brown University. During the spring of 1862 almost the entire student body marched off to the Civil War, specifically to help guard Washington, DC. Although Ward fell seriously ill and was unable to remain in military service, he recovered enough to return to his studies at Brown University, and during summer months he participated in wartime activities as a chaplain in the U.S. Christian Commission, a philanthropic organization dedicated to the care of the sick and wounded.

Ward graduated from Brown in 1865 and returned to Andover for enrollment in the Theological Seminary, where he remained until completing his program in 1868. The Seminary at that time was an exciting place. Missionary spirit was strong and many young men planned lives of service in foreign or American mission fields. Also, faculty members began a strong liberal movement that would later involve Ward in a significant way.

Early in 1868 he received an invitation from the American Home Missionary Society to preach at the newly organized Congregational Church in Yankton, Dakota. He declined, out of a commitment to finish his degree, at the same time turning down an offer to go as a missionary to Turkey. Once he completed his degree, he was called to preach at the First Congregational Church in Oakland, California. He accepted and was ready to go when he got word that the invitation had been rescinded; another man had been offered the position. "Yet," as his biographer put it, "no sooner was the door closed in that direction than, strange to say, it opened again in the direction of Yankton."[3] To Ward it was the hand of Providence working in his life, and this time he eagerly accepted.

He did not go alone, for, on August 12, 1868, he married Sarah Wood of Providence, Rhode Island, whom he had known since his first year at Brown and to whom he had been engaged since 1864. The newlyweds were able to go as far as Sioux City by rail and traveled the rest of the way on muddy roads by stage coach. Their arrival in Yankton was remembered in later years by Ephriam Miner, one of the original members of the Congregational church:

> On the 6th. of Nov. 1868 a young man came into the store and walked back to where I was standing. He was something over 6 feet in height,

broad shouldered, well proportioned, plainly but well dressed. He looked as if he might be a traveling man, or a young preacher; at all events he looked like a man who could do things.

He said he was looking for a man named Miner, I told him my name was Miner and then he told me his name was Ward, and somehow we got hold of each others hands and for twenty [sic] one years and one month we walked and worked together hand in hand as closely as any two brothers could until I sat at the bedside and held his hand and felt the life go out of it.[4]

Taking over the new congregation was difficult for Ward, but he had ample cooperation from members to get him through the early stages. When the Dakota Legislature came into session, he and his flock had to vacate the capitol building and occupy a small house on Cedar Street. At Christmas a tree was brought in and hung with presents. Included was a note from former Delegate to Congress John B. S. Todd, offering the gift of a lot on the corner of Fifth and Walnut, where the Yankton Congregational Church has stood ever since. In his first quarterly report, submitted during February of 1869, Ward observed optimistically that attendance at his services was steadily increasing, ranging from a low of eighteen to a high of 140. It was by no means a homogeneous group: "There are Norwegians, Germans, Danes, Jews, Indians & Africans," he wrote. "There are graduates of Bowdoin, from Union & from West Point. Generals, Doctors, Lawyers, Indian traders & agents." Even so, he sensed general indifference to religion, especially on the part of some of the "prominent men," who "almost boast that they leave religious matters to their wives."[5]

As the congregation grew and prospered, so did Joseph and Sarah Ward's family. Seven children were born between 1871 and 1885, two of whom died in infancy. With money from Sarah's father, they built a large house at 512 Mulberry Street, into which they moved in November, 1873. Featuring steep twin gables and bay windows, it is well known as a landmark in Yankton's historic district. Its present owners have restored it to its original condition and operate it as a hostelry under the name "Mulberry Inn."

The work of the Church began to expand beyond Yankton. A year or so after the Wards came to Dakota, Joseph's sister and brother-in-law, Sarah and Stewart Sheldon, arrived with their son Charles. (Charles became one of the nation's foremost Congregational ministers and a writer of international fame for his modern allegory, *In His Steps*, one of the most popular books ever published in America.)

Stewart Sheldon was assigned as a missionary pastor and church organizer to the communities of southeast Dakota. New congregations sprang up and by 1876 fourteen churches and ten ministers served southeastern Dakota Territory. By definition, Congregationalism did not require a superstructure like that in most mainline Christian denominations, but the need for mutual support among congregations was strong, resulting in the founding of the General Association of Congregational Churches. Among the goals of the Association was education, and its members began a movement to found a college as early as 1875.

Ward had shown his interest in education as a teenager back in New York when he taught in his own private school. During the fall of 1869, his second year in Dakota, he founded and taught in a private school at Yankton, which enrolled the children of William H. H. Beadle, John B. S. Todd, Andrew J. Faulk, and Newton Edmunds, as well as those of other prominent citizens. In 1872 Ward organized Yankton Academy, the forerunner of both Yankton High School and Yankton College. His concern extended to public education and he was closely associated with General Beadle in the effort to prevent the sale of school lands at low prices. Beadle later recalled Reverend Ward as "my first convert, if indeed he required conviction at all and had not always thought substantially the same way."[6]

Yankton College got off to a slow start and nearly failed in its first decade, but for many years it was among the strongest liberal arts colleges in the Upper Midwest. In those years, especially the 1920s and 1930s, none in the community of Yankton would have believed it would close in 1984 due to a drop in enrollment and an increase in expenses, or that it would be offered to the U.S. Government in 1988 for conversion into a minimum security prison. In light of these developments, what Joseph Ward said at the laying of the cornerstone in 1882 takes on a tone of bitter irony:

> We shall live long enough to look back with gladness and pride to this day. . . . Children not yet born will tell the story of this corner stone and draw from it lessons for the encouragement of those who are to come after them—for we cling to the thought that this institution is to endure as long as the hill shall last and the river run.[7]

In the founding of Yankton College, Ward was clearly the prime mover, although it was ostensibly a cooperative effort by the General Association of Congregational Churches. The Association met in Canton during May of 1881 and voted to place the college in Yankton, which had offered not only a site but also eleven thousand dollars, nine thousand of which came from the local Congregational Church. Originally the name was to be Pilgrim College, but somehow the town's name was attached instead. A charter was issued in August, 1881. Classes began on October 4, 1882, ahead of the University of Dakota at Vermillion by twelve days. Sessions during the first year were held in the Congregational Church, while the first building was under construction.

Ward found it necessary, in light of his new duties as president of the College, to resign as pastor of the Congregational Church. Much of his time went to the tedious task of raising money, which required numerous trips to New England to speak on behalf of the new and struggling College. As a fund-raiser he was successful and was well on the way to making the College financially secure when a crisis, brought on by a theological dispute, almost destroyed it.

Liberal groups within the Congregational Church, led by faculty members at Andover Seminary, had begun to talk of "Progressive Orthodoxy." The issue that seemed most controversial was what is known as the hypothesis of "Future Probation," a "hope or possibility" that salvation is possible "for infants and heathen who died without the saving knowledge of Christ."[8] Conservatives who opposed the idea saw it as a threat to the whole missionary endeavor. What was the need of taking the message of Christ to the heathen world if God held out the promise of salvation at some future time? Ward's support for the Andover faculty came as a result of his friendship more than because he felt strongly about the theological implications, but this support almost cost him the College. A showdown came at a meeting of the American Board of Missions at Des Moines during October of 1886. Conservatives were in the decided majority during the "Great Debate," and many of them, New Englanders and Dakotans alike, who had supported Ward and Yankton College in the past, withdrew their support. One conservative from New England came to him at the meeting with these words: "We will make your college pay for this when you come East to collect funds."[9] Even support in Yankton diminished, for townspeople also divided over this issue. What saved the College was the Wards' house, which he mortgaged for $7,500 as collateral for the debt against the institution. The controversy finally settled down and support resumed by the time Ward died three years later.

Throughout his career in Yankton he found time for political matters.

Indeed, his concerns with religion, education, and politics came together in a symbolic, almost mythic, way, during an episode that took place in November, 1879. On Thanksgiving Day a group of men met for dinner at the home of Stewart Sheldon on West Sixth Street. Gathered around the table, along with Sheldon and Ward and others, were William A. Howard, Governor of Dakota Territory; William H. H. Beadle, Territorial Superintendent of Public Instruction; and Hugh J. Campbell, U.S. Attorney for Dakota Territory. All were members of Ward's First Congregational Church. Here this group of latter-day Pilgrims began the first serious discussion on the topic of statehood.

Ward remained active as the movement took shape through the formation of Statehood Clubs, probably the creatures of Ward himself. Their purpose was to bring together those interested in the movement. The division of the Territory so its southern communities would gain statehood separate from northern Dakotans was the main purpose. This demand for division may have slowed the process of admission for either South or North Dakota. After 1882 Congress was controlled by Democrats, who were opposed to admitting two Republican states. There was also the school land matter, which both Ward and Beadle wanted to resolve. Finally, there was the issue of prohibition, which churchmen of all denominations wanted to see written into the constitution. The upshot was a convention in Canton during June, 1882. The gathering was not sanctioned by any governing body; it was primarily a group of citizens, dominated by clergy, devoted to the concept of statehood. Ward, who wrote the report of the Committee on Resolutions, said: "It is not boasting to say that in subsequent generations men will quote the work of to-day [sic] as similar to that done by the Pilgrims in the cabin of the Mayflower when they put their names to the compact which was afterwards expanded into the Constitution of Massachusetts."[10]

Although there were no tangible results from the Canton convention, the next year brought the movement another step toward statehood. Judge Campbell and many others, including Ward, were ready to declare: "We are a State," without the approval of Congress. An important convention was held at Huron in June and most important citizens were there. Ward, though a prohibitionist himself, saw to it that the prohibition issue was separated from the more crucial issues of school land and geographic division. A constitution evolved, but Congress refused to accept it. Meanwhile, there was a reaction against dual statehood, which resulted in the movement of the capital from Yankton to Bismarck.

The constitution drafted at Huron was essentially the same as the one finally approved in 1889. Ward, as Chairman of the Committee on Arrangement and Phraseology of the Constitution, wrote a substantial part of it. Certainly he also wrote the sentence that remains the motto of South Dakota: "Under God, the People Rule."[11] His statement summed up the ideals of this Congregational clergyman, educator, champion of democracy, and politician.

President Benjamin Harrison signed the statehood proclamation on November 2, 1889. Joseph Ward lived in the State of South Dakota for only five weeks. On December 11, attended by his wife Sarah, his five young children, and his old friend Ephriam Miner, he died at age fifty-one of blood poisoning brought on by the diabetes that had stricken him just a few years before. Tolling of College and Church bells announced his death, and the public schools closed in his honor. Clergymen, politicians, and educators from around the state attended his funeral.

Now that Yankton College, Joseph Ward's longest lasting monument, is passing away, little remains as a reminder of the presence of this multi-faceted and influential citizen of Dakota Territory. No town or county bears his name. The little community of Academy in Charles Mix County once boasted a school called Ward Academy, named in his honor after his death, but now that school is closed and there is little left of the community. People like Ward, who work behind the scenes, are builders. They establish the foundations on which the structure can be built. Ward's influence on his own times was such that the foundation of this state was built firmly on the footings of sound government, religious values, and liberal education.

In Dakota Territory during those early days the opportunists outnumbered the idealists. The cynicism of the period after the Civil War, the "gilded age" as Mark Twain called it, infected the West as well as the rest of the country and made the exploitation of land and people seem almost respectable. Ward did not share that spirit of the times, but seemed truly to be guided by the sense of idealism that brought him to Yankton and that formed his vision of what Dakota might become. Further, he was able to convince others, in both West and East, of Dakota's future, a land not to be exploited for its wealth but to be cultivated for the next century and the centuries beyond. He carried this idealism into everything he did, whether working for the Church, the College, or the State. And he was able to articulate his idealism in numerous speeches before religious and political forums, and in some of the most respected intellectual journals of the day.

Though never a flashy figure, he was widely known and greatly respected. Knox College in Illinois awarded him an honorary doctorate and he was welcome in many homes and at many pulpits and lecture halls in New England. Until the Des Moines crisis, which slowed but did not stop his efforts, he had only to mention his Church or his College and his wealthy friends would offer their financial support. For many people in the East his very presence in Dakota lent credibility to the statehood effort. In his extensive and demanding travels and in his dedicated and continuing concern with church, school, and state, Ward never lost sight of his motivating vision of Dakota's future. His energetic involvement with nearly every facet of territorial life and his immeasurable influence on the actions and attitudes of others have left a significant legacy to the people of South Dakota.

Notes

1. Dorothy Holloway, "Kennedy Praises Ward in Unveiling of Statue," *Sioux Falls Argus Leader,* September 29, 1963.

2. George Harrison Durand, *Joseph Ward of Dakota* (Boston: Pilgrim Press, 1913), p. 3.

3. *Ibid.,* p. 70

4. Ephriam Miner, "The Mother Church," *The Monthly South Dakotan,* I (January 1899), p. 140.

5. Ward to Executive Committee, American Home Missionary Society, Yankton, February 5, 1869, *Joseph Ward Letters, 1868–1873* (Madison L. Sheely, ed.; Yankton, SD: First Congregational Church, [1968]), p. 7.

6. Durand, *Joseph Ward,* p. 157.

7. *Ibid.,* p. 137.

8. *Ibid.,* p. 189.

9. *Ibid.,* p. 193.

10. *Ibid.,* p.162.

11. *Ibid.,* p. 171; W. H. H. Beadle, "The Building of the State," *The Monthly South Dakotan,* III (April 1901), p. 390.

William Henry Harrison Beadle.

*Statue of Beadle in the state Capitol,
Pierre.
Courtesy U.S. Representative Tim
Johnson.*

Territorial Surveyor General, Protector of School Lands, Educator: William Henry Harrison Beadle

Thomas J. Gasque

General Beadle! This almost Dickensian name conjures an image of stuffy pomposity, a self-important Colonel Blimp. In the history of South Dakota, however, the peculiar name of William Henry Harrison Beadle appears again and again in association with important developments, and some observers have regarded him as the most outstanding citizen in the entire history of the state. A careful look into his life suggests that he was in ways a comic, pompous figure, but he was, as a participant in the early development of South Dakota, also a man who earned abiding recognition.

In his own time General Beadle seems never to have captured the imaginations of most of his fellow Dakotans. Honors were never spontaneous. Rather, they came from individuals who admired his work and staged events to make of him a folk hero in the image of George Washington. In 1910, for example, the South Dakota Education Association unveiled a life-size statue of General Beadle in the Capitol Building at Pierre. On the pedestal is this inscription:

W. H. BEADLE—EDUCATOR
HE SAVED THE SCHOOL LANDS

At age seventy-two, the General was present for the occasion, which was planned and staged by Doane Robinson, State Historian for the South Dakota Historical Society. Just as Mason Locke "Parson"

Weems created a memory of General Washington more favorable than he deserved, so did Secretary Robinson fashion an historical image of General Beadle to make him larger than life.

In 1938, the centennial of Beadle's birth, attention again focused on his contributions, this time one suspects at the direction of his biographer, Barrett Lowe, who chaired the Beadle Centennial Committee. He had produced a silent movie called *Dakotah* based on Beadle's life in 1929, had published a book-length biography in 1937, and had written a master of arts thesis about Beadle at the University of South Dakota in 1938. Lowe then became the prime mover in getting a replica of the Beadle statue at Pierre placed in the National Statuary Hall in Washington, DC, in 1938, and was instrumental in changing the name of Eastern State Normal School to General Beadle State Teachers College.

Material about the General's life is accessible enough. Lowe's biography is comprehensive and full of detail, and it is a wild and wonderful book with a strange but effective pattern of organization. An earlier biography by O. W. Coursey came out in the first edition before Beadle died. The General also wrote an autobiography, at the request of Doane Robinson, who included it in the third volume of *South Dakota Historical Collections* in 1906. Yet there has appeared no critical biography. One can only sift through the self-aggrandizement of Beadle or the adulation of his two biographers in search for a portrait of the man as he really was.

William Henry Harrison Beadle was born on January 1, 1838, in Parke County, Indiana, less than sixty miles from where his namesake had fought Tecumseh at the Battle of Tippecanoe in 1811. Harrison, who served about a month in the White House while young William was only three years old, may have been related to the family. Beadle attended local schools in Parke County until 1857, when he entered the University of Michigan. In his first two years, he studied Latin, Greek, and Mathematics, and in 1861 he received a baccalaureate degree with a specialty in civil engineering. At Michigan Beadle came into contact with Rev. John D. Pierce, whose ideas about state-supported education were far ahead of his time. At one lecture Beadle's imagination was stimulated by his mentor's argument that the Michigan school system had been damaged from the mismanagement of funds and by the sale of federally granted school lands too cheaply. This became a lesson of value later on in the formulation of Beadle's public policy on school land.

His senior year drew to a close as the Civil War began, and Beadle signed up as a First Lieutenant. His service in the Union Army was honorable but not illustrious enough to justify his displaying the title of General as though he had earned it with distinguished service. His unit, of Company A, 31st Indiana Volunteer Infantry, fought in western Tennessee and in Mississippi. For this he was promoted to the rank of Captain, then returned to Michigan to recruit and train sharpshooters. On January 1, 1863, he was commissioned Lieutenant Colonel in the First Michigan Sharpshooters. After some combat action and exposure to severe snowstorms in December of 1863, Beadle and his regiment were ordered to travel in unheated box cars to Maryland. From exposure he fell sick and nearly died in an Annapolis hospital. When he recovered enough to return to duty, he was assigned at the rank of Major in the Veteran Reserve Corps to guard the area around Washington, DC, and he commanded the honor guard when Abraham Lincoln gave his Second Inaugural Address. After Lincoln's assassination in April, 1865, Beadle went with the funeral train part of the way to Illinois. According to some sources, on March 13, 1865, he was "brevetted Colonel and Brigadier General of Volunteers 'For gallant and meritorious service during the war.' "[1] According to other sources the brevet rank of General came as late as March of 1866, when he was mustered out of the Army.[2] Whichever is correct, the rank was more honorary than real; Beadle was no war hero when he returned to civilian life at the age of twenty-eight.

While recruiting for the Michigan Sharpshooters, he had married a young widow named Ellen Chapman on May 18, 1863, in her hometown of Albion, Michigan. Ellen, a few months younger than her husband, had two small daughters by her previous marriage, and the Beadles had one child named Mae, born in August of 1865. Throughout the General's career the members of his family, especially his wife, remained shadowy, background figures with little influence on his thinking; they seldom surfaced to share in his public image.

He returned to the University of Michigan after separation from military service and in 1867 received a law degree. Beadle practiced at Evansville, Indiana, then in Boscobel, Wisconsin, as he toyed with politics. Possibly the U.S. Representative from his district perceived him as enough of a threat to arrange for Beadle to get a federal appointment far from Boscobel. Whether this was the reason, or President Ulysses S. Grant wished to reward him for his campaign support, is hard to say. In any event, Beadle won appointment as Surveyor General of the United States for the Territory of Dakota with a commission signed by Grant on April 7, 1869. He came to the Sioux City, Iowa, railhead in April and entered a frontier career.

What was the nature of his job? For nearly eighty-five years surveyors had carefully divided the United States into square mile sections, as prescribed by the Land Ordinance of 1785, and prepared the sections for sale to land speculators or settlers. The rectangular survey was the most efficient way to divide the land, since usually only two sides of the square had to be marked. The method used by the first surveyors was nearly the same as that employed in Beadle's time. With compass and Gunter's chain (sixty-six feet, or eighty chains to the mile), a party followed a direct, westward line. Every six miles, one party would head south, and another north, to mark off each mile. Six miles on each side constituted a standard township; thus, there were thirty-six square miles to each township. Every one of these square miles or sections was numbered, beginning in the northeast corner and going to the west side, then turning as a plowman does and finishing in the southeast corner, at the section numbered thirty-six. Surveyors did not build up a series of townships one after another. First they established a sequence of base lines and principal meridians. From these lines marking Ranges the smaller divisions could be made. The original line, running west from the Ohio border beyond Pittsburgh, became the first base line. As settlement caught up with surveys, new base lines and principal meridians were established. Beadle's surveys, like all of those in eastern Dakota, were based on the Fifth Principal Meridian, a line running north and south from the baseline in eastern Arkansas.[3]

When General Beadle arrived in Dakota during 1869, the process of surveying in the Territory was well underway. As early as 1859, surveyors had entered to lay out townships in the southeast. By late 1860, the surveying of the first "tier" of townships along the Missouri river had been completed. There was much to be done, however, before the survey of the whole state was finished in 1920. Beadle's task was to supervise the whole process while sometimes helping with surveys himself.

In his autobiography he commented on the job. The General praised the early explorers and cartographers, especially Joseph N. Nicollet and Gouverneur K. Warren, as map makers. Through careful measurements and astronomical observations, they had pretty well fixed the positions of rivers, lakes, and hills. But "the details between the determined points were inaccurate until progressive surveys defined every part."[4] Beadle told of running new standard parallels and guide meridians into the northern part of the Territory, often laying out townsites after a railroad had pushed through.

Seeing so much of the Territory and meeting so many of its early settlers gave Beadle "a great confidence in the future of the country and an enduring enthusiasm for its progress."[5] His belief in the future of Dakota and his ideas about how to shape that future come together in his autobiography. When he arrived at Sioux City late in April of 1869 to take up the post of Surveyor General, he met William Tripp, his predecessor. On the long journey to Yankton over muddy roads with stops to clean the gumbo off the wheels, Beadle and Tripp talked at length about many things. Beadle remembered saying that territorial citizens should not give up school lands carelessly, as had happened in many states further east. "The schools and this endowment were live issues in my mind on the first day I saw Dakota."[6]

Soon this became a complicated issue. In Dakota Territory federal officials designated, as an addition to the original grant of Section 16 in each township, Section 36 for the development of schools. Two sections were thus available to generate revenue through sale or rent for a fund to support public education. Territorial officials east of the Mississippi River had sold their school lands at the prevailing rates of $1.25 to $2.50 per acre to create a school fund. Beadle feared similar, hasty sales would deny future generations valuable support for their schools, and found the chance to put this idea into action when Governor William Howard asked him in 1878 to serve as his private secretary, then as the Superintendent of Public Instruction. Beadle accepted the appointment as Superintendent contingent upon the Governor's agreement to support the idea that the education laws be reformed, and that "no school lands should ever be sold for less than their appraised value, and never for less than ten dollars an acre."[7] In 1878 land was cheap. Doubtless ten dollars appeared exorbitant. It still seemed excessive in 1885, when Beadle managed to get the ten-dollar minimum written into the proposed constitution that gained ratification at statehood in 1889 bearing the same provision.

A look at advertisements in newspapers gives a sense of the relative value of the land. In Vermillion during 1873, for sixty-five dollars one could buy a Secor sewing machine, complete with cover, from William L. Owens, agent, who also published the *Clay County Register*, a subscription to which cost two dollars per year. In 1886, H. E. Hobbs in Sioux Falls sold "reliable" bicycles, the kind with the high front wheel, for prices ranging between twenty-five and ninety dollars. I. P. Lounsbury sold pianos for 198 dollars. C. Listman had suits for as low as twenty-five and as high as forty-five dollars. A traveler could stay at the Merchants Hotel for two dollars a night.[8] The amount of money to support a family of five, like that of Beadle, was around sixteen hundred dollars a year. For that amount Beadle might have bought 160 acres of school land at ten dollars an acre. That was a substantial price, considering other land acquired through federal laws was free as homestead or cost either $1.25 or $2.50 per acre under special legislation. Beadle cut a good deal in the public interest as he charged a fee for state school land several times as great as the highest price fixed on the general offerings of federal lands.

The General was also a force behind congressional legislation in 1881 that set aside seventy-two sections (two townships) in each of five territories (Dakota, Montana, Arizona, Idaho, and Wyoming) to fund professional universities as suggested by the Northwest Ordinance of 1787. Indeed, he was invited to select these sections for Dakota because of his knowledge of the Territory. Settlement was occurring so fast that some of the land in the sections he chose was occupied by squatters before legal details could be taken care of to protect them, and he had to choose others. "The final selection," he recalled, "was not so good, but was much more valuable than could have been made after statehood."[9]

The problem of squatters on designated school lands was serious and Beadle used as much influence as possible to prosecute the trespassers. Many individuals went to trial, with U.S. Attorney Hugh Campbell prosecuting. In the northern part of the Territory, bonanza (corporation) farm operators became a serious threat, too. Beadle and Campbell brought several to court and won most attempts to keep the lands clear of settlement or unauthorized corporate farming.

Success came in the face of stern opposition. His insistence on keeping land prices high meant delay in the development of a school fund. With thousands of settlers pouring into eastern counties during the Dakota Boom, two out of thirty-six sections, or about five and a half percent of territorial acreage, was a significant amount to withhold from general entry, and newcomers were incensed. The threat from speculators was serious. In a supplementary note to his autobiography, Beadle revealed that a group of influential businessmen approached him early in 1884, proposing to buy one million acres of school land at five dollars an acre, once statehood was attained, if no price limitation were written into the state constitution. "I refused to have anything to do with it," Beadle wrote, and he also "promised not to expose them by name and not to publish the plan" until the chief spokesman was dead. In 1906, the man had died, allowing Beadle to reveal the plan, but he never identified the man.[10]

He resigned as Superintendent of Education in 1883 but remained active in territorial affairs. Representatives of southern Dakota met in two constitutional conventions. Documents from both sessions reveal Beadle's tenacity and his success in preserving ten dollars an acre as the minimum charge for school land, under constitutional authority.

In February, 1889, Beadle was appointed Superintendent of an Indian training school near Salem, Oregon, where he remained only until August, returning eagerly to accept the presidency of the Dakota Normal School at Madison. His career as an administrator and teacher at Madison was distinguished and, by the time of his retirement at age sixty-seven in 1905, he bore the image of a "Grand Old Man." Yet, the South Dakota Board of Regents removed him from administration at that point and he served out his career as a professor of history. This forced retirement, called by some the "Crime of 1905," has been blamed on a governor, on a "militant, plotting," on an unnamed regent, and even on a discontented faculty member.[11] The General remained at Madison until 1912 as a professor, when ill health finally forced him into full retirement. (His name was later attached to the state college at Madison until it was re-named Dakota State College in 1969.)

Honors began to come with old age. In 1902 the University of Michigan awarded an honorary Doctor of Laws degree. In 1908 Beadle delivered the main speech at the laying of the Capitol cornerstone in Pierre. In 1910 came the crowning honor, when his statue was authorized by the South Dakota Education Association. Citizens and school children were invited to make small contributions to meet the cost. It was unveiled on January 21, 1910, with Beadle in attendance.

In 1912 the General went to live at the Soldier's Home in Hot Springs, South Dakota. His small income came from a fund set up with an excess over the amount needed to pay for the statue plus the soldier's pension paid for his keep. In 1915 he visited his step-daughter in San Francisco. While there, he died a month and a half short of his seventy-eighth birthday. Later his body was taken to Albion, Michigan, for burial beside that of his wife.

There has been little pressure to keep the name of William Henry Harrison Beadle before the public late in the twentieth century. Beadle County, fourth largest in population in South Dakota, commemorates him, even though he had no special connection to that county or to its county seat at Huron. The college he led no longer bears his name, but educators remember him with the Beadle Club, an organization of professional educators, and a special room in the School of Education at the University of South Dakota in Vermillion is a shrine to his memory. His statue stands in the Capitol buildings at Washington and in Pierre. One of the ironies of his career, and of his personality, is his allowing himself to be called *General* Beadle. The temper of the times encouraged such honorifics, but the title was misleading in light of his major contributions, which were most definitely not of a military nature. His work as a surveyor was significant, but it was not really special. His presence as an educator was most important, for he exerted lasting influence over the development of the public schools— both as the Superintendent of Public Instruction, and later as the President of the College at Madison.

Beadle's twenty years in Yankton, from 1869 to 1889, were crucial to the development of statehood and he was at the center of power. He influenced governors, judges, and ministers—most significantly Joseph Ward—in a number of intangible ways, and he was one of the chief architects of the state constitution. Beadle's major impact on that document was his insistence that it should prohibit school lands from ever being sold at less than ten dollars an acre. This policy also found its way into the constitutions of other western states. Beadle was obsessed with the issue, almost to the point of absurdity, but it was this that earned him a place of honor in the history of the state. His struggle was almost heroic, and, even though the results may have seemed lost in the complexities of subsequent educational financing, his legacy had remained. From a grant of more than three and a half million acres in school lands, the state has preserved a permanent school fund in excess of sixty-two million dollars, plus nearly a million acres in residue to produce additional income.

Beadle regarded himself as a statesman and his statue, with its stern manner and military bearing, projects the image. He was, however, not a statesman of the first rank and, despite his involvement in so many of the activities of the territory and early statehood, his accomplishments, beyond the school lands issue, were minimal. Yet, among that first generation of public figures in the development of Dakota Territory, William Henry Harrison Beadle deserves to be considered one of the most influential.

Notes

1. Barrett Lowe, *Twenty Million Acres: The Story of America's First Conservationist, William Henry Harrison Beadle* (Mitchell, SD: Educator Supply Company, 1937), p. 42.

2. R[aynor] G. W[ellington], "Beadle, W. H. H.," *Dictionary of American Biography*. II (1929), p. 86; O. W. Coursey, *A Complete Biographical Sketch of General William Henry Harrison Beadle* (3rd ed.; Mitchell, SD: Educator Supply Company, 1916), p. 34. For the portion of his biography dealing with the war years, Coursey reprints a sketch written by Beadle's daughter, Mae Beadle Frink.

3. For a good discussion of the land survey, see Hildegard Binder Johnson, *Order Upon the Land: The U.S. Rectangular Land Survey and the Upper Mississippi Country* (New York: Oxford University Press, 1976).

4. W. H. H. Beadle, *Autobiography of William Henry Harrison Beadle* (Pierre: South Dakota State Historical Society, 1938), pp. 16–17.

5. *Ibid.,* p. 20.

6. *Ibid.,* p. 8.

7. *Ibid.,* p. 77.

8. *Clay County Register* (Vermillion), August 21, 1873; Daily Argus (Sioux Falls), May 4, 1886.

9. Beadle, *Autobiography,* p. 33. The two-township land grant was authorized by XXI, *Statuses at Large of the United States,* p. 326.

10. *Ibid.,* p. 158.

11. Lowe, *Twenty Million Acres,* pp. 200–201.

Arthur Calvin Mellette.

From Territorial Status to Statehood:
Arthur Calvin Mellette

William O. Farber

Among the many noteworthy South Dakota pioneer leaders, Arthur
Calvin Mellette occupied a unique position. As the last Governor of
Dakota Territory and the first Governor of South Dakota, he played a
pivotal role at the end of one era and the beginning of the next. He was
territorial Governor during a dramatic period of rapid growth and
optimism, exciting and romantic as only the western frontier could be.
He was state Governor in the initial years of statehood confronted by
all the ordinary difficulties of a fledgling governmental organization
with niggardly resources, and bedeviled by an unusual variety of
adverse economic and political problems. Mellette's troubles were
complicated by the high expectations of the migrant pioneers, many
lured recently from the East by extravagant promises from land devel-
opers. Indeed, Dakota Territory seemed fated as a place confounded
by persistent problems and unanticipated challenges, and subject to
continuous instability. Vagaries of weather may have been the underlying factor, but man-made political and social influences, and technological developments, were to prove significant, as well.

South Dakota leaders have never had an easy task. This was especially true of the state's first Governor. Arthur Mellette earned a place
in its history as a leader for the remarkable way he met crisis after
crisis with honesty and integrity, and his steadfast determination to do
the best that could be done with the resources available. As the
historian Doane Robinson said in 1910 while reviewing the Mellette
administration: "The way was uncharted and he displayed a patience

and wisdom which will always distinguish him and commend his memory."[1]

Mellette was, of the ten territorial governors, one of few who had much Dakota background; most of the others were appointees from outside the state. When he came to Dakota in early 1879, settling in Springfield, he had much to offer the Territory. At thirty-six years of age he had a superior education, had experience as a lawyer, and had served as a county superintendent of schools, newspaper editor, publisher, and member of the Indiana Legislature. He was a recognized authority on school law and common school district organization. Furthermore, he was a Civil War veteran, an important frontier credential.

Mellette was born in Prairie Township, Henry County, Indiana, June 23, 1842, the son of Charles and Mary Moore Mellett. His parents had moved to Indiana from Virginia in 1830. Of French Huguenot descent, the first Mellett in America had been a soldier in Marquis de Lafayette's army. The name was usually spelled "Mellett" until after the Civil War, when Arthur as well as some of the other family members added the "e."

Arthur had two brothers, James Thomas ("Jim") and Josiah Edmund ("Si"), and two sisters, Aletha Elvina ("Lethe") and Melinda Ann ("Linda"). His frequently used nickname, derived from his middle name, was "Cal." He was somewhat of an infant prodigy and learned to read at an early age. He attended a log cabin school about a mile from his farm home. He saved a little money, purchasing a "fiddle," which he hid in an old hollow tree, since in those days music was considered the "instigation of the devil." Unfortunately, his father, a strict Baptist, discovered his hiding place and he lost his "treasure."

Young Mellette demonstrated early his independence of thought. His wife recorded in a biography of her husband in 1908:

His Father and all the neighbors were Democrats and were strong believers in slavery. In some mysterious way "Uncle Tom's Cabin" (Mrs. Stowe's book) fell into Arthur's hands—this he read over and over. It made him want to know more. He questioned his Father—and after many long talks on the subject, he decided slavery was wrong—and he declared himself to be a Whig-from this through life he never changed, his next money was saved for a flag, and a very proud boy he was when a little flag floated from a pole he had placed in the yard. Gradually his Father and brothers changed their politics and all became Republicans.[2]

When Arthur was sixteen, he was sent to the Academy at Marion, Indiana, where he studied for two years. His greatest ambition was to attend college but, since his father was sending his older brother to Indiana University, he felt he must earn his own way. The result was serving as a country school teacher for a year. With his savings he entered Indiana University as a sophomore in 1861.

Mellette made a remarkable record at the University during his years as an undergraduate. He was highly regarded by his professors, was an able orator, received a Latin award, and was a member of a literary society as well as Phi Delta Theta social fraternity. He graduated with distinction in 1864, receiving an A.B. degree, converted later to an A. M. after he pursued professional studies.

Following his graduation on June 30, 1864, Mellette decided that duty compelled him to enter military service. The Civil War with its ominous developments had long haunted him. In a letter to Maggie, the daughter of an Indiana University professor whom he had met as a student and who later would become his wife, he wrote: "It almost seems to me sometimes that our cause is hopeless. And I even felt and said that if the nation must fall I hope to be in the number who would not live to bear the disgrace due an American who had not *fought* for it." In seeking the "path of *duty* for *me*," he thought of the "horrors of death on the battlefield . . . [and] too of that death seizing me probably with the blood of a murdered human being on my hands. It was to me a hard, *hard* problem." Arthur continued, "I have gone to the orchard at home night after night and studied about it. I sought every means at my command of communication with the unerring voice of nature and nature's God. . . . Well all I could do served to make clear the path of duty, and that was the path to battle—to death—that others might live and be happy."[3]

When he first sought to enlist, he was offered a first lieutenancy. After he returned home to say goodbye, he learned that his brother Jim had been drafted. Their parents, who seemed to favor the older boy, did not think Jim physically able to stand the rigors of army life and, since money to secure a replacement was not readily available, Arthur volunteered to go in his place. Referring to this act, his wife later wrote that his life was often one of self-sacrifice. Mellette went to Company "H", Ninth Indiana Volunteers, in which he served from October 12, 1864, to September 28, 1865. His military career was an almost continuous hell and he often doubted his ability to survive his perpetual bouts with diarrhea. He wrote in his "will" (November 12, 1864): "Never go in the Army."[4]

When he was mustered out, he returned for a final year of legal training at Indiana University, receiving his LL.B. degree on June 28, 1866. His marriage to his college sweetheart, Margaret "Maggie" Wylie, took place on May 29, 1866. The Mellettes settled in Muncie, Indiana, not far from his childhood home. There Arthur commenced the practice of law with his long time friend, Colonel T. J. Brady. All of his children, four sons, were born in Muncie. He was a popular attorney and in 1868 he was elected District Attorney for Delaware County. He proved to be a vigorous prosecutor and was known for his antagonism to the liquor interests.

Mellette's interest in politics grew as his work as editor of the *Muncie Times* involved him in the issues of his era. During the fall of 1870 he was elected County Superintendent of Schools. This was followed in October 1872 by election to the Indiana Legislature as a member of the House of Representatives representing Delaware County.

A month after Mellette took office, the Governor called a special session of the General Assembly, and the new legislator had an immediate opportunity to express his ideas in bill form. This he did in an amazing fashion for a freshman legislator. Indeed, the very first bill introduced was by Mellette: House Bill No. 1 proposed a constitutional amendment changing the general election date from the second Tuesday in October to the more orthodox Tuesday after the first Monday in November.

Mellette's political concerns at the time centered on public schools, perhaps because he had seen how education had enabled his brothers and sisters as well as himself to advance, and perhaps, too, because his own children were about to begin their schooling. His service as County Superintendent had undoubtedly convinced him of the drastic need to reorganize the Indiana system. The legislative output of the General Assembly in 1873 is a testimonial to his efforts. His wife recorded in the biography of her husband: "[H]e was Father to the Indiana school system, which is said to be the best in existence, and which has been adopted in nearly all the Western States. He often said of all his work he was proudest of this."[5]

The Muncie years were both politically and economically successful. With so many members of both the Mellette and Wylie families close by, the decision in 1878 to leave Indiana must have been agonizing. In the previous year the printing office burned and the business itself was sold. Rather than reestablish himself in Indiana, a geographical change seemed opportune. This was reenforced by the need to find a climate better suited to Maggie's failing health. Apparently the consequence of nursing a tubercular brother, her illness made a change seem imperative. The Mellettes, after careful investigation and visiting several places including Colorado, selected Dakota Territory. This choice became more attractive after a visit to Washington, DC, where Arthur secured an appointment from President Rutherford B. Hayes as Register of the Public Lands Office in Springfield.

The Indiana chapter in Mellette's life thus came to an end in 1878 and the people of the Dakota Territory were to be the big winners. They acquired an eager, ambitious, well-educated, honest, and capable leader with an amazing variety of successful experiences for one who was only thirty-six years of age.

The Mellette family arrived in Dakota Territory during January, 1879. Slightly more than a decade later, in 1889, Arthur Mellette was to become the Territorial Governor, and in the same year the Governor of the new State of South Dakota. The decade was thus to witness his phenomenal rise as a politician and statesman, partly because of the frontier nature of a territory experiencing rapid development and partly due to Mellette's own considerable abilities.

Dakota Territory was an exciting place in 1879. Optimism based on certain growth was pervasive. Population had spiraled from 5,000 in 1860 to 14,181 in 1870, and had advanced by 12,000 per year or more during the seventies, so that by 1880 the official count was 135,177. There was every indication that the rate of growth would continue.

As the newly appointed Register of Public Lands at Springfield, Mellette was in an ideal position to observe developments and evaluate future potential. The Springfield assignment was to prove of short duration, however, and on May 1, 1880, Mellette transferred to the newly established Watertown Land Office. Even his new post proved relatively temporary. As a consequence of political changes in Washington, DC, the Watertown appointment came to an end in 1883. Both events were probably fortunate. The transfer to Watertown brought Mellette to an area that was to serve as an appropriate base to launch a political career, and the surrender of his office enabled him to participate privately in territorial economic development.

Arthur's experience in the Watertown Land Office had revealed his abilities as an administrator. The office was swamped but, by employing extra help and working long hours, delays were eliminated. After several months he was able to resume his reading of history and almost immediately to become involved in local politics, which presented a challenge since local Republicans were quarreling among themselves.

Upon leaving government service Mellette practiced law in Watertown with his brother Jim. The land office experience proved invaluable as a guide to profitable investment. He purchased land in Huron, Redfield, Watertown, and Mitchell. His judgment was good and he was regarded as a successful businessman. He had come to Dakota Territory with $10,000 but soon enough that multiplied. He invested in local enterprises, including a brick business. "Mellette Block" was constructed in Watertown, and it was here the Mellette law office was located.

Almost immediately upon his arrival in Watertown, Mellette was drawn into politics. His Indiana experience had prepared him for a quick entry and in 1883 he was elected delegate to the Sioux Falls constitutional convention that met in September of that year. According to Doane Robinson, "This finally successful movement had its inception at a little gathering at the home of Rev. Stewart Sheldon, in Yankton, on the evening of Thanksgiving Day, 1879, and was attended, among others, by Dr. Joseph Ward, Dr. William H. H. Beadle, General Hugh J. Campbell, and Hon. Edward P. Wilcox." Motive for "the movement was the preservation of the school lands, a proposition having been advanced for the sale of all the school lands to a syndicate at a low price. . . . General Beadle was the territorial superintendent of public instruction, and he worked unceasingly upon the proposition that no portion of the school lands should be sold for less than ten dollars per acre."[6]

As a result of the Yankton meeting, a convention met in Canton on June 21, 1882, and an executive committee was appointed to prepare a bill for a constitutional convention and present it to the Territorial Legislature. The convention also adopted a report on school lands and school funds, stressing the importance of a permanent school fund and fixing the minimum sale price at $10 per acre. The bill providing for a constitutional convention was subsequently passed by a wide margin in both territorial houses but was vetoed by Governor Nehemiah Ordway. This greatly inflamed the public. There was widespread protest and the statehood movement was organized under the name "Dakota Citizens' League."

With no favorable actions from Congress in response to repeated petitions by the territorial assemblies, activities prior to 1883 lacked legitimacy. As a result, the executive committee of the Dakota Citizens' League called a delegate convention for Huron for June, 1883. Almost all counties were represented and it was this body that called the Sioux Falls Constitutional Convention, with delegates apportioned

among the counties to be elected on August 1. Mellette was a participant at both Huron and Sioux Falls. Both houses in the Territorial
Legislature during its 1882–1883 session authorized, by almost unanimous votes, a constitutional convention for that portion of the Territory south of the forty-sixth parallel, but the Governor did not approve
the bill. Thus, a "purely extra-legal convention" had met in Huron,
June 13, 1883, and arranged for the historic and productive September
Sioux Falls convention.

These initial developments had little encouragement from either the
national Congress or Governor Nehemiah Ordway. Beginning with the
Yankton meeting, however, the preservation of school lands became a
strong motive for statehood. Since Mellette was concerned with the
same objective in Indiana, it was not difficult for him to relate to the
movement. Furthermore, statehood was certain to assist in inducing
greater investment and, as an investor himself, Mellette was anxious
to see statehood come as quickly as possible.

For one who had been in Dakota less than five years, his unanimous
election as temporary chairman of the Sioux Falls Convention was a
great tribute and symbol of personal esteem. Upon taking the chair he
did not give a lengthy address, but merely thanked convention members for the honor and asked them to lay aside all of their prejudices.
Under his leadership they produced the comprehensive document that
was to endure with some minor modifications through subsequent
conventions in 1885 and 1889 and withstand all attempts at comprehensive revision for almost 100 years. The constitution, as adopted in
1889, contained 258 sections compared with 215 in the draft of 1883.
Many of the additions were required by the need to provide for
separation from North Dakota and to incorporate the conditions imposed by the Enabling Act. From the beginning it was clear the
philosophy espoused and vigorously defended by Mellette was to
prevail; namely, if one knew what was right, one placed it in the
constitution even though it was more properly the subject of legislation.
The state constitution as framed in 1883 was lengthy, in striking
contrast to the 4,543—word Constitution of the United States.

Mellette later explained and defended his approach to constitution
making:

> [I]f it is right, if you know what is the proper thing to embrace in your
> legislation, the more there is in the constitution the better for the people.
> One of the greatest evils is excessive legislation—the constant change
> every two years of the laws, and the squabbles and debates over the

different questions that constantly arise. It is wise, in my judgment, after the people have decided in which direction their interests lie, to embody them in the fundamental law of the land and make it permanent. Here is one of the greatest evils from which we have suffered as a territory. Every Legislature has had power to undo what all the Legislatures had done before.[7]

The 1883 constitution contained some unique features. Included was part of the so-called "Dakota Plan," which embodied the constant involvement of the people in government and a limited role for the State Legislature. The amending process provided that legislators could propose constitutional amendments only if they were approved by two successive legislative sessions (Art. XIX, sec. 1). "If five thousand legal voters shall petition the Legislature . . . ," however, "to amend the constitution in any particular, then the Legislature shall submit such proposed amendment or amendments to the people at the next general election thereafter, or at a special election to be held not less than ninety days nor more than six months after the session of said Legislature shall be terminated, . . . and if the people shall approve and ratify such amendment or amendments shall become part of the constitution." While this provision of Article XVIII did not survive in the 1889 constitution, a provision for the initiative and referendum of "measures" was adopted by law in 1899, and South Dakota became the first state to adopt these devices. Noteworthy is the fact that the word "measures" was not interpreted subsequent to 1896 as including constitutional provisions, although the intended use of the word might well have been to include more than laws. It was not until 1972, on the recommendation of the Constitutional Revision Commission, that the use of the popular initiative for constitutional amendments was authorized by constitutional amendment.

A unique feature that has survived to the present was the power of the Governor "to disapprove of any item or items of any bill making appropriations of money . . . " (Art. IV, sec. 10). Women were given the right to vote "at any election held solely for school purposes, and may hold any office relating to schools . . . " (Art. III, sec. 7). A cause of great importance to Mellette was the establishment from the sale of school land of a permanent school fund, which "may be increased, but never shall be diminished" (Art. VII, sec. 4) and "in no case shall be sold at less than $10 per acre" (Art. VII, sec. 4)—the so-called Beadle provision. Another provision of special interest to him was that total state indebtedness could not exceed $500,000 (Art. XII, sec. 2).

Among the many other provisions surviving to the present: "The blessing of a free government can only be maintained by a firm adherence to justice, moderation, temperance, frugality and virtue, and by frequent recurrence to fundamental principles" (Art. II, sec. 26). The great seal was described in considerable detail, as it still is, but the state motto as set forth in 1883 was "Fear God and Take Your Own Part." By 1889 this had become "Under God the People Rule," replacing the allegedly irreverent "By God the People Rule," and the seal no longer had to include "an Indian and tepees."

From 1883 onward Mellette was an active proponent of statehood. The arguments were convincing. Territorial government had been dominated by politics and inefficiently administered. Territorial finances were in bad shape. Admission would result in more rapid population growth and economic development. It was estimated that statehood would add twenty-five percent to the value of all property and attract large amounts of outside capital. Furthermore, a state constitution could safeguard a permanent school fund and prevent the sale of school lands at a low price.

The adoption of the constitution in 1883 by the overwhelming vote of 12,366 to 6,814 was a strong endorsement of the statehood movement but it was obvious from the size of the vote that many of the new inhabitants were not concerned with politics. Territorial legislators again authorized a constitutional convention, which met in Sioux Falls, September 8, 1885. After only sixteen days of deliberation to make a number of improvements in phraseology and some substantive changes and additions, a revised document emerged and gained acceptance by the margin 25,226 to 6,535. The document provided for the election of a full slate of state officers in the hope that, if an organized government was in place, Congress would accept South Dakota as a going concern.

An example of the awareness of the delegates with developments in constitution making elsewhere came by the inclusion in the 1885 document of a provision giving the Governor the power "to require the opinion of judges of the supreme court upon important questions of law involved in the exercise of his executive powers and upon solemn occasions" (Art. V, sec. 13). Colorado had earlier that same year adopted such a provision and, without much debate, the 1885 Dakota convention did the same.

On October 21, 1885, subsequent to the constitution's acceptance, the Republican Party convention met in Huron. Mellette was elected Chairman and was nominated for Governor by acclamation. In the November, 1885, general election, he received an overwhelming vote.

His message on December 14, 1885, was a tribute to his skill as a debater and orator. He ably presented the case for statehood, arguing that precedent was clearly in favor; both the Northwest Ordinance and the Louisiana purchase treaty had guaranteed it.

Since Nebraska had been admitted as a state with only 100,000 inhabitants and Kansas with only 112,000, the Dakota case was convincing. Nevertheless, the political climate in Washington, DC, continued to be unfavorable. Democrats in control were fearful that admission to statehood for southern Dakota would result in the choice of two more Republican U.S. Senators. Only after the election of 1888 was it clear that the two Dakotas would be admitted soon. The Enabling Act, also called the Omnibus Act, was passed by a lame duck Congress. It provided for the admission of North Dakota, South Dakota, Montana, and Washington, and was signed by retiring President Grover Cleveland on February 22, 1889. In the case of South Dakota, the delegates to a constitutional convention were required to meet in Sioux Falls, July 4, 1889, and incorporate by "ordinances irrevocable" certain provisions with respect to religious freedom, taxation of government and Indian lands, maintenance of a system of public schools, and payment of an appropriate share of the territorial debt. A referendum on the constitution of 1885 was also required. The stipulated convention was held incorporating the congressional requirements and at the subsequent election held October 1, 1889, the constitution was accepted by a vote of 70,131 to 3,267. There was no strong disposition to modify the 1885 convention draft despite the rising tide of Populism. Such overwhelming approval was considered a conservative victory.

At the same time the South Dakota Constitution was adopted, Arthur C. Mellette was elected Governor for a second time and now it was legitimate. On November 2, 1889, South Dakota and North Dakota were formally admitted as states by the proclamation of President Benjamin Harrison. The admission documents were purposely shuffled so that neither state could claim priority. Nevertheless, North Dakota was regarded as the thirty-ninth state, and South Dakota as the fortieth state to enter the Union.

Before Mellette took the oath of office as South Dakota's first Governor, he served a brief term as Dakota Territory's last Governor. His predecessor, Louis K. Church, a Democrat and an appointee of President Cleveland, had been confirmed by the U.S. Senate February 4, 1887, and served until March 22, 1889. Benjamin Harrison, a Republican, was elected President in 1888 and a change in territorial

Governor was certain. Harrison, as a young lawyer educated in Ohio, had gone to Indianapolis in 1853 at the age of twenty-three. It was inevitable that the careers of the two politically motivated and like minded Republicans, Mellette and Harrison, should become intertwined. Mellette became an ardent Harrison supporter. Indeed, in 1876, in Indiana, Mellette had campaigned on Harrison's behalf when he ran for Governor. Both were members of Phi Delta Theta fraternity. In the United States Senate, Harrison served as Chairman of the Committee on Territories and as a member of the Committee on Indian Affairs. Thus a close personal relationship of the two men had evolved. On March 4, 1889, Mellette, the Republican national committeeman for Dakota Territory, attended Harrison's inauguration in Washington, DC. Appointment as territorial Governor followed shortly; on March 22, 1889, Mellette took an oath as the tenth and last Governor of Dakota Territory.

Since the legislature did not meet during the seven months Mellette served as territorial Governor, he did not address a territorial session. Nor was he called upon to make policy recommendations. Nevertheless, he took his duties as territorial Governor seriously and, while maintaining his Watertown home, Mellette also had a residence in Bismarck. His family took advantage of the move north to travel extensively, making two trips to the North Dakota badlands, which were famous because of the ventures of the Marquis de Mores. They visited Fargo, Grand Forks, and Devil's Lake as well as the large Indian school near Fort Totten.

During his governorship, Mellette was of necessity very active in preparations for statehood for both South and North Dakota. The North Dakota constitutional convention met on July 4, 1889, in Bismarck, which since 1883 had served as territorial capital. His principal preoccupations as Governor of Dakota Territory were administrative. He was plagued by appointment problems, for, although only a short time remain until statehood, job hungry Republicans beseeched him for positions. Even General Beadle, writing from Oregon, sought unsuccessfully a return to his old post of Superintendent of Public Instruction.

Much time went to statehood preparations. Republicans held their convention at Huron on August 28, 1889, and Mellette accepted nomination for Governor by acclamation. The general election was held in October 1889, and Mellette won with 53,964 votes over his Democratic opponent's 23,840.

The Governor spent much time in Bismarck closing out territorial affairs. One of his major activities was to submit a comprehensive survey of the progress and development of the Territory of Dakota for the year ending June 30, 1889, entitled *Report of the Governor of Dakota to the Secretary of the Interior* (Washington, DC: U.S. Government Printing Office, 1889). This remarkable document contains extensive data on Dakota at the eve of statehood. The optimistic nature and tone of the report, embodying Mellette's own thinking relative to the future, are demonstrated in the following quotes:

> It is specially worthy of note that Dakota has been totally free from the ravages of disease usually prevalent in the settlement of a new country, and the past year has fully sustained her character in this respect.
>
> The healthy, invigorating properties of the atmosphere, consequent upon its richness of ozone, its dryness, purity, and above all its favorable electrical condition, perform cures in pulmonary, malaria, and general chronic debilities that are a constant and joyful surprise to the afflicted and a mystery to the medical profession.
>
> It is believed that no error is so prevalent and universal throughout the country as the general misconception concerning the climate in Dakota.
>
> The very low temperature and violent storms occasionally prevailing for a few hours during winter are accepted abroad as the normal climatic condition throughout that season, while in truth there is not perhaps an area in the United States that can boast so many perfect, sunshiny, pleasant days during the winter season as Dakota.

At this early date, Governor Mellette met the South Dakota image problem head-on. He was prescient in anticipating climatic conditions as a barrier to economic development—a problem that persisted throughout the next century. What must have been especially disturbing to Mellette in 1889 was his strong conviction that Dakota's many assets were not properly appreciated across the nation. He pointed out that South Dakota was large; it was eighth in size among the states in the Union. Soil was "of unquestioned fertility. . . . The entire surface of Dakota is well watered. . . . The James or Dakota River . . . is the longest unnavigable river in the world." He pointed out that "the growth of population in the Territory of Dakota has been singularly rapid and stable. . . . In no other country of the world are there larger areas of fertile land, level as a floor, easily worked, and as fruitful as the valley of the Nile."

Mellette's report is replete with data about wheat, corn, livestock, vegetables, fruit, mining, tin, gold, silver, coal, and timber. He noted that "A good way to judge the character of a new country is to read its newspapers.'' At the time Dakota had 400, more than Minnesota, and five times as many as Vermont. In 1889 the South Dakota portion of the Territory had 607 post offices, more than Colorado or Connecticut. The territorial educational system was progressing satisfactorily; there were more than 4,000 schools and 5,000 teachers.

Mellette downplayed the importance of problems with Native Americans and failed to anticipate the unfortunate events of the next several years. He asserted:

> There is nothing to fear from the Indian population of Dakota. A few are farmers, and the rest are more or less accustomed to white man's labor, for which a large majority, however, have as yet a sovereign contempt. They are peaceably disposed toward their white neighbors, and as but little is seen of them anyway their presence in the Territory on the Government reservations is hardly observed, and of no concern to the people of Dakota generally.

Concluding his report, the Governor saw a bright future for both South and North Dakota, observing of Dakota Territory: "While her material development, which is chiefly the work of a decade, has been phenomenal, she is proud chiefly of the fact it has been accomplished without the bloodshed usual upon the establishment of civilization in the wilderness."

On November 2, 1889, with the advent of statehood, Dakota Territory ceased to exist and Governor Mellette's term came to an end. In accordance with the 1889 constitution, the newly elected South Dakota Legislature met on October 15, 1889, at 12 o'clock noon in Huron and Governor-Elect Mellette, with all other state officers, took the oath of office. Two U.S. Senators were elected by the Legislature. Thus, on November 2, 1889, after the certification of these actions by the Governor, President Harrison proclaimed South Dakota a new state with full readiness to assume the duties and responsibilities of government.

The constitution provided that the first session of the State Legislature should begin on the first Tuesday after the first Monday of January in 1890 (January 7). Governor Mellette presented his views about public policies on January 8. This, the first "State of the State" message, along with his second message of January 7, 1891, and his farewell message of January 3, 1893, constitute the major keys to Mellette's thinking with respect to needs and problems as South Dakotans faced their challenging, uncertain future.

The new Governor served slightly more than three years. They were trying, vexing years. Starting a new government would have been difficult under the best of circumstances but from the very beginning the inadequacy of tax revenues was especially frustrating. The 1883 constitution had limited indebtedness to $500,000 but because the territorial debt exceeded that figure, the 1889 constitution had changed the limit to $100,000, excluding the territorial debt. This still permitted little fiscal maneuverability. Property taxes would produce no revenue in the first year. Keeping government in operation was thus a major feat. Furthermore, while territorial government could assess a 3 mill tax, the constitution limited state property taxes to 2 mills, cutting potential revenues by one-third. The maximum $100,000 debt was immediately incurred, depriving future legislatures of this revenue source.

Financial needs received major emphasis in all of Mellette's messages. He believed in dedicated public service at some sacrifice. The annual salary of the Governor and of each judge on the Supreme Court was fixed by the constitution at $2,500, although after 1890 the Legislature could raise the compensation of each to $3,000. With respect to the South Dakota Board of Regents, he recommended that there be "no pecuniary compensation whatsoever . . . in order to prevent the suspicion that the sacred trust is being discharged for other than the highest considerations of honor and citizenship."[8]

In his first message Mellette stressed the need to insure that "no single dollar" should be lost from the permanent school fund. He expressed his strong determination to enforce prohibition, which had been approved in the 1889 election. He introduced measures to promote irrigation and mining, and concluded his first message in a philosophical vein:

> In legislation it is easy to tear down, hard to build up, easy to find fault, hard to find a remedy, and nothing ever known to political science was so delicate and intricate as the fabric of free government. . . .
>
> The modern sentiment in contempt of rights of property, would stifle human enterprise and paralyze civilization and is but the dream of drones in the hive of industry. . . .
>
> Your work is to become a precedent, whether established in wisdom or folly, diligence or slothfulness, economy or extravagance, selfishness or patriotism. . . . When we know the best we can and do the best we know, mistakes must still strew our pathway, as the work of man at its best is fallible and experimental, and only approaches perfection through the reflected light of divine revelation.[9]

The State Legislature was quick to react to the Governor's message. To provide for an orderly transition to statehood, emergency legislation was passed and approved February 6, 1890, providing "All laws, in force in the Territory of Dakota at the date of admission of the State of South Dakota into the Union and not repugnant to or inconsistent with the Constitution of said State, shall continue and be in full force and effect until altered, amended or repealed."[10]

Mellette's concern about education was manifest in one of the important measures passed during the first session, a thirty-two section law regulating the disposal of school lands and establishing a Board of School and Public Lands, with the Governor, Commissioner of School and Public Lands, and State Auditor its members. In addition, the powers of the Superintendent of Public Instruction were strengthened. Teaching in the public schools was required on the subject of the effects of alcoholic drinks and narcotics upon the human system. A comprehensive "incorporation of cities" act was passed, establishing three classes of cities: those over 10,000 population; those over 2,000 but less than 10,000; and those less than 2,000. This three-fold division has persisted for almost a hundred years, but with a downward revision of required numbers.

Although the constitution had been in effect fewer than six months, three amendments were proposed: (1) raising the debt limitation from $100,000 to $500,000; (2) giving women the right to vote; and (3) denying Indians still enrolled in tribes the right to vote. In the 1890 election all were to be overwhelmingly defeated.

The negative mood of the times was clearly demonstrated in the election that year. Discontented farmers had organized in the early eighties into farmer alliances, from which the Dakota Alliance emerged in 1889. Members gave up in their attempt to find relief from problems through the Republican Party. In June, 1890, they founded the Independent Party. Independents nominated state candidates and drew much of their strength from the Republicans. So in the 1890 election Mellette, while reelected, received only 34,497 votes, nearly 20,000 votes less than a year before. An added feature in the election was the contest for state capital. Pierre defeated Huron for the location as the permanent site by a vote of 41,969 to 34,610.

In light of the constitutional restriction on indebtedness, it is not surprising that Governor Mellette began his 1891 State of the State message with these words: "The first and most important subject for your consideration is the PUBLIC FINANCES. The State's financial condition could scarcely be more embarrassing, and her revenue system could scarcely be worse.'' What was needed was "a systematic, comprehensive and efficient code of revenue laws, and rigidly restricting current expenditures.''[11] The fiscal year was yet to be defined. Expenditures had been made at institutions without regard for appropriations. Mellette advocated eliminating and consolidating positions and possibly closing down some institutions. He recommended that all receipts for educational fees and tuition payments should go into the general fund.

The Governor endorsed a recommendation by the South Dakota Board of Regents that the normal department at the University of South Dakota be abolished. As for the School of Mines: "It is suggested that what might be called luxuries, such as music, and the fine arts, and superfluous employees and teachers be the first to go, and the substantials be preserved in the educational curriculum and in instructors.'' Indeed, with respect to the educational system in general he said: "Too many school officers, too many school buildings, too many school teachers and too many expensive state educational institutions are now faults with our present system that should be at once remedied.''[12] To encourage students to pursue higher education, he recommended that all who finished high school as certified by a county authority should be admitted without further examination.

To complicate governmental problems, the state inherited persistent difficulties with the Indian population. Mellette noted the "growing discontent resulting from the vexation of having to leave their lands." He bared his feelings:

> From more than ordinary insolence and theft everywhere, in many places, notably on the upper Cheyenne, White and Bad rivers, they became open and defiant in their depredations, pillaging and robbing the settlers and conveying their plunder to a general rendezvous in the Bad Lands between the forks of the upper White River. The prompt action of United States troops in breaking up the lesser camps and the timely death of Sitting Bull, the prince of the disaffected, as he was starting with his band from the Grand river to join the camp in the Bad Lands, has, it is believed, dampened their warlike ardor, although the main camp is yet to be captured. The affray at Wounded Knee creek a fortnight since wherein 32 soldiers and a number of Indians were killed shows the trouble is not yet settled.[13]

Mellette concluded his 1891 message to the Legislature with a sentence that embodied the principles that had guided his own life— hard work, high moral principles, and education. He said: "The province of legislation is not to foster idleness, but to stimulate effort; not to destroy ambition, but to elevate and direct it; to preserve with jealousy the social institutions which ennoble human nature; to foster religion, which furnishes divine ideals, and to promote a common education, which is the preserver of us all."[14]

The 1893 Mellette message to the Legislature was an optimistic report of developments during the previous two years. He noted with pride that substantial progress had been made in reforming the state's financial system. The debt was finally under control. Institutions were not spending beyond authorized appropriations. Mellette retained his confidence in the state's potential. He observed, "The development of the great artesian basin of the James river valley continues to disclose new wonders and possibilities." He noted, "The State has preserved its usual notoriety for freedom from epidemics." He was able to report the adoption of the Australian ballot system and substantial progress in most administrative areas.[15]

What the 1893 report failed to include was the critical economic condition that prevailed during Mellette's entire administration. The drought of 1889 continued and no amount of optimism could hide the hardship of homesteaders. Determined not to violate the constitution by imposing illegal taxes or incurring illegal debt, he sought $100,000 in private subscriptions both within and outside the state to alleviate suffering. Less than half the amount was raised.

In his 1891 message to the Legislature, Governor Mellette had attempted to secure an appropriation for a state building at the Columbian Exposition to be held in Chicago in 1893. The Exposition offered a great opportunity for publicity. The temper of the times was manifest in legislative refusal to approve the request. Mellette called this a "great embarrassment" to him and, as a result, in May, 1891, a convention of more than 200 delegates from all over the state met in Yankton for the purpose of "devising ways and means to have our State properly and modestly represented."[16] Sixteen gentlemen attended as commissioners. In an interesting procedure reflecting the times, the commissioners met and selected nine women, including Mrs. Mellette, to constitute the South Dakota World's Fair Commission. The commissioners failed in their attempt to secure funds by a call for a special legislative session, but funds were acquired privately to sponsor a South Dakota exhibit at the Columbian Exposition.

The 1893 message to the Legislature was Mellette's farewell to public life. He had already decided for personal and business reasons to retire. The gubernatorial salary, fixed by constitutional provision at

$2,500 (and remaining at that level until 1899), did not encourage savings. With a family of four boys, his return to law practice and real estate development was attractive. Mellette thus inaugurated a tradition that the Governor should serve no more than two terms. The tradition was respected until 1972, when it was formalized by a constitutional amendment restricting governors to two consecutive terms, but providing that each term should be four years in length.

A review of Mellette's thirty-eight months as Governor shows his great talent as both policy-maker and administrator. His seemingly boundless energy permitted searching examination of policy issues, and first hand investigations. When he left the office of Governor in 1893, Mellette bequeathed a high standard for future governors to emulate. He had been honest, hard-working, able, compassionate, and dedicated. The problems facing the new state had been difficult. He was aware that what he did made precedent. Hence, every action should be taken only after careful deliberation.

The final three years of Mellette's life were anticlimactic and tragic. He returned to Watertown to resume his previous career as a lawyer and a developer. But by July an earlier illness returned. He made a trip to see a physician in Cincinnati, who could find nothing seriously wrong with his health.

His personal business affairs had been so neglected that he had to borrow money and planned eventually to sell much of his South Dakota property. As if in search of new worlds to conquer, however, he went to Kansas and Missouri, receiving offers for his South Dakota investments if he would move south. On returning from Kansas, while in Chicago, he received word that his oldest son, Wylie, had committed suicide. This was a severe blow.

It was at this time that the Taylor scandal was uncovered. The circumstances were complicated, and the consequences to the Mellettes were devastating. W. W. Taylor had served as State Treasurer, and in his departing January 3, 1893, legislative message Governor Mellette had stated: "Too much credit cannot be given the Hon. W. W. Taylor, State Treasurer, for the diligence and ability with which he has labored to enhance the credit of the State."[17] Mellette was one of Taylor's bondsmen; the defalcation was in excess of $350,000. When Mellette learned that Taylor had absconded, he went to Pierre immediately and arranged that his property might be used to take care of the loss.

Mellette's own illness, the tragic death of his oldest son, the Taylor defalcation, and his own lack of financial resources were to compel the decision to leave South Dakota. It is a tribute to his character that he had the confidence and enthusiasm in the face of adversity to begin a new career. A much impoverished Mellette borrowed $5,500 and went to Pittsburg, Kansas, in 1895. There his talents were quickly recognized and his prospects for a time seemed good. He was selected as part of a delegation to Washington, DC. Just as his fortunes seemed to be improving, however, his old illness returned. On a visit to St. Louis in April, he was forced to run to catch his train. He never seemed to recover from the exertion and he grew steadily weaker. On May 14, only eleven days before his death, he wrote:

> My life has been a checkered one. I have had more pleasure than falls to most mortals & I know most of the trials of life. I have hope that the latter have been sent to do me good. I am by nature all sin & worldly & it is necessary to hold me in check—if I can only feel it is done with a father's loving hand. I have suffered much from my disease. More than most people know, I am thankful that the near future promises relief.[18]

Mellette died at three o'clock, Monday morning, May 25, 1896. He was buried in Mt. Hope Cemetery, Watertown, South Dakota. At the time of his death, he was fifty-two years and eleven months of age. The cause of his death seems uncertain. Possibilities include heart disease and gall bladder infection.

As one surveys Mellette's life, one is amazed at how much he accomplished in a relatively short time. He was able to inspire almost immediate confidence in his abilities and character. Through it all he retained a sense of perspective not only of his place in history, but of his personal life, as well. His early upbringing was in a staunchly religious environment. Christ's Sermon on the Mount was his religious treatise and his guide, and he studied it continually and lived by it.

Mellette exemplified the best of leadership. His background and training provided the basis for achievement. He possessed a breadth of intellectual curiosity, which compelled him to be ever the student. He was action oriented. His enormous energy stimulated his associates. He was a man of principles, but his deep convictions in such matters as prohibition, education, and scope of government did not prevent him from being the compromiser for what he considered the greater public good. Thus, to secure public approval of the new state constitution, controversial issues were submitted separately in order to avoid a negative response to the entire document. He was not adverse to political deals whereby his friend, Judge Alonzo Edgerton, was assured a federal judgeship upon Edgerton's withdrawal from the U.S. Senate race.

Mellette was a strong believer in limited government. This was the reason he whole-heartedly supported the South Dakota Constitution as adopted in 1889 with its extensive limitations on legislative power. He also stressed frugality as a virtue in government. These ideas were to predominate in South Dakota politics almost to an extreme. An historian has summed up what became the basis for Mellette's problems:

> It became a fashion for politicians and all others seeking public favor to raise a hue and cry about economy. In fact the officials often seemed to vie with each other in cutting down to the bone important appropriations that were necessary for the life and prosperity of state institutions and state progress. All of this cry of economy was in a measure a necessity under the constitution, but was also a political dodge for the officials to curry favor with the people. All agreed that the state must have whatever was necessary to carry on legitimate expense and propel the commonwealth on its stride upwards.[19]

The tragedy of Mellette's governorship was the denial to him of opportunities to implement his vision of South Dakota greatness. On the one hand, he was confronted by a growing political negativism and limited financial resources. On the other hand, he faced economic and social problems of monumental proportions. He never had the chance to innovate and build. He remains a leader deserving both admiration and sympathy, and, while most leaders in public life wish to be remembered for their honesty, in Mellette's case it was undoubtedly true. The reason he rose so quickly to the top of the Republican Party in South Dakota, and why he was so personally popular, was not only because he was hard-working and able, but also because he was a man of conscience who could be trusted.

Mellette's final words in his address to the State Legislature upon retiring in 1893 were: "May God bless the people of South Dakota and their children forever and make them all worthy representatives of a great and grand State."[20]

Notes

1. George W. Kingsbury, *History of Dakota Territory* (6 Vols.; Chicago: S. J. Clarke Publishing Company, 1915), III, p. 118. The author wishes to

acknowledge the helpful assistance of Joanita Kant, Kampeska Heritage Museum, Watertown, in preparation of this manuscript.

2. Margaret Wylie Mellette, "Arthur Calvin Mellette," handwritten biographical sketch, 1908, Mellette Papers, South Dakota Historical Resource Center, Pierre, SD, p. 3.

3. Arthur C. Mellette to Maggie, August 12, 1862, Mellette Papers, South Dakota Historical Resource Center.

4. Arthur C. Mellette to Dearest Father and Brothers, November 12, 1864, in Gerald W. Wolff and Joanita Kant, eds., *The Civil War Diary of Arthur C. Mellette* (rev. ed.; Watertown, SD: Codington County Historical Society, Inc., Kampeska Heritage Museum, 1983), p. 75.

5. "Arthur Calvin Mellette," Mellette Papers, South Dakota Historical Resource Center.

6. *Dakota Constitutional Convention* (2 Vols; Huron: Huronite Publishing Company, 1907), I, pp. 5–6.

7. John D. Hicks, *The Constitutions of the Northwest States* (Lincoln: University of Nebraska, University Study Series, 1923), XXIII, p. 45.

8. "The Governor's Message" *Journal of the House of Representatives of the First Session of the South Dakota Legislature* (Pierre: Free Press Company, 1890), p. 35.

9. *Ibid.*, p. 53.

10. *Laws Passed at the First Session of the Legislature of the State of South Dakota* (Pierre: State Bindery Company, 1890), C. 105.

11. "Governor's Message," *Journal of the House of Representatives of the Second Session of the South Dakota Legislature* (Pierre: Free Press Company, 1890), p. 9.

12. *Ibid.*, p. 11.

13. *Ibid.*, p. 35.

14. *Ibid.*, p. 40.

15. "Governor's Message," *Journal of the House of Representatives of the South Dakota Legislature, 1893, Third Session* (Pierre: Carter Publishing Company, 1893), p. 33.6

16. *Ibid.*, p. 26.

17. *Ibid.*, p. 14.

18. A. C. Mellette to Mother, May 14, 1896, Mellette Papers, Mellette House, Watertown, SD.

19. Kingsbury, *History of Dakota Territory*, III, p. 119.

20. "Governor's Message" in *Journal of the House of Representatives of the South Dakota Legislature, 1893, Third Session*, p. 33.

R.F. Pettigrew (ca. 1900).
Courtesy Siouxland Heritage Museums.

Andrew E. Lee.
Courtesy South Dakota State Historical
Society.

Coe I. Crawford.
Courtesy Richardson Archives, USD.

Queen Bee Mill.
Courtesy Siouxland Heritage Museums.

The Populist-Progressive Era: Richard Franklin Pettigrew, Andrew E. Lee, and Coe I. Crawford

Kenneth E. Hendrickson, Jr.

The man who would one day be first full-term United States Senator from South Dakota arrived in Dakota Territory nearly a decade after its founding. Born in Vermont in 1848, Richard Franklin Pettigrew migrated to Wisconsin with his family in 1854. There he went to public school and attended Beloit College, but because of family financial difficulties he never earned a degree. To help make ends meet, he joined a surveying party bound for Dakota in June of 1869. He was so impressed by the potential opportunities available in this vast land that he staked a claim to 160 acres near the hamlet of Sioux Falls in November and returned to take permanent residence less than a year later.

Having read law, Pettigrew was qualified to practice as an attorney during his early years in Dakota, but he made his living as a surveyor. Traveling about, he befriended many people and learned the ways of territorial politics. Key factors in political relationships were, on the one hand, competition between federal officials and, on the other, contests between groups led by politicians in personal bids for power. Ordinarily, one major faction revolved around the territorial Governor, while another worked in the network of the territorial Delegate to Congress, an elected official whose success depended heavily on the effective use of patronage.

Nearly all territorial politicians were Republicans at the time of

Pettigrew's arrival. Quickly, he entered a faction of the party head-quartered at Yankton through an alliance with Gideon C. Moody—an alliance that was to remain fairly constant over the years and lead to major triumphs for both political partners and their associates. Petti-grew regarded his affiliation with Moody as an avenue to power and wealth. Not only would he climb as high in elective office as it would take him, but he would also use politics to open doors to improve his financial opportunities.

Pettigrew's initial excursion into politics came in 1872, when he ran for the Territorial Legislature. He won but never served, due to the involvement of the Moody faction in an intra-party dispute over public printing contracts. Moody lost the dispute and his adversaries used the issue successfully to challenge Pettigrew's qualifications for office.

Nearly five years elapsed before he entered the political arena again. During that period he did surveys, practiced law, and dabbled in real estate to earn a comfortable living. In 1876 he served in a territorial convention that endorsed the presidential aspirations of Rutherford B. Hayes. Later the same year he was elected to the Legislature that organized the first counties in the Black Hills. By that time Pettigrew had come to believe there was virtually no limit to the success he might achieve if he maintained his personal popularity and expanded his role in the Republican Party. The platform he offered to his constituents included economic development, pressure upon federal officials for the division of the Territory, and statehood for southern (South) Dakota.

During the next four years Pettigrew maneuvered carefully through the maze of territorial politics, always protecting his political alliances and personal friendships. By 1880 he had enough support to run successfully for the office of Delegate. No sooner had he been elected, however, than he found himself locked in a battle against the newly appointed Governor, Nehemiah G. Ordway—a struggle that was to vex him constantly for several years.

Historical assessments of Ordway vary because evidence concerning his career is scanty. From appearances he, like Pettigrew, looked upon public office as a stepping-stone to power and wealth and he was even less scrupulous than the Delegate. A native of New Hampshire, Ord-way had served for many years as the Sergeant-at-Arms in the U.S. House of Representatives before his integrity was called into question during the Credit Mobilier scandal. Congressional investigators exon-erated him but he emerged with a shady reputation. Following his appointment to the office of Governor in Dakota, Ordway planned to establish complete control over territorial affairs by monopolizing patronage. This brought him into a conflict with Delegate Pettigrew that finally ended in Ordway's removal from office in 1884.

Controversy between the two men began in a dispute over postmasterships; both desired to control all appointments and neither would compromise. They attacked each other through the press. Pettigrew called Ordway an incompetent fraud; the Governor referred to the Delegate as the "leader of a gang of speculators."[1] At length, Pettigrew went beyond verbal abuse and brought formal charges of nonfeasance against Ordway on grounds that he left the Territory while in office. Ordway sidestepped this move, but the controversy intensified as it came to involve the statehood issue. In 1881 Pettigrew submitted legislation to Congress calling for the division of the Territory and statehood for its southern district. It failed, but publicity as a champion of statehood helped him win re-election and emerge as the principal leader of the Dakota Republican Party. Ordway was not ready to quit. In an effort to recover his political losses and improve his financial prospects, the Governor undertook the relocation of the territorial capital from Yankton to Bismarck. By this means he would gain political support in the north while he made a profit on the real estate he owned in the Bismarck area.

To oppose Ordway's removal scheme, Pettigrew depended on his alliance with Gideon Moody, which had grown into the so-called "Yankton Ring" that included William H. H. Beadle, and George W. Kingsbury. Presenting themselves as anti-removalists, the four men gathered information concerning Ordway's activities in hopes of charging him with some criminal offense. They found evidence of possible bribery and presented it to a grand jury.

While Ordway arranged a defense, the anti-removalists redoubled their campaign for statehood. In May of 1883, at a convention in Huron, they adopted a proposal drafted by U.S. Attorney Hugh J. Campbell, which declared that Congress must confer statehood because southern Dakota met all of the legal requirements. Known as the "we are a state doctrine," Campbell's plan gained considerable popularity for a time. Using it as their rationale, anti-removalists demanded action from Congress and called for a constitutional convention.

Meanwhile, Governor Ordway's troubles continued to multiply. Some of his officers balked at removing their records to Bismarck. The anti-removalists intensified their attack against him. A grand jury indicted the Governor and he went to trial in June of 1884. His attorneys argued that because he was a federal official he could not be tried by a territorial court. Judge A. J. Edgerton agreed and Ordway went free. By then public opinion was so hostile to him that he soon was removed from office.

Politics were especially turbulent through the years of the Ordway administration, because his tenure of office as Governor coincided with the height of the Great Dakota Boom (1878 to 1887), a period of expansion that brought thousands of newcomers who were vulnerable to the machinations of ambitious men like Ordway and Pettigrew. The two politicians and their friends spent considerable time and effort attempting to enrich themselves through various speculative schemes involving, for the most part, land transactions and transportation. Deep-rooted hatreds evolved from fierce battles over federal patronage and the relocation of the territorial capital because the outcome of each issue affected the vested interests of every political group.

In this controversy Pettigrew emerged as the leader of the "home rule faction." Its members exploited the image of longest residence in Dakota Territory with campaigns to check the self-serving efforts of newer arrivals like Governor Ordway. In venomous exchanges Pettigrew and his allies claimed for themselves the right to distribute political favors and to plan the economic development of the Territory. They succeeded. Yet, as they entered the last phase of their drive for statehood, the "home rule Republicans" began to fight among themselves over the distribution of favors and economic benefits. Farmers especially demanded a greater voice in party affairs and their spokesmen emerged to claim positions of leadership in the Republican Party.

Thousands of farmers and ranchers immigrated to Dakota during the boom years seeking economic independence. Led by the advertising campaigns of railroads and territorial officials, they hoped to make their fortunes in the production of cattle, wheat, and corn. Without regard for increasing world competition that weakened their markets, they borrowed heavily to put hundreds of thousands of acres into agricultural production. Overproduction, falling prices, and rising operational costs drove many into debt so far that they lost all hope of recovery. Most debtors could not comprehend the abstractions of market economy and turned in frustration against adversaries they could see and understand. Mainly, they blamed railroads, banks, and grain elevators, whose managers charged high rates without restraint. Soon they were convinced their problems could be solved only by gaining control of governmental agencies that could impose regulations on the activities of businessmen. To that end they formed pressure groups within existing political parties—groups led by professional politicians whose primary motivation was desire for office.

Such a man was Henry L. Loucks, a Canadian who immigrated to a homestead in Deuel County early in 1884. As a participant in the Great Dakota Boom he experienced all of the hardships common to newcomers and took up their cause by organizing a political club, which soon took the name of Dakota Territorial Farmers' Alliance. In 1885 this group affiliated with the National Farmers' Alliance. Its strategy was to elect men to the Legislature who would support the group's demands. Such a bloc met in every session from 1885 to 1889, but it had limited success with regulatory legislation. Failure resulted not only because of the powerful influence of railroad lobbyists in the Republican Party, but also due to the reluctance of Republican leaders to allow a farm bloc to seize control of the Party. Loucks, Alonzo Wardall, John W. Harden, A. D. Chase, and other Alliance leaders represented a threat to party control exercised by Pettigrew, Moody, and their associates—who now were known as the "Combine." A clash between the farm bloc and the Combine was inevitable.

When Pettigrew took a seat in the territorial Legislature of 1885, Alliance men were there in force. Pettigrew watched closely as the Alliance men worked for the passage of far-reaching legislation to control railroad rates and practices and was relieved when they failed. Although legislators created a new railroad commission, its powers were so limited that railroad owners had little to fear. Of greater interest to most residents, in any event, was the statehood movement. The Legislature adopted a resolution based on the "we are a state doctrine," demanding that Congress recognize sovereign status for South Dakota.

This demand was rejected by a Democratic majority in Congress, but it marked the beginning of an intense drive for statehood that finally succeeded in 1889, after Republicans regained control of both the White House and Congress. Leaders of the statehood movement in Dakota were Republicans Pettigrew, Moody, Campbell, Edgerton, and Arthur C. Mellette. Opposing them were most Democrats led by Governor Louis K. Church (1887–1889) plus those who desired to admit Dakota Territory to the Union as a single state according to ex-Governor Ordway's plan.

A critical turn in the statehood movement came at a convention in Sioux Falls during September of 1885, when delegates considered a new state constitution. During November the voters approved the document in a very light turnout. By the same election the Combine asserted its "we are a state doctrine" and elected state officers and legislators, even though its members knew full well the officials held no legal authority. Meanwhile, U.S. Senator Benjamin Harrison of Indiana, a friend of Arthur C. Mellette, introduced a statehood bill to Congress without success.

As Delegate to Congress, Pettigrew played no active role in the events described above, but beginning in 1887 he emerged from background politics to participate in the final drive for statehood. He was confident of success and felt certain that statehood would carry him into the United States Senate. Accordingly, he watched with great interest as delegates representing all major interest groups including farmers gathered for a statehood convention at Huron in July of 1887. The Pettigrew-Moody Combine abandoned its ''we are a state doctrine'' and concentrated instead on the unification of factions through intensive public relations campaigns. At first the results were not promising. In an election held during November, voters of southern districts favored the division of the Territory, and single statehood for South Dakota. Delegates from the northern districts opposed it for fear they would live as territorials indefinitely. To appease them, Oscar Gifford proposed the creation of two states, and statehood became an issue in the campaign of 1888 acceptable to nearly all White Dakotans.

Events moved rapidly as Pettigrew and his friends worked toward dual statehood. Through the press and in numerous local gatherings, they wore down the opposition by the time Republicans gained victory in national elections. On February 20, 1889, the Omnibus Bill (Enabling Act) to admit South Dakota, North Dakota, and two other states passed in Congress. On March 9, 1889, President Benjamin Harrison appointed Arthur C. Mellette to serve as territorial Governor until an acceptable constitution was approved and state officials were elected. During July a convention assembled in Sioux Falls. Alliance men, fearing that Combine leaders might ignore them in the distribution of offices, tried to seize control of proceedings, and with help from Democrats and Prohibitionists they nearly succeeded. Only by the careful manipulation of delegates did Pettigrew and Moody have their way.

After their failure at the convention, leaders in the Farmers' Alliance considered complete withdrawal from the Republican Party and the establishment of an independent organization dedicated to the interests of the farmers alone. This did not happen at once because influential Alliance men took their cues from Loucks, who preferred to stay with the Republican Party for a time. As statehood approached, however, Alliance men continued to discuss their role. On June 19, 1889, they held their last territorial convention and asserted their right to control state government. Two months later, at the first state Republican convention in Huron, they learned they were not strong enough to prevent the Combine from dictating nominations. Alliance men supported regular party candidates only after the platform was amended to allay some of their fears with planks that called for fair elections, just taxation, equitable transportation rates, and prohibition.

With Alliance support, Republicans enjoyed overwhelming success in the election of 1889. Mellette became Governor and his party won a large majority of seats in the State Legislature. Once in office, Republican legislators associated with the Yankton Combine proved their ability to proceed without support from Alliance men in the selection of U.S. Senators. Pettigrew and Moody competed with Alliance leaders Edgerton and Wardall. Pettigrew and Moody had ample votes to win and a party caucus endorsed them unanimously.

As a U.S. Senator, Pettigrew entered the most difficult era of his career. He was lucky enough to draw the long term of six years by lot, but he knew Mellette intended to challenge Moody's bid for re-election in 1891. Because that would weaken the Combine and encourage embittered Alliance men, Pettigrew urged the Governor to reconsider. He agreed, but the threat that he might change his mind without warning mirrored the fragility of the Combine's dominance in Republican politics. There was doubt that Pettigrew and Moody could control the affairs of the state for long.

There was adversity in Pettigrew's private life all the while. To the substantial real estate holdings in Minnehaha County that he acquired over the years he added various business dealings, most important of which concerned railroads. Between 1878 and 1888 Pettigrew became a leader among the men who made Sioux Falls the hub of a regional transportation network by bringing five rail lines to the city. Late in 1888 Pettigrew expanded his interests with other investments in transportation. First he and his brother, Fred, organized the Sioux Falls Railroad and Transit Company, a trolley car line that ran from the town's business district to an industrial area on the south side. It operated for four years before collapsing in bankruptcy during the Panic of 1893. In 1892 Pettigrew also founded the Yankton, Sioux Falls and Southwestern Railroad Company, which he operated for approximately a year before he sold it to make up other losses.

While the Yankton line was still under construction, Pettigrew launched his grandest scheme—construction on a transcontinental rail line, called the Midland Pacific, projected from Sioux Falls to Seattle. Using funds derived from the sale of stock, Pettigrew took options on land along a proposed route between Sioux Falls and Pierre and funded considerable grading before the project was abandoned in financial collapse during 1893. When the Panic set in, nearly every property owner along the route on which Pettigrew had taken options demanded payment. The Senator could not meet his obligations. By selling the Yankton line to James J. Hill he was able to cover his debts, but the dream of heading his own transportation empire was gone.

He retained lesser interests. Pettigrew built the Queen Bee Mill to produce flour with water power from the Big Sioux River. His mill ran at partial capacity from 1881 to 1883 before it went bankrupt because there was seldom enough current in the water of the Big Sioux to keep it in operation. Pettigrew planned a stock yard tied to a meat packing plant and by 1893 invested more than $370,000 in this project. The Panic forced suspension until 1895. Gradually, construction was completed. Pettigrew's plant finally opened in 1899 but it remained in operation only three months. Through many years of planning and building, he and his associates had neglected to provide adequate sewage disposal. When they began to dump waste into the Big Sioux River, local residents got a court injunction. The plant shut down for good and its investors lost more than $1,000,000. Yet another project was a woolen mill, which Pettigrew built in Sioux Falls with the belief that he could obtain federal contracts for the manufacture of blankets. The woolen mill failed, too, along with other business interests due to the Panic of 1893.

The collapse of each venture he launched at great expense between 1883 and 1893 had a telling affect on his political posture. Before 1893, Pettigrew behaved like a typical frontier politician-promoter. After, he changed his views and altered his behavior dramatically. The bankers, lawyers, financiers, and regular Republicans with whom he had dealt and accepted so readily now were suspect as potential adversaries. He questioned the gold standard, if not the entire capitalist system. As an inflationist in favor of unrestricted silver coinage, he turned first to the Populists, then to the Democrats, and finally to the Socialists. While shifting his political stance, Pettigrew won re-election to the United States Senate in 1895, but after that his career went rapidly downhill.

To be sure, his second term in the Senate was eventful. There was embarrassment over patronage. Shortly after his arrival in Washington, DC, Pettigrew demanded the summary dismissal of all Democratic U.S. Indian Agents in South Dakota so he could replace them with Republicans. Several new appointees were men of so little competence and ethical standing that President Harrison was forced to intervene.

Because any loss of power over appointments would diminish his prestige and influence, the Senator lashed out at Harrison and his Secretary of Interior, John W. Noble, and opposed them openly.

As his career suffered from affiliation with inept and crooked Indian Agents, Pettigrew became a victim of dynamic political change. By 1890 even conservative Alliance leaders such as Henry L. Loucks had come to favor the formation of some new political organization in South Dakota, contending the older parties had paid no heed to demands by farmers for appropriate voice in political affairs. A new Independent Party, founded in the summer of 1890, offered a platform calling for the abolition of the national banks, inflation through the direct issue of currency by the federal government, an income tax, a levy on real estate mortgages, the Australian ballot, and the government ownership of railroads. It affiliated with the national People's Party (the Populists) in 1892. For a time, Pettigrew viewed the new organization with disdain and criticized it harshly. Yet, he warned that Republicans must take farmers' demands seriously and even suggested that Republicans familiarize themselves as thoroughly as possible with the silver issue.

Independents attracted a substantial following from the outset. In the election of 1890 Mellette was re-elected Governor, but he lost more than 20,000 votes to Loucks while Republicans lost their majority in the State Legislature. In addition, Independents combined forces with Democrats as "Fusionists" to elect their man, James Henderson Kyle, to the United States Senate in place of Moody. Kyle's election enraged Pettigrew, but he was the least of the senior Senator's problems. Worse was a threat to Republican unity caused by Governor Mellette who, as Pettigrew himself put it, was "crazy to go to the U.S. Senate."[2] The Combine all but collapsed. Pettigrew and Moody were able to salvage their control of Republicans, but Independents made clear their probable alliance with Democrats.

Pettigrew responded by advocating relief for debtors from inflation by the free and unlimited coinage of silver. The appeal of free silver was spreading rapidly, as evidenced in the strong showing of Populists during the national election of 1892. Unless South Dakota Republicans accepted monetary expansion to reduce the real value of rural indebtedness, they could be doomed. Pettigrew's political philosophy changed, too, because he became a primary victim of bankers and other businessmen supported by Republicans during the Panic of 1893.

The change in Pettigrew's outlook became clear when he criticized an effort by Democratic President Grover Cleveland to deflate the currency by the repeal of the Sherman Silver Purchase Act. "With silver demonetized, and the world on a gold basis," he said, "there will be a constant decline in the value of credit to the ruin of the debtor."³

This placed Pettigrew in a peculiar position. He was convinced the issue of inflation through unrestricted silver coinage would prevail but was reluctant to abandon the Republican Party. As an alternative, he identified with propaganda groups in South Dakota known as "bimetallic leagues." If he could bring Republicans, Democrats, and Populists together in support of currency expansion, he could retain his affiliation with the Republican Party. When this movement failed, Pettigrew confided to friends his fear that Republicanism had passed its zenith. "I am sure," he said, "that the . . . party will never again elect another President and never again control either house of Congress."⁴

As his confidence in the Republican Party faltered, Pettigrew faced opposition from Mellette as well as the specter of fusion between Democrats and Populists. In frustration, he courted Republican candidates for the State Legislature, warned Democrats against assimilation if they combined with Populists, and asked friends across the state to do everything possible in opposition to political fusion.

Republicans won the election of 1894 and Pettigrew went back to the Senate as a Republican. Yet, political organizations, like economic conditions in South Dakota, were unsettled. More than ever Pettigrew put his energy into the free silver campaign and came out publicly in favor of greater power for the state railroad regulatory commission. Indeed, he supported a Populist bill in the Legislature to empower the commission to regulate rates. It failed, but Pettigrew was so adamant in his support that Populist leaders predicted he would soon quit the Republicans and join them.

By the spring of 1895 Pettigrew all but made the transition; he was the major spokesman in the state for "Silver Republicans." Regular party leaders in Washington viewed him with suspicion. South Dakota conservative Republicans withdrew from his camp over the issue of railroad regulation. As his Republican support diminished, his Populist connections grew and he became increasingly open in his support of a downtrodden constituency. He favored regulatory legislation aimed at railroads and other large businesses. He believed in the inflationary economics of free silver as a key to the survival of debt ridden farmers and laborers. He said the banking system was organized to rob the producer of the fruits of his efforts, and to restrict the volume of currency to the advantage of the bankers and investors. There was no hope for farmers and workers as long as regular Republicans remained in power.

Overcoming vigorous opposition, Pettigrew went as a delegate to the Republican national convention of 1896. Party leaders in South Dakota believed he and the other delegates were committed to support William McKinley and endorse restriction on the enlargement of currency, but Pettigrew intended to support McKinley only if an inflationary silver plank were placed in the platform. When he recognized that silverites were not likely to control Republican monetary philosophy, he began to confer with Henry L. Loucks about a possible alliance with Populists.

A majority of delegates to the Republican national convention endorsed sound money as they nominated William McKinley and Pettigrew left the convention with Henry Moore Teller of Colorado and other advocates of inflation to announce the formation of the Silver Republican Party. At first, they intended to nominate Teller for President, but instead they joined Populists and Democrats in support of William Jennings Bryan. In South Dakota they abandoned the state Republican convention when it endorsed sound money and went to the Peoples' Party convention in Huron to endorse the Populist candidates. Pettigrew addressed the assembly, declaring that he would not resign from the Senate but would continue to use his office in the fight against "Wall Street criminals and gamblers" under the banner of Populism.[5]

In national elections the Democrats dominated fusionism. In South Dakota the reverse was true. Fusionist nominations were dictated by Populists, and Fusionists supported the Populist candidate for Governor—Vermillion merchant Andrew E. Lee. He was acceptable to Pettigrew and the Democrats as well as the Populists. Thus a three-way merger of forces pointed to the probable success of reformers in gaining control of government.

Fusionists campaigned hard in South Dakota yet won a marginal victory in the election of 1896. Bryan carried the state by only 183 votes; Lee defeated his Republican opponent, A. O. Ringsrud, by a margin of 319 votes. Populist candidates were elected to Congress. Fusionists held a majority of nineteen in the State Legislature. But Republicans won the offices of Lieutenant Governor, Secretary of State, Treasurer, Superintendent of Public Instruction, and Commissioner of School Lands. Republicans failed to prove a charge of fraud at the polls against Fusionists and settled for the satisfaction of knowing that fusionism had not achieved the overwhelming victory expected by its advocates. Republicans also recognized that reform was the real issue and reduced their losses with a commitment to railroad regulation.

Senator Pettigrew's relationship with Republicans deteriorated steadily through the fight over reform and was all but lost when he came out in opposition to imperialism in the U.S. Senate. In his view there was a clear connection between the forces of economic privilege in the United States and the movement for expansion abroad. It was a conspiracy to rob American farmers and workers of their rightful share in the nation's wealth and to subjugate helpless foreigners. "Plutocrats of Wall Street" were obsessed with the idea of using overseas operations and the vehicle they used to support them was the Republican Party.[6]

Pettigrew opposed the annexation of Hawaii after a coup deposed Queen Lilioukalani in 1892. He argued that annexation would be expensive and would endanger American security by causing jealousy among other nations. With some justification, he charged that the American Sugar Refining Trust was behind the annexation scheme and that Hawaii was controlled by "monied interests" in the United States. When annexation failed and Hawaiian leaders created a constitution requiring high property qualifications and a literacy test for the exercise of the franchise, Pettigrew was sure he was right.[7]

The Senator opposed the passage of the Wilson-Gorman Tariff of 1894, which perpetuated the practice of allowing Hawaiian sugar to enter the United States duty free in exchange for American port privileges at Pearl Harbor. Not only did he believe this tariff law was calculated to promote monopolies in America, he also thought a bounty on sugar provided in the law would be injurious to South Dakota farmers who were going into sugar beet production.

There was some racism in Pettigrew's attitude toward Hawaiian expansion. When the question of annexation came up in 1895, he said there were already enough "dark-skinned people" in the United States. "We cannot afford to add more. . . . With the Negroes in the South, the Chinese . . . , and the 'dagoes' . . . , every problem we are able to solve will be presented to us in the near future."[8] Partly on this basis, he railed against a joint resolution for annexation in 1898 and renewed his charge that the quest for Hawaii was a plutocratic conspiracy. The steel industry wanted naval contracts. Other business interests sought new sources of raw materials, better markets, and cheap labor. All the while he harped on the alleged inferiority of indigenous people. "Our aggressive energetic, active, dominating race is not suited to inhabit tropical lands," he said. "The natives are unable and unfit to govern themselves so that controlling such land is more trouble than it is worth."⁹

In 1898 he could favor the war against the Spanish Empire as long as it remained a fight for freedom among colonials. When it was clear that the United States intended to annex the Philippines and other Hispanic islands, however, he vented his rage. In this he was not alone. The debate went on across the United States until the Senate ratified a peace treaty with Spain in 1899. Then came the Philippine Insurrection, which Pettigrew could blame on Republican leaders in Washington, DC. Troops from South Dakota had volunteered to fight in Cuba, but had been transferred to Asia by federal order.

Pettigrew openly said he was ashamed of his country, labeled McKinley a "puny president" with a corrupt administration, called the American flag a rag, and attacked the character of such military heroes as Elwell S. Otis and George Dewey. Most damaging of all, he earned the undying hatred of Republican leader Marcus Alonzo Hanna by accusing him of bribery. By 1900 his days in political office were numbered; he met defeat in his bid for re-election by Republicans, who recovered a majority in the South Dakota Legislature.

After leaving office, Pettigrew put money in mining operations to recoup his fortune. For a time he lived in New York City, where he practiced law and dabbled in politics as a Democrat. He stayed with the Democrats until 1912, when, in dissatisfaction over the nomination of Woodrow Wilson, he gave his support to the Progressive Republicans who followed Theodore Roosevelt. After Roosevelt's defeat, Pettigrew abandoned the Progressives and through the remaining years of his life he flirted with Farmer-laborites, Socialists, and Communists. He died in Sioux Falls on October 5, 1926.

Succeeding him as a force in the reform politics of South Dakota was Andrew E. Lee, who served as Governor from 1897 to 1901. Born in Norway in 1847, Lee came to the United States with his family in 1851 and grew up on a farm in Wisconsin. As a young adult he moved to Dakota Territory and settled in Vermillion, where he made a living as a merchant, farmer, and stock breeder. He entered politics in 1892 as a Populist and ran for the Vermillion city council. After one year of service he was elected to the office of mayor, which he held until he won the office of Governor in 1896.

During Lee's term at Pierre, Fusionist reformers enjoyed their initial opportunity for success. Because of major obstacles they could not entirely overcome, they never gained complete control of state government. To be sure, Lee was elected to two terms as Governor, but while he served most of the other elective offices remained in the hands of Republicans. Fusionists held a majority in the Legislature of 1897 but were unable to unify their control sufficiently to enact Lee's entire reform agenda, to elect a United States Senator from their own ranks or distribute patronage in a manner satisfactory to their constituents. Fusionist efforts were impaired, too, by internal divisions. They included Populists, Democrats, and Silver Republicans, who never fully trusted each other and never melded into a cohesive political unit. Governor Lee added difficulty to the arrangement by retaining appointive officers who were either incompetent or corrupt.

At the time, South Dakotans were especially sensitive to the problem of dishonesty in public office because of the bizarre case of Treasurer W. W. Taylor, who in 1895 had stolen the entire state treasury. Governor Lee had campaigned on a promise of honesty and efficiency in government. With determination to ferret out wrong-doers, especially if they were Republicans, Lee appointed Maris Taylor as a special investigator. First to fall under scrutiny was the office of State Auditor, where Taylor found that thousands of dollars had been mishandled. The Auditor, his predecessor, and a clerk all went to trial and, at length, were released on a technicality.

Next to be examined was the office of Insurance Commissioner. Lee's own appointee, J. H. Kipp, was removed for corruption when it became clear he was guilty of faults similar to those for which his predecessor had been fired. Subsequently, Lee found it necessary to replace a state oil inspector named R. E. Dowdel for the falsification of expense accounts. The Governor found that the Board of Regents for Higher Education, which he appointed to replace a politicized Republican Board, was ineffective. Superintendents at the state penitentiary, the asylum for the insane, and the reform school, as well as members of the Board of Equalization, were uncooperative if not corrupt.

Despite these problems Lee and his Fusionists left some noteworthy legacies in reform legislation. Most spectacular was the passage of the Palmer-Wheeler Bill, which increased the powers of the railroad commission substantially and gave it the right to establish rates. Railroad officials fought the law in the courts and eventually saw it struck down. Nevertheless, the Palmer-Wheeler Bill was a significant expression of the zeal for reform that eventually led to the passage of such major federal regulatory measures as the Eklins Act of 1903, the Hepburn Act of 1906, and the Mann-Eklins Act of 1910. Moreover, in the wake of a costly court fight over the Palmer-Wheeler Bill, railroaders voluntarily reduced their freight and passenger rates. Regarding railroads, Lee also enjoyed moderate success in his effort to increase the valuation of railroad property for tax purposes near the end of his administration.

Another reform of which Lee could be proud was the regulation of illegal liquor traffic—a major problem in the region from the inception of the fur trade late in the eighteenth century. Under legislation passed by Fusionists, liquor could be sold only through county dispensaries, which paid high license fees for the privilege. Fusionists also passed legislation controlling elections. Most important, they adopted the initiative and referendum. Regarded by many as a tool for control of state government by the people, these were prime objectives in many western states during the Populist-Progressive Era. In 1899 South Dakota became the first state to legislate them into effect.

Although they were in many ways dissimilar, Lee and Pettigrew worked closely together. The Governor informed the Senator about affairs in the state and Pettigrew was loyal to Lee's Fusionist alliance. They were not always successful. They failed to engineer the defeat of Senator James Henderson Kyle in 1897, failed to satisfy all Fusionist elements in the distribution of appointive offices, and failed to gain the abiding support of Populist leaders. The return of Henry L. Loucks to the Republican party in 1898 was a major blow. The victory of Fusionists in the election of 1896 was, at best, a sign of limited success and after that they suffered decline.

Through personal popularity Lee won his second term in 1898, despite the resurgence of conservative Republicans. He was strengthened in office by raising troops to liberate Cuba during the Spanish-American War. He gained credit across the state for his resistance to the placement of South Dakota volunteers in the Philippines, and for his demand that they return in 1899.

A fairly successful, honest, and popular Governor, Lee left office in 1901 with confidence that he had governed well. After retirement from public life, he returned to his home in Vermillion and resumed control of business interests. He ran unsuccessfully for Governor in 1908 as a Democrat. Otherwise, Lee had little more involvement with public life before he died on March 19, 1934, at Vermillion.

Coe I. Crawford succeeded Lee as principal leader of South Dakotans who carried their support of the Fusionist platform into the twentieth century. Crawford was born in Iowa in 1858, reared in a strict Presbyterian household, educated in Iowa public schools, and awarded a law degree from the University of Iowa in 1882. Soon, he set out to make his fortune in Dakota Territory, arriving at Pierre in December of 1883. He quickly established a law practice and entered politics. Working up from the Hughes County Republican organization, he entered the upper house of the territorial Legislature in 1886, and served to its last session at Bismarck. From there he moved directly to the State Senate, where he displayed unusual skill as a lawyer and demonstrated oratorical ability to rival that of William Jennings Bryan. As a state legislator, he chaired a committee on revenue and drafted the original revenue laws of the State of South Dakota. For his success, he was elected Attorney General in 1892.

The Taylor scandal broke during his tenure and cost him some political support. Crawford hired Pinkerton Agents to capture Taylor, prosecuted him, and saw him sentenced to two years in prison. Because a substantial amount of some $367,000 taken from the state was never recovered, Crawford won settlements from Taylor's bondsmen, the principal of whom was Governor Mellette. Many South Dakotans thought Crawford was unfair to Mellette and withdrew enough support to cost him an election.

Crawford campaigned as a Republican candidate for the U. S. House of Representatives in 1896. He belittled Fusionist demands for better government and spoke out against the inflationary economics of free silver. For this stand, plus the loss of support he suffered due to his treatment of Mellette, he received fewer votes than any major office seeker that year.

After this humiliating defeat he abandoned politics for a time. First, he accepted a partnership in the law firm of Gideon C. Moody. He became general counsel for the Chicago and Northwestern Railroad Company and moved to Company headquarters at Huron. As railroad counsel, Crawford became thoroughly familiar with techniques by which railroaders gained inordinate influence in the state. He learned how lobbyists operated: for example, how railroad officials decided upon which politicians they would support, and which they would oppose, and how they could best use the distribution of favors—mainly free passes—to cultivate support among influential people. No evidence exists to indicate that Crawford was immediately offended by these practices, but eventually he used knowledge from the experience to attack the railroads vigorously.

Crawford found the work of general counsel to be routine and often boring. Possibly for this reason his political ambition revived when U.S. Senator Kyle died in office in 1901. Crawford asked Governor

Charles N. Herreid to appoint him as Kyle's successor. Herreid refused, and named instead the rich and powerful Alfred B. Kittredge, of Sioux Falls, to complete the term.

This marked the beginning of Crawford's alienation from regular Republicans in South Dakota and set the stage for his emergence to leadership among Progressive Republicans. In 1903 he cast his lot with the political forces of reform—openly terminating his association with regular Republicans and declaring his place among Progressives. Herreid's refusal to appoint him to the U.S. Senate was only a catalyst for the transition that evolved from several causes. One was the realization that since his defeat in the congressional election of 1896 he had never been able to re-establish himself as a force in the Republican inner circle. Another was the gradual development of a distaste for political manipulation of economics to an extent that offended his Presbyterian morality. A third was personal ambition and independence, which drove him to seek higher goals.

As a Progressive, Crawford patterned his activities after those of Robert M. LaFollette of Wisconsin and Albert B. Cummins of Iowa. Because a seat in Congress seemed out of reach, he set his sights on the office of Governor in Pierre. Looking ahead to the next election, in December of 1903 he resigned his position as railroad attorney and launched an attack against the regular Republican machine that served corporations. Crawford's platform called for political democracy and equal economic opportunity. As the date of the Republican nominating convention approached and his candidacy gained momentum, the regular Republicans marshaled forces of delegates sufficient to assure his defeat. The nomination went instead to Samuel H. Elrod of Clark.

Crawford's supporters responded with agitation for a state primary election law that would weaken the control that a convention of delegates could exert over partisan nominations. Interest in such legislation was not confined to South Dakota, of course; it was a goal of Progressives across the nation. Leader of the movement in South Dakota was Richard O. Richards of Huron, a wealthy landowner and banker, who fast became one of Crawford's principal backers. Richards formed the Republican State Primary League and financed its activities with personal support.

The League forced the South Dakota Legislature to consider a primary election bill in 1905 on an initiative petition. This was the first use of the initiative and referendum law passed earlier by the Fusionists. The bill passed in the lower house of the Legislature but lost in the Senate, where regular Republicans held a majority of seats. Defeat notwithstanding, Progressives went ahead with their plans to nominate Crawford for Governor and he opened his campaign in September of 1905. For several months he traveled across the state and used his oratorical ability to rally the people to the Progressive cause. In orations he linked South Dakota progressivism to the national progressivism of the popular President Theodore Roosevelt. Behind the scenes, Crawford's supporters sought alliance with Republicans who were not on good terms with their party machine. At the Republican convention in May of 1906, Crawford defeated Governor Elrod for the nomination. In November, he won easily at the polls.

At his inaugural Crawford spelled out principal legislative objectives: laws to forbid the distribution of free passes by railroad officials for favor among influential people; to forbid corporations from making political contributions; and to require the public accounting of campaign funds. He also asked for legislation to extend the regulation of railroad corporations beyond restrictions on free passes and lobbying efforts—to include such things as compensation for the widows and orphans of men killed in rail accidents, and the more accurate assessment of railroad property for tax purposes.

Not only did legislators pass all laws requested by Governor Crawford, they also fixed maximum passenger rates, made railroad companies responsible for late shipments and property damage, and limited the continuous service of train operators to sixteen hours per day. In addition, legislators created a state food and drug commission and prohibited unfair competition and discrimination in commerce. They provided for the distribution of free textbooks to school children and established a telephone commission with the power to regulate rates. In the realm of morality they submitted a proposed county option law to referendum (which was defeated), prohibited theatrical performances or baseball games on Sundays, forbade the sale of cigarettes to minors, and required one year of bona fide residence before divorce could be granted in South Dakota.

In scope, this was a reform agenda comparable to those of other states where Progressives came to power and one in keeping with the Progressive philosophy of Theodore Roosevelt's Square Deal. Obviously, Progressives succeeded where Fusionists had failed. Unlike their predecessors, they had no alliances with other political organizations and no taint of political corruption to overcome. Moreover, Governor Crawford and Progressive leaders in the Legislature understood each other and worked harmoniously together. The result was dramatic achievement.

Using popularity accrued from this, Crawford announced his intention to win the seat in the U.S. Senate held by A. B. Kittredge, leader of the regular Republican machine in the state. The Governor proclaimed his support for President Roosevelt in the regulation of corporations and railroads, and endorsed a downward tariff revision to benefit consumers. He encouraged the completion of the Panama Canal under the exclusive control of the United States. His battle against Kittredge prior to the primary election of 1908 was bitter. The Senator maligned the Governor's character and condemned his politics. Crawford defeated Kittredge, nevertheless, then won election to the U.S. Senate by the State Legislature with relative ease.

In Washington, DC, Crawford made some unnerving discoveries. Contrary to his naive expectations, he found no one took oration on the floor of the Senate very seriously. Robert M. LaFollette, his idol, was an unlikable fellow who demanded loyalty if not subservience from political allies. There was the complex and vexing issue of tariff. When the bill that eventually became the Payne-Aldrich Act found its way to the Senate, Crawford studied every provision carefully and voted according to conscience more than to LaFollette's demands. Accordingly, he voted "nay" when the entire bill first passed the Senate; then he voted "yea" with only two other Progressives when the final version came back from the conference committee. In the latter instance, Crawford sided with President William Howard Taft in the belief the inadequate downward revisions it contained were the best that Congress would allow at the time. With this stance, he not only alienated LaFollette, but many of his constituents, as well. Moreover, the image of inconsistency bared him to a charge of "wobbling" on principle in a way that soon came back to haunt him.

Through the year 1910, Crawford was steadfastly loyal to Taft, but after that the two men parted ways. The most significant cause was the Canadian reciprocity agreement of 1911, which was inimical to the agricultural marketing interests of South Dakotans. Gradually, Crawford moved back towards an alliance with LaFollette, although he never went so far as to become a member of the National Progressive Republican League. In 1912 he supported LaFollette's presidential aspirations until they collapsed, then shifted his support to Theodore Roosevelt, who, as a third-party candidate, lost to Woodrow Wilson.

Political conditions for Crawford deteriorated similarly in South Dakota. Progressives fought regular Republicans as they quarreled among themselves. Difficulties began with an agreement among Progressive leaders in 1908 to support Robert S. Vessey for Governor over all other candidates. The agreement, to which Crawford was a party, was viewed by many as a violation of the spirit of the primary election law. Problems multiplied when Richard O. Richards withdrew support from Crawford, charging that the Senator had abandoned his idealism for personal political gain. Richards's ire had been raised by the deal concerning Vessey and he was chagrined because Crawford did not support his proposed amendments to the primary election law. The break between Crawford and Richards led directly to a rupture in the Progressive organization which was never fully repaired.

Regular Republicans tried to gain advantage from the rift, but Progressives held their ground in party affairs to the considerable disadvantage of both factions. By the time Crawford ran for re-election, in 1914, senatorial candidates were subjected to the scrutiny of voters not only in partisan primaries, but by constitutional amendment in general elections, as well. Amid this change of political process, Progressive Crawford lost in the primary to regular Republican Charles H. Burke and Burke was defeated in the general election by Edwin S. Johnson, the first Democratic U.S. Senator from South Dakota.

When Senator Crawford's term expired in March, 1915, he returned to his law practice at Huron, where he retired in 1934, and died of a heart attack on April 25, 1944. In retirement, with Pettigrew and Lee he shared the onus of rejection by the South Dakota electorate. With them, however, he also shared the image of success. They had led a predominantly rural, Republican society into the acceptance of reforms promoted by Populism and Progressivism, and had set the stage for still more dramatic change under Peter Norbeck and William McMaster.

Notes

1. Dakota *Herald,* March 26, 1881.
2. Kenneth E. Hendrickson, Jr., "The Public Career of Richard F. Pettigrew of South Dakota, 1848–1926," *South Dakota Historical Collections, XXXIV,* pp. 146–311.
3. Pettigrew to W. S. Bowen, September 19, 1893, *ibid,* p. 230.
4. Pettigrew to William N. Sterling, September 9, 1893; Pettigrew to A. B. Kittredge, September 13, 1893, Pettigrew Papers, the Pettigrew Museum, Sioux Falls.
5. Sioux Falls *Press,* July 15, 1896.
6. Richard F. Pettigrew, *Imperial Washington* (Chicago: Charles Kerr and Company, 1922), pp. 12–24.

7. *Ibid.*, pp. 317–318.

8. Richard F. Pettigrew, *The Course of Empire* (Chicago: Boinwright, 1920), pp. 197.

9. *Ibid.*, pp. 166, 180, 189.

Norbeck at desk, Senate Chamber (1909).
Courtesy Richardson Archives, USD.

William Henry McMaster.
Courtesy Richardson Archives.

South Dakota State Cement Plant.
Courtesy Richardson Archives, USD.

Gutzon Borglum in front of Mt.
Rushmore before carving.
Courtesy Richardson Archives, USD.

An Experiment in State Sponsored Economy: Peter Norbeck and William Henry McMaster

Larry Remele

The actions of Governors Peter Norbeck and William Henry McMaster between 1917 and 1925 expanded the economic base and shifted the political direction of South Dakota substantially. During their terms in office, South Dakotans accepted a progressive philosophy that brought state government into partnership with private interests. Although the relationship began to falter as it was forged, and was all but abandoned in the end, its legacy remains an unusual dimension in the political tradition of the state.

During the Norbeck-McMaster era, officials in Pierre established state owned industries and state sponsored services to meet some needs that had not been satisfied by Populist, Fusionist, or Progressive Republican precursors. To boost the economy, they built tourism into a leading industry, for example, and sponsored a rural credit system to liberate farmers from the vagaries of the money marketplace. These and other initiatives brought South Dakota's Populist-Progressive philosophy to its highest point of development.

The plan of the two governors for economic recovery was bound to fail because so many of their constituents were deeply opposed to the ownership and operation of industries by the state. Inspired by Norbeck's strong leadership and McMaster's activism, South Dakotans accepted state ownership initiatives for a time to stave off the intrusion of more radical agendas set by the Nonpartisan League in North

Dakota. Soon the resurgence of conservatism coupled with a rise in operational costs during hard times forced the abandonment of most state programs. By the late 1920s South Dakotans returned to a free enterprise credo, leaving under state control only the cement plant in Rapid City as a reminder of the Norbeck-McMaster experiment in state owned industries and state sponsored services.

The two Governors were contemporaries who had been steeped in the progressive goals of rural Republicanism from childhood years. Peter Norbeck was born at Vermillion on August 27, 1870, to Norwegian immigrant parents. Largely self-educated, he attended public schools and the "pre-freshman course" at the University of South Dakota. To overcome his scant education, Norbeck read widely throughout his life, especially major works on history, philosophy, religion, science, and Scandinavian studies. After moving with his family to Charles Mix County in 1886 to homestead, he took an interest in well-drilling and in 1892 entered the business in partnership with a cousin. Norbeck perfected drilling apparatus for deep artesian wells. Within two years he became the head of an expanding company that eventually operated dozens of gasoline-powered drilling rigs and employed more than 100 men. In 1901 he moved his operation to Redfield. By 1908 he was one of South Dakota's wealthiest businessmen.

Norbeck was elected constable of a township in Charles Mix County in 1892 but otherwise refrained from active participation in politics until the gubernatorial campaign of Progressive Coe I. Crawford in 1906. Soon, Norbeck became a local Republican Party leader and accepted nomination for a seat in the State Senate. He waged a strong campaign, calling for federal and state laws to protect bank depositors, to regulate public service companies, and to control the fares charged to passengers by railroads. Using tried-and-true political techniques, which included the transportation of drilling crews in his company to polling places, Norbeck won the race with ease.

During the session of 1909 he established his reputation as a forceful, if unschooled, debater. In 1910 he was re-elected easily for his advocacy of reform legislation and gained the attention of Progressives in search of candidates for higher office.

Norbeck fit the mold of Progressivism nicely. He was a self-made success and an innovator. He supported the presidential candidacy of Robert LaFollette in 1911 and that of Theodore Roosevelt in 1912. Norbeck's active campaign and his own reelection to the South Dakota Senate assured his place in the inner circle of the state's Progressive movement.

In 1914 he was elected Lieutenant Governor. Although the role of a legislative presiding officer little suited his temperament, he continued his study of the political economy and developed his interest in using the power of government to aid the economically distressed. Norbeck's biographer, Gilbert C. Fite, asserts that by 1916, "[h]is desire to help the common man was the ultimate of his progressiveness." In particular, Norbeck advocated state-financed rural credits, a bank deposit guarantee law, and the regulation of securities sales. Says Fite, Norbeck "knew practical politics . . . , was an experienced legislator," and had "some understanding of the major forces which were influencing American life."[1]

Just as the successful well-driller had readied himself for high public office, so had his contemporary, William H. McMaster. A native of Ticonic, Iowa, born on May 10, 1877, McMaster demonstrated throughout his career the gritty determination to succeed. In his youth, his family moved to Sioux City, where he worked as a newsboy, an inconvenient and arduous occupation that helped support his family and provided early evidence of his business acumen. Orphaned at age seventeen, McMaster still managed to graduate from high school in 1895 and to complete an undergraduate degree at Beloit College of Wisconsin in 1899. He entered banking in Yankton County, South Dakota, in 1901 and from there developed a substantial chain of local banks. By his fortieth year, McMaster had obtained economic security and the wherewithal to sponsor a political career.

Quickly, he gained a reputation as one who "always played to win."[2] A convert to the Progressive Republican principles of Coe I. Crawford, McMaster first sought public office as a candidate for the South Dakota House of Representatives in 1910, and served through the following session. He moved to the South Dakota Senate in 1912, where he commenced an association with Norbeck that would last through the ensuing decade. McMaster's progressive credentials were not so well established as those of Norbeck, but he added support to their aggregate following with the image of being much more conservative than the roughhewn well driller from Redfield.

McMaster was re-elected in 1914, and became the Republican candidate for Lieutenant Governor in 1916 on the ticket with Norbeck. The careers of these two men, which had been yoked in the politics of Progressivism from about the year 1910, thus merged in the task of leading South Dakota Progressive Republicans to a stage of greatest achievement.

After winning Republican endorsement for Governor, Norbeck car-

ried the 1916 general election by more than 20,000 votes, running far
ahead of his ticket. On January 2, 1917, he became the first native-
born Governor of the state.

With a noteworthy mandate to initiate reform, he asked the Legislature to consider a variety of laws. Foremost among them was a rural
credits system, whereby the State would provide real estate loans to
farmers. Long a part of his legislative agenda, this measure addressed
a perennial problem for small farmers—the need to borrow money at
short term for low interest to finance their seasonal operations. It was
an old idea proposed to Congress by Farmers Alliance leaders without
success late in the nineteenth century. South Dakota's legislators
enacted the measure readily in February. Doubtless their support came
as a response to the popular appeal of the Governor as much as their
desire to bring state government into the banking business.

Norbeck's other initiatives attracted similar support among legislators. He asked for money to match funds available through the Federal
Highway Act of 1916 for the construction of arterial roads, to establish
a wildlife refuge system, and to supply the free textbooks for school
children authorized in the session of 1907. He called for the creation
of a state office to help farmers market their crops. To pave the way
for further reforms, Norbeck requested studies for a system of work-
men's compensation, state hail insurance, state-owned flour mills and
terminal elevators, state development of water power resources, and a
state-owned coal mine. He supported prohibition and advocated the
creation of a unicameral legislature. With the exception of the latter,
Norbeck won every fight; his success left his opponents scratching
their heads.

While moving South Dakota's government in the direction of state-
owned enterprises, Norbeck doubtless responded more to political and
economic necessity than to a personal desire. Many of his initiatives
mirrored the ideas introduced earlier by the Nonpartisan League, the
insurgent movement that swept North Dakota in 1915 and 1916 by
linking socialists with cooperative organization activists. The five-point
League platform had called for stateowned terminal elevators, flour
mills, cold storage plants, and packing houses; state inspection of grain
and grain dockage; exemption of farm improvements from taxation;
state hail insurance; and rural credit banks operated at cost. The
Nonpartisan platform derived largely from demands voiced by the
American Society of Equity, a cooperative organization that featured
marketing strategies and had considerable strength in northeastern
South Dakota. Although many South Dakotans were attracted to the

Nonpartisan League, most elected to stay beneath the banner of Progressive Republicanism.

No evidence links the Norbeck program directly to the Nonpartisan platform, even though his crews were often in touch with League spokesmen as they traveled to drill wells across south-central North Dakota from their headquarters at Redfield. The Governor doubtless developed his legislative reforms mainly in response to appeals from farmers and ranchers who favored state participation in economic activities. A smart and ambitious politician, Norbeck understood the threat of popular insurgency. His studies on the state's involvement in economic enterprises were calls for action within the Progressive Republican tradition of collective action more than efforts to enhance his own political career. To Norbeck, the urgency for action on behalf of constituents in need was simple: "When the water gets too high, let a little of it over the dam."[3]

His plans for the direct involvement of state government in economy caused a stir among South Dakotans. Republican leaders, whose intraparty battles pitted stalwarts against Progressives, were stunned to discover they had put a businessman in the governorship who evidently had the heart of a socialist. Stalwarts could not attack Norbeck openly for this because he was so popular. Democrats were placed in the difficult position of either presenting a "me, too" program or finding some candidate with equal appeal. Left wing insurgents saw their program usurped by the Governor. As a result, there was a shift in South Dakota politics to the ideological left and the initiation of a new political debate.

World War I augmented Norbeck's strategy. Winning the war became an encompassing national goal. Any hint of "anti-Americanism" became grounds for local repression. Emotional fervor that evolved after the United States declared war on Germany in April, 1917, provided a political lever that could be used against the League, whose national leader, Arthur C. Townley, had "radical" affiliations with the Socialist Party. When some of Townley's friends declared their opposition to America's entry into a foreign war, the Nonpartisan League's opponents sensed an opportunity to discredit the entire organization.

Accordingly, Governor Norbeck used Townley as a convenient target in South Dakota. He banned the Nonpartisan leader from speaking engagements during the 1918 campaign for his alleged seditious comments, and acted slowly, if at all, to stop local mob attacks on League meetings and organizers. Gilbert Fite believes that Norbeck "made a sincere effort to protect" Nonpartisan gubernatorial endorsee Mark P.

Bates, but Bates reported otherwise. Through Nonpartisan media he called the Governor insincere in his public advocacy of free speech.[4] Sporadic violence eventually led Norbeck to ban all campaign meetings in October, 1918, using the onset of the influenza epidemic as justification for the order. Norbeck won re-election handily, perhaps as much through this strategy as his abiding popularity. Along with the victory came public approval for constitutional amendments, which went before a special legislative session in March, 1918, to invite South Dakota's government officially into the world of business.

The Governor and the Legislature both waffled at that point. The suggestion of state-owned packing plants, terminal elevators, and flour mills received no endorsement in Norbeck's inaugural address. Instead, he chose to follow the recommendations of the South Dakota Farmers Union, whose leaders rejected state ownership of business establishments. Norbeck restricted the introduction of his experiments in socialism to those that could pass easily in the Legislature. The rural credit system, which was initiated in 1917, received additional funds and added staff. At the same time, the Governor gained authorization for the development of the state-owned cement plant, the opening of a state coal mine, and the initiation of a state hail insurance system. Moreover, the Legislature gave him authority to lay plans for a major hydro-electric development on the Missouri River. A progressive agenda suitable to Norbeck's moderate ideas about the role of the state in the economy was in place.

Several measures forecast the greater importance of tourism to South Dakota and Governor Norbeck devoted large amounts of time to laying a foundation for this through the remainder of his second term. A vast increase in the private ownership of automobiles brought many travelers to the region during the World War I era. As the owner of an automobile, Norbeck understood its possibilities and the need of its better use. He knew especially that motor vehicles required better roads and their development became a major goal. He established a new highway commission that laid plans for the allocation of $10,000,000 to road improvements throughout the state in 1919 and 1920. He accelerated plans to supply materials for hard surfaced highways from a state-owned cement plant. Better roads would both spawn a major market for the cement plant's product and serve to attract additional tourists.

Still more significant among Norbeck's efforts to develop tourism was his work on the creation of a park in the Black Hills. Although sometimes featured as an example of his interest in the conservation of natural resources, this effort better served his plans for the diversification of state economy. In addition, it provided an opportunity for Norbeck to claim a middle-of-the-road philosophy that linked public business directly to private enterprise.

He had advocated a Black Hills park since 1905 and led a movement to set aside 61,440 acres in Custer County as a state game preserve in 1913. Local leaders opposed the idea but Norbeck persevered. He was able to arrange the addition of 30,000 acres of federal lands to the park in 1920. The expansion brought Sylvan Lake, Needles, and Harney Peak under state control. Norbeck labored personally on the design of a scenic road into the area that was completed by 1922 under Governor McMaster.

Norbeck's involvement with the greater development of the Black Hills as a national tourist attraction continued. After his election to the United States Senate in 1920, he promoted federal highway bills, backed the idea of sculpting a monument to America's heritage on Mount Rushmore, and succeeded in attracting President Calvin Coolidge to vacation in the Black Hills. The combination of his efforts established an image of the Hills in the national mind and contributed enormously to making them into a tourist mecca later on.

Not so successful was his program of state industries. Its cornerstone, rural credits, became law in February, 1917. The statute established a five-person board to be appointed and headed by the Governor. It was empowered to borrow money against state revenues and lend the proceeds to farmers for expansion, improvements, machinery, livestock, or operating expenses. The maximum loan to a single borrower was not to exceed $10,000. Rural credits bonds were issued for funding. At the beginning the system enjoyed wide acceptance because it extended assistance to South Dakota's primary industry at a time when farmers and ranchers entered a post-war depression.

Unfortunately, the rural credits system was managed more through personal contacts and recommendations than objective analysis. Abuses resulted. Applicants were not investigated adequately. Loans to the maximum limit were granted without adequate security. As long as farm prices and land values remained as high as they had been during wartime, faulty management mattered little. The rural credits board failed because it did not adjust its lending procedures to deflated land values and agricultural commodity prices in postwar years. Its collapse was almost inevitable.

Norbeck's other initiatives in state ownership generated similar enthusiasm and expectations. Commissions to develop and govern the state coal mine, the state cement plant, and a state sponsored hydro-electric facility appeared in 1919. Each was created to eliminate the cost of middlemen from production and distribution and establish competition that would keep the prices for coal, cement, and electricity as low as possible.

All of the initiatives commenced operation by the end of Norbeck's second term in Pierre. The coal mine commission bought a mine near Haynes, North Dakota, because it was near the main line of the Chicago, St. Paul, and Milwaukee Railroad. Norbeck closed the deal in August, 1920, and the mine operated as a state industry until it was sold for $5,500 in 1934. It probably lowered the wholesale price of coal but, in the end, it cost the state more than $174,000. At best, it was a qualified success.

A similar conclusion may be drawn with regard to state hail insurance. A governing agency funded it by a premium tax on crop land, which was levied from 1919 to 1933. State insurance absorbed the risk of hail damage at low cost to farmers. By the late 1920s, however, the problems of poor administration and decreasing farmer participation made it a losing proposition. At its demise, the agency disbanded with a debt of more than $263,000.

The hydro-electric initiative suffered a different fate. The commission in charge grappled earnestly with a task that was far too big for management by any one state with limited resources. The commission made a contribution to future efforts when it inspired the investigation of sites for dam construction along the Missouri River—one site at the Mulehead, for example, and another at Mobridge—but it never overcame the inability of South Dakotans to provide enough money to meet the enormous costs.

Norbeck's only success in state owned industry came at the cement plant. It got underway slowly. A commission appointed by him placed it at Rapid City in 1920 and put it in operation in 1925. Thereafter, it was managed conservatively and effectively. The plant had little impact on the cement market but, in time, it made a profit for the state because it operated at low capitalization with exemption from state taxation. The plant benefitted, too, from the massive relief projects of the federal government during the 1930s, selling a high-quality product for the construction of public buildings and highways across the region. By any standard, the part it played in the improvement of public facilities justified its existence.

The probable demise of Norbeck's other initiatives had not become apparent in 1920. At the end of his second term as Governor, Norbeck could claim that his goals had been met. The Limited state participation in business had been institutionalized to cushion the negative effects of monopoly or collusion by private interests; yet, state owned industries would stimulate individual initiative. The time had come for the operational phase of every state enterprise to get fully underway.

The Progressive Republican machine dominated the 1920 election. "Old Pete" moved to the United States Senate with a large margin of votes over two challengers. Extensive debates between gubernatorial candidates, mandated by the Richards Primary Law of South Dakota, brought life to an otherwise dull campaign. When the dialogue ended, Lieutenant Governor William H. McMaster moved to the Governor's chair and pledged to carry out all programs established by his popular predecessor. Most observers interpreted McMaster's election as evidence of wholehearted endorsement for Norbeck's brand of progressivism.

McMaster outlined several priorities in his inaugural address. He offered state assistance for the development of cooperative marketing organizations, going so far as to advocate the creation of a state agency to finance foreign commodities sales and offer state accounting and auditing services to rural cooperative organizations. There was ample support for this in the growing influence of cooperative buying and selling systems operated or endorsed by the South Dakota Farmers Union. To assist organizations, McMaster also recommended the licensure and inspection of stockyards. He called for the increased regulation of livestock and commodities sales and asked for higher taxes on all corporations with headquarters outside South Dakota. He promoted, too, greater economy in government, the investigation of state bonding to finance home construction, and a commitment to the continued support of state industries already in operation.

Unfortunately, most of McMaster's ideas fell victim to the postwar depression that rippled across rural America in 1921 and 1922. In South Dakota an economic slump put heavy pressure on banking and credit systems. Early in his administration, McMaster announced he would not foreclose on rural credits mortgages as long as operators tried to make their payments. His declaration was based on an urgent need. A 1922 report from the rural credits board, prepared at the Governor's request, noted more than $41,000,000 in outstanding bonds and acknowledged considerable difficulty in collecting even the interest due from many borrowers. Clearly, the rural credits system was in difficulty.

This problem forestalled any new initiative for state industry, but

McMaster retained a progressive faith. He called on the Legislature to encourage the local consumption of South Dakota commodities, foster cooperative marketing, and develop a system of intermediate credits for farmers. In these ideas, he reacted to the changing mood of the people and their declining faith in government ownership. The new posture became obvious during the election of 1922, when South Dakota voters soundly rejected an initiative to fund the construction of a hydroelectric dam near Mobridge, and by a 4-to-1 majority negated an attempt to create a state-owned bank.

The progressive tide was waning. Yet it did not diminish rapidly enough to threaten McMaster's reelection in 1922. He defeated two candidates by a smaller margin than he won in 1920, largely on the strength of his reputation as an able manager of state funds, and of the continued power of the Republican Party of South Dakota.

During his second term, McMaster fought to retain state initiatives, but the continuing recession in rural economy made his task very difficult. His most spectacular success, which became the moment in his public career for which he is best remembered, came after August of 1923 when he took on a fight with the Standard Oil Company in particular, and the petroleum industry in general. Noting that retail gas prices far exceeded the costs of production and shipping, the Governor ordered the South Dakota Highway Department to purchase supplies on the wholesale market and sell them at state-owned stations for two cents per gallon above cost. Public acceptance was immediate and overwhelming. After failing to get state courts to enjoin the Governor, oil companies lowered their prices to meet the competition. McMaster continued to use the stations to control prices in South Dakota and, in 1925, claimed that his actions saved some $5,700,000 for his constituency.

This singular triumph ended the reign of Progressive philosophy at Pierre. McMaster followed Norbeck to the United States Senate in 1924, knowing that the hegemony of Progressive Republicans in South Dakota had passed. A change was foretold by the inability of state institutions created after 1917 to stave off financial collapse in the rural depression of the early 1920s. Approximately 175 banks closed in South Dakota. A depositor's guarantee fund created during Norbeck's tenure at Pierre did little to protect either bank owners or their patrons. In frustration over the clash between promises and realities, the Legislature repealed the measure in 1925.

Likewise, an investigation of the rural credits system demonstrated that one-third of the loans were in default, that members of the governing board had manipulated its funds for personal benefit, and that record keeping had been handled in the most unusual ways. At first, the legislature stopped negotiation of new loans. In 1925, a grand jury at Pierre accused Norbeck and McMaster of "dereliction and malfeasance" during their respective stewardships of the rural credits operation. The charge brought no indictment, but rural credits board treasurer A. W. Ewert was later convicted of criminal behavior and sentenced to prison. The liquidation of all rural credits obligations cost more than $57,000,000 that South Dakotans paid gradually until the late 1950s.

The most disturbing evidence of decline in the popularity of progressive philosophy was a factional feud within the South Dakota Republican Party as a result of state fiscal problems. Resurgent conservatives, teamed with disaffected progressives led by Governor Carl Gunderson, maligned the initiatives of Norbeck and McMaster. This split in the Republican majority led to the election of the conservative Democrat William G. Bulow as Governor in 1926.

There was considerable irony in such a result. Norbeck had supported Gunderson over McMaster as the Republican candidate for Governor in 1920. Yet he watched his successor faithfully institute a program of "Norbeck Socialism." That the man he had backed as his most legitimate heir would become a bitter antagonist in 1925 so enraged him that he announced his plans to go "before the public . . . with a defense."[5] That Norbeck, as the Governor who had received the largest vote of confidence in state history, had to plan such a rearguard action denoted a changing mood in public opinion and the inevitable demise of Norbeck's dreams.

Both Norbeck and McMaster remained in politics. Norbeck won re-election to the U.S. Senate in 1926 and 1932, where he developed the reputation of a stern advocate for conservation and federal farm program legislation. He voted as a member of the Farm Bloc in Congress and after 1933 added the policies of President Franklin D. Roosevelt to his personal creed. While a U.S. Senator, Norbeck also fought for development of the monument at Mount Rushmore and contributed greatly to the expansion of America's national parks. He died in office on December 20, 1936, an honored and revered leader whose positive reputation has not suffered over time.

The Great Depression stopped McMaster's political career abruptly. Known as a traditional progressive, he worked within the Farm Bloc of Congress to promote relief measures for farmers. He called for high protective tariffs on commodity imports, opposed militarism (once attempting to amend a military appropriations bill to mandate the conscription of corporate leaders and congressmen in time of war), and introduced legislation beneficial to Indian peoples. Despite the admirable quality of his platform, a poor campaign in 1930 against the astute William Bulow, coupled with some lingering resentment about McMaster's program in Pierre, brought him defeat in his bid for re-election. McMaster retired from politics, moved to Illinois in 1933, re-entered the banking business, and lived a productive life. He died on September 14, 1968, long after the struggles of his political years had become faint memories.

The general legacies of these two progressive leaders have diminished with time. Just as the progressive domination of the Republican Party that they fostered languished in factionalism by the middle 1920s, so did most of their programs end in collapse. South Dakota Republicans withdrew their support from state involvement in the economy, thereby rejecting a credo they had inherited from Alliance men, Populists, and Fusionists. In frustration and disgust, they returned to conservative principles. Leaders of the same party that sent two progressive ex-governors to the U.S. Senate in the 1920s replaced them with conservatives Karl Mundt and Francis Case no more than a decade later.

The contributions of Progressive Republicans Peter Norbeck and William McMaster were not diminished by the reversal of philosophy in their party. State industries nurtured from 1917 to 1924 brought tangible benefits to a majority of the people for a time. The cement plant survived to become an important institution. Experiments with state-owned business activities established interest in governmental services to stimulate and assist lagging areas of state economy. Progressives laid a foundation for the diversification of South Dakota's economy with aid for road construction, promotion of tourism, and conservation of natural resources. An unsuccessful effort to build a hydroelectric plant along the Missouri River failed for the lack of adequate financial support, but the investigation of probable sites and the promotion of public acceptance became important to the completion of mainstem dams under authority from the Flood Control Act of 1944. Overall, these two leaders taught South Dakotans the virtue of making state government more responsive to requests from people in need than to demands by special interests. For this, Peter Norbeck and William H. McMaster are to be honored as prominent persons in the history of their state.

Notes

1. Gilbert Courtland Fite, *Peter Norbeck: Prairie Statesman* (Columbia: University of Missouri, 1948), p. 49.

2. Charles J. Dalthorp, ed., *South Dakota's Governors* (Sioux Falls: Midwest-Beach Company, 1953), p. 37.

3. *Nonpartisan Leader* (St. Paul, MN), June 9, 1918, p. 8.

4. Gilbert C. Fite, "Peter Norbeck and the Defeat of the Nonpartisan League in South Dakota," *Mississippi Valley Historical Review,* XXXIII, no. 1 (June 1946), pp. 217–236; Robert L. Morlan, *Political Prairie Fire: The Nonpartisan League, 1915–1922* (Minneapolis: University of Minnesota Press, 1955), pp. 212–213.

5. Peter Norbeck to Doane Robinson, April 4, 1925, Doane Robinson Papers, South Dakota Historical Resource Center, Pierre, Box 10, Folder 162. In a second letter, dated March 3, 1925, located in the same file, Norbeck writes: "Of course, you know I did not want McMaster to succeed me as governor. . . ."

The four Pyle children in surrey with fringe on top.
Courtesy Richardson Archives, USD.

Gladys, May and Nellie (1909).
Courtesy Richardson Archives, USD.

Mrs. John L. (Mamie) Pyle.
Courtesy Richardson Archives, USD.

Gladys Pyle during her teaching career.
Courtesy Richardson Archives, USD.

Gladys Pyle in recent years.
Courtesy Richardson Archives, USD.

The Emergence of Women in Public Life: The Family of John L. Pyle

Jeannette Kinyon

Several members in the family of John L. Pyle, whom Cleata B. Thorpe in her book about them called "Dakotans Extraordinary," made "outstanding contributions" to every community of which they were a part.[1] Born to be leaders, they grew up in surroundings where public affairs, church activities, human rights, and compassion for others were subjects of dinner table conversations. Believing in their parents' involvement with life beyond the home, all members of the family lived up to the bright promise of their heritage.

Red-haired John L. Pyle numbered colonial Quakers among those in his paternal background. His father, Levis Pyle, was an underground railroad activist. His mother, Mary Dean Pyle, was known for her "remarkable gentleness and self-control." John was the ninth of thirteen children, only six of whom lived to maturity. Born at Coal Run, Ohio, in 1860, he moved with the family to Raritan, Illinois, where his parents farmed until 1882.

He received a formal education in Illinois. At age thirteen he went to work for money to support a normal course at Westfield Academy (later re-named Western Illinois University at Macomb). In 1879 he obtained a Second Grade Teacher's Certificate, which was valid for one year in McDonough County, Illinois. He did not teach but, like many another young man, he planned to go West. As preparation, he set out to make enough money to study law at the University of Michigan Law School and become a lawyer.

John worked in the mines of Montana for three years and saved his wages. Then he became ill with lead poisoning, and fate stepped in. Through weeks of recovery, he used up his savings. Undaunted by this misfortune, young Pyle resolved to study law on his own.

He traveled by river boat from Montana to Dakota Territory, after his parents had already arrived. Having no money for a trip from Pierre to Miller, he borrowed from a fellow passenger and gave his watch as security. In 1882 he filed on a homestead near Miller and began to read the law.

John studied as he worked in the office of attorney M. E. Williams at Miller and by 1886 he passed the bar examination and began a private practice. Six months after his admittance to the territorial bar, he was elected Hand County State's Attorney on the Republican ticket. At age twenty-six, he began an extraordinary career that would have a profound effect not only upon his immediate family, but also on the future state of South Dakota.

About the time John Pyle entered Dakota Territory, members of a family named Shields journeyed to Miller. They were of Irish background: Harry, Sarah Jane, and their daughter Mamie (Mary Isabella), who was born in 1866 in Orange, New Jersey. Mamie was seven years old when she moved with her parents to Pleasant Grove, Minnesota. Harry and Sarah came to Miller in 1882, but Mamie stayed with her mother's brother in Brookings County, where she had a teaching job at a rural school in Richland Township. During the fall of 1883 she went to Hand County to teach the rural school south of Miller that was later named the Golden Shield School in her honor.

On May 26, 1886, John L. Pyle and Mary Isabella Shields were married at the bride's parents' home. The book by Thorpe contains the following account:

> The groom is one of Miller's brightest young attornies [sic]. The bride is one of Miller's favorite young ladies and looked very bewitching in a lovely cinnamon-brown silk dress. After the ceremony the evening was spent with music and lively conversation. Harry Shields, father of the bride, sang several new songs that delighted the guests. Delicious refreshments were served. They are a worthy couple, worthily mated, and worthy of each other.

John and Mamie lived for a time in Miller before they moved to Huron. During the next four years they became the parents of four children: John Shields (born March 12, 1887), May (May 1, 1888), Nellie (August 1, 1889), and Gladys (October 4, 1890).[2]

The home that John and Mamie Pyle built in 1894 was, at the time of its construction, "one of the finest in Huron."[3] It was a nine-room, story-and-a-half house of Queen Anne style that had golden oak woodwork, carved window ornamentation, antique furniture, rugs, and glass chandeliers. For some ninety years it was to be the home of Gladys Pyle. Since 1974 it has been on the National Register of Historic Places.

Here, members of the extended family found a welcome home and the four Pyle children spent their childhood, adolescence, and teen years. They became young adults surrounded by love, discipline, patriotism, religion, and a sense of great responsibility for making the world around them a better place. All members of the Pyle family were active in the First Presbyterian Church. All four children graduated from Huron College.

John Pyle had a successful career in Huron. He served as attorney for various farmland sales in an era of mortgage foreclosures on land in South Dakota. He became President of the Board of Directors of the First National Bank in Huron, which he also served as attorney. In 1898 he formed a law partnership with Alva E. Taylor. On June 4, 1901, John was appointed Major and Judge Advocate of the South Dakota National Guard by Governor Charles Herreid.[4]

Twice he was elected to the office of Attorney General of South Dakota, in 1898 and 1900. At the capital city he was active in temperance reform as head of the state Anti-Saloon League and took a firm stand against the use of alcoholic beverages. John was a believer in young people and their higher education. Not surprisingly, he supported little Pierre University, which was established by the Presbyterian Synod in 1883, and helped it through hard times in the 1890s. He was the chief contributor to a fund to buy the unoccupied Royal Hotel as a home for the University, for example, and instrumental in an effort to bring it to Huron. With the help of his wife and others, he saw the realization of this dream. Pyle became the President of its Board of Trustees when it was newly established as Huron College, and he awarded the first diplomas from the College to normal school students and two commercial school "graduates."[5]

As Attorney General, John Pyle was involved with important litigation. He won a suit against the Chicago, Milwaukee & St. Paul Railway, whose attorneys contended before the Supreme Court of the United States that no state had a right to interfere with rates charged by a railroad. He worked on the North Carolina case, which established the right of one state to sue another.

While he was in Helena, Montana, meeting governors and attorneys general on the landmark Great Northern Merger Case, he contracted typhoid fever and died on February 21, 1902, at age forty-two. As the former Judge Advocate General of the South Dakota National Guard, he received a military funeral. Governor Charles Herreid ordered flags at half-mast, and state offices were closed during the funeral. At the First Presbyterian Church in Huron, where John Pyle was eulogized, guardsmen were in attendance and appeared at the site of his grave in Riverside Cemetery.

About Pyle's legal career, a biographer quoted his professional associates and friends:

> Governor Herreid said: 'Mr. Pyle was an efficient officer, an able conscientious lawyer, and an honorable Christian gentleman who was respected by all classes and loved and admired by all who had the privilege of his personal acquaintance. In his untimely death his family, the legal profession, the public service and all the people of the state have suffered unmeasureable [sic] loss.' Resolutions of the Beadle County Bar Association said in part: Mr. Pyle was 'a man of high character and worth; as a public official he served the people of the state with fidelity; as a private citizen he was zealous in the discharge of every civic duty; as a husband he was faithful and kind; as a father he was patient, gentle and indulgent; as a lawyer he was able and conscientious; steadfast in his relations with clients, and earnest and careful in the protection of their interests; as a man he was mild and sincere, true in his friendships, dignified in his bearing, and in all conduct governed by a lofty sense of duty. . . . Few men have been in the public eye who loved right and justice with such a passionate love.' Summing it all up were the words of the Rev. Richard A. Vander Las of the First Presbyterian Church in his funeral sermon for Mr. Pyle: In him could be found all those sterling qualities that go to make up true and noble manhood.'[6]

John's widow, Mamie, felt the loss keenly. At age thirty-six, she accepted responsibility not only for the rearing and education of four children, ranging between ages eleven and fifteen, but also for the work of her husband in support of a struggling Huron College. Mrs. Pyle (as she preferred to be called by then) replaced him on the Huron College Board of Trustees and served as a member for forty-six years. First she organized the Ladies College Association, later renamed the Huron College Women's Association. In her work with this group, which gave extensive financial help, Mrs. Pyle enlisted the aid of every congregation in the Dakota Presbytery. Church groups raised $5,000.

Yet Mrs. Pyle knew it was only a fraction of the $30,000 needed to build on land offered by the Western Town Lot Company, an affiliate of the Chicago & Northwestern Railway. Working with many others, she persuaded Mrs. Ralph Voorhees of Clinton, New Jersey, to give $15,000. While appealing for personal contributions, the Women's Association held bake sales, rented dormitory rooms during South Dakota State Fair week, and launched a Huron College Endowment Campaign in 1911. While in Chicago with her three daughters (all of them Huron College graduates who went on to attend graduate schools), Mrs. Pyle received a wire from the College President asking her to see Mrs. Cyrus McCormick. Working through a secretary, she acquired a gift that arrived in time to meet the challenge set in the endowment campaign. After adequate funding was in place, she worked toward making Huron College a center of Christian culture by hiring faculty members with adequate credentials.

Away from home, Mrs. Pyle was best known for her work in the suffrage movement. Because the state constitution of 1889 permitted women to vote only in school elections and because subsequent suffrage amendments proposed by the State Legislature were defeated in referenda, she became President of the State Equal Suffrage Association, known after 1911 as the South Dakota Universal Franchise League. In the elections of 1912, 1914, and 1916, Mrs. Pyle and co-workers saw the suffrage amendment go down to defeat, but they continued the fight. Finally in 1918, two years before women gained the right to vote under a universal franchise amendment to the Constitution of the United States, Mrs. Pyle and her colleagues saw a suffrage amendment added to the state constitution by approval from a large majority of South Dakota voters.

She received wide recognition beyond state boundaries as a delegate to the National Suffrage Convention in 1915, 1917, and 1919. She was on the Honor Roll of the Association in 1920 as one who had given "distinguished service" to the cause of women's suffrage across America. Through her efforts and those of other women as well as South Dakota legislators, the state ratified the suffrage amendment to the federal Constitution on December 4, 1919.

Mrs. Pyle received recognition in other areas of interest. For example, she served as a presidential elector and, on behalf of five electors from South Dakota, carried word of the state's presidential preference to Congress. She was well-known for her service in community affairs as President of the South Dakota League of Women Voters and as a resource person in the Huron chapter; as President of the Presbyterian

Women's Association of the Huron church; and as a member of the Twentieth Century Study Club, the Women's Christian Temperance Union, and the Young Women's Christian Association, which she served through its board of directors at Huron.

In 1947, at age eighty-one, Mrs. Pyle received recognition as South Dakota Mother of the Year, after nomination by the Huron Branch of the American Association of University Women. She had worked with determination for years on behalf of Huron College, women's suffrage, and the Presbyterian Church, but she had given the most dedicated service to her role as a mother. After parenting beside her husband during the formative years of her children, she became a single parent when her children were in their teens. Their upbringing and education became the motivating force in her life. She hitched up a horse to the carriage and accompanied them on outings for fishing and fun and went with them by train on debate trips and other school-related activities.

After all three daughters graduated from Huron College, she closed the Huron house and joined them in Chicago, where May and Nellie did graduate work at Chicago University in English and mathematics, respectively, and Gladys studied at the American Conservatory of Music. John Shields Pyle attended the University of Michigan Law School. May and Nellie came back to teach in Huron High School, and Gladys taught at Miller High School.

Three of the Pyle children left South Dakota. John, who married his Huron College sweetheart, Florence Bruce, practiced law in Huron and Belle Fourche, SD; worked in Pennsylvania for the Internal Revenue Service as a Prohibition Raiding Squad Leader and Enforcement Officer; then entered private law practice in Pittsburgh. May taught school at Vista, Colorado, and served as Dean of Women at Whitworth College, at Spokane, for two years before she married Harold E. Andrews, a Presbyterian minister, who served churches in Iowa and Ohio. For forty years, May taught English in Ashland College in Ohio. Nellie met her future husband, Wilson L. Miser, at the University of Chicago, while they both did graduate work in mathematics. In 1916 they married and went to Fayetteville, Arkansas, where he taught at the University. Later, they moved to Chicago, where he taught mathematics at Armour Institute of Technology. From 1925–1951, Miser was Professor of Mathematics in the School of Engineering at Vanderbilt University in Nashville. After their four children reached school age, Nellie taught mathematics, first at Ward Belmont College and later at Vanderbilt University.

Only Gladys, the youngest child, remained in South Dakota. When asked about the greatest influence in her life, she credited her father. Although he died when she was only eleven years old, she adored him as a child and cherished his memory throughout her life. He had personal magnetism and a fine physique, she said. "He was 6'2" in his stocking feet" and "weighed 220 pounds and had red hair."[7]

After a year at Miller, Gladys taught in Huron High School, then became Superintendent of Schools at Wessington, commuting on weekends to Huron to be with her mother. When schools closed because of the influenza epidemic in the years 1918–1919, she served as a volunteer nurse. Gladys returned to Wessington, but when her brother John needed someone to look after a sick wife and a child she left her job to help. Altogether, she taught for eight years—two in Miller, four in Huron, and two in Wessington. When asked many years later what she regarded as the most significant part of her life, Gladys said, "Teaching."[8]

Like her parents, she enjoyed dealing with people. She was endowed with a friendly and outgoing personality and with ambition, courage, and general competence. During 1921–22, she spoke on citizenship at summer institutes for the South Dakota Department of Public Instruction. After that, she lectured in Indiana, Kansas, Nebraska, and South Dakota for the League of Women Voters, training women to become active in political parties. Taking her own advice, in 1922 Gladys filed a petition for the primary election. When the ballots were counted, she received the most votes by a margin of fifty-three and became a legislative candidate in the fall. She led the Republican ticket by 350 votes to win election as one of Beadle County's three members to the State House of Representatives and became the first woman ever to sit in the South Dakota State Legislature.

Gladys had the opportunity to find out what *she* could accomplish. In 1923 she fought for the ratification of a child labor amendment to the Constitution of the United States, which failed. She "worked diligently but unsuccessfully" for a bill to permit women to serve on juries in the state.[9] This bill failed by a margin of 46 to 50 votes. When it was reconsidered with a change to make jury service for women optional, she opposed the bill. Later Gladys would see her call for the inclusion of women on juries expressed as law.

Near the end of her first term in the Legislature she accepted appointment as Assistant Secretary of State, when through "a complex bit of law interpretation" Attorney General C. E. Coyne asked her to serve. By the appointment she became the first woman assistant in a state constitutional office and served until she resigned to run for a second term in the Legislature.

During her second term Gladys proved herself "an ideal legislator" on all counts. She was "modest, but not shrinking, level-headed and self-possessed, riding no hobbies, broad-minded and practical on all legislation, speaking only when she had something to say and then saying it in concise language . . . doing her share of committee work painstakingly and with no idea of shirking," wrote Dick Halliday, editor of the *Iroquois Chief*.[10]

At the end of her second term she again accepted appointment as Assistant Secretary of State and held the office until she won election as South Dakota Secretary of State in 1926. Through two terms in this constitutional office, from 1927 to 1931, she demonstrated competence. Gladys sponsored the bill that became a statute to provide a Certificate of Title and Safety Code for motor vehicles, including motorcycles.

As the result of her service in state offices during the 1920s, Gladys grew to express concern about financial problems in South Dakota, especially as they related to farm prices, mortgages, foreclosures, and bank closings. At the urging of friends and political mentors, she allowed the circulation of petitions nominating her for Governor. Thus, she became one of five candidates for the office in the Republican primary election of 1930. On May 2, 1930, over WNAX Radio in Yankton, she made one of few formal campaign speeches:

> The most urgent need in the fiscal affairs of South Dakota is the liquidation of the general fund overdraft. . . . The financial condition of the state and the requirements of the law should be such that sinking funds would be a separate and a sacred trust fund, available for no purpose other than the retirement of bonds. They should be placed on long-time deposit at a higher interest rate, or invested in income producing government or state bonds. For the state to be paying as high as 6% interest on several issues of bonds and to be securing only 2% on the money accumulating to retire those bonds would be both unnecessary and unreasonable, could the overdraft be wiped out.[11]

She built her platform around the reorganization of the banking department and in the primary election received 33,153 votes, thirty-three percent of the total cast. This was not the necessary thirty-five percent required for nomination. Thus, if she were to become the Republican candidate for Governor she would have to be selected by the state party convention.

When Leo Temmey, a Huron attorney and future state Republican Chairman, placed her name in nomination, he summed up her political career with these words:

"She first entered the field of politics in 1922 as the first woman member of the House of Representatives from Beadle County. She found herself in a position unusually hard to fill. The eyes of the state were upon her. Her every word or gesture was news. . . . Into this position she came with rare tact and ability and soon taught her associates and the state at large that she was to be considered, not as a woman simply, or as a novelty or fad, but as an unusually able legislator from Beadle County."[12]

After twelve ballots, Gladys lost to Warren Green, the candidate with the fewest votes in the primary election. She took a defeat called by many "a raw deal" with grace and poise. Gladys supported Warren Green after she received his assurance that he would investigate the banking department. Although unsuccessful in her effort to become Governor, she succeeded in bringing "about disclosures of irregularities in the state banking department" that resulted in "the prosecution and conviction of the department head for embezzlement."[13]

From Governor Green, she received appointment as Secretary of the Securities Commission of South Dakota and served in this position from 1931 to 1933. Thereafter, she entered a business career that would continue for fifty years. Beginning in 1933 she became an insurance agent for the New York Life Insurance Company and retained her affiliation until her mother took sick. After Mrs. Pyle's death in 1949, Gladys went to work for Northwestern Mutual Life of Milwaukee and continued her affiliation with this firm as agent or emeritus agent until the 1980s.

She had other responsibilities. Gladys served as guardian for two growing orphaned boys, whose grandparents felt unable to manage the business affairs of their grandsons. She managed a 640-acre farm near Huron after her mother became unable to do so. Through help from federal programs for farmers, Gladys weathered the Great Depression of the 1930s and made a profit from farming through the 1940s. In 1959, when "all mortgages, back taxes, and other financial obligations on the land were at last cleared away," she sold the farm to a renter.[14]

Meanwhile, Gladys continued to serve the state, for she was elected to a short term in the United States Senate. Following the death of Peter Norbeck in 1936, Democratic Governor Tom Berry appointed Herbert Hitchcock to fill the vacancy. In 1938 Berry defeated Hitchcock in the Democratic senatorial primary election for a regular six-year term. At the November election, Republican Chan Gurney defeated Berry for the long term, while Gladys Pyle defeated the Democrat J. C. McCullen for a short term. Gladys served as United States Senator from South Dakota for only two months, but in that time she gained recognition as the first Republican woman elected to the United States Senate and the first South Dakota woman elected to a seat in either house of Congress. Furthermore, Gladys Pyle "was the first woman of either party to be elected without first being appointed to fill an unexpired term in the Senate."[15]

Although her term in the Senate was short, she made the most of it. Her work consisted primarily of correspondence, all of which she answered. Her most interesting communications were those involving the American visit of the Crown Prince and Princess of Norway, Heir Apparent Olaf and Princess Martha. Senator Pyle worked with Sioux Falls officials to arrange an overnight stop in the city for the royal couple. On June 14, 1939, she was at hand for festivities—a parade, a luncheon, and a banquet.

While in Washington, DC, Gladys attended several White House functions. At one, she spoke extemporaneously for Eleanor Roosevelt's "At Home at the White House" program for the Newspaper Women's Club. In humorous remarks, Senator Pyle endeared herself to listeners when she related why her white gloves were both for the same hand: dry cleaners had delivered them just before she left for the party. On January 12, 1939, with Congressman and Mrs. Francis Case of South Dakota, she attended another White House reception, hosted by Franklin and Mrs. Roosevelt.

In 1940 Gladys began another phase of her political career when, at the urging of friends, she ran for mayor of Huron. She lost the election but, as the only woman candidate, she received the second highest number of votes in a race with four contenders. As a delegate to the National Republican Convention in Philadelphia the same year, she placed the name of second-term Governor Harlan J. Bushfield in nomination for the presidency.

Many positions of honor and responsibility followed. In 1941 Gladys Pyle began a six-year term on the Board of Charities and Corrections, as an appointee of Governor Harlan Bushfield. Reappointed in 1947 by George Mickelson and again in 1953 by Sigurd Anderson, she served on the Board until 1955, when Joe Foss replaced *all* members because they had supported a Board member for Governor. She regarded her tenure as one of special accomplishment and great personal satisfaction. She saw schools for industrial and agricultural training established at the penitentiary. She also worked for the establishment of a four-year accredited high school at the state training school in Plankinton.

When South Dakota legislators finally passed a law permitting women to serve on juries in 1947, Gladys and six other women served on a federal grand jury of the United States District Court at Deadwood. Gladys was foreman. In 1952 she became Huron's First Lady of the Year. In 1955 she became an honorary international member of Beta Sigma Phi at Huron. In 1956 she received the Huron College Alumni Association's Distinguished Service Award. In 1958 she received an honorary doctorate of letters degree at Huron College.

In 1963 she became the First Citizen of Huron and in 1965 received the Y.W.C.A. Christian Citizenship Award. The same year she became the first woman to receive the Huron Chamber of Commerce Distinguished Civic Service Award for Community Activity; was the recipient of a life membership in the Huron Chamber of Commerce; and became an honorary member of the Delta Kappa Gamma International honorary society for women teachers.

As she enjoyed these and other moments of honor and recognition, Gladys continued to take an active part in numerous organizations. In 1972, for example, she served as Chairman for the Beadle County Senior Citizens to Reelect the President. She participated in the activities of the First Presbyterian Church, where she had been a Sunday School teacher, choir member, and elder as well as an active member of the Presbyterian Women's Association.

Shortly after her ninetieth birthday, she was the honoree of the Huron Business and Professional Women's club. On that occasion, she received a "cup commemorating her participation in the Huron College jogging marathon (she walked two and one-half miles!) and a cake for her history of support of the proposed Equal Rights Amendment to the United States Constitution."[16]

Finally, on her ninetieth birthday, October 4, 1980, she attended Gladys Pyle Day in Huron. From morning to night for three days she reigned. She was the grand marshal in the Huron College Pow Wow parade. In the afternoon, she received "state and local dignitaries," relatives, friends, and Huronians at the Huron College Campus Center, where all came to honor a foremost citizen. In a proclamation, the mayor of Huron referred to her as "one of our most illustrious citizens"; in a proclamation, Governor William Janklow called her a "truly 'grand' lady," who "symbolizes the spirit and vigor of an involved citizen, whose great contributions illustrate her genuine love for people.''[17]

Gladys Pyle deserved the high regard of South Dakotans and others outside the state not only for her specific contributions in city, state, and national affairs, but also for the quality of life she had lived. With others in the family, she served ably in education. As an administrator and legislator, she contributed to state government. As a leader among women at a time when their opportunities were limited, she like her mother championed political as well as social equality. She became first among women in South Dakota to attain high offices and first among women of unqualified success in public life.

Notes

1. Cleata B. Thorpe, *The John L. Pyle Family: Dakotans Extraordinary, 1882–1973* (Huron, SD: Creative Printing Company, 1973), pp. 75.

2. Several years after Gladys was born, Mrs. Pyle's parents, Mr. and Mrs. Harry Shields, also moved to Huron and lived near the Pyle family. When his wife died, Harry Shields spent the last ten years of his life in the Pyle home, where he died on February 28, 1927, after a productive life that included amateur theatricals and painting as well as singing.

Mrs. Pyle's sister Nellie, who had moved to Huron as a young woman and was for a while a secretary for the Pyle and Taylor law firm, returned to Huron when her husband died. She, too, lived at the Pyle home, where she died in 1942. Nellie had been the wife of John H. Albright, the architect for the Pyle home at 376 Idaho Avenue, Huron.

3. Thorpe, *Pyle Family*, p. 9.

4. *Ibid.*, p. 17.

5. *Ibid.*, p. 22.

6. *Ibid.*, p. 24.

7. Interview with Gladys Pyle by Jeannette Kinyon at Huron, SD, April 25, 1986.

8. Jeannette Kinyon and Jean Walz, *The Incredible Gladys Pyle* (Vermillion, SD: Dakota Press, 1985), p. 24.

9. Thorpe, *Pyle Family*, p. 61.

10. Kinyon and Walz, Gladys Pyle, p. 38.

11. Thorpe, *Pyle Family*, p. 64.

12. *Ibid.*, p. 65.

13. *Ibid.*

14. *Ibid.*, p. 67.

15. *Ibid.*, p. 68.

16. *The South Dakota Business Women*, January, 1981.

17. Kinyon and Walz, *Gladys Pyle*, p. 65.

Seth Bullock.
Courtesy South Dakota State Historical
Society.

Deadwood looking north (1876)
photographed by Stanley J. Morrow.
Courtesy W.H. Over State Museum.

First jail in Deadwood (1876) photographed by Stanley J. Morrow.
Courtesy W.H. Over State Museum.

Black Hills Entrepreneur: Seth Bullock

David Miller

Western South Dakota was exploited little by White people until the last quarter of the nineteenth century. Non-Indian influence previously had been restricted to intrusions by fur traders, explorers, United States Army units, and agency personnel or negotiators who dealt with Sioux tribes on behalf of the U.S. Department of the Interior. Following their migration from east central Minnesota during the eighteenth century, Teton, Yanktonai, and Yankton Sioux people claimed West River country as an area of permanent settlement as well as a place to hunt and gather natural bounty. The 1868 Treaty of Fort Laramie affirmed their claim until such time as three-fourths of the adult males in every signatory tribe permitted additional White people to enter. But the gold rush and a resulting confrontation between Indians and federal forces brought negotiations that resulted in the general opening of the region. This process began with the controversial Black Hills Agreement of the mid-1870s and ended in the Sioux Agreement of 1889. By the early 1890s tribal reservations were in place, and great tracts of land were under survey for settlement by White people from the Missouri River to the foothills of the Rocky Mountains.

Seth Bullock and James "Scotty" Philip were among the earliest immigrants to envision West River country as a suitable place for development by pioneers with interests in livestock, agriculture, urban development, and commerce. Parallel in some respects, and different in other ways, Bullock and Philip personified the ambitions, attitudes, triumphs, and failures of pioneers who came from eastern states and European countries seeking opportunities on a shrinking frontier. Some aspects of their careers were paradoxical. Bullock and Philip were willing to use almost any method to exploit the natural wealth of the region. They were restless and daring in their efforts to effect change. Yet they were dedicated to the preservation of bits of a vanishing frontier.

Seth Bullock was born at Sandwich, Ontario, in 1847. A biography written by his grandson, Kenneth Kellar, describes Seth's father, George Bullock, as "an irascible retired major in the British Army," and his mother as a "sweet natured, docile woman who had emigrated from the River Dee country."[1] According to family tradition, which contained some inaccurate details, Bullock ran away from home to live with a sister who was the wife of an army officer. In 1867 he entered Montana to begin a pioneering apprenticeship in the vicinity of Helena when it was little more than a placer mining camp.

Quickly, Bullock learned pioneering techniques from seasoned frontiersmen as he worked to gain power through commercial interests and territorial politics. A photograph of the Helena business district taken in 1870 contains the image of a sign on the side of a single-story, stone building: "Costling and Bullock Wholesale and Retail Grocers" and "auction and commission."[2] In public service Bullock established close relations with influential men. He served in the Territorial Council from 1871 to 1873. As one of two Republicans in a Democratic body, he stood firm in partisan battles to attract railroads to the Montana gold fields with funds raised by bonds subscribed by county governments. Bullock argued in favor of moving the Territorial capital from Helena. Neither of his proposals was successful but the controversy taught him how to use politics for economic development.

Later, he left his mark on Rocky Mountain affairs with a prominent role in the movement to create Yellowstone National Park. A Yellowstone Park bill, drafted for consideration in Congress by explorer/geologist Ferdinand V. Hayden after his 1871 expedition, passed in the United States Senate quickly but was held up in the United States House of Representatives. Bullock joined Judge Cornelius Hedges of Montana to draft a resolution for submission by members of the Territorial Council to Congress. Although he was new to the legislative process, Bullock wrote a letter to the Speaker of the House in Washington, DC, recommending the Yellowstone region be added to Montana Territory and be "dedicated and devoted to public use, resort and recreation, for all time to come, as a great national park, under such care and restrictions as to your honorable bodies may seem best calculated to secure the ends proposed."[3] Massachusetts Representative Henry L. Dawes employed Bullock's letter for leverage in the

House committees on territories and public lands as he used the creation of Yosemite Park in 1864 as a precedent. Persuaded by "the urgent and ardent support of the legislature of that [Montana] Territory" expressed in Bullock's letter, House members approved the bill and President Ulysses S. Grant signed it into law on March 1, 1872.[4] With a sense of satisfaction, Bullock explored the new park on an expedition that lasted from August 24 to September 20, noting in his journal a favorable response of tourists and recording the hope expressed by some visitors that Yellowstone National Park might accommodate settlers as well as "invalids" seeking cures in its mineral springs.

Bullock's journal also portrayed his interest in potential for economic development at other locations. Certain passages reflected his sense of humor. Describing a campsite where several rattlesnakes had been killed, Bullock wrote that none in his party had slept well and described the attempts by other members to deal with the problem:

At night our slumbers were troubled with horrible dreams of snakes. Mr. White and myself being unable to sleep . . . amused ourselves by frightening Teller. This gentleman had crawled into one of the four dog tents. In one of the larger ones, he made his bed secure as he supposed from snakes. We took the rattles from the snake killed first, succeeded in getting up a good counterfeit of the noise made by those beasts, so much so that Teller came rushing out very much alarmed. Toward morning, our hisses becoming quieter, we dozed away.[5]

While he was in Montana, Bullock worked in other facets of public life. He ran unsuccessfully for Sheriff of Lewis and Clark County shortly after he arrived at Helena, but he won the office in an election on August 4, 1873, and later served as Chief Engineer in the Helena Fire Department. The latter position was especially significant due to Helena's unenviable record of disastrous fires.

Bullock made many friends and useful business contacts with powerful men in Montana, but his most important alliance was one with Solomon Star, who became his partner at Deadwood. The two may have become acquainted during the 1871–1872 session of the Territorial Legislature, when Star showed up as a lobbyist for Deer Lodge, where he operated a mercantile business. Their friendship grew as flush times of placer mining around Helena fell into decline, and they witnessed the disappearance of prospectors, observed the evolution of hardrock mining, and watched the growth of urbanization. Historian K. Ross Toole described it:

These western settlements of which Helena was typical, were in no sense 'villages' or 'towns' in the Eastern or particularly the New England sense. It is not a matter of mere pretension that the word 'village' had no place in the western lexicon. There was an intensity and vitality about these communities that was all out of proportion to the actual number of people participating. Such population centers served a tremendous area with their needs, and they themselves were particularly cosmopolitan and independent.[6]

Equipped with experience in frontier Montana, Bullock pooled what resources he had with those of Sol Star and the two men braved the danger of the Great Sioux War when they set out to establish a mercantile business in Deadwood. It was an obscure placer camp barely four months old, situated some 250 miles from the nearest railroad, where it was served mainly by cargo wagons from Fort Pierre, Bismarck, and Sidney, Nebraska. Deadwood rested precariously on land set aside by the 1868 Fort Laramie Treaty under the provision that Whites were not to enter without permission from the signatory tribes. Bullock and Star loaded a wagon with hardware, traveled down the Missouri by steamboat past Ft. Benton, and entered Deadwood by the Bismarck-Deadwood Trail on August 1, 1876.

The Star-Bullock hardware store did its business on the corner of Main and Wall Streets. The night of their arrival, Bullock worked as an auctioneer to sell a large number of chamber pots they brought from Helena. Subsequently, their business featured conventional hardware plus furniture, wallpaper, and various household items. For a time, Star and Bullock sold liquor, too, which helped to build up their volume of business. On September 25, 1879, the great Deadwood fire dealt them a loss near $18,000, of which only $13,000 was covered by insurance. Using the insurance payment as seed money, they created a still larger store in Deadwood. They also opened branches in Lead, Sturgis, and Spearfish, and operated the Deadwood Flour Milling Company, which was capitalized at $60,000. When the construction of the Northern Pacific Railroad created a boom in the Yellowstone River Valley, Star and Bullock went back to Montana and opened stores at Miles City and Billings. *Montana: A State Guide Book*, published by the Federal Writers Project, contained this account of Bullock's return:

It is told that when the town was only two or three months old, one Seth Bullock, approaching over a miserable trail on a dark rainy night, asked a citizen the distance to Billings. 'You're in Billings now', said the citizen. 'The devil I am', said Seth. 'Can you tell me where the Star, Bullock and

Company store is?' 'Keep right on this street', said the citizen, 'the store is on the left-hand side twenty-six miles from here.'[7]

Back in Deadwood Bullock entered politics again after smallpox broke out at the town and mining camps. The threat of disease and the unauthorized use of streets as town lots stimulated a movement to form some sort of government. The Board of Health and Street Commissioners became the first governing body and Bullock was chosen as one of the original five commissioners. As a community leader he accepted whatever responsibilities came his way. After the itinerant Methodist minister Henry Weston "Preacher" Smith was murdered in nearby Centennial Valley, on August 20, 1876, Bullock arranged his burial. Using the *Book of Common Prayer*, he put the Methodist to rest with Episcopal procedures, and wrote a letter of condolence to Smith's superior at Louisville, Kentucky.

Action in the Dakota Territorial Legislature during February of 1877 drew him further into public life. Governor John Pennington, during whose term Lawrence County was organized, appointed a group of temporary county officials that included Bullock as Sheriff. They were to serve until permanent county officials were chosen by election the following November. Bullock and most of his fellow Republicans were defeated by a Democratic constituency and he never ran for the office of Sheriff again.

Nevertheless, he commanded respect from an image he developed through his brief tenure as Sheriff. There is no evidence that Bullock ever shot anyone. As his biographer put it, "When Bullock went out into the streets of Deadwood in the blazing sun of high noon, he was looking for his lunch, not someone to shoot."[8] He dealt with violence by other means. During the Keets Mine riot, unpaid miners refused to work or leave the mine without their wages. Bullock threw burning sulfur down the mineshafts to drive gasping protesters out. In an attempt to stop a jail break by Barney Jordan, he acted on a tip to catch Jordan and his cohorts in the act. He and his deputies broke into the section of the jail where Jordan held a hostage. A. M. Willard, one of the deputies, doctored up his account to better fit the image of the wild west:

> Bullock and others had to climb the fence and break down the door to the bullpen. Barney had Tracy [a deputy] down. Very much to his surprise he was facing the sheriff and his deputies, all with drawn revolvers. Bullock said in his soft low drawl: 'Hands up, Barney. These boys are pretty nervous, something might happen.'[9]

Bullock was not a gunfighter. He used other methods to solve community problems without violence.

Far more dramatic was his entry into ranching. By 1878 the Star-Bullock partnership was well enough established to support a new venture. The valleys of the Belle Fourche and lower Redwater Rivers, north of the Black Hills, offered ample water, grass, and farm land superior to any available around Deadwood. As Indians surrendered their ponies and guns to accept confinement on reservations after the Great Sioux War, federal officials opened the land they abandoned for development by non-Indians, because of a growing demand in West River country for food and forage. Drawing on the Montana experience, Star and Bullock extended the activities of their partnership in 1878 to include a ranch at the junction of the Belle Fourche and Redwater on unsurveyed land.

They started their ranching operation in partnership, using an "S-B" brand for the "Star Ranch," or the "S-B Outfit." Charles C. Haas, who ran a large ranching operation in the neighboring Whitewood Valley, described it candidly:

> Bullock 'squatted' on his ranch in 1878 'by proxy'. You know, of course, that the land had not been surveyed at this time and no filings were made till this was done and, of course, Bullock did not homestead his large ranch, but like all large ranchers furnished the money to build up and stock his location, and those ranches were run by a foreman who was usually a married man and as many ranch hands as needed. After the land was surveyed their men filed homesteads on the land and were grubstaked until they made final proof when it was turned over to the ranchman. Bullock himself spent only a small part of his time at his ranch.[10]

Bullock brought sound business methods to the S-B Outfit. He experimented with selective cattle and horse breeding. He introduced alfalfa—perhaps the first ever grown on the Northern Great Plains. Bullock had seen it before and asked Thomas Russell, the Union Pacific and Wells Fargo Agent at Deadwood, to arrange the purchase of seed in the Bear River Valley of Utah, where farmers called it "Lucerne." The seed arrived in time for planting on the S-B Ranch in 1881. Later, Bullock claimed proudly that "this seed, I am satisfied, is the parent seed of the hardy alfalfa grown in the Whitewood and Belle Fourche Valleys at this date [1914]."[11] He also insisted that alfalfa seed taken from his Belle Fourche Valley ranch was important to the cattle industry in Montana.

As an owner of the S-B Outfit Bullock became involved in one of the most hotly contested county seat controversies in Black Hills history. Lasting almost a decade, the conflict involved town development, stagecoach lines, railroad construction, and the futures of the towns of Belle Fourche and Minnesela. The episode began in 1884, when the Marquis De Mores announced a plan to open a stagecoach line from his ranch on the Northern Pacific Railroad at Medora to Deadwood. Promoters of a Minnesela townsite included Azby Chouteau, from the fur trade family at St. Louis, and George W. Kingsbury, the leading territorial historian. Presumably, the stage line would pass through Minnesela on the Redwater River and continue to Deadwood via Spearfish. When it was routed west of Minnesela to a stage station on the junction of the Redwater and Belle Fourche Rivers, at the S-B Ranch some three miles away, Bullock was declared the enemy of Minnesela boosters.

The new stage station, named De Mores, quickly took on the appearance of a rival townsite. Efforts to convince the Marquis to re-route his line through Minnesela failed and Bullock was held responsible. Of course, Bullock's Montana experience with legislation in an era of railroad promotion made him suspect, and there was the whiskey issue. Minnesela was dry, and the De Mores station had a saloon before the Deadwood-Medora stage made its first run. Boosters of Minnesela responded by inviting traffic in liquor and the stage line was short-lived. It appeared that De Mores station might close. Even the S-B Ranch continued to purchase some supplies in Minnesela.

A greater threat to Minnesela's survival came at the building of a railroad. Construction on the Fremont, Elkhorn & Missouri Valley line to Sturgis in 1887 created much excitement. Reports that it would run to some distant point cast Deadwood and Minnesela in the roles of rivals. Minnesela boosters believed the railroad would come to them and expanded their town boundaries to include space for yards and station grounds. They thought railroaders would pay handsomely for space in their town, for it was the Butte County seat and it promised to be a gateway to grass range country in the north and west. They were mistaken. The Star Ranch offered land around the De Mores station site for rail yards and grounds. A second opportunity for access to a major transportation route had passed Minnesela by.

Bullock and Sol Star granted station and yard grounds near the De Mores site on the condition that railroaders would agree to build their line up Whitewood Canyon to Deadwood. Minnesela partisans were furious. Bullock and his partner opposed them for the purpose of promoting the future growth of Deadwood and the establishment of a new town called Belle Fourche. They offered free lots in Belle Fourche to all merchants at Minnesela who were willing to relocate and a classic county seat battle between leaders at the two towns persisted into the early 1890s. It included the theft of Butte County records by Belle Fourche partisans in 1893, and the relocation of the county seat in 1894. The published history of Minnesela accuses Bullock and Star of key roles in the demise of the town.

Bullock's role in the Minnesela controversy set a tone for his future influence on the Black Hills frontier. That he demonstrated prestige and power sufficient to break an entire town is doubtful. When leading citizens of Rapid City, for example, failed to offer space for a railroad depot in 1886, the Elkhorn located its depot outside of city limits. A similar thing happened at Sturgis in 1887. The Pioneer Townsite Company, a subsidiary of the Fremont, Elkhorn & Missouri Valley Railroad, created a whole new community at Whitewood and bypassed Crook City as the Whitewood Canyon gateway to Deadwood. Minnesela boosters who called upon railroads to pay for access showed bad judgement. Nevertheless, the episode at Minnesela demonstrated that Bullock was experienced enough to know that town builders were somewhat at the mercy of railroaders and responded to railroaders' demands with a view toward long range development.

He displayed similar insight as a frontier entrepreneur in the Black Hills mining industry. During the mid–1880s the future of mineral extraction around Deadwood was uncertain. The deposits initially exploited by gold prospectors in the 1870s represented what mining experts called free-milling ore. After miners brought ore to the surface for crushing, an amalgamation process using mercury drew gold from crushed rock. The rapid exhaustion of the freemilling ores around Deadwood created interest in other sources, called refractory-gold ores. They could be refined, but existing processes were too expensive, considering the quantities of gold they produced. Several Black Hills mining enterprises attempted to export ores to distant points, such as Omaha and Black Hawk, Colorado, for processing. Because the cost rendered profit margins very slim, it became apparent that development of refractory ores around Deadwood would require a new refining process.

In June, 1887, the Deadwood Smelting and Reduction Works Company was organized. Among its founders was Seth Bullock, who hoped to raise capital to attract engineers who could process refractory ores at a profit. The group tried several processes that had been used successfully elsewhere without encouraging results. Engineers came to Deadwood from mining communities across the West. Faculty at the new School of Mines in Rapid City worked to solve the puzzle. As Deadwood's economic growth stalled in the late 1880s, it became clear that the issue was more than one of geological identification, chemistry, and mining engineering. The future of Deadwood was at stake.

Seth Bullock watched with interest. By 1889 Dean Franklin R. Carpenter of the School of Mines had developed a promising technique. His design used a smelting process that employed an iron-sulfide matte from which gold and silver could be extracted. Bullock invested heavily in properties with suitable ores. When Carpenter was ready to try his process outside the laboratory, Bullock offered ore from his Iron Hill Mining Company mine. Initial runs were unsuccessful but, with modifications, Carpenter developed a matte that could produce gold at a profit. Boasting, Bullock proclaimed that "to the Iron Hill company belongs the credit of inaugurating the process of pyritic smelting" according to specifications prescribed by Carpenter.[12]

This proclamation was somewhat premature. The pyritic smelting process worked on some ores, but not on others. Carpenter's procedure remained in use sporadically until 1903 but never achieved the goal of smelting with materials drawn exclusively from the Black Hills. Yet, Bullock's claim to success through his promotional efforts was eventually justified. A boom around Deadwood in the early 1890s, triggered by the development of refractory ore mines and the arrival of railroad service, led to the survival of the town. By 1895 Deadwood's population grew to more than 4,000. In large degree, Seth Bullock was responsible.

The Deadwood boom created other opportunities. New growth and commerce brought a stream of visitors and the city's hotel accommodations became inadequate. The Deadwood Board of Trade responded by purchasing downtown property and raising a $20,000 bonus to use as incentive for builders. Several groups worked out plans, without success. Bullock bought the holdings of the Deadwood Hotel Company in 1895, ordered improvements, and opened the Bullock Hotel. Thoroughly modern for its time, the three-story stone structure cost $40,000. The facade was constructed of white and pink sandstone, highlighted by an ornamental iron balcony. It contained sixty rooms with steam heat. When it opened, it was the most modern hotel structure in the northern Black Hills and remained the premier lodging place at Deadwood until the Franklin Hotel opened in 1903.

As the United States approached its war with Spain in 1898, Bullock was fifty years old. Although he appeared to be healthy and robust from hunting and other outdoor activities, he was past the age when men ordinarily enter military careers. But the Spanish-American War offered young men who had been entertained by thirty years of Civil War stories a chance for their own adventure. When South Dakota Attorney General Melvin Grigsby took appointment as Colonel in the 3rd U.S. Volunteer Cavalry, Bullock volunteered to raise a company. At first, he failed the physical examination. Later, he had his deficiency waived to allow enlistment. Bullock's company, Troop A, consisting of volunteers from Deadwood, Lead, and Spearfish, joined "Grigsby's Cowboys," a regiment comprising volunteers from the two Dakotas, Montana, and Nebraska. The entire unit was ready in less than a month and left the region for Chickamagua Park, Georgia, May 20, 1898. Because the war ended before the regiment could embark for Cuba, Bullock and most of his company were back in the Black Hills by December, after having suffered nothing worse than poor rations and considerable frustration. Bullock took the title of "Captain," which he flaunted proudly for the rest of his life.

After his military career ended, he returned to government service for a time. Bullock became Supervisor of the Black Hills Timberland Reserve and, during his tenure, saw it transformed into the Black Hills National Forest. Created by proclamation from President Grover Cleveland on February 22, 1897, the Reserve created a stir from the outset. Loggers demanded access to the million-acre tract because of ready markets for lumber. Existing regulations required that any timber sale from the Reserve on a tract larger than 160 acres be approved through the Regional Superintendent's office at Sheridan, Wyoming, then in Washington, DC, where the application would be reviewed and sometimes sent back through bureaucratic channels for revision. After the creation of the Black Hills Reserve, there were lengthy delays. The Homestake Mining Company paid trespass fees and carried on illegal logging operations. Timber shortages forced the closing of the Holy Terror Mine at Keystone. In 1899 authorization for the famous Case #1 near Este, South Dakota, allowed the first sustained yield logging contract issued in any U.S. forest reserve. This made Black Hills timber more accessible. It came about with the institution of new procedures designed by Bullock.

Early in 1901 he was invited by officials in the U.S. General Land Office to become the Black Hills Reserve Supervisor. Bullock agreed, subject to four conditions: he would report only to the Washington office, to reduce administrative delays; hire local people who knew the Black Hills; be allowed administrative staff sufficient to process applications and permits at the local level; and have local authority to authorize small timber sales. With the exception of local control over small sales, he received authority to proceed according to these guidelines.

By the time Bullock took over the Reserve, Chief U.S. Forester Gifford Pinchot had begun to introduce new policies regarding conservation and had made clear his intention to use the Black Hills Reserve as a laboratory for testing new ideas. The Case #1 sale to Homestake Mining Company, noted above, marked the beginning of sustained-yield logging for American forest reserves, according to Pinchot's design. As Black Hills Reserve Supervisor, Bullock had to administer Case #1, which was plagued from the outset by delays from cumbersome evaluation and reporting processes. To expedite administration, he arranged the transfer of inspection procedures from personnel based in Washington, DC, to local employees. Bullock cut through red tape and demonstrated that sustained yield contracts could be handled to the satisfaction of private interests.

He also dealt handily with an unprecedented problem of disease. By 1903 mountain pine beetle infestations had killed thousands of ponderosa pine—the Black Hills' principal lumber tree. The spread of an epidemic could be controlled only by cutting diseased trees. Officials assumed that infected trees should be removed almost immediately for effective disease control and that the trees should be sawed into lumber quickly before they rotted. Bullock simplified administrative procedures to encourage the logging of diseased timber. Salvage operations would have been impossible without the local autonomy Bullock had demanded in asserting the prerogatives of his supervisory office.

Preservation instincts that had drawn Bullock into the Yellowstone Park movement were beneficial while he served as Black Hills Reserve Supervisor. In 1903 he initiated the removal of 1,920 acres of timber land from private use around Wind Cave and, in this effort, he originated a process that led to the establishment of Wind Cave National Park. He took an interest in preserving Devil's Tower and Jewel Cave and created administrative procedures for their withdrawal from public entry. On September 24, 1906, Devil's Tower became the first National Monument in the United States. On February 7, 1908, Jewel Cave took National Monument status.

There is some evidence to suggest that Bullock initiated the idea of exchanging forest reserve lands for South Dakota's scattered school sections (#16 and #36 in each township) throughout the Black Hills Reserve. If credit is due him for this, he was an originator of a movement that led to the establishment of Custer State Park. Negotiations between the South Dakota Commissioner of School and Public Lands and forest officials began in 1911 and under their agreement came the transfer of land creating Custer State Park on May 10, 1912.

Not all of Bullock's policies for the management of the Reserve were successful. A scheme to harvest pine seeds from cones on trees in the winter of 1901–1902 resulted in seeds costing $1.36 per pound. Black Hills natives ridiculed the effort because youngsters could collect seed cones from squirrel caches at a fraction of the cost. Bullock was frustrated by trespass on the forest. Black Hills residents who were accustomed to doing as they pleased required constant supervision and education about forest regulations.

Bullock's tenure as the first Supervisor of the Black Hills National Forest ended abruptly in 1906 because of a new threat to forest reserves. He had long been troubled by scattered tracts of private land in the forest that encumbered effective management. As public land available for homesteading diminished across the West, political pressure to open forest reserve meadowlands to homesteading grew stronger. The introduction of a bill that took the colloquial name "Forest Homestead Act of 1906" convinced Bullock it was time to leave. He sought another government appointment. For having served earlier as a peace officer, he was invited to become U.S. Marshal and on July 1, 1906, he took the oath of office in Sioux Falls.

Needless to say, the appointment was no accident. His influence in Washington, DC, had increased greatly after the death of President William McKinley on September 14, 1901. For McKinley's demise placed a man in the White House with whom Bullock had very close ties. The origin of his friendship with Theodore Roosevelt was a chance encounter sometime between 1884 and 1893 near the S-B Outfit, or at Spearfish. Roosevelt recalled years later that he and his traveling companions had been on the trail from his ranch at Medora for several days when they encountered Bullock, who suspected them of being a "tin-horn gambling outfit."[13] Social calls that Bullock paid on Roosevelt in Washington, DC, helped cement their friendship. Roosevelt's influence as Vice-President contributed to Bullock's appointment as Forest Reserve Supervisor. After Roosevelt became President, an invitation to the White House for dinner made Bullock a frequent correspondent on political and policy matters. A high point in Roosevelt's inaugural parade of March, 1905, was the appearance of a delegation of fifty Dakota, Wyoming, Montana, and Nebraska "cowboys," which Bullock assembled and led to the event. The delegation comprised a combination of working cowboys, including future film star Tom Mix, and several prominent ranch owners. They traveled in their own railroad cars with horses and loaded pistols. There were roping demonstrations and firing salutes. "Cowboys" provided an inaugural parade spectacle that no coordinator could have allowed in a more recent celebration.

The families of Roosevelt and Bullock were close. Beginning in 1902 the President's children, cousins, and friends made annual pilgrimages to Deadwood, with Bullock as their host, to hunt and fish and live the "strenuous life" that Roosevelt fondly remembered from his Medora days. To the end of Bullock's life in 1919, "the boys" corresponded regularly with him. In a 1907 letter to son Kermit, the President described his delight at an unexpected encounter with Bullock aboard the steamer U.S.S. *Mississippi* at Keokuk, Iowa: "I seized him at once and have him on the steamboat going down the Mississippi, and will take him to St. Louis or Cairo, or for the matter of that Memphis, if he so desires."[14] Bullock was seated next to Roosevelt at the final ceremonial meeting of his White House "tennis cabinet," on March 1, 1909. He was to preside over the award of a bronze cougar to Roosevelt, but Henry L. Stimson finished the ceremony after Bullock choked with emotion.

Bullock enjoyed a command performance in London. After Roosevelt returned to Europe from his African safari, in the spring of 1910, he asked the Bullocks to meet him. One version of the request suggests that the idea occurred to Roosevelt while he was discussing Bullock as "a fine example of Western American" with the King of Norway.[15] In *Old Deadwood Days*, Estelline Bennett recalls a conversation with Roosevelt and his statement that he asked Bullock to come to London "because I wanted those Britishers to see my ideal typical American."[16] In any event, the Bullocks traveled in the company of the former President to a number of social engagements. Bullock returned with a repertoire of "while we were in England" stories, which he delighted in telling for the rest of his life.

The bond between the Bullocks and the Roosevelts typified the integrity of Bullock's domestic life. Martha was a conventional Victorian wife and mother—mistress of the house, club and church woman, ever in her husband's shadow. Almost always described as "Mrs. Bullock," she was at her husband's mercy in reaching decisions about the three children, house guests, business arrangements, and travel plans. Visits by the Roosevelt children were in Bullock's purview. Perhaps Martha's greatest accomplishment was the conversion of her husband to support womens' suffrage in 1914. She was a leader in the fight for the suffrage amendment in Lawrence County. Martha also attracted attention as a musician. After Bullock died in 1919, she lived a quiet life until her death in March, 1939. The Bullocks' gravestone in their plot above Mt. Moriah Cemetery bespeaks their relationship. It says of Bullock, appropriately, "Pioneer," and of Martha, simply, "His Wife."

Through his waning years, Bullock dabbled in various activities. During the presidential election of 1912 he recruited support for Theodore Roosevelt's Bull Moose candidacy and the former Rough Rider-President carried the state. He remained active as a charter member of the Society of Black Hills Pioneers. He was a charter member of the South Dakota State Historical Society. He composed "An Account of Deadwood and the Northern Black Hills in 1876." With emphasis on economic development and civil government, it lay in manuscript until it was recognized as an original document of value by inclusion in the *South Dakota Historical Collections* in 1962.

From this Bullock might have stepped into full retirement had Theodore Roosevelt not issued a final call. As the Bull Moose party collapsed in the election year of 1916, Roosevelt drew up plans to raise a volunteer force for service in France. He asked Bullock: "Are you too old to raise a squadron of cavalry in South Dakota?"[17] Bullock took up the challenge. As Roosevelt requested, he laid plans for a unit of 1,200, which would have included as officers his son, Stanley Bullock, and Kermit Roosevelt. Composed of cowboys, railroaders, and miners from the Black Hills and surrounding regions, the unit would have been almost a carbon copy of Dakota Rough Riders who volunteered for service in the Spanish-American War. When the United States finally entered the war in April, 1917, President Woodrow Wilson declined to accept such a volunteer division. Saddened and frustrated, Roosevelt called twenty key officers together. Bullock looked on from the Trophy Room at Sagamore Hill as the former President signed an order disbanding the division.

During the war, Bullock chaired the Home Service Section of the Red Cross Civilian Relief for the Black Hills region. He served on a three-member committee in the attempt to persuade Governor Peter Norbeck to locate the state cement plant that he had in mind at Deadwood instead of Rapid City. After Theodore Roosevelt died in January of 1919, Bullock worked earnestly on the creation of a monument for him on Sheep Mountain in the Black Hills. He foiled efforts to place the monument at the center of Deadwood and persuaded local leaders to construct a road to the summit. On July 4, 1919, a cavalcade of thousands moved to the top. General Leonard Wood and Governor Peter Norbeck presided over the re-naming and dedication of the site as "Mt. Theodore Roosevelt."

From there he turned to the endeavor of dedicating parts of Spearfish Canyon as the "Theodore Roosevelt Bird and Wildlife Sanctuary." Before the work was finished, Bullock died on September 23, 1919. His remains were taken for burial above Mt. Moriah Cemetery, on a plot he had donated to Deadwood, in full view of Mt. Theodore Roosevelt.

Maybe Seth Bullock was the "ideal typical American." Surely he merited the epithet carried by the *Pioneer-Times*: "Deadwood's most prominent citizen." He was the prototype of entrepreneur who led in the development of rugged areas in the West that were as luring as they were inhospitable. Bullock was a contributor of many talents as a business competitor, politician, public official, conservationist, preservationist, romantic, urban developer, strategic investor, and publicist. Only James "Scotty" Philip and a few others earned a place among those who contributed leadership of such high quality toward the development of non-Indian society in the region of the Black Hills.

Notes

1. Kenneth C. Kellar, *Seth Bullock: Frontier Marshal* (Aberdeen, SD: North Plains Press, 1972), p. 7.

2. Photograph reproduced in Tom Stout, ed., *Montana: Its Story and Biography* (3 Vols.; Chicago and New York: American History Society, 1921), I, p. 756.

3. Louis Crampton, *Early History of Yellowstone National Park and Its Relationship to National Park Policies* (Washington, DC: U.S. Government Printing Office, 1932), p. 25.

4. Aubrey L. Haines, *The Yellowstone Story: A History of Our First National Park* (2 Vols.; Denver: Colorado Associated University Press, 1977), I, pp. 155–173.

5. Bullock's Yellowstone Journal, quoted in Kellar, *Seth Bullock,* p. 25.

6. K. Ross Toole, *Montana: An Uncommon Land* (Norman: University of Oklahoma Press, 1959), p. 81.

7. Works Progress Administration, Federal Writers Project, *Montana: A State Guide Book* (New York: Viking Press, 1939), p. 128.

8. Kellar, *Seth Bullock,* p. 77.

9. *Ibid.,* p. 93.

10. Charles C. Haas to Doane Robinson, February 17, 1925, "Seth Bullock-Alfalfa File," South Dakota Historical Resource Center, Pierre, SD.

11. Seth Bullock to Charles C. Haas, December 13, 1914, *Ibid.*

12. Black Hills *Daily Times,* June 4, 1890.

13. Theodore Roosevelt, *Theodore Roosevelt: An Autobiography* (New York: The Macmillan Company, 1916), pp. 119–120.

14. Will Irwin, ed., *Letters to Kermit from Theodore Roosevelt, 1902–1908* (New York: Charles Scribner's Sons, 1946), pp. 216–218.

15. Lawrence A. Abbott, ed., *The Letters of Archie Butt* (New York: Doubleday, Page and Company, 1924), p. 243.

16. Estelline Bennett, *Old Deadwood Days* (New York: Charles Scribner's Sons, 1935), p. 54.

17. Kellar, *Seth Bullock,* pp. 177–178.

Scotty Philip.
Courtesy South Dakota State Historical
Society.

Pierre to Deadwood wagon train.
Courtesy Richardson Archives, USD.

Scotty Philip's funeral.
Courtesy W.H. Over State Museum.

Pioneering Black Hills Cattleman: James "Scotty" Philip

David Miller

James Philip was an immigrant, born on April 30, 1858, in Dallas, Morayshire, Scotland. He retained some ties throughout his life to family and old country roots east of Inverness on the coast of Scotland. The son of George Philip and Christina (Smith) Philip, he had only four years of formal schooling at a nearby stone schoolhouse and spent his youth working in the fields and tending livestock. His older brother, George, was the first Philip to make the crossing to America, emigrating to Victoria, Kansas, in 1873. George's letters described a colony of transplanted English aristocrats on a rich land in need of labor. At age fifteen James left with his older brothers, Alexander and David. After traveling in the winter of 1873–74, the three joined George at Victoria.

James worked as a laborer on farms and ranches nearby until the winter of 1875. Seeking other opportunities, he went first to Dodge City, Kansas, then to Cheyenne, Wyoming Territory. After working briefly near Cheyenne as a ranch hand through the spring and early summer of 1875, he decided to join the Dakota gold rush as soon as he earned enough money to purchase supplies. On August 28, 1875, he left Cheyenne with a party bound for the Black Hills gold camps.

There was more dream than reality in his plan. Philip intended to find gold with little effort in the Black Hills. That failing, there was always the lumber business, or he could earn a living from the pelts of poisoned wolves and other predators. Like many early settlers and entrepreneurs, he was willing to take whatever opportunities came to him.

His career as a Black Hills gold prospector was short-lived. A camp he occupied near the original discovery site east of present-day Custer was on land from which U.S. Army units had expelled miners for infringing on areas that rightly belonged to the Sioux. Philip was in a party escorted out to Fort Robinson, Nebraska, and was released after most of his supplies were confiscated. He went to Cheyenne with determination to return to the Black Hills but doubted that mining held the key to success. He wrote his brother George from Cheyenne on October 8, 1875, that he still expected to make "a big thing in the Hills" but urged George not to leave the security of Victoria.[1] In late October, Philip and a companion left Cheyenne, traveling light and away from main routes to the Hills. After losing their horses to Indians, the two separated in an evening raid to get them back. Philip was able to catch his mount and reach Custer on horseback in a train of gold seekers. Again, he was evicted, this time by George Crook on an expedition to clear miners from the Hills in the fall of 1875. Once more he returned to Cheyenne.

The lack of success did not dull his enthusiasm for mining. Philip continued to believe there would be opportunities when he could return. After passing the winter of 1875–1876 doing odd jobs, he came back in mid-July of 1876 and prospected around Deadwood without success. Through the winter of 1876–1877 he drifted from job to job. By the spring Philip abandoned mining, left for Fort Laramie, and hired on as a teamster.

During a trip to Fort Robinson in search of work for the summer of 1877, Philip learned that the U.S. Army was contracting for hay. Creek bottoms in the unsurveyed, unsettled region were full of tall grass for the taking. He formed a partnership with a man named George Clark, purchased stock, mowing equipment, and a hay rack on credit, and contracted to deliver hay at Fort Robinson. The partners lived in a small cabin eight miles north of Red Cloud Agency as they worked.

By the fall of 1877 Philip and his partner were in the freighting business. Using a contract with Red Cloud Agency to secure a loan, they bought a wagon and additional stock and began hauling agency supplies from Fort Pierre to Red Cloud. Philip did scouting part time for the Army out of Fort Robinson. When the first great open range cattle herds came into the region, in the spring of 1878, he took part time work with Edgar Beecher Bronson's Three Crows (range cattle) Outfit.

Apparently, Philip remained undecided about his future in 1878. He had proven he was adaptable enough to survive, but he was far from committed to any enterprise. During the preceding winter, he had written his brother George: "I would like to go anywhere south. At any rate I won't stay another winter in this northern country."[2] In another letter to George he wrote during the summer of 1878: "You spoke of a 1/4 section of land you will file for me. Do it if you can for I intend to come home. This is what I call Victoria."[3] Within a year Philip's situation changed substantially, however, as he made the decision to cast his lot with the shortgrass country between the North Platte and the Missouri somewhere in the vicinity of the Black Hills.

A crowded year from mid-1878 to mid-1879 brought new direction to Philip's life. His freighting business remained profitable. During late summer and early fall he traveled the freight trails from Sidney and Fort Pierre to Deadwood and became increasingly impressed with the ranching potential of the country he crossed. Livestock on a small ranch that Philip acquired seemed healthy. His participation as a scout at Fort Robinson in the capture and confinement of some Cheyenne between October, 1878, and February, 1879, brought additional income and made him a minor participant in a great tragedy for the Cheyenne people.

His marriage influenced the decision to continue ranching. Early in the summer of 1879 Philip wed Sarah Larabee, fourth daughter of Joseph Larabee, a former fur company employee who lived with an Indian wife near the fort. Her oldest sister, Helen, had married Crazy Horse. The other girls, Suzie and Zoe, married non-Indians named Mike Dunn and J. E. Utterback. Sarah, whom Philip called "Sally," had been previously married to a man named Moran and had a son named Louis, or "Posey." The wedding certificate, dated January 1, 1882, bore the names "John Phillips [sic]" and "Sally Larabee." The two moved to Philip's ranch without Posey, who went to live with his mother's relatives.

In his marriage to Sally, Philip found added incentive to remain in the region, for her Indian connection opened new opportunities. Range cattle operations were filling the area between the North Platte and the Black Hills. Lacking capital and livestock, Philip had no hope of claiming enough unsurveyed grassland to acquire room for expansion. As a squatter at his little place on White Clay Creek, he could only control as much area as he could find cattle to graze. Unlike Seth Bullock, with the S-B Outfit backed by capital to hire hands and stock to graze public range, Philip faced the prospect of being crowded out by competition. There was an area, however, in which Philip's marriage to Sally gave him a leg up. The Great Sioux Reservation, which stretched east from the 103rd Meridian and the fork of the Cheyenne to the Missouri River, contained vast tracts of land not open to non-Indian operators. But through marriage to Sally, Philip had the right to occupy an allotment on her reservation. From that quarter-section their ranching operation gained access to thousands of acres of reservation grassland free from competition. The construction of railroads into the new river towns of Chamberlain and Pierre in 1880 gave access to transportation for the shipment of cattle to eastern markets.

By the time he settled on the ranch, Philip had acquired the nickname "Scotty," for his thick Scottish accent. To friends and acquaintances he remained "Scotty" for the rest of his life.

He and Sally settled on Sioux Country in 1881 along the Bad River near the mouth of Grindstone (Butte) Creek east of the present-day city of Philip. The Fort Pierre to Deadwood Trail passed a few miles to the north. The site was well watered and contained excellent grass. Philip's stock completed the trip from the White Clay ranch to Grindstone Creek in good condition.

The Grindstone Creek ranch was ideal. Located near the center of the Great Sioux Reservation, there was little chance for immediate infringement by any ranchers except those enrolled or married into a tribe. In 1881 the Office of Indian Affairs issued an interpretation of policy that prohibited the lease or sale of reservation lands by Whites without the approval of three-fourths of the adult male members of the tribe as stipulated in Article Twelve of the Fort Laramie Treaty of 1868. Shortly thereafter, all non-Indians ranching on the Reservation were ordered to leave unless they could prove marriage to an Indian. James and Sarah Philip were secure with their official marriage certificate in hand.

Soon the cattle industry around them grew. Zoe and J. E. Utterback opened a ranch between the Bad and White Rivers. Suzie and Mike Dunn began to run cattle along the White River. Scotty and his brothers-in-law resisted the organization of stock growers, for they feared the loss of special treatment in the use of land through their marriages to Indian women.

Marriage to tribal members gave them marketing advantage, too. Demand for beef at Indian agencies was reliable because the terms of Sioux treaties required U.S. Indian Field Service employees to keep livestock on hand for slaughter and issue as annuity rations due every enrolled member of a signatory tribe.

Even with ready markets available, cattle operations such as that of Scotty Philip did not expand rapidly enough to use all available range. Repeated efforts to open reservation range land to non-Indian ranching operations were unsuccessful until 1889. Philip purchased some additional cattle in Minnesota and convinced a group of Minnesotans to furnish capital and additional livestock. He provided knowledge of the range and crews to work the cattle. This arrangement, called the Minnesota and Dakota Cattle Company, was formalized in the summer of 1890 as a partnership between Philip and Charles Stube of New Ulm.

Philip's efforts to expand during the early 1890s came in response to change in the status of range land due to the breakup of the Great Sioux Reservation. An act of Congress signed by the President on March 2, 1889, opened approximately 9,000,000 acres between the Cheyenne and White Rivers to non-Indian settlement. Philip's ranch on the Bad River was protected by a provision exempting allotments taken under the 1868 Fort Laramie Treaty from homestead entry, but most of the range land he used was in jeopardy of loss to newcomers. Now he was forced to face competition similar to that which he had faced on the range near Fort Robinson in the late 1870s. By 1889 Philip had some collateral of his own, contacts with capital resources outside the area, and a proven record as a cattleman. His principal problem was competition for the range from big cattle outfits and individual settlers. He had to get big or get out.

Other issues associated with change on the Great Sioux Reservation affected Philip. He was involved in events related to the Messiah Movement and the Wounded Knee tragedy. Evidently, Ghost Dancers living near his Bad River ranch began to take livestock. Federal troops appeared. South Dakota Governor Arthur Mellette recommended to General Nelson A. Miles that Philip be retained as a scout. "I know Philip well and will take his judgment on the situation in preference to anybody I know."[4] Accordingly, Philip served as a scout and courier from Pine Ridge to the Cheyenne River from November, 1890, to March, 1891.

The 1889 congressional act opening Sioux Country created obvious opportunities. The opening of West River land allowed the organization of counties in the area. Stanley County, an unorganized entity since 1873, was organized in 1890. Philip and several associates created the Town of Stanley on 160 acres located partly on a homestead that Philip had filed. It was the temporary county seat. Philip and Buck Williams built a frame hotel. Partisans of Stanley campaigned against Fort Pierre as a permanent county seat during an election on April 15, 1891. Scotty Philip argued that Fort Pierre had no designated courthouse site, but Fort Pierre proponents complained that Philip was not a U.S. citizen. He responded by applying for citizenship before the election. Fort Pierre won by a narrow margin, however, and the town of Stanley went rapidly into decline.

The creation of the Philip Post Office became much more significant. It was established at Scotty's request near his Bad River ranch on April 27, 1891. This postal station was moved several times, but it provided the name of Philip for the townsite when it later became a municipality.

Comparisons of the Philip and Stanley experiences provide some insight into West River town development. The promoters of Stanley had no leverage derived from the previous appearance of a railroad or a county seat and, without such an advantage, could not survive competition from the boosters of Fort Pierre. The sponsors of Philip had only a simple country post office as an attraction until the Chicago & Northwestern Railroad came and insured their town's development in 1906.

Even in the absence of an urban settlement or a railhead nearby, Scotty's stockgrowing activities expanded rapidly through the 1890s into a complicated combination of individual enterprises, joint ventures with friends and neighbors, and partnerships involving investors from outside the region. By 1893 Philip ranged stock from his home on the Bad River northward to Fort Pierre, and to the Cheyenne River breaks northwest of present-day Hayes. In the late 1890s Philip formed the Native Cattle Company, an organization funded by out-of-state investors, mostly from Omaha. The Company imported stock from Texas and sold to the federal government for delivery on Indian reservations. After the turn of the century Philip leased Indian land on the Lower Brule Reservation and ran a cattle operation there under management by Si Hiett.

Philip's expanding interests included business activities outside ranching and a brief career in politics. He bought a home in Fort Pierre and an interest in the Stockgrowers Bank situated there. He traded town lots and other real estate for a profit. When the Chicago & Northwestern Railroad began construction west from Fort Pierre in 1905, Philip leased a gravel pit to the Company and convinced railroad executives to build a spur to his ranch land north of Fort Pierre. Scotty sponsored the drilling of some artesian wells in the area, and spent a good deal of time tinkering with well-drilling machinery. Access to

warm mineral water led to a warm-water heating business in Fort
Pierre and an indoor swimming pool that was featured as an attraction
in the town for many years. There were experiments with large-scale
potato growing, and ditch irrigation using Missouri River water on
Scotty's ranch. He served as a Stanley County Commissioner during
the 1890s, and won election as a Democrat to the State Senate from
Stanley County in 1898.

A pattern that characterized Philip's business activities for the rest
of his life had emerged by 1900. He saw diverse opportunities, but
confined his business activities mainly to ranching and dabbled in other
activities in tentative fashion. Philip's management style may have
been responsible for this. Apparently he kept few records. Several of
his joint ranching ventures were dissolved when he became angry at
partners who insisted on keeping cattle tally books. Frequently he
commented that he could keep better books in his head while watching
his livestock than clerks could maintain when sitting over ledgers in
their offices. A dispute about this issue was a cause of the sale of his
"73 Brand" interests in the winter of 1899–1900.

As his ranching interests grew, Philip delegated increasing responsibility to foremen, but he was never completely satisfied with the
results. His nephew George Philip remembered how ranch crews with
whom he worked had expected Philip to appear anywhere at any time.
Scotty's judgment in choosing foremen was not always good. George
recalled the hiring and firing of one of his uncle's old friends. Tom
Beverly was given responsibility for hiring ranch hands, buying wagons, and assembling supplies and other equipment for a new cattle
operation. Philip left on a cattle-buying trip to Fort Worth. Beverly's
reputation for drinking and unreliability caused experienced cattlemen
to view his appointment with justifiable skepticism. Soon after the
operation was organized, Beverly got drunk. Philip learned of this and
demoted him to the role of ranch hand.

Sentiment and friendship sometimes undermined managerial judgment, but Scotty's image grew as one of prominence in the region.
After reservation lands were opened, Philip became interested in
organizing cattlemen's associations. He helped create the Missouri
River Stockmen's Association, and the Western South Dakota Stock
Growers Association, which later became the South Dakota Stock
Growers Association. By 1900 Philip was a regular participant in
national livestock association meetings. Fellow South Dakota ranch-
man Ed Lemmon recalled Philip's ability to become the center of
attention: "Scotty was of the Buffalo Bill type, a good mixer, much

admired by the ladies, and always a leader in any group he was a part of."[5]

Philip attracted attention with his buffalo herd. In the biography *Scotty Philip: The Man Who Saved the Buffalo*, Wayne C. Lee implied that Philip's purchase of the Dupris buffalo herd saved the animals from extinction. This was doubtful, but it was certain that Philip capitalized on the bison after he bought them. In 1906 cigars went on sale across the United States with the label "Scotty Philip, the Buffalo King, New York, Pierre, San Francisco." The cigar box lid featured a likeness of Philip on one side, and a buffalo bull on the other. Philip's buffalo near Fort Pierre became a tourist attraction; many dignitaries who visited the state capital crossed the Missouri River to see them.

One such excursion became a bizarre chapter in South Dakota history. A delegation of Mexican officials visiting Pierre observed the buffalo and compared them unfavorably to Mexican fighting bulls. Philip and some of his friends were outraged. Controversy led to an arrangement that pitted Mexican fighting bulls against Philip's buffalo bulls in a bull ring at Juarez. A life-long gambler, Philip made large wagers. His buffalo bulls, "Pierre" and "Pierre, Jr.," traveled on a reinforced stockcar in January of 1907. "Pierre" managed to best four fighting bulls with no assistance from "Pierre, Jr.," who was pitted against Mexican bull fighters a week later with similar results.

Philip's reputation as the savior of buffalo was probably inevitable, but other aspects of the relationship gained greater attention. His "last buffalo hunt," with South Dakota Governor Charles Herreid in 1904, gained national attention. It was a successful quest for several old bulls who refused to be driven out of rough country on the Dupris Ranch. According to some accounts, buffalo even came out of the Missouri River breaks to gaze impassively through a buffalo pasture fence during services at Scotty's funeral in the family cemetery.

All of these buffalo-related activities have obscured the fact that Scotty was little involved with saving the buffalo. His herd was gathered by Frederick Dupris, several of his sons, and Basil Claymore on a hunt in the early 1880s. Evidently, the hunt lasted several months, and ranged from Dupris' ranch on Cheyenne River north and west into the Slim Buttes and Little Missouri River areas along the Montana-Dakota border. Eventually the party found a small herd, captured five buffalo calves, and carried them back to the Dupris Ranch in wagons, where they were kept in a specially-fenced pasture. By 1886 this foundation herd had grown to include nine animals. In 1901, when Philip bought the herd, it contained approximately ninety head. It was not the only one of substantial size, but it grew to contain some 900 head, the largest privately-owned buffalo herd in the world at the time.

Scotty became involved in other activities during the final decade of his life. The opening of surplus Indian reservation land to White settlers, and the construction of the Chicago & Northwestern Railroad from Fort Pierre to Rapid City in the years 1905–07, created competition for dwindling supplies of range land. Records in the Stanley County Register of Deeds Office at Fort Pierre indicate that Philip struggled to gain ownership of more land as the West River boom progressed. Land acquisitions must have placed a strain on his financial resources. The land became security for large promissory notes. Eventually, Philip and Sarah controlled more than 10,000 acres of range land, and most of them were mortgaged.

James and Sarah Philip had ten children, five of whom died in childhood or as young adults. In addition to their own children, they raised Scotty's nephew George, whose relationship to Scotty was as close as that of any son or daughter. Sarah was a traditional homemaker who shunned the activity in which Philip was involved. She stayed at home when Scotty and nephew George visited their ancestral home in Scotland. She rarely went along on trips to buy cattle, or to attend stock growers association meetings. Sarah never learned to write; her signature was a mark, usually witnessed by one or more of her daughters on mortgage agreements or land transactions. After Philip's death, the family faced financial crises in the depression of the early 1920s, and Sarah lived quietly in Fort Pierre until she died in 1938.

Circumstances surrounding Philip's death contained some irony. His attempts to preserve the buffalo, elk, and other wildlife, and his zeal for rehabilitating old cowboys, were tinged with romance or nostalgia. This became evident in his family cemetery project. Beginning in 1908 Philip planned and landscaped his own family plot on a site overlooking the Missouri River near his buffalo pasture north of Fort Pierre. From this site, scenes associated with much of Philip's life in West River were visible. Four of his five deceased children were reburied at the cemetery. Philip insisted there be no visitors to the cemetery until landscaping and other work was done to his satisfaction. On the evening of July 22, 1911, he drove into Fort Pierre to announce that work on the cemetery was finished. After midnight that evening, he died unexpectedly of a cerebral hemorrhage. He was only fifty-three years old.

Notes

1. James Philip to George Philip, October 8, 1875, in George Philip, "James 'Scotty' Philip, 1858–1911," *South Dakota Historical Review,* I, no. 1 (October, 1935), p. 13.
2. James Philip to George Philip, November 30, 1877, *Ibid.,* p. 19.
3. James Philip to George Philip, May 13, 1878, *Ibid.,* pp. 20–21.
4. Governor Arthur C. Mellette to General Nelson A. Miles, November 26, 1890, Arthur C. Mellette Papers, South Dakota Historical Resource Center, Pierre, SD.
5. Statement by Ed Lemmon in Nellie Snyder Yost, *Boss Cowman: The Recollections of Ed Lemmon, 1857–1946* (Lincoln: University of Nebraska Press, 1969), pp. 203–204.

M.J. Smiley.

Herding sheep.
From Vallery et al., 1964.

Marketing wool in Sturgis (ca. 1908).
From Vallery et al., 1964.

Pioneering Black Hills Sheepman: Myron John Smiley

Jami Huntsinger

The sheep business has been important to Dakotans since territorial times, especially west of the Missouri River. One pioneer who developed and influenced its growth through early stages was Myron John Smiley. His life story and his business dealings illustrate the beginnings and characteristics of the sheep industry from the early years of statehood to the 1920s.

Smiley, who was known to friends and close associates as "M. J.," was born in Ithaca, New York, on December 17, 1872, to John George and Parmelia Adelaide (Addie) Weed Smiley. He attended Ithaca public school until his father moved west in 1882 to pursue his interest in the livestock business. John, Addie, and their two boys, M. J. and Lee, packed a wagon and headed for Wyoming.

The Smileys settled in the Fort Steele/Rawlins area, where John built up a herd of cattle. A sagging national economy coupled with the overproduction of livestock and glutted international markets soon brought his business to the brink of collapse. Consequently, John was forced to raise vegetables for sale to support the family. In September of 1882 Addie wrote this: "Two or three weeks ago John took a load of turnips to Rawlins, so Lee and I went with him to see the town and for a ride."[1] The sale of vegetables was not enough to keep the livestock business solvent, however, and like many other farmers and ranchers he was forced to abandon his land. The Smileys moved to Omaha and opened a mercantile store.

A frustrating experience with the boom and bust economy was

259

important in the long run. The Smileys learned about livestock production in Wyoming Territory and gained insight into the pitfalls of frontier economy. John and M. J. both fell in love with ranching. Financial failure was a hidden blessing, for at Omaha M. J. had the chance to resume his formal education, and he enjoyed success. In the spring of 1885 Addie wrote about his experience:

> Myron is in school; it commenced Monday. He passed his examinations and ranked highest of anyone in his class. He came home last night and said he had got to have all new books as he goes into sixth grade. I am glad he is so much interested and hope he will be able to make up for the year he was out.[2]

M. J. made up the year he had missed and advanced sufficiently in his studies to qualify for entry into a business college at Stromsberg, Nebraska. Thus an early pioneering experience blended with formal training to generate a degree of business acumen necessary for financial success.

During M. J.'s years in school, his brother Lee died in 1884 of diphtheria and his mother passed away in 1886 due to complications of giving birth. The infant, Bertha, was sent back to New York to live with Addie's sister. John Smiley died in 1894, and M. J. was alone to pursue a career. Saddened by the personal loss but unencumbered by family obligations, M. J. returned to Rawlins in 1893, at age twenty-one, where he worked for others a year or so and later married Catherine Ling. Little evidence survives about their activities except that he invested in the sheep business and "had been ranging his sheep on the Red Desert [in Wyoming], but decided to make a change."[3]

The name of Smiley appeared next in records for 1904, when M. J. moved a great herd toward Belle Fourche, South Dakota. Perhaps the change of location came for the reason explained in George Alton's account of the sheep industry:

> [S]heepmen from Wyoming and Nebraska were looking for new locations because of crowded conditions and poor grass on their home range. The newly opened Black Hills region presented opportunities which owners of both classes of livestock [sheep and cattle] were quick to seize.[4]

Range land west of the Missouri had been tested earlier by sheepmen. A couple of head appeared on an inventory from Fort Pierre as early as 1844 and other small herds were reported from time to time.

When J. D. Hale had trailed three thousand woollies into the Black Hills in 1878, however, he became the first to place a large herd in the area set aside as the Great Sioux Reservation by the Fort Laramie Treaty of 1868 and opened to non-Indians by an Act of Congress in 1876. J. D. Hale's example of success coupled with crowding on grasslands of Wyoming may have prompted M. J.'s decision to enter western South Dakota. The cession of more land for non-Indian entry by the Sioux Agreement of 1889 and the opening of pastures for lease on Sioux reservations in the 1890s made the region more attractive.

Doubtless, pressure from cattlemen was a factor, too. Sheepmen ran their herds in bands or clusters for protection from predators as they moved about or slept at night. Drifting as great herds in this fashion, the woollies cropped or trampled grass, leaving barren ground in their wake. Cattlemen resented apparent devastation to vast areas of open range, which became more crowded every year. In Wyoming, where the Cattlemen's Association was almost as influential as organized government, cattlemen were strong enough to push even the largest of sheepmen out of their state.

M. J. Smiley must have been one of the biggest operators among sheepmen in the West by the time he moved. In the summer of 1904 he owned approximately fifty thousand head, which he drove in bands of about five thousand head each along trails "through northern Wyoming and across southeastern Montana."[5] In good weather, his drovers progressed at the rate of ten to fifteen miles a day. To move ten bands of sheep over so great a distance, M. J. hired numerous sheepherders, assigning them to guide the various bands. He also employed "Mexican gunslingers" to lead the way across the South Dakota border. As Smiley's herds drew near, Dakota cattlemen, who were in competition for almost every available acre of grassland, spread the word:

> Sheep are odorous animals and this odor to a cattleman was worse than that of a 'spice kitty' as cowboys called skunks. It was claimed that cattle would not graze where sheep had been, nor drink from the same water-holes, and that their small, sharp hooves cut the roots of the prairie grass and would ruin the range.[6]

Black Hills cattlemen lined up on the border to block Smiley's entry, and a leader rode out with the intention of intimidating the Mexican gunslingers. Suddenly, a rope swung out across a band of sheep, entangling the lead cattleman, and a Mexican dragged him around the herd until all the cattlemen backed off and allowed M. J.'s herd to pass

unmolested into South Dakota. "Thus by 1905," wrote Alton, "sheep
. . . had spread over the area contained in Fall River, Meade, Butte,
Harding, Perkins and part of what is now Dewey and Corson counties."[7] M. J. was at the vanguard of the movement, as he wintered his
sheep near Castle Rock at a place later called Smiley Springs.

On arrival, he conducted "his operations on a more extensive scale
than ever before, as his income from that source is [was] gratifying."[8]
For the family that followed six months later—Catherine, Florence
Kay, John Clinton, and Robert Alamanzo—he built a three-story home
on National Street in Belle Fourche, elegantly furnished with chandeliers, oak hardwood floors, expensive furniture, and running water.
The house was managed by servants, who did all of the cooking,
serving, and cleaning. The grounds on which the house was built
provided ample space for a large garage that contained M. J.'s collection of five cars, of which he was very proud.

His "gratifying income" was evident both in his conspicuous consumption and in his public life. Often he gave his time as well as his
money to projects for the improvement of the region around him.
Smiley was one of the ranchers who brought pressure to bear upon the
U.S. Bureau of Reclamation to make the Belle Fourche Dam and
irrigation project one of the first ever sponsored by the revolving fund
set up under the Reclamation Act of 1902. M. J. was a prominent figure
in the establishment of the Belle Fourche Round-up. He was a founder
of the U&I Sugar Beet Factory. He was also involved in local projects
and activities, such as founding President of the Commercial Club in
1911, President of the Tri-State Fair and Sales Association, President
of the Butte County Bank, and President of the Redwater Irrigation
District. M. J. was a primary stockholder in the Belle Fourche Cream-
ery, the Smiley-Gay Hardware Company, and the Belle Fourche
Hospital Association. In addition, he was active in the Elks Club, the
Shriners, and the Masonic Order.

Financial success was apparent in the way he supported his children.
Surprisingly, he did not want any of them to take over the family
business. Instead, he urged each one to receive a good education and
learn how to run some business successfully. As entrepreneurial training, M. J. set his boys up in a pony business. They were to be
responsible by feeding and caring for the animals as well as buying and
selling the stock. The boys kept a ledger account, which was approved
by their father. M. J. taught his boys business acumen without ever
involving them in the strenuous work of a sheepman.

The ranch that supported this lifestyle consisted of three main units.

A home place called "Westkota Ranch" was situated six miles east of Belle Fourche. This was a diversified operation on 480 acres:

> Starting with an ordinary set of ranch buildings, he built the farm into a modern dairy and livestock feeding farm. Among the improvements that he constructed were two large dairy barns with electric milkers, two calf barns, two large sheep feeding sheds with self feeding facilities and an elevator, feed grinding, mixing, and storage building. In addition there were granaries, horse barns, and hog houses. Housing on the ranch consisted of two modern dwellings, a bunk house for single employees, and four semi-modern dwellings for married couples. Employees [for this home base] numbered from twelve to fifteen. This farm helped to pioneer the sugar beet industry in the area, and for a number of years prior to the sugar beet growing in this country, he grew mangles, a feed beet for his cattle. When this development was taking place, his motive power was Shire horses—beautiful horses which he prized very highly. At one time the work horses numbered in excess of sixty head. The produce from this 480 acre farm was extensive enough in fed lambs, sugar beets, hay and grains, that the railroad company constructed a siding and stock yards on land furnished by Mr. Smiley, and on which the sugar company later constructed a beet dump.[9]

For his second unit M. J. "leased a large tract of land in the same locality" as Westkota Ranch "which is [was] also devoted to the same business," but was operated under separate management. "A third ranch somewhat farther east near Nisland was also given over to stock."[10]

As spring arrived, all three units were alive with activity. The careful management of lambing and shearing was essential, as Archer B. Gilfillan pointed out in his book *Sheep*:

> Those of you who know the devastation that may be wrought in a hitherto peaceful and well ordered household by the arrival of one little nine pound stranger are asked to stretch your imaginations and envision the arrival of a thousand or fifteen hundred little strangers at one address within a period of twenty days. It sounds improbable, and yet this is what happens every spring on hundreds of sheep ranches throughout the West. It takes place about the time the green grass has become abundant enough to supply the ewes with milk. As might be expected, all other activity on the ranch ceases while lambing is going on. Extra help is hired, extra hours are added to the working day. The days themselves are at their longest and the boss's temper at the shortest.[11]

As the ewes were lambing, M. J. traveled almost continuously between bands of sheep in one of his cars, which was driven by a youth from the Belle Fourche area. It was imperative that he be actively involved, for the lambing season could make or break a sheepman. He had to oversee the pairing of mother with offspring, as George Alton explained:

> [T]here is one basic principle upon which all lambing operations must be founded; namely, that for several days after its birth the ewe knows her lamb only by its smell. It is necessary then that the ewes and the lambs be a part of a small bunch for the first few days because, if a ewe has to smell too many lambs to find her own, her sense of smell becomes confused and she stops searching. If this occurs, the lamb will die.[12]

Pairing was difficult, but sheepmen worked to accomplish the task throughout the lambing season, often without a day off, and more often with little or no sleep.

Of course, range lambing also took place. If a winter was mild, and there was a range full of lush grass to help the ewes produce milk, sheepmen sometimes decided to lamb on the open range. In M. J.'s operation, this was the usual procedure when weather conditions allowed. A sheepherder held together all pregnant ewes in a band. As a ewe gave birth to a lamb, the sheepherder separated the two from the rest of the herd, which he referred to as the "drop bunch." The drop bunch moved on, leaving mother and baby behind to "mother-up." Sometimes a sheepherder placed a teepee-like structure over the mother and baby for twelve to fourteen hours to make sure the mother learned the smell of her lamb. If the mother had twins or triplets, only the strongest was saved; the other baby or babies were killed. Two lambs were unduly stressful to the ewe. If she were left with two or more lambs, all could die.

After lambing there were other jobs. At six weeks of age, all male lambs were castrated. (Smiley imported his rams, which he kept in a separate pool.) The little lambs were separated from the herd, and grabbed one by one. The sheepherder cut the sac surrounding the testicles, pushing it down with his fingers. He bent over, clenched the testicles in his teeth, and with a swift turn of his head he removed the testicles. Supposedly, this was easier on the lambs than was the use of pliers. As part of the same operation, the sheepherder "docked" all of the lambs—cut off their long tails. That prevented the catching of burrs in the tails and diminished anal irritation from diarrhea.

After that came shearing; it had to be accomplished at precisely the right time. The sheep needed their wool to protect them until cold weather passed. In addition, ewes had to be treated carefully while with lamb. Dropping a pregnant ewe to the ground, as sheepshearers sometimes did, could injure both mother and unborn lamb. If the sheep were allowed to become too heavy with wool and roll on its back, it could bloat and die. Shearing had to be accomplished during early summer because in hot weather maggots sometimes infested the wool. Shearing time was also governed somewhat by the location of the sheep. Bagged wool was heavy; it was easier to transport wool from an area close to Westkota Ranch where the railroad siding was located, for instance, than to wait until summer when the sheep were hundreds of miles away on the open range.

M. J. hired large crews of men to shear when his herd numbered fifty thousand head, for the best of them could shear only "100 to 150 sheep a day."[13] A shearer dropped the ewe to the ground. The trick was to hold a manually operated tool as close to the sheep's hide as possible, to shear the wool not in pieces but in large hunks, and to keep from cutting the skin of the ewe. Once the fleece was removed, much care was taken:

> Hand shearers usually tie their own fleeces but machine crews carry an extra man to tie the fleeces. The wool is tied with paper twine so as not to get foreign material mixed with it. [This was important if the producer were to receive top dollar for his wool.] The fleeces are packed into large burlap bags by another member of the crew, the wool tramper. These bags are hung on wooden frames high enough so they do not touch the ground and as the fleeces are put into them the tramper walks around in the bag, tramping them solidly. A well trampled bag of wool weighs from 300 to 500 pounds.[14]

The wool was then transported to the railroad siding and shipped to market.

After lambing and shearing came open range management. Sheepmen like Smiley used vast acreages of grassland. After lambing and shearing, his herds trailed from Belle Fourche through Faith to Eagle Butte. Until the end of summer he kept his ewes and lambs on leased Indian land, and in early fall he trailed them back toward Rapid City.

Once at Rapid City, sorting and marketing procedures were critical. The ewes were sorted. Because many sheepmen shared the open range the brands painted on their ewes were carefully inspected. If a ewe did not have M. J.'s brand, it was returned to the rightful owner. Once the herds were sorted, M. J.'s ewes were trailed back to Belle Fourche, while sheepherders held the lambs for loading into railroad cars and shipment to Sioux City, Iowa, for slaughter. M. J. was personally involved in this entire operation. He even followed the lambs to market in his own railroad car, which contained elegantly furnished sleeping and dining areas.

After sheepherders trailed the ewes back toward Belle Fourche, they prepared their bands for winter between the Moreau and the Grand Rivers. There was good shelter in the area, which was essential because ewes could perish in harsh weather. "Breaking wool" was also a consideration, for unless the ewes were well fed through the winter months the wool growth stunted, limiting its value on the market in springtime. They had to be in good condition at their return to the home place for lambing, too, when the annual cycle began anew.

Sheepherders who guided the bands through an annual cycle all followed standard procedures. As sheep were trailed to prime grazing land, a herder tightened his bands and lighted lanterns at night and placed them in a circle around the band. With help from a sheep dog and lanterns, a herder could discourage predators such as wolves and coyotes. The death of ewes meant lower wool production and fewer lambs.

Because dedicated sheepherders were essential to the success of the operation, M. J. offered to any who remained with him for seven years the reward of three hundred to four hundred ewes to start his own ranch. This plan benefited both parties. M. J. received loyalty and hard work from his herders, and the herders received financial support to open their own ranches. Many a rancher started his business this way. "From these various bands Billy Marty, James Tidball, Ole Locken and others obtained sheep."[15]

Although M. J. Smiley was affluent enough to stimulate the growth of the industry by helping loyal sheepherders into ranching for themselves, he was not immune to financial hardships due to blizzards, springtime floods, and faltering markets. After one such financial setback, M. J. stood outside the Belle Fourche Bank in the fall after the lambs had been sold. He had his hands in his pockets while gazing at the ground when Billy Marty, his former employee, spotted him. Marty was shocked to learn that M. J. was "broke"; he had lost it all! Marty, who owed his own success to M. J., offered fifty thousand dollars, his entire savings. M. J. took it, and by spring he had built his assets back up into an operation worth millions of dollars.

Over the years M. J. lost his fortune several times, only to win it back; however, in 1927, he lost it for good. During the previous winter he had suffered heavy losses of sheep as well as cattle due to harsh weather and heavy snow cover. In early spring, M. J. rode out to assess the condition of his herds. While he searched for his sheep, his horse spooked and bucked him off. As he fell to the ground, his tailbone landed on the saddle horn, and he was severely injured.

The next two years were a struggle. He labored to bring his business back to a solvent condition by mortgaging his land, by selling his Redwater Irrigation investment, and by liquidating his Butte County Bank stocks. All the while his health grew steadily worse. From the effects of injury he became weaker and weaker and, finally, lay dying of cancer. M. J. passed away on July 4, 1929, knowing his business was at the verge of bankruptcy.

What remained of his assets went at public auction on the steps of the Butte County Court House on October 27, 1932. Billy Marty purchased the land, stocks, and all other ranching assets for $83,000, which went to the bank to cover mortgage debts. Katie was forced to sell the house M. J. had built for her, and her youngest son, R. A., spent the next ten years paying the balance of the indebtedness that M. J. left behind.

Several aspects of his experience made him important enough to rank among leaders in South Dakota history. The lure of a bonanza in open range grassland attracted him into West River country soon after the general opening of the Great Sioux Reservation by the Agreement of 1889, and his herders drove in from Wyoming one of the largest herds of woollies ever assembled in this region of the trans-Mississippi West. The role of Mexican gunslingers at the border portrayed his deep involvement in a war between cattlemen and sheepmen for graze, and exemplified the animosity between the two groups that has lingered in the livestock business of the state. Smiley may have lived as lavishly as the Marquis de Mores of North Dakota while his ranching operation was at its zenith, and he gave as generously as the Marquis of his resources toward the development of the region around him.

Perhaps the most striking aspect of his life was how typically it fell victim to the boom and bust economy to which he subscribed. Hundreds of others with smaller livestock operations suffered a similar fate in the same era. James Galette Rogers showed up at Midland on the Bad River in 1906 to purchase land and assemble a herd of some 5,000 sheep in a growing economy over the next fifteen years. While serving as the founding President of the South Dakota Sheep and Wool

Growers Association, he went broke during the agricultural depression
of the 1920s. Like M. J. Smiley, he died of effects from an injury; on
July 4, 1924, Rogers stepped on a rusty nail as he helped a neighbor
pen his sheep for shearing, and died of "lock jaw" at Pierre a few days
later. Soon the sheriff sold his assets at auction on the steps of the
County Court House at Philip, and the Midland Live Stock Loan
Company accepted the properties as compensation for the amount of
$44,323.23 in default. Like Smiley, Rogers became the victim of a
risky business that led him into bankruptcy because of circumstances
almost entirely beyond his control.[16]

Smiley, Rogers, and smaller operators added an important dimension to livestock production, the leading industry of the state. Characterized by some sheepmen as a "hard times industry" that affords
easy entry and abandonment at small investment, sheep production
has cushioned the livestock industry through periods of great economic
stress. Sheep production has also grown to an industry of significant
potential by itself. South Dakota has gained rank as the fifth state in
the nation for mutton and wool production. Belle Fourche remains a
center for sheep culture of national importance, and its emergence
must be attributed in large degree to the efforts of M. J. Smiley.

Notes

1. William Heidt, Jr., *Addie Smiley's Letters from the West 1882–1886*
(Ithaca, NY: DeWitt Historical Society, Inc., 1955), p. 23.

2. *Ibid.*, p. 60.

3. Philip Vallery, et. al., *Pioneer Footprints* (Sioux Falls, SD: Midwest-
Beach Co., 1964), p. 177.

4. "The Sheep Industry in South Dakota West of the Missouri River"
(Unpublished master of arts thesis, University of South Dakota, 1943), pp. 7–
8.

5. Vallery, *Pioneer,* p. 177.

6. *Ibid.*, p. 165.

7. Alton, "Sheep Industry," pp. 13–14.

8. George W. Kingsbury, *History of Dakota Territory* (6 Vols; Chicago: S.
J. Clark Publishing Company, 1915), V, p. 941.

9. Vallery, *Pioneer,* p. 177.

10. Kingsbury, *History, V,* p. 941.

11. (Boston: Little, Brown and Company, 1929), pp. 102–103.

12. "Sheep Industry," p. 37.

13. *Ibid.*, p. 41.

14. *Ibid.*
15. *Ibid.,* p. 13.
16. Herbert T., Karolyn J., and Christopher J. Hoover, *James Galette Rogers: Pioner Rancher at Midland* (Vermillion: Published Privately, 1987), pp. 1–8. The South Dakota Sheep and Wool Growers Association was founded in 1920 as the first major wool marketing cooperative organization in the region. Later reorganized and enlarged to encompass five state cooperative wool marketing agencies, it gave rise to the North Central Wool Marketing Corporation of Minneapolis.

Niels Hansen at Omsk, Siberia (1908).
From Taylor, 1941.

Doctor Hansen standing in grass gathered
in the Caucasus Mountains.
From Taylor, 1941.

Feeding yellow-flowered alfalfa to camels at Semipalatinsk, Siberia (1913).
From Taylor, 1941.

Eminent Horticulturalist:
Niels Ebbesen Hansen

John E. Miller

Niels Ebbesen Hansen and Emil Loriks stood out among agricultural leaders in the history of South Dakota, a state whose economy has depended heavily upon farming and ranching. Born a generation apart, they dedicated themselves to the improvement of agrarian industries, one as a scientist and teacher, the other as an organizational and political leader. Both established national reputations while earning high regard among people in the state. Both were idealists. Both were energetic and indefatigable in the pursuit of their goals. Hansen gained attention for his travels to find better crops and livestock. Loriks obtained a following for his efforts to improve the agricultural economy. They were patriotic sons of immigrants who wanted people elsewhere to understand the strengths of the United States as well as its deficiencies. The two men worked at the left of center on the political spectrum to gain a fair deal for farmers and suffered criticism for being "soft" on Communists—Hansen because of his liking for the people of Russia and personal relationships with its scientists, and Loriks for his political associations with labor leaders, farm organizers, and radical politicians.

From childhood, Hansen was regarded by his teachers as a brilliant student and spent his career in academia researching and teaching the results of his investigations to students in college classrooms, horticulturists across South Dakota, and agriculturalists around the world. Loriks did some high school teaching but decided against a college faculty career, preferring to follow in his father's footsteps as a farmer

271

while he became increasingly involved with rural organizations and political activities.

Niels Hansen's route to South Dakota resembled that of many other European immigrants in that he made several stops along the way before he settled in the state. Born on a small farm near Ribe, the oldest city in Denmark, on January 4, 1866, he retained memories of seven childhood years along the Danish coast before emigrating to the United States in 1873. His mother, Bodil Midtgaard, the daughter of a large landholding farmer, died while Niels was an infant. His father, Andreas Hansen, later remarried to raise Niels and his two older sisters, Helene and Kristine.

Andreas was an altar painter and mural decorator who transmitted to Niels an artistic temperament and a lifelong interest in art. Finding it difficult to pursue his craft where threats of war with Germany upset social conditions, Andreas left for America in 1872 and the family joined him later. They spent three years in New York and New Jersey. Andreas helped decorate a Vanderbilt mansion and assisted with mural decorations at the Philadelphia Centennial Exposition. He moved the family to Iowa in 1876 and worked on decorating the dome, ceilings, and walls of the Iowa state capitol building at Des Moines.

The Hansens spoke Danish at home, but Andreas encouraged his children to learn English from other Americans. A precocious pupil and an avid reader, young Niels finished the first eight grades in five years. As much as reading, he loved to run and explore the woods and fields near his home. He was especially intrigued by butterflies and by all kinds of fruits, flowers, and plants. He loved to play chess and became an expert. He joined a Turnverein club and took up gymnastics and wrestling. At age twelve he wrote his first poem and worked on a novel until his teacher confiscated the first three chapters. "This ended my literary career," he noted later on, but the skill was not wasted. Niels published letters in a children's magazine, wrote poems for a college literary journal, and as a professor at South Dakota Agricultural College wrote a school song entitled "The Yellow and the Blue."

After two years of high school, Niels worked for sixteen months in the office of Iowa Secretary of State John A. Hull, who introduced him to interesting people and encouraged the pursuit of independent study. Privately, Niels took a reading program in literature, philosophy, history, psychology, and six languages. The freedom was exhilarating; "to him all routine was confining and annoying," his biographer noted.[1]

In March of 1883 he enrolled at the Iowa Agricultural College in

Ames, intending to become an editor. Soon he came under the influence of two outstanding educators, Charles E. Bessey and Joseph L. Budd, who directed him down a different path. Bessey presented botany with inspiration from his belief in service-oriented science, providing a model for his young student to follow. Budd, who was known as "the Columbus of western horticulture" for his path-breaking investigations, encouraged Hansen to experiment with new areas of knowledge. Hansen listened carefully as he cultivated other interests. He taught part-time at a Danish Folk School, served a year as secretary to the college president, and published in a literary magazine. He also enjoyed courses in psychology, sociology, literature, and art. Professor Budd praised him as the most brilliant student he had ever taught: "Hansen, you can think of more new things in one week than many can think of in a hundred years."[2]

After graduation came four years of work at commercial nurseries, which enlarged his knowledge about a variety of plants and the practical problems of horticulture. In 1891 Budd summoned him to Ames as a first assistant. While serving in that capacity for the next four years, he worked on a master of science degree in botany and horticulture as he developed a goal that would shape all of his work later on. During a trip in 1894 to Russia and nine other countries, which was arranged by his mentor, Hansen gained exposure to a great variety of plant life and decided to make his mark by bringing diversity to agriculture back in the United States. He toured fields, orchards, and experiment stations across Europe and Russia. Along the way he perceived that the best way to bring hardiness to a plant was not the process of selection alone; "if hardiness is to be gotten into perennial plants, it must be by hybridizing or crossing with some plant that nature through several millenniums has made hardy. Man must work with nature, not against her." He credited the flash of inspiration to reading De Candolle's "The Origin of Cultivated Plants," which asserted that "The northern limits of wild species . . . have not changed with historic times, although the seeds are carried frequently and continuously to the north of each limit. Periods of more than four or five thousand years, or changements of form or duration, are needed apparently to produce a modification in a plant which will allow it to support a greater degree of cold."[3]

It would be better, thought Hansen, to search for sturdier plants able to withstand cold climates through cross-breeding native species with high quality cultivars found elsewhere than to engage in the slow, laborious process of developing native varieties with superior characteristics through gradual selection. On the trip arranged by Professor Budd in 1894 he sharpened this insight. Then he spent half a century exploring its implications.

The new science of genetics was under development across the country. Federal officials, college faculties, and agricultural experiment station personnel cooperated in the search for better plant varieties. Through connections at college, Hansen became a leader in the movement. At Ames, he worked with Professor James Wilson, Director of the Iowa Experiment Station. Wilson supported William McKinley in the presidential campaign of 1896. When McKinley became President, he appointed Wilson Secretary of Agriculture and Wilson used his office to support the pioneering work of Hansen.

Niels completed a master of science thesis entitled "The Crossing and Hybridizing of Our Native Fruits: A Study of Apples" in 1895, and accepted appointment as Professor of Horticulture at South Dakota Agricultural College in Brookings, near the center of the northern country he affectionately referred to as "American Siberia." For the remainder of his life he served as a member of the faculty at Brookings while he won worldwide renown for his scientific discoveries and accomplishments.

In November, 1898, Hansen married Emma Elise Pammel, the youngest sister of Dr. L. H. Pammel, Head of the Botany Department at Ames. With a degree in chemistry and botany, she had taught school in Des Moines and in Wahpeton, North Dakota. To the Pammels, Hansen wrote, "You know that your daughter Miss Emma and I have been corresponding for a long time and that we are good friends. I write this letter now to tell you that I have loved Emma ever since I first met her at Ames and that Emma's friendship has ripened into love. . . . As you know, college professors are seldom wealthy men. I have no fortune to offer Emma but she is willing to keep house in the same modest fashion that is customary among the faculty here and at Ames. My prospects are good and I think we will get along well together."[4]

To Emma he wrote, "I remember your father took me out to the orchard to show me his fruit trees at the time of my visit. Now at all other times I am interested in fruit trees, but that day I wasn't at all interested because I had come especially to see a certain blue eyed girl with a queenly bearing and very good looking. But I had to appear interested in the fruit trees all the same."[5]

Around their house in Brookings Niels and Emma planted trees, shrubs, and flowers to beautify the place. A daughter, Eva, was born in 1899 and a son, Carl Andreas, two years later. Tragically in 1904, while she was expecting another child, Emma died. For several years, the children spent much of their time in La Crosse, Wisconsin, with grandparents and Emma's sister Dora cared for them. By the time Niels and Dora married in 1907, she had taken care of the children so long that to them she already seemed like a mother.

At Brookings, Hansen taught college classes and carried on his research. Meanwhile, U.S. Secretary of Agriculture "Tama Jim" Wilson made one of his top priorities the establishment of a special administrative unit to locate and introduce new plant species from around the world for the purpose of improving varieties native to the United States. Hansen was engaged in the search for hardy varieties of plants that could survive both the cold and aridity of northern Great Plains environment. Wilson needed personnel to send abroad for plant specimens that could be used to improve agricultural productivity. The purposes of the two men meshed nicely. No wonder Hansen was chosen as the first plant explorer to be sent out by the newly created Section of Seed and Plant Introduction. "I have twelve thousand men under me, but none who knows how to work like Hansen," wrote Secretary Wilson. "There is only one Hansen."[6]

Hansen thus became the first in a succession of plant explorers sent out by the Department of Agriculture. Soon to follow were Mark A. Carlton, searching Russia for durum wheats; Seaman A. Knapp, looking for commercial rice varieties in Japan; Walter T. Swingle, collecting in southern Europe and northern Africa; David Fairchild and Barbour Lathrop, foraging through South America; and many others. The idea of introducing plants from other climes and places originated in prehistory among the Indian tribes of the Western Hemisphere, and among Egyptians of Western Civilization. Many grains and other crops grown in colonial America came from Europe. While representing their colonies and a new United States before European courts, Benjamin Franklin and Thomas Jefferson searched for seedlings to send back home for cultivation and experimentation.

Wilson and Hansen built on a well-established tradition as the intrepid South Dakotan set out on his journey in 1897. Hansen's task was to find forage crops and other plants that could flourish in an inhospitable climate on the northern Great Plains. Siberia, Turkestan, and northern China were the principal places of his search. His adventure may have been a subject appropriate for publication in the dime novels that were so popular in his time, but every aspect of Hansen's travel related to scientific discovery. With license to set his own itinerary, he traveled from June in 1897 to March of 1898. Landing at Hamburg, he proceeded to St. Petersburg, went down the Volga, and moved eastward across the Black and Caspian Seas to the Chinese border. He rode horses, walked, and sometimes traveled in a tarantass—a springless wagon that rattled his bones. Everywhere he made observations and inquiries, took notes, and shipped plants and seeds back to Brookings. Hansen was especially interested in finding alfalfa better suited to the northern Great Plains environment than had been the North African varieties introduced to South America three centuries earlier by Spaniards and carried northward into the United States.

To communicate with the citizens, he engaged three interpreters— one to translate Chinese into Tartar, one to convert that into Russian, and another to translate Russian into German, which he could understand. Once he was accused of being a spy but managed to talk his way out of it. Following some delay during the investigation, he learned that alfalfa was grown further northward than he was traveling, but winter was coming on. After 1,300 miles of travel, he made it to Kopol, where alfalfa flourished. Still 700 miles south of Omsk on the Trans-Siberian Railroad, he set out by sledge. A blinding snowstorm and temperatures of fifty degrees below zero temporarily halted the party and almost killed Hansen. After a week of recuperation at a small military post, the party finally made it to Omsk, then headed home. Following him came several carloads of seeds and plants for experimentation by the U.S. Department of Agriculture. Included were the first crested wheat grass in the United States and specimens of alfalfa that grew at a latitude further north than Americans had previously realized it could be grown.

Some bureaucrats in Washington, DC, looked askance at Hansen's informal procedures and resented some of his activities. The hardships of his journey impressed them little, and the publication of his reports was squelched. Some detected in Hansen a penchant for self-promotion, for he was a master of publicity. Indeed, over forty years he built up a loyal following outside as well as within his state of residence among people who admired him for his contributions to science and his service to South Dakota. If he promoted himself, doubtless it was in the cause of advancing professional goals. In his travels around the state, one of his first stops at each town was the newspaper office. The South Dakota newsmen often wrote about his activities. "Between Prof. Hansen and the Electric Short Line the Brookings headline is getting into the dailies pretty regular these days," the editor of the Brookings *Register* noted in 1913.[7] Frequently he was called upon to speak before service clubs and women's societies. Sometimes he was asked to address the Legislature at Pierre. Everywhere he established good will for himself, for the College, and for the Experiment Station at Brookings. Evidently it was the propensity to publicize his activities in other nations as well as his research at Brookings that caused ranking officials in the U.S. Department of Agriculture to withdraw their support for the publication of Hansen's reports.

Nevertheless, federal officials endorsed his travel on another venture abroad in 1906. The Russo-Japanese War of 1904–1905 and the Russian Revolution of 1905 were among factors that caused delay. While waiting, he tramped the Dakota and Canadian prairies in search of hardy wild fruits as he continued doing research on campus. He sent a request to Secretary Wilson in 1905 for Departmental support. Wilson's subordinates opposed the idea, but the Secretary overruled them. That fall, in a speech at the state fair in Huron, Wilson surprised Hansen and his audience with the announcement that there would be a second trip to Asia in search of hardy alfalfa specimens at federal expense.

This trip lasted six months, picking up the search along the Trans-Siberian Railroad. To Hansen's delight, he found that beyond the northern limit of blue-flowered alfalfa a yellow-flowered alfalfa flourished. "This find," wrote his biographer, "was more precious and more priceless than the diamond mines of Africa. Its value to the farmers of the northwest was beyond price."[8] Out of the discovery came the famous Cossack alfalfa. Travel through England, Denmark, Norway, Sweden, Finland, Siberia, Manchuria, and Japan on the same trip netted more than 300 lots of seeds and plants for experimentation.

Hansen now could present justification for a third expedition, the need to collect more yellow-flowered alfalfa seed. The third trip took place over nine months, in 1908 and 1909, and produced the seeds of two yellow-flowered alfalfas. Given a $10,000 congressional appropriation and the freedom to go where he wanted, Hansen planned a route that brought him home through the Mediterranean and North Africa, where he searched for additional varieties of alfalfa.

Now it was time for South Dakota to pay his way. In 1911 the State Legislature appropriated $2,000 for alfalfa research. Two years later the figure escalated to $25,000, of which $10,000 was designated for Hansen's return to Russia. From a trip that lasted five months he brought back several Siberian fat-rumped, tailless sheep, which J. W. Wilson, a son of Secretary Wilson and Professor of Animal Husbandry at the College in Brookings, used to attempt to develop a new breed of sheep.

Eleven years passed before the Legislature sent Hansen back on his fifth expedition—one that lasted three months in 1924. Hardy pears were among the plants he obtained from China. Six years later he toured Western Europe while attending the International Horticultural and Botanical Congresses. His final trip overseas came in 1934 on invitation from officials in the Soviet Union to represent the United States at a four-day celebration sponsored by the Lenin Academy of Agricultural Sciences.

Over the years Hansen focused his attention on almost every plant he could find that was suited to the Great Plains environment. He was undeterred by hazards on the trail of some specific plant group, such as alfalfa, and acquired expertise of amazing breadth. A glance through current seed catalogs provides abundant evidence of the value of his search. For years his discoveries were advertised and sold by the Gurney Nursery in Yankton. Often his picture appeared in advertisements that carried information about his proven varieties. Among Hansen's contributions listed in a recent Gurney catalog were the Dolgo Crab and Anoka Apple; the South Dakota Plum as well as the Tecumseh, the Sapa, and the Kaga; bush cherries; Tartarian Honeysuckle; the Siberian Pea Shrub, or Caragana; the Hopa Flowering Crab; sand cherries; hedge roses; and the Manchu apricot.

His energy was boundless. Besides traveling abroad, teaching classes, and directing Experiment Station research, he visited frequently around the state to supervise ongoing research operations. He laid plans for a landscaping project in Watertown, gave advice for plantings around the new state capitol in Pierre, formed exhibits at the Brookings County Fair, lectured at farmers' institutes, judged fruit displays at the State Fair, and assisted with flower shows at Sioux Falls. Hansen lent his services to the state and local communities for myriad projects. Clubs and organizations extended invitations for speaking engagements. Lectures about his Asiatic explorations were especially popular. He used lantern slides to illustrate talks about his journeys and researches. He did not feel obliged to hew closely to his special areas of expertise. On one swing through Aberdeen he addressed the Social Science Club on the subject, "A Psychoanalytic View of the Russian Situation"; lectured on "Evolution as Guided by Man" at a convocation at Northern Normal and Industrial School; and at a noon meeting of the Lions Club discussed "The Sublimation of the Libido."[9]

Hansen attended scholarly meetings and conferences both in and out of state. For thirty-three years he was a fixture as Secretary of the South Dakota Horticultural Society, and served as President for three years before becoming President Emeritus of the organization. Frequently, he addressed or presented papers at the Minnesota State Historical Society, the Missouri Valley Society of Horticulturalists, the American Pomological Society, the American Congress of Horticulture, the National Dry Farming Congress, the American Society for the Advancement of Science, and other scholarly organizations. Somehow he found time to manage all the responsibilities associated with teaching, research, and service at the College. He supervised research on plant varieties at the greenhouse, which was said to be the first of its kind ever built, and spoke often at biweekly chapel sessions (assemblies) for faculty and students.

Hansen visited Canada, North Dakota, and other states many times. After his last tour abroad, he made yearly pilgrimages to follow the first buds of spring northward from Oklahoma to Canada. He would be on hand to gather pollen to pollinate other varieties in experimental crosses, which he followed up on with the help of labels carefully tied to the twigs so apples could be identified properly when harvested in the fall. It was all painstaking work but the kind Hansen reveled in. Onlookers were not surprised at seeing a white-bearded professor pop into their orchards at almost any time of year to see how crosses were progressing. Strangely, he never learned how to drive a car but relied on his son Carl, his grandson, numerous students, or various others to do the driving.

Carl used the experience of many trips with his father to set himself up in the nursery business at Brookings in 1922. He sold many of the varieties his father had helped develop, specializing in hardy fruits and shrubs. He and his wife, the former Gladys Manbeck of Armour, had four children. The Hansens' daughter Eva married David Gilkerson in 1921. They ran a dairy farm near Armour from 1921 until 1944, and for six more years near Brookings before retiring. They had four daughters and a son.

At Niels Hansen's home in Brookings, pots of apples simmered on the stove as samples to be tasted by the master of regional horticulture. Dora superintended the activities but left the rest of the research up to her husband, having, in the words of one magazine writer, "long ago ceased to be disturbed over her husband's wanderings, either abroad or at home."[10] In his later years, Hansen was an inveterate movie goer, enjoying B-grade thrillers and arty films the most. He liked to walk three or four miles a day. He had a reputation of being quite a dancer. He knew a great deal about Indian culture, possessed enormous admiration for tribal civilization, and gave some of his new plant varieties Indian names. He became a member of Kiwanis and an active participant in the activities of the Episcopal Church. Dora hosted meetings of the St. Paul's Guild at their home on the southeast corner of Eighth Avenue and Ninth Street, two blocks west of the College campus.

Bookshelves lined the walls of his home. Stacks of magazines cluttered the floor. Omnivorous reading tastes he acquired as a youth never flagged. Piles of magazines, books, and scientific bulletins filled his office. Retirement to emeritus status in 1937 did not slow him a bit; a reduction in teaching duties only allowed more time for research and study. During the thirties and forties, as people became more and more concerned about Stalin's tight control over the Soviet system, Hansen's expressions of good will for fellow researchers in Russia and his unwillingness to accept the fashionable anti-Communist line annoyed some South Dakotans. But he was by that time such an institution in the state that no one could bring him discredit.

His inquiring mind probed questions to the day of his death at the age of eighty-four on October 5, 1950. The "Burbank of the Plains" had transformed the ecology of a major physiographic region of North America. A sparkling personality with commitment to community and state had enriched Brookings and South Dakota for more than half a century and had left an abiding legacy for the state's most important industry.

Notes

1. Mrs. H. J. Taylor, *To Plant the Prairies and the Plains: The Life and Work of Niels Ebbesen Hansen* (Mount Vernon, IA: Bios Press, 1941), p. 9.

2. *Ibid.,* p. 12.

3. William P. Kirkwood, "The Romantic Story of a Scientist," *World's Work,* XV (April 1908), p. 10110.

4. N. E. Hansen to Mr. and Mrs. Pammel, April 28, 1898, in possession of David and Naomi Gilkerson, Brookings, SD.

5. Letter, N. E. Hansen to Emma Pammel, May 1, 1898, in possession of David and Naomi Gilkerson, Brookings, SD.

6. Taylor, *To Plant,* p. 19.

7. Brookings *Register,* December 4, 1913.

8. Taylor, *To Plant,* p. 29.

9. Brookings *Register,* February 23, 1922.

10. Arnold Nicholson, ''Burbank of the Plains,'' *Country Gentleman,* CX (December 1940), p. 55.

Emil Loricks.
Courtesy Sioux Falls Argus Leader.

Dust drifts along the south side of Lake Byron during the 1930's.
Courtesy Richardson Archives, USD.

Agrarian Exponent: Emil Loriks

Elizabeth Evenson Williams

Carl Emil Loriks created a legacy in public service on behalf of farmers and ranchers before he died at age ninety on Christmas morning in 1985. He exerted strong influence as a state legislator and farm organization leader from the 1920s to the 1960s. After retirement he spoke out on a wide variety of issues and wrote voluminous correspondence to ordinary citizens as well as to political leaders.

Loriks was born on the farm of his parents in Kingsbury County between Arlington and Oldham on July 18, 1895. His father, Carl Loriks, was a Swedish immigrant who entered Dakota Territory at the beginning of the Dakota Boom, worked on a crew that built the Chicago & Northwestern Railroad to Pierre, and filed his claim on a homestead. Because the Loriks family conversed exclusively in Swedish, Emil did not learn English at home. But "I mastered English quickly" after starting school, he recalled, and later he refined his grasp of proper usage with practice in public speaking.[1]

The final year of high school was not available near his home, so Loriks finished at Huron while boarding with an aunt. He also spent five years at Eastern Normal (Dakota State) College in Madison, South Dakota, then enrolled at the University of Nebraska and earned a baccalaureate degree in agriculture before the United States declared war on Germany in 1917. With his degree in hand, he trained as a biplane pilot in the U.S. Army but saw no combat duty because the war ended before he could get to Europe. On his return after discharge, Loriks turned down the chance to teach at Eastern Normal College in Madison and moved to the family farm. He married Ruth Dahlen, the

Oldham postmistress, in 1924. They had one daughter, Ruth Ann, in 1930.

Two years after his marriage, Loriks entered public life as a Democratic member of the South Dakota State Senate from Kingsbury County, in "the election surprise of the state."[2] Before he resigned from the seat in 1934, he became involved with the Farm Holiday Association as its leading organizer and Executive-Secretary. Legislative duties and Farm Holiday activities were closely intertwined; through both affiliations, Loriks worked continuously to improve conditions for the rural society he represented. After entering the Senate, "I sensed the lack of representation that agriculture had," he recalled. "As a farmer, I knew what their gripes and their needs were. I had the feeling that farmers weren't adequately represented and that they had an inferiority complex."[3] Because they were emerging from a post-war agricultural depression, they had grave economic problems, too, which were not resolved before they entered the Great Depression a few years later. In the legislature, Loriks sponsored no particular bill designed to alleviate the distress of his constituents but, after Democrats gained control in 1932, he served as Co-chairman of the Joint Appropriations Committee that charted a course of austerity for state government through depression times.

Recognizing that state officials could do little for rural people in distress, Loriks sought to defend their interests through the colorful Farm Holiday Association. President Franklin Roosevelt declared a bank holiday to save the banking industry of the United States from collapse. Agricultural leaders borrowed Roosevelt's nomenclature and called for a moratorium or holiday on farm foreclosures until new marketing strategies and production quotas could raise agricultural product prices enough to save the business of farming and ranching from bankruptcy. In his history of the South Dakota Farmers Union, Robert Thompson described the movement after it came out of Iowa to sweep across East River communities:

The Farm Holiday in South Dakota never became well organized in the strict sense of the word at any level, local, state or national. It was made up from, and supported by, five separate state organizations. From each one of these organizations came one member to make up the board of directors of the South Dakota Farm Holiday. The membership included the Farmers Union, the Grange, the Farm Bureau, the South Dakota Chamber of Commerce, and the Bankers Association. Emil Loriks, who was vice president of the South Dakota Farmers Union at this time, was selected by the directors to be the executive secretary, a post he held until he became president of the Farmers Union.

Taking the board of directors as a whole, the membership and the organizations they represented comprised a somewhat conservative element. The conservative blending showed itself in many ways in the activities of the South Dakota Farm Holiday when compared to the movement in other states. Except in a few isolated cases in South Dakota, it was more conservative than one would expect from such an organization.[4]

According to Thompson, Emil Loriks said that in South Dakota the Association was invited by some merchants to come into their counties to bring the discontentment of farmers under control. Evidently the strategy was successful; historian John Miller called the movement one of "Restrained, Respectable Radicals," in a recent article.[5] Miller went on to say that Holiday participants in South Dakota were more restrained than those in Iowa due to the quality of leadership supplied by Loriks and others in participating organizations.

Loriks and South Dakota Farm Holiday President Barney McVeigh, who had been Republican Speaker of the South Dakota House of Representatives during its 1931 session, insisted that farmers not seek "class legislation," although literature distributed by the state Farmers Union organization suggested otherwise. That Loriks was a Democrat and McVeigh a Republican gave the Association a moderate tone as well as a broad appeal. Loriks logged thousands of miles in his own car during 1932 and 1933, driving from town to town to organize local meetings. He was active in the role of mediator between farmers with delinquent loans and lending agencies seeking repayment. Miller observed that "Loriks' delicate position in the organization and his desire to retain credibility with both sides in disputes led him to avoid penny sales, but he was informed about them when they did occur."[6] "Cooperation with Main Street businessmen was a frequent theme of Emil Loriks, and the methods used by him and his colleagues in the Holiday movement to attract resources and support constitute the final explanation for the general moderate tone" of the South Dakota Holiday.[7]

That McVeigh, the President, and Loriks, the Executive Secretary and principal organizer, were both members of the South Dakota Legislature brought "circumspection in their actions."[8] For example, as a public official, Loriks opposed violent picketing, but he acknowledged that peaceable pickets might be necessary if other means of protest were unsuccessful. During an interview for the *South Dakota*

Union Farmer in 1978, Loriks admitted some tactics used by Holiday participants may not have been legal, but they were "the only expedient way to dramatize the farmers' plight so that the nation would be aware of the seriousness of the situation."[9] Evidently, he and McVeigh worked often at the fringe of legality, sometimes using spirited rhetoric or even veiled threats in their effort to prevent a general movement of constituents into such radical camps as that of the Communist-affiliated United Farmers League.

Loriks was far more comfortable in his leadership role after he became South Dakota Farmers Union President in 1934, following the elevation of E. G. Everson to the national Farmers Union presidency. This liberal organization had been founded by the newspaperman Isaac (Newt) Gresham of Texas near the outset of the twentieth century. A South Dakota chapter was established in 1914. Within its ranks the national Farmers Union always had a "split personality—with one group within the organization having faith in the power of farmers to work themselves out of the agricultural dilemma by encouraging the growth of cooperative marketing, while the other group felt there had to be major federal assistance."[10]

In the South Dakota Farmers Union there was a similar, ideological division. According to Thompson, some members favored cooperative marketing strategies free from government involvement while others called for helpful legislation. Personally, Loriks sided with the former group; despite some rhetoric to the contrary, he supported a free enterprise credo. Publicly, however, he gained a reputation for his role in introducing a change of tactics on state legislation; by the "introduction of a vigorous legislative program, Loriks began to work for more harmony by supporting desirable legislation and actually formulating a legislative program."[11] His blend of government support and cooperative action was described in the *South Dakota Union Farmer* during 1942, after his election as national Farmers Union Secretary-Treasurer:

> During the many years Loriks was state president of the South Dakota Farmers Union, he never chose the easy, negative road of blind denunciation and fault finding. He did not waste his time merely talking about our problems. Loriks is a positive personality, a builder, a man of action. He led the fight against the powerful Hearst interests, resulting in an ore tax of over a million dollars a year for the state of South Dakota collected from the Homestake Gold Mine. Other legislative victories followed, resulting in lower taxes and lower interest rates, all designed for the benefit of the family type farmer.

Acting in harmony with his conviction, he launched a most ambitious program of building cooperative oil companies during 1934, 1935 and 1936, just at the time our people were hardest hit by drought, grasshoppers and hard times.[12]

Loriks's fight for a tax on gold ore at the Homestake Mine was a push for equity in the distribution of wealth that gained publicity for him and other Farmers Union spokesmen. For their visible roles, Loriks and Oscar Fosheim were dubbed the "Gold Dust Twins." In the depths of farm depression during the 1930s, when the agricultural economy suffered gravely, the Homestake Mining Company flourished because of profits from gold sales under the new Gold Reserve Act of 1934. "The Company sold sixteen and a half million dollars worth of gold and its corporate stock reached $430 a share from a pre-Depression level of $50."[13] Farmers Union leaders called for a severance tax to extend some benefits to more depressed parts of the economy:

The ore tax bill was introduced in the Senate by Emil Loriks during the 1933 session. Oscar Fosheim introduced an identical proposal in the House. Although neither bill was enacted, Farmers Union officials were determined to secure an enactment at the next legislative session and continued their campaign to that end. . . . Loriks insisted that the mining interest had removed over $300,000,000 from South Dakota gold mining but had never paid one cent of tax on this production. He insisted that the state legislature was controlled by "Special Interests," which thus far had made the enactment of ore tax legislation impossible. When the legislature refused to enact an ore tax measure, the Farmers Union carried the fight to the people to arouse the electorate into action. The Union members circulated an ore tax petition which proposed an initiated bill if the legislature should again fail to enact an ore tax law. . . . Legislative members closely identified with the two major political parties hesitated to assume any leadership for ore tax legislation but the Farmers Union kept the issue before the public.

Representative Oscar Fosheim, then vice president of the South Dakota Farmers Union, introduced the ore tax bill again in the 1935 legislative session. This time, after a long and bitter fight, the measure was enacted. . . . Under provisions of the measure, gold, silver, tin and all other minerals in the state were taxed on the basis of four percent on the value of the ore mined. . . . During the session of 1937 the tax was increased to six percent.[14]

In a single year, $750,000 collected from the Homestake provided one third of the state's operating budget.

From farm organizational service in his native South Dakota, Loriks moved into other arenas, one being political during an unsuccessful bid for a seat in the U.S. House of Representatives when he ran against Republican Karl E. Mundt in the election of 1938. Loriks' defeat was followed by his service as state, then regional, administrator for the New Deal Farm Security Administration.

Major emphasis for the second half of his public service career, however, was on the goal of the Farmers Union Grain Terminal Association (GTA), which he helped to found while he was still President of the state Farmers Union. Loriks joined the board of directors of GTA in 1940, as it became the world's largest grain marketing cooperative organization. From 1957 to 1967 he served as GTA President, assuming a position of regional importance. Annual reports during his ten-year tenure as President reflected continuous expansion. There was, for example, the acquisition of "the world's largest processing plant for soybeans and flaxseed" at Mankato, Minnesota.[15] In the 1960 report, which announced the close of operations for the Association after twenty-two years, Loriks remarked:

> We must not let our pride paralyze us. It is a demonstration of what farm people can do. . . . GTA was not built by timid souls, nor by those who are fearful of the future and believe only in maintaining the past. GTA was built by men of vision and courage, with a determination to go forward, to move ahead, to keep abreast with the new area. . . . This may seem like a bold vision, but its success is likely to depend on how well each of us do our part in planting the idea of peace through abundance in our own land, so that the world can reap the harvest.[16]

Loriks went on to explain the need for both a cooperative approach to marketing and a political process to bring about favorable change in agriculture. In his 1961 annual report, he said, "We must have a political, as well as economic, awareness. We must know how to use our coops. And above all, we must understand that farm prices are made in Washington."[17]

Loriks believed Americans should assist each other and should reach out to help others:

> We must find ways to use this nation's enormous productive agricultural capacity to provide for an expanded abundant life in other nations, as well as in our own nation.
>
> Our agricultural resources can be weapons for peace. We can substitute the tools of production for the tools of destruction.[18]

To that end, he labored more than thirty years toward "a change from concentration on marketing to the new era of diversification and expansion in the processing of grain. . . . GTA has been transformed from a grain commission and storage operation into an integrated marketing and processing enterprise."[19]

Loriks was successful in agricultural leadership in large measure because of his skills as a communicator. Speech-making started early in his career and, during his term as South Dakota Farmers Union President from 1934 to 1938, he gave biweekly addresses over radio station WNAX in Yankton. He presented annual convention addresses and spoke often to small groups. Loriks was a fiery orator who relied heavily upon emotion. This was evident in the radio tribute he gave to Senator Huey P. Long, who was widely regarded as a testy demagogue, after Long had been shot:

Is the assassin's bullet, the cross, or the hemlock ever going to be the reward for faithful service to humanity? Since Socrates was forced to drink the fatal hemlock, Jesus Christ crucified upon the cross, history has been a chronology of such events. Our own Abraham Lincoln, the Great Emancipator, was murdered at the hands of an assassin. Today, the outstanding friend of the downtrodden, the exploited, the destitute, lies at death's door.[20]

He spoke with similar passion as he pronounced against corporation barons on behalf of poor farmers. "Those who own America (the Morgans, the Hearsts and the Mellons) are the dominant economic interests and they also control prices. They are the exponents of the profit system. They make laws, they declare war—Anything For Profit!" Loriks went on: "We must build a new economic order through cooperation. We can build this right within the present structure, without violence, without bloodshed and without the sacrifice of human lives."[21]

In his fight for a tax on gold ore in 1935, Loriks lashed out at the "Hearst-Homestake interest":

We have had a taste of it in South Dakota—how the dominant economic interest (the Hearst-Homestake mining interest) situated in one county has dominated our state for half a century.

Today we behold Hearst in the role of America's Facist [*sic*] No. 1 with the largest newspaper empire in the world to promote the selfish, avaricious cause of a decadent capitalism. Hearst is leading America on the road to Facism [*sic*], to capitalistic dictatorship.

South Dakota is helping to nourish this beast whose tentacles reach into every corner of the land. . . . Do you know that this gold is helping to nourish the Hearst Octopus to finance his poison propaganda to be spread through the columns of the largest newspaper empire in the world?[22]

The same theme was evident in a similar address some three decades later: "If we permit corporations, chains and monopolies to take over our political life, then our hopes for survival will indeed go glimmering."[23] That he drew inspiration from Populist leader William Jennings Bryan was clear enough when he spoke before the 1937 Convention of the South Dakota Farmers Union: "Shall we crucify mankind upon the Cross of Profits, or can we save mankind through economic democracy?"[24] In this same speech, there was Populism in his approach to government:

We have a right to ask the federal government for aid and assistance in times of great emergencies such as drought and flood and other catastrophes beyond our control. It is the duty of government to come to the aid and assistance of any area that is so stricken![25]

In the traditions of Populist philosophy and emotion, Loriks carved a niche in state history for a steady performance in farm leadership. Longtime South Dakota Farmers Union President Ben Radcliffe put it succinctly in 1985: "Emil Loriks has been both a leader and a stabilizer. . . . He knew how to be aggressive and outspoken without alienating others who might not agree with him. In the end, more often than not, Emil's judgment proved sound. It would be hard to separate the man, Emil Loriks, from the history of South Dakota agriculture during the past half-century."[26]

Notes

1. Emil Loriks to Elizabeth Evenson Williams, September 4, 1972.
2. Gerald Lange, "Americanism over Radicalism: Mundt's First Election, 1938," in *Selected Papers of the First Nine Dakota History Conferences 1969–1977* (Madison: Dakota State College, 1981), p. 312.
3. Interview with Emil Loriks by Elizabeth Evenson Williams, July 19, 1982.
4. Robert S. Thompson, "The History of the South Dakota Farmers Union,

1914–1952," (Unpublished master of arts thesis, University of South Dakota, 1953), pp. 54–55.

5. John E. Miller, "Restrained, Respectable Radicals: The South Dakota Farm Holiday," *Agricultural History*, LIX, no. 3 (July 1985), p. 429.

6. *Ibid.*, p. 440. "Penny sales" referred to the practice of farmers attending foreclosure auction sales and banding together to bid pennies for the foreclosed farmer's holdings. The holdings were then returned to the bankrupt owners.

7. *Ibid.*, p. 444.

8. *Ibid.*

9. Betty Burg, "Emil Loriks: Family Farm Trailblazer," *South Dakota Union Farmer*, September, 1978.

10. Theodore Saloutos and John D. Hicks, *Agricultural Discontent in the Middle West, 1900–1939* (Madison: University of Wisconsin Press, 1951), p. 238.

11. Thompson, "Farmers Union," p. 29.

12. *South Dakota Union Farmer* clipping, n.d.

13. Robert F. Karolevitz, *Challenge: The South Dakota Story* (Sioux Falls: Brevet Press, Inc., 1975), pp. 259–260.

14. Thompson, "Farmers Union," pp. 77–80.

15. Emil Loriks, "The President's Report," *The Annual Report for 1960*, Farmers Union Grain Terminal Association, St. Paul, Minnesota.

16. *Ibid.*

17. Emil Loriks, "A Report to the Members," GTA *1961 Annual Report*.

18. *Ibid.*

19. Emil Loriks, "Report of the President," *GTA Digest*, December, 1967.

20. Emil Loriks, "Farmers Union State President Pays Tribute to Huey Long Who Was Genuine Friend of Humanity," *South Dakota Union Farmer*, September 18, 1935, p. 1.

21. Emil Loriks, "Report of the State President," *Minutes of the Farmers Union Educational and Cooperative Union of America (South Dakota Division)*, Sioux Falls, South Dakota, October 13–15, 1936, pp. 6–7.

22. *Ibid.*, pp. 7–8.

23. Emil Loriks, notes for a 1962 speech to grain meeting at Brady, Montana, Loriks Papers, Center for Western Studies, Augustana College, Sioux Falls.

24. Emil Loriks, "State President's Report," *Minutes of the Farmers Educational and Cooperative Union of America (South Dakota Division)*, Huron, South Dakota, October 12–14, 1937, p. 5.

25. *Ibid.*, p. 8.

26. Interview with Ben Radcliffe by Elizabeth Evenson Williams, January 6, 1985.

*Francis Case holding South Dakota
Highway map (with U.S.S. South Dakota
in foreground). Courtesy Loren Carlson.*

*Karl E. Mundt (behind Lyndon Johnson's left shoulder) at swearing in of Joe Bottum as
U.S. Senator. (Administrative Assistant Loren Carlson third from right.)
Courtesy Loren Carlson.*

Platte-Winner bridge across the Missouri River.
Courtesy Richardson Archives, USD.

I-90 and I90 interchange north of of Rapid City.
Courtesy Richardson Archives, USD.

The Republican Majority:
Francis Higbee Case and Karl E. Mundt

Loren Carlson

Francis Higbee Case and Karl E. Mundt had similar careers as Republicans in South Dakota politics. Neither ever held an elective position in state or local government. Both began in the United States House of Representatives and later served in the United States Senate. Both voted with isolationists in Congress on international affairs until the Japanese attack on Pearl Harbor, after which both vigorously supported the entry of the United States into war. For two decades thereafter, Case and Mundt worked together as leaders of the Republican majority in state politics as well as in the South Dakota congressional delegation.

Francis Case was once called "the ideal Congressman."[1] His campaigns were conducted in a folksy, personal manner. He was a hardworking, conscientious member who took pride in typing his own weekly news letters. Among peers he earned the reputation of being a "comma-chaser" for his attention to detail. A man of simple tastes and intense loyalties, Case introduced new ideas and worked on countless projects to benefit South Dakotans. In self-deprecation, he once called himself "just a water and roads Senator."[2]

He was born in Everly, Iowa, on December 9, 1896, the son of Reverend Herbert and Mary Case, In the family of a Methodist minister, he moved to Sturgis, South Dakota, at the age of twelve, in 1909. He had three sisters (Joyce, Caroline, and Esther) and one brother (Leland).[3] The Reverend Case moved later to a pastorate at Hot Springs, where Francis graduated from high school and from there

293

went on to earn a baccalaureate degree in history from Dakota Wesleyan University at Mitchell in 1918.

After graduation, Case joined the U.S. Marine Corps and began a long and warm association with the government of the United States. In 1937 he received the commission of Lieutenant in the Corps. The previous year he entered the U.S. House of Representatives, where he served until 1950, when he moved to the U.S. Senate. There he served until his death in 1962.

After World War I Case enrolled at Northwestern University and earned a master of arts degree in history as a means to the development of a professional career. To finance study in a doctoral program he became assistant editor of the *Epworth Herald*, a Methodist newspaper. The experience whetted his appetite for journalism, and soon he left doctoral studies and returned to West River South Dakota where he became a part-owner and a reporter for the *Rapid City Journal*. Case sold his interest in the *Journal* three years later and, with his brother, Leland, acquired the *Hot Springs Star*. Some six years later they sold the *Star* and acquired the *Custer Chronicle*.

Journalistic experience led Case into the promotion of numerous causes and countless projects that he pursued throughout a long political career at the forefront of a post-Norbeck, moderate Republican movement in the state. He was almost obsessed with boosting the Black Hills. The most successful of his promotional schemes was having Calvin Coolidge spend the summer of 1927 at the Custer Game Lodge. Case had written numerous editorials urging the President to make the Black Hills a summer White House. U.S. Senator Peter Norbeck and U.S. Representative William Williamson joined the effort by extending their personal invitations. Coolidge accepted and later made history by announcing from his Black Hills retreat: "I do not choose to run."[4]

On many other occasions Case drew attention to the Black Hills. He was instrumental in getting President Dwight Eisenhower to visit. He joined Karl Mundt in the promotion of the Rapid City area as a prospective headquarters site for the United Nations. He worked for a "Christ on the Mountain" statue near Spearfish. Cooperating with U.S. Senator Chandler Gurney, he was successful in the location of the U.S. Army Air Base, later named Ellsworth Air Force Base, at Rapid City. Case played an important role in getting federal appropriations to complete Mount Rushmore. Through untiring effort, he arranged the location of a cloud-seeding experimental project at the South Dakota School of Mines.

The face of the state changed immeasurably because of him. Numerous bridges, national guard armories, flood control and irrigation projects, and federal highway improvements may be attributed to Case's success as a member of the Senate Public Works Committee, where he served as Chairman of the Roads and Highways Subcommittee. While a member of the Senate Armed Services Committee, Case had a key role in the Minuteman site selection in Western South Dakota. His work in arranging the construction of Fort Randall Dam has been recognized by his name on the reservoir as well as on the bridge across the Missouri River west of Platte. The name of Francis Case also appears on the auditorium at Hot Springs and on buildings at Sturgis and Ellsworth Air Force Base. Even the Washington Channel bridge on I-395 in Washington, DC, was named in his honor.

Legislation he co-sponsored with Senator Burton Wheeler of Montana opened two irrigation projects—Deerfield in Rapid Valley and Angostura on Cheyenne River south of Hot Springs. Because of him, dams were constructed at Pactola above Rapid City, Shadehill on the Grand River, and Bixby on the Moreau. General Lewis Pick, Chief of the U.S. Army Corps of Engineers, complimented Case for "attracting his attention to the possibilities of the Missouri River" at a Rapid City meeting in 1941.[5] In his capacity as a member of the House Appropriations Committee, he helped obtain funds for the construction of the five dams authorized by the Flood Control Act of 1944. Case stated in 1946 that he had spent more time and effort on Missouri River development than on any other single thing since he had entered Congress.

Early in his congressional career Case earned a reputation for overcoming strong opposition in the passage of legislation. Senator Mike Monroney of Oklahoma, for example, credited him as being the "moving spirit behind the War Renegotiation Act which resulted in billions" in fiscal recoveries from cost-plus contracts negotiated by the federal government.[6]

Roads and bridges became symbols of the soft-spoken Senator's numerous contributions to his state's transportation system. The construction of Interstate Highways 29 and 90 across South Dakota came about in large degree because of his work as a freshman Senator in 1956. Harry McPherson, a staff aide of Senator Lyndon Johnson, credited Case as the builder of the Interstate Highway System which he called "a monument . . . of our productive genius."[7]

Despite the many contributions he made over two decades in Congress, Case and his supporters began to meet a serious challenge in

1956 when he faced the popular young farmer Ken Holum from Groton in the election. An agricultural depression combined with drought presented a political problem to every western incumbent Republican. The Democratic Party rebounded from the disastrous election of 1952, when Dwight Eisenhower and an entire slate of state Republican officeholders had been elected. Indeed, only two Democrats served as legislators in the 1953 South Dakota legislative session. Thereafter, Republicans quipped that "the Democrats could hold their caucus in a phone booth." After a low-key campaign in 1956, during which Case often found himself defending Republican policies, he emerged as a narrow victor. His margin was only 4,620 votes in a total of 290,622. That year the Democrat George McGovern unseated the incumbent Harold Lovre to enter the U.S. House of Representatives.

In 1958 Republican fortunes slipped further when the Democrat Ralph Herseth won election as Governor over Phil Saunders, the husband of Case's niece, Lois Wilson. Most state constitutional offices and seats in the South Dakota Senate went to Democrats. By 1960, however, the farm revolt had passed. Republicans recaptured the governorship, all of the constitutional offices, both houses of the Legislature, and all four seats in Congress.

In 1962, Case perhaps would not have had any opposition in the primary election had not a heart attack in March led to speculation that his health would not permit him to endure the rigors of a political campaign. With ease, he defeated A. C. Miller, the State Attorney-General and longtime politician from Lyman County. Case's health remained suspect. The fall election loomed large. With support from the White House, George McGovern supplanted former Lieutenant Governor John Lindley at the last minute as the Democratic candidate for the U.S. Senate, setting the stage for a major challenge. Case suffered a fatal heart attack, however, and died on June 22, 1962, after brief treatment at the U.S. Naval Hospital in Bethesda, Maryland.

To his death, Case liked to consider himself a moderate Republican, even though others viewed him as a conservative. He was a strong advocate of projects that involved generous federal spending, especially for South Dakota. Working with Karl Mundt from leadership positions, particularly membership on the Senate Public Works and the Senate Appropriations Committees, Case wielded enormous power on Capitol Hill. He always prided himself on being fiscally responsible. To those who criticized his support of so many projects in South Dakota, he replied that when the money was allocated to states under cost-sharing, or for public works and military projects, his obligation was to get a fair share for his own constituency.

This complex, quixotic, unpredictable man was known for his integrity. He wrote poetry and took pride in his literary and oratorical skills. He typed his own newsletters to the time of his death. He expressed concern about the condition of American Indians from the time of the very first bill he introduced as a member of Congress in 1937 and over the years amassed a voluminous file of letters that sought to redress Indian policy mistakes and administrative errors.

Even more prominent was his work on conservation, and for this he was regarded as a "progressive."[8] Raised in arid Meade County, his interest in water projects was almost instinctive. Before the 75th Congress, in 1937, he said:

> When every ranch has permanent stock water and a watered garden, our folks will get by these dry years. We are adjusting our herds to the amount of summer range and winter feed. Let us store our run-off waters and we will be willing to take our chances on the years as they come.[9]

Subsequently, the Flood Control Act of 1944, coupled with legislative efforts in desalination and weather modification, became evidence of Case's lifelong dream of "a dam, some trees, and a prairie garden for every farm."[10]

The legislative record alone earns Case a place in history among leaders in South Dakota's congressional delegation—one similar to that of Richard Pettigrew, Peter Norbeck, Karl Mundt, or George McGovern. This alone, however, does not reveal the qualities of the man in public service. As a legislative assistant through his last years, the writer was continuously exposed to dimensions of political life about which little information is preserved in documents. Some examples may be instructive.

Case was aware of the potential threat Governor Herseth posed to his re-election in 1962. Under South Dakota law, Herseth was prohibited from serving more than two successive two-year terms following his election in 1958. This appeared to place him on a collision course with Case. Threatened by a close margin of victory in 1956, when West River votes saved him in the late hours, Case was sensitive to the valuable opportunities that could strengthen his support in other parts of the state. Early in 1959 he set in motion some political wheels that led to the construction of the bridge over the Missouri River reservoir west of Platte. The site of the Wheeler Bridge, located some fifteen miles upstream from Fort Randall, had been inundated by the reservoir after the Bridge had been floated upstream on barges to Chamberlain, where it was put in place beside an older bridge to accommodate four lanes of traffic across the Missouri on U.S. Highway 16. In May, Case wrote to officials in the Corps of Engineers suggesting that surplus bridges upstream scheduled for removal from reservoir sites at Mobridge and Whitlock's Crossing might be installed as a replacement for the Wheeler Bridge to carry traffic between Platte and Winner. In his letter, he pointed out that the Fort Randall crossing was inadequate compensation for the loss of the Wheeler Bridge because it forced travelers to drive many extra miles. General Wilton B. Person replied that the cost of moving the surplus bridges was too high. It would be cheaper to build a whole new structure. The State of South Dakota and the Corps had entered into a contract on April 5, 1949, however, by which Governor George T. Mickelson agreed to the construction of Fort Randall Dam together with state responsibility for highway and bridge modifications resulting from the creation of a reservoir. Accordingly, the Corps had no obligation for the construction of an additional bridge.

In July of 1959 Case wrote to Commissioner Ellis L. Armstrong of the Bureau of Public Roads and asked for copies of all memoranda exchanged between the Bureau and the State Highway Commission regarding the responsibility of the Corps of Engineers for providing an adequate crossing to replace the Wheeler Bridge. Armstrong replied that there was no such agreement in the files. Case wrote E. F. McKellips, Secretary of the State Highway Commission, asking for the same information. McKellips replied there was no firm agreement.

When the Senator received a copy of the 1949 contract from the Corps of Engineers, he studied it and concluded that it did not specifically deal with the Wheeler crossing. In September of 1959, Case told S. D. Wright, editor of the *Platte Enterprise*, that he would bring this up next year in the Public Works Committee as an amendment to the Omnibus Flood Control bill under consideration. I recall that Case was cognizant of strong Democratic leanings among constituents in the area around Platte, especially in Charles Mix County, which was considered one of the strongholds of the Democratic Party. Governor Herseth had apparently commented in a local appearance that a crossing at Platte was needed.

When Congress reconvened in 1960, Case put in a bill to fund the construction of such a new bridge at the cost of $6,375,000, the estimate of the Corps of Engineers. He knew that Corps personnel would oppose the bridge and asked his staff to assemble data for its support. We contacted Chambers of Commerce in Platte, Winner, Parkston, and even Sioux Falls, knowing we had to find economic justification for such a large expenditure, which was not in the President's budget. The Sioux Falls Chamber of Commerce was especially helpful. Because the Fort Randall crossing routed truck traffic near the southern border of the state, livestock from West River would be shipped to Sioux City rather than Sioux Falls. A crossing at Platte, on the other hand, would make the Sioux Falls livestock market the most accessible and economical destination. We developed estimates of the miles driven to cross from West River either at Fort Randall or at Chamberlain and compared them with the distance across the Missouri near Platte. The advantage of a new bridge near Platte was obvious.

Meanwhile, the bill had been routinely referred to the Bureau of the Budget for comment. On March 1, 1960, the Bureau's interim report said the Fort Randall crossing was adequate and gave a negative report on the bill. A few days later, the Secretary of the U.S. Army made an opposing statement. Usually, the combination of negative recommendations by the Bureau of the Budget and the Corps of Engineers would have doomed any legislative proposal.

Case refused to take "No" for an answer. With a powerful ally in Senator Robert Kerr of Oklahoma, a wealthy oil man and Chairman of the Public Works Committee, Case began his legislative "end run." Kerr operated from a strong power base. Case did the nitty gritty work of negotiating and drafting the committee report. The Senate Public Works Committee document of June 6, 1960, contained this language: "We, the Committee, believe that a crossing at the Wheeler site is economically justified and the Committee further believes that local interests should construct the necessary approaches."[11] The bill passed the Senate in this form, and provision for a Platte-Winner Bridge was inserted into the Omnibus Flood Control bill.

When the bill went to conference, there was strong opposition from the House tacitly backed by personnel of the Corps of Engineers and the Bureau of the Budget, and I remember negotiations orchestrated by the Bureau of the Budget. Deputy Director Elmer Staats, later named U.S. Comptroller General, visited Case's office and told the Senator that the Eisenhower Administration could not authorize construction because "It's over the President's budget and there is some question as to whether we're even obligated to do this in face of the Corps agreement." Case called upon Kerr for assistance. He had a conference with Budget Director Maurice Stans. Case told me that he asked Stans: "How much would the Administration go for?"[12] Stans responded that if the cost were lowered to $4 or $4.5 million, the Bureau might go along with the project. Already, Case had conferred with state Bridge Engineer Kenneth Scurr and learned that he felt the estimate of the Corps was high. Scurr had designed a similar bridge at a lower cost. Stans apparently felt there was little chance his offer would be accepted, for he had only the Engineers' estimate of $6.75 million in hand. Surely Case would not want to build only part of a bridge. The Senator surprised him, however, when he agreed to the $4.5 million without hesitation. He enjoyed telling this story—of how he gambled that the bridge could be built for only $4.5 million.

A few days later the conference committee agreed but stipulated that the state must assume any cost in excess of $4.5 million and pay for the construction of approaches to the bridge. On July 14 President Eisenhower signed the bill into law. There was still work to be done. The bridge site was not on the highway system. Case called upon a former South Dakotan, Senator Clinton Anderson of New Mexico, to have highway approaches written into a state system that qualified for federal aid. The South Dakota Legislature approved a bill, written by Senators James Ramey and F. E. Manning, to provide matching funds as partial payment for the approaches.

Case was still worried that Corps of Engineers personnel would sabotage the project—that the Corps' bridge plan would come in with a high bid, which would force a supplemental appropriation. Since there was by then a new national Democratic administration, Case was fearful the proposed bridge at Wheeler might be doomed. He convinced Corps personnel that the State of South Dakota, represented by his ally and friend Kenneth Scurr, should design and build the bridge. The Corps agreed.

Inasmuch as the Corps had opposed a replacement for the Wheeler Bridge, its spokesmen had no detailed plans for a bridge or even a probable site. A small delegation from the Corps came to Case's office to seek his advice and approval for a location. Large maps were spread over the desk in the Senator's office. Using a ruler and a sharp eye, Case picked the location, which appeared to be the shortest distance across the reservoir. His was anything but a scientific decision.

The project was let to contract a few months later. Formal groundbreaking took place on July 17, 1962. The Senator's untimely death in June denied him the opportunity to enjoy any political benefit. I have no doubt that his success with the Platte-Winner Bridge would have won over support in an otherwise Democratic area to assure his reelection. At his death, the Senator knew, however, that his meticulous work had arranged a vital crossing between East and West River, South Dakota, over the Missouri River reservoir bearing his name.

He was as careful about answering constituents as he was about legislative strategy. More often than not, they sent copies of single letters to every member of the congressional delegation. Nevertheless, Case wanted their correspondence answered accurately and completely; he was not satisfied with a form letter of acknowledgement. Once he told me that he was more interested in having the *best* response, not necessarily the *first* response. Careful research and draftsmanship were his long suits and he demanded the same from his staff.

This caused frustration for a legislative staff that prepared mass mailings. Countless drafts were submitted, returned, rewritten, and often delayed for days or weeks. By then, the letter would have to be revised because the situation had changed. Case did not believe in the value of mass-produced correspondence anyway. He wanted to put his personal imprint on every letter. During my three years in his office he never accepted a signing machine like the ones that came into use among other Senators at the time. Rather, he laboriously signed each letter and often added a personal note. At the least, he crossed out a formal salutation and wrote in the addressee's first name.

Much of the correspondence a Senator receives is service mail. Constituents write about problems with federal agencies, regulations, or interpretations. Most of these are sent to the offending agency for a response. Naturally, a letter from a Representative or Senator is given more attention than one from any constituent. An elaborate congressional reply system exists in each agency to deal with inquiries in writing. Sometimes, a phone call is made to obtain a quick answer. Agency personnel do not like to admit their mistakes. The odds of reversing an agency decision are one or two in a hundred. Case knew this. Yet, he also understood that if he wrote an agency's decision in his letter, the constituent would look upon the Senator as the bearer of bad news. By sending a letter from the agency with his cover letter, he avoided direct association with an unfavorable response. His letter would point out how disappointed he was with the outcome. Invariably, he offered to pursue the request further if he felt there was a chance for success. On those rare occasions when the agency reversed its position in favor of a constituent, Case's personal letter would only cite excerpts from correspondence of the agency and would reserve credit for the Senator himself.

Sheer political power was exercised when South Dakota "stole" the interstate. Case had been impressed by the German Autobahn as a defense system when he served on the Herter Committee after World War II. With Americans buying cars in record numbers and with deepening suspicions about the intentions of the Soviets, the time was ripe for a national, four-lane highway system. Dwight Eisenhower established the Clay Commission, which recommended a 40,000 mile interstate system under a bill entitled the National Defense Highway Act. At the time, Case was the ranking minority member on the Public Roads Subcommittee of the Senate Committee on Public Works, which conducted hearings on the National Defense Highway Act.

A proposed map showed a highway crossing the state (I-90) served by a branch route from Sioux Falls to Sioux City (I-29), but there was no provision for a four-lane highway into North Dakota. Case bided his time, supporting the administration's bold road plan. He had penciled in a Sioux Falls to Fargo route, however, on his personal copy of the map. After some adroit lobbying of the federal highway administration on a South Dakota trip and enlisting the assistance of Senator Robert Kerr, Case pushed through an amendment that added a thousand miles to the original 40,000 mile system.

Meanwhile, Senator Hubert Humphrey, a leader in the Democratically controlled Congress, worked to move the I-29 extension to Fargo into western Minnesota. Humphrey was not a member of the Public Works committee, however, and did not have the Kerr connection. It is perhaps no accident that Oklahoma and South Dakota got the lion's share of interstate extensions. I-29 north of Sioux Falls was scheduled for construction in South Dakota. As a bonus, the I-229 bypass was approved around Sioux Falls, making it one of the smallest cities in the country to enjoy such a luxury.

Tucked away in Case's kit of future plans was an interstate connection to the state capital. I recall his working with the Pierre Chamber of Commerce on a connection with I-90 at Vivian, for he thought all state capitals should be on the interstate system. It was a source of irritation that South Dakota's capital was one of the very few in the nation not served in this way.

Case left this and other projects undone when he died, but he earned the eulogy of Senator Albert Gore, leading Democrat from Tennessee, who rose to say that he doubted "the (interstate highway) bill could have been written or enacted" without the work of South Dakota's "water and roads Senator."[13]

U.S. Senator Larry Pressler has called Case's senatorial colleague

Karl Earl Mundt a "superb politician and an unbeatable votegetter."[14] For his tenure in the U.S. Congress over a third of a century, Mundt set a record in South Dakota. He served five terms in the House of Representatives and four in the U.S. Senate. This remarkable record of support came mainly through his reputation as a public speaker, a conservationist, and an agrarian spokesman with Populist leanings.

Mundt was born in Humboldt, South Dakota, on June 3, 1900, the only son of Ferdinand and Rose Mundt. His grandfather, Johann Mundt, was a Methodist pastor who had emigrated to the United States in 1868 and settled in the small northeast Iowa community of Girard. The Senator's father was a South Dakota businessman with interests in real estate, investments, banking, and insurance whose penchant for politics is evidenced by his voluminous letters and speeches on political subjects. While under this influence, Karl attended high school in Bryant, South Dakota, and went on to earn a baccalaureate degree at Carleton College in Northfield, Minnesota, in 1923. There he was active in oratory and debate, making speeches that emphasized religious themes or focused on pacifism and the abhorrence of war.

After graduation he returned to Bryant High School, where he taught speech and social studies, and served as the Principal. A year later Karl became Superintendent, and his wife, Mary, took the office of Principal. From these positions, Karl and Mary improved their institution while Karl published tracts that boasted the quality of teaching in Bryant and extolled the virtues of education.

Following the completion of a master's degree in speech at Columbia University in 1928, Mundt joined the faculty at Eastern Dakota Normal College in Madison, which later was named General Beadle State Teacher's College, then Dakota State College. Besides teaching, Karl worked as a junior partner in his father's business, the Mundt Loan and Investment Company. A political career became a logical outgrowth of his growing reputation as a public speaker. In 1930 Karl gave public addresses on behalf of U.S. Representative Royal Johnson. In 1933 he helped organize the Young Republican League. Meanwhile, Mundt became a member of numerous lodges, clubs, and associations, often serving in positions of leadership. In 1931 he accepted his political novitiate as a member of the South Dakota Game and Fish Commission by appointment from Governor Warren Green, and during a six-year term on the Commission Mundt won national recognition as a speaker and writer in support of conservation.

At last in 1936 his national political career began when he ran for Congress against the incumbent Democratic Representative Fred H.

Hildebrandt. Despite the presence of Franklin Roosevelt on the ticket and the continuing agricultural depression, Mundt came within 2,800 votes of unseating his opponent. In 1938 his long streak of victories in South Dakota congressional contests began when he defeated Emil Loriks, the Farmers Union activist who could boast a state legislative triumph in increasing the ore tax on the Homestake Mine.

In the 1938 campaign Mundt aligned himself with the progressive wing of the Republican party that had been developed by the late Peter Norbeck. From the 1936 campaign he also bore a commitment to isolationism through his support of U.S. Senator William Borah for the presidency. By his victory in 1938, too, he became a central leader in the resurgence of Republicans more conservative than himself that brought them back into control of the South Dakota State Legislature and all of the state's constitutional and congressional seats.

As a freshman in Congress Mundt began his career by casting his votes against a mandatory draft bill and the Lend Lease Act. He claimed to be neither an isolationist nor an interventionist, but an "insulationist." His goal was to avert the entry of the United States into war. This view changed, however, with the bombing of Pearl Harbor. Mundt became a vigorous supporter of the war effort and a careful student of international affairs. With appointment to the House Foreign Affairs Committee in 1941, Mundt began to shift his focus to international relations. Later he would support the Fulbright resolution urging post-war international cooperation and U.S. participation in the United Nations Relief and Rehabilitation Adminstration.

Mundt was assigned to a special investigating committee under the Chairmanship of U.S. Representative Martin Dies of Texas. In this service, particularly at the 1948 hearings on charges of spying against Alger Hiss, he first gained the national limelight. Later, cartoons of the historic event covered the walls of his senatorial office. Mundt emerged as a national political figure, along with Richard M. Nixon, upon Hiss's conviction for perjury. Mundt and Nixon also teamed up to co-sponsor the controversial Internal Security Act of 1950, which was passed over the veto of President Harry Truman.

Concern about international Communism and its infiltration of federal agencies led to the passage of the Smith-Mundt Act. It was a unique coalescence of the South Dakotan's interests in education, patriotism, and internationalism. The Act established the U.S. Information Agency as the successor to the wartime Voice of America and provided for an exchange of scholars. The goal was to counteract Soviet propaganda initiatives.

Mundt's influence in international policies diminished sharply after he left the House Committee on Foreign Relations by his election to the U.S. Senate in 1948. U.S. Senator Harlan Bushfield suffered a stroke and early in the year announced he would not be a candidate for re-election. This set the stage for Karl Mundt. He won handily and, by the early resignation of Bushfield's wife, who had been appointed by Governor George T. Mickelson to serve out her husband's term after his death, Mundt began his career in the U.S. Senate a few days early. That gave him seniority over others who entered the Senate by the same election.

Mundt used his office as a forum for some proposals that never came to fruition. He pressed for a Freedom Academy, which would establish a school to train Americans in the methods of cold war and guerilla tactics. His bill passed the Senate in 1960, but the House took no action. Despite subsequent efforts and the enlistment of bipartisan support, his various bills failed to win. By the time he gained enough seniority for a seat on the prestigious Senate Foreign Relations Committee, times had changed and his dream of the Freedom Academy was lost.

Mundt attended his first NATO Parliamentarians' Conference at North Atlantic Treaty Organization headquarters in Paris during 1961 and was honored with an assignment to the Cultural Affairs and Information Committee. This coincided with his interest in the International Exchange Act, which he co-authored. When Mundt became Chairman of the Conference on Cultural Affairs, he selected Professor William O. Farber from the University of South Dakota as his principal aide to develop a NATO Foreign Service Academy. Successful seminars in public administration for NATO public servants were held in 1969 and 1970 in Brugges, Belgium.

Mundt worked in foreign affairs at an historic period for international communication. I once traveled to Washington, DC, from Sioux Falls on the same plane with him. At the old Joe Foss airport, a high school student who had won a trip to the national capital also boarded our plane. At the approach, her parents recognized the Senator and asked if he would help her make connections in Chicago, and see that she made it safely to her destination. Mundt was happy to oblige. When we arrived at O'Hare Field in Chicago to transfer to another airline, we walked several blocks through the terminal. Moving along corridors that were lined with temporary plywood partitions, the young lady asked: "Senator, are they just building this airport?" Mundt responded: "I've traveled all over the world and every airport in the world is under construction."

Mundt's election to the Senate coincided with Truman's surprise victory over Thomas E. Dewey. Fresh from experience on the House Un-American Activities Committee, the South Dakotan brought with him a conviction that the Communist threat required attention. Although his views paralleled those of Joe McCarthy, Mundt eventually served as temporary Chairman of the Permanent Investigating Sub-Committee when McCarthy stepped down to be a prosecuting witness. The hearings, which began in the spring of 1954, were covered on live television by the major networks. Mundt gained national prominence for his role as Chairman even though the hearings were inconclusive. Before a committee report was complete, a resolution was introduced to censure Senator Joseph McCarthy for "bringing the Senate into disrepute."[15]

Arthur Watkins, the Republican from Utah, headed a select committee to consider the resolution, and Francis Case was a member. Case supported while Mundt opposed the censure. Years later, while writing about his first quarter century in Congress, Mundt said this was his most difficult assignment ever. "This experience made the tough spot of chairing the Hiss-Chambers episode seem easy by comparison."[16]

While Mundt had attained national stature as he gave his attention to legislative investigations, he also found time for the interests of agriculture and his South Dakota constituents. He kept in close contact through a weekly newsletter and a radio show entitled "Your Washington and You." This resulted in abiding support from constituents, despite the agrarian depression and drought of the 1950s, and brought him victory in the election of 1960.

The challenge came from George McGovern, who had just finished two terms in the U.S. House of Representatives. The young Democratic historian built a political career by concentrating upon the plight of farmers and ranchers under the policies of Ezra Taft Benson, Dwight Eisenhower's U.S. Secretary of Agriculture. Both Mundt and McGovern were members of Agriculture Committees in Congress. Mundt claimed support for his constituents equal to that given by McGovern and claimed to share with Francis Case stern opposition to Benson's farm policies, which had brought crop parity payment levels down.

An important feature in the campaign was a series of three debates. The challenger felt he was the clear winner of the first one in Sioux Falls: "I just slaughtered him," McGovern boasted. Mundt was the apparent victor at the second debate, in the Huron Arena, where the hall was packed with the advocates of both candidates.[17]

The McGovern-Mundt contest of 1960 was in ways a microcosm of the presidential contest between John Kennedy and Richard Nixon. McGovern actively campaigned for the Kennedy-Johnson ticket while Robert Kennedy came to Watertown in the effort to help McGovern. Polls had shown Nixon in the lead with sixty percent of the support of South Dakota voters even though McGovern held an edge over Mundt. Yet the incumbent won by 15,000 votes, while Nixon defeated Kennedy in the state by some 50,000 votes.

Mundt's influence in the South Dakota Republican Party was evident during the interregnum between the death of Francis Case on June 22, 1962, and the appointment of Lieutenant Governor Joe Bottum as interim U.S. Senator on July 10, 1962. Even before the final rites were held for Case in Rapid City, there was discussion about whether the interim Senator chosen by Governor Archie Gubbrud should merely be a caretaker to fill out an unexpired term for approximately six months or should assume the role of candidate for a full six-year term. The name of the widow of Francis Case came up, but she had never been active in the Senator's public life. There was a suggestion made that I, as Case's Administrative Assistant, might be appointed. I demurred that I felt honored but reluctant to consider this at a time before the Senator's burial. Indeed, as a staff member involved in arrangements with the Sergeant-at-Arms of the U.S. Senate for the funeral and memorial services, I was deeply offended. Case had mentioned the former Governor Sigurd Anderson and U.S. Congressman Ben Reifel as possible successors while he recuperated from his first heart attack, and they were given careful consideration. Gubbrud declined the suggestion that he might appoint himself and resign as Governor. For some time, the issue was under debate.

At length, the politically saleable argument advanced by Karl Mundt was accepted. Gubbrud delayed appointing a successor until after the meeting of the Republican Central Committee, which held responsibility for filling vacancies in the state party ticket for the fall election. More than one hundred members went through twenty ballots before they chose Joe Bottum over five other candidates. When Bottum arrived in Washington, DC, Mundt ushered him to the Senate for swearing in by Vice President Lyndon Johnson. I accepted the request to remain as Bottum's Administrative Assistant and other members of the staff of Senator Case stayed on with me.

Mundt and his staff were helpful. The Senator and Bob McCaughey, his long-time Administrative Assistant, became Bottum's main advisors on strategy and tactics for the campaign against George McGovern. In the latter stages of the McGovern-Bottum race, a rumor circulated that Bottum and his wife, Nellie, were alcoholics. For a time, Bottum ignored the accusation on advice from his campaign staff and advisers. He thought it was unfair, however, privately attributed blame to McGovern, and belatedly decided to go on the attack. McCaughey suggested he should give a Nixon-like "Checkers" speech, recalling that this approach had saved the Californian's renomination for Vice President in 1956. Accordingly, a self-pitying television appearance by Bottum was aired a few days before the election. Many political experts felt the speech backfired, and in retrospect thought it a major factor in Bottum's defeat.

After the defeat by Mundt in 1960, McGovern had been appointed by John Kennedy as Director of the Food for Peace program. His late entry into the 1962 senatorial race was believed to have been at the urging of White House advisors whom, it was suspected, had made the decision based on inside medical information about Case's deteriorating health.

Mundt counseled Bottum on what might be expected from McGovern, now that he enjoyed the blessing of a sitting President, and the veteran Senator himself joined the political fray after Congress adjourned late on October 13, 1962. By this time, the Cuban missile crisis had become an issue and Bottum tried to use it to his advantage by demanding a blockade on October 9. McGovern responded by calling Bottum a self-styled, arm-chair general, and warned that a blockade could lead to war.

Meanwhile, McGovern had become ill and was sidelined from the campaign; one *Argus Leader* editorial noted this "unhappy and sad development," which "required his hospitalization in Sioux City."[18] He cancelled many scheduled appearances and was forced to conduct a campaign from bedside. His advisers announced that Ethel Kennedy, wife of Attorney General Robert Kennedy, would come to South Dakota to campaign on his behalf while he was "recovering from a recent illness."

The Cuban crisis became McGovern's ally. On Monday, October 22, the President went on national television, announced that Soviet missile bases had been established in Cuba, and disclosed a seven-point program of action, including a naval blockade. Karl Mundt reacted by saying that the blockade was late in coming. Yet, he joined both Republican and Democratic congressional leaders in support of

President Kennedy. At this point McGovern seized the opportunity to demonstrate close ties with the White House by announcing that he was "enroute to Washington for consultations on the international crises and emergency planning of food reserves."[19]

Mundt and other strategists in the Bottum campaign grew suspicious. McGovern had not been able to campaign due to his illness except for occasional appearances on television and radio; hence, they could not believe that the ailing candidate was up to a flight to the national capital. A top Mundt aide in the Washington office, James Smith, was alerted to have incoming flights from Minneapolis and Chicago monitored to see if McGovern actually appeared. The watch continued without success until McGovern's press release appeared in the Thursday, October 25 *Argus Leader*. It contained an unusual statement from Minneapolis, where he retracted an earlier remark that implied he had been called to a White House conference, and McGovern admitted he had called Secretary of Agriculture Orville Freeman and offered to come to Washington for a one-day conference session on emergency food policy. The release explained that a friend had picked him up Tuesday morning in a private plane and that he had flown by commercial airline to Washington and back. The meeting with Freeman had lasted only two or three hours before his return to Minneapolis. The release implied that McGovern had also called at the White House for discussions.

Mundt led a campaign attack, charging that another press release by McGovern had implied he was called back for conferences at the White House when he had in fact invited himself. Using inconsistencies in the releases, Republican campaign aides became more convinced than ever that McGovern's illness may have prevented his ever leaving Minneapolis. Because no one had seen him in Washington, it seemed unlikely that he ever made the trip, for McGovern was a well known public figure who knew how to attract attention. Bottum's staff aides debated the risks of charging that McGovern had not gone to Washington but, instead, had issued self-serving press releases. Mundt cautioned that the White House staff would cover for him. Such a charge could back-fire. In the end, the use of McGovern's suspected ruse was abandoned.

It was weeks after the campaign when I was talking with the candidate's staff member. "Did McGovern really go to Washington?" I asked. "No, but we didn't think anyone would ever find out," he replied, "or if they did it would be too late to affect the election." A KELO newsman later confirmed my suspicions, claiming that a picture, supposedly released at the press conference in the Minneapolis Airport showing McGovern with Secretary Freeman at the conference, was an old file photo. In any event, McGovern became Mundt's seat-mate in the U.S. Senate after narrowly defeating Joe Bottum in the 1962 election.

Mundt handily won re-election to an unprecedented fourth term in 1966. Recognizing his long and distinguished service, President Nixon came to Madison, South Dakota, on the Senator's birthday in 1969 to dedicate the Karl and Mary Mundt Library on the Dakota State College campus. Karl Mundt's public career came to an end a few months later when he suffered a disabling stroke from which he never fully recovered. Most serious was his inability to speak. In the fall of 1970, after Governor Frank Farrar's defeat by Richard Kneip, there was an effort to have him resign so Farrar could appoint a successor. Despite pressure from his long-time Administrative Assistant Bob McCaughey and from Senator Barry Goldwater and other Senators, neither Karl nor his wife would accede. Mundt remained in the office until his term expired on December 31, 1972.

One of the major accomplishments of that interim period was the location of the Earth Resources Observation Station (EROS) Data Center near Sioux Falls. The Mundt staff, headed by McCaughey, worked closely with Nixon's White House advisers, Senator Milton Young of North Dakota, Governor Frank Farrar, and Sioux Falls promoter Al Schock. The placement of EROS in South Dakota was dictated partly by geography but even more by desire for a tribute to Mundt for his long-time work on the Senate Appropriations Commit-tee.

In 1971 Republican leaders made the unprecedented move of reliev-ing Mundt of his committee assignments because there was no chance for his recovery. On August 16, 1974, he died, leaving no children behind. He was buried in Madison near the campus of Dakota State College, the site of the Karl and Mary Mundt Library. Mary Mundt died in 1985.

No two political leaders have had greater impact on the affairs of South Dakota than Francis Case and Karl Mundt. If one were to take a satellite picture of the state today, their imprints would be evident. There would be patches of green irrigation plots on the fringes of the Black Hills, blue-water lakes behind earthen dams on the Missouri, and white ribbons of interstate highways crossing the state. These are the legacies of two men who dominated the South Dakota political scene through the Republican Party for a third of a century.

Notes

1. Larry Pressler, *U.S. Senators from the Prairie* (Vermillion: Dakota Press, 1982), p. 140.
2. *Ibid.*
3. Francis Case Re-election Brochure, 1962. Copy in possession of Author. Case was proud of his family and its achievements, noting these at length in a legend appearing beside an old photograph taken at the homestead in Meade County. Case was especially close to his brother Leland, who was for many years editor of *The Rotarian,* later editorial director of Methodist Publications, and of *The Pacific Historian.* In 1944, Leland Case was the originating force behind "The Westerners," an organization of history buffs devoted to the preservation of the history, lore, and legends of the vanished frontier. See article by Leland D. Case, "The Westerners: Twenty-five Years of Riding the Range," *Western Historical Quarterly,* I (1970), pp. 63–76.
4. Pressler, *Senators,* p. 140.
5. Richard R. Chenoweth, "Francis Case: A Political Biography," *South Dakota Historical Collections,* (1978), p. 321.
6. *Memorial Addresses Delivered in Congress in Eulogy of Francis H. Case* (Washington: U.S. Government Printing Office, 1962), p. 50.
7. Harry McPherson, *A Political Education* (New York: Little, Brown and Company, 1972), p. 71.
8. Nancy Lee Lamport, "Francis Case, His Pioneer Background, Indian Legislation and Missouri River Conservation" (Unpublished master of arts thesis, University of South Dakota, 1972), p. 47.
9. *Congressional Record,* 75th Cong., 1st Session, p. 9540.
10. Lamport, "Case," p. 62.
11. *Congressional Record,* 86th Cong., 2nd Session, p. 13058. Senate Report 1524.
12. Harold Schuler, Remarks at Dedication of Francis Case Bridge, July 17, 1962, cited in *Memorial Addresses,* pp. 181–184.
13. *Memorial Addresses,* p. 59.
14. Pressler, *Senators,* p. 131.
15. Scott Heidepriem, "Karl Mundt," unpublished manuscript, 1987, p. 501.
16. *Washington Star,* August 17, 1974.
17. Robert Anson, *McGovern: A Biography* (New York: Holt, Rinehart, and Winston, 1972), pp. 96–97. There is some question as to the number of debates scheduled. After the third debate in Sioux Falls, Anson wrote, the fear of violence caused cancellation of the rest of the debates. The Heidepriem manuscript identifies on p. 663 two debates at KELO Television Station in Sioux Falls and at Huron. A debate at Washington High School, sponsored by the Sioux Falls Jaycees, is reported in the Sioux Falls *Argus Leader,* October 5, 1960. Copies of three debates are on file in the Mundt Archives.
18. Sioux Falls *Argus Leader,* October 14, 1962.
19. Sioux Falls *Argus Leader,* October 23, 1962.

George S. McGovern.
Courtesy Richardson Archives, USD.

George McGovern conversing with constituents.
Courtesy Herbert T. Hoover.

The Democratic Minority:
George McGovern

Alan Clem

A remote, thinly populated state must husband its resources and cherish its heroes. South Dakota's foremost political leaders have included progressives such as Peter Norbeck and conservatives such as Karl Mundt. Senator Norbeck died in 1936, two years before Mundt entered the U.S. House of Representatives and initiated a period of conservative dominance for the state. In 1956 Liberal Democrat George McGovern won election to the House to usher in a new era of balance between partisan forces. McGovern served two terms in the U.S. House of Representatives, three terms in the U.S. Senate, and ran as the presidential candidate for the Democratic Party in 1972. He was a significant force, too, in Democratic presidential politics during 1968, 1976, 1980, and 1984.

As the leader of South Dakota's minority political party, McGovern reaffirmed many of the social, economic, and political philosophies initiated by Populists and Progressive Republicans two generations earlier. The interspersion of liberal with conservative political leadership in South Dakota history has been important. The Republican Party has long claimed more registered members than has the Democratic party, and it has won the lion's share of election victories. The ratio of Republican to Democratic victories in major contests has been approximately four to one. The infrequent Democratic victories serve as convenient benchmarks to set off eras in state political history.

In the first decade of statehood, gubernatorial victories by Andrew Lee, in 1896 and 1898, resulted as Democrats allied with Populists in

313

the "Fusion" ticket. Twice during the same decade, the State Legislature chose Democrat James Kyle as U.S. Senator because Republican factions and candidates could not work together. Democrat Harry Gandy was elected to the U.S. House of Representatives from the West River district for three successive terms, in 1914, 1916, and 1918. Democrat Edwin Johnson earned one term in the U.S. Senate in the 1914 election, defeating stalwart Republican Charles Burke when the Republican Party split into stalwart and progressive factions.

Democrats became prominent for a time in the period between the two World Wars. William Bulow, a conservative isolationist, was elected Governor in 1926 and 1928, and U.S. Senator in 1930 and 1936. Tom Berry was elected Governor in 1932 and 1934. When Berry and Bulow faced each other in the Democratic senatorial primary of 1942, they cleared the way for the election of Republican Harlan Bushfield, however, and a period of Republican domination. Democrats came back with the election of McGovern as Congressman in 1956 and the election of Ralph Herseth as Governor in 1958. Herseth lost to Republican Archie Gubbrud in gubernatorial elections in 1960 and 1962, but Democrat Frank Denholm was elected to Congress from the first congressional district in 1970 and 1972, and George McGovern was out of Congress for only two years between his first victory in 1956 and his defeat in 1980. Other Democrats were successful during and after the McGovern era: Governor Richard Kneip, Congressman and U.S. Senator James Abourezk, Congressman and U.S. Senator Tom Daschle, and Congressman Tim Johnson. Like Loucks, Pettigrew, Lee, Crawford, and Norbeck, McGovern and his fellow Democrats have made use of local agrarian movements to build a political machine for use as a forum on state as well as national and world affairs. Previous essays explain how the progressives used similar strategy when they solicited endorsement from rural constituents. Crawford, Norbeck, and McMaster especially made use of agrarian distress in developing their Progressive Republican platforms.

Liberals had little success for a time after the mid-1930s. South Dakotans were disillusioned because several of the Norbeck-McMaster initiatives failed. Bulow's isolationist voice between the wars won him votes because it reflected the attitudes of many South Dakotans. Urban unrest and radical pressure for social welfare programs were practically non-existent in the state. Indian people, estimated from five to eight percent of the population, presented no political challenge that required a response from the political parties or their leaders. Generally, politicians were most successful when they remained at a distance from issues fashionable elsewhere and concentrated on the special interests of the state.

Liberals became successful again in the mid-1950s because George McGovern understood provincial attitudes and how to use them to win elections. A prairie background gave him insight into "South Dakota thinking." His father, Joseph McGovern, was a professional baseball player turned Methodist minister. George was born in Avon, South Dakota, on the Republican (western) side of Bon Homme County. In his youth, he followed his father in his ministry to Canada, then back to Mitchell. The elder McGovern made a thoroughgoing Christian of his son. George learned the Bible well enough to display his favorite passages in political speeches. He was a voracious reader, an avid movie fan (to the displeasure of his parents), and a successful debater. One important influence on the direction of his life was a high school forensics coach, Bob Pearson. Another was a rival debater, Eleanor Stegeberg of Woonsocket, who became his wife.

McGovern joined the U.S. Army Air Corps in 1942 and, after brief training, became a B-24 bomber pilot. While based in North Africa, he flew thirty-five combat missions over Germany, Austria, and Italy, earning the Distinguished Flying Cross and the Air Medal with three oak leaf clusters.

He graduated from Dakota Wesleyan University with a B.A. degree in 1946 and entered graduate school at Northwestern University, where he received M.A. (1949) and Ph.D. (1953) degrees in history. McGovern returned to teach at Dakota Wesleyan in 1949, while he worked on a doctoral dissertation. Published in book form many years later, it concerned the labor strike at Coalfield, Colorado, in 1913–14. With doctoral degree finally in hand, the ambitious McGovern began to search for a more prestigious academic position. He was in the final running—one of nearly one hundred applicants—for a position at the University of Iowa, but lost to a graduate of an Ivy League institution. The experience had a chilling effect on McGovern's plans for an academic career.

The disappointment also influenced McGovern's decision to enter politics as a serious candidate during the mid-1950s. From religious upbringing and debate experience, he nurtured deep interest in public affairs. While teaching at Mitchell, he immersed himself in civic and statewide issues. When Ward Clark, a former state Democratic chairman, approached McGovern about the possibility of becoming the first full-time executive director of his party, he found a receptive listener.

McGovern left the academic world and accepted the challenge to revive the Democratic Party in the state.

The Democratic organization of South Dakota was in a sorry condition. There were no Democrats in state elective offices, except the two in the Legislature, where they served with 108 Republicans. Democratic strength in South Dakota was an aggregate of scattered counties—including Charles Mix, Brule, Roberts, Miner, Beadle, Aurora, and Brown—where Democrats controlled most if not all of the county offices.

In the elections of 1952, Democratic candidates won only sixty of the 366 county officer positions statewide (sixteen percent), but the percentage improved considerably during subsequent elections. Competing for 412 positions, twenty-five percent of the Democratic candidates were victorious in 1954, thirty-eight percent in 1956, and forty-seven percent in 1958. The enhancement of Democratic fortunes was noticeable in state legislative results, too. Twenty-four Democrats were elected to the State Legislature in 1954, forty-four in 1956, and fifty-two in 1958. McGovern led the Democratic ticket when he won a seat in the U.S. House of Representatives in 1956 and gained re-election in 1958. His organizational and inspirational efforts contributed heavily to the growing success of Democrats in county and legislative races across the state.

Republicans fought back in the face of Democratic inroads. In 1956 Republican Governor Joe Foss gained re-election in a race against the Democrat Ralph Herseth, and Republican U.S. Senator Francis Case won a second term over Democratic contender Kenneth Holum. Republicans were vulnerable, nevertheless, because of distress among rural constituents. McGovern unseated incumbent Harold Lovre in the first congressional district, which contained about three-fourths of the state's population, many of whom lived in urban communities. Rural candidates Herseth and Holum gave the Democratic ticket a rural flavor, and all three leading Democrats made the programs of Dwight Eisenhower's Secretary of Agriculture a principal focus. Farmers assembled to throw eggs at Secretary Ezra Taft Benson during his visit in the state. Eisenhower carried South Dakota by a margin of some 49,000 votes in spite of it. Foss won by 25,000 votes. Yet, Case earned his second term in the U.S. Senate by fewer than 5,000 votes, and McGovern defeated Lovre handily, with a margin of more than 10,000 votes, to become the state's first Democratic representative in Congress since the 1930s. During the same election, several other Democratic candidates defeated incumbent Republican congressmen from rural districts in the upper Plains area.

Democrats followed up their 1956 victory by securing the re-election of Congressman McGovern in 1958 against a strong challenge by Governor Foss. They also elected Herseth to the governor's chair and took control of the South Dakota Senate.

The year John F. Kennedy won the presidency, 1960, was the watershed of George McGovern's political career, for it brought him out of local and regional into national and international affairs. He decided to take on the powerful, veteran U.S. Senator, Karl Mundt, who had already served five terms in the House and two in the Senate. Mundt was an experienced debater and a leading Republican spokesman for the Middle West. He was a conservative on economic and social issues and an internationalist and anti-Communist in foreign policy. Like some other senior midwestern Republicans, he had kept his distance from Secretary Benson's farm proposals. The race against Mundt brought McGovern to the attention of national liberal leaders in the Democratic party, who were more concerned about the development of candidates for the U.S. Senate than for governorships or seats in the House. McGovern's intelligence and energy had been well known, and now his ambitions became clear. McGovern gained access to national financial resources, media attention, and political influence. The Kennedys were especially aware of him. All of this made the Mundt-McGovern race one of the most significant and interesting general election campaigns in the state's political history. Mundt won, 160,181 to 145,261, while Nixon drew some 50,000 votes more than Kennedy in the state. But, after his inauguration, Kennedy saved McGovern's political career by appointing him director of the Food for Peace program.

The Food for Peace position was transitory. Francis Case's second term was to expire in 1962, and his health was faltering. With overt blessings from the White House, McGovern announced his intention to run against Case. A few weeks after the primary elections, on June 22, 1962, Case died. Several weeks later, members of the Republican state central committee met in Pierre to fill the vacancy on the November ballot. The list of candidates consisted of Sigurd Anderson, Nils Boe, Joe Bottum, Joe Foss, A. C. Miller, and the Rosebud Sioux leader, Congressman Benjamin Reifel. To win the nomination, a majority in the state Central Committee was required; each county's voting power was equal to the votes it had cast for the Republican gubernatorial candidate, Archie Gubbrud, in the 1960 general election. On the twentieth ballot, because of a switch by a committee member from populous Minnehaha county, the nod went to Bottum. Governor Gubbrud then appointed Bottum to fill out the remaining six months of Case's term. As a result, McGovern had to run against an appointive incumbent.

The McGovern-Bottum contest was so close that an official state-wide recount was required. The result was narrowly in McGovern's favor, 127,458 to 126,861. McGovern arrived in the U.S. Senate during January of 1963—he final year of "Camelot." The South Dakotan wasted little time finding the core issues of his national reputation—opposition to defense spending, particularly for nuclear weaponry, and resistance to growing involvement in the Vietnam War. His speech in the Senate on August 2, 1963, was considered by Senator Frank Church of Idaho "the most important address of the session":

> Every patriotic citizen desires that this country be prepared to defend itself against attack. Even the most ardent economizers—men who vote with zeal to cut funds for education, conservation, and health—are quick to shout "aye" for more billions for arms. . . .
>
> But . . . has the time not come to question the assumption that we are adding to defense and security by adding more and more to the nuclear stockpile. . . ?
>
> For this fiscal year, we are asked to approve a Department of Defense budget of $53.6 billion, plus additional billions for the Atomic Energy Commission and the space program. That is well over half of our entire federal budget. . . .
>
> My limited effort to prepare myself for this forthcoming vote as a senator whose chief concern is the security of our country and the peace of the world has led me to certain tentative conclusions. I set them forth now, not as final judgments, but simply as one person's convictions about a most complex problem. . . .
>
> In that spirit, I suggest the following propositions:
>
> First. The United States now has a stockpile of nuclear weapons in excess of any conceivable need.
>
> Second. Bringing the arms race under control involves risks less dangerous than the proliferation of nuclear warheads and the acceleration of the arms race.
>
> Third. Present levels of military spending and military foreign aid are distorting our economy, wasting our human resources, and restricting our leadership in the world.
>
> Fourth. Diverting some of our present and proposed military spending to constructive investments both at home and abroad will produce a stronger and more effective America, improve the quality of our lives, and strengthen the foundations of peace.

There are powerful options of peace as well as options of war. Still alive in the world is a faith that can move mountains if we will only seize upon it. From our own heritage the philosophy of Jefferson and Lincoln speaks with a voice that is more effectively heard in Asia, Africa, and Latin America than any number of nuclear explosions or moon shots. A conscientious effort on our part to eliminate excessive nuclear stockpiling will give that voice of peace and reason an even clearer and more compelling tone.

I pray that our country will in every possible way use its unique power and influence on the side of peace. I know that is what President Kennedy and his administration seek. I am sure that is the sense of the Congress and the American people. I even dare to believe that is what Mr. Krushchev and his people have come to accept as the only condition of their survival.[1]

Through this speech, McGovern gained attention for his views on foreign policy, even though he did not become a member of the Foreign Relations Committee of the Senate until 1973.

The presidential election year of 1968 was a remarkable year in American politics. It was the year when an incumbent president, Democrat Lyndon Johnson, thought to be unbeatable two years before, dropped out of the race after a few early primaries showed him to be vulnerable. It was the year in which two of America's most well-known public figures, Martin Luther King, Jr., and Robert Kennedy, were assassinated. It was the year of George Wallace's significant third party candidacy for the White House. It was the year George McGovern missed his first good chance to win the Democratic nomination for President.

Kennedy was killed on the night of the primary elections in California and South Dakota. In the hectic weeks after his assassination, McGovern reached the decision to enter the race with encouragement from both South Dakota and national party leaders. On August 10, two weeks before the Democratic national convention in Chicago, he made a formal announcement from the Senate Caucus room:

I wear no claim to the Kennedy mantle, but I believe deeply in the twin goals for which Robert Kennedy gave his life—an end to the war in Vietnam and a passionate commitment to heal the divisions in our own society. . . . If I have any special asset for national leadership, it is, I believe, a sense of history—an understanding of the forces that have brought this country to a position of power and influence in the world and an appreciation of what is important in our own time. For five years I have warned against our deepening involvement in Vietnam—the most disastrous political and military blunder in our national experience. That war must be ended now—not next year or the year following, but now. . . . Beyond this, we need to harness the full spiritual and political resources of this nation to put an end to the shameful remnants of racism and poverty that still afflict our land. Just as brotherhood is the condition of survival in a nuclear world, so it is the condition of peace in America. . . . It is for these purposes that I declare myself a candidate for the presidential nomination.[2]

At an unruly convention in riot-torn Chicago, McGovern received 146½ votes for the Democratic presidential nomination. Most delegates preferred Hubert Humphrey, as the tried-and-true inheritor of Johnson's policy, to Senators Eugene McCarthy or McGovern, whose antiwar demands appeared too radical to win the presidency.

Many observers thought McGovern could have won the nomination through an earlier attack on Johnson's administration. McGovern's biographer reported a remark delivered to McGovern at the end of the Democratic convention by the journalist Theodore H. White, author of the *Making of the President* series: "How does it feel to be the guy that booted away the presidency of the United States?"[3]

A consideration that troubled McGovern was that he was up for re-election to the U.S. Senate in 1968. Was it feasible to run for both offices in the same year? Several of his closest South Dakota political backers, including Peder Ecker and Bill Dougherty, felt the more talk there was about McGovern's presidential candidacy the harder it would be to get him re-elected in the state. The issues that might propel McGovern to the Democratic presidential nomination, and even to the White House, were issues that might cost him votes in South Dakota.

After his failure to stop Humphrey's nomination, McGovern returned to South Dakota to run a campaign against a well-known and respected but somewhat colorless Republican challenger, former Governor Archie Gubbrud. In running for the Senate, McGovern was not required to emphasize concerns about urban problems, the poor, civil rights, and Vietnam. He could conduct a personal campaign on other issues, address voters through quality media, and work with an experienced organization as well as personal friends in almost every community. It was, after all, McGovern's fifth major candidacy, and his third statewide contest in eight years. He won, 158,956 to 120,930. Meanwhile, Richard Nixon made it to the White House, narrowly defeating Humphrey in a race in which the Independent candidacy of

Alabama's Governor George Wallace became a significant factor in several states.

Secure in his Senate seat for another six year term, McGovern could look forward to 1972 as "his" year. McGovern's biographer has written that he believed "the ideas he had been talking about for the last twenty-five years had at last won majority acceptance. In the interval he had built a public career on a willingness to be oddly out of kilter with his time. Now, he felt, had come the moment to act on what he had been warning about."[4]

But the Democratic presidential nomination was not his for the asking. There were other ambitious and experienced potential candidates, most notably Humphrey; the 1968 Democratic vice-presidential candidate U.S. Senator Edmund Muskie of Maine, who was at first regarded as the front-runner; U.S. Senator Henry Jackson of Washington; Mayor John Lindsay of New York, a former Republican Congressman; and Governor George Wallace of Alabama.

Gary Hart, McGovern's campaign manager for 1972, summarized events and attitudes of the period between 1968 and 1972:

For the anger, frustration, and alienation weren't directed simply at government. *Nothing* worked anymore. All the institutions were failing. None could solve the problems of crime, of drugs, of the war, of taxes. Worst of all, none of the traditional institutions could return a sense of direction and purpose to America, or restore the ruling values by which our national life had always been gauged. Offered only two alternatives out of the past in 1968, the frustration of the people only deepened. Thus, we entered the 1970s. A sundered nation, an alienated citizenry, our prospective leadership in near-rebellion, our existing leadership badly out of touch, and a system of failing institutions. The people wanted change. The leadership didn't bring change, but rather exploited fear and apprehension to avoid it. And the country drifted along.[5]

Hart continued:

George McGovern then entered the scene. He had come to national prominence on that great divisive issue, the war, the issue which contributed more to the social fragmentation than any other. McGovern's genius was both in correctly reading the longing for change and in realizing the only hope for its success was in a leader who could bridge the national divisions-the generation gap, the racial distrust, the bitterness over the war. He spoke of himself and his campaign as "a bridge over troubled waters." He used phrases like "healing," "reconciling," "bringing together," and "restoring."[6]

It was McGovern's good luck to be the only significant opponent to Muskie in the New Hampshire presidential primary. Perhaps New Hampshire's proximity to Muskie's Maine discouraged other Democratic hopefuls from committing their resources to the early primary contest. Through the year 1971, Muskie had appeared the likely nominee; he ran far ahead in contributions, organization, visibility, and name recognition. With abundant liberal credentials and close contact with party and media influentials, he was the man to beat. Sensing this, he adopted a centrist approach to the electorate. In retrospect, Hart saw it this way:

> By all traditional political measures, Muskie should have been his party's nominee and should have had a reasonable chance at defeating Nixon. But Muskie failed because he offered nothing new. He offered more solidity and stability, when for ten years people had longed to recapture energy and movement, direction and purpose.[7]

This image, combined with an emotional response to newspaper attacks on his wife, became Muskie's undoing. His victory in the New Hampshire primary, where he received only forty-six percent of the vote, did not approach expectations raised by the media. McGovern's thirty-seven percent, on the other hand, surprised almost everyone.

On April 4, McGovern came in first in the Wisconsin primary, followed by Wallace, Humphrey, and Muskie. On April 25, he won fifty-three percent of the vote in the Massachusetts primary, against only twenty-one percent for Muskie. Humphrey won in Pennsylvania, Indiana, Ohio, and West Virginia. Wallace led the Democratic list in Tennessee, North Carolina, Maryland, and Michigan. But the shooting of Wallace in Maryland ended his candidacy.

The last primaries of May and June cemented McGovern's position as front-runner; he led the balloting in Oregon with fifty percent, in Rhode Island with forty-one percent, in California with forty-four percent, in New Mexico with thirty-three percent, and was unopposed in South Dakota. The California campaign was costly in two ways. During a televised debate, Humphrey damaged McGovern's reputation severely by egging him into a pledge to guarantee family income through an expanded federal welfare program. Subsequently, Humphrey's staff used McGovern's close margin of victory, which under Democratic rules gave McGovern all the state's delegates, as an argument to demand the proportional allocation of California delegates, which might have denied McGovern a convention majority on the first nominating ballot.

With the defeat of anti-McGovern Democrats over the division of the California delegation, McGovern felt confident in his nomination. But his victory was undermined by three glaring errors. First, because of a lack of sensitivity among Democratic convention leaders to the importance of prime time on national television, McGovern's acceptance speech did not come until early morning, after millions of viewers had gone to bed.

Second, the choice of U.S. Senator Thomas Eagleton of Missouri as McGovern's running mate, and the subsequent revelation of Eagleton's record of mental instability, suggested weakness in McGovern's capacity to make critical personnel decisions. As Hart wrote later, the Eagleton affair "shattered any chance McGovern may have had to emerge as a competent leader."[8] Since Eagleton had served in the Senate with McGovern for four years, it was difficult to accept White's assertion that McGovern "was persuaded to accept a man unknown to him," but certainly there is little reason to quarrel with White's subsequent statement that the Eagleton affair amounted to "the erasure of McGovern's already almost hopeless candidacy."[9]

Third, under pressure late in the convention week, McGovern dismissed Lawrence O'Brien from a proffered appointment to run the presidential campaign and, instead, appointed the Democratic party's first national chairwoman, Jean Westwood, who, in White's words, "would mismanage the most mismanaged campaign in modern history."[10] In retrospect, these misplays seemed to have doomed McGovern's November chances in midsummer.

McGovern's 1972 presidential campaign was beset by several misfortunes, some unavoidable, and some brought on by the McGovern team itself, but there is no doubt that the McGovern movement represented the aspirations of millions of Americans, particularly those committed to ending the Vietnam War and the attendant arms buildup, and to broadening economic opportunity in the United States. Blacks, women, and young professionals were notably prominent in the McGovern movement. White noted that "the rising Democratic group of career women" had first asserted themselves "at the McGovern convention of 1972." And of "the earnest youngsters of the 1968 insurgency of Eugene McCarthy and Robert Kennedy, as well as most of the youngsters of the McGovern campaign of 1972," White said most would go on to start careers and families, "with the insurgency only a romantic memory. . . . But thousands would not give up the memory," wrote White, and would go on in later campaigns using field organization, computers, television, and polling as vital tools in vote gathering.[11] Hart had written that McGovern's candidacy had "brought hope to millions. . . . It was the occasion for the emergence of new activists." Further, Hart predicted that these activists from the McGovern campaign would "stay active in party affairs all across the nation." Hart characterized the McGovern campaign as a "bridge over troubled waters for those who supported him. . . . His courage, his refusal to accommodate to 'the establishment center' and to become simply another politician, restored faith and hope for the disillusioned. It won for him not only the nomination but, more enduringly, the respect and admiration of millions of Americans."[12]

McGovern attacked the establishment center of his own party repeatedly, blaming the Johnson administration, especially, for leading "us into the stupidest and cruelest war in all history," for seeing the planet "engaged in a gigantic struggle to the death between the free world and the communist world," and for constructing a "vast military colossus based on the paychecks of the American worker."[13] McGovern's campaign was often negative, according to Hart. He wanted to withdraw from Vietnam and reduce defense spending. A McGovern team plan to revise the welfare system was abandoned because of internal inconsistencies. There was enthusiasm, organization, and technological innovation in the campaign, according to Hart, but little creative thinking. "The fields of liberalism failed to provide a crop in 1972. The soil is worn out."[14]

McGovern called for the return of Americans to traditional practices and ideals. In his acceptance speech before the Democratic convention, he put it simply: "Come home, America." This was an attempt to bring the country together after its riotous divisions in the 1960s, with emphasis on ending the war and spreading the wealth. A majority of voters felt more comfortable with Richard Nixon.

It has been said there is nothing so powerful as an idea whose time has come. Unfortunately, McGovern's strategists did not see clearly what most citizens were ready to accept. They failed to fit the party's platform and candidate's personality to national aspirations and expectations. Gary Hart summed it up eloquently:

Edmund Burke said that the march of the human mind is slow. Any evaluation of the McGovern phenomenon must finally decide whether it was marching a half-step faster than the collective national mind or marching to the beat of a different drummer—whether the McGovern campaign was simply ahead of its time, or out of step.[15]

Close observers of, and participants in, McGovern's campaigns commented on how his dislike of his bestknown opponents, Karl Mundt and Richard Nixon, had a negative effect on his ability to campaign effectively. About his 1960 contest with Mundt, McGovern said:

> It was my worst campaign. . . . I lost my sense of balance. I was too negative. I made some careless charges. When the media in the state turned against me, the television and the radio stations and almost all the newspapers, I got kind of rattled. I got on the defensive. I started explaining and answering things I should have ignored. It was hard to get a hook in Mundt.[16]

If McGovern made a similar error in 1972, he at least retained the admiration of those who supported him. Wrote Gary Hart, "About George McGovern I can only say, he is the finest man I have ever met in politics."[17]

McGovern became something of an elder statesman after 1972, in the nation as well as in South Dakota. He continued to speak and write effectively, but he no longer represented the wave of the future. Perhaps it would be unfair for historians to judge that from 1972 McGovern's political career went steadily downhill, but certainly his role as a leader in the national Democratic Party did not extend much beyond November of 1972.

Other campaigns remained. McGovern's second term in the U.S. Senate ended in 1974, when he confronted an inexperienced but oddly disconcerting candidate, Vietnam War prisoner Leo Thorsness, who came home to espouse the conservative side of most issues and to attract voters who had opposed McGovern's unequivocal anti-war posture. In an occasionally bitter campaign, the veteran incumbent was equal to the task. He was helped by Republican troubles with the Watergate scandal and by the image of the popular Democratic Governor, Richard Kneip. McGovern defeated Thorsness by only 17,000 votes, while Kneip beat Republican John Olson by some 20,000 votes. In the same election, Democrats retained control of the South Dakota Senate. As McGovern's popularity waned, however, Republicans made significant gains. They won a majority in the House of Representatives at Pierre, and vociferous William Janklow ousted the incumbent Democratic Attorney General by a margin of 86,000 votes.

At the 1980 Democratic national convention in Detroit, McGovern played a significant role in U.S. Senator Edward Kennedy's attempt to take the Democratic presidential nomination away from President Jimmy Carter. Ironically, the South Dakotan argued in favor of a change in convention rules that would allow pledged delegates to ignore their constituents' wishes and vote from "conscience"—a change that might have cost him the nomination in 1972.

A Republican tide ran against both McGovern and Carter. The great issues that earned McGovern a special place in history counted little. Struggles for peace and civil rights were no longer useful to politicians, and markedly divisive. The social welfare programs and agriculture supports that had been touted so long by Democrats seemed on the verge of bankruptcy. In the opinions of most voters, throwing money at symptoms brought only limited relief. Underlying problems of poverty, ignorance, and rural depression had not abated. President Carter had remarkable success in bringing Sadat of Egypt and Begin of Israel together at Camp David. Yet people across the country were in doubt about his leadership. Inflation, unemployment, interest rates, and fuel prices appeared to be out of control. American hostages were trapped in Tehran. Russian troops occupied Afghanistan.

As McGovern watched the image of the Democratic President grow steadily worse, he found himself on a political "hit list." He was one of five liberal senators targeted for defeat by the National Conservative Political Action Committee (NCPAC). The Republican opponent of 1980 was not a sluggish candidate like Joe Bottum or Archie Gubbrud, or an inexperienced ideologue such as Leo Thorsness. He was a four-term Republican Congressman with emotional ties to South Dakota's soil as well as to its people. Strangely, a three-term U.S. Senator with an international reputation became the underdog in a bid for re-election against James Abdnor.

McGovern had the greatest resources, by a considerable margin. He flaunted his valid claim to the title of "Prairie Statesman." Yet, he won only forty percent of the vote, losing by a margin of 61,000 votes in the year that President Carter lost South Dakota by 94,000 votes. McGovern could not overcome the personal affection voters had developed for Abdnor, whose reputation for fairness and sensitivity was well deserved. Conservative Republicans in South Dakota recovered the dominance they had lost in the 1960s. A similar trend gave Abdnor's Republican Party control of the U.S. Senate for the first time since 1954; McGovern lost his seat to Abdnor in the year Republicans also gained Senate seats in Alaska, Washington, Idaho, Iowa, Wisconsin, Indiana, North Carolina, Alabama, Georgia, Florida, and New Hampshire.

This marked the end of McGovern's political career as a candidate for office, except for his half-hearted offer to become the alternative to Walter Mondale as the Democratic presidential nominee of 1984. His departure from the Senate came gracefully, with little rancor. In a post-election interview with the Associated Press, he admitted he may have lost touch with his constituents—with "South Dakota thinking." He said he did not feel betrayed by the voters who had sustained him in office for so long. "I don't think they owe me a lifetime job."[18]

Many of McGovern's Senate colleagues gave him warm tributes on his departure. Majority Leader Robert Byrd of West Virginia said that McGovern's "courage and foresight are recognized as legendary."[19] Senator Patrick Moynihan of New York noted that McGovern "brought us decency, compassion, integrity, and the fiery spirit of Plains States populism."[20] Senator Edward Kennedy noted the respect and affection he and his brothers John and Robert felt toward McGovern. Said Kennedy:

> In a conservative constituency, he has always had to sail against the wind and always he has kept the rudder true. . . . He has been one of the great Americans of a generation in the Congress and in the country.[21]

A survey of index entries in fifteen college textbooks on recent politics and campaigns in the United States ranks McGovern behind only President Jimmy Carter among Democratic leaders. This confirms the importance attached by scholars to McGovern's place in recent American politics.

Through the same era, he created a legacy in the state as the leader most responsible for the renewal of the Democratic Party as a significant contemporary force. Richard Kneip, a state legislator from the 1960s, was elected Governor in 1970, 1972, and 1974. During his tenure came the professionalization of state government in the reorganization of the executive branch, as authorized by a revised executive article in the Constitution of South Dakota. Kneip resigned from office during the middle of his last year (1978) to accept appointment by President Carter as U.S. ambassador to Singapore. He attempted a return to politics by entering the Democratic gubernatorial primary of 1986 but was defeated by Lars Herseth. When Kneip died a short time later, he was eulogized as one of the state's most successful Democrats.

James Abourezk won a primary race narrowly in 1970 against Don Barnett and Elvern Varilek for the Democratic nomination for the state's second congressional (West River) district, barely reaching the minimum thirty-five percent required for nomination. In November, he won the general election with fifty-two percent of the vote. Two years later, Abourezk won the seat in the U.S. Senate vacated by an ailing Karl Mundt, after a campaign against Republican Robert Hirsch. For six years, South Dakota had two liberal Democratic Senators. Abourezk was known best for his defense of American Indians, his support for Arab causes vis-a-vis those of Israel, and his attacks on President Nixon. When Abourezk declined to run for re-election in 1978, his seat went to the Republican Larry Pressler.

After Abourezk's retirement, only McGovern and Tom Daschle remained as Democrats in high elective office. Daschle defeated McGovern's foe of 1974, Leo Thorsness, in the first congressional (East River) district race of 1978 to take Pressler's seat in the U.S. House of Representatives. Daschle won reelection easily in 1980, then in 1982 defeated fellow Congressman Clint Roberts by some 9,000 votes, when South Dakota lost one seat in the House on the basis of the 1980 census. Daschle defended the single seat against a challenge from Republican Dale Bell in 1984, then faced the man who had defeated McGovern in 1986. In effect, Daschle risked the only high elective office retained by a Democrat to win back the seat in the U.S. Senate held by James Abdnor. Mainly for this victory, U.S. Senator Daschle merits special recognition among leaders. His presence, in a sense, extends the legacy of McGovern. Because of their economic condition, South Dakotans have long raised political voices to receive special consideration from federal agencies. As citizens on the hinterland, they have been partial to frontier reforms. When during a 1974 senatorial campaign address before some 600 peers in the history profession at Rapid City, George McGovern presented himself as a "Neo-Populist," he acknowledged his link with the old forces of progressivism.

In the aftermath of his defeat by Jim Abdnor in 1980, McGovern said he felt no bitterness and was somewhat relieved "at being out from under the tremendous pressure of the office." At the time, he considered the major achievements of his Senate career were his efforts to end U.S. involvement in the Vietnam conflict and his work to relieve world hunger. Although he did not return to South Dakota to reside, he said that "As long as I live, I'll claim Mitchell as my home town."

Notes

1. *Congressional Record,* 88th Cong., 1st Session, pp. 13986–13995.
2. George S. McGovern, *Grassroots: The Autobiography of George McGovern* (New York: Random House, 1977), p. 121.

3. Robert Sam Anson, *McGovern: A Biography* (New York: Holt, Rinehart, and Winston, 1972), p. 2.

4. *Ibid.*, p. 291.

5. Gary W. Hart, *Right from the Start: A Chronicle of the McGovern Campaign* (New York: Quadrangle, 1973), p. 325.

6. *Ibid.*, pp. 325–6.

7. *Ibid.*, p. 325.

8. *Ibid.*, p. 329.

9. Theodore H. White, *America in Search of Itself: The Making of the President, 1956–1980* (New York: Warner Books, 1982), p. 320.

10. *Ibid.*, p. 118.

11. *Ibid.*, pp. 115, 232.

12. Hart, *Right from the Start*, p. 330.

13. Gordon L. Weil, *The Long Shot: George McGovern Runs for President* (New York: W. W. Norton, 1973), p. 239.

14. Hart, *Right from the Start*, p. 328.

15. *Ibid.*, p. 323.

16. Weil, *The Long Shot*, p. 223.

17. Hart, *Right from the Start*, p. x.

18. Associated Press dispatch from Washington, *Sioux City Journal*, December 5, 1980, page A5.

19. *Congressional Record, Senate*, December 5, 1980, p. 32719.

20. *Congressional Record, Senate*, December 30, 1980, p. 34379.

21. *Congressional Record, Senate*, December 10, 1980, p. 33349.

Ben Reifel.
Courtesy Aberdeen American News.

Ben Reifel, with wife Frances, being sworn in as the last Commissioner of Indian Affairs
by Secretary of the Interior Thomas Kleppe.
Courtesy Williams Library, Northern State College.

Ben Reifel.
Contributed from Myrtle Miller Anderson's Sioux Memory Gems *(1929), Courtesy Steve Emery*

Transitional Sioux Leader:
Benjamin Reifel

John S. Painter

The citizens of eastern South Dakota recognized Benjamin Reifel as a proven leader when they elected him in 1968 to a fifth consecutive term in the United States House of Representatives. Born of German-American and Sioux lineage, he was the only enrolled tribal member with a commitment to Sioux heritage ever elected to Congress from the state and the only member in Congress of Native American ancestry during the 1960s.

The Congressman was a member of the Brule or Burnt Thigh tribe of Sioux whose Indian forebears had settled around the U.S. Agency at Rosebud less than a century earlier, when the tribe was under the leadership of Spotted Tail. It comprised Upper Brules who gathered along river and creek beds of the upper White River basin in bands identified on early reservation maps as "camps," which usually took their group names from prominent local leaders. Every band contained *tiyospayes*, each of which included from five to twenty extended families, and every *tiyospaye* had its principal leader. Born in the year 1906, Ben grew up as part of such a community that observed traditional standards changed little by the presence of non-Indians.

His was a band identified in early Rosebud Agency records as that of Black Crow, who set up his camp at *Wososo*, on Cut Meat Creek. The father of Reifel's maternal grandmother, Yellow Hair, was a *tiyospaye* leader in Black Crow's camp. Reifel's grandfather, Burning Breast (*Ceska Ile*), came from another camp near Cut Meat Creek, led by Hollow Horn Bear. According to family tradition, Burning Breast

331

got his name from the reflection of the sun off a large gold medallion hanging by a thong on his chest. Federal officials often issued such medals to participants in treaty councils.

Burning Breast and his wife, Spring or Swamp (*Weeweela*), set up their tipi at her *tiyospaye* camp circle in time-honored fashion. There were no great buffalo hunts or Crow camps nearby to raid for horses. Otherwise, life went on as before; the social structure remained intact. A close-knit, supportive *tiyospaye* community continued to function under leadership from Weeweela's father, Yellow Hair, as it had for centuries before.

Out of this cultural setting came Ben Reifel's mother, named Small (*Ciscila*), who later took the name Lucy Burning Breast. Born in 1879, she was educated from childhood in her own *tiyospaye* by traditional means. Featured were the values of Lakota tradition: intense religious commitment, selflessness for the good of the group, and a strong sense of community. Gradually, however, these values were confronted by the new ideals imposed by missionaries and agency employees: individualism, self-support by family farming, and other Anglo-American practices sifted through day or boarding school training and Christian teaching. In her band, Lucy was among the first of the youngsters to grapple with the contradictions in biculturalism.

To aid in the transition to reservation life, agency personnel opened Issue Stations near their camps for the convenient distribution of rations purchased largely with treaty funds set aside in tribal accounts. At first, federal officials issued food and clothing plus a few luxuries to the *tiyospaye* chiefs for distribution at their discretion. By the end of the 1870s annuity benefits were issued directly to family heads. Thus, agency officials used ration issues to undermine traditional Lakota leadership while providing sustenance and encouraging individualism. Subsequently federal officials replaced traditional Chiefs with appointed, "progressive" individuals who were friendly to federal policy goals.

Following a congressional mandate to engender rapid assimilation, U.S. Indian Field Service employees undermined the cohesiveness of *tiyospayes* and broke up communal real estate by allotting tribal acreage to individual Indians. White settlers moved in as neighbors to occupy "surplus land" within reservation boundaries. In less than a quarter century, a spate of changes took place that brought Upper Brule people into frequent contact with cultural ways that were new to them.

Members of Burning Breast's family took their land allotments within a mile or two of the Cut Meat Issue Station, but there is no evidence to indicate that Burning Breast himself ever left his *tiyospaye* camp circle to live on his allotment acreage or to farm any part of it himself before his death in 1899. Yet, as a teenager Lucy was continuously in contact with non-Indians. She accepted Christian baptism and remained a devout Episcopalian throughout her life. For at least two years she attended Rosebud Agency's Cut Meat Day School, where she learned the alphabet, did a little reading, spoke some English, and dabbled in domestic arts. The curriculum required young girls to take instruction in home economics: sewing, washing clothes, baking and cooking on stoves, housekeeping, and other skills taught according to habits in White culture that were foreign to Lakota women. Customarily the wife of the Day School teacher taught domestic arts. Lucy Burning Breast learned from Maggie Reifel, the wife of the German-American John Reifel, who was one of the first civil servants hired to teach in federal schools on the Rosebud Reservation.

After leaving school at age nineteen, Lucy worked for the wives of several traders and other federal employees at Cut Meat. She also used her homemaking skills at the residence of Jack Whipple, a prominent rancher in the neighborhood who had married into the tribe. At the Whipple's ranch she met William M. "Shorty" Reifel, the younger brother of Lucy's day school teacher, who had followed his older brother John from Indiana to South Dakota.

Although Lucy spoke little English, the language barrier was no obstacle to romance. She and William Reifel married. "Shorty" built a dirt-roofed log cabin on her allotment approximately a mile and a half from the Whipple's ranch. Lucy's mother and younger brother, William Burning Breast, lived with the young couple when Benjamin (*Wiyaka Wanjila*, or Lone Feather), the first of their five sons, was born on September 19, 1906. He and his brothers grew up hearing some German and English but mainly Lakota language at home or out in the community. The social ways of the *tiyospaye* continued even though Christian mission personnel, and to a lesser extent day school teachers, infringed on the purity of Indian values and activities.

Ben began his schooling at the age of five. "I just kind of stumbled in," he recalled. "I had a friend who was going to school by the name of Robert Whipple, who was a year older than me. One day in the fall, my mother and father were going to Valentine, Nebraska, to get groceries and do some trading. I was playing with Bob, and he said, 'Well, come on to school with me.' So I went to school with him. I just stayed the rest of that year."[1]

"A schooling" did not easily become a routine thing for Ben. By the time he was sixteen he had completed the eighth grade through enrollment at several places. He attended an integrated district school and the small federal day school at Parmalee. He spent a year at the Rosebud Boarding School. From the third grade on, Reifel dropped "in" and "out." At age fifteen, however, he decided to enter full time at Parmalee, where he finished the sixth grade because "they had a pool hall down there and I could play pool," he said jokingly, and "my father used to give me heck when I'd come home late in the evening."[2] With the aid and encouragement of a teacher at Cut Meat Day School, Ethel Kraus, Ben went on to finish the seventh and eighth grades in less than a year.

Influenced by some books he read during spare time while working the family farm, Ben had "visions of being a great rancher, a college educated rancher on the reservation."[3] He had no training beyond the eighth grade, and there was no high school for him to attend on the Rosebud Reservation. With encouragement from the new teacher at Cut Meat, Roy Grubb, he enrolled at the Secondary Agricultural School on the campus of the College of Agricultural and Mechanical Arts at Brookings. The "Aggie" winter school, which was in session from October to March, enabled youngsters from the ranches and farms of South Dakota to get intensified high school education along with some courses in agriculture.

Encouragement came from the John Andersons, owners of a trading store in Rosebud, for whom both Ben and his father had worked. U.S. Superintendent at Rosebud James McGregor and his wife urged him on. Although the Reifel family had no money to help with expenses, Ben, as a tribal member at eighteen years of age, could take his share of the proceeds from the sale of "surplus" tribal land to non-Indians. This "Sioux Benefit" of $550 had not been processed by the time he had to leave for Brookings. Fortunately, Superintendent McGregor took Ben to his bank in Crookston, Nebraska, and co-signed a note for $100 so Ben could begin school in October of 1925.

In the quest for knowledge, Reifel left the reservation at age nineteen armed with determination to learn how agricultural practices could be improved around his home. More important than an eighth grade diploma and the borrowed $100 in his pocket was his commitment to hard work, which he had learned through his mother's Lakota culture as well as his father's German-American habits. With rigorous effort, he finished enough high school credits in three winter terms to begin regular courses at the College of Agricultural and Mechanical Arts.

Reifel majored in chemistry and dairy science, took ROTC military training, and became a campus leader as well as an Honor Society student. Except for the Sioux Benefit and a $900 federal loan, he financed his education with the money he earned doing part time jobs and the funds he saved doing summer work.

Things went well in Brookings. Ben's peers nominated him for President of the Student Association. He passed his initiation into the arena of politics with flying colors by winning the election and serving with distinction during his senior year. Awarded a baccalaureate degree in June of 1932, he took the commission of Second Lieutenant in the U.S. Army and spent the summer in Reserve Officers training camp, where he advanced to the rank of First Lieutenant.

Romance for Reifel began during the 1929–1930 school year, when he met Alice Janet Johnson, a slightly-built, blue-eyed, blond of Norwegian-American heritage from Erwin, South Dakota. Alice trained to be a home economics teacher and, like Ben, she received an undergraduate degree in June of 1932. The depth of the Great Depression was discouraging to both graduates as they searched for jobs. Ben no longer had "great visions of being a . . . college educated rancher on the reservation." Rather, he wanted to join the U.S. Indian Field Service, where his education would benefit his people.

No vacancies were available at the time. By then he had become an active Episcopal church worker and Lay Reader and, partly as a result of that activity, he found a job for the 1932–1933 school year as Boys' Advisor in the Episcopal Hare School at Mission, South Dakota. Alice Johnson landed a country school teaching position near Parmalee. With only thirty miles between them, their romance flourished. Meanwhile, Ben's longtime friend and mentor James McGregor became Superintendent on the Pine Ridge Sioux Reservation. Through his effort, Reifel received an appointment as U.S. Farm Extension Agent during July of 1933.

Ben and Alice planned their wedding for December 26th. Alice moved to Pine Ridge where she took an interim job as a live-in tutor for a nurse who needed to complete high school credits for job advancement in the federal service. Until suitable quarters could be built at Oglala, a tiny community where Ben would be stationed, he also lived in Pine Ridge. With the title of Farm Agent, Reifel served as a field administrative representative for the Superintendent. He had responsibility for federal program activities in the Oglala Farm District, at the southwestern edge of the reservation, which was occupied by people of traditional Indian disposition.

The Oglala Farm District near Pine Ridge had evolved in much the same way as the Cut Meat District on the Rosebud Reservation. It originated as an Issue Station. The Superintendent had assigned an Issue Clerk to keep track of rations parceled out to family heads through various *tiyospaye* leaders. As his responsibility for federal policy implementation had increased at a local level, especially in agriculture and education, the Superintendent had assigned regular agency personnel to the issue stations. Re-designated Farm Districts, they had come under the supervision of "Assistant" or "Additional" district U.S. Farmers. Called "Boss Farmers" by most Indians, these men had become the personifications of the federal government. Each Boss Farmer had promoted education and assisted the Day School teacher. He had supervised a District Policeman, who worked mainly as truancy officer. The Boss Farmer had coordinated the activities of all government personnel in his district as he procured supplies and served as the field liaison to individual Indians or families. He had helped to initiate land leases, made out wills, and performed the functions of a social worker. In many instances, a Boss Farmer had decision making power over expenditures from Individual Indian Money Accounts held in trust by the U.S. Secretary of the Interior.

Reifel's appointment came early in the 1930s as the U.S. Indian Office phased out Boss Farmers of the previous era and replaced them with Farm Extension Agents. The change reflected new policy initiated during the Hoover Administration to improve personnel and to reform reservation programs. The U.S. Commissioner of Indian Affairs worked toward these goals by creating a Division of Extension and Industry to govern local activities.

Reifel was familiar with the duties of the old Boss Farmer before taking charge of federal programs at the Oglala Farm District. Although he still considered himself a Boss Farmer, he understood the new obligation to offer instruction about such matters as scientific land-use practices. Just as a State Extension Agent supplied information to White farmers and ranchers, so did the Extension Division Farm Agent work directly with Indians to provide technical aid for the improvement of reservation agriculture. Undeniably aided by the influence of Superintendent McGregor, Reifel's appointment resulted from his academic training and because of a directive from the new Commissioner, John Collier, who from the time of his appointment in 1933 stressed the hiring of qualified tribal members in the U.S. Indian Field Service.

Due to his reservation background, Ben thought of himself as a Boss

Farmer of the traditional sort as much as an Extension Division Farm Agent and blended paternalism with scientific instruction according to the philosophy of John Collier's "Indian New Deal." In much the same fashion as other federal officials helped non-Indians through the Great Depression, so did Collier and his staff offer assistance to Indians with a combination of direct and self-help relief. During the winter of 1933–1934, Superintendent McGregor put Reifel in charge of direct relief in the distribution of clothing and surplus food commodities acquired through the Federal Emergency Relief Administration.

Once the threat of starvation had passed, there was increasing emphasis on self-help. As White ranchers in dire economic straits sold their foundation herds to the Agricultural Adjustment Administration, Reifel and other Farm Agents acquired cattle with money allocated by Congress for as little as twenty-five dollars a head to establish or enlarge Indian-owned livestock operations. Ben also assisted Indians in taking advantage of numerous other self-help programs: the Civilian Conservation Corps—Indian Department, Civil Works Administration, Public Works Administration, Works Progress Administration, National Youth Administration, and others. Not only did such programs as these enhance reservation economy by the improvement of living conditions, they also brought meaningful employment with an opportunity to learn new job skills.

Reifel met John Collier for the first time when the Commissioner made a swing through Sioux Country in December of 1933, presenting talks to tribal leaders and Indian Field Service personnel at Rosebud and Pine Ridge. It seems doubtful that anyone in the audience had anticipated the revolutionary nature of Collier's proposed reforms. Beginning with the concept that Indians were equal to all other citizens, and that Indian culture had validity equal to that of other cultures, Collier said that without coercion on either side the peoples of different cultures could come together for an exchange of ideas to find accommodation with each other. Therefore, he fashioned an Indian policy to enable tribal members to find their places in mainstream society without suffering cultural loss, either as individuals or as tribal groups. It should be possible for Indians "to earn decent livelihoods and lead self-respecting organized lives in harmony with their *OWN* aims and ideals, as an integral part of American life."[4]

This pleased and intrigued Ben Reifel, of course, because he understood from long experience the negative impacts of previous policies on Indian people. As the Flathead Indian leader D'Arcy McNickle put it:

Collier began his commissionership at a time when law and policy extended back 100 years and had wrought incalculable damage to Indians, their property and their societies. . . . Tribal religious practices when they were not proscribed outright were treated as obscenities. Land losses were catastrophic, while the failure of government to provide economic tools and the training for proper land use left the land untenable or put out to white farmers and ranchers at starvation rates. The bureaucratic apparatus had penetrated the entire fabric of Indian life, usurping the tribal decision-making function, obtruding into the family, demeaning local leadership—and yet was totally oblivious of its inadequacies and its inhumanity.[5]

Reifel has told a story to illustrate the impact of that policy on life in his own Farm District. Community leaders had always come to the Boss Farmer for permission to hold their dances:

They could have dances only on Saturday night. Bert Kills Close to Lodge came in and said, 'I want to get permission to have a dance tonight for our group in the village.' I had just received a copy of a telegram signed by John Collier, Commissioner of Indian Affairs. It said, 'If the Indian people want to have dances, dances all night, all week, that is their business.' So I read it to him. Bert sat there, stroking his braids, looking off in the distance, and he said in Lakota, 'Well, I'll be damned.' The interesting part of it was, if they did not have the dance Saturday night, they would have a dance a month later, because they felt they were on their own. The Indian police were not going to police anybody, and it was just too much for them to have self-determination about their own dances.[6]

Reifel heard Collier in person a second time when the Commissioner held the first in a series of Indian congresses at Rapid City in early March, 1934. Wanting to find out more about Collier's ideas, Reifel took annual leave to attend the three-day meeting, where more than 200 representatives of northern Great Plains tribes along with some U.S. Field Service employees listened while Collier and other officials explained the new Wheeler-Howard Bill recently under consideration by Congress. Reifel had no idea that he was destined to play a major role in implementing what soon became the Indian Reorganization Act (I.R.A.).

Congress enacted the Wheeler-Howard Bill into law during June of 1934 to encourage tribes to incorporate for economic development under newly reconstituted tribal governments guided by elected officials and written constitutions and bylaws. With these governments recognized by law, self-governing tribes would play more active roles in decisions affecting reservation affairs. The I.R.A. authorized expenditures of monies to help restore part of each tribe's land base, establish a revolving loan fund for economic development, and fund scholarships for Indians to gain the education that would aid them in their new decision-making roles. A most unique and historic feature of the I.R.A. was the allowance of tribes to elect whether or not they wanted to organize tribal governance and economic development under the provisions of the Act.

Two other features put great pressure on a tribe. The I.R.A. allowed only one year for a decision on whether or not the voting members would be part of the procedure for governance it offered. This hampered decision-making, especially for the more traditional tribes, because all documents had to be translated into native languages. For most tribes that still made decisions by consensus, a legitimate decision making process could not be hurried that much.

The other negative feature of the Act was the absence of money for the first year of operation. A shortage of funds required the Office of Indian Affairs to implement the Act with existing personnel, who already were spread thin with depression relief demands. Accordingly, Indian Field Service personnel were assigned enormous responsibility without enough staff or money to give it the attention it deserved.

Commissioner Collier named various Field Service employees as regional coordinators and sent some officials from his national office to assist. Agent Reifel later described how he went about the work in his district:

> I could speak and write the Sioux language and took one of these old ABC charts that they used to use in Indian schools on a little stand. And on one side I would write a little synopsis of each section. . . . And right along side of it, I would put the Indian translation and draw some pictures to illustrate what it meant.[7]

When Superintendent McGregor noticed that Oglala District leaders seemed better informed than others and heard about Reifel's educational technique, he requested his Farm Agent to repeat the explanation before central tribal officials. Reifel's talk, using the visual aid written on the back of an old ABC chart, again was so successful that McGregor scheduled Reifel's appearance before meetings in all of the reservation districts.

After learning of Ben's ability as an instructor, Joe Jennings, Superintendent of Indian Education for South Dakota and newly designated I.R.A. regional coordinator, asked him to assist in an educational program for other tribes in South Dakota, North Dakota, and Nebraska. Reifel spent the better part of a year explaining the Indian Reorganization Act to tribal members across the northern Great Plains and his educational program was acclaimed as being crucial to the success of Collier's whole policy for the region.

Officials involved in the educational program faced opposition from several sources that undermined tribal acceptance. Old-line Indian Office personnel, especially the Superintendents, opposed the I.R.A. They feared a loss of influence over reservation activities and the lives of tribal members if newly constituted tribal governments took on greater decision-making powers. Non-Indian agricultural and business interests opposed the plan. They wanted to protect the economic advantages they had enjoyed under the old system. Most church leaders lashed out at Collier's new plan. They recognized in his New Deal for Indians a degree of religious freedom that could eliminate their privileged ecclesiastical status on the reservations. Some tribal members and many outsiders spoke out against the I.R.A. as a "back to the blanket" policy, if not a form of communism that would retard the absorption of Indians into mainstream society. Many tribal elders also believed the acceptance of the I.R.A. would result in the loss of tribal financial claims against the United States.

Despite such diverse opposition, the I.R.A. educational program in Sioux Country, where Reifel played a prominent role, was successful. Majorities of the members of most tribes voted in special elections to bring their tribes under the provisions of the Act. Realizing that such referendum elections constituted only the beginning of tribal economic development and self-government, Office of Indian Affairs personnel established a new branch called the Indian Organization Division to promote the goals of the Act.

Reifel became one of the first two regional Field Agents for the new Division. After training three months in Washington, DC, during July of 1935, he entered this field of service with responsibility for North and South Dakota, Nebraska, Montana, and Kansas. As an I.R.A. Field Agent, he had to function within the contexts of both Indian and White cultures, and for this he was exceptionally well qualified. Reifel had demonstrated this capacity during college days, while serving as Farm Agent, and especially when setting up the I.R.A. educational program. His bicultural insight now became essential to the restoration of tribal governments that could function in agreement with Anglo-American democratic concepts.

Tribes that chose to create governments under the Indian Reorganization Act all followed the same pattern of development as their Field Agent worked among them as a facilitator, educator, and liaison to the Office of the Commissioner of Indian Affairs. First, the tribe chose a committee to write a constitution. Some revised documents that had been prepared to guide their affairs before 1934, but most modified a model constitution developed by the Indian Organization Division staff in Washington, DC. Reifel spent countless hours at meetings with tribal committees explaining the sovereign powers of tribes and how they could be safeguarded by the new constitutions. Once a committee's members agreed on the contents of a new instrument, its chairman sent a final draft to the U.S. Secretary of the Interior for approval.

Next, tribal leaders explained their constitution to members in reservation community meetings prior to referendum elections. On the northern Great Plains, Reifel played a crucial role by assisting the leaders with this educational activity. Then, after tribal members chose officials by rules described in their new constitution, they exercised freedom of choice regarding whether to create a corporate charter. As outlined by the Indian Reorganization Act, such a document would enable a tribe to conduct its own business enterprises without close supervision from the Indian Office. Reifel assisted his own Rosebud Sioux in writing one of the first I.R.A. charters and it became a model for use by other tribes throughout the country.

The process of advisement continued for several years. At the same time, Reifel and other Organization Field Agents lent assistance to tribal groups as they placed their new institutions of governance into operation. Law and Order Codes and Land Lease Forms, for example, were essential from the start. Because so many tribal leaders were unfamiliar with practical aspects of government based upon Anglo-Saxon political principles, the Field Agent was called upon almost continuously for detailed information. Reifel held meetings with tribal leaders across the region to help them develop numerous skills: maintaining appropriate minutes and records; establishing tribal budgets; and generally carrying out tribal business within constitutional boundaries.

Thus, his role shifted from one of concern with organization under the I.R.A. to one of assisting tribes with the development of organizational tools. To this end in 1940, Reifel and other Organization Field Agents planned and managed four-day regional conferences to assist tribal officers at Minneapolis, Minnesota; Billings, Montana; Carson City, Nevada; and Pierre, South Dakota. For the first time in the history of Indian-White relations on the northern Great Plains, leaders from various tribes came together for discussions about mutual problems and common concerns at federal expense with U.S. employees standing by to help.

These conferences demonstrated not only the revitalization of tribal governments, but also the deeper meaning of the whole Indian New Deal as the basis for a new relationship between tribal groups and federal officials. The conferences revealed how thoroughly Reifel and other Field Agents had succeeded in the facilitation of tribal self-government and economic development while leaving all decisions of abiding importance to the tribal members themselves. In addition, the conferences played an important role in the continuing education of Whites as well as Indians regarding the erosion of paternalism and tribal dependence, and the right of Indians to tribal self-reliance and cooperative self-sufficiency.

By the end of the 1930s the complexity of reservation affairs under the aegis of the United States led to the establishment of the Branch of Planning and Development. Field Agents like Ben Reifel had been vital to the improvement of reservation life under New Deal programs, which required the involvement of Indians themselves. Reifel especially had insisted that reservation communities as well as tribal leaders be active in planning for the future. Although Field Agents, including Reifel, had assisted in the planning of various economic projects for the tribes, the absorption of the Division of Indian Organization into the Branch of Planning and Development during November of 1941 greatly enlarged tribal responsibilities.

Unfortunately, new developments from outside Indian Affairs converged to undermine Collier's concept of Indian self-determination. Late in the 1930s and early in the 1940s congressional conservatives sought to undermine New Deal programs through the reduction of appropriations. As funding grew scarce, there came great demand for national resources in the war effort after the Japanese attack on Pearl Harbor. Federal sources of funds dried up. The Office of Indian Affairs moved to Chicago, where it was restyled as the modern U.S. Bureau of Indian Affairs. Developments during World War II did not undo recent progress toward tribal organization, revive the tribal dependence of the past, or place any obstacle in the way of viable self-government and self-help. Nor did the War diminish the value of the personal contributions made by Reifel and others in the Organization

Division. Successes in tribal self-determination convinced many in the Division that tribes needed a national forum to collectively influence Indian policy and discuss solutions to common problems. As a result, former Field Agent Archie Phinney orchestrated the establishment of the National Congress of American Indians in 1944.

By then Ben Reifel was in military service. During March of 1942 he went on active duty as a Second Lieutenant in the regular U.S. Army, and spent most of his tour states-side with the Military Police. After V-E Day he went to France and Germany for nine months to retrain combat troops for military police duty in Europe. He rose to the rank of Major by the time he mustered out in April of 1946.

When Reifel went back to work for the Bureau of Indian Affairs in July, its new role and marked reductions in congressional appropriations necessitated changes in administrative structure. The BIA was regionalized into five districts. Reifel became the first District Tribal Relations Officer for the Northern Great Plains states of Montana, Wyoming, Nebraska, and the two Dakotas. Headquartered in Billings, he was assigned to do essentially what he had done as an Organization Field Agent before the war.

He had hardly settled at Billings when he was promoted to the office of Superintendent on the Fort Berthold Reservation in central North Dakota. Administrators in the Commissioner's office had long recognized his leadership ability. As early as 1937 Reifel's name had appeared on the "recommended Superintendent candidate's list." In 1941 he was offered the Superintendency at Crow Creek Reservation in South Dakota, but chose to continue his work as a Field Agent instead. At last, circumstances enabled him to assume total responsibility for the affairs of a reservation on behalf of the United States.

Fort Berthold, the home of the Three Affiliated Tribes (Arikaras, Hidatsas, and Mandans), was a most difficult place to manage in 1946, not due to the dispositions of the tribes but because of the impact of recent national legislation. Congress had passed the Flood Control Act of 1944 to authorize the management of the Missouri River basin by the U.S. Army Corps of Engineers. The Garrison Dam was scheduled for construction downstream from the Fort Berthold Reservation. Eighty-five percent of the reservation population lived in the "taking area," which would be inundated by the reservoir. All of these tribal members would be relocated onto barren uplands. The destruction of flood plain economy would upset the entire existence of the Mandans, Arikaras, and Hidatsas.

Chaotic conditions existed at Fort Berthold when Reifel took over as Superintendent in November of 1946. In addition to the normal duties of administering federal programs, he had a responsibility to convince members of the tribes and their leaders to accept the Garrison Dam without protest, and to devise a plan for change. Administrative skill and experience were his primary assets. Through long meetings he assisted tribal leaders in communicating with tribal members; with citizens of nearby communities; with officials of local, county, and state governments; with ranking BIA officials; and with members of Congress. As compensation for inundated land, Congress mandated the U.S. Department of War to offer areas of comparable size and quality before January 1, 1947. This "lieu lands" proposal already had been submitted to the Three Affiliated Tribes for approval. Reifel quickly became involved in whirlwind community meetings to explain the offer to tribal members. Reflecting the people's sentiment, the Tribal Council rejected the War Department's offer. Few of the proposed lieu land areas were adjacent to the reservation and most were of questionable quality as prospective agricultural acreages.

While many still hoped to prevent the construction of the Garrison Dam, failure to secure lieu lands compelled Fort Berthold Indians to shift their efforts toward getting a sizable cash settlement as compensation for their losses. In July, 1947, Congress passed a law to stipulate that when the Three Affiliated Tribes accepted a contract with the United States, $5,105,625 would be paid to them for the loss of land plus the cost of relocation. After lengthy deliberations the Fort Berthold people accepted the contract. In a tearful ceremony Tribal Chairman George Gillette and the several councilmen signed it on May 20, 1948. One thing was clear: federal officials had forced contract terms upon the Three Affiliated Tribes. The Eightieth Congress added $7.5 million to the settlement as conscience money. Declaring it to be neither a "just" nor a "moral" settlement, North Dakota U.S. Representative William Lemke called the Garrison Dam Project yet another treaty-breaking chapter in the history of federal relations with Indian tribes.

Superintendent Reifel had to oversee Fort Berthold Agency personnel who, while working in partnership with staff from the Missouri River Basin Investigations (MRBI) agency, were planning for the inevitable. The BIA had established the MRBI as a specialized unit to assist tribes and local Bureau administrations in dealing with the impact of dams and reservoirs upon reservations along the Missouri River. Together, BIA and MRBI employees developed detailed strategies for relocation and economic reconstruction in reservation communities. Again, Reifel drew upon valuable experience as he bridged the gap between the two cultures.

During a meeting with officials from Washington, DC, the Superintendent learned of a graduate scholarship offered by Harvard University. With an inquisitive mind and the encouragement of his wife, Alice, he applied and won the award to enter Harvard's Littauer School of Public Administration. In September, 1949, Reifel took leave from the Indian Service for graduate study. Questions gnawed at his mind as he completed requirements for a master's degree in Public Administration. "I wanted to know why the Indians did not respond to advantages made available to them through churches, schools, and so on."[8] Financial aid in the form of a Harvard Faculty Scholarship and a John Hay Whitney Fellowship enabled him to continue. Thus by 1952 Reifel received a doctorate in Public Administration. The dissertation title was: "Relocation on the Fort Berthold Reservation: Problems and Programs." The writing helped him formulate answers to why Indians did not take greater advantage of available opportunities, and to realize that only by the better use of available economic avenues could Indians begin to solve their own problems.

The problems pertained to cultural difference. Reifel said that Indians again had to be flexible as they had been in the past, and he outlined four cultural adjustments necessary for their adequate adaptation to mainstream economic and social systems. While preserving their resources, Indians had to learn to save, plan for the future, adjust to the time perceptions imposed by White society, and adapt to regular wage-labor work, if they were to take advantage of opportunities and survive in the world of non-Indians. Incorporating these changes into an Indian way of life would be difficult, but Reifel believed Native Americans could do so if they desired, and still remain Indians.[9]

By the time he returned to the Indian Service in 1952, after three years on leave, important changes had occurred. The administrative structure of the BIA had been refined by the establishment of eleven regional offices. The Aberdeen Area Office assumed responsibility for the tribes in North Dakota, South Dakota, and Nebraska. In addition, official Indian policy had reverted to the pre-Collier assumption of need for rapid assimilation. To save money as well as to end federal trusteeship over Indians, congressional conservatives formulated the notion of "termination."

When the Commissioner of Indian Affairs reappointed Reifel as Superintendent at Fort Berthold, in October, 1952, the Harvard University graduate brought to his job new knowledge in public administration as well as confidence that Native Americans could take advantage of opportunities and become wholly self-sufficient. The task was tortuous at Fort Berthold, where it entailed the relocation of families from wooded bottom lands to treeless prairie. Education and health facility replacement became snarled in federal efforts to end federal responsibility for these functions. The Agency moved from Elbowoods to New Town in August, 1953, before work on the construction of administration buildings was complete. In the midst of turmoil, Reifel and tribal leaders negotiated a contract to salvage four million board feet of cottonwood lumber. Its sale not only provided a temporary source of income for tribal operations, but also afforded jobs for individuals. Meanwhile, internal factionalism grew over how tribal compensative monies appropriated by Congress ought to be used. Some members in financial straits sought per capita payments while others argued in favor of the investment of the money in a program of reservation economic development. The controversy continued beyond Reifel's tenure as Superintendent.

In January of 1954 the Commissioner of Indian Affairs appointed him as the first Indian ever to hold the office of Superintendent at Pine Ridge. Except for the Navajo Superintendency, the post at the largest Sioux reservation was considered the most demanding in the Bureau. Almost immediately Reifel returned to Pine Ridge, where he had begun his BIA career twenty-one years earlier.

Freed from the burden of worrisome details at New Town, Reifel was better able to implement his strategies of administration while he fine tuned his philosophy regarding successful adaptation by Indians. This was a challenge. Oglalas were among the most traditional of Sioux peoples. They retained a large degree of dependence upon federal support. Their tribal government contained vocal minorities that often created difficulties not only for the tribal council, but also for the Superintendent as he worked to administer federal Indian policy. Reifel's style of administration was well suited to deal with Oglalas. While he was determined to enforce the rules and regulations of the BIA, he also was even handed in his effort to avoid favoritism or interfactional distress. He established a strong chain of command, delegating authority to agency staff members with responsibility for federal programs.

The Superintendent made his personal contribution mainly with communicative skills. He kept lines of communication open to tribal officials and invited a representative of the tribal council to attend agency staff meetings. He scheduled informational sessions with agency program staff in the districts. Reifel participated in such community activities as church, 4-H club, and Parent Teacher Association meetings. More than forums to impart information, local gatherings gave members of reservation communities the opportunity to exchange ideas and to voice opinions.

Reifel informed tribal members through the publication of *The Pine Ridge*, a monthly news bulletin. He printed a one-page Agency *Daily News Sheet* within two weeks of his becoming Superintendent. It carried information on agency programs, staff activities, and policy changes. Most popular was a daily local news column about deaths, health tips, activities of the tribal council, reservation programs, and community organizations, especially those involving the younger members of the tribe.

Skillfully, Superintendent Reifel employed traditional Lakota traits combined with communicative skills to engender a new spirit of optimism at Pine Ridge. He recognized that defeatism would continue as long as Oglalas depended on the Bureau of Indian Affairs for support. He also realized that it would take a change of attitude for Indians to make the cultural adaptation necessary to function within the economic and social systems of the mainstream society. He worked with tribal leaders and individual tribal members alike to help them solve their own problems. He appealed to their sense of pride, imploring them to restore the strength Oglalas had demonstrated under leadership from Red Cloud and Crazy Horse. He boastfully lauded individual and group accomplishments, but, when the occasion demanded, Reifel quickly shamed any detrimental behavior.

Education was the cornerstone for revitalization as well as a necessary ingredient in cultural adjustment. Whenever possible, the Superintendent attended commencement exercises at both the eighth grade and high school levels. Exemplary educational achievement by youngsters received prominent mention in agency publications. Reifel printed daily school attendance figures and gave special praise for perfect attendance. Parents who did not keep their children in school were exposed in a list of names that appeared in the *Daily News Sheet*.

Educational youth organizations—4-H, church, or school related— were central to the Superintendent's plan. Reifel's interest in youngsters prompted him to accept a position on the Board of Directors of the Black Hills Council for the Boy Scouts of America in hopes of providing an opportunity for Pine Ridge boys to take part. For his effort to introduce Boy Scouts on the reservation and dedicated work on both the state and national level, he received Scouting's highest awards, the Silver Beaver, Silver Antelope, and Silver Buffalo.

Stark reality added credence to Reifel's focus on education. Following the passage of House Resolution 108 in Congress during 1953, the U.S. Department of Interior had relaxed a moratorium on the sale of individual Indian land allotments established during the New Deal era. Reifel reported in mid-1954 that through land sales the Oglalas had lost nearly 100 acres of land per day during the previous year, and that a burgeoning reservation population reported requests for land sales of an aggregate acreage three to four times as large as that sold in the previous year. At a time when only 200 out of 1700 families could earn adequate livings off the land or other employment on the reservation, there was no hope that more than a few of the remaining 1500 families could benefit from any long-range land-use program. He concluded that, although in the past the livelihood of Sioux people had come from their land, in the mid-twentieth century the future for many Oglalas depended upon their ability to secure off-reservation employment. Only through education could they obtain the knowledge and skills needed to secure jobs and develop the understanding necessary to make cultural adjustments in a non-reservation environment. Accordingly, Reifel supported the Voluntary Relocation Program of the Bureau of Indian Affairs.

A major deterrent to effective education and self-esteem was alcohol abuse. Although in 1953 Congress had made it legal for all Indians to drink, the tribes had been given local option to decide whether liquor could be consumed or sold on their reservations. The Oglalas had continued prohibition and Reifel declared war on bootlegging because he deplored the degenerative effects of alcohol consumed in excess. Both in speech and in print, he exposed the effects. In an address following the inauguration of a new tribal council, for instance, the Superintendent pleaded for tribal leaders to look into the innocent faces of young people. In *The Daily News Sheet* he graphically reported on automobile accidents and family tragedies caused by excessive drinking. He published the names of individuals who ran afoul of the law in a state of drunkenness, described their offenses, and identified their sentences in a daily Jail Report for everyone to see.

Reifel's efforts to bring rebirth to Oglala spirit extended to improving the image of Indians to outsiders. He initiated a reservation-wide cleanup campaign. He became a liaison between Pine Ridge and off-reservation groups and communities. More than just a promoter of good relations between Pine Ridge and reservation border towns,

Reifel became an educator for Indians and Whites alike. To all who would listen, he explained the complexities of federal Indian policy, the role of the BIA, the cultural differences between Indians and non-Indians, and the problems that those differences created. He addressed business, civic, church, and service club groups. He spoke at commencement proceedings for numerous Indian Schools and for such public institutions as Chadron (Nebraska) State Teachers' College. He addressed high school students and teachers. He appeared before district church convocations, Chambers of Commerce, and even state-wide conventions containing groups as different from each other as the Veterans Administration Nurses and the South Dakota White House Conference on Education.

By the time the Commissioner of Indian Affairs appointed Reifel to the position of Area Director for the Aberdeen Area Office in July, 1955, his administrative philosophy had matured. As the Director he served as a mid-level administrator for Indian policy in the BIA regional structure. He was directly responsible to the Commissioner of Indian Affairs in Washington, DC, and often served as the Commissioner's Bureau representative with other federal agencies and state governments. Area Office staff directors for various BIA programs, and field superintendents of twelve reservations, three schools, and several hospitals scattered across the states of Nebraska, South Dakota, and North Dakota, all worked under Reifel's direction.

In straightforward manner, Reifel used a chain of administrative command as he oversaw and coordinated those responsible for carrying out Indian policy at the Area Office and the reservation level. From prior experience, he understood the parts that were played by administrators under his supervision and used their individual talents while providing expert guidance.

Reifel became Aberdeen Area Office Director at the height of the "Termination Era" and remained in that position for some time after the Secretary of the Interior announced in 1958 that the withdrawal of federal support for Indians was more an objective for the future than a policy for immediate implementation. Administering a plan designed to save money by getting the BIA out of the "Indian business" often produced contradictory and controversial results. Terminationists in Congress as well as in the Eisenhower administration faced the reality that many individual Indians and tribes were not yet prepared for so drastic a change. Congress had never funded the BIA sufficiently to prepare all Indians to survive on their own. As a result, policy makers in Washington had never fashioned their assimilationist ideas or termination strategies to prevent failure.

Mounting opposition among high ranking officials finally forced the terminationists to slow the process of federal withdrawal from tribal affairs. This gave Area Director Reifel the time and opportunity to prepare Indians for adverse consequences by using new programs initiated for this purpose late in the 1950s and early in the 1960s. The Community Services programs under Bureau management underwent considerable improvement. Partially out of a concern about juvenile delinquency, Congress increased appropriations to up-grade Law and Order personnel and equipment. Two-way radios were installed. Law and Order programs no longer had to rely upon vehicles cast off from other BIA programs. There was concerted effort to introduce preventive law enforcement. Reifel took special interest in youth groups and in chapters of Alcoholics Anonymous on reservations.

The welfare section of BIA Community Services was broadened and improved. Although Aberdeen Area Office funding remained fairly constant, the number of professional social workers more than doubled between 1953 and 1958. Adoption and foster care programs improved through greater support from state agencies and cooperation from leaders in the BIA with those of the Child Welfare League of America. For families affected by the Missouri River Development Program, the BIA expanded its range of services to assist in making the plans and adjustments required by changing reservation conditions.

Commissioner of Indian Affairs Glenn Emmons supported Reifel in the belief that education was the most essential ingredient in the preparation of Native Americans for survival in mainstream society. As early as October, 1955, the Commissioner launched a pilot project in Adult Education among five tribal groups identified for having the greatest need. Inasmuch as two of the groups were in the Aberdeen Area (The Turtle Mountain Chippewa in North Dakota and the Rosebud Sioux in South Dakota), Area Office Director Reifel became involved in the pilot project. From the outset, he provided wise counsel at the national as well as the regional and reservation levels. He not only participated in the planning and early implementation of the program for his Area, but also contributed to Bureau-wide Adult Education conferences.

Because this educational plan reinforced Reifel's own thoughts concerning modern Indian adaptation, he grasped its broadest implications. In July, 1956, only six months after the Adult Education program began, he told a joint meeting for the leaders of pilot projects on three reservations that this vocational training program for all adult Indians was the first in the history of tribal education. Speaking in July of 1956, he called not only for English literacy, but also for economic, social, and cultural literacy. Through his encouragement and counsel, by 1959 Aberdeen Area adult education programs were operating at several reservations and at the Sioux Sanatorium in Rapid City.

Reifel's role in the Adult Education program epitomized his administrative accomplishments as it reflected his contribution to the improvement of public relations. Relying on experience and Harvard University training, he applied modern management practices that enabled him to emphasize public relations more than had any other Area Director in memory. Reifel was a persuasive speaker with the oratorical skills to reach a variety of audiences. He spoke at banquets, conferences, meetings, and workshops. He talked to agricultural organizations, church and professional groups, service clubs, teachers, student and youth groups, and commencements. For nearly five years, he averaged approximately ten engagements a month, delivering his messages on a variety of issues, broadening general understanding of intercultural problems.

Accomplishments by Ben Reifel to the year 1960 made his decade of service as a South Dakota Republican in the U.S. House of Representatives seem almost anticlimactic. With a sterling record of achievement in administration, policy design and implementation, public communication, and intercultural relations, he announced his candidacy for Congress. His qualifications far exceeded those of most others who had sought candidacy for Congress in South Dakota with the exception of a few outstanding men such as Coe Crawford and Peter Norbeck.

He attracted support from various constituencies. Reifel's public relations activities of the 1950s gave him considerable name recognition in eastern South Dakota. As an outstanding alumnus of a South Dakota State College and its "Winter School," he drew support from a network of friends and associates he had maintained throughout the years. Sacrificing the security of a lucrative federal position just three and a half years short of a full retirement salary to run for elective office convinced many voters that he was sincere in his purpose. Reifel's past reputation plus his positive straightforward, people-to-people campaign made "A Straight Shooter" image more than a slogan. "A departure from the well-known political figure," he brought a "breath of fresh air" to South Dakota's political scene.[10] Reifel was the right man at the right hour; had the times not been right, he might never have been elected to Congress.

Neither political party had a candidate to rival Reifel's public appeal in 1960, when Democrat George McGovern abandoned his seat in the U.S. House of Representatives to make his first bid for the U.S. Senate, where Republicans Francis Case and Karl Mundt were firmly entrenched. Reifel won the election not by support from Indians alone but also as the overwhelming choice of non-Indians in the First Congressional District east of the Missouri River. Some South Dakotans gave him support because of his unwavering image as a successful tribal member who could win favor in Washington, DC, without risking damage to the interests of mainstream society in his state. Loyal Democrats could continue supporting party leader McGovern in the senatorial contest and still voice their concern about Indian issues by voting for Reifel in his race for a seat in the U.S. House of Representatives. Businessmen could support him because of his reliability and ethical standards.

Once in office, Reifel demonstrated his commitment to personal integrity and public responsibility without the quest for recognition. He authored no famous legislation and sponsored no flamboyant investigations. Yet, he received many special appointments, awards, and honorific degrees—including doctorates from the universities in Vermillion and Brookings and the college at Aberbeen—which recognized his many achievements.

The quality of service to his constituents was more important to Reifel than was personal aggrandizement. He was dedicated to communication with all people at all levels just as he had been while holding offices at New Town, Pine Ridge, and Aberdeen. His colleagues in Congress found him always dedicated to promoting greater understanding of Indian culture and the complex problems of Indian affairs. Many admired his strong belief in equality expressed through his staunch support for civil rights legislation during the 1960s. With depth of understanding, he was instrumental in the passing of congressional legislation to establish the National Endowment for the Arts and the National Endowment for the Humanities.

As a freshman congressman on the Agriculture Committee, Reifel authored and won passage for three bills beneficial to state agricultural economy, and throughout his tenure sought in other ways to aid South Dakota agribusiness. His expertise and interest in Indian Affairs won him membership on the Subcommittee on Interior and Related Agencies of the powerful House Appropriations Committee. There he had an opportunity to shape federal Indian policy toward providing greater educational opportunities for tribal members and to facilitate the construction of cooperative school plants at Mission and Sisseton, South Dakota.

Most of all, Reifel gave his unwavering support to the management of congressional appropriations that gave advantages to South Dakotans during the era of Lyndon Johnson's Great Society programs. Through the period 1962 to 1970, the state possessed an inordinate amount of influence regarding congressional appropriations due to the committee assignments of Reifel in the House and Karl Mundt in the Senate. Projects ranging from Missouri River Development to the establishment of the EROS Data Center northeast of Sioux Falls fostered economic growth.

Reifel retired voluntarily from political life after a decade in Congress, but he continued to give his expertise to the promotion of a better intercultural understanding. Maintaining a primary residence in his home district, Reifel's influence continued in matters both on and off the Indian reservations, and his presence was ever obvious because of the Airstream recreational vehicle in which he enjoyed relief from the stressful demands of public service.[11] There came a brief return to active administration after December 7, 1976, when President Gerald Ford chose him to fill a vacancy in the office of Commissioner of Indians Affairs. Called the "best-qualified person ever appointed to head the Bureau," he easily brought calm to a troubled bureaucracy through a term better measured in days than in months or years of service.[12] Reifel then resigned as the last Commissioner of Indian Affairs, for when he vacated the office its responsibilities were transferred to an Assistant Secretary of the Interior. A brief appearance by a person whose image invited no controversy accomplished this transition in federal Indian relations. Thereafter, Reifel retired quietly for a second time to be revered as one of the most distinguished leaders in the history of his state.

He should be remembered best for his contributions in facilitating tribal adjustments to twentieth century conditions, and for his continuous effort to promote intercultural understanding. With personal experience, advanced education, administrative skill, and communicative acumen, he educated all who would listen. Reifel was successful at every turn in his career because he transcended the problems of the past and present to address the needs of the future with deep bicultural understanding emanating from his own dual cultural heritage.

Notes

1. Interview with Ben Reifel by John S. Painter, May 30, 1979.
2. *Ibid.*

3. *Ibid.*

4. U.S., Department of the Interior, *Annual Report of the Secretary of the Interior, 1938* (Washington, DC: Government Printing Office, 1939), p. 210. Emphasis added.

5. *They Came Here First: The Epic of the American Indian* (Revised Edition; New York: Harper & Row, 1975), p. 212.

6. Benjamin Reifel, "Federal Indian Policy, 1933–1945," *Indian Self-Rule: First-Hand Accounts of Indian-White Relations from Roosevelt to Reagan* (Kenneth R. Philp, ed.; Salt Lake City: Howe Brothers, 1986), p. 54.

7. Interview with Ben Reifel by Joseph H. Cash, Summer, 1967, *The Plains Indians of the Twentieth Century* (Peter Iverson, ed.; Norman: University of Oklahoma Press, 1985), p. 109.

8. Quoted in Mildred Fielder, *Sioux Indian Leaders* (Seattle: Superior Publishing Co., 1975), p. 138.

9. Ben Reifel, "Cultural Factors in Social Adjustment," *Indian Education,* (April 15, 1957), pp. 1–10.

10. Editorial comment, *Redfield Press,* reported in the *Aberdeen American News,* April 24, 1960.

11. Approximately a year after Reifel retired from Congress, Alice died of influenza and pneumonia. She was survived by their only child, Loyce Reifel Anderson, born in 1935 during Ben's Organization Field Agent days. On August 21, 1972, Reifel married longtime friend Francis Ryland Colby. Francis, her late husband, Irvin Colby, Alice, and Ben had been colleagues in college. Ben's younger brothers all had successful careers. John was a carpenter and maintenance engineer prior to his death in an auto accident in 1969. George was an educator, Alexander was an engineer. Albert was a medical doctor.

12. Michael T. Smith, "Benjamin Reifel, 1976–1977," *The Commissioners of Indian Affairs, 1824–1977* (Robert M. Kvasnicka and Herman J. Viola, eds.; Lincoln: University of Nebraska Press, 1979), p. 347.

Charles Eastman.
Courtesy W.H. Over State Museum.

Elaine Goodale Eastman. Courtesy South
Dakota State Historical Society.

Normal Training School, A.L. Riggs,
Principal, photographed by W.R. Cross.
Courtesy W.H. Over State Museum.

Crow Creek Agency, D.T.
Courtesy W.H. Over State Museum.

Building a Cultural Bridge:
Elaine and Charles Eastman

Ruth Alexander

On June 18, 1891, in New York's Church of the Ascension, Elaine Goodale, "child poet of the Berkshires" and supervisor of Indian education in the Dakotas, married Dr. Charles Eastman, Dartmouth-educated Santee Sioux known as "Ohiyesa" ("the winner") during his boyhood among Mdewakanton people. These attractive, intelligent young inheritors of two different cultures had met the previous November at Pine Ridge Agency in South Dakota. Their love was born in the turmoil of the Ghost Dance movement and nurtured in the blood and death of the Wounded Knee Affair.

Neither individual had planned on marrying at this time and both recognized theirs as a union dedicated to something more than romance. "I had not given due weight to the possibility of love," Charles wrote. "I had planned to enter upon my life work unhampered by any other ties, and declared that all my love should be vested in my people and my profession. At last, however, I had met a woman whose sincerity was convincing and whose ideals seemed very like my own."[1] Of this decisive time in their lives, Elaine later wrote, "The gift of myself to a Sioux just at this crisis . . . followed almost inevitably upon my passionate preoccupation with the welfare of those whom I had already looked upon as my adopted people. . . . I embraced with a new and deeper zeal the conception of life-long service to my husband's people."[2]

In many ways the lives of Elaine and Charles were expressions of federal Indian policy in the late nineteenth century. Each represented

355

the best in a culture. Elaine, descended from Puritans, was nurtured on Emersonian plain living and high thinking, and Thoreau's nature in the twilight of New England's greatness. Charles, fleeing the defeat of the Minnesota Sioux War with his uncle, led the traditional Native American life, training as a warrior and hunter in the Canadian woods and on the plains and prairies of Saskatchewan until he was fifteen. At that time, his father came to claim him and to encourage him to follow the White man's way.

Elaine and Charles explored each other's culture. Imbued with a missionary spirit, Elaine traveled to Indian Country in the 1880s to bring education and Christianity to Indian young people, to learn their language, and to live closely with them. Encouraged by teachers and driven by desire to succeed in the White world, Charles traveled to New England to attend Dartmouth College and Boston University, where he acquired a medical degree and an immersion into New England culture. When he returned to South Dakota as the United States Physician at Pine Ridge, and Elaine concluded her visit to Indian schools around the Agency, their marriage might have seemed almost predestined. Certainly, the wedding signified the destiny that Indian reformers of the 1870s and 1880s envisioned for every tribal member—transformation into an educated, Christian, middle class citizen. Together, according to this idealized plan, Elaine and Charles would lead the way into the happy assimilation of Indians.

The dream never materialized, either personally for the hopeful couple or nationally for Indian-White relations. Some thirty years and six children later, Elaine and Charles separated, and each pursued a life independent of the other. Although their union had produced a wealth of publication about Sioux people, it had not achieved for either of them the personal satisfaction or fulfillment they had anticipated. Simultaneously, the federal Indian Peace Policy, which had been designed to give concrete expression to reformers' ideas, had ended in failure, too. Reservation surveys of the 1920s revealed that Sioux tribes had lost most of their land to White people, had grown dependent on federal support, yet had clung stubbornly to remnants of their traditional culture.

In recognition of these conditions, the Indian New Deal of the 1930s called a halt to the loss of land, re-established tribal governments, and encouraged cultural activities. Out of their failure to create a lasting marriage and life together, Elaine and Charles Eastman salvaged a cultural bridge between Whites and Indians based on increased under-standing of Indian culture and greater respect for the customs, religions, and languages of all Native Americans. Because Charles had difficulty earning a living for his growing family in a competitive White world, and because Elaine was already a widely-published author when she wed, she encouraged him to write and publish his own astonishing story, assisting him with her talent and experience when necessary. The dream of a fully assimilated Indian people might not have been realized, but together Elaine and Charles produced an extraordinary series of popular books that enabled general readers, young and old, to understand and appreciate Sioux culture. The books revealed the Indians' humanity, treating them neither as "savages" nor as anthropological objects. Each was written with sympathy, insight, and affection drawn from the writers' own experiences.

To Sioux readers, *Indian Boyhood* (1902), *Old Indian Days* (1907), *Smoky Day's Wigwam Stories* (1909), *The Soul of the Indian* (1911), *The Indian Today* (1912), and *From the Deep Woods to Civilization* (1916) provide a bridge to self-respect. Charles Eastman was one of their own, expressing their stories, beliefs, and customs in the language of White men.[3] To other Americans, Eastman's books opened the lives of Plains Indians, providing a bridge to greater knowledge and understanding of their habits and religious beliefs. Some critics might think these works are too romantic in their view of traditional life or too heavily filtered through the perceptions of Christian reformers.[4] But the books are still popular and widely read, holding up well after more than half a century.

The Eastmans' unique combination of talent and experience formed the basis for literature that has lasted so well. Indeed, their early lives so prepared them for their task that publication became an historical inevitability. Both grew up in the best that their cultures had to offer. Elaine's gifts as writer and editor, and Charles' wealth of material, blended to create a series of books that retold Charles' life and ideas in a way that appealed to White as well as to Indian readers.

In *Indian Boyhood*, Charles recounts "the freest life in the world" of hunting, of training for Indian warfare by mimicking the great warriors of the tribe, of studying the habits of animals and the wilderness. The flight from the Minnesota River Valley after the War of 1862 across Dakota Territory and the Missouri River, then north to the Canadian Plains, must have been torturous for Mdewakanton bands. According to the factual details, Hadakah (or "pitiful last one," as he was called until he was renamed Ohiyesa) suffered great loss and hardship. His mother died soon after his birth, and he was left in the care of Un-cheedah, a grandmother. His father was separated from the band when, as a warrior in the Minnesota War, he was arrested and imprisoned and, as far as his family knew at the time, hanged at New Ulm with other leaders. The Leaf Band struggled to survive in the face of diminishing game and a contest for territory that was also claimed by Metis (mixed-bloods) as well as Gros Ventres and Crows. Always they were threatened by American "Big Knives" who seemed powerful, treacherous, and incomprehensible to them.

But Eastman's account of his first fifteen years acknowledges neither deprivation nor bitterness. He tells of his experience as a boy growing up in a traditional Indian life with nostalgic affection: "I was now an exile as well as motherless, yet I was not unhappy," he writes. "Our wanderings from place to place afforded many pleasant experiences and quite as many hardships and misfortunes."[5] He regarded Uncheedah as "the wisest of guides and the best of protectors."[6] From her he learned the power of Wakan, the Great Mystery, and the wonders of the natural world. He loved and respected his uncle, Mysterious Medicine, who took responsibility for his training as a warrior and hunter. At age fifteen, Mysterious Medicine gave him a flint-lock gun with which he expected to avenge the death of his father and other warriors of the Leaf Band.

Although Eastman reveals the hardships and rigorous training of fasting, silence, and solitude that would develop his bravery, endurance, and patience, he spends much more time on the joyous tribal activities: games and sports, maple sugar making, wild rice harvesting, story telling, tribal gatherings, celebrations, and hunts. Some of the ways he learned stayed with him throughout his life: his love of the wilderness, his enthusiasm for stories, his devotion to physical activity. Yet all of these moorings in Ohiyesa's life were abruptly torn loose when his father reappeared in the band one day during the boy's fifteenth year. Released from prison where he had converted to Christianity and committed to the "White man's way," he had left the Santee Reservation in Nebraska and taken up a homestead near present-day Flandreau on the Big Sioux River. In 1872 Jacob Eastman persuaded his son to return to the United States with him to become Christian and "civilized."

It was less than a month since I had been a rover and a hunter in the Manitoba wilderness, with no thoughts save those which concern the most free and natural life of an Indian. Now, I found myself standing near a rude log cabin on the edge of a narrow strip of timber, overlooking the fertile basin of the Big Sioux River. As I gazed over the rolling prairie

land, all I could see was that it met the sky at the horizon line. It seemed
to me vast and vague and endless, as was my conception of the new trail
which I had taken and my dream of the far-off goal.[7]

Meanwhile, back in Massachusetts, Elaine grew to womanhood in
the close family circle at "Sky Farm" in the Berkshires. Born to old
New England families that traced their lineage to colonial days and
named for Tennyson's heroine, the oldest daughter of a literary family
spent a happy childhood among the mountain meadows and forests
reflected in Elaine's later writing.[8] Her literary talents were encouraged
at an early age. She read fluently at three and her father published the
poems of Elaine and her sister Dora in 1877 in *St. Nicholas Magazine*.
Two years later their book *Apple Blossoms: Verses of Two Children*
achieved considerable fame for the precocity demonstrated by the two
budding authors.

The whole emphasis of Elaine's childhood was upon "plain living
and high thinking" and "the beauty of service" in the best Puritan
tradition.[9] Her mother found the "rustic simplicity" of carrying water,
sleeping in unheated bedrooms, churning butter, preparing sausage
and head cheese, and trimming, cleaning, and filling kerosene lamps
an arduous undertaking for one used to more genteel and urban life in
Connecticut. Yet Elaine remembered the pastoral life with great affection. In spite of her letters from the poet Longfellow, and her reading
Shakespeare, MacCauley, Gibbon, and lots of writing, there was not
enough money to send Elaine to college. She had only two terms at a
boarding school in New York City. When she was twenty, her family
left Sky Farm, her mother returning to a family home in Connecticut,
and her father taking a salaried position in New York City. Like that
of Charles Eastman, her life at the beginning of adulthood took a
sudden new direction.

Elaine was certainly ready at that time to make her way in the world.
She was not interested in romance, and later described herself as a
non-conformist of fashion. "I cared little about what I wore, seldom
thought about my looks, was socially abrupt and awkward—a fault I
have never been able entirely to overcome. I had no small talk, no
particular desire to please."[10] In addition to her independent spirit,
Elaine claimed literary ambition and an almost missionary-like desire
to serve humanity. With her mother's encouragement, she accepted a
teaching position at Hampton Institute, where Samuel C. Armstrong
and Richard Henry Pratt assembled liberated Black children and
Indian youngsters for practical training and cultural instruction. By

serving there, Elaine Goodale was launched on a path that would lead her to Wounded Knee and Charles Eastman.

After growing up deep in their respective cultures, both Charles and Elaine immersed themselves thoroughly in each other's culture before they met and married. When Charles accompanied his father Jacob to the Indian homesteading community near Flandreau, the entire direction of his life changed. Academic education and Christianity were the requisite attributes of White culture that Charles had to accept, according to his father. At first it was difficult. Cutting his hair, wearing White man's clothes, being laughed at for not knowing English, Charles sought solace in the woods and fields. Yet, with his father's and brother's encouragement, he persevered. He learned English at the local school, walked 140 miles to attend Santee Normal Institute, the reservation boarding school in Nebraska supervised by the Reverends John P. Williamson and Alfred Riggs. Charles's ability to learn, and adapt quickly, became apparent.

Slowly, but inexorably, he moved East to further his education. Shortly after the Battle of the Little Big Horn, Charles went to Beloit College in Wisconsin, where Alfred's father Stephen Return Riggs retired. From there, he moved to Knox College in Illinois. Finally, through the efforts of Alfred Riggs, he took the train to New Hampshire—ogling the wonders of houses and comforts that the *Washechu* had—to attend Dartmouth, the college haven for Indian students. Charles was a popular and successful scholar at Dartmouth, deep in Elaine's home country. He played football, worked, studied, and joined a fraternity—adopting all the external paraphernalia of White students. It was a happy and hopeful time. Finally, he moved to the intellectual citadel of nineteenth century America, Boston, where he entered Boston University Medical School, graduating in 1889. By this time he had all the accoutrements of a White young man—education, culture, the Christian religion.

While he was soaking up New England's culture, Elaine had become enraptured with the free, natural life of the Sioux people. Ever an eager learner, she was not content for long to teach Indian students at Hampton Institute. She wanted to *know* them. Already she had been encouraged by Samuel Armstrong to write articles about the school and the philosophy that motivated its Indian work. Education, Christianity, individualism, the work ethic, and property ownership were seen as the necessary tools by which the Indian would be remodeled in the White man's image. Elaine felt genuine devotion to her work. She admired and liked the students, and was deeply committed to racial equality. She became a public spokesperson for Indian education, but she wanted to see Indian Country for herself.

Such a determined young woman was bound to succeed! In 1885, she traveled with friends to the Great Sioux Reservation in Dakota Territory. Beginning at Pierre, the party attended a church convocation at Crow Creek Reservation with Bishop William Hobart Hare. The group crossed the Missouri to Lower Brule Agency and visited a camp near the mouth of the White River. Here Elaine saw an empty federal day school (to which she returned to teach through the following three years). By steamboat and covered wagon, the party continued to Standing Rock Reservation, then by buggy and horseback to Rosebud and Pine Ridge. Although it was an arduous and rough journey, Elaine commented: "Indians are experts at outdoor living and their primitive arrangements delighted me."[11]

During her teaching she became a participant in Indian life. She became fluent in the Sioux language. Elaine was permitted to attend, in the role of reporter, the "Big Council" of Sioux leaders in 1888, as they opposed the reduction of the Great Sioux Reservation through the modification of the 1868 Fort Laramie Treaty. She was "definitely" on the side of the Indians in their deliberations, as she stated to Richard Pratt, Head of the Commission. In 1889, she persuaded Whirling Hawk to let her accompany his band on an antelope hunt in the Nebraska Sand Hills. Wearing moccasins and Indian dress, sleeping in a tipi, eating the game they killed, and riding her pony, Elaine traveled with former Sioux warriors and their families, who spoke no English. It was a joyous experience. She remarked on the friendliness, humor, and cleanliness of the women, the modesty and courtesy of the men. One night the band entertained Chasing Crane, who told of the New Messiah and the Ghost Dance that would bring back the buffalo—intimating the troubles to come.[12]

As a result of her experiences, Elaine Goodale developed immense respect for and admiration of the Indians she had come to know. Wherever she went, she wrote. She sent articles, letters, and stories to more than twenty periodicals and newspapers during these years. She told of the Indians' struggle to survive in spite of diminishing annuities, poor land, sickness, and government treachery. She was even privately adopted into the Lame Horse band. By the end of the decade she was well-known for her championship of the Indians' cause. When she returned East in late 1889, she spoke at the Mohonk Conference, at schools, and at other gatherings on their behalf, always advocating the necessity of assimilation, of turning these people whose culture so delighted her into educated, Christian, individual property owners. She supported the destruction of tribal land through individual allotment under the Dawes Act of 1887, and was a particularly ardent advocate for education, especially at day schools like the one she served on Lower Brule Reservation.

Not surprisingly, this vocal champion was appointed supervisor of all Indian schools on western Sioux reservations, beginning in 1890. She purchased a team and wagon, hired an Indian couple to accompany her, and set out in good weather to inspect the schools. Her earlier experience traveling across the empty land and her knowledge of the language stood her in good stead. She tirelessly worked for better food, fresher air, better trained teachers, less harsh discipline for Indian pupils in the schools. In the course of her journey, she dined with Sitting Bull on the Grand River just weeks before his death, and breakfasted with the ill-fated Big Foot's band on the way to Pine Ridge just weeks before the disaster. She heard and saw the Ghost Dancers, but regarded their "craze" as a "passing novelty"—a diversion from the drought, poverty, and depression of the plains—with no threat of violence.[13] Yet, the stage for the ominous background against which the romance of Elaine and Charles would be played out was set.

Death at Wounded Knee came on December 29, just four days following the Christmas upon which they announced their engagement. The Wounded Knee Affair was devastating to both of them, but particularly shattering to Charles. Worried as the first terrified wounded were brought in, he joined the search party after a blizzard and discovered many snow-covered, weaponless bodies that had been chased and shot by White soldiers. Among them were some wounded, which they rescued, carrying them into Pine Ridge where the church was converted to a make-shift hospital, and where Elaine helped nurse the victims—mostly women and children. "All of this was a severe ordeal for one who so lately put all his faith in the Christian love and lofty ideals of the White Man," wrote Charles later, but he was too busy using his professional skills to express himself at the time.[14] Elaine, however, turned to her pen and sent an account to the New York papers, laying blame for the slaughter squarely on the U.S. Army and federal government, maintaining that Big Foot's band was not "hostile" but frightened, and that women and children were killed deliberately.[15]

Although life quieted down and the two were wed, this ugly event presaged a married life that for more than a decade was troubled and unstable. Within a year, Charles was embroiled in a dispute with the

Agent at Pine Ridge over the payment of Sioux claims for losses of property and livestock incurred during the Ghost Dance troubles. The Commissioner of Indian Affairs upheld the authority of the Agent and Charles was forced to resign in 1893. The family moved to St. Paul, where he attempted to establish a private practice, but he soon accepted a position heading the Young Men's Christian Association program for Indians. This job required travel to Indian reservations and strained the marriage just as the addition of two more children drained the family finances. When a few years later the YMCA work proved unsatisfactory, Charles attempted to lobby for Santee claims in Washington, DC, moving his family there in 1898. But he was not an attorney, and was opposed by others in the tribe. So his two years of work, largely unremunerated, went for naught. After a stint at Carlisle Indian School in Pennsylvania, during which Elaine was apparently the primary family breadwinner as editor of *The Red Man*, and after Charles' serious bout with pneumonia, he succeeded in 1900 in obtaining a position as U.S. Physician at Crow Creek Reservation. This lasted two years before he was again asked to resign over serious differences with the U.S. Agent.

Family circumstances were strained indeed! Out of these difficult times, Elaine turned to the talent that had succored her in the past. When the family had first moved to St. Paul in 1893, she had urged her husband to write down recollections of his early life, which she had carefully edited and submitted to *St. Nicolas Magazine*, publisher of her own work years earlier.[16] These were readily accepted and, during the years at Crow Creek, revised into the first book, *Indian Boyhood* (1903). Living once again in Minnesota and pressed for funds, they worked on a second book, *Red Hunters and the Animal People*, which was published in 1904. A pattern was established and seven other books followed. Although Elaine revised and edited all of Charles' work, she is listed as co-author of only one: *Smoky Days' Wigwam Evenings: Indian Legends Retold* (1910). The others recounted Charles' life after his Indian childhood, *From the Deep Woods to Civilization* (1916), or dealt with Indian life and customs: *Old Indian Days* (1907); *The Indian Today* (1916); *Indian Heroes and Chieftains* (1918). The work usually regarded as his best and most profound, *The Soul of the Indian* (1911), describes Indian religion and beliefs.

The books changed the courses of the Eastmans' lives. For one thing, in 1903 they moved back to New England at Elaine's insistence, and she never lived in Indian Country again. For another, Charles became famous. His books made him a celebrity much in demand as a lecturer, and Elaine managed the publicity and arrangements for as many as twenty-five lectures a year. Other accolades followed. He attended a dinner for Mark Twain in New York in 1905; he was selected to attend the North American Race Congress in London in 1911; and he was elected President of the Society of American Indians in 1918. In the next decade, he lectured at Oxford.[17] All of this required much traveling and absence from home.

During these years, Elaine remained at home with the six children. In spite of her husband's success and her own efforts in achieving it, she lived in obscurity. "He travelled widely, even to London, and met hosts of interesting people. I was inevitably house-bound," she wrote.[18] She created and published some work of her own: *Little Brother o' Dreams* (1910), *Yellow Star: A Story of East and West* (1911), and *Indian Legends Retold* (1919). Her writing never achieved the acclaim that her husband's had received-even though she was the principal writer in the family.

Financial problems continued to plague the Eastmans. Elaine desired excellent education for her children, and this need encouraged the family to open a camp for girls at Granite Lake, New Hampshire, in 1915. The older girls acted as counselors, the younger children were general helpers, and Charles taught swimming and archery, told stories, and entertained the campers. But the main work of the camp fell on Elaine. In 1917 tragedy struck the family in the death of their beautiful and talented daughter Irene during the flu epidemic. Additional troubles surfaced in 1921, when a counselor accused Charles of fathering her child. Although the charge was neither believed nor proved, the event irreparably ruptured the marriage, which had been disintegrating for years. In August of 1921, Charles and Elaine separated.[19] Although they never divorced, nor even publicly admitted the failure of their marriage, the separation represented the end of the dream they had followed since Wounded Knee. In some respects, the very ambivalence of their relationship symbolized America's ambivalence in her relationship with Indian people. Just as Elaine and Charles were neither wholly compatible in legal marriage nor ever formally divorced, so were Whites and Indians neither assimilated nor independent of each other.

In the remaining years of his life, Charles maintained his position of honor in American eyes as a spokesman for the Indian. He lived sometimes with his son, Ohiyesa II, in Detroit. He worked as U.S. Inspector for the Office of Indian Affairs for a time, continued to lecture, and became embroiled in a dispute over Sacajawea's birth place. But he never published anything again. Furthermore, he grew out of touch with issues on Indian reservations. The ideas he espoused—education, individual property ownership, citizenship—no longer seemed pertinent to twentieth century Indians who were struggling to survive as a cultural entity in the face of poverty, disease, alcoholism, and loss of tribal land. In the final years he appeared to find the greatest joy at his cabin in Ontario, alone in the Canadian woods where he had always felt at home.

Elaine, on the other hand, continued to write both books and articles from her home in Northampton. She published two works of fiction, *The Luck of Oldacres* (1928), and *Hundred Maples* (1935). The first was based on the family's camp experience; the second explored Elaine's struggle to be both writer and traditional wife and mother. She also returned to her first love in a history of the Wounded Knee affair, and her biography of the head of Carlisle Indian School, *Pratt, the Red Man's Moses* (1935). She was astonishingly productive even as a very old woman, surrounded by children and grandchildren.

In spite of the apparent failure of their marriage and their hopes, the books they wrote remain a substantial monument to their union and their dreams. Neither Charles nor Elaine could have produced the best of them—*Indian Boyhood, Soul of an Indian, From the Deep Woods to Civilization*—without the other. Essential were Charles' intelligence, education, and experience, and Elaine's literary skill, resourcefulness, and energy. Together, they created a cultural bridge that has enabled White Americans to begin to know, respect, and admire their Indian compatriots, and which has enabled the Sioux to express their culture in language and form that White Americans can understand. The creation of such a bridge is a major achievement for which South Dakotans and all Americans can be grateful!

Notes

1. Charles A. Eastman, *From the Deep Woods to Civilization: Chapters in the Autobiography of an Indian* (Boston: Little, Brown and Company, 1916), p. 87.

2. Kay Graber, ed., *Sister to the Sioux: the Memories of Elaine Goodale Eastman, 1885–91* (Lincoln: University of Nebraska Press, 1978), pp. 169, 172.

3. Interview of Father Andy Weston by Ruth Alexander, Flandreau, South Dakota, July 20, 1986.

4. Raymond Wilson, *Ohiyesa: Charles Eastman, Santee Sioux* (Urbana, Ill.: University of Illinois Press, 1983), p. 192.

5. Charles Eastman, *Indian Boyhood* (Rapid City, SD: Fenwyn Press, 1970, Reprint from 1902 edition), p. 16.

6. *Ibid.*, p. 21.

7. Eastman, *Deep Woods*, p. 14.

8. *Little Brother o' Dreams*, 1910; *Luck of Oldacres*, 1928; *Hundred Maples*, 1935.

9. Graber, *Sister to the Sioux*, p. 14.

10. *Ibid.*

11. *Ibid.*, p. 27.

12. *Ibid.*, pp. 90–113.

13. Elaine Goodale Eastman, "The Ghost Dance War and Wounded Knee Massacre 1890–91," *Nebraska History*, XXVI (January 1945), pp. 32–33.

14. Eastman, *Deep Woods*, p. 114.

15. Graber, *Sister to the Sioux*, pp. 163–164.

16. Elaine Goodale Eastman, "All the Days of My Life," *South Dakota Historical Review*, II, no. 4 (July 1937), p. 182.

17. Wilson, *Ohiyesa*, pp. 150–165, 185.

18. Eastman, "All the Days of My Life," p. 182.

19. David Reed Miller, "Charles Alexander Eastman: One Man's Journey in Two Worlds" (Unpublished master of arts thesis, University of North Dakota, 1975), pp. 267–270.

Vine Deloria, Sr.
Courtesy Center for Western Studies.

Philip Deloria.
Courtesy Center for Western Studies.

Ella C. Deloria.
Courtesy Institute of Indian Studies, USD.

St. Elizabeth's School.
Courtesy Center for Western Studies.

A Legacy in Sioux Leadership: The Deloria Family

Leonard Rufus Bruguier

Successful leadership in Native American society requires a conspicuous and continuous effort to help the poor, the weak, and the elderly
without boasting. In Indian tradition, leaders are persons who give
away many material possessions. Leaders are those who share knowledge or spiritual guidance and remain available to give helpful words
of encouragement. Among the families of Dakota (Sioux) society that
have demonstrated these qualities for more than one hundred years is
the one named Des Laurias (Deloria).

The first person of this name to live among the Dakota was Francois
Des Laurias, "Saswe," the son of a French fur trader and an Indian
mother. After Ihanktonwan (Yankton) Dakota leaders relinquished
more than 11,000,000 acres by their Treaty of 1858 and accepted a
reservation containing 430,000 acres of land, Saswe moved with the
White Swan *tiyospaye* (extended family) into an area located across
the Missouri River from Fort Randall. With great courage and keen
intellect, Francois flourished in a bicultural milieu as Ihanktonwans
made their adjustment to the ways of White people. There, he was
recognized by officials in the United States Department of the Interior
as the founder (called Chief by non-Indians) of the Ihanktonwan "half-
breed band."

A division took place in the tribe because of a need to provide for
members of fur trade heritage, especially those who received special
benefits under Article 7 of the 1858 Treaty. Later, an Indian agent at
Greenwood would report that Deloria's band contained a greater

percentage of full-blood, traditional Indians than did some of the other seven bands. Deloria did not shrink from his duty as the principal spokesman for the group while he encouraged its members to retain their Indian ways. Negesa (Simon Antelope), whom Ella C. Deloria interviewed in 1936, had this to say about Saswe: "He was a leader. All men flocked to him. He was always surrounded by older men who knew and related these things (the traditional customs)."[1]

Federal officials recognized Deloria as head of the band because he understood the beliefs and practices of both cultures and because band members accepted him for his obvious abilities. As much as any band leader, he could work effectively for peaceful coexistence. The Agent at Greenwood listed his group with the flexible "lower bands" that made the most rapid adjustment to reservation life. Only Mad Bull and John Ree were accorded as much respect as Saswe for the acceptance of Christianity and the practice of domestic and social habits taught by missionaries.

The Minnesota Sioux War, which broke out in 1862, broadened Deloria's influence in tribal politics. Many eastern Sioux seeking refuge came to join their Ihanktonwan relatives. General Alfred Sully heard of this, held council with the tribe, and reminded its leaders of their obligations under the 1858 Treaty. The General warned Ihanktonwans to drive refugees off the reservation. When they refused, he replied: "If you shoot one of these refugees, I'll report [to President Lincoln] that the Yanktons are allies. They have killed Isanti."[2] Chief Struck By The Ree asked Francois to fulfill this distasteful assignment in the interest of protection against further military harassment. Francois responded:

Yes . . . I have killed two Sioux and this will make the third. I had that in a dream. I saw four purification lodges in my vision. At the end was a great big black hawk. And on the side was a big white owl. And they stood there. They told me that by passing those purification lodges, I was going to kill four of our own people. I've killed two and this is the third. I'll kill him.[3]

Alfred Sully wanted a full-blood to commit the deed, but he was forced to accept Saswe's reaction. Later, when Deloria's daughter married Sully, a bond of marriage became a means of tribal security.

Like his father Francois, Philip Joseph Deloria (Tipi Sapa) became a man of bi-cultural understanding. Born in 1854, and known as "P.J." to family and friends, he spent his childhood in freedom during pre-reservation days. When the Ihanktonwans signed their Treaty of 1858 and moved to their reservation along the Missouri Hills, the independence of tribal members was curtailed. Philip witnessed upheaval and turbulence as they struggled with transition to reservation existence.

Because of the tribe's close proximity to Fort Randall, young P.J. learned of depredations. A White soldier killed a Ihanktonwan on the parade ground, for example, when he refused to surrender his wife to sexual abuse. Soldiers from the Fort rode their horses through tribal fields and destroyed their crops. There was suffering due to inadequate food supplies, disease, whiskey traffic, greedy settlers, and dishonest agency personnel. Because of U.S. Indian Agent Walter Burleigh's corrupt and dictatorial regime, factionalism grew in the bands during the 1860s. A breakdown in traditional leadership sometimes set family against family, band against band, in the scramble to receive benefits due the tribe from its treaty.

Along with heavy-handed and sometimes corrupt administration there came an assault on traditional religion and philosophy. In 1869 Presbyterian minister John P. Williamson became the first resident missionary on the reservation, despite heated opposition from traditional leaders, such as Feather-in-the-Ear. Feather led the movement against assimilation. Santee Episcopal leader Paul Mazakute moved in and began proselytizing among Ihanktonwans. The Reverend Joseph Cook arrived in 1870 and established Holy Fellowship Church at Greenwood. Bishop William Hobart Hare arrived three years later, and from Holy Fellowship grounds they expanded the Episcopal movement across Sioux Country. Old ways were threatened. New ways gave different men the reins of leadership. Understanding through education was, thought P.J. Deloria, the best way to deal with federal agents, non-Indian clergy, and adjustments that lay ahead.

The personal transition was not easy. Previously, P.J. earned his position in a warrior society and became the apparent heir to his father's role as leader of the half-breed band, but the young man made his decision in 1870 to join the ranks of "White Robed" Episcopal clergy. Through education and religious life, he could better serve the process of adjustment. Deloria cut off his long hair and accepted baptism by Reverend Cook on Christmas Day. He went away to attend the White man's schools in Nebraska and Minnesota, where he learned to read, write, and speak English. He fulfilled his internship at Holy Fellowship Church in Greenwood, under the Episcopal Bishop William Hobart Hare, rising to the rank of Deacon in 1883. P.J. held other offices in denominational affairs over the next several years and was finally posted by Bishop Hare to the Standing Rock Reservation by the end of the 1880s.

Tribal members at Standing Rock Reservation seethed in anger under the regime of U.S. Agent James McLaughlin, a controversial figure intent on subduing the will of his charges. McLaughlin advocated agrarian and Christian adjustment as the best solution to the "Indian problem." Part of his plan was to discredit traditional Indian leaders, especially those in Sitting Bull's Hunkpapa band. McLaughlin's determined effort to overshadow Indian leaders met sullen resistance.

By previous experience with his Ihanktonwan people, Philip was prepared for conditions at Standing Rock. The same disintegration of leadership in politics and religion was obvious. As a substitute, he brought strong faith in the Great Spirit through the new way of the Episcopal church. Internal strength alone helped him withstand bitter taunts thrown at him for wearing White man's clothes and cutting his hair.

When Deloria took over all activities at St. Elizabeth's Mission near Wakpala, he became the first enrolled Indian in charge of an Episcopal reservation mission. He imparted feelings of peace and good will among the people of the four satellite churches he served: St. Thomas, St. John the Baptist, Good Shepherd (in Sitting Bull's area), and Grand River Station. For a time, he was caught at the middle of the power struggle between Sitting Bull and McLaughlin. Sitting Bull opposed the sedentary, agricultural way of life required by the Agent. Reverend Vine Deloria, Sr., son of P.J., remembers his father's account of a meeting with Sitting Bull on the eve of his assassination:

My father [Philip] said Sitting Bull was the smartest man he ever talked to. He visited him the day before he was killed. And he went there. . . . They wanted Sitting Bull to go and camp inside the compound of the Fort [Yates]. He wouldn't go because he was afraid he would be imprisoned under subhuman conditions until he died. He had heard about the Apaches by moccasin telegraph and he wouldn't go. They sent out a Catholic Bishop [Martin Marty, O.S B.] first to try to talk him into it. But he wouldn't do it. And then they sent Episcopal Bishop Hare. He still wouldn't do it. So the government and the military wanted to send a minister. They knew there was a young Indian minister at Wakpala, Gall's community. His name was Philip Deloria. He was in his thirties. They said, 'send him.' So he went there and Sitting Bull said, '*Hau, hau, misun, misun, iyotaka, iyotaka. Winuhcha, wochuwa.*' They offered him coffee and so he drank. Then Sitting Bull said, 'well, I know what you want.' And he told my father about the Apaches and why he didn't want to go to the Fort. He tried to get Sitting Bull to talk but the only thing he said was, 'in the first place they [White people] think I dominate these people just as they dominate theirs. They have kings, emperors, dictators. They think that is what I am. But no, I am just a member of this family, Hunkpapa. But it is true that from the time I was young the people said, Sitting Bull, go for us, *unkciapi*. And then if there is a confrontation, Sitting Bull, see if you can stop those people from acting like that. So I am a diplomat. When I come home I don't get any special reward or recognition. I am just one of the people. I'm Hunkpapa. If they [the government] want, if they are worried, go down and pull a whisker out of Gall. He will give them a fight. He is absolutely fearless. I have been with him in wars. It seems like he wanted to get killed, but he never got touched.' My father tried to get Sitting Bull to talk more, but he said, 'Sitting Bull was so brilliant that he had me talking.' He just sat there and listened.[4]

It was a hectic life for an Indian Episcopalian leader. Deacon Philip J. Deloria was ordained into the priesthood during September, 1892, and from that position carved out a lasting place for his family within the Hunkpapa Nation. His daughter, Ella Cara Deloria, thought her father pushed too hard for assimilation—the move away from older customs and traditional ways. But Deloria worked to encourage adaptation at Standing Rock Reservation. The Hunkpapas adopted him and his family by formal enrollment. Reverend Deloria was pleased that the respected leader Gall received baptism and proud that, because of a strong Christian faith, he helped to open the way for many others who joined the Episcopal Church on the Standing Rock Reservation.

After retirement, P.J. returned to the Ihanktonwan Reservation and remained politically and spiritually active. He represented the White Swan band during the Pipestone Reservation claims meetings in the 1920s.

Yet Reverend Deloria's principal contributions were in the past. At age nineteen, he had worked with Felix Brunot and David Tateopa to found the Brotherhood of Christian Unity. They "got to talking. And they said, 'the country is going to be overrun by Whites. Our people shouldn't be trying to run and lead the old life. They ought to settle and learn how to live on the land.' " At the same time, they talked about an "ecumenical movement. . . . Many Yanktons who joined the Christian church were either Romans or Episcopalians, Congregationalists or Presbyterians. . . . It was causing the people to become aloof from one another. And they said, 'Let's have a Sioux united movement.' They were talking about the Brotherhood." At the time, "there was a great deal made of the idea of whatever each church taught, it was the only way to Heaven. . . . Christianity is a wonderful religion, but with that attitude, somebody is wrong." Clergymen taught: " 'Oh, be careful of the Presbyterians, be careful of the Romans, be careful of the Congregationalists, be careful of the Episcopalians, and so on.' That's making even relatives aloof—that feature the life of American Indian religion. Let's just live with God every day," said the three young Ihanktonwan men. "They were three-dimensional people. Here is the physical, the intellectual, and the spiritual. So they weren't lopsided guys. . . . And so it was they started the Brotherhood. . . ." It was going to elevate people, he went on, above denominationalism to a place that acknowledged virtue in one religious way under God.[5]

The Brotherhood established a philosophy expressed in many ways through the Delorias by the time Philip's daughter, Ella Deloria (*Anpetu Waste Win*, or Beautiful Day Woman), was born in 1890. Like her father, Ella grew up in turbulent times for Indians. Her legacy was to carry on traditional ways through new tools of Indian existence, especially education. Ella began her schooling at St. Elizabeth's Mission on the Standing Rock Reservation, then transferred to All Saints School in Sioux Falls to finish high school. Her intellectual promise caught the attention of officials and she received a scholarship at Oberlin College in Ohio. From there, Ella matriculated at Columbia University, where she earned a Bachelor of Science degree. For a time Ella returned to serve as Superintendent at St. Elizabeth's. In 1929 she went back to Columbia University for graduate work with the anthropologist Franz Boaz. Ella's influence "Indianized" his work, making it palatable to Indian people.

Anpetu Waste Win served tribal members in many other ways, but perhaps her contributions to Indian literature were most important. She recorded stories and legends uncovered by personal interviews and field trips. From her notes she composed numerous articles and books for publication under her own name, while contributing to the quality of works published by Franz Boaz. Foremost among Ella's books are *Dakota Texts* (1932), an authoritative collection of sixty-four Sioux stories on mythology and historical developments; and *Speaking of Indians* (1944), a portrait of life among Sioux people before its replacement by reservation culture.

Ella Deloria perceived the importance of written Dakota and Lakota dialects of Sioux language and set about collecting and recording materials necessary to write a dictionary. In these ways she dispelled the myth that Indian language did not possess nuances essential to

clear thought. Beyond linguistics, Ella helped to change movie carica-
tures from downcast "end of the trail savages," limited in vocabulary
to "ugh," to people with culture equal to that of any in the United
States.

Ella's impact on education in South Dakota was considerable, for
she worked at a time when racial and sexual discrimination presented
great obstacles. She served on project staff at the University of South
Dakota when Indians were barely represented in the faculty or student
body. As a productive scholar, she was highly instrumental in bringing
attention to the importance of Indian studies on the campus in the late
1950s. Ella's linguistic research with Franz Boaz, aided by further
inquiries funded through the National Science Foundation, led to the
establishment of the Ella C. Deloria Project at Vermillion. Her materials contributed to better understanding of Indian-White relationships.
Her name brought credence to the Ella C. Deloria Scholarship Fund
for Indian Women, established in 1969. After 1975, when Reverend
Vine Deloria, Sr., presented her papers to the University of South
Dakota, Dr. Agnes Picotte (Oglala) began collating and interpreting
their contents. Through Ella's efforts, *Dakota Texts* and *Speaking of
Indians* went into a second printing in the late 1970s. Miss Deloria's
papers, which contain a wealth of information about tribal cultures,
remain the focus of attention for Dr. Picotte, who has moved her office
to Chamberlain for its closer proximity to the reservations. Dr. Picotte
approaches the completion of the dictionary that was in manuscript
when Anpetu Waste Win passed away in 1972.

A second leader appeared in the Deloria household in 1901. Vine
Victor Deloria (*Ohiya*, or Champion) was born at St. Elizabeth's
Mission near Wakpala. Like his sister, he received an early education
at the Mission. Vine's life changed abruptly after his mother's death in
1916. Reverend Philip, still active in the ministry, arranged for his son
to attend Kearney Military School in Nebraska. There, under the
watchful eye of Bishop George Beecher, a close friend of his father,
Vine was an attentive student. From Kearney he moved to matriculate
at St. Stephens (Bard) College, in Poughkeepsie, New York.

Vine was precocious. He made friends easily, enjoyed all sports,
and played football, baseball, and basketball. Later, he coached and
taught for a year at Fort Sill Indian School in Lawton, Oklahoma.
Between semesters at St. Stephens he took a job in a coal mine, which
reinforced his understanding of the value of discipline. At the time he
was undecided about what to choose for a lifelong career. Among his

many interests he especially liked working with wood and seriously considered carpentry as a vocation.

Then came a fateful twist in his life; the decision was taken out of his hands. Reverend P.J. Deloria took ill in the late 1920s and expressed the wish that Vine follow him into the priesthood. Vine did not especially like this calling. Yet, he respected his father's desire and began the career that made him an inspiration to many others, both Indian and White. Soon after the completion of Vine's training and ordination at divinity school in 1931, Reverend Philip Joseph Deloria passed away.

Young Father Vine went first to work among Dakota kinsmen at the Indian Mission in Pine Ridge, South Dakota. He went after that to serve on the Sisseton Reservation, where an incident taught him a very valuable lesson. One day, while walking near a hatchery, he and his children found some discarded eggs. From the outside, they looked alright. An inquiry revealed they had been heated on only one side, however, and would not yield good chicks. This set him to thinking about Christians who were only half-heated and thus were half-prepared to reach the greater grace of God. To help his people, Father Vine served the first twenty years of his career in Indian Country, making many visits to Niobrara Deanery Convocations, and performing other church functions. He also served on countless occasions as the voice of Indian Episcopalians to outsiders.

With remarkable success in the mission field, Ohiya drew an assignment at national Episcopal Church headquarters in New York City, where he served as Indian Secretary for the Episcopal Church of America. This proved his most frustrating experience. Vine's ideas were not heard by the Episcopal hierarchy; it was a fruitless effort to work for improvement in Indian life through people who ignored his advice. He spent four frustrating years on the assignment before moving to Durant, Iowa, for two years, and then to Pierre, where he served eight years as Archdeacon. Reverend Deloria finally retired in 1968, at age sixty-eight, after devoting thirty-seven years to the ministry. In retirement, he served for a couple of years as priest at St. Paul's Episcopal mission in Vermillion. Then he left the ministry for full retirement at Pierre. In 1986, Father Vine and his wife, Barbara, moved to Tucson, Arizona, to be near their sons, author/professor Vine, Jr., and Sam.

An aura of respect has always surrounded Father Vine Deloria, Sr. Many Indians claim a relationship, calling him Grandpa (*Tunkashina*) and naming their children after him. He has ranked among the strongest personalities to emerge from Indian society in the twentieth century. He sees the Holy Bible as a man some two thousand years old. It contains knowledge we need to know. One has only to look there and the answer will be revealed. Although Father Vine assumed an assimilationist vocation, he maintained his Indian cultural integrity— preserving in use both Indian language and oral tradition and, while preaching Christian truth, teaching also the power and usefulness of traditional Indian religion. He gained recognition far and wide for depth and diversity as a premier orator—a teller of stories with purpose. He successfully translated the best qualities of each culture for use in bringing peace to human relations, and seeking grace under God.

During an interview conducted in 1984, at his home in Pierre, Grandpa Vine reflected back on his ministry:

> For thirty-seven years I preached the Christ of the Church, the Son of God. The whole of Christianity does that, emphasizes the Christ of the Church, the Son of God, and pays little attention to the history of Jesus, the Son of *Man*. You see, I want to look at him entirely as a man, none of this divine business. And so I read through the Four Gospels and kept doing that, and then I ran into John Collier's book, *Indians of America*. I read through that. And I read Helen Hunt Jackson's *A Century of Dishonor*. And so I read all of those, and boy, since then, I haven't been happy. At the time of Columbus there were three million Indians [or more] occupying what we call the United States. Columbus, after praising the character of those Indians, turned around and worked them all to death in the mines and those who didn't want to work were hunted down and shot. They depopulated the island we now call Haiti. Then by 1890, at Wounded Knee, there were only 250,000 Indians left. I am just absolutely, totally disillusioned about Christianity. I think I'm right. They didn't understand the fraternalism, humanitarianism, altruism, and universalism of Jesus. And they don't know that every human being was meant to develop mentally, physically, spiritually, and morally. So they didn't teach them that; if you neglect any one of these just a little bit, to that extent you are really lopsided. So we are a nation of lopsided people. And that's why Christianity is so ineffective and inefficient. Where is the peace, peace on earth goodwill to men?[6]

Still active and influential among Sioux people, in June of 1986 Reverend Deloria attended the 114th Niobrara Episcopal Convocation, at Santee Agency, Nebraska. During the business session, it was proposed that mission land be sold to raise money to keep St. Mary's

Indian School at Springfield, South Dakota, in operation. At the end of the debate, Ohiye rose and slowly walked to the front. People waited expectantly for his opinion:

> I inherited land from Francois Deloria [Saswe]. So did Ella and Susie. They sold theirs. I kept mine. I get an income every year.[7]

The message was clear: Keep the land!

Reverend Vine Deloria, Sr., has perpetuated the aura of leadership inspired by his father in two sons, Vine, Jr., and Sam. Vine Deloria, Jr., was born at Martin, South Dakota, in 1933. After serving in the United States Marine Corps, he graduated from Iowa State University and Lutheran School of Theology, then earned a Law Degree at the University of Colorado. Now serving as Professor of Political Science at the University of Arizona, Vine, Jr., proudly carries on the leadership qualities of his father, grandfather, and great grandfather. For this he has been recognized as a principal leader in the fight for the rights of Indians in the United States.

As a foremost Indian author, he writes books that address tribal existence in modern society, offering plausible alternatives for improving the quality of Indian life for the future. Backed by historical research, his voice stands out against injustice. To recognize a major source of influence on his life, Professor Deloria quoted Chief Seattle in his book *God is Red*:

> It matters little where we pass the remnant of our days. They will not be many. A few moons; a few more winters—and not one of the descendants of the mighty hosts that once moved over this broad land or lived in happy homes, protected by the Great Spirit, will remain to mourn over the graves of a people once more powerful and hopeful than yours. But why should I mourn at the untimely fate of my people? Tribe follows tribe, nation follows nation, like the waves of the sea. It is the order of nature, and regret is useless. Your time of decay may be distant, but it will surely come, for even the White Man whose God walked and talked with him as friend with friend, cannot be exempted from the common destiny. We may be brothers after all. We shall see.[8]

As a political activist, Vine Deloria, Jr., has used education to fight for Indian land, water, and civil rights. Offices he has held include the Executive Directorship of the National Congress of American Indians, the National Office for Rights of the Indigent, and a membership on the Board of Inquiry on Hunger and Malnutrition in the United States.

He has been a magnet and an inspiration to Indian and non-Indian people alike who have been interested in changing a system that has excluded tribal members from rights accruing to a White majority. As an abiding legacy, Professor Vine Deloria, Jr., has published many books. His earlier works included: *Custer Died for Your Sins* (1969), a look at Indian-White relations; *We Talk, You Listen* (1970), a call for the return of land and perpetuation of corporate tribalism; *Of Utmost Good Faith* (1971), a review of the legal history of tribes; *God is Red* (1973), the espousal of Indian religious beliefs; *Behind the Trail of Broken Treaties* (1974), a call for the creation of tribal enclaves with greater sovereign authority; *The Indian Affair* (1974), an assessment of tribal relationships with government, religious, and educational institutions; and *The Metaphysics of Modern Existence* (1979), pointing to danger in a world view that distorts reality. Overall, his publications have presented an appeal to non-Indians while they have inspired pride and cultural revival in tribes.

As important to the endeavor of cultural adjustment have been the efforts of Sam Deloria. His contributions have centered on Indian law, and have been expressed through the founding of the American Indian Law Center at the University of New Mexico. This organization played a vital role in updating Felix Cohen's seminal treatise, *Handbook of Indian Law*.

The original inhabitants of the Western Hemisphere greeted the White man with generosity and sustenance. Through centuries of warfare, broken treaties, and reservation confinement, tribal members chose leaders dedicated to the preservation of Indian cultural ideals. The Delorias, whose ancestral blood runs throughout the Sioux Nation, are prime examples of the Indian leadership that helped with survival in a transitional period of 150 years. They have been architects of social and political change. Francois Des Laurias led Ihanktonwans through difficult reservation adjustments. Reverend Philip Deloria used his strong religious faith to find safe ground for adjustment through hard times following the Massacre at Wounded Knee. Vine Deloria, Sr., helped his people cope with changes through the Great Depression and two wars while earning the respect of non-Indian society. Ella C. Deloria gave leadership and encouraged intercultural understanding through the preservation of oral tradition and language—leaving for future generations a precious heritage. Vine Deloria, Jr., called to the attention of the literate world a need to defend tribalism for the benefit of non-Indians as well as all Red Nations. Sam Deloria facilitated change through education, encouraging Indian students to enter legal careers to protect tribal rights.

The Deloria family has earned both loyalty and respect. Largely because of leaders such as these, Sioux people will continue to adapt and survive as Indians. Young men and women—Ben Kitto, Kevin Locke, Deacon Stanley Jones, Jr., Steve Emery, Charlene Thornton Stuhlmacher, and Reverend Joseph Bad Moccasin—draw inspiration from the Delorias to carry on their own careers in helping their relatives. In this and other ways to many different people—White as well as Indian—the Deloria family represents the best of Indian leadership.

Notes

1. Ella C. Deloria Research Notes, Oral History Center, University of South Dakota.

2. Renee Sansom Flood, *Lessons From Chouteau Creek* (Sioux Falls: Augustana College Center For Western Studies, 1986), p. 61–62. "Isanti" is a term assigned to eastern Sioux in early records that was changed to "Santee" later on. In either case, it pertained to one or more Minnesota Sioux tribes situated east of the middle group named Ihanktonwan.

3. *Ibid.,* p. 62.

4. Interview with Vine Deloria, Sr., by Leonard R. Bruguier and Renee Sansom-Flood, 1984.

5. "Father Vine Deloria," *To Be An Indian* (New York: Holt, Rinehart and Winston, 1971), p. 28.

6. Interview with Vine Deloria, Sr., by Leonard R. Bruguier and Renee Sansom-Flood, 1984.

7. 114th Annual Niobrara Episcopal Convocation, at Santee, NE, June 22, 1986.

8. Vine Deloria, Jr., *God is Red* (New York: Grosset and Dunlap, 1973), p. 115.

Ole Rolvaag in front of Holland Hall, St. Olaf College.
Courtesy Ella Rolvaag Tweet.

Frederick Manfred photographed by Larry Risser.
Courtesy Frederick Manfred.

The Andrew Berdahl home near Garretson (1925) where Rolvaag's wife Jennie grew up and where Rolvaag heard many of the stories he wrote into Giants in the Earth. *Courtesy Karl Rolvaag.*

Master Tellers of Prairie Tales:
Ole E. Rolvaag and Frederick Manfred

Arthur R. Huseboe

More than any others, two writers of fiction have contributed to American literature the richest and most accurate picture of life in what is now South Dakota: Ole E. Rolvaag, best known for the classic novel *Giants in the Earth* and two sequels; and Frederick Manfred, author of four novels about South Dakota, including the national best seller *Lord Grizzly*. Other well-known novelists have written about South Dakota, including Hamlin Garland, who was the first fiction writer to bring farm life on the northern prairies to national attention, and Laura Ingalls Wilder, author of the Little House series of children's stories about prairie life in the settlement period. Rolvaag and Manfred, however, take on added significance because they lived in and near the state for all of their adult lives and because they wrote about important ethnic groups that inhabited the region, Rolvaag the Norwegians and Manfred the Dutch-Frisians and the Sioux Indians.

The older of the two novelists and the spokesman for the Norwegian immigrants, as well as for the pioneer settlers in the northwest prairie states, was Ole Edvart Rolvaag, born in Norway in 1876 and brought up with a deep respect for the literature and culture of his homeland. This love of his Nordic heritage led Rolvaag to believe that for most of the Norwegians the cost of immigration was greater than its benefits. What was lost besides the spectacular landscapes of the homeland were religion, language, literature, folkways, and the love of cleanliness that mattered so very much to the Norwegians. As Harold Simonson expresses it, for Rolvaag, much of the immigrant experience in America could be characterized as a "tragedy of deracination, of cultural uprootedness."[1] Moreover, Rolvaag believed that as the various national groups fell out of touch with their European heritage, America was the less for it, losing a rich and dynamic diversity and substituting a pallid and uninteresting cultural uniformity in which the almighty dollar was the principal unifying element.

From childhood on, Rolvaag was an apt student of Norwegian culture. Once he had learned to read—a particularly difficult task as it turned out—he became an eager patron of the small library on Donna Island, where the family lived. He walked often with his brother Johann to the parish library seven miles away in order to borrow more books. Among the novels Ole read in translation was James Fenimore Cooper's *The Last of the Mohicans*. From it he contracted "America fever," as did 800,000 of his countrymen before the emigration period ended, and at age seventeen he decided to go to America.

In addition to his fascination with a wild new land, Rolvaag determined to emigrate because the occupation for which he had been prepared from age fifteen and on was extremely dangerous. The men in the Rolvaag family had been fishermen for six generations. It was expected that Ole Edvart would follow in their wakes. He went to sea for the first time in January, 1891, sailing north to the distant Lofoten Islands as an apprentice, counting as "half a man" in the distribution of the profits.[2] In the winter of 1893, when he was still a novice, the fleet experienced the worst storm ever recorded at the Lofoten banks. As Rolvaag described it later: "I've seen storms strike suddenly before. . . , but never with the suddenness of this one—it was as if it had been let out of a sack! Although three men—strong men all—sat at the oars keeping the boat steady, the first fierce gust of wind threw her sideways as if she had been a matchstick. And then came a blinding blizzard and darkness."[3] Rolvaag would remember that storm later on when he described a South Dakota blizzard on the prairie in *Giants in the Earth*. Many of his friends died in that storm at sea, and not long after he wrote to his uncle Jakob Jakobsen at Elk Point to ask for a ticket to America. It finally came, but not until Rolvaag had spent three more winters with the fishing fleet at Lofoten.

In the last analysis, Rolvaag's decision to emigrate to America came from something more than fear of storms at sea, or even fascination with a mysterious new land. As a child he had decided in secret to devote himself to a life of creative accomplishments. On one occasion his mother had asked him what he wanted to be. "Either a poet or a professor," he responded promptly.[4] Although his mother laughed at him, a poor fisherlad from just below the Arctic Circle, his mind was made up. "Perhaps," he thought, "I may still have the opportunity to laugh at Mother because she once thought her own boy talked rank nonsense."[5] These high ideals must have lain behind his decision to leave Norway. As Rolvaag tells the story, a few days before his departure he and his friend and skipper, Kristian Andersen, were looking over some sleek fishing boats. When Andersen learned that Rolvaag was about to emigrate, he offered to buy the best of the boats on display for his young friend, with the expectation that it could be paid for after only one good fishing season. Rolvaag was stunned by the proposition and begged for a little time to think it all over. Sitting on a mountainside above the fjord, he mulled over his dilemma: "If I decided to refuse this wonderful offer, what reasonable excuse could I make? You see, I *had* no valid excuse, or none that could be put into words. I just felt that I wasn't fulfilling myself."[6] When he came down from the mountain, his mind was made up: he would go to South Dakota. The night before his departure he wrote in his diary, quoting the great Norwegian author Bjornstjerne Bjornson: "Some day, I believe, I shall reach the goal, far far beyond the high mountains."[7] He would attain both of his high goals—to be a poet and a professor, and to live a life of creative achievement.

After an arduous journey across the Atlantic by steamship and across middle America by train, Ole Rolvaag arrived in Elk Point, South Dakota, in late August, 1896. He thought the landscape west from Chicago very monotonous, "almost nothing but prairie."[8] His greatest disappointment was in not seeing any Indians. "This seems quite odd," he wrote. "From all the Indian stories we read at home I should have thought that every grove would be swarming with them."[9] This was only the first of many misconceptions that Rolvaag would learn to correct during his five years in South Dakota.

The life that Rolvaag led as a farm hand and later as an academy student is told most fully in the diary he kept and in his first South Dakota novel, *Amerika-Breve* (America Letters), in 1912. The two accounts deal with the same events, but the purpose of each is quite different: in the diary, Rolvaag confesses his emotional and spiritual struggles, whereas in the novel he presents a light-hearted picture of his adjustments to American life.

In the diary Rolvaag recounts a succession of unhappy affairs of the heart. He reminds himself from time to time of his high ambitions and almost as often despairs of reaching them. He occasionally meditates on the nature and future of the soul: one June day in South Dakota is so perfect, he decides, that the contemplation of nature's purity makes his soul ashamed. Perhaps most interesting of all, Rolvaag speculates about the transformation that electricity might someday bring to the homestead frontier. As the Augustana College bell rings on December 31, 1900, to usher in the twentieth century, he tries to imagine electrical power "so well regulated that with its help all types of machinery can be driven. If that be the case, then the twentieth century inhabitants will have done more for mankind than has been accomplished from the time of Adam up to the present."[10] That dream began to take shape even before Rolvaag's death in 1931. By the mid-twentieth century rural electrification had indeed wrought the miraculous changes that Rolvaag envisioned for South Dakota and the prairie West.

Rolvaag's first novel is a story of the Norwegian immigrant's adaptation to a new way of life in a rugged land, where the language and the customs were strange, and where values were sometimes radically different. In *America-Breve* (translated as *The Third Life of Per Smevik* in 1971), Rolvaag tells his own story, of arriving at Elk Point in the heat of an August afternoon, of discovering a fanatical intensity in the way Americans tackled work, of learning to make one seriocomic cultural adjustment after another (even accepting the American nickname *Pete* in place of *Per*), and of deciding to attend a Norwegian-American academy in the fall of 1898 to learn English. It was a fortunate decision for Per Smevik, for he began to discover the full range of his intellectual potential, as well. Rolvaag's own decision, in real life, was even more fortunate. Enrolling in the Preparatory and Parochial Course at Augustana College (in Canton), he became acquainted with the Berdahl family of Garretson. He would eventually marry Jennie Berdahl. Equally important, from the members of that family he would hear most of the stories that would later go into the making of *Giants in the Earth*.

During his three years at Augustana, Rolvaag studied hard. His best grades were in English and history, his worst in arithmetic and handwriting. He did well enough to graduate with honors and be selected as one of the speakers at the graduation exercises in 1901, a remarkable achievement for one who had arrived less than five years earlier with scarcely a word of English. The title of his talk, given in Norwegian, was "True Culture on a National Foundation." According to a newspaper account of the time, Rolvaag argued that by giving up one's native language one becomes "a sort of international vagrant." With the loss of religious faith, "the morals of the person or race degenerates.''[11] He would return to that theme again and again in his teaching and writing.

Following graduation from the Preparatory and Parochial program at Augustana, Rolvaag entered St. Olaf College, in Northfield, Minnesota. There he would remain for the rest of his life, first as a student and then as a member of the faculty. But he returned to South Dakota from time to time, first to court and then marry Jennie Berdahl, and then visit his inlaws and friends.

Out of his South Dakota experience came his most important writings. After the printing of *Amerika-Breve*, which sold only 471 copies in spite of favorable reviews, Rolvaag published *Paa Glemte Veie* (On Forgotten Paths) in 1914. It is the story of Chris Larsen, the richest farmer in the Elk Point settlement, and his daughter Mabel, a fully committed Christian. While Chris makes the conquest of the prairie an obsession, Mabel devotes herself to converting her stubborn father from his godless ways. The end of the novel is tragic for the long-suffering Chris: crippled previously by a farm accident, he dies when a fire breaks out in his room. Mabel, however, has the consolation of hearing his dying prayer for forgiveness. Moreover, her choice of an uncompromising religious faith will be rewarded, Rolvaag implies, by marriage to a young Norwegian Lutheran pastor who is equally devoted to the faith of their fathers.

Quite a different tone is found in Rolvaag's next novel, *To Tullinger* (Two Fools, 1920), also written in Norwegian and published by Augsburg Publishing House in Minneapolis. Instead of the likelihood of a happy life for the committed Christian, there is a tale of continuous greed that ends in hopeless and miserable death. In the six years between the two novels, Rolvaag's vision of the world of the immigrant had grown a good deal darker, in part because of a series of deaths in his family and in part because of the anti-foreigner hysteria of the first world war. The young couple who begin their marriage in the expectation that hard work and frugality can bring happiness turn into confirmed and life-long misers, substituting coins and bills for the children they never had. In Louis and Lizzie Houglum, Rolvaag intended to show what could happen to immigrant farmers, like those around Elk Point, when they substitute shallow materialism for their cultural heritage.

The reaction of many Norwegian-Americans to Rolvaag's sermon on greed was an unfavorable one. Others recognized the unfortunate truth about many of their countrymen. Professor H. M. Blegen recalled that as a young man in Churchs Ferry, North Dakota, he overheard a group of his mother's friends complaining about the exaggerated picture of greedy Norwegians in *To Tullinger*. When his mother named a couple in their own community whose stinginess was even more extreme, one of the women responded: "I believe you're right, Maret. I think perhaps he has not drawn the picture true enough."[12] When the book was issued in an English translation as *Pure Gold* in 1930, American reviewers were most impressed by the novel as a record of the sterility of prairie life, and they tended to find it less powerful and less interesting than *Giants in the Earth*, which had appeared three years before to national acclaim. In both versions, *To Tullinger* is Rolvaag's darkest vision of the cost of immigration to those unable to retain their ethnic identity while seeking the American Dream.

In the year following *To Tullinger* Rolvaag published his most personal novel, *Laengselens Baat* (The Boat of Longing), continuing the theme of the tragedy of immigration. As the story moves from Norway to Minnesota and back again, from the lyricism of scenes set in Nordland to the empty futility of immigrant lives in Minneapolis, Rolvaag elaborates on the idea that creativity cannot flourish in a society made up of insecure people set culturally adrift. It was an odd novel, praised by reviewers for the beauty of the portions laid in Norway, criticized for the realism of the scenes set in Minnesota, but not quite complete. As Einar Haugen has said, the story of Nils Vaag "is a fairy tale about the soul of the immigrant, which ends in midstream, long before he has won his princess and his kingdom."[13] The explanation for Rolvaag's failure to complete the second portion of the tale is clear: he was already planning what would become *Giants in the Earth*.

Early in 1922 Rolvaag learned that despite many favorable reviews by Norwegian-American critics and reviewers, only 600 copies of *Laengselens Baat* had been sold, and only 1150 copies of *To Tullinger*. It was, he wrote to friend Simon Johnson, "the saddest hour I have experienced in America."[14] A year later he wrote to Johnson, even more convinced that the Norwegian-American community was not going to support its own writers: "Even if the angel Gabriel came down from on high . . . and wrote a first-rate book with the topic and theme from heaven itself, our people would only shrug their shoulders and wonder what new stupidity is now afoot."[15] That fear continued to haunt Rolvaag as he began to plan and to write his masterpiece of settlement life in South Dakota, *Giants in the Earth*.

Rolvaag was spurred to begin work in earnest on the new book when he learned from the newspapers that the Norwegian writer Johan Bojer was about to start a novel about immigration. Rolvaag immediately asked for a leave of absence from St. Olaf College and began to write, first in northern Minnesota and then briefly in Sioux Falls, London, and Oslo, where he finally finished the book in the spring of 1924. By chance a young scholar from St. Olaf, Gunnar Malmin, was in Oslo that spring and was passing Aschehoug and Company at the moment Rolvaag learned his novel would be published there. Rolvaag rushed out, embraced the astonished Malmin, and exclaimed, "Aschehoug is going to publish my book!" Malmin looked blank. "Don't you see? When my book is published here in Norway, it will come to the attention of America's publishers and will be translated and published in America. I'll be famous!"[16]

In Norway the new book appeared during 1924 and 1925 as two volumes, *I de Dage: Fortaelling om Norske Nykommere i Amerika* (In Those Days: A Story of Norwegian Immigrants in America) and *I de Dage: Riket Grundlaegges* (In Those Days: The Founding of the Kingdom). Both were well reviewed in Norway but largely ignored in America. Very early, however, novelist Lincoln Colcord contacted Rolvaag about a possible translation into English and Rolvaag agreed. In 1927 the one-volume translation appeared, jointly prepared by the two men, and very quickly became a Book-of-the-Month Club selection and national best seller.

What captured most critics of *Giants in the Earth* was that the westward movement, usually depicted as triumphant, was seen as a costly and even tragic event for many who settled the prairies and plains. Rolvaag's protagonists, Per Hansa and his wife Beret, are psychologically mismatched partners, and that fact adds greatly to their other difficulties. Per Hansa sees the high ground west of the Big Sioux River in eastern South Dakota as the ideal place to establish his prairie kingdom. He works with a passion to accomplish that end, breaking the sod, building the largest house in the settlement, trading with the Indians of Flandreau, and in many other ways demonstrating ingenuity and strength of will.

He would appear to be the ideal pioneer, but he cannot win his kingdom without a supportive mate, a woman who shares his goals and his triumphs. And this he does not have. In his determination to conquer the new land, he tries to abandon his Norwegian heritage and his fathers' God, but these are the very ingredients that give Beret's existence meaning. For her the prairie becomes a demonic force with its terrible summer storms, blizzards, plagues of grasshoppers, and isolation. Most significant, the prairie is a threat to the moral nature of its inhabitants, she believes; it threatens their very souls. Beret's madness is Rolvaag's expression of the worst that can happen to the immigrant who loses the power of her Norwegian past. Only after the first minister arrives at the Spring Creek settlement is Beret restored to sanity.

The tragic death of Per Hansa in a blizzard, when he again dares the forces of nature singlehandedly, has an ironic sequel. In *Peder Seier* (1929), published in English the same year as *Peder Victorious*, Beret becomes the strong one. She successfully manages the family's farm, rears the four children alone, and devotes herself to the task of preserving the Norwegian heritage she sees disappearing from the Spring Creek community. In the third novel in the series, *Den Signede Dag* (1931), published as *Their Fathers' God* the same year, the struggle intensifies between Beret, the preserver of tradition, and her son Peder, the rebel against all the old values. When Peder's marriage to the Catholic girl Susie Doheny ends in divorce, the one note of hope that sounds for Peder is his recognition that he cannot abandon his heritage; he is both Norwegian and American. Remaining true to one's culture, Rolvaag is saying in his last novel, is the truest way of becoming an American.

For Ole Edvart Rolvaag the experience of Norwegian immigrants in South Dakota was one of crisis and confrontation. Old World values were in conflict with New World values; the older generations were in conflict with the younger; and always there was the endless struggle with an uncompromising nature, a nature of drought, insect infestations, and destructive storms. In *Giants in the Earth* Rolvaag created a timeless masterpiece that records the experience of many who immigrated to South Dakota and the other prairie states, and who laid the groundwork for the society of comfort and convenience that is enjoyed today by their descendants.

When Frederick Manfred discovered O. E. Rolvaag's *Giants in the Earth*, he realized that it was a story about his own place, that the wagon tracks of Per Hansa's little caravan might have crossed his family farm in northwest Iowa, and that he lived in a region that was worthy of a novelist's effort. As a young man growing up, Manfred often wondered who the people were who had lived on and traveled over that land before his people settled there. He wondered, too, as he contemplated a career as a creative writer, whether anything was worth writing about in the farm country around his home near Doon.

From that time on, northwestern Iowa and adjacent Minnesota and South Dakota were sacred soil for him, The land had been written about by a master writer, and someday he might follow in the footsteps of Rolvaag and other admired novelists in telling the story of his own land and people.

That youthful wish has long since been fulfilled, and Manfred stands out today among American novelists as one of the few who have given unique identity to a particular region of the country. William Faulkner and Yoknapatawpha County in Mississippi come to mind, as do Herbert Krause and Pockerbrush in the Fergus Falls area of western Minnesota. For Manfred's own territory, the drainage basin of the Big Sioux River in South Dakota and the country west of it, he created the name *Siouxland*. He has been writing about that region for more than forty years and has brought it to national prominence. Moreover, his teaching in the art of writing for more than fifteen years at the University of South Dakota and at Augustana College has helped dozens of young writers to find literary voices that express their own sense of the land.

The man who invented Siouxland was born Frederick Feikema on January 6, 1912, north of Doon, a village located on the fertile banks of the Rock River in northwest Iowa and eighteen miles east of the Big Sioux, the river that marks the boundary between Iowa and South Dakota. The Rock River flows into the Big Sioux some thirty winding miles south, and still farther on the combined rivers join the Missouri at Sioux City, Iowa, the point where Iowa, Nebraska, and South Dakota meet. This is the southern boundary of Siouxland. One of the campgrounds of the Lewis and Clark Expedition of 1804 is not far away to the east, and the site of the first homestead filing in the United States is a little way to the north.

Of Frisian and Saxon background, Manfred grew up to the sort of rigorous farm life shared by most inhabitants of Siouxland—the Dutch and Frisians of northwest Iowa and southwest Minnesota, the Norwegians scattered the length of the Big Sioux valley in South Dakota, and the Germans and Swedes and other European nationalities that settled throughout the region. Out of the hardest experience that a farm boy could ever have in this area would come Manfred's first novel, *The Golden Bowl*, a poetic tale of the 1930s Dust Bowl in South Dakota.

As the eldest of six sons, Manfred felt himself alone, oftentimes, in spite of a warm and supportive family. His early interest in reading may have developed out of that feeling but, whatever the reason for his precocious absorption in books, he was much encouraged to be a reader by his schoolteacher aunt, Kathryn Feikema, and by his gentle mother Alice. He recalls that whenever the family went visiting, his

first hope was that there would be a boy his own age to play with. If
there was not, he would search out a book to read until it was time to
go home. Because his father could not read or write, the responsibility
for reading the Bible at family worship fell to young Frederick. By the
time he left home for college he had read the English Bible through
seven times, besides reading everything else he could lay his hands on.

As a baptized member of the Christian Reformed Church, Manfred
was sent to Western Academy in Hull, Iowa. Following graduation at
age sixteen, he worked for two years on the farm and then entered
Calvin College in Grand Rapids, Michigan. There he began to write in
earnest, first poems for student publications, then short stories and
sketches. One of these latter he considered to be the first good thing
he had written. It was a description of his desperate race, back on the
farm, to cut 120 acres of ripe grain before a storm: "My brothers
brought a change of horses for me, but I just cut night and day until I
had all of it cut. Before a storm. I never forgot the beauty of that on-
coming storm."[17] His college writing, however, proved to be only
apprentice work; it would be ten more years before his first book
would appear in print, a period during which he wandered and worked
around America, exploring a variety of careers, including some in
sports. He was a natural athlete, six-foot-nine inches tall with great
strength, and that made him a formidable competitor. His wanderings
were nearly ended, however, when he contracted a severe case of
tuberculosis and spent two years, from 1940 to 1942, in a Minneapolis
sanatorium. When Manfred emerged, cured, he brought with him the
desire to devote himself completely to a life of writing. Soon after, he
married Maryanna Shorba, a fellow patient at the sanatorium with
whom he had fallen in love.

In 1943 Manfred quit the writing job he had taken with *Modern
Medicine* and launched into a full-time career as a novelist. It was a
decision that over the next forty-four years would lead to the writing
and publishing of twenty novels and six other books of poetry and
prose. The most successful of them would be the novels set in South
Dakota, or in neighboring northwest Iowa, in particular the much-
praised and widely read Buckskin Man Tales.

The very first novel grew out of a hitch-hiking trip Manfred took in
the summer of 1934 across drought-parched South Dakota to Yellowstone National Park. Encouraged by his fellow newspaper writers and
by Minnesota author Meridel Le Sueur, Manfred wrote the first version
of *The Golden Bowl* in 1937. It went through seven more rewritings
before its publication by Webb Press of St. Paul in 1944.

The story of *The Golden Bowl* is that of Maury Grant, a young wanderer who is determined never to return to the farming life that had ruined his parents. On his way to the Black Hills, however, to work in the gold mines, he is talked into helping the Thors, a family trying to eke out a dust-plagued living on the edge of the Badlands. In them, and in Pa Thor in particular, Maury discovers an abiding faith in the land that convinces him to stay: "They say it's a dust bowl now," says Pa Thor. "But I can close my eyes and see the golden bowl it's been."

The warm critical reviews that welcomed *The Golden Bowl* became more mixed the next year when *Boy Almighty* appeared, Manfred's powerful and somewhat bitter retelling of his two-year stay in the sanatorium. Two years later, however, Manfred's reputation soared with the publication of *This Is the Year* (1947). The hero of the novel is Pier Frixen, a Frisian farmer modeled after Manfred's own father. Pier loves his land in northwest Iowa, but he also abuses it, as do so many of his neighbors. Their attitudes and actions contribute, in fact, to creating the dust bowl conditions that form such a powerful background for the action in Manfred's first novel.

This Is the Year became a national best-seller, was praised by Sinclair Lewis and Van Wyck Brooks, and was selected unanimously by the Associated Press book reviewers as "Novel of the Year." It was followed, however, by a seven-year period in which Manfred's popularity slumped and his publishers became doubtful about his potential as a best-selling novelist. The works of that period were *The Chokecherry Tree* (1948), a comic account of little Elof Lofblom, a mediocre man who through suffering manages to maintain a kind of common-man dignity; and the three ambitious volumes that make up the *World's Wanderer* trilogy. In these autobiographical novels or *rumes—The Primitive* (1949), *The Brother* (1950), and *The Giant* (1951)—Manfred traces the growth of a creative artist, Thurs Manfred Wraldsoan. Thurs shares many of Manfred's own traits, and many of his experiences as well: like Manfred he goes to college in Michigan, works in New Jersey and New York, and ends up in the Minneapolis-St. Paul area. Like Manfred, too, he explores Christianity, Marxism, and Science.

In general the reviews of the trilogy were very mixed, with Eastern critics in particular complaining about Manfred's experiments with language, his name coinages, and the frequent mixing of burlesque with serious subjects. A characteristic reaction to the trilogy was that of the *New Yorker* critic, who described *The Primitive* as having an "impassioned, headlong style" and "immense detail."[18]

At this low point in his popularity, Manfred decided two things: to change his difficult-to-pronounce pen-name from Feike Feikema to Frederick Manfred, and to choose for his next novel a subject that had first intrigued him in 1943, the story of fur trader Hugh Glass, his desperate battle with a grizzly bear, and his miraculous return to safety. Both decisions were the right ones. Manfred's new novel (over his new name) would rescue a languishing career and launch him in a new direction—toward the Old West of South Dakota and neighboring states, and toward the series called the Buckskin Man Tales that has since made Manfred's name synonymous with serious western fiction.

As early as 1940 Manfred had had in mind a series of from six to ten books about the farming Midwest, and in 1950 he had considered several series of novels. In the meantime, however, Manfred had been gathering materials related to the Hugh Glass story. He had first read about the mountain man and the grizzly bear in 1943 in the *South Dakota Guide*, and shortly thereafter he began to collect items in preparation for a story. By early fall in 1952, he was ready to write. By the summer of the following year, he was well along in the writing and made a trip from his home in Minneapolis to northwestern South Dakota where he recreated part of Glass's crawl from the Grand River to the Cheyenne.

In casting about for a name for the work, Manfred tried various combinations, and at last hit upon *Lord Grizzly*, a translation from the Latin *horribilis imperator*, a scientific name that he had found in his reading. Thus the title refers specifically to the grizzly bear who mauls and maims Hugh Glass on the Grand River. It also applies to Glass himself, who wears the grizzly's hide on his long journey home, who lives like the grizzly, close to the earth, and who is pursued during his long crawl by a ghostly grizzly. It represents the guilty thoughts that finally alter his decision to take revenge on the two companions who had left him for dead.

The success of the novel with the unusual name was immediate and complete. More than a million copies were printed. Literary critics like William Carlos Williams and Walter Havighurst lavished it with praise. Robert Penn Warren voted for it in the National Book Award competition and it very nearly won. Only a negative vote by Malcolm Cowley, who believed that a novelist should write about his own time, kept *Lord Grizzly* from the esteemed prize.

In 1954 Manfred began planning other western books, notably *Con-*

quering Horse and *Riders of Judgment*, and throughout 1955 he wrote alternately at the two. By 1956 *Riders* took precedence. By the end of the year Manfred had decided on an Old West series that could have its own identity. He hoped as well that a single publisher would take over *Lord Grizzly* and the three books in progress and publish them as a set.

The final shaping of the Buckskin Man Tales took place in the spring of 1958, when *Riders of Judgment* was in print, *Conquering Horse* was written, and *Scarlet Plume* and *King of Spades* were in the planning stages. "I think it a really worthwhile project," wrote Manfred to his editor, "one that will someday be known as a very fine literary project, possibly even a famous one."[19]

The second of the Tales was *Riders of Judgment*, which appeared in 1957, the story of the range wars of 1892 in Wyoming between the small ranchers and the big-time cattlemen. Although it was praised by critics and reviewers for seriousness and powerful realism, it was far outshadowed two years later by the reception given *Conquering Horse*.

Many readers consider the story of No Name and his vision quest to be Manfred's finest work and one of the most faithful accounts of Sioux life ever written by a non-Indian. *Conquering Horse* is an effort to explore and celebrate the lives of the earliest of the peoples who had inhabited Siouxland and parts west. It is the story of a young Sioux brave in pre-White times who belongs to a band living at the falls of the Big Sioux River, at present-day Sioux Falls. Because he is unable to attain his holy vision, No Name believes himself unworthy to be the son of a chief. But when he finishes the first part of his vision ordeal, the young man learns not only how he will obtain his name but also that he must kill his father in order to complete the promise of the dream. In the process of accomplishing his mysterious task, No Name is reunited with Leaf, the girl he made pregnant, captures the white horse of his vision, and returns—triumphant—to his village, bearing the white horse's colt and his own new-born son. There he receives his new name, Conquering Horse, and his vision is fulfilled when his father, Redbird, follows his own vision and dies when struck by lightening.

From the rush of favorable reviews that followed, Manfred was encouraged to continue to explore the world of the Sioux Indians who had inhabited the land before him. He tried his hand at a novelette, *Arrow of Love* (1961), the love story of a Sioux brave and a Chippewa maiden, and the tragic pattern of vengeance that destroys them. The theme of troubled Indian-White relations also plays an important part in *Arrow of Love*, and it was that theme that Manfred determined to explore in his next full-length book. He chose the story of the Minnesota Sioux War of 1862, which ended in the mass exodus of non-Indians, the expulsion of Minnesota Sioux people, several hundred deaths, and the hanging of thirty-eight Sioux men charged with crimes in the War. As the central character in *Scarlet Plume* (1964), he created Judith Raveling, a captive of the Sioux, who sees her daughter and neighbors killed and mutilated, who escapes to Sioux Falls, and falls in love with a Dakota Indian. She bitterly mourns the capture and death of Scarlet Plume, despite the disapproval of military officers and other returned captives. In frequent and sometimes shocking contrasts thus portrayed between Indian and White cultures, Manfred created his most profound exploration of the question of how harmony between the two races might someday be attained.

The final novel in the Buckskin Man Tales, also with a South Dakota location, is *King of Spades* (1966), Manfred's remarkable fable about the gold mining boom in the Black Hills and a young man's painful growth to manhood—and early death. The plot of the story centers on young Roddy King, later named Earl Ransom, who believes that his mother is dead and that he has killed his father. The mother is not dead, however, but turns up in Wyoming, where the unknowing Earl Ransom enters into an affair with her. Besides the Oedipal theme, Manfred also illustrates once again the destructive power of the White man's lust for riches, as shown by the exploitation of the mineral wealth of the Black Hills. As if to compact all of the White man's failings into one person, Manfred has Ransom kill several men, choose gold in preference to the idyllic Indian life he might have entered, take up with a prostitute, and finally kill his mistress, learning only at the end that she is his mother. It is a powerful story, one that Manfred himself says led him to plumb his own psychological depths more fully than in any other novel.

As Robert C. Wright points out in his biography of Manfred, the reviewers and critics tended to take extreme positions on the novel. Victor P. Haas wrote: "It has been a long time since I have read a novel as distasteful, absurdly violent, and luridly melodramatic." E. C. Kiessling, on the other hand, wrote that we overlook the "implausibility of the plot in the intensity and excitement of the story." Manfred's good friend Herbert Krause, a prize-winning novelist himself and writer in residence at Augustana College, wrote, "The book will shake the vitals of any reader who accepts the traditional picture of Deadwood and the gold field. Never before has this region been portrayed as it is in this rambunctious pistol jetting novel.''[20]

On the way to becoming the state's most distinguished novelist, Frederick Manfred has written fifteen novels that do not have a South Dakota setting. Besides those already named are *Morning Red* (1956), a romance set in Minneapolis; *The Man Who Looked Like the Prince of Wales* (1965) and *Eden Prairie* (1968), contrasting character studies set in small-town Iowa; *Milk of Wolves* (1976), the study of a ruffian artist; *The Manly-Hearted Woman* (1976), a probing examination of Indian psychology and sexuality; *Green Earth* (1977), an epic retelling of Manfred's growing up; and *Sons of Adam* (1980), a study of paired male characters. The list is long and convincing. There are short stories, too, and essays and poems, an autobiographical sketch, and a book made up of Manfred's incomparable conversation moderated by John R. Milton. In these as well are the recurring themes already noted: the maturation of individuals as well as of the geographic region Siouxland, a persistent argument for a responsible partnership between man and nature, and a deep interest in the ties that hold people together. As Robert Wright says of much of Manfred's work, he has "consistently devalued isolation and recognized the importance of natural bonds."[21]

A dozen years ago Manfred's popularity reached a significant high point when all of his Buckskin Man Tales in inexpensive editions were selling by the hundreds of thousands of copies. A *New York Times* Review by Madison Jones carried the headline, "Frederick Manfred— Parallels with Homer."[22] It was a startling claim, but it was close to the goal Manfred once established for himself: to create for Siouxland the "first classics of our Homeric culture." He would not have achieved it, chances are, had Ole Rolvaag not inspired him many years before with *Giants in the Earth*. The Buckskin men of Frederick Manfred and the dirt farmers of Ole Rolvaag will serve to inspire new generations of Siouxland readers and writers, and to remind them of the struggles for survival that lie behind us as well as some that continue to lie ahead.

Notes

1. Harold P. Simonson, "The Tragic Trilogy of Ole Rolvaag," *The Closed Frontier: Studies in American Literary Tragedy* (New York: Holt, Rinehart, and Winston, Inc., 1970), p. 85.

2. Ella Valborg Tweet, "Introduction," *The Third Life of Per Smevik,* by O. E. Rolvaag, translation of *Amerika-Breve* by Ella Valborg Tweet and Solveig Zempel (Minneapolis: Dillon Press, Inc., 1971), p. xi.

3. Rolvaag, cited in Tweet, pp. xi–xii.

4. Rolvaag to Jennie Berdahl, September 22, 1904, cited in Paul Reigstad, *Rolvaag, His Life and Art* (Lincoln: University of Nebraska Press, 1972), p. 8.

5. *Ibid.*

6. Rolvaag, quoted in Tweet, "Introduction," pp. xiii–xiv.

7. Rolvaag's *Diary,* translated by his wife Jennie Berdahl Rolvaag, after August 4, 1896, Norwegian-American Historical Association Collections.

8. *Diary,* August 20, 1896.

9. *Amerika-Breve,* translated as *The Third Life of Per Smevik,* p. 3.

10. *Diary,* January 2, 1901.

11. Quoted in Einar Haugen, "Rolvaag and the Norwegian Heritage," *The Prairie Frontier,* (Sandra Looney, Arthur R. Huseboe, and Geoffrey Hunt, eds.; Sioux Falls: Nordland Heritage Foundation, 1984), p. 110.

12. Quoted in Helmer M. Blegen, "O. E. Rolvaag—A Reminiscence," *The Prairie Frontier,* p. 101.

13. Einar Haugen, *Ole Edvart Rolvaag* (Boston: Twayne Publishers, 1983), p. 53.

14. Letter to Simon Johnson, January 21, 1922, Norwegian-American Historical Association Collections.

15. Letter to Simon Johnson, December 27, 1922, *ibid.*

16. Quoted in Arthur R. Huseboe, "*Giants in the Earth* at Aschehougs," *The Nordlander* VI (June 1983), p. 4.

17. *Conversations with Frederick Manfred.* Moderated by John Milton. (Salt Lake City: The University of Utah Press, 1974), p. 24.

18. *New Yorker,* XXV (September 17, 1949), p. 106.

19. Letter to David McDowell, April 19, 1958, Manuscript Division, University of Minnesota Libraries.

20. Quoted in Robert C. Wright, *Frederick Manfred* (Boston: Twayne Publishers, 1979), p. 88.

21. Wright, "The Myth of the Isolated Self in Manfred's Siouxland Novels," *Where the West Begins* (Arthur R. Huseboe and William Geyer, eds.; Sioux Falls, S.D.: Center for Western Studies, 1978), p. 110.

22. *New York Times Book Review* (February 16, 1975), p. 6.

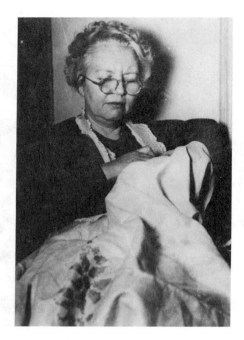

Laura Ingalls Wilder

Rose Wilder Lane.

Ingalls home at De Smet, South Dakota.
Courtesy Laura Ingalls Wilder Memorial Society, Inc.

*"Pa and Ma" (Charles and Caroline)
Ingalls.*

Pioneer Authors from South Dakota: Laura Ingalls Wilder and Rose Wilder Lane

William T. Anderson

South Dakota plainswoman Laura Ingalls Wilder concluded her pioneering experience in 1894, the year after historian Frederick Jackson Turner delivered an hypothesis to suggest that the American frontier had closed. She was twenty-seven when she left South Dakota; for more than two decades, she had been a participant in the rapid expansion of non-Indian society across the American West, first as the daughter of pioneers Charles and Caroline Ingalls, then as the wife of homesteader Almanzo Wilder. After fifteen years on the Dakota prairie near the town of DeSmet, she left the open country for the hills and hollows of the Missouri Ozarks.

Like the historian Turner, Laura was a native of Wisconsin. She was born at Pepin on February 7, 1867. While Turner made a place for himself among eminent historians when he defined the collective society of the frontier in American history, and explained its relationship to national character, Laura carved a niche for herself among writers who brought into focus the life of the pioneering family on the frontier. For her, the West meant the agricultural frontier on the prairie. She shared with her pioneering family what she termed "the fascination and the terror of homesteading." She was part of the human "wave" that pushed back the frontier line in trackless lands ceded by Indians and opened to pioneering homesteaders.

After leaving a birth place about seven miles east of Lake Pepin,

Laura spent nearly all of her ninety years in the Mississippi River basin and the Great Plains. Summing up her early years, she wrote:

> I was born in the *Little House in the Big Woods*. . . . From there, with my parents and sisters, I traveled in a covered wagon across Minnesota, Iowa, Missouri, and Kansas into Indian Territory, where we lived in the *Little House on the Prairie*. Then, after traveling back to western Minnesota, we lived for several years *On the Banks of Plum Creek*. From there, we went West again to live *By the Shores of Silver Lake* and through *The Long Winter* in Dakota Territory. We lived at DeSmet, *Little Town on the Prairie*, and I married Almanzo Wilder of *Farmer Boy*, just as I told about in *These Happy Golden Years*.[1]

The book titles in her autobiographical sketch, which have become synonymous with her life as a pioneering author, chronicled her personal experiences from the early 1870s to the middle of 1890s. While Turner sociologically defined the actions of pioneers like the Ingalls and Wilders, Laura concretely explained the grass roots experience for audiences of all ages around the globe. Readers have read her books in more than forty languages. Through the television series "Little House on the Prairie," her fans have seen a distorted version of Wilder's accurate portrayals of pioneer life. Despite deviations from fact, the television versions have enhanced her reputation as a writer of unusual popularity.

Laura's writing was inspired by life on the prairie at the height of the homesteading era. In her literature she recorded the trials and privations of prairie settlers and described the wide-open stretches of prairie land:

> All around them to the very edge of the world, there was nothing but grasses waving in the wind. Far overhead, a few white puffs of cloud sailed in the thin blue air.
>   Laura was very happy. The wind sang a low, rustling in the grass. Grasshoppers' rasping quivered up from all the trees in the creek bottoms. But all these sounds made a great, warm happy silence. Laura had never been in a place she liked so much as this place.[2]

Eastern Dakota Territory awakened full-blown in her the mystical qualities of land and sky and water. Describing the sunrise at Silver Lake, which adjoined the townsite of DeSmet, she expressed with awe and appreciation a morning spectacle that she witnessed daily while she drew water from a well:

Beyond the lake's eastern shore the pale sky was bordered with bands of crimson and gold. Their brightness stretched around the south shore and shone on the high bank that stood up from the water in the east and the north. Night was still shadowy in the northwest, but Silver Lake lay like a sheet of silver in its setting of tall wild grasses. Ducks quacked among the thick grasses to the southwest, where the Big Slough began. Screaming gulls flew over the lake, beating against the wind. A wild goose rose from the water with a ringing call, and one after another the birds of his flock answered him as they rose and followed. The great triangle of wild geese flew with a beating of strong wings into the glory of the sunrise. Shafts of golden light shot higher and higher in the eastern sky, until their brightness touched the water and was reflected there. Then the sun, a golden ball, rolled over the eastern edge of the world.[3]

As a citizen of Dakota from 1879 to 1894, she experienced prospering times through boom years as well as hard times and depression. There were near-famines, deaths, droughts, grasshopper plagues, diseases, and physical maladies. Laura's older sister, Mary, was stricken blind before the family entered Dakota Territory in 1879. Charles Ingalls told Laura she must be her sister's eyes, relating the world of movement, light and color. By accepting the charge to narrate events for Mary, she served an apprenticeship in the use of words.

After the Ingalls family arrived on the Chicago & Northwestern Railroad, Charles became a timekeeper and paymaster for a Big Sioux Railroad camp, near present-day Brookings, and moved west with rail construction to the Silver Lake camp, near the future site of the town of DeSmet. Here, Caroline's "no farther" edict prevailed. Charles filed on a quarter section within a mile of the town site and established a farmstead. When DeSmet was formed, in 1880, he became active in its early development, and until his death in 1902 he was respected as a town patriarch.

Laura found it hard to reconcile the gradual loss of an unfettered prairie surrounding DeSmet. "Wild birds did not like the town full of people, and neither did Laura," she wrote. "I would rather be out on the prairie with the grass and the birds and Pa's fiddle. Yes, even with wolves! I would rather be anywhere than in this muddy, cluttered, noisy town, crowded by strange people."[4]

It was DeSmet, however, that offered the Ingalls family a refuge from their drafty claim shanty during the hard winter of 1880–1881. Snow stranded a community of less than one hundred, miles from the nearest source of supplies. Blizzards curtailed train service. The Ingalls family huddled in the kitchen of their store building, and survived by twisting hay into sticks for fuel, and grinding wheat in a coffee mill for use to bake a daily loaf of bread. Laura mused that "there is something about living close to the great elemental forces of nature that allows people to rise above small annoyances and discomforts."[5]

She surrendered her freedom-loving spirit to become a school teacher, beginning at age fifteen in an abandoned claim shanty a dozen miles from DeSmet. She taught three terms. "I never graduated from anything," she noted, for at age eighteen she wed Almanzo Wilder.

The Wilders' marriage in 1885 was unusual, even by Dakota territorial standards. The couple took up wheat farming in partnership, and Laura set a four-year limit on the experiment, insisting that if it were unsuccessful Almanzo would pursue another career. The attempt at wheat farming was doomed from the outset; good years of the early 1880s gave way to a drought cycle late in the decade. "How heart-breaking it was," Wilder remembered, "to watch the grain we had sown with such hope wither and yellow in the hot winds. And it was back-breaking, as well as heart-breaking to carry water from the well to the garden only to see it dry up despite all my efforts."[6]

Other set-backs were devastating. Hail storms drove their only bountiful wheat crop into the ground. Fire destroyed their home. The Wilders battled diphtheria, which left Almanzo with a crippled foot. A few pleasures intervened to ease the pain of tragedy. Although pregnancy made Laura dizzy and despairing, her only surviving child was born on December 5, 1886. Laura named her daughter Rose because she symbolized a hope and longing that all of Dakota could be as flowerful as the mass of wild roses that covered the land during the month of June. The second child, a son, died soon after his birth in 1889.

Because Almanzo was permanently weakened by his bout with diphtheria, the Wilders were forced to leave South Dakota in search of a recuperative climate. In 1890 they lived with Almanzo's parents in Minnesota. During 1891 they journeyed to Florida, where they spent a year hoping the mild climate would restore Almanzo's vigor. In 1892 they returned to DeSmet. Successive dry years and the Panic of 1893 drove hundreds from the prairie land, from their independent roles as homesteader-yeomen. The Wilders decided to abandon South Dakota permanently.

Because prairie conditions had twice caused their failure, they sought surroundings more like Laura's woodlands birthplace. Farmland in the Ozark Hills of Missouri was being promoted as a prime location for small-scale fruit farming, dairying, and poultry raising. For Almanzo, it was attractive as a milder climate; he was still partially lame and weak from the effects of diphtheria.

With a team and wagon carrying all of their remaining household goods, their seven-year-old daughter Rose, and a $100 bill to stake a new start, the Wilders pulled out of DeSmet in 1894. They left Laura's family behind. Drought years had driven Charles Ingalls from his farm into DeSmet, where he worked as a carpenter and minor public official.[7]

As the Wilder's wagon headed south toward "The Land of the Big Red Apple" in Missouri, Laura opened a nickel notebook and in pencil recorded her observations of the last journey in search of a home. She described a barren countryside in Dakota, the burnt-out fields, and the roads filled with displaced travelers. She reveled in the green oasis of a camping spot near the James River, and a prosperous group of German-Russian "colony" people, who were hospitable to the Wilders. When describing the picturesque river bluffs, Wilder expressed strong empathy for Native Americans who, like her own family, were displaced from their homes by circumstance. "I would have scalped a lot more white folks before I would have left," she noted in her diary.[8]

When the Wilders reached Yankton and prepared to cross the Missouri River to take leave of South Dakota, a violent storm rose in the sky like a final jeering blow. The wind howled and threatened to uplift the wagon. Almanzo tied the wagon wheels to secure them. Laura and Rose watched angry lemon-colored clouds of dust billow above the Missouri. "That's your last sight of Dakota," Laura grimly told her wide-eyed daughter.

After traveling 650 miles, they arrived at a small town tucked away in the Ozark hills: Mansfield, Missouri. "This is where we stop," Laura said in a voice full of hope as they rounded a bend into town. The bitter experience of homesteading was over.

Near Mansfield, Laura and Almanzo established Rocky Ridge Farm, which eventually contained 200 productive acres, and specialized in orcharding, dairying, and poultry raising. Over the years, the couple cleared a stony woods, created fields and pastures, and built a ten-room farmhouse as they grew prosperous in their new environment. Their South Dakota experience became the stuff of story-telling, and anecdotal repartee among their new neighbors in the Ozark hills. Laura felt a compulsion to ruminate over her experiences as a pioneer child and prairie wife.

She longed to express herself in words and to see her experiences in print. The chance finally came at age forty-four, when she published her first article in *The Missouri Ruralist*, a weekly publication for farm families. The by-line "Mrs. A. J. Wilder" became familiar to subscribers after she became the Household Editor for a column labeled "As a Farm Woman Thinks."

In the position of Editor for a regular column, Mrs. Wilder overcame her usual modesty and sometimes wrote autobiographically. Between her columns on Ozark sunrises, vignettes of farm life and advice on how to prosper in the Ozarks, Laura occasionally wrote of her experiences as a homesteader's daughter. Such writing was a prelude to her later career as the author of the Little House Books.

While her parents farmed, Rose Wilder attended school in Mansfield. She recalled that her parents were "courageous, even gaily so. They did everything possible to make me happy, and I gallantly responded with an effort to persuade them that they were succeeding."[9] As the Wilders' financial condition improved, Rose went to school dressed as well as any of her classmates. But she struggled to learn from unqualified, semi-literate, Ozark mountain teachers.

To improve her education, Rose left Mansfield to attend high school in Crowley, Louisiana, where she lived with relatives. Then she became a "bachelor girl" telegrapher in Kansas City. Independent pioneering instincts inspired her through participation in a walk-out during the first Western Union labor strike, in 1904. Her wardrobe changed to include the serviceable shirt-waist and she became a suffragist. The wanderlust that had enticed her parents lured Rose across the United States, as a Western Union operator, until she reached the shore of the Pacific Ocean at San Francisco.

In California, Rose Wilder blazed new trails in life-style. She was the first female real-estate agent in the northern part of the state, where she sold thousands of acres of farmland in the San Francisco area. She married businessman Gillette Lane in 1909. When the land business slackened at the outset of World War I, the couple moved to Telegraph Hill in San Francisco, where Rose went to work as a newspaper woman. By 1915 she was a star reporter for the *Call-Bulletin*, and the darling of its crusading editor, Fremont Older.

While with the *Bulletin*, Rose Wilder Lane perfected a crisp, descriptive, journalistic style, and received plum assignments that included coverage of a burgeoning movie business. She wrote a series about the famous star Charlie Chaplin. She created serials on the lives of Jack London, Herbert Hoover, Henry Ford, and the aviator Art Smith, a daredevil performer at the 1915 World's Fair.

Meanwhile, the Wilders of Rocky Ridge Farm prospered enough to release Laura for a 1915 visit with the Lanes in San Francisco. While in California, she learned from her daughter the subtleties of writing and the strategies of publishing articles in outlets beyond the *Missouri Ruralist*. In a letter to her husband, she expressed the desire to "do a little writing with Rose to get the hang of it a little better so I can write something that perhaps I can sell."[10]

By the end of World War I, Rose had divorced her husband, published her first novel, enlarged her list of literary accomplishments with newspaper and magazine features, and engaged in service to the American Red Cross as a publicist. For nearly a decade, she worked in Europe and the Middle East, traveling as a freelance writer, a tourist, a correspondent, and a reporter of conditions in refugee centers for the Near East Relief organization as well as the Red Cross. From her desk flowed a steady stream of books, short stories, translations, and dispatches that made her an important force in American media.

In 1928 Rose returned to live with her parents at Rocky Ridge Farm, intending to use Ozark folkways as literary materials. Through a close daily relationship with Rose, Laura learned more about submitting her writing, and she entered mainstream magazine markets when Rose helped her polish two articles on the family home at Rocky Ridge for publication in *The Country Gentleman*.

For a decade, Laura had toyed with the idea of writing her childhood experiences into a book. Knowing the richness and authenticity of her mother's recollections, Rose offered encouragement. Collaboration between mother and daughter, which had evolved steadily since 1919, led to the formulation of a working plan:

> If I were you I would jump directly, after the transition paragraph, into "when I was a girl—" and draw the contrast clearly. Only one generation ago, Indians and forests and half a continent were practically untouched by the white race. Free land, free fuel, food for the hunting it—"Go west, young man, and grow up with the land," That sort of thing. And do it all concretely—don't *say* those things were so, *show* that they were so. Your log cabin in the Great Woods . . . your trip through Kansas . . . the buildings of the railroad through the Dakotas. . . . Make it real, because you saw it with your own eyes.[11]

Laura Wilder's first book length manuscript was the autobiography she completed in 1930, entitled *Pioneer Girl*. In it she told the story of childhood from its beginnings in the Big Woods of Wisconsin to her wedding in Dakota Territory. Rose took time from assignments with *Country Gentleman*, *Ladies Home Journal*, and other periodical publications to edit and type for her Mother, and Rose sent the manuscript to her agent in New York.

When it was rejected, Rose helped Laura give her story a different form. In the flowing phrases of a story-teller, Laura re-wrote the section of her book on the Wisconsin experience, and it appeared as *Little House in the Big Woods* in 1932.[12] This was an immediate success, and at age sixty-six Laura published a second work. *Farmer Boy* was about Almanzo Wilder's boyhood in Malone, New York, published in 1933.[13]

Enthusiastically, Laura and Rose continued their work on the saga of pioneering experience; collaboration on "Little House" manuscripts kept both women busy for a decade. Laura drafted material. Rose edited and dealt with agents and publishers. Laura explained her plan:

> I began to think what a wonderful childhood I had had. . . . I had seen the whole frontier, the woods, the Indian country of the great plains, the frontier towns, the building of railroads in wild, unsettled country, homesteading and farmers coming in to take possession. I realized that I had lived and seen it all—all the successive phases of the frontier. . . . Then I understood that in my own life I represented a whole period of American history. I wanted children now to understand more about the beginnings of things, to know what is behind the things they see—what it is that made American as they know it. Then I thought of writing the story of my childhood in several volumes. . . . [14]

In rapid succession, the books appeared: *Little House on the Prairie* in 1935 and *On the Banks of Plum Creek* in 1937. Librarians, educators, and historians applauded each volume as a valuable historical record, and the isolated Wilder farm became a center for literary production. Almanzo added his recollections of people, places, and events to those of Rose and Laura. As Laura explained: "My series of stories are literally true, names, dates, places, every anecdote and much of the conversation are historically and actually true."[15]

South Dakotans took immediate interest in the two women from DeSmet, focusing initially on the writings of Rose. Aubrey Sherwood, publisher of *The DeSmet News*, kept his readers informed about all of her books and articles. There had been a flurry of interest since "Let the Hurricane Roar" appeared as a *Saturday Evening Post* serial, in 1932, for it featured the homesteading era around DeSmet. The book version became a best-seller. South Dakotans were especially proud because the story it told mirrored the hardships they endured during the "dirty thirties."

Frequently, Rose used childhood memories, prairie settings, and pioneering tales in her popular fiction. To many South Dakotans she became as much the pen woman of the state as Willa Cather was the spokes person of Nebraska. In 1938 her serial "Free Land," in *The Saturday Evening Post*, brought national acclaim, and South Dakota newspaper editors acknowledged the positive image it elicited in an era when the state was otherwise portrayed as a wasteland. Former homesteaders and their descendants corresponded with Rose Lane, sharing their experiences and corroborating her stories. Howard Mumford Jones wrote in *The Saturday Review of Literature* that:

> The writing is simple, honest and direct. The quiet heroism of the Dakota settlers is, of course, appealing, but the novel seems more important as a document than as a work of art. Thus, indeed, one says to himself, did they toil to create another American state.[16]

Rose wrote *Free Land* partly as an expression of antagonism for the New Deal policies of Franklin Roosevelt, which she and her parents regarded as dangerous assaults on American ingenuity and independence. The Wilders remembered the sacrifice they made to occupy "free land." They believed that in hard times—during the homesteading era as much as the Great Depression—Americans should survive by their own will and initiative. Rose explained:

> I wrote "Free Land" because I could no longer bear hearing people say, "But everything is changed now; there's no more free land." Everything certainly is changed now, but as to really "free" land, there never was any. . . . I usually write because I need the money. Sometimes I write because I get mad. I wrote "Let the Hurricane Roar" and "Free Land" because I got mad.[17]

While Rose Wilder Lane was lionized in South Dakota for writing about the state, Laura continued to make further contributions. In the spring of 1939, she and Almanzo drove to DeSmet and attended an "Old Settler's Day." They talked to old friends and refreshed their memories about names, locations, and facts. Laura was ready to begin the last group of Little House books, each set at DeSmet. She visited at length with Aubrey Sherwood, toured the countryside (in a Chrysler instead of horse and buggy), and visited her sisters Carrie and Grace.

The first of Laura Ingalls Wilder's Dakota books was *By the Shores of Silver Lake*, published in 1939. She recounted the building of a railroad in Dakota Territory, and described the founding of DeSmet in 1880. Rose remained active in her mother's work, despite a move from Mansfield to establish a home in Danbury, Connecticut. Their author-editor relationship continued through the exchange of correspondence and manuscript drafts.

In *The Long Winter*, which appeared in 1940, there was a minor title change that amused the Wilders. Blizzards through the winter of 1880–1881 had long been referred to as "The Hard Winter," which Laura used as a title in draft. Her editors at Harper and Brothers cringed, however, at the notion of presenting anything as "hard" for young readers. They insisted upon the use of *The Long Winter*, instead.

The last two books, *Little Town on the Prairie* (1941), and *These Happy Golden Years* (1943), concluded the saga. Her books described the founding and growth of the town of DeSmet and the rich social history that surrounded it. Accuracy in relating events, describing people, and reporting a sense of place was impeccable. Correlation with the factual contents of *The DeSmet News and Leader* was apparent.

In her desire to write books as historical accounts as well as readable fiction, Laura Ingalls Wilder carefully checked details and facts. She wrote to people who remembered, including a letter to DeSmet pioneer Henry Hinz that asked about the time a train departed during the Hard Winter. She corresponded with Aubrey Sherwood to ask that he refresh her memory about sites. In her penciled manuscripts, Laura drew detailed maps of DeSmet as she remembered it. With marginal notes to Rose, she elaborated from her own recollections, revealing extraneous details about Dakota history. Regarding the building of the Dakota Central Railroad, she said that "contractors expected to be cheated on the surveying and the R.R. companies expected the contractors to steal all they could get away with. This *was* the way the R.R. was built!"[18]

Aubrey Sherwood helped bring the name of Laura Ingalls Wilder to South Dakotans. He had known of the Ingalls family all his life and his father had taught Carrie Ingalls the printing trade at *The DeSmet News*. His admiration for Rose and Laura surfaced often in editorials. After the publication of *These Happy Golden Years*, in 1943, *The*

DeSmet News began reporting the many honors accorded Laura's work. Libraries in Detroit, in Pomona, California, and in Mansfield were named after her. Literary awards were bestowed. Little House books reached an international audience through translations. After World War II, State Department officials ordered translations of Wilder books into German and Japanese as an acculturation technique.

The impact of Little House books in South Dakota was extensive. In 1944 Laura Ingalls Wilder, Carrie Ingalls Swanzey, and Rose Wilder Lane presented Charles Ingalls' violin to the South Dakota State Historical Society in Pierre. "Pa's fiddle" drew thousands of visitors to the Memorial Hall museum. Many went on pilgrimages to the sites mentioned in Wilder's books. DeSmet residents noticed out-of-state cars stopping along Main Street, and tourists began photographing the Ingalls store building and other familiar places. They went to *The DeSmet News* office, where Aubrey Sherwood often had recent letters from the author to show wide-eyed children. He became the unofficial historian for Ingalls-Wilder lore.

In November, 1951, Laura wrote Sherwood from Rocky Ridge Farm that "Quite often I have a letter telling of some tourist's visit to DeSmet, of how nicely they have been treated by you and shown around to places of interest."[19] She expressed appreciation for a copy of *The DeSmet News*, saying "I read every word of it for it carries me back. Now and then I find a familiar name, children and grandchildren of those I used to know, I suppose."[20] Nostalgia for the old days in Dakota intensified, she said, especially after the death of Almanzo Wilder at age ninety-two in 1949.

As interest increased in the area around DeSmet because of Laura Wilder's books, a memorial to the Ingalls family was discussed. In 1953, Hazel Gilbert Failing, the daughter of a friend of the Wilders, visited the Mansfield home. On her return to South Dakota, Mrs. Failing proposed a replica of the Ingalls' claim shanty at their homestead a mile east of DeSmet. "It is fine of you and Mr. Sherwood to attempt to commemorate the memory of DeSmet pioneers," wrote Mrs. Wilder to Mrs. Failing. "In your choosing my family I am greatly honored," she added," but "I fear a duplicate of the claim shanty would not be attractive to sight-seers."[21]

When the author died at age ninety near Mansfield on February 10, 1957, admirers in DeSmet were determined to honor her. They formed the Laura Ingalls Wilder Memorial Society, dedicated to preserving the Little House lore and extending hospitality to readers. Two of the Ingalls homes are now restored and opened for visitors. Rose Wilder

Lane appreciated the tributes to her mother, and encouraged the group when she published *On the Way Home*, in 1962, giving DeSmet another book with a local setting. The book related the Wilders' final days in DeSmet, in 1894, and included the diary Laura had kept on the journey to Mansfield.

Rose continued to express the wanderlust of her family. In 1965, at age seventy-eight, she became America's oldest war correspondent when she flew to Viet Nam to report for *Woman's Day*. Three years later, she planned an itinerary for a tour around the world, but she died on October 30, 1968, at her home in Danbury, Connecticut. Because she was the only grandchild of Charles and Caroline Ingalls, and the only child of Laura and Almanzo Wilder, her death closed the odyssey of two generations in a family of Dakota pioneers. But the popular body of work by both Laura Ingalls Wilder and Rose Wilder Lane remains as a rich South Dakota literary legacy.

Notes

1. Stanley Kunitz and Howard Haycraft, *The Junior Book of Authors* (New York: H. W. Wilson Company, 1951), p. 292. A ninth volume, *The First Four Years,* found among the author's papers after her death in 1957, was published posthumously in 1971. It is the story of her early married life on a South Dakota homestead.

2. Laura Ingalls Wilder, *Little House on the Prairie* (New York: Harper and Row, 1935), pp. 48–49.

3. Laura Ingalls Wilder, *By the Shores of Silver Lake* (New York: Harper and Row, 1939), pp. 71–72.

4. *Ibid.,* pp. 71–72.

5. Laura Ingalls Wilder, "Energy Shortage: Winter of '80–81," *Laura Ingalls Wilder Lore* VI, no. 2, (Fall–Winter 1980), p. 5.

6. William Anderson, "It is Better Farther On," *The American West,* XXI, no. 3 (May–June 1984), p. 37.

7. The remainder of the Ingalls family remained in South Dakota after Laura's 1894 departure. Charles Ingalls died at DeSmet in 1902; Caroline in 1924. Their blind daughter Mary never married or regained her sight; she died in 1928. Carrie Ingalls was an early female homesteader when West River lands opened to settlement in the early 1900's. As a newspaperwoman, she operated several final proof newspapers in the Black Hills before her marriage to mine owner David Swanzey. She lived at Keystone until her death in 1946. Grace Ingalls married Nate Dow, a homesteader's son, and they farmed at Manchester. She died in 1941.

8. Laura Ingalls Wilder, *On the Way Home* (New York: Harper and Row, 1962), p. 24.

9. Rose Wilder Lane, "I Discovered the Secret of Happiness," *Cosmopolitan* (June 1926), p. 42.

10. Laura Ingalls Wilder, *West from Home* (New York: Harper and Row, 1974), p. 54.

11. Rose Wilder Lane to Laura Ingalls Wilder, April 11, 1919, Rose Wilder Lane Papers, Herbert Hoover Presidential Library, West Branch, Iowa.

12. (New York: Harper and Brothers, 1932).

13. (New York: Harper and Brothers, 1933).

14. Laura Ingalls Wilder, Book Week Speech [1937], Wilder Papers, Hoover Library.

15. Mary Phraner Warren, "An Exciting Letter," *Cobblestone* (February 1986), p. 30.

16. Howard Mumford Jones, *Laura Ingalls Wilder Lore* (Fall–Winter 1984–1985), p. 8.

17. "Iron Men, Iron Sod," *Saturday Evening Post* (March 5, 1938); *Laura Ingalls Wilder Lore,* p. 8.

18. Laura Ingalls Wilder to Rose Wilder Lane, January 25, 1938. Wilder Papers, Hoover Library.

19. Laura Ingalls Wilder to Aubrey Sherwood, November 19, 1951. In the collection of the recipient.

20. *Ibid.*

21. Laura Ingalls Wilder to Hazel Gilbert Failing, July 27, 1953. Laura Ingalls Wilder Memorial Society Collection, DeSmet, SD.

Oscar Howe and painting.
Courtesy Richardson Archives, USD.

Oscar Howe with students.
Courtesy Richardson Archives, USD.

Sioux Artist: Oscar Howe

John Milton

For an artist, the art often takes precedence over the life, making his true biography a discussion about the development of his work rather than a narration of events in his life. Oscar Howe was a serious artist, ranking with Allan Houser and Blackbear Bosin, perhaps, as the best of traditional Indian painters during the earlier phase of his work, then surpassing R. C. Gorman and Fritz Scholder in a later and more distinctive phase of Indian painting. His treatment of tribal themes and subjects was quite different from those of Gorman and Scholder. His lifestyle was also different, his personality showing up in the meditative and precise paintings that characterized his work in the 1950s and 1960s. Although Howe's art was of the utmost importance to him, and eventually brought him fame and respect, it cannot be separated entirely from his personal history as a Sioux Indian in South Dakota working against the odds imposed upon him by physical ailment and ethnic prejudice.

At various times in his life, Oscar Howe was attacked by his own Sioux people as well as by the White society he partially espoused, apparently leaving him in the difficult position of a man without a country. Yet he remained loyal to both cultures. As for his art, it began in physical and psychological pain and ended with the onslaught of Parkinson's disease. Even during the productive middle years, he faced obstacles not shared fully by his counterparts in the Southwest. With Gorman he shared an admiration for Picasso, but there the similarity ended. Gorman's father, a respected artist himself, surely encouraged his son and provided practical assistance until Gorman could stand on his own. Furthermore, Gorman's personality differed greatly from

Howe's, Gorman being flamboyant, self-promoting, given to entertaining celebrities, and always the center of attention, whereas Howe was reserved, private, living within his thoughts. Howe's relationship to Scholder was that of teacher to pupil for a few years in the 1950s at Pierre, but Scholder soon moved to the Southwest and began painting playful exaggerations of Indian themes and attitudes that often seemed comic, and which Scholder once called Pop Indian Art. One sees no influence of teacher upon pupil. Yet, curiously, the teacher's style began to change during that time, a rather precise, semi-abstract style emerging in 1956, shortly after Scholder left South Dakota.

These brief references to the Southwest only hint at a larger problem faced by artists on the Northern Great Plains region, White as well as Indian. In New Mexico, for example, the headquarters of Gorman and Scholder, three cultures have existed together for a long time, enriching the possibilities of art. Pueblo traditions and established communities go back a thousand years in contrast to approximately 250 years that have passed since the Sioux left their life where the prairie meets the Woodlands around Mille Lac and spread out on the Dakota plains. Spaniards were well settled in New Mexico 200 years before Lewis and Clark came through Sioux Country on their journey of exploration.

Historically, then, South Dakota is still a child. Even after 100 years of statehood, it remains a frontier state in many ways. Its artists are still molding their heritage in relative isolation, partly because of distances between them, and partly because they are few in number. The northern climate demands a large share of survival energy, and artists like Scholder left for the kinder climate of the Southwest. Oscar Howe went south to study, but he returned to his northern home and found few painters with whom to talk or to exchange ideas. It is to his credit that he prevailed, becoming one of the most respected and influential Indian painters in the United States.

When Oscar Howe was born at Joe Creek, on the Crow Creek Indian Reservation, May 13, 1915, he had in his favor a fairly distinguished lineage, including several hereditary chiefs. His great-grandfather Chief White Bear signed the 1876 Agreement, which transferred ownership of the Black Hills to the United States. Ownership of the Hills was a rather tenuous matter, depending on possession; the Cheyenne held claim a century earlier until driven out by the Sioux, and soon after the Custer debacle at the Little Big Horn it became clear that the Sioux, deprived of horses and weapons and facing starvation, had to yield to stronger forces. White Bear was only one of many chiefs to sign the federal Agreement, and was not one of the distinguished chiefs. Yet, he made a speech and is remembered for his oratory.

Howe's other great-grandfather of distinction was Bone Necklace, head chief of the Lower Yanktonai and eloquent spokesman for his people at the 1886 meeting of the Northwestern Indian Commission in South Dakota. In his own middle-age memories, Oscar spoke fondly of Bone Necklace. This great-grandfather's oratorical skill had not been passed down to him. On certain occasions with close friends, where perhaps he was warmed by a highball or two, Oscar spoke freely and with a sense of humor, but he was more often characterized by reticence. What he may have inherited from his ancestor chiefs was a sense of pride, even an aloofness, that did not allow him to bend in the presence of others. (As a bowler in the University of South Dakota faculty league for many years, he did not bend to set the ball gently upon the lane but threw it out from a straight and tall posture. The ball landed with a loud thud and his colleagues knew who had just bowled. Whether he did well or poorly, his expression never changed, and he did not take part in the team's banter. However, he was respected both as a man and as a bowler—with an average score in the 150s—and was missed when Parkinson's forced him to retire from the sport.)

Howe's grandfathers were also chiefs, Unspesni (paternal grandfather), the last hereditary chief of the Yanktonai Sioux and Fearless Bear (maternal grandfather), made a chief when the general council of his tribe met in 1876. Some of the artistic traditions of the Sioux came to Oscar through his mother, Ella Fearless Bear, and through forebears who had kept the "winter counts" on tanned buffalo hides. But the mother died when Oscar was nine. So it was Shell Face, the maternal grandmother, who wielded the greatest influence on the boy, drawing in the sand with her fingers the symbols of the Sioux tribes that Oscar was to use later in his paintings.

Aside from that early training in Sioux symbolism, Oscar Howe's life was difficult for many years. His father tried to discourage the boy's drawing with either a pencil someone had given him or with charcoal that he pulled from the stove, forcing Oscar to go outside by himself where he could make lines with a stick in the dry dirt, lines that the wind took away all too soon. At about the time he was sent to the federal boarding school in Pierre, he developed a skin disease for which the doctor said there was no cure. Open sores discouraged the other school children from coming near him, adding to the isolation caused by a language problem. Oscar spoke only Sioux language, but the rules of the Office of Indian Affairs required that only English be spoken. While in the boarding school hospital, Oscar, age ten, considered ending it all by jumping out of a second-story window. Instead, he was sent back to his reservation home as a hopeless case, both physically and psychologically, having suffered near-blindness (as a result of trachoma) in addition to the skin disease and the shame of having his abnormalities exposed to his fellow students.

There followed a year of physical healing. For the sores on his skin, Oscar tried strong commercial soap. At least several times a day he covered his body with soap, let it dry, and then washed it off. To compensate for his faulty vision, he turned inward and saw in his mind the facts and symbols of the old Sioux stories told to him by Shell Face. After many months the body sores began to heal; the scars that blackened his face did not last nearly as long as the scars on his head that were the result of repeated beatings at the school in Pierre.

In 1926 Oscar returned to the boarding school, his mother now dead and his father still trying to discourage the interest in art. It was his artistic talent, however, that kept him from feeling ashamed at school. Although there were no classes in art, there were contests, and Oscar won them. He was still shy and unhappy, but he finished the eight grades when he was eighteen. Finding a job in 1933 in South Dakota was next to impossible, the national depression and the local dust bowl conditions having nearly destroyed economies in most agricultural states. He managed at last to get a part-time job as a laborer on his reservation for the Roads Division of the Office of Indian Affairs.

After two years of breathing dust and eating inadequate meals, he was diagnosed as having tuberculosis. The bad news probably saved his life. Federal officials sent him to New Mexico where the higher elevation and the dry air would be good for his lungs. Because of his talent for painting he was enrolled in the recently opened (1932) art department of the Santa Fe Indian School—a school soon to gain national attention as the Institute of American Indian Arts. Academic necessities for a high school diploma were combined with individual responsibilities in the art program. Supervised by Dorothy Dunn, later a critic and historian of Southwest Indian art, the students were encouraged to work out their own problems of form and design without lectures or theories or regimented drawing exercises. Oscar flourished under this system. By the time he graduated in 1935 as salutatorian of his class, several of his paintings had been exhibited in San Francisco and Brooklyn as well as with a traveling exhibit of American Indian art that included London and Paris in its itinerary. Not only had Oscar learned self-reliance and discovered his ability to create intuitively without inhibitions, but he was also on his way to a measure of fame.

However, he had only a high school diploma at age twenty-three and returned to the reservation in South Dakota to do what little road labor remained available through Indian Office work relief assistance. He felt that he had come back to where he started. False hopes were raised by the replies to a brochure sent out by the Santa Fe school advertising the work of its art students. Oscar received perhaps 500 letters, many of them orders for paintings, but he could not afford to buy the necessary art materials. So he packed the letters in a box and hoped that he could get back to them later. Before that could happen, his aunt burned the box and letters, thinking them trash as she cleaned house.

In 1939 Howe took a job as art instructor at the Pierre Indian boarding school with board and room being the pay. A year later he was assigned by the Works Progress Administration to paint designs on the domed ceiling of the Mitchell Library. WPA artists and writers' projects kept many talented and later famous persons from starving during the 1930s, and for Howe, as it turned out, the Mitchell project was only his first acquaintance with the city that was to become his home for a while after World War II. For this first project he was awarded a scholarship to the Indian Art Center in Lawton, Oklahoma, where he studied mural painting with Olaf Nordmark.

Having learned the special techniques of mural painting, such as cartoon scaling and the use of egg tempera, Howe was commissioned by the town of Mobridge to do ten historical murals in a new auditorium. As he had done in Pierre, he painted, sculpted, and carved for himself also, but these items did not sell very well; he had to rely on the murals for financial support. Before he completed them, in the first part of 1942, he was drafted into the United States Army. Mobridge officials obtained a two-week induction delay for him so that the murals could be finished. He worked twenty hours a day, had food sent in, and slept briefly on the floor of the auditorium in an effort to get the job done before he reported to the draft board in June.

Older than most of his fellow soldiers (at twenty-seven), still shy and quiet, of a minority race, and having art as his chief interest, Oscar Howe was hardly a good candidate for Army life except that he had already undergone military discipline and drills at the Pierre Indian school. Much to his consternation, he was immediately assigned as a drill corporal and found himself in the company of regular army noncommissioned officers. When his overseas unit was formed (the

442nd Anti-Aircraft Battalion) Howe was the only American Indian in it, yet he did not sense any racial prejudice during the three and a half years he served. During those years his art work consisted of illustrations for training lectures and, in North Africa, painting camouflage on army equipment. After surviving also in Italy and France, Corporal Howe was in Germany just after the fighting ended in Europe, and it was there, in Biedenkopf/Lahn, that he met Adelheit Karla Margarete Anna Hampel in her father's clothing store. Heidi, as she came to be called, accepted Oscar's proposal of marriage before he returned to the United States to be discharged from the army in October, 1945.

Although Heidi, like many military wives, was prevented by various restrictions from coming to the United States until July, 1947, her meeting with Oscar and their subsequent marriage made his military service extremely fortuitous. She was to encourage him in a way that no one else could, fully loyal to her husband's dedication to painting. The war also benefited Howe in another way—the G. I. Bill of Rights that enabled returning servicemen to get education. Howe settled in Mitchell, home of Dakota Wesleyan University, freelancing in art for a year and a half. In 1947 he entered a painting in the Second Annual American Indian Art competition at the Philbrook Art Center in Tulsa, Oklahoma, winning the grand award of $350.00, enough money to bring Heidi to America. They were married July 29 in Chicago and went immediately to Mitchell. Unfortunately, remembering the recent war, many townspeople were still prejudiced against Germans, and perhaps to some it was even worse that the German woman should be married to an Indian. Out of work, and with little money, the Howes faced a dismal future when, unexpectedly, Oscar was asked to go to Oklahoma and work with Dr. O. B. Jacobson, head of the art department at the University of Oklahoma, on a two-volume portfolio, *North American Costumes*. The portfolio was later published in France and quickly became a collectors item. While in Oklahoma the Howes had their only child, Inge Dawn, born June 9, 1948, at the Talihina Indian Hospital. Back in South Dakota, Oscar was asked to design and supervise the installation of the large murals made of colored corn on the outside walls of the famous Corn Palace in Mitchell. Almost coincidentally, he enrolled as a student at Dakota Wesleyan and was named Artist-in-Residence at the same time, an unusual appointment.

Howe's new life, one he could hardly have dreamed of just a few years earlier, began at this point. The next ten years, however, would be a mixture of success and personal failure. Money was still scarce and although Howe began painting in earnest, he had a tendency to pay bills with his paintings or to give them to friends—the Sioux custom of sharing. Gradually, and necessarily, Heidi took over the business arrangements. During the early 1950s the prices for Howe paintings were in the price range of $25.00 to $125.00—paintings to be worth one hundred times more in the latter part of the artist's life.

During the four years at Wesleyan, Howe won six prizes in art competitions and served as acting head of the school's art department during his senior year. After graduation in 1952, and a local exhibition at which every painting was sold, Howe was offered a full-time position in the art department at Dakota Wesleyan, but he chose to begin work on a Master of Fine Arts degree at the University of Oklahoma. After a year of studies he became art director in the Pierre public school system, working with junior and senior high school students. During his first three years in South Dakota's capital city, Howe won four prizes in Colorado and Oklahoma competitions, received his M.F.A. from the University of Oklahoma, and, perhaps not the least of his accomplishments, instructed young Fritz Scholder who later became as well-known as his teacher and who himself taught at the Santa Fe Institute of American Indian Art during the 1960s. Clearly, Oscar Howe had by this time decided to be teacher as well as painter. His former instructor, Dorothy Dunn, wrote to him in Pierre: "In your paintings I see the record of the triumph of an artist over the devastation of the Plains People."[1] The same thing might have been said about his teaching.

In spite of increased acceptance, both as artist and as Indian, by the people of South Dakota, and thankful for the prizes he had won, Howe nevertheless grew bitter during the 1950s. His awards had come from Indian competitions. He was proud of his Sioux heritage, and his paintings never ceased to reveal Sioux legends, symbols, and beliefs; but he did not want to be considered an Indian curiosity rather than a painter *per se*. It angered him that he was not able to show his work in eastern galleries or in nearby city art museums such as the Walker Art Center and the Minneapolis Art Institute.

In May, 1956, while still teaching at Pierre High School, Howe was invited to speak and to exhibit and sell his paintings at the annual meeting of the Minnesota-Dakotas American Studies group at the University of Minnesota. While awaiting his turn, he listened to a White anthropologist "explain" Indians. Their difficulty in adjusting to White society, said the anthropologist, lay in their peculiar concept of time, probably held over from old hunting habits and making it difficult, if not impossible, for the Indian to work responsibly—meaning, of course, according to the rules of another culture. Because the moveable tipi had been the traditional housing, Indians did not take care of houses and did not see in them a symbol of status. Rather, they collected old cars as their ancestors had acquired horses. Furthermore, farming was considered women's work. The picture drawn by the anthropologist was bleak and unflattering.

Oscar Howe was concerned with a different kind of picture, the paintings produced by American Indians as well as by other American painters and by Europeans. He insisted that Pablo Picasso, often held to be the greatest painter of the twentieth century, and much admired by Oscar, had adopted some of the techniques of Indian painting. After all, Indian art was the only true American art. Why, then, should major galleries and museums show little interest in it? Slowly and methodically, as though he were indeed oblivious to time, Howe tried to explain Indian art to his audience, emphasizing pattern and space, flatness and non-realistic coloring. Patiently and almost simplistically, he said: "The problem is space. I have studied space. How do you study space? You take a piece of paper. You study the paper. The paper is space."[2]

Not everyone understood this stoic Sioux painter who was actually seething inside, although they picked up on the ceremonial use of the straight line as truth and the circle as unity. The paintings Howe had brought with him proved very popular. The prices were low, so sales went at a brisk pace. More importantly, perhaps, most of the audience went away wondering why, indeed, more galleries were not interested in exhibiting Indian art.

The problem was yet to be resolved when Howe was recognized in another way, a 1957 appointment as Artist-in-Residence and Assistant Professor of Art at the University of South Dakota in Vermillion. Elbert Harrington, Dean of the College of Arts and Sciences, was interested in the Sioux artist and his undeniable talents. The professorship gave the Howe family the social status and acceptance that made living and painting easier. Because there were at that time no appropriate facilities on the campus, Oscar opened a creative arts laboratory in a converted apartment in downtown Vermillion, the lab also serving as his studio. For several years he worked hard at establishing an art program, at the same time preserving several days a week for his own painting.

During the mid-1950s the style of Howe's painting began to change from the traditional designs and illustrative scenes to a more abstract rendering of figures and a greater use of symbols and bright, hard colors. The painting he submitted to the Philbrook competition in 1958 was different from anything either he or the other Indian artists had attempted, and it started a controversy during which Howe finally vented his anger. Perhaps without meaning to, the Philbrook Art Center had set standards of style for its national Indian exhibits, the style Fritz Scholder called "Traditional" when he complimented his former teacher in 1971. Howe's new work departed from that style and was too individual and distinctive for the Philbrook. The work was rejected. Howe fired back a letter that brought to the surface much of what he had suffered under for too many years:

> Who ever said that my paintings are not in the traditional style has poor knowledge of Indian art indeed. There is much more to Indian art than pretty, stylized pictures. There was also power and strength and individualism (emotional and intellectual insight) in the old Indian paintings. Every bit in my paintings is a true studied fact of Indian paintings. Are we to be held back forever with one phase of Indian painting, with no right for individualism, dictated to as the Indian always has been, put on reservations and treated like a child, and only the White Man knows what is best for him? Now, even in Art, "You little child do what *we* think is best for you, nothing different." Well, I am not going to stand for it. Indian Art can compete with any Art in the world, but not as a *suppressed* Art. I see so much of the mismanagement and treatment of my people. My father died there about three years ago in a little shack, my two brothers still living there in shacks, never enough to eat, never enough clothing, treated as second class citizens. This is one of the reasons I have tried to keep the fine ways and culture of my forefathers alive. But one could easily turn to become a social protest painter. I only hope the Art World will not be one more contributor to holding us in chains.[3]

No one can be sure of the extent of influence of that letter, but the following year the Philbrook revised its rules, Howe took the Grand Purchase Prize, and former student Scholder received an honorable mention for an abstract painting. Howe continued to take prizes at the Philbrook during the 1960s as two more national competitions in Indian art were established, these in Arizona—the Scottsdale National and the Heard Museum Annual. Scholder, part Sioux, and R. C. Gorman, Navajo, both striking off in nontraditional directions, were featured often in the Arizona exhibits after 1969. All three of these Indian painters stressed the necessity of being recognized as artists, original painters, and not just Indian curiosities. In doing so, they changed Indian art from what Scholder called the Bambi Syndrome to a fine art.[4]

Oscar Howe is rarely given full credit for his leadership in this movement. Nevertheless, by 1960 he could be considered successful in his career. That year he was appointed South Dakota Artist Laureate by Governor Ralph Herseth. He was also named a Fellow in the International Institute of Arts and Letters. In April he was the honored person on the television show, "This Is Your Life," with Vincent Price and Ralph Edwards. Price pointed out that Oscar Howe paintings hung alongside work by Picasso, Gauguin, and Van Gogh in some of the major museums in the United States.

Honors, one-man shows, and inclusion in special exhibitions followed one another in rapid succession after 1960. Howe was given an honorary doctorate at South Dakota State University, Brookings, in 1968. Four years later he was awarded a similar degree by Dakota Wesleyan as the Oscar Howe Art Center opened in Mitchell. In 1973 a third honorary doctorate was given him by Hamline University in St. Paul, and he also became the first recipient of the annual South Dakota Governor's Award for Creative Achievement. Meanwhile, in 1971, he was appointed Lecturer to the Near East and South Asia, this tour for the U.S. Department of State taking him to nine different countries.

The activity tired him, and while in New York City in 1974, readying himself to appear on national television again ("To Tell the Truth"), he suffered a severe heart attack that drastically curtailed his work. The subsequent illness of Heidi took more of his energy, and the onset of his own Parkinson's disease stopped his work altogether. His style of painting demanded a steady hand and fine, carefully drawn lines. When friends urged him to draw in any way that he could, allowing the disease to alter his style, he refused. Oscar Howe was stubborn and proud to the end. In his own way, having overcome great obstacles, he had become an internationally known artist and a full professor of art at the University of South Dakota. He would not settle for less.

Howe retired from the University in 1980 because of his disease, spent several years in a nursing home, unable to straighten his once-proud back, and died on October 7, 1983. His legacy is the beauty of his paintings and the preservation of what he deemed significant in his native cultural heritage, a legacy that is available to Indian and non-Indian alike.

Notes

1. Oscar Howe Papers, in the possession of the author.
2. *Ibid.*
3. *Ibid.*
4. Fritz Scholder, "The Emergence of the New Indian Painting," *South Dakota Review* IX (Summer 1971), p. 83.

Harvey Dunn.
Provided by Robert Karolevitz,
courtesy South Dakota Memorial Art
Center.

Harvey Dunn in his studio.
Provided by Robert Karolevitz,
courtesy South Dakota Memorial Art Center.

Artist, Teacher, Poet: Harvey Dunn

Robert F. Karolevitz

Some South Dakotans never leave their native state and, as a result, lack a yardstick of comparison to measure its unique virtues. Others have gone away and, in absentia, developed lifetime love affairs with the land they left behind.

Harvey Thomas Dunn was one of those whose career took him to distant places but whose loyalty to the Dakota prairies grew in intensity with each passing year. When asked about this magnetic attraction to the land of his birth, he simply borrowed his answer from the Bible, Matthew 6:21: "where your treasure is, there will your heart be also."

He was born on March 8, 1884, in Kingsbury County, Dakota Territory. His parents—William Thomas and Bersha Dow Dunn—had homesteaded some three miles south of the rail line connecting the villages of Manchester and DeSmet. Two other children—an older daughter, Caroline, and a younger son, Roy—shared the primitive home on the 160-acre claim between the meandering Redstone Creek and a hoof-packed buffalo trace over which huge herds of the shaggy beasts had traveled in their nomadic wanderings in search of forage, salt licks, and water.

When the time came, the Dunn children were enrolled in the single-room District One rural school of Esmond Township. Like its counterparts throughout the frontier country, the tiny school offered the rudiments of education but little else. Although he was an avid reader and better-than-average student, Harvey seemed to be more impressed by the box-like building itself and its setting than the reading, writing, and arithmetic he studied inside. He imprisoned vivid pictures of the place in his memory—scenes of cavorting children and raging blizzards that one day his talented hands would recreate on expansive canvas. As a youngster, when he was not forced to cipher or do ovals and push-pulls, he sketched endlessly on the blackboard. He drew oxen and flowers and gnarled cottonwood trees and, now and then, his version of a Chicago & North Western locomotive he occasionally saw in Manchester. Finally, to conserve her supply, the teacher had to hide the chalk box from him.

For nine years Harvey attended the Esmond Township school. During that time he grew tall and muscular. By age fourteen he was capable of doing a man's work on the farm: following a walking plow, planting, cultivating, and traversing the family fields with a stone boat to remove the ever-appearing glacial rocks and an occasional bison bone. All these things, too, were indelibly imprinted on his young mind.

To what degree his talent for art was recognized and encouraged in those early years is little known. He probably was even chastised for carving pictures on the walls of the Esmond school's entryway. His mother, who was described as sensitive and poetic, unquestionably knew that he had ability, and years afterward Harvey told of the many evenings he and Bersha sketched by the light of a kerosene lamp.

In 1901 young Harvey had completed all available courses at the rural school and had passed the examinations necessary for him to be accepted as a preparatory student at South Dakota College of Agricultural and Mechanical Arts (as South Dakota State University was then known). With his mother's backing, he convinced his skeptical father that he should enroll, and on November 1, the seventeen-year-old boy boarded the train for the forty-five-mile trip to Brookings and the campus of South Dakota A & M.

With just one year of study beyond the eighth grade, Harvey was not eligible for the college course. He was there mostly because he wanted to learn more about art, but it was necessary for him to take other classes, too. In the fall term of 1901 he earned a 76 in algebra, which at that time was a C grade in the school catalog. He got a D in military, a 95 (or A) in advanced drawing, and no credit in a non-required course known as Buehler's English. In the winter term of 1902 he scored a 96 in free-hand drawing and a 94 in English classics (both A's). His elementary physics teacher gave him a D. Far more important than grades, though, he met Miss Ada B. Caldwell, a talented young art teacher who herself had studied at the Chicago Art Institute, the Pratt Institute, and the Chase School of Art. To Harvey Dunn she was the ideal person to help him.

"She opened new vistas for me," he wrote later after her death. "For the first time I had found a serious, loving and intelligent interest in what I was vaguely searching for. She seemed to dig out talent where none had been, and she prayed for genius. She was tolerant and the soul of goodness. With my eyes on the horizon, she taught me where to put my feet."[1]

When it became apparent to her that Harvey possessed unusual, innate abilities, Miss Caldwell suggested that he go on for additional study at the Chicago Institute of Art. Bersha readily concurred, but Tom Dunn was not convinced, simply because he felt that a strong young man should be thinking of making a living and not making pictures. To his credit, though, he did not stand in his son's way when the decision to "seek new vistas" was finally made. What extra clothing and personal gear Harvey possessed were packed in a round-topped traveling trunk. Then a proud but saddened mother and a dubious, unbending father said their farewells to the young man who in spirit never really left his native state, but who was never to live in South Dakota again.

On November 21, 1902, the hopeful youngster stood before the inspiring structure at the foot of Adams Street on Michigan Avenue in Chicago. He gazed at the majestic bronze lions guarding the entrance, squared his broad shoulders (on which he had hauled his trunk from the train station to save express charges), and walked resolutely up the concrete steps. He stared open-mouthed at the statuary and the magnificent paintings. It was a dream world beyond his comprehension; this was where Miss Caldwell had said his talents could be nurtured and fully developed. With mixed feelings of awe, excitement, and apprehension, he presented himself for enrollment.

Harvey Dunn's stay at the Institute was not notably auspicious in the beginning, but during the two years from 1902 to 1904 the transition from farm boy to man-of-the-world began to take place. It was not an easy process, however. On one occasion, after his first three months of study, a group of older students visited him in his shabby room in the run-down Arundel Hotel with the intention of discouraging him "for his own good." Art, they insisted, presupposed not only a certain amount of talent, but a high degree of culture and bearing on the part of the artist himself. In their estimation the raw boned farmer from South Dakota could never acquire the necessary personal attributes and, therefore, he should go back to his plow before he spent too much money worthlessly and suffered any bitter disappointments.

The mild-mannered Dakotan thanked his visitors for their thoughtfulness on his behalf but, because he was having such a good time, he guessed he would just stay on regardless of the consequences. Harvey continued to draw and paint, uninterrupted by agricultural chores or the cares of day-to-day living. The unlimited opportunity to express himself on paper and canvas was a joyous circumstance, and young Dunn didn't worry at all about whether he would ever look or act like an artist. There was too much work to be done.

For two years he labored incessantly at the Art Institute, not only at his sketch pad and easel but also in doing janitorial and other chores to earn his tuition. He even made a few dollars posing in the nude for a sculpting class, but he quit abruptly when a young woman on whom he had a brief crush enrolled in the course. The $17.50 he paid to enroll at the school was, he later insisted, the only cash he ever invested in art training. During the summer months between sessions, he hired out as a farm hand near his mother's birthplace in Wisconsin for room, board, and $100. All the while Harvey Dunn enjoyed himself immensely, never doubting that the path he had chosen was the right one. No longer were the more esthetic students belittling the ruggedly handsome, six-foot one-and-a-half inch, still-growing country boy from the prairie. He could draw and paint, and they knew it.

Staff members of the Institute knew it, too, and counseled with him about the next step in his career. At that time, Howard Pyle was recognized as the foremost illustrator in the United States, and Dunn's realistic approach to art marked him as a potential talent in that particular field. In Wilmington, Delaware, Pyle was generously sharing his knowledge and experience with a small, select group of students whose work he carefully screened before admitting them to his studio. When Pyle saw the twenty-year-old Dakotan's work, he accepted Harvey as a pupil. From that moment on the tutelage of the great illustrator shaped his future not only as an artist, but as a teacher and humanist as well.

When he himself became an acknowledged success, Dunn wrote: "Howard Pyle did not teach art. Art cannot be taught any more than life can be taught. He did, however, lay constant stress upon the proper relationship of things. . . . His main purpose was to quicken our souls that we might render service to the majesty of simple things."

For two years Dunn remained under the guidance of the watchful master, savoring the luxury of such elite instruction in Wilmington and at Pyle's summer studio at Chadds Ford, Pennsylvania. At the same time he burnished off a few of the rough edges of his homestead upbringing, enough so that he attracted the attention of Johanne Louise

Krebs, daughter of a Danish immigrant who had achieved considerable success as founder of the Krebs Pigment and Chemical Company which later was sold to DuPont for considerable profit. Tulla (a Danish term for endearment with which Harvey always referred to her) was an added inspiration for the young painter who was beginning to grow more and more confident, not only professionally but personally.

In 1906 Howard Pyle advised Dunn, who was then just twenty-two, that he should begin his professional career. Harvey took his mentor's advice, and because he was not yet entirely familiar with the commercial centers of the East—and because Tulla Krebs was there—he decided to open his first studio in Wilmington, using the name H. T. Dunn. He had reached the end of his training period. It was time to see if it were possible, as his father had doubted, to make a living by making pictures.

He was almost an immediate success as an illustrator. He presented himself and his paintings to the commercial art buyers of Philadelphia, New York, and other sophisticated eastern markets, and they put him to work. With a tendency to belittle his own achievements (whether he really meant it or not), Dunn credited his good fortune to an accident of timing when he explained:

> I cannot claim that it was due to my wisdom that I picked the best time since the Civil War to enter upon the activity I did for [then] it was just beginning to be realized by advertisers that the weekly and monthly periodicals offered a splendid field, and a great wave of advertising swept the country on a flood of new magazines . . . [and] to supply these, illustrators were in great demand. The long-haired, flowing-tie artist disappeared, and in his place was a business man making $10,000 or more a year.

The first painting he ever sold apparently was a commercial illustration for the Kieffel and Esser Company of New York. After that, assignments began to come from such popular magazines as *Scribner's, Harper's, Collier's Weekly, Century,* and *Outing.* "The Silver Horde," a novel by Rex Beach, was enhanced by his work, and other books, with illustrations by H. T. Dunn, followed. Of even greater significance to his career, however, was the fact that *The Saturday Evening Post* under its dynamic editor, George Horace Lorimer, had emerged as a forceful vehicle of opinion and a medium of fictional entertainment. It also became a leading showcase for the talents of Harvey Dunn.

His practical, business-like approach to illustration gave him a jump on the "velvet pantaloon artists," as he called the bohemian painters of his day. He wouldn't have been caught dead in a beret, according to one of his friends; nor would he adopt any other affectation of artistry. He was a man's man—too sentimental sometimes by his own admission, but a craftsman who had no use for sham or phonies.

On March 12, 1908, Harvey Dunn and Tulla Krebs were married in a Unitarian Church with N. C. Wyeth as their best man. With new responsibilities, he plunged into his work as an established illustrator. He had an almost unbelievable capacity for production. "He literally attacked a canvas," a contemporary said. "Sometimes I thought he would impale the painting with his brush." With his huge but sensitive hands, he applied oils boldly and with gusto. Often he used his palette knife almost more than his brushes. The result was the powerful, dramatic style which characterized his paintings through the years.

Buyers learned they could depend on him, not only for good work, but also for punctual delivery. He was neither a procrastinator nor an esthete who had to wait until an inspiration dawned. No wonder he was able, on one occasion, to turn out fifty-five completed illustrations in just eleven weeks for various clients.

It was because of the growing demand for his services that he and Tulla decided to leave Wilmington and move closer to the art markets of New York City. In 1914 he established his studio in Leonia, New Jersey, directly across the Hudson River from The Bronx. From this vantage point he was able to provide even better service to advertising agencies and magazine production offices. He became what he himself called "a businessman-artist."

Harvey Dunn's great admiration for Howard Pyle (who died in Italy in 1911) and for Ada Caldwell began to stir within him a desire to help others as they had helped him. He discussed this feeling with fellow artist Charles S. Chapman, who was similarly inclined. As a result, in the summer of 1915 they established their Leonia School of Illustration in a converted Civil War vintage farm house to offer their experience and talents to aspiring young painters as they themselves had been just a few short years before.

The Leonia experiment was the beginning of a second concurrent career for Harvey Dunn. As he grew older, he also grew more loquacious (even to the point of brashness, according to some). Teaching offered an escape valve for his pent-up energies and for the philosophies of art and of life bubbling within him. Also, he had a penchant for minor theatrics, and this, too, found an outlet in the process of instruction. As it turned out, he and Charles Chapman were dissimilar teachers and not entirely compatible, so their association was short-lived. However, the Leonia school was the genesis of other classes that came to be known as the Dunn School of Illustration and which were to leave lasting impressions on scores of future artists. In the meantime, another event occurred on the global scene which was to play an important part in further shaping the career of Harvey Dunn.

When the United States declared war on Germany on April 6, 1917, Harvey Dunn was thirty-three years old and reasonably secure from military conscription. His career as an illustrator had been unusually successful to that point and his future was even more promising. In Leonia he and Tulla lived quite comfortably, a far cry from his beginnings in a Dakota claim shanty. Before they had moved from Delaware, they had been joined by a son, Robert Kruse, born on July 3, 1911, and a daughter, Louise, who arrived on November 3, 1912. (A third child, a son, had died in infancy, so they had known tragedy, too.) Theirs was an uncomplicated, unwanting existence, and the busy artist could well have continued the pattern without disruption, but the wave of patriotic fervor which engulfed the nation also reached him.

At that time the Pictorial Publicity Division of the Committee on Public Relations—headed by Charles Dana Gibson, one of the nation's foremost illustrators—was given the responsibility for selecting eight volunteers to be the official artists of the American Expeditionary Force. Chosen were Harry Townsend, Walter Jack Duncan, George Harding, William J. Aylward, Wallace Morgan, J. Andre Smith, Ernest Clifford Peixotto, and Harvey T. Dunn. The men were commissioned as captains in the Engineers and issued orders which permitted them wide-ranging freedom on the battlefields of France. Dunn entered the service on March 7, 1918, and by the end of the month he was on his way overseas.

Captain Dunn accepted his orders as a great challenge, and he went to Europe with a fervent desire to picture the war as it really was: "the shock and loss and bitterness and blood of it." With a portable sketch box—almost too big for an ordinary man to handle—he roamed the front lines, the shell-torn villages, and the rear sectors, endlessly sketching the battle-weary soldiers, the spiritless refugees, and the physical ravages of war. From his vast reservoir of sketches, he painted many dramatic pictures, most of which eventually ended up in the National Collections of the Smithsonian Institution.

In oils, watercolors, pastels, crayon, and charcoal he portrayed the places and the events he had seen and experienced. Then, with the coming of the Armistice, he envisioned several years of work at the War College, committing to canvas the pictorial record captured in his sketching scrolls. However, in this desire he was keenly disappointed. In the great national urge for demobilization, he was returned to the United States on February 9, 1919, and discharged on April 26 the same year, long before he could do justice to what he considered a gigantic and important mission. According to Dean Cornwell, one of his first students, it was "the big heartbreak of his life." After his battlefield experiences in France, Cornwell noted, illustrating a mere manuscript was too tame for him, and his commercial paintings tended to show it. Although he resumed his professional career with his usual energy, he began more and more to turn to his second role: that of a teacher.

Like his own mentor, Howard Pyle, Harvey Dunn taught a philosophy of life more than he taught art. He paid little attention to techniques, emphasizing instead the qualities which separated an artist from a draftsman. "Paint a little less of the facts and a little more of the spirit," he would say. "Paint more with feeling than with thought . . . when intellect comes in, art goes out. To hell with the rules and the mathematics . . . the spirit of the thing should rule."

He taught in his own studio, at the Grand Central School of Art, the Art Students League in New York, and even in the public schools of Tenafly, New Jersey, where he and his family had moved in 1919. He was a hard taskmaster. He didn't believe in namby-pamby art or namby-pamby artists. "I believe in discouraging all I can," he said, "because if I can discourage them, it will save them from floundering around about ten years of their lives before finding out they are in the wrong profession. The *real* ones can't be discouraged!"

Dunn himself was a prolific painter and a versatile one, but each picture, even those he considered bad, came from within him. He was not an artistic automaton by any means, however. He demanded substance in his own work, just as he did in the work of his students. Some paintings he worked on for months and even years before he was satisfied with them. He worked with models, sketches, and an occasional photograph (though he had an inborn dislike for cameras), but he believed firmly in painting in a studio, using his aids only as reminders or mental refreshers. If he wanted to paint a specific tree, he went out and looked at the tree, studying it with his keen sense of observation. Then he would return to his easel and paint it as his mind had captured and translated it. So-called artists who roamed about and erected their easels at scenic locales generally displeased him. He felt they were merely looking for a good place to snooze or to steal apples from the farmer under whose tree they professed to paint.

While he taught, he continued with his commercial work. He illustrated advertisements for such major firms and products as Maxwell House Coffee, Coca Cola, White trucks, Texaco gasoline, Ticonderoga pencils, the Sinclair Refining Company, and the John Hancock Mutual Life Insurance Corporation. His pictures appeared with stories and articles in *Collier's, American Magazine, Cosmopolitan, McCall's* and other leading publications. (His thirty-year association with *The Saturday Evening Post* eventually was to end over an argument about one of his paintings.) A special edition of Charles Dickens' "A Tale of Two Cities" was embellished by his work. As further proof of his versatility, he won top honors in a competition sponsored by the Guild Artists Bureau of Manhattan for a delicate painting of a reclining nude which *Time Magazine* for June 9, 1941, said received the most votes in all five categories of judging: (1) Best company on a desert island, (2) Best company on a desert, (3) Best company, (4) Best, and (5) Whew!!!!

For a brief period after World War I Dunn apparently had some second thoughts about his own career. He felt his commercial work was not of a lasting nature, so he tried sculpting for a time. He also painted an expansive, five-panel mural for the Lord and Taylor Department Store of New York. As some solace for his disappointment in not being able to complete his war paintings, *The American Legion Monthly* featured many of his battle pictures on its covers. William MacLean, the assistant art editor of the veterans' publication who appealed to Dunn to make his war art available to the magazine, became a close friend of the artist and eventually became aware of Harvey's nagging desire to produce a body of work which would perpetuate his name and talent. Although he may not have known it at the time, that urge was to be fulfilled because of the nostalgic and gripping ties he maintained with the prairies of South Dakota.

In the excitement and hard work of his earlier years on the East Coast, there was little time to think about bullheads and turtles in Redstone Creek or the daily jawing of men at the Manchester town pump. But when he was past forty and the demands and attraction of commercial illustration waned, Harvey Dunn's thoughts turned westward again. "My search for other horizons had led me around to my first," he wrote.

He began to make almost annual trips back to his beloved flatlands. Once he brought Tulla out to Kingsbury County in a luxurious DuPont automobile which caused the local citizens to gawk in admiration and awe. But the prairies held no particular attraction for his wife who, in fairness to her lack of interest, had been born and raised in a totally different environment. Thereafter, his periodic visits to the land of his birth were generally alone or with an artist friend.

Actually, Harvey could have traveled to the most romantic and majestic regions of the world, but, for him, the elbow-room countryside of South Dakota possessed all the majesty and romance he desired. He could read more of life in a lightning-scarred cottonwood tree, a tumble-down barn, or a rusted well pump than most sophisticated tourists would ever find in the Taj Mahal or the Eiffel Tower. In his slouch hat and country work clothes (he sometimes wore belt *and* suspenders), he coursed the plainsland for which he had such fondness, experiencing again the big-sky sunrises and sunsets, the mildly acrid smell of ripening grain in the evening heat, and the distinctive song of the meadowlark (which no Dakotan can ever forget).

On one occasion he wrote: "I remember when there were no fences and the prairie flowers nodded to each other under the winds to the far horizon, which was broken by the black humps of sod houses and the yellow gleam of pine claim shanties. The creak of an oxbow and the voice of a driver could be heard a long way off on still evenings after a rain, and the air was pungent with the odor of fresh turned earth."

During his visits he sketched scenes reminiscent of his earlier years, usually with brown and blue crayons and occasionally using the steering wheel of his Ford or Mercury station wagon as a temporary easel. These he took back with him to Tenafly where, when he wasn't busy with commercial work, he painted pictures depicting life on the Dakota frontier. These were *his* pictures as differentiated from those for which he accepted payment. He worked on them with loving care and the immense sentimentality which was both his strength and his weakness.

When he finished a Dakota picture, he usually stored it away in what he called his "morgue." Most of the easterners did not understand, and Harvey never foisted his prairie art on anyone. Several times he dusted off a few canvases and took them across the Hudson to the annual meeting of the South Dakota Society of New York City. There he found men and women who recognized and appreciated what he was doing, not as art dilettantes but as Dakota natives like himself who had seen and been part of the earthy existence his pictures portrayed.

Then one day in 1950 Aubrey H. Sherwood, publisher of *The DeSmet News* who had become acquainted with Harvey as the result of the artist's yearly visits, came to see him at the Tenafly studio.

Dunn showed the newspaperman some of his pioneer paintings, and Sherwood said: "I wish the folks back home could see what I am seeing." It was not a baited remark at all, but Harvey showed an immediate interest and soon the unplanned conversation turned to the discussion of a possible exhibit in DeSmet.

At that time the town's population was officially listed as 1,184, and the availability of buildings suitable to house such a showing was extremely limited. Dunn rejected the high school gymnasium because he did not like the idea of his paintings in a roomful of bleachers. Sherwood then suggested the Masonic Temple, and the artist, himself a Master Mason since 1930, said that if it were as suitable as it sounded he would bring more canvases than the walls would hold.

Dunn flew to South Dakota, approved the Temple as an exhibit site, and returned home. At Tenafly he selected forty-two framed pictures which were packed in four huge wooden crates for the trip westward at his expense. Harvey then journeyed again to DeSmet, this time to supervise the hanging of the paintings in time for the Old Settlers' Day festivities on June 10. The one-time country boy, whose chalk drawings on the rural school blackboard had been a harbinger of the greater things to come, had at last brought the products of his huge, talented hands back to the land he loved.

The people—probably not a half dozen sophisticated art connoisseurs in the lot—were delighted to see what Aubrey Sherwood had seen in Tenafly. More than 1,500 viewers registered on the opening day, shaking hands and visiting with the famed artist whose works covered the Temple walls. The exhibit was such a success that instead of terminating it as planned at the end of a few days, Dunn remained in DeSmet for the summer; for fourteen weeks his paintings were on display daily. More than 5,000 visitors signed the guest book, but many of them came back time and time again to admire the inspiring pictures, born of events and homely activities which Harvey Dunn had seen or participated in just a few short miles from the Temple building.

One of the visitors during the final week of the exhibit was Fred H. Leinbach, president of South Dakota State College. Doctor Leinbach's appearance could not have been better timed. The pictures impressed him deeply, and when he learned that Harvey Dunn (with Aubrey Sherwood's gentle nudging) might be willing to leave his paintings in South Dakota if a proper display site could be arranged, the school official promptly offered the College's Pugsley Memorial Union as a repository. The artist responded quickly to the suggestion. After all, it was on the same campus where he had met Miss Caldwell and where his art career had really begun exactly half a century before. In typical Harvey Dunn fashion, he asked for a sheet of paper, and then, on the seat of a Temple chair, he wrote out a transmittal letter granting to "the people of South Dakota" in perpetuity his magnificent gift.

With the presentation of his paintings to the citizens of his native state delivered, Harvey Dunn returned to Tenafly and his easel. There were other pictures he wanted to add to the prairie collection, and he seemed to have a premonition that time was running out. During the summer of the exhibition in DeSmet, his health began to concern him. Except for a slight wheeze (which he attributed to a battlefield gassing in France), he had always been physically robust and vigorous. In his younger years he had been a heavy smoker, but he quit perfunctorily in the early 1940s, saying that "I've lived in a burning building long enough." In time his ailment was diagnosed as cancer, and he faced an unpredictable future, resolutely and with the strength of his great spirit.

He made his annual pilgrimage to DeSmet and Manchester in the summer of 1951. His routine was much the same, and he sketched as though there were years of painting time ahead of him. Unfortunately he had but a short palette of life remaining. A year later—on June 9— he was awarded an honorary Doctor of Fine Arts degree by South Dakota State College at the 1952 commencement exercises. But the honoree was not on the stage, and had he been, he probably would have been fidgety and uncomfortable in a cap and gown. Instead, he was in Chicago, being strengthened there throughout the summer according to the Christian Science precepts to which he had been introduced by his mother and to which his wife was a devoted adherent. Earlier he had undergone surgery at the Mayo Clinic. Finally, the dying artist was moved back to his home in Tenafly, where the end came on October 29, 1952.

Several days after his death, a memorial service was held in his immense studio, from which had come so many paintings to enrich the lives of untold thousands. Members of the family, fellow artists, former students, and grieving friends gathered around the massive fireplace (where he had burned an unknown quantity of his paintings which he considered inferior) to pay their respects to his memory. Outstanding illustrators like Dean Cornwell, Grant Reynard, and Harold von Schmidt were in attendance to honor their departed mentor. Following the informal ceremony, von Schmidt returned to his home in Westport, Connecticut, where he wrote a personal tribute encompassing all the experiences of sadness and the bittersweet memories he had heard at the memorial gathering:

> Harvey Dunn—illustrator, teacher, poet, man. It was my privilege to know him as all four. Seldom was he only one of these. He gave freely of himself to all who sought him with honest inquiry. His high intolerance matched his honesty in the keeping of his code. This code was service— service as he saw and knew it. Gentle as only a big man can be, he could use both quirt and spur when needed. . . . Not only did he make us better illustrators, he made us better men. He asked only for our best and it was heart-rending fun to give it. . . . Though the gesture and the voice are stilled, the idea of Harvey Dunn flows strong with those of us who loved him and will ever continue.

Harvey Dunn had erected his own monument, in the form of an artistic legacy which eventually was to go on permanent display in the South Dakota Art Museum built principally for that purpose on the campus at South Dakota State University. Those who saw him in the late summer of 1950 knew he had found fulfillment when he left his prairie paintings behind him to his beloved state. The collection spanned the seasons, from springtime colors of his recognized master-piece, *The Prairie Is My Garden*, to the chilled tones in *After the Blizzard*. He depicted the great arc of life in *Bringing Home the Bride*, in *Dakota Woman*, in *Old Settlers*, and in the homesteaders' funeral scene he titled *I Am the Resurrection and the Life*.

To his students he had once said: "Take the subject of man in despair. Let the sky be lowering, weeping in sympathy, the hill will be bleak and barren, and shrubbery and trees bending with the same grief." So it was that Harvey Dunn, poet as well as artist, had—in his own words—described the day in which he once again would set out in search of new horizons.

Notes

1. All quotations in this chapter came from Robert F. Karolevitz, *Where Your Heart Is*. (Aberdeen: North Plains Press, 1970), passim.

Doane Robinson (1928).
Courtesy South Dakota State Historical
Society.

Painted portrait of W.H. Over.
Courtesy W.H. Over State Museum.

Herbert S. Schell.
Courtesy Richardson Archives, USD.

Over's museum in Slagle Hall (1918).
Courtesy W.H. Over State Museum.

W.H. Over and others in the field.
Courtesy W.H. Over State Museum.

Keepers of the Past: Doane Robinson, William Henry Over, and Herbert S. Schell

Larry J. Zimmerman and Mary Keepers Helgevold

Most of us function as if the past has little impact on our daily lives, but most are aware that history at least influences our customs and institutions, and some recognize that our individual personalities, attitudes, and decisions are formed by people and events that preceded us. The past comes to us in many ways. Our grandparents might tell us tribal stories with content of myth, action, and tradition, or they might just talk about "the good old days." We might read history textbooks as an assignment in a classroom, but most of us have little more than a passive role in creating and recording the events that swirl around us everyday. Some do, however, and they are the "keepers of the past," the individuals who provide the rest of us with a record of our accomplishments as a people.

In South Dakota we have been fortunate to have many keepers of the past, and three of them—Doane Robinson, William Henry Over, and Herbert Samuel Schell—stand out. Their active involvement in history writing spans nearly the entire one hundred years of South Dakota statehood. Over that span of time, keepers of the past have expanded the preservation of historical evidence from an interest of amateurs to a professional service. Robinson and Over exemplified the high quality of scholarship that may be achieved by a self-educated historian, while Schell provided the first examination of history in South Dakota by an accomplished academician. Robinson and Over were contemporaries, largely self-educated; Schell was a generation younger, professionally trained.

Doane Robinson was born on a farm near Sparta, Wisconsin, on October 19, 1856. Although he was christened "Jonah Leroy," his little sister pronounced his name as "Donah," which became Doane, the name he preferred. His boyhood and teen years were spent working on the farm and he had little time for formal schooling, not completing the eighth grade. He was studious, though, and eventually became qualified to be a teacher. He left Wisconsin to homestead near Marshall, Minnesota, when he reached his majority. In addition to his work on the homestead and teaching school, he worked as a copyist in a lawyer's office, which sparked an intense interest in the law. He was admitted to the bar in 1882 before attending any law classes. In the academic year 1882–1883 he attended senior law classes at the University of Wisconsin, but dropped out due to failing eyesight.

Robinson remained a practitioner of the law in spite of vision problems and moved to Watertown, Dakota Territory, in 1883 to set up a practice. He met and married Jennie Austin in 1884. To this union two sons, Harry Austin (December 4, 1888) and Will Grow (May 11, 1893), were born. His meager earnings as a lawyer were supplemented with work as a free-lance writer for newspapers in Minneapolis and St. Paul, and for the *Watertown Courier*.

Many early lawyers became involved in territorial politics and Robinson was no exception. Although he never ran for office, he was frequently involved in political machinations. He became Chairman of the Republican Central Committee of Codington County due in part to his support of an old Montrose County, Wisconsin, friend, William McIntyre, who became the leading Republican politician in the county. Robinson also became a friend of Arthur C. Mellette, who came to Watertown in 1880 as Register and Receiver of the Territorial Land Office. This friendship led to an appointment as the last territorial and first state Secretary of the Railroad Commission in the years 1889–1891. The job was a political "plum" with low pay, but it led to important contacts around the state. Travel on the job aroused his interest in South Dakota history and led directly to contact and interviews with several Indian leaders, eventually culminating in *A History of the Dakota or Sioux Indians* (a feat in historical writing not duplicated by anyone else in the United States until the appearance of another Indian federation history nearly half a century later).

During the same period, Robinson was editor of the *Watertown Courier News* and at the same time of *The Public Opinion*. He became something of an entrepreneur in 1892 when he was involved with an English mining syndicate in publishing a newspaper in eastern Kentucky, but the venture was a financial disaster. He returned to South Dakota in 1894 and purchased the *Gary Interstate*. In commenting on Robinson's purchase of the newspaper, the *Watertown Kempeskian* noted, "Gary can congratulate herself upon having not only one of the best known newspaper writers and all around hustlers in the State but one of the best known newspaper correspondence [sic] in the West and a literary genius of national repute."[1] When Gary lost the Deuel County seat to Clear Lake in 1895, Robinson, perhaps because of his own vision problems, convinced the State Legislature to use the empty courthouse as the state's School for the Blind. During this time he also began to see his poetry, first put into the volume *Coteaus of Dakota*, become widely accepted outside of the region.

Poetry is probably the gift and accomplishment for which Robinson is least remembered, but during his lifetime that for which he was most widely known. In 1898 he traveled under the auspices of the Northwest Lyceum Bureau of Minneapolis. A flyer for that program carried reviews of his readings. A clip from the *Minneapolis Journal* noted: "the interest of the audience never flagged, and when the curtain went down expressions of satisfaction were heard from all sides." The *Minneapolis Times* noted that, "Mr. Robinson read in excellent taste in simple straight-forward fashion so little understood by professional elocutionists, but so highly appreciated by people of refinement who cannot bear to see the actor's art diverting attention from the poet's sentiment." Doane's particular skill was apparently his ability to capture both the sentiment and the dialect of the Upper Midwest and eastern Plains in his poems. A reviewer in *The Arena*, a journal of opinion published in Boston, asked his readers to allow him to be a literary Columbus and introduce them to "a new world in the great Northwest by a short sketch of its first authentic singer. There is no following of old models in the productions of our poet. The informing touch is his own; the metrical forms, sometimes rude and crude, are generally his own and cunningly adapted to his themes; and the quiet humor, with apparently unconscious pathos, is decidedly original."[2]

During the next ten years Robinson was involved in a variety of publishing enterprises. He moved to Yankton to become editor of the *Yankton Gazette*, and on May 1, 1898, he began publication of *The Monthly South Dakotan*, devoted to literature and history. He moved the magazine to Sioux Falls in hopes of getting more advertisers and subscribers, but was not successful. He then moved to Aberdeen and purchased the *Aberdeen Democrat*, which he renamed the *Brown County Review*, and continued to publish his magazine. It was *The Monthly South Dakotan*'s popularity that prompted the reorganization of the State Historical Society in 1901.

Governor Charles Herreid, Charles DeLand, and Doane Robinson put their names on postcard notices about a meeting to organize the Society and sent them out to interested persons. Due to an illness, the Governor could not preside at the meeting so the Lieutenant Governor appeared. Among others in attendance were Thomas L. Riggs, De-Lorme Robinson, DeLand, T. N. Shanafet, and Robert F. Kerr. The State Historical Society was chartered on January 21 of 1901, and the Department of History was created by the State Legislature during its 1901 session. The Society selected Robinson to fill the newly created position of State Historian (Superintendent of the Department of History) and Collector of Vital Statistics. His role was to collect facts and figures regarding state and federal government as well as genealogy and census information. It was also to preserve newspapers from around the state, historical photographs, and relics of historical interest, and to set up the State Library. Finally, it was to explore the archaeology of the state, a task delegated to W. H. Over. The tasks were myriad, and the accomplishments of the Society and Department impressive during Robinson's tenure. He was personally a major contributor to the success of the organization. This was due both to his energy and to his belief about what a historical society should do.

He thought that a historical society should first collect, verify, and preserve materials within its field, but chief among its auxiliary functions was "the vitalizing of local history, to the end that it may be reflected in the better citizenship of the community." In his almost poetic style he wrote:

> There is something in the antiquarian history of a locality that intrigues the imagination of the normal citizen and inspires him to walk with a bit of a strut when he contemplates the deeds done upon his soil, even though those deeds were of no high import. In such things is pride of locality founded; a sort of pride that is ever conducive to civic satisfaction. Knowledge of such deeds finds permanent lodgment in the consciousness of the citizen, exalts his spirit, and spreads a halo over the countryside.[3]

The philosophy that local history should be popularized, and that historical source material should be made available to the public, guided most of his historical endeavor.

The State Historical Society began publication of *South Dakota Historical Collections*, which he edited through volume XII and for which he often wrote. Robinson also published an "Annual Review of the Progress of South Dakota" full of statistics and facts for real estate men and prospective residents (from which he made money for his own pockets). In slightly more than a decade he wrote numerous books, including *The Green Butte Ranch; History of he Dakota or Sioux Indians; A History of South Dakota from the Earliest Times* (later revised as *The Sunshine State*); *History of South Dakota*; and *History of Leavenworth's Expedition and Conquest of Ree Indians*. During his years as Secretary of the Society, he also drafted laws for legislators until a legislative research branch with an assistant was added to the Department of History and took over the task. He worked with W. H. Over to organize an archaeological society, and he helped to create the South Dakota Academy of Science. For his efforts, he was awarded an honorary masters degree from the University of South Dakota in 1915, and an honorary Doctor of Literature from Yankton College in 1922.

He took his role as citizen very seriously and, for his time, probably had as thorough an understanding of South Dakota's land, its citizens, and its needs as anyone in the state. He served as *ex officio* member and Secretary of the Free Library Commission for thirteen years, the same positions on the State Hydroelectric Commission from 1919 to 1926, and as a trustee of Yankton College. He was President of the South Dakota Academy of Science and President of the History Teachers Section of the South Dakota Education Association.

Robinson's ideas about citizenship went into action beyond the confines of the Department of History. While residing in Yankton and Pierre, he studied the history of the Missouri River. He became convinced that harnessing the River for power would greatly aid in navigation and restore the Missouri to the prominence it had during the century before. He concluded that private enterprise could not do the job in South Dakota, and that state officials would have to take on the task. He found a willing listener in Peter Norbeck, and plans were eventually advanced for the state to enter a public power project at Mobridge. Although the project was defeated at the polls, it may well have provided impetus for the subsequent construction of dams under the Flood Control Act of 1944.[4]

Robinson's own feeling about his greatest contribution to the material development of the state also involved the River, not in its development, but in bridges across it.[5] During the 1923 legislative session, five cities contended for the construction of Missouri River bridges: Mulehead, Pierre, Chamberlain, Mobridge, and Forest City. All but Mobridge and Pierre were disgruntled and pushed the idea of a state referendum that would have delayed any construction for more than two years. During a sleepless night, Doane contacted his son Will, then a practicing lawyer in Pierre, to see if there was some constitutional way for counties to bond and advance money for construction. Indeed, Section 11 of Chapter 204 allowed such a privilege, and a compromise was approved which permitted the bridges to be built without referenda, almost simultaneously.

The era of Peter Norbeck contained an accomplishment that some South Dakotans consider Robinson's most lasting contribution, the construction of Mount Rushmore. Norbeck became interested in the Black Hills in 1901 and conceived the idea of a state park and game sanctuary in the southern Hills. As Governor, he worked toward the development of what eventually became Custer State Park. Norbeck saw the tourist potential of the Black Hills, and in this he was not alone. Robinson had always been an advocate of the Black Hills as a recreational ground. He was heavily involved in advocating the Black and Yellow Trail as an alternative route to the Hills, and in locating some of the first tour and camp groups in the area. At the end of the first decade of the new century, he was responsible for the development of Pierre Lodge in the Hills, a venture that was successful until the automobile opened more private camping areas to the public. No one knows exactly how he came up with the idea for a stone sculpture for the Hills, but he may have been influenced by a carving, "The Lion of Lucerne" in Switzerland, which brought "to that municipality . . . not less than a half million gold marks annually."[6] He may also have been influenced by the ongoing relief carving on Stone Mountain in Georgia by Gutzon Borglum, the eventual sculptor of Mount Rushmore. His first inclination was to see figures carved in the Needles, and historical figures were always the subject matter, ranging from such persons as Red Cloud, Meriwether Lewis, William Clark, and John C. Fremont.[7]

There was no small amount of controversy about the possibility of carving the figures, and it was one of the few times that Robinson actually bucked the considerable public sentiment against the project and pursued his idea. Enlisting the help of Peter Norbeck (after he entered the U.S. Senate) and others, including J. B. Greene and various Rapid City businessmen, Robinson eventually was able to continue his agitation to convince the public. In August of 1924 he made contact with Gutzon Borglum and received a promise of active aid. The eventual construction of a monument, which became one of the "sacred symbols" of the United States, is well documented.[8] In a sense, the carvings are monumental testimony to Robinson's ideas about how history links us to a sense of pride in place.

In 1926, at the age of seventy, he retired from his role as Secretary of the State Historical Society and Superintendent of the Department of History. In his twenty remaining years, he was active. Robinson continually pushed for Mount Rushmore's completion; he wrote a column for the Sioux Falls *Argus Leader*, called the "Cockloft"; and he authored an *Encyclopedia of South Dakota* plus a three volume *History of South Dakota*. He served briefly as State Historian again. In his ninetieth year, on November 27, 1946, he died in Pierre. Perhaps little can be said that is more fitting of this keeper of the past than was said by his biographer for *Who's Who in South Dakota*. Calling him "a symmetrical man," O. W. Coursey said:

> Farmer 10 per cent, teacher 8 percent, lawyer 14 per cent, editor 18 per cent, poet 22 percent, historian 28 percent; total 100 per cent, of symmetrical manhood; such is our analysis of Doane Robinson. . . .[9]

William Henry Over was a contemporary of Doane Robinson, and the two crossed paths many times and cooperated on many ventures regarding the natural history of South Dakota. While Robinson's contributions were largely from the period after the coming of the White man, Over's contributions were essential to our understanding of the prehistory of human occupation of the northern prairie and Great Plains.

W. H. Over was born on June 10, 1866, in a log cabin near Albion in Edwards County, Illinois. His education was limited; he attended a rural, one-room Illinois school and did not complete the eighth grade. Although his schooling was limited, he had a variety of boyhood interests that allowed him to educate himself. He had both an insect and seashell collection, but his arrowhead collection, begun when he discovered an arrowhead in a field, was displayed at local fairs. His collecting interest continued into adulthood and eventually became the focal point of his work. He migrated to Minnesota in 1888 at age twenty-two and worked as a general store clerk in Lake Crystal and in Garden City, eventually becoming a store manager. He and Clem F. Johns were married on October 4, 1891, a marriage that was to bring them two children, Florence and Clarence. He became a favorite speaker for civic organizations while still in Minnesota on topics ranging from "Primitive Man" to "Potatoes." At the 1901 Pan American Exposition in Buffalo, New York, he won honorable mention for his display of yellow dent corn, blue stem wheat, and German spletz (a wheat). Over worked for a Minneapolis real estate firm for a short time before migrating to Clear Lake in Deuel County, South Dakota, in 1902 or 1903, where he set up a general store. In 1908 he homesteaded in Perkins County, but maintained his outside interests.

These interests began to draw attention when, in 1908 in Deuel County, his knowledge of shells led to his discovery of two previously unknown species. A snail was named *Pisidium overi* in his honor, and a bivalve clam was named *Anodonta dakota*. His article on the discoveries was published in *Chonchology*, a magazine devoted to the science of shells. Seven years later he discovered a fossil crab, which was named *Dakotacaner overana*. His article in a 1912 issue of the *Curio Collector* magazine about the wildlife in Perkins County impressed the right people and resulted in his employment as an assistant curator of the museum in Vermillion in 1913.

The museum had been established in 1893 for the display of material collected by the State Geological and Natural History Survey. It was located in one room of Science Hall, which also served as a general storeroom for the University of South Dakota. The museum was something of a mess. Nothing was on display. Specimens were unlabeled and consisted of twelve mounted animals, fifty mounted birds, four cases of minerals, and many unmounted and unprotected plant specimens. Over's task was to bring order to the collection.

He prepared several displays and added his own collections to the museum holdings. All items were catalogued and labeled. Plant specimens were mounted and stored in an insect-proof herbarium. This work done, Over was appointed full-time Museum Curator and began a job at which he spent the next thirty-five years. He continually added to the collections by purchasing some specimens, but mostly by accepting donations and collecting on numerous field trips. He also began the continual struggle for better housing for the collections.

Over often kept live animals in the museum along with the mounted specimens. Among these were rattlesnakes, which he would periodically defang in order to prevent serious injury to anyone. One day, while attempting to defang his largest and most difficult rattler, he was bitten. His scientific nature demanded that he keep records of both his symptoms and his treatment, which he published in a 1928 issue of the *Bulletin of the Antivenin Institute of America*.

In 1927 the Museum was administratively moved from the State Geological and Natural History Survey to become a department of the University, with Over as its Director. His shift was appropriate in that Over viewed himself as an educator, not just a curator. He believed the best way to educate was to entertain while he taught. Using the available formats of his day, he built a variety of museum displays, conducted guided tours, and went on the lecture circuit within the state. He also developed a museum newsletter, magazine, and special publication series. He worked hard to write newspaper articles and give radio interviews.

One of his particular goals in education was to promote a better understanding of the state's natural resources. He was especially interested in wildlife conservation, which he felt lagged ten to twenty years behind that of other states. Over thought if he could increase public awareness of natural resources the Legislature would be compelled to write protective laws. His museum publications were never "slick," but they were very popular. All had some kind of illustrations, usually line drawings. Many of them saw reissue.

His most popular publication was South Dakota Geological and Natural History Survey Bulletin number 9, co-authored with Craig Thoms, entitled *Birds of South Dakota*. Issued in 1921, it was so well received that it was revised and reissued in 1946. In 1923 he also wrote both *Trees and Shrubs of South Dakota* and *Amphibians and Reptiles of South Dakota*. Over and E. P. Churchill combined talents to produce three volumes: *A Preliminary Report of a Biological Survey of the Lakes of South Dakota*, in 1927; *Fishes of South Dakota*, in 1933; and *Mammals of South Dakota*, in 1941. To these volumes he added *The Flora of South Dakota: An Illustrated Check-list of Flowering Plants, Shrubs and Trees of South Dakota* (1932), *Mollusca of South Dakota* (1942), and *Wild Flowers of South Dakota: Describing and Illustrating 52 Common Wild Flowers of South Dakota* (1942). Over's most lasting contributions, however, were made to our understanding of the archaeology of the state and the region.

His interests in archaeology stemmed from finding his first arrowhead in Illinois, mentioned above, and while Museum Director he was able to pursue them with some vigor. Doane Robinson, from his position as leader of the Department of History, supported Over's interest and essentially turned the investigation and survey of the state's prehistory over to him. Early human remains in the region at that time were considered to be part of natural history, so the allocation of the tasks seemed appropriate.

Over often organized collecting trips for plant, animal, and fossil specimens for the museum, and on his trips he encountered the remains of many prehistoric human activities, including mounds and villages. After a trip to Indian village sites near Pierre and the Grand River, he became convinced of the need for a broader archaeological survey of the state, especially along the Missouri River. He then spent part or all of several summers traveling down the River in a homemade boat with a variety of companions, including Charles DeLand, State Geologist Freeman Ward, and Doane Robinson, to discover and record archaeological sites between Mobridge and Vermillion.

Over actively promoted the preservation of the state's archaeological resources. He helped organize a state archaeological society in 1917, affiliated with the South Dakota Academy of Science. Papers were given at Academy meetings for two years, but the fledgling organization failed. In spite of this, Over had generated enough publicity so he received reports and locations of numerous archaeological sites across the state, many of which he visited. He kept his site locations, notes, and maps in a black notebook. The notebook has since been published and is still frequently consulted by contemporary archaeologists in the state.

Over not only conducted extensive surveys to locate archaeological sites in the state, but also excavated or directed the excavation of several important sites. In 1920 he dug a rock shelter called Ludlow Cave in the Cave Hills area of Harding County. This site had three levels of human activity going well back into prehistoric times. He published a very well received paper about it in the prestigious professional archaeological journal *American Antiquity*, an article which helped to bring him and South Dakota's archaeology to the attention of many other archaeologists across the nation. That work brought him into correspondence with archaeologists interested in the Plains and adjacent regions. In particular, he came into contact with Charles Keyes of Iowa, also a non-professional archaeologist, who was undertaking a survey of sites in his state. Over also worked with Albert Jenks from Minnesota, A. T. Hill from Nebraska, William Meyer from the Bureau of American Ethnology, Matthew Stirling from the U. S. National Museum, and Alfred Bowers from Wisconsin. Keyes's work in western Iowa on the Mill Creek culture especially interested Over. The area in which Keyes worked was only twenty miles from Vermillion, so Over could visit the excavations on Mill Creek culture sites along tributaries of the Big Sioux River.

The two became increasingly aware of possible links between Mill

Creek and the village sites near Brandon and Mitchell, which Over believed to be ancestral Mandan, but they were not sure of what to make of it. Keyes told Over about the work of a young professional archaeologist newly arrived at the University of Nebraska, William Duncan Strong, who might be able to help answer their questions. Over's special interest was the migration of the Arikara into the state, but he found none of their sites in the southeast part of South Dakota where the ancestral Mandan sites were located. Strong agreed to work on the problem with Over and others.

Ultimately, the information they gathered made archaeologists understand the need for a meeting to discuss their various findings and ideas. Consequently, Over offered the facilities of the University for what became known as the Plains Conference. On August 31, 1931, twenty-two participants gathered to exchange ideas on terminology, origins, and a variety of other issues. Over's contributions to the first Plains Conference were many.[10] The organization has survived and prospered into one whose annual meeting draws several hundred archaeologists and anthropologists from the United States and Canada, and whose journal, *Plains Anthropologist*, is read world wide.

Among the ideas Over proposed, to better understand the origins of Plains groups, was a technique called the "direct historical approach." This suggests that the best way to understand the origins of a group is to carefully study the historic group and then move back in time using decorations on pottery, oral history, and any other evidence to link known historic sites to those of the more ancient past. W.D. Strong is usually given credit for the approach and, in truth, he did first publish it and use it effectively. But Over first proposed it and most certainly shared his thoughts about it with Strong.

The coming of the Great Depression was in some ways beneficial to Over's efforts. After several years of trying, Over finally received funds for excavations from a public works project under the Works Projects Administration in 1938. The University Museum excavated the village site at Mitchell under the supervision of Elmer Meleen. This work, on a complex of what eventually became known in Over's honor as the Over Focus, sparked interest by outsiders who wanted to come to South Dakota and use WPA funds to dig sites. Over expressed reservations about eastern institutions "carrying off artifacts,"[11] a concern that was to cause him and others consternation during the coming decades, especially during the archaeological salvage of sites about to be inundated by reservoirs along the Missouri River.[12]

After World War II, as the construction projects associated with reservoir development along the Missouri geared up, the River Basin Surveys projects to salvage prehistoric sites were set up as a jointly managed project of the National Park Service and the Smithsonian Institution Bureau of American Ethnology. Headquarters were established in Lincoln and the project was staffed by a cadre of professional archaeologists overseeing projects. Excavations were carried out by archaeologists and institutions from all across the country, and the significance of Over and the University Museum were eclipsed in their importance by a general investigation of the archaeology of the northern Great Plains. Many of Over's ideas were simply overlooked. Nonetheless, he contributed in numerous ways to the thinking of those working in the state.

By the time W. H. Over died on February 20, 1956, he had amassed a collection in the University Museum in excess of 75,000 items. He had been named a member of Sigma Xi, the national scientific research honorary; had been awarded an honorary Doctor of Science by the South Dakota Board of Regents; and had received honorary membership in the South Dakota Academy of Science and the South Dakota Ornithologists' Union. In tribute, the Board of Regents renamed the University Museum the William H. Over Museum on his retirement as Director in 1949. A new museum building that opened in 1988 on the campus of the University of South Dakota also carries his name.

Over's contributions were pioneering in the natural history and even more in the archaeology of the state and northern Great Plains region. His work and ideas have influenced interpretations about the first inhabitants of South Dakota made by many professional archaeologists working in the region. This keeper of the past gave us our earliest comprehensive view of South Dakota's ancient peoples.

Born a generation later than Robinson and Over, Herbert S. Schell was to become the state's first professionally trained historian. In his work he was ever in the company of his wife, Mildred Schell, who was also a professional historian. Schell began his life on April 12, 1899, at a farm in the Pennsylvania Dutch and German country near Bernville. His parents, William and Mary Staudt Schell, sent him to a country school near his home, from which he graduated in 1916. Nothing particular in his early career motivated him toward the study of history, except, perhaps, the rich ethnic heritage of the region in which he lived. From 1916 to 1917 he pursued a college preparatory course at Kutztown Normal School (now Kutztown State College) and was admitted to sophomore classes at Muhlenberg College in 1917. He majored in English and received his A.B. degree in 1920, even though his studies were interrupted in 1918 by a brief two-month term of military service near the close of World War I.

After graduation from college, he taught high school at Bethel, Pennsylvania, from 1920 to 1921 and at Metuchen, New Jersey, from 1921 to 1923. He also did course work to complete a master of arts degree at Columbia University in 1923. This convinced him he wanted to teach at the college level, so he enrolled in the Department of History at the University of Wisconsin. He attended classes from 1923 to 1925, then accepted an offer to teach at the University of South Dakota in 1925. Schell eventually returned to the University of Wisconsin during the 1928–1929 academic year on a leave from South Dakota to finish his degree requirements. His dissertation on American financial history, "The Inflation Movement, 1862–1879," earned him a Ph.D. Except for summer sessions at the University of Cincinnati (1929) and the University of Nebraska (1939), he served steadily in Vermillion until his retirement in 1968. His tenure at the University has seen enrollment rise from approximately 900 students to more than 6000 per year, and a department faculty shift from three members to twelve at the time of his retirement. He served as Chairman of the Department of History from 1946 to 1955. He also administered the Graduate School of the University from 1936 through 1964, serving as its Director until 1952, when he was named its Dean.

After the completion of his dissertation, which occupied a great deal of his time during his first years in South Dakota, he shifted to the study of the local history. Part of the reason he accepted the position at Vermillion was because a professor, Carl R. Fish, had suggested that the first settlers of the region were getting old; their reminiscences should be gathered. Schell traveled across the state and looked up old timers to get their stories, but his interests turned more toward documents than oral history.

Schell's first article on the state, which appeared in 1931, documented the impact of drought on agriculture in eastern South Dakota during the 1890s. His interests in economic and political history became the focal point in his work, but he always seemed to view those areas from the perspective of local history. His first book was an elementary history of South Dakota for grades four through six, an effort to replace Doane Robinson's "Little Red School House" volume with a more professional work. Schell's history, first published in 1942, had seen its third edition by 1960. He contributed a variety of other articles to regional and national journals, all oriented toward the state's economic and political history or the writing of local history.

In 1939, on the occasion of South Dakota's fiftieth anniversary, he contributed the chapter "The Evolution of a Commonwealth" to a volume *South Dakota: Fifty Years of Progress*. He had articles in other South Dakota anthologies, as well. In 1949 he wrote on the role of the state's schools during World War II; subsequently he chronicled the governorship of Andrew E. Lee for the book *South Dakota's Governors*, which celebrated the centennial of Dakota Territory; and in 1961 he contributed the chapter "Politics—Palaver and Polls" to the popular *Dakota Panorama*. In 1954 he published a monograph entitled *Dakota Territory During the Eighteen Sixties* for the University Governmental Research Bureau, and in 1955 he wrote *South Dakota Manufacturing to 1900* for the Business Research Bureau. His most lasting achievement, however, was his *History of South Dakota*, published initially in 1961.

History of South Dakota was the first full-length history of the state to appear since Doane Robinson's effort some thirty years earlier. The twenty-five chapters encompass the entire span of the state from the time of the last glaciation and the coming of the first Indian people through developments up to 1960. Persistent themes—Indian-White relations, manufacturing, agricultural adaptations, and cultural life— reflect the impact of a harsh and changing environment on the people of the state. Schell's perspective in the book is not provincial; however, he makes the effort to give these themes broader regional and national perspective—something little done in the earlier histories of the state. Schell himself views the volume as his most memorable work. Now in its third edition, it is not an easy volume to read, for its academic vernacular and an emphasis on political and economic history, but the treatment of those issues is thorough.

During these productive years, Schell taught nearly 9,000 on a variety of subjects, and he was apparently a memorable teacher who motivated students. In response to his reminiscences in the November issue of *The Dakotan* in 1967 just before his retirement, a former student remembered Schell's lecture on Andrew Jackson in American History 20b. He wrote, "When you finished the lecture, we gave you a well-deserved standing ovation." He concluded his letter by writing, "Multiply 42 years of teaching by the number of students upon whom you left your mark each semester, and it adds up to an enormous quantity of good."[13]

His career spanned several difficult periods in American education for social scientists, but one of the hardest came during the anti-Communist hysteria of the McCarthy period in the early 1950s. Schell was asked to deliver the second lecture on Liberal Education (later called the Harrington Lecture) of the College of Arts and Sciences on February 25, 1954. The title was "The Professor Under Fire: 1954 Version." He used the historian's perspective to analyze attacks that had occurred on higher education across the United States. His philosophy of what it meant to be a professor and a historian appears throughout.

One of his major concerns was to help students acquire the ability to interpret historical data with objectivity. To do this he had to deal with several problems. The first was to remain objective in a way as to express himself freely in a discrete, wise, and inoffensive manner. A second was the danger of forcing his own opinions upon the student, believing he had no right to indoctrinate. A third problem, he felt, went to the heart of the teaching function; he had to have something to teach that was fortified with sufficient data. Finally, he believed that propriety demanded of the professor a certain sense of equilibrium that, on one hand, needed to curb the zeal for debunking and cynicism and, on the other, to protect students from so much idealism that the realistic and practical worlds were not touched. Being aware of these problems was critical to the maintenance of independent, original thought and inquiry.

Professor Schell translated these ideals into most of his academic endeavors. During his career he was a member of numerous educational and historical organizations, including Phi Beta Kappa, the Beadle Club, the South Dakota Education Association, and both the Minnesota and South Dakota Historical Societies. He was a member of the Executive Committee of the Mississippi Valley Historical Association (1946–48), chairman of the Midwest Conference on Graduate Study and Research (1959–60), and Vice President of the South Dakota Historical Society (1961–63). He also participated in educational workshops in modern world history for German elementary teachers in Heidelberg and Stuttgart in 1949, and served as a consultant in the establishment of the University of the Ryukyus at Shuri, Okinawa, in 1950.

Professor Schell retired from active classroom teaching in July of 1968, but his retirement, like that of both Robinson and Over, was almost as active as his earlier years. He served as the first University Archivist during the 1968–1969 academic year and retired with the titles of Dean Emeritus and Professor Emeritus in 1969. He also continued writing, with *South Dakota: A Student's Guide to Localized History* published by Columbia University's Teachers College Press, in 1970; a third edition of his *History of South Dakota*, in 1975; *History of Clay County, South Dakota*, published by the Clay County Historical Society in 1976; and *Clay County: Chapters Out of the Past*, published by the Vermillion Area Chamber of Commerce in 1985. These works were award winners, and Schell was named the "South Dakota Writer of the Year" in 1976 by the South Dakota Cowboy and Western Heritage Hall of Fame. His Clay County history won an award of merit from the American Association of State and Local History as a model publication in county history. From 1979 through 1983 he also managed to write ninety-four weekly columns on various aspects of local history in southeast South Dakota for the Vermillion *Plain Talk*. In 1988 he continues to work on a number of smaller projects.

The historian has provided an impressive volume of professional writings about South Dakota's past, and it is in that endeavor that his major contribution to keeping the past resides. His arrival in the state marked the transition to professional history from the important early amateur histories of the region like those written by Robinson and Over. Professional history, while perhaps less enthusiastic in tone than that written by amateurs, is history tempered by greater accuracy in documentation plus a perspective that sees the history of a locality or state in the broader contexts of the region or the nation. It is also interpretive, seeking causes or trends in events. As a professional, Schell viewed local history with different intent than did the amateur. Robinson, as noted earlier, saw local history as something to generate pride in place and motivation to good citizenship. Schell, on the other hand, viewed the history of a community as representing a cross section or microcosm of the country at large.[14] Schell's work was no less optimistic about South Dakota, however, or about the accomplishments of its people than were the works of his amateur predecessors.

Doane Robinson, W. H. Over, and Herbert S. Schell were all immigrants to the state who found events moving around them as well as those that happened before their arrival to be both fascinating and important. All three were prolific researchers and writers, but they were very different as men. Robinson was a "superbuff," active in everything from poetry to politics. He was the most popular of the three with a wide following in South Dakota. He was dedicated to seeing progress in the state and saw what an important contribution the study of history could make toward that goal.

Over was more a quiet, dedicated amateur who provided South Dakota with greater understanding of its natural heritage, especially of the state's first inhabitants. Self educated and extremely versatile like

Robinson, he found his way to a university campus, where he was continuously in contact with professional scholars of both history and archaeology. His interests, like those of Robinson, were provincial in that he promoted state control of South Dakota's archaeology for the sake of the people of the state. Yet, his position tempered his enthusiasm and he was less given to hyperbole than Robinson. Over made lasting intellectual contributions to our ways of understanding the distant past.

Schell was university trained. He viewed history in a way very different from Robinson and Over. His concerns were to understand local history in the broadest context, and he was little concerned for the political ramifications of the past. Rather, he focused on understanding the state's past in an intellectual way as a manifestation of broader processes at work in the nation.

In some ways the three were alike. All were teachers. Robinson and Over lectured widely on their work, promoting the understanding of history. Schell transmitted his information to students in classrooms as well as to a broader audience through newspapers and scholarly publications. All three understood the importance of history to the people of the state, no matter what particular view of history prevailed. As Professor Schell noted, South Dakota has at times aptly been called a "political and sociological laboratory in which new ideas may be put to the experimental test to determine their practicality or workability." He also recognized that the success of a state history rests largely upon the efforts of a whole corps of researchers, a group that would surely include both professional historians and "buffs."[15] Understanding who we are as a people stems largely from the efforts of that corps, who like Robinson, Over, and Schell, have been and remain important keepers of the past.

Notes

1. Will G. Robinson, "Builders of the Dakotas: Doane Robinson," *Young Citizens* (1912), n.p.

2. James Realf, Jr., "A Poet of the Northwest," *The Arena,* XII, no. 3 (1895), pp. 308–309.

3. Doane Robinson, "Functions of a Historical Society," *South Dakota Historical Collections,* XII, p. 121.

4. Anonymous manuscript on file, South Dakota State Historical Society, c. 1955, attributed to Will G. Robinson, p. 12.

5. *Ibid.*, p. 13.

6. Letter to the Editor, Sioux Falls *Argus Leader* dated February 8, 1924.

7. Robinson to Lorado Taft, January 26, 1924.

8. Gilbert Fite, *Mount Rushmore* (Norman: University of Oklahoma Press, 1952), pp. 9–11.

9. O. W. Coursey, "A Symmetrical Man," *Who's Who in South Dakota,* (Mitchell, SD: Educator School Supply Company, 1913), I, p. 88.

10. Mary K. Helgevold, *A History of South Dakota Archaeology* (Vermillion, SD: South Dakota Archaeological Society, 1981), pp. 21–27.

11. W. H. Over to M. Stirling, January 3. W. H. Over Museum Files, Vermillion.

12. Larry Zimmerman, "Paranoia, Polemic, and Prehistory: CRM and the Development of South Dakota Archaeology," *Perspectives on Archaeological Resources Management in the Great Plains* (A. Osborn and R. Hassler, eds.; Omaha: I & O Press, 1987), p. 357–359.

13. K. G. Melgaard to H. S. Schell, December 20, 1967.

14. Herbert Schell "Writing State History," *Minnesota History XXXVI* (September 1958), p. 84.

15. *Ibid.*, p. 88.

Bibliography

The editors and the University of South Dakota Press disclaim any responsibility for the accuracy of details, citations, or quotations in the text; a publication schedule for this state centennial volume alone places the entire burden on the contributors. Each has supplied citations for quotations, and has prepared a list of published works for use by readers who wish to learn more about the life of a subject. Some contributors have also supplied descriptions of manuscript and documentary collections of greatest value, which the most careful readers may employ for the verification of details as well as the further exploration of subjects that arouse their interests. In this way the contributors offer guidance to both primary and secondary sources of greatest value to the histories of South Dakota and the upper Missouri River region.

Additional direction is readily available in recent bibliographical publications: Jack W. Marken and Herbert T. Hoover, eds., *Bibliography of the Sioux* (Metuchen, NJ: The Scarecrow Press, Inc., 1980); Herbert T. Hoover, ed., *Planning for the South Dakota Centennial: A Bibliography* (Vermillion: University of South Dakota, 1984), printed in limited edition for the libraries of South Dakota; and Sue Laubersheimer, ed., *A Selected Annotated Bibliography* (Brookings: South Dakota Library Association, 1985), with the companion volume *A Selected Annotated Bibliography: Supplement*, a "browser's guide" containing the lists of titles submitted by public and academic libraries in South Dakota not included "in the original bibliography *but* which in some way also shed light on the South Dakota experience."

Pierre Chouteau, Jr.

No one has attempted a professional biography of Pierre Chouteau, Jr., or a major study of the commercial network he sponsored along the upper Missouri

River basin. Information must be derived mainly from the Pierre Chouteau, Jr., and Company Papers preserved by the Missouri Historical Society in St. Louis, which appeared on microfilm during 1986; and from such manuscript collections housed by the Minnesota Historical Society in St. Paul as the Alexis Bailly Papers, the Lawrence Taliaferro Papers, and the Henry H. Sibley Papers. Important, too, are germane War Department documents preserved by the National Archives, many on microfilm; and some scattered sources held by the South Dakota Historical Society in Pierre.

In addition to the general literature on trans-Mississippi fur trade, several publications are useful in piecing together the life story of Pierre Chouteau, Jr., and the history of his influential Company:

Denig, Edwin Thompson. *Five Indian Tribes of the Upper Missouri*. Norman: University of Oklahoma Press, 1961.

Foley, William E. "The Laclede-Chouteau Puzzle: John Francis McDermott Supplies Some Missing Pieces," *Gateway Heritage: Quarterly Journal of the Missouri Historical Society*, IV, no. 2(Fall 1983), pp. 19–25.

Foley, William and C. David Rice. *The First Chouteaus: River Barons of Early St. Louis*. Urbana: University of Illinois Press, 1983.

Whishart, David J. *The Fur Trade of the American West, 1807–1840*. Lincoln: University of Nebraska Press, 1979.

Newton Edmunds

Bloom, John P., ed. *The American Territorial System*. Athens: Ohio University Press, 1973.

"Ending the Outbreak." *South Dakota Historical Collections*. IX, pp. 409–470.

Karolevitz, Robert F. *Yankton: A Pioneer Past*. Aberdeen, SD: North Plains Press, 1972.

Lamar, Howard R. *Dakota Territory, 1861–1889: A Study of Frontier Politics*. New Haven: Yale University Press, 1956.

Owens, Kenneth M. "Frontier Governors: A Study of the Territorial Executives in the History of Washington, Idaho, Montana, Wyoming, and Dakota Territories." Unpublished doctoral dissertation, University of Minnesota. 1959.

Pomeroy, Earl S. *The Territories and the United States, 1861–1890*. 2nd ed.: Seattle: University of Washington Press, 1969.

Prucha, Francis Paul, SJ. *American Indian Policy in Crisis: Christian Reformers and the Indian, 1865–1900*. Norman: University of Oklahoma Press, 1976.

Rau, John Edward. "Newton Edmunds: Dakota Territorial Statesman." Unpublished master of arts thesis. University of South Dakota, 1985.

Robinson, Doane. "A Composite History of the Dakota or Sioux Indians." *South Dakota Historical Collections*. II, part 2, pp. 1–523.

Schell, Herbert S. *Dakota Territory During the Eighteen Sixties*. Vermillion, SD: University of South Dakota, Government Research Bureau, 1954.

———. *History of South Dakota*. 3rd ed., rev.; Lincoln: University of Nebraska Press, 1975.

———. "Newton Edmunds: Second Territorial Governor." *The Wi-iyohi*, XI (1958), pp. 1–8.

Ward, Rev. Joseph. "Governor Newton Edmunds." *The Monthly South Dakotan*, I (1898), pp. 8–12.

Original documents are essential to the study of the Governors of Dakota Territory. Most important are newspapers published in Yankton, the ancestors to the present-day *Press and Dakotan*, and the microfilm edition of the Dakota Territorial Records in eighty-six reels. Both the I. D. Weeks Library at the University of South Dakota in Vermillion and the South Dakota State Archives in Pierre have copies of the two collections. The State Archives at Pierre has the largest body of microfilmed newspapers in the state. Information regarding federal policies is available in the Congressional Serial Documents, Letters of the Office of Indian Affairs (microfilmed by the National Archives), and the published *Annual Reports of the Commissioner of Indian Affairs*. All are available at I. D. Weeks Library. Pertinent treaties are compiled in Charles A. Kappler, comp., ed. *Indian Affairs Laws and Treaties*. Washington: U.S. Government Printing Office, 1904, 1941, 1972.

Sitting Bull, Spotted Tail, and Crazy Horse

Burdick, Usher L. *The Last Days of Sitting Bull: Sioux Medicine Chief*. Baltimore: Wirth Brothers, 1941.

Fiske, Frank Bennett. *Life and Death of Sitting Bull*. Fort Yates, ND: Pioneer-Arrow Print, 1933.

Hinman, Eleanor. Interviews with He Dog, "Oglala Sources on the Life of Crazy Horse," *Nebraska History*, LVII (1976), pp. 1–52.

Hoover, Herbert T. "Sitting Bull," *American Indian Leaders: Studies in Diversity*. Lincoln: University of Nebraska Press, 1980.

Hyde, George. *Spotted Tail's Folk*. Norman: University of Oklahoma Press, 1974.

Josephy, Alvin M. "Crazy Horse, Patriot of the Plains," *The Patriot Chiefs:*

A Chronicle of American Indian Leadership. New York: The Viking Press, 1961.

Knight, Oliver. "War of Peace: The Anxious Wait for Crazy Horse," *Nebraska History*, LIV (Winter 1973), pp. 521–544.

Olson, James C. *Red Cloud and the Sioux Problem.* Lincoln: University of Nebraska Press, 1975.

Sandoz, Mari. *Crazy Horse: The Strange Man of the Oglalas.* Lincoln: University of Nebraska Press, 1961.

Stewart, Edgar. *Custer's Luck.* Norman: University of Oklahoma Press, 1955.

Turner, C. Frank. *Across the Medicine Line.* Toronto: McClelland and Stewart, Limited, 1973.

Vaughn, J. W. *With Crook at the Rosebud.* Harrisburg, PA: The Stackpole Company, 1956.

Vestal, Stanley. *Sitting Bull: Champion of the Sioux.* Norman: University of Oklahoma Press, 1957.

————. *Warpath.* Boston and New York: Houghton Mifflin Company, 1934.

Worcester, Donald E. "Spotted Tail: Warrior, Diplomat," *The American West*, I, no. 4 (Fall 1964), pp. 38–46.

Archival collections contain manuscript correspondence that directly relates to the activities of Sitting Bull and Spotted Tail. Records of the Office of Indian Affairs and Old Army-Navy Branch of the National Archives have extensive holdings. The state historical societies of North and South Dakota possess valuable papers that pertain to both men. An important source on the life of Crazy Horse is the Ricker Collection at the Nebraska State Historical Society. Other valuable materials are found in the military records preserved by the National Archives, especially the collection known as the Sioux War Papers in the Adjutant General records.

Annie D. Tallent

Scattered biographical information on Annie D. Tallent is found in Jesse Brown and A. M. Willard, *The Black Hills Trails* (Rapid City: Rapid City Journal Company, 1925), pp. 565–571; O. W. Coursey, *Beautiful Black Hills* (Mitchell: Educator Supply Company, 1926), pp. 37–55; Clay D. Curran, "Annie D. Tallent: Her Life Story and Contributions," *SDEA Journal* (January 1962), pp. 25–29; Nancy Niethammer Kovats, *Annie Tallent* (Hermosa, SD: Lame Johnny Press, 1983); and *Memorial and Biographical Record: The Black Hills Region* (Chicago: George A. Ogle & Company, 1898), pp. 243–244.

Collections of original documents pertaining to Annie's life are located in the public libraries of Deadwood, Lead, Rapid City, and Sturgis. The Minnelusa Pioneer Society Museum in Rapid City contains memorabilia, and the Adams Museum in Deadwood has the records of the Society of Black Hills Pioneers. Documents relating to Annie's career in education are in the Archives of the Pennington County Courthouse. The most valuable accumulation of documents is the Clay Curran Collection, Leland D. Case Library for Western Historical Studies, Black Hills State College, Spearfish.

The following newspapers contain articles about the Tallent family and the 1874 expedition: *Black Hills Press, Black Hills Weekly Journal, Custer Weekly Chronicle, Daily Pioneer Times, Elgin Daily Courier, Rapid City Daily Journal, Rochford Miner, Sioux City Weekly Times,* and *Sturgis Weekly Record.* Several of these are on microfilm in the Rapid City Public Library, or in the Archive of the South Dakota Historical Society in Pierre.

Literature about the 1874 expedition includes Annie D. Tallent, *The Black Hills: Or, The Last Hunting Ground of the Dakotahs* (Sioux Falls: Brevet Press, 1974); David Aken, *Pioneers of the Black Hills* (Fort Davis, TX: Frontier Book Company, n.d.); O. W. Coursey, *The First White Woman In The Black Hills* (Mitchell: Educator Supply Company, 1923); and "The Russell-Collins 1874 Gold Expedition to the Black Hills of Dakota," a handwritten manuscript in the Deadwood Public Library attributed to Thomas Russell.

Readers interested in the development of Black Hills history should see Richard Hughes, *Pioneer Years in the Black Hills* (Glendale, CA: Arthur H. Clark Company, 1957); John S. McClintock, *Pioneer Days In The Black Hills* (Deadwood: The Author, 1939); Peter Rosen, *Pa-Ha-Sa-Pa, or the Black Hills of South Dakota* (St. Louis: Nixon-Jones Printing Company, 1895); and Agnes Wright Spring, *The Cheyenne and Black Hills Stage and Express Routes* (Glendale, CA: Arthur H. Clark Company, 1949).

The Williamson and Riggs Families

Barton, Winifred [Williamson]. *John P. Williamson: A Brother to the Sioux.* New York: Fleming H. Revell, 1919.

Creswell, Robert J. *Among the Sioux: A Story of the Twin Cities and the Two Dakotas.* Minneapolis: University Press, 1906.

Meyer, Roy W. *History of the Santee Sioux: United States Indian Policy on Trial.* Lincoln: University of Nebraska Press, 1967.

Pond, Samuel W. *Two Volunteer Missionaries among the Dakotas: or The Story of the Labors of Samuel W. and Gideon Pond.* Boston: Congregational Sunday-School and Publishing Society, 1893.

Riggs, Stephen R. *Dakota Grammar, Texts, and Ethnography.* Washington, DC: U.S. Government Printing Office, 1893.

———. *Mary and I: Forty Years with the Sioux.* Chicago: W. G. Holmes, 1880.

————. *Tah-Koo Wah-Kan; or The Gospel among the Dakotas*. Boston: Congregational Publishing Society, 1869.

Willand, John. *Lac Qui Parle and the Dakota Mission*. Madison, MN: Lac Qui Parle County Historical Society, 1964.

William Hobart Hare

Girton, Polly W. "The Protestant Episcopal Indian Missions of Dakota Territory." Unpublished master of arts thesis, University of South Dakota, 1960.

Graves, E. Norman. "History of the Episcopal Church in South Dakota to Statehood." Unpublished master of arts thesis, University of South Dakota, 1932.

Green, Charles Lowell, "The Indian Reservation System of the Dakotas to 1889." *South Dakota Historical Collections*, XIV, pp. 307–415.

Hare, William Hobart. *Reminiscences*. Philadelphia: Press of William F. Pell & Company, 1888.

————. *The True Policy Toward the Indian Tribes*. Omaha: Herald Steam Book Bindery and Publishing House, 1877.

Howe, M. A. De Wolf. *The Life and Labors of Bishop Hare: Apostle to the Sioux*. New York: Sturgis and Walton, 1914.

Marrs, James David, Sr. "Grants' 'Quaker' Policy and the Bishop of Niobrara." Unpublished master of arts thesis, University of South Dakota, 1970.

Peabody, Mary. *Life of the Right Reverend William Hobart Hare*. Hartford, Connecticut: Church Missions Publishing Company, n.d.

Woodruff, K. Brent, "Episcopal Mission to the Dakotas, 1860–1898." *South Dakota Historical Collections*, XVII, pp. 553–603.

The primary source of greatest value to scholarship on the life of Bishop William Hobart Hare is the Episcopal Archive preserved by the Center for Western Studies at Augustana College in Sioux Falls. The papers and diaries of Hare and Reverend Joseph Cook are especially helpful. Sources scattered in congregations founded by the Bishop contain additional information plus useful photographs. This collection includes a vast amount of primary source material relating to the Bishop, and it is an essential starting point for anyone wishing to write a new and much needed treatment of his life. The collection is described fully in Harry Thompson's excellent *Guide To The Archives Of The Episcopal Church In South Dakota*. Nevertheless, it may be useful, here, to outline its general contents. The *Guide* indicates that the William Hobart Hare Papers are contained in seven regular boxes, eight Hollinger boxes, and three front drop boxes. They are divided into twelve series: (1) Incoming

Correspondence, 1873–1909; (2) Letterpress Copybooks, 1873–1880; (3) Outgoing Correspondence, 1873–1909; (4) Subject Files, 1876–1909; (5) Sermons and Speeches, 1870–1908; (6) Japan and China Files, 1887–1892; (7) Official Journals, Ledgers, Diaries, Etc., 1878–1909; (8) Personal Journals, 1871–1909, (9) Personal Account Books, 1873–1909; (10) Clippings Scrapbook, 1864–1878; (11) Photographs, 1890–1903; (12) Photo Scrapbook, 1870–1878.

Martin Marty

Duffy, Consuela Marie. *Katherine Drexel: A Biography*. Cornwells Heights, PA: Sisters of the Blessed Sacrament, 1966.

Duratschek, Claudia, OSB. *Under the Shadow of His Wings*. Yankton: Sacred Heart Convent, 1971.

Karolevitz, Robert F. *Bishop Martin Marty: The Black Robe Lean Chief*. Yankton: Published Privately, 1980.

Kessler, Ann, OSB. "Assimilating the Contemplative II," *Benedictines*, XXXVIII, no. 2 (Fall/Winter 1983–1984), pp. 16–27.

———. *Benedictine Men and Women of Courage, A Fifteen Century History*. Scheduled for publication in 1989.

Prucha, Francis Paul, SJ. *American Indian Policy in Crisis: Christian Reformers and the Indian, 1865–1900*. Norman: University of Oklahoma Press, 1976.

Rippinger, Joel. "Martin Marty, Monk, Abbot, Missionary and Bishop," *American Benedictine Review*, XXXIII, no. 4 (December 1982), pp. 376–393.

Mothers Superior Joseph Butler, Raphael McCarthy, and Jerome Schmitt

Duratschek, Claudia, OSB. *Under the Shadow of His Wings: History of Sacred Heart Convent*. Yankton, SD: Sacred Heart Convent, 1970.

Fry, Timothy, ed. *RB 1980: The Rule of Saint Benedict*. Collegeville, MN: Liturgical Press, 1981.

Hausman, Dixie, "The Benedictine Sisters of the Sacred Heart: An Administrative History of their Roles in Nursing and Health Care for South Dakota, 1897–1986," Unpublished master of arts thesis, University of South Dakota, 1986.

Kessler, Ann, OSB. *Benedictine Men and Women of Courage: A Fifteen Century History*. Scheduled for publication in 1989.

Magaret, Helene. "Marty," *Catholic World* (December 1944), pp. 220–225.

Peterson, Susan C. "The Presentation Sisters in South Dakota, 1880–1976," Unpublished doctoral dissertation, Oklahoma State University, 1979.

———. *Women With Vision: The South Dakota Presentation Sisters, 1880–1985*. Champaign: University of Illinois Press, 1988.

———. "From Paradise to Prairie: The Presentation Sisters in Dakota, 1880–1896," *South Dakota History*, X, no. 3 (Summer 1980), pp. 210–222.

———. "Religious Communities of Women in the West: The Presentation Sisters' Adaptation to the Northern Plains Frontier," *Journal of the West*, XXI, no. 2 (April 1982), pp. 65–70.

———. "A Widening Horizon: Catholic Sisterhoods on the Northern Plains, 1874–1910," *Great Plains Quarterly*, V, no. 2 (Spring 1985), pp. 125–132..

———. "Adapting to fill a Need: The Presentation Sisters and Health Care, 1901–1961," *South Dakota History*, XVII, no. 1 (Spring 1987), pp. 1–22.

Primary sources most useful for research about the lives and communities of the Mothers Superior include: the Presentation Archives in Aberdeen, SD, containing letters, minutes of community meetings, newspaper clippings, photographs, and oral history transcriptions; the Presentation Sisters Collection at the Oral History Center on the campus of the University of South Dakota in Vermillion; the Benedictine Archives in Yankton, SD, preserving letters, minutes of community meetings, newspaper files, photographs, Sister Claudia Duratschek's Collection, and a substantial holding on the history of health care delivery and higher education; the Catholic Chancery Office in Sioux Falls, SD, containing correspondence between the Mothers Superior and Sioux Falls Diocese officials as well as manuscripts pertaining to the works of the Presentation and Benedictine Sisters.

Joseph Ward

Beadle, W. H. H. "The Building of the State." *The Monthly South Dakotan*, III (1901), pp. 387–391.

Durand, George Harrison. *Joseph Ward of Dakota*. Boston: Pilgrim Press, 1913.

Ehrensperger, Edward C., ed. *History of the United Church of Christ in South Dakota, 1869–1976*. n.p.: United Church of Christ in South Dakota, 1977.

"Joseph Ward." *The Yankton Student*, V (1890), pp. 1–13.

McMurtry, William J. *Yankton College: A Historical Sketch*. Yankton, SD: n. p., 1907.

Miner, Ephriam. "The Mother Church." *The Monthly South Dakotan*, I (1899), pp. 139–142.

Nordness, Reinhart L. *Joseph Ward the Builder*. Sioux Falls: R. L. Nordness, 1957.

Parsons, Horace Wells. "The Development of Congregationalism in South Dakota, 1868–1928." Unpublished doctoral dissertation, University of Chicago Theological Seminary, 1937.

Rowe, Henry K. *History of Andover Theological Seminary*. Newton Centre, MA: Andover Theological Seminary, 1933.

Sheely, Madison L., ed. *Joseph Ward Letters, 1868–1873*. Yankton, SD: First Congregational Church, [1968].

S[tewart], E[dgar] I. "Ward, Joseph." *Dictionary of American Biography*, XIX (1936), pp. 429–30.

Thompson, Harry F. *Guide to the Archives of The South Dakota Conference of The United Church of Christ*. Sioux Falls: The Center for Western Studies, 1986.

Ward, Joseph. "Government Aid to Education in the New West: A Communication from President Ward." *Andover Review*, I (April 1884), pp. 448–451.

———. "The Territorial System of the United States." *Andover Review*, X (July 1888), pp. 51–62.

Williams, Daniel Day. *The Andover Liberals: A Study in American Theology*. Morningside Heights, NY: King's Crown Press, 1941.

See also manuscripts and documents housed by the Center for Western Studies at Augustana College in Sioux Falls and by the Yankton College Archives and the United Church of Christ (Congregational) in Yankton.

William Henry Harrison Beadle

Beadle, W. H. H. *Autobiography of William Henry Harrison Beadle*. Pierre: South Dakota State Historical Society, 1938. Reprinted from *South Dakota Historical Collections*, III.

Coursey, O. W. *A Complete Biographical Sketch of General William Henry Harrison Beadle*. 3rd edition; Mitchell, SD: Educator Supply Company, 1916.

Dykstra, Harry, *et al.*, eds. *Permanent School Fund in South Dakota and the Beadle Club*. Aberdeen, SD: North Plains Press, 1976.

Lange, Gerald. "William Henry Harrison Beadle: Standing Tall in Statuary Hall." *Papers of the Fifteenth Annual Dakota History Conference, April 7–9, 1983*. Madison, SD: Dakota State College, 1984, pp. 460–470.

Lowe, Barrett. "The Public Activities of General William Henry Harrison

Beadle, 1869–1889.'' Unpublished master of arts thesis, University of South Dakota, 1938.

————. *Twenty Million Acres: The Story of America's First Conservationist, William Henry Harrison Beadle*. Mitchell: Educator Supply Company, 1937.

W[ellington], R[aynor] G. "Beadle, W. H. H." *Dictionary of American Biography*. II (1929), pp. 86–87.

The Karl E. Mundt Library at Dakota State College in Madison holds the Beadle Papers, a rather small collection of letters, documents, and memorabilia representing Beadle's South Dakota career. Most of it pertains to his tenure at the College.

Arthur Calvin Mellette

"Arthur Calvin Mellette" *The Wi-lyohi*, XXII, no. 12, (June 1, 1969), pp. 1–3.

Hicks, John D. *The Constitutions of the Northwest States*. Lincoln: University of Nebraska, 1923, XXXIII, nos. 1 & 2.

Kant, Joanita. *Maggie: The Civil War Diary of Margaret Wylie Mellette*. Watertown: Codington County Historical Society, Kampeska Heritage Museum, 1983.

Kingsbury, George W. *History of Dakota Territory*. 6 Vols.; Chicago: S. J. Clarke Publishing Company, 1915.

Lamar, Howard R. *Dakota Territory, 1861–1889*. 2d ed.; New Haven: Yale University Press, 1966.

Lowe, Barrett. *Twenty Million Acres*. Mitchell: Educator Supply Company, 1937.

Mellette, Margaret Wylie. "Arthur Calvin Mellette," a twenty-one page handwritten biographical sketch, Mellette Papers, Robinson State Library, Pierre, SD, 21 pp.

————. "Love Story," Mellette Papers, Mellette House, Watertown, SD, 8 pp.

————. "Personal Recollections of Wild Life," Mellette Papers, Mellette House, Watertown, SD, 5 pp.

————. Untitled, handwritten data for biographical sketch of Governor A. C. Mellette, Mellette Papers, Mellette House, Watertown, SD, 10 items.

Robinson, Doane, ed. *Dakota Constitutional Conventions*. 2 Vols.; Huron: Huronite Publishing Company, 1907.

————. *History of South Dakota*. Chicago: B. F. Bowen and Company, 1904.

————. *History of South Dakota*. Chicago: American Historical Society, Inc., 1930.

———— and Willard C. Lusk. "Arthur Calvin Mellette," *The Monthly South Dakotan*, I (February 1898), pp. 183–186.

Robinson, Will G. "Arthur C. Mellette, Tenth Territorial Governor," *The Wi-lyohi*, XII, no. 12 (October 1, 1958), pp. 1–6.

Schell, Herbert S. *History of South Dakota*. 3rd ed; Lincoln: University of Nebraska Press, 1975.

Schuler, Harold H. *The South Dakota Capitol in Pierre*. Pierre: State Publishing Company, 1985.

Tarbell, Wright. "Arthur Calvin Mellette, 1889–1893," *South Dakota Governors*. Sioux Falls: The Midwest-Beach Company, 1953; reprinted in Oyos, L. S., ed. *Over a Century of Leadership*. Sioux Falls: Center for Western Studies, 1987, pp. 51–59.

————. "Louis K. Church, Ninth Territorial Governor," *The Wi-lyohi*, XII, no. 4 (September 1, 1958), pp. 1–6.

Turchen, Lesta, and James McLaird, comp., "Messages of Dakota Territorial Governors to the Legislative Assemblies," *South Dakota Historical Collections*, XXXVIII, pp. 159–438.

Wolff, Gerald W., and Joanita Kant. *The Civil War Diary of Arthur Calvin Mellette*. Rev. ed.; Watertown, SD: Codington County Historical Society, Kampeska Heritage Museum, 1983.

Richard Franklin Pettigrew, Andrew E. Lee, and Coe I. Crawford

Armin, Colin P. "Coe I. Crawford and the Progressive Movement in South Dakota". *South Dakota Historical Collections*, XXXII, pp. 23–231.

Brooks, Arthur F. "The Administration of Andrew E. Lee, Governor of South Dakota, 1897–1901." Unpublished master of arts thesis, University of South Dakota, 1939.

Drake, Lois M. "The Influence of the Newspapers of Dakota Territory on the Administration of Governor Nehemiah G. Ordway." Unpublished master of arts thesis, University of Missouri, 1941.

Hendrickson, Kenneth E., Jr. "The Public Career of Richard F. Pettigrew of South Dakota, 1848–1926". *South Dakota Historical Collections*, XXXIV, pp. 143–312.

Kingsbury, George W. *History of Dakota Territory*. 6 Vols. Chicago: J. S. Clarke Publishing Company, 1915.

Lamar, Howard R. *Dakota Territory*. New Haven: Yale University Press, 1956.

Lindell, Terrence J. "Problems of Populists in Power: The Andrew E. Lee

Administration in South Dakota, 1897–1901.'' Unpublished manuscript preserved in the I. D. Weeks Library, University of South Dakota.

Pettigrew, Richard F. *The Course of Empire.* Chicago: Boinwright, 1920.

———. *Imperial Washington.* Chicago: Charles Kerr, 1922.

Robinson, Doane. *History of Dakota Territory and South Dakota.* New York:
American Historical Society, 1930.

Schell, Herbert S. *History of South Dakota.* Lincoln: University of Nebraska
Press, 1961.

Schlup, Leonard. "Coe I. Crawford and the Progressive Campaign of 1912,''
South Dakota History, IX (Spring 1979), pp. 116–130.

Sobel, Robert and John Raimo, eds. *Biographical Directory of the Governors
of the United States, 1798–1978.* Westport: Meckler Books, 1978.

Detailed information not included in the publications listed above is available
in the Andrew E. Lee Papers housed by the archives in the I. D. Weeks
Library at the University of South Dakota, Vermillion, and in the Richard F.
Pettigrew Papers preserved at the Pettigrew Museum in Sioux Falls. (A copy
of the Pettigrew Papers is available on microfilm at the Center for Western
Studies, Augustana College, in Sioux Falls.) See also the newspapers Dakota
Herald, Sioux Falls *Press, Huronite; and* the *Congressional Record,* 53 Cong.,
1 Sess., XXV, 1893, and *South Dakota Journal of the Senate,* 1895.

Peter Norbeck and William Henry McMaster

Bellamy, Paul E. "Peter Norbeck: A Biography.'' Unpublished paper, South
Dakota Historical Resource Center, Pierre.

Dalthorp, Charles J., ed. *South Dakota's Governors.* Sioux Falls, SD: Midwest-Beach Company, 1953.

Fite, Gilbert C. "The History of South Dakota's Rural Credits System.''
South Dakota Historical Collections, XXIV, pp. 220–275.

———. " 'The Only Thing Worth Working For': Land and Its Meaning for
Pioneer Dakotans.'' *South Dakota History,* XV, nos. 1 & 2 (Spring/Summer
1985), pp. 2–25.

———. "Peter Norbeck and the Defeat of the Nonpartisan League in South
Dakota.'' *Mississippi Valley Historical Review,* XXXIII, no. 1 (June 1946),
pp. 217–236.

———. *Peter Norbeck: Prairie Statesman.* Columbia: University of Missouri,
1948.

Morlan, Robert L. *Political Prairie Fire: The Nonpartisan League, 1915–1922.*
St. Paul: Minnesota Historical Society Press, 1985.

Norbeck, Peter. "For the Whole Family: How South Dakota's Sane Legislation Helps Ambitious Farmers to Succeed." *The Country Gentleman*, LXXXV, no. 7 (February 14, 1920), pp. 3–4, 34, 36.

"Peter Norbeck: Well Driller, Statesman," *Water Well Journal*, XXVIII, no. 10 (October 1974), pp. 34–37.

O'Brien, Patrick G. "William H. McMaster: An Agrarian Dissenter during 'Normalcy'." *Emporia State University Studies*, XX, no. 4 (June 1972), pp. 24–39.

Olsgaard, John N. "Dakota Resources: The Peter Norbeck Papers at the University of South Dakota." *South Dakota History*, X, no. 2 (Spring 1980), pp. 147–151.

Olson, Richard O. "The Public Career of Peter Norbeck, 1908–1921." Unpublished master of arts thesis, University of South Dakota, 1941.

Remele, Larry. "The North Dakota Farmers Union and the Nonpartisan League: Breakdown of a Coalition, 1917–1920." *North Dakota Quarterly*, XLV, no. 4 (Autumn 1978), pp. 40–50.

Saloutos, Theodore. "The Expansion and Decline of the Nonpartisan League in the Western Middle West, 1917–1921." *Agricultural History*, XX, no. 4 (October 1946), pp. 235–252.

———. "The Rise of the Nonpartisan League in North Dakota, 1915–1917." *Agricultural History*, XX, no. 1 (January 1946), pp. 43–61.

Schell, Herbert S. *History of South Dakota*. 3rd ed., rev.; Lincoln: University of Nebraska Press, 1975.

Tingley, Ralph. "The Crowded Field: Eight Men for the Senate." *South Dakota History*, IX, no. 4 (Fall 1979), pp. 316–336.

Inaugural Addresses for Governors Norbeck and McMaster for 1917, 1919, 1921, and 1923, and McMaster's 1925 farewell address are held by the South Dakota Historical Resource Center at Pierre. Also available there are *South Dakota Legislative Manuals* and manuscript collections covering Norbeck's and McMaster's gubernatorial terms; archival collections for both are at the University of South Dakota at Vermillion. The Doane Robinson Papers at the South Dakota Historical Resource Center are also very useful.

The Family of John L. Pyle

Huron Daily Plainsman, Centennial Edition, June 15, 1980.

Inserillo, Tom. "Spirit of the Dakotas," a proposed film project about the Pyle Family. Pyle Archives, Ella McIntire Library, Huron College, Huron, SD.

Kinyon, Jeannette and Jean Walz. *The Incredible Gladys Pyle*. Vermillion, SD: Dakota Press, 1985.

Purple and Gold, February 1902. Eulogy for John L. Pyle, Pyle Archives, Huron College.

The South Dakota Business Women. January, 1981.

Thorpe, Cleata B. *The John L. Pyle Family: Dakotans Extraordinary, 1882–1973*. Huron, SD: Creative Printing Company, 1973.

Seth Bullock

Bennett, Estelline. *Old Deadwood Days*. New York: Charles Scribner's Sons, 1935.

Brown, Jesse and A. M. Willard. *The Black Hills Trails*. Rapid City, SD: Rapid City Journal Company, 1924.

Bullock, Seth and Harry Anderson, ed. "An Account of and the Northern Black Hills in 1876," *South Dakota Historical Collections*, XXXI, pp. 287–364.

Irwin, Will, ed. *Letters to Kermit from Theodore Roosevelt, 1902–1908*. New York: Charles Scribner's Sons, 1946.

Kellar, Kenneth C. *Seth Bullock: Frontier Marshal*. Aberdeen, SD: North Plains Press, 1972.

Kollar, Joe. "Minnesela Days," *South Dakota Historical Collections*, XXXIV, pp. 1–113.

Lawrence County Historical Society. *Some History of Lawrence County*. Deadwood, SD: Lawrence County Historical Society, 1981.

Lee, Robert H., ed. *Gold, Gals, Guns, Guts*. Rapid City, SD: Rapid Printing Company, 1976.

McClintock, John S. *Pioneer Days in the Black Hills*. Deadwood, SD: J. S. Mclintock, 1939.

Parker, Watson. *Deadwood: The Golden Years*. Lincoln: University of Nebraska Press, 1981.

Rezatto, Helen. *Mount Moriah*. Aberdeen, SD: North Plains Press, 1980.

Tallent, Annie D. *The Black Hills; Or Last Hunting Ground of the Dakotahs*. St. Louis: Nixon-Jones Printing Company, 1899.

Toole, K. Ross. *Montana: An Uncommon Land*. Norman: University of Oklahoma Press, 1959.

Wolff, David A. "Pyritic Smelting at Deadwood: A Temporary Solution to Refractory Ores," *South Dakota History*, XV, no. 4 (Winter 1985), pp. 312–339.

James "Scotty" Philip

Baye, Elsie H., ed. *Haakon Horizons*. Pierre, SD: State Publishing Company, 1982.

Blasingame, Ike. *Dakota Cowboy: My Life in the Old Days*. New York: Putnam's Sons, 1958.

Bye, J. O. *Back Trailing in the Heart of the Short Grass Country*. Everett, WA: Published Privately, 1956.

Dary, David A. *The Buffalo Book: The Full Saga of the American Animal*. Chicago: The Swallow Press, Inc., 1974.

Gard, Wayne. *The Great Buffalo Hunt*. New York: Alfred A. Knopf, 1959.

Hall, Bert L. *Roundup Years: Old Muddy to the Black Hills*. Pierre, SD: Published Privately, 1954.

Lee, Robert and Dick Williams. *Last Grass Frontier: The South Dakota Stock Grower Heritage*. Sturgis, SD: Black Hills Publishers, 1964.

Lee, Wayne C. *Scotty Philip: The Man Who Saved the Buffalo*. Caldwell, ID: The Caxton Printers, 1975.

McHugh, Tom. *The Time of the Buffalo*. New York: Alfred A. Knopf, 1972.

Nebraskaland Magazine. *Fort Robinson Illustrated*. Lincoln: Nebraska Game, Fish and Parks Commission, 1986.

Philip, George. "James 'Scotty' Philip, 1858–1911," *South Dakota Historical Review*, I, no. 1 (October 1935), pp. 1–48.

Robinson, James M. *West from Fort Pierre: The Wild World of James (Scotty) Philip*. Los Angeles: Westernlore Press, 1974.

Sandoz, Mari. *The Buffalo Hunters: The Story of the Hide Men*. New York: Hastings House, 1954.

Veglahn, Nancy. *The Buffalo King: The Story of Scotty Philip*. New York: Charles Scribner's Sons, 1971.

Yost, Nellie Snyder. *Boss Cowman: The Recollections of Ed Lemmon, 1857–1946*. Lincoln: University of Nebraska Press, 1969.

Myron John Smiley

Alton, George. "The Sheep Industry in South Dakota West of the Missouri River." Unpublished master of arts thesis, Unversity of South Dakota, 1943.

Belle Fourche Bee, Belle Fourche, South Dakota, newspaper.

Gilfillan, Archer B. *Sheep*. Boston: Little, Brown and Company, 1929.

Heidt, Jr., William, ed. *Addie Smiley's Letters from the West 1882–1886.* Ithaca, NY: DeWitt Historical Society, Inc., 1955.

"The History of the Chamber of Commerce in Belle Fourche." Smiley Collection.

Huntsinger, Jon D. "Smiley." Smiley Collection, in the possession of Jon D. Huntsinger.

Interview with James D. and Marilyn S. Huntsinger by Jami Huntsiger, November 22, 1987, Oral History Center, University of South Dakota.

Interview with David Rathbun by Jami Huntsinger, November 29, 1987, Oral History Center, University of South Dakota.

Kingsbury, George W. *History of Dakota Territory.* 6 Vols; Chicago: S. J. Clark Publishing Company, 1915.

Morrison, Frank B. *Feeds and Feeding.* 22nd Ed.; Clinton, IA: Morrison Publishing Company, 1959.

Smiley Bros. Ponies. Ledger, Smiley Collection.

Smiley Family Tree. Smiley Collection.

Vallery, Philip, et. al. *Pioneer Footprints.* Sioux Falls: Midwest-Beach Company, 1964.

Niels Ebbesen Hansen

Friggins, Paul. "His Plants Transformed the Plains." *Coronet,* XXVI (July 1944), pp. 58–61.

Gurney's 1986 Spring Catalog. Yankton: Gurney's Seed and Nursery Company, 1986.

Harding, T. Swann. *Two Blades of Grass: A History of Scientific Development in the U.S. Department of Agriculture.* Norman: University of Oklahoma Press, 1947.

Hodge, W. H. and C. O. Erlanson. "Federal Plant Introduction–A Review." *Economic Botany,* X (October–December 1956), pp. 299–334.

Interview with David Gilkerson and Naomi (grandson of Hansen and wife) by John Miller, December 29, 1986.

Isern, Thomas D. "Niels Ebbesen Hansen: Plant Explorer for the Northern Plains." Paper presented at Northern Great Plains History Conference, Moorhead, Minn., October 3, 1985.

Kirkwood, William P. "Hansen, America's First Plant Explorer." *Review of Reviews,* XLVIII (October 1913), pp. 443–48.

———. "The Romantic Story of a Scientist." *World's Work,* XV (April 1908), p. 10109–10120.

Lowe, Barrett. *Heroes and Hero Tales of South Dakota.* Minneapolis: E. M. Hale and Company, 1931, pp. 140–154.

Nicholson, Arnold. "Burbank of the Plains." *Country Gentleman,* CX (December 1940), pp. 11, 54–55.

Rumbaugh, M. D. "N. E. Hansen's Contributions to Alfalfa Breeding in North America." Agricultural Experiment Station *Bulletin #665;* Brookings: South Dakota State University, [1980].

Ryerson, Knowles A. "History and Significance of the Foreign Plant Introduction Work of the United States Department of Agriculture." *Agricultural History,* VII (July 1933), pp. 110–128.

————. "Plant Introductions." *Agricultural History,* L (January 1976), pp. 248–57.

Taylor, Mrs. H. J. *To Plant the Prairies and the Plains: The Life and Work of Niels Ebbesen Hansen.* Mount Vernon, IA: Bios Press, 1941.

Emil Loriks

Burg, Betty. "Emil Loriks: Family Farm Trailblazer," *South Dakota Union Farmer,* September 1978.

Lange, Gerald. "Americanism over Radicalism: Mundt's First Election, 1938," paper presented to Fifth Annual Dakota History Conference, April 1973, reprinted in *Selected Papers of the First Nine Dakota History Conferences* (1969–1977). Madison: Dakota State College, 1981, pp. 311–320.

Miller, John E. "McCarthyism Before McCarthy: The 1938 Election in South Dakota," *Heritage of the Great Plains,* XV, no. 3 (Summer 1982), pp. 1–21.

————. "Restrained, Respectable Radicals: The South Dakota Farm Holiday," *Agricultural History,* LIX, no. 3 (July 1985), pp. 429–447.

Thompson, Robert S. "The History of the South Dakota Farmers Union, 1914–1952," Unpublished master of arts thesis, University of South Dakota, 1953.

Williams, Elizabeth Evenson. *Emil Loriks: Builder of a New Economic Order,* Sioux Falls: Center for Western Studies, Augustana College, 1987.

Emil Loriks's South Dakota Farmers Union speeches and President's reports are on file at South Dakota Farmers Union headquarters in Huron. His Grain Terminal Association (GTA) reports and speeches are preserved at Harvest States Cooperatives (formerly GTA) headquarters in St. Paul. Loriks's Papers, the source of most writings about him, are available at the Center for Western Studies at Augustana College in Sioux Falls.

Francis Higbee Case and Karl E. Mundt

Arneson, William. "I Remember Bryant (Circa 1915–1925)." Unpublished manuscript, 1986.

Chenoweth, Richard R. "Francis Case: A Political Biography," *South Dakota Historical Collections*, XXXIX, pp. 288–433.

Heidepriem, Scott. *Karl Mundt: Prairie Politician and Statesman*. Unpublished Manuscript, 1987. At press by the *Madison Daily Leader*, it will be published by the Karl Mundt Historical and Educational Foundation.

————. "Karl Mundt: 1900 to 1939." Unpublished master of arts thesis, University of South Dakota, 1983.

Lamport, Nancy Lee. "Francis Case, His Pioneer Background, Indian Legislation and Missouri River Conservation." Unpublished master of arts thesis, University of South Dakota, 1972.

Lange, Gerald. "Mundt vs. McGovern: The 1960 Senate Election," *Heritage of the Great Plains*, XV, No. 4 (Fall 1982), pp. 33–42.

Pressler, Larry. *U.S. Senators from the Prairie*. Vermillion: Dakota Press, 1982.

The Francis Case Collection of correspondence, newsletters, and office files is located at the Layne Library, Dakota Wesleyan University, Mitchell. The Karl Mundt Collection is located in Madison, on the campus of Dakota State College, in the Karl E. Mundt Library, which houses the Karl E. Mundt Foundation and Archives. It includes personal memorabilia as well as tapes, films, manuscripts, correspondence, and published materials acquired by the Foundation on the life and contributions of Mundt. Both repositories contain extensive collections of government documents, including committee reports, bills, hearings, and copies of the *Congressional Record* for the period of service by the two men in Congress.

George McGovern

Anson, Robert Sam. *McGovern: A Biography*. New York: Holt, Rinehart, and Winston Company, 1972.

Clem, Alan L. *Prairie State Politics: Popular Democracy in South Dakota*. Washington, DC: Public Affairs Press, 1967.

————. *South Dakota Political Almanac*. 2nd ed.; Vermillion: Dakota Press, 1969.

Hart, Gary W. *Right from the Start: A Chronicle of the McGovern Campaign*. New York: Quadrangle, 1973.

McGovern, George S. *Grassroots: The Autobiography of George McGovern.* New York: Random House, 1977.

"McGovern, George S(tanley)." *Current Biography.* 1967.

Weil, Gordon L. *The Long Shot: George McGovern Runs for President.* New York: W. W. Norton Company, 1973.

White, Theodore H. *America in Search of Itself: The Making of the President, 1956–1980.* New York: Warner Books, 1982.

Public Affairs, the bulletin published by the Governmental Research Bureau at the University of South Dakota, frequently covers current political and party developments in South Dakota. The following issues devoted considerable attention to various stages of McGovern's career, particularly his re-election campaigns:

Clem, Alan L. "The 1962 Election in South Dakota," *Public Affairs*, No. 12, February 1963.

———. "The 1968 Election in South Dakota," *Public Affairs*, No. 36, February 1969.

———. "The Submerging Republican Majority: The 1972 Election in South Dakota," *Public Affairs*, No. 52, February 1973.

———. "The 1974 Election in South Dakota," *Public Affairs*, No. 60, February 1975.

———. "The 1980 Election in South Dakota: End of an Era," *Public Affairs*, No. 80, March 1981.

Benjamin Reifel

Few printed sources exist on the life and career of Benjamin Reifel, but his own words appear in: "The Problem of Relocating Families on the Fort Berthold Indian Reservation," *Journal of Farm Economics*, XXXII (November 1950), pp. 644–646; "Cultural Factors in Social Adjustment," *Indian Education* (April 15, 1957), pp. 1–10; "Federal Indian Policy, 1933–1945," "Felix Cohen and the Adoption of the IRA," and "The Trust Obligation," in Kenneth R. Philp, ed., *Indian Self-Rule: First-Hand Accounts of Indian-White Relations from Roosevelt to Reagan* (Salt Lake City: Howe Brothers, 1986), pp. 54–58, 76–78, 309–310; "Relocation on the Fort Berthold Reservation: Problems and Programs," Unpublished doctoral dissertation, Harvard University, 1952, a copy at the Beulah Williams Library, Northern State College, Aberdeen, SD; Interview with Ben Reifel by Joseph H. Cash, "The New Deal and the Years that Followed: Three Interviews," in Peter Iverson, ed., *The Plains Indians of the Twentieth Century* (Norman: University of Oklahoma Press, 1985), pp. 108–120; lengthy press interviews such as James Denney,

"That Poor Indian Boy in Congress," *Los Angeles Times*, February 21, 1971, Sec. A, p. 23. There is a useful biographical article on Reifel in the journalistic chapter by Mildren Fielder, "Ben Reifel, Sioux Congressman," *Sioux Indian Leaders* (Seattle: Superior Publishing Company, 1975), pp. 127–148. A profile of his life and philosophy appears in an article presenting him as one of the "South Dakota 99" most distinguished leaders down to the state centennial year. *Sioux Falls Argus Leader*, May 1, 1988.

Substance for this chapter came mainly from materials gathered by the author, which are in use for the composition of a biography in book length. With only spotty records for part of the 1950s and because Reifel's office files for his Organization Field Agent years (1935–42) and his congressional career (1961–71) were not preserved, the story of his life and career had to be pieced together from a wide variety of sources. Included are more than one hundred oral history interviews with Ben Reifel, his surviving brothers, his contemporaries, and his colleagues, which are housed by the American Indian Oral History Research Project at Northern State College in Aberdeen. Information also came from government records at the National Archives in Washington, DC, and five of the National Archives' Regional Centers at Kansas City, Seattle, Ft. Worth, and San Bruno and Luguna Niguel, CA, printed federal documents, newspaper accounts, letters from presidential libraries, materials in congressional collections including the papers of Karl Mundt at Dakota State College in Madison, SD, Francis Case at Dakota Wesleyan University in Mitchell, and E. Y. Berry at Black Hills State College, Spearfish. Of particular interest are papers contained in the Harriet Montgomery Water Resources Collection at Northern State College in Aberdeen, and in materials and insightful letters written by Dr. Robert Ruby while he served as a physician at Pine Ridge from 1953 to 1955. The author's collection on Ben Reifel will become available at Northern State College for general use following the publication of a biography in book length.

Elaine and Charles Eastman

Eastman, Charles. *From the Deep Woods to Civilization*. Boston: Little Brown and Company, 1916.

––––––. *Indian Boyhood*. 1902. Reprint. Rapid City: Fenwyn Press Books, 1970.

––––––. *The Indian Today: The Past and Future of the First American*. Garden City: Doubleday, 1915.

––––––. *The Soul of the Indian: An Interpretation*. Boston and New York: Houghton Mifflin Company, 1911.

Eastman, Elaine Goodale. "All the Days of My Life," *South Dakota Historical Review*, II, 4 (July 1937), pp. 171–196 (reprinted from the introduction to the author's book of poems, *The Voice at Eve*. Chicago: The Bookfellows, 1930).

————. "The Ghost Dance and Wounded Knee Massacre of 1890–91," *Nebraska History*, XXVI (January 1945), pp. 26–42.

————. *Pratt, the Red Man's Moses*. Norman: University of Oklahoma Press, 1935.

————. *Yellow Star: A Story of East and West*. Boston: Little Brown and Company, 1911, 1931.

Graber, Kay, ed. *Sister to the Sioux: The Memoirs of Elaine Goodale Eastman, 1885–1891*. Lincoln: University of Nebraska Press, 1978.

Meyer, Roy. *History of the Santee Sioux: United States Indian Policy on Trial*. Lincoln: University of Nebraska Press, 1967.

Miller, David Reed. "Charles Alexander Eastman: One Man's Journey in Two Worlds." Unpublished master of arts thesis, University of North Dakota, 1975.

Wilson, Raymond. *Ohiyesa: Charles Eastman, Santee Sioux*. Urbana: University of Illinois Press, 1983.

The Deloria Family

From its founding in 1923 to the year 1982, an organization in Chicago named Indian Council Fire issued an Achievement Award almost every year to recognize "quality of Indian initiative and leadership." The fifty-four recipients included Commissioners of Indian Affairs Robert L. Bennett and Louis R. Bruce, U.S. Representative Benjamin Reifel, author Charles A. Eastman, physician George Frasier, and ethnologist Alfonso Ortiz. Among the other forty-eight were three Delorias: Ella, Vine, Sr., and Vine, Jr. Biographical sketches contained in an ICF anniversary publication outline the major achievements for which these eminent persons have received international recognition. See *The Indian Achievement Award of the Indian Council Fire* (Chicago: Indian Council Fire, 1982), pp. 13, 17, 26.

No previous essay summarizes the history and contributions of the entire family. Most publications by the Delorias that appeared before 1980 are included in *Bibliography of the Sioux* (Metuchen, NJ: The Scarecrow Press, 1980), by Jack W. Marken and Herbert T. Hoover. Following is a list of the most important works:

Deloria, Ella C. *Dakota Texts*. New York: G. E. Stechert and Company, 1932.

————. *Speaking of Indians*. New York: Friendship Press, 1941.

————. *Water Lily*. Lincoln: University of Nebraska Press, 1988.

Deloria, Vine, Jr. *American Indian Policy in the Twentieth Century*. Norman: University of Oklahoma Press, 1985.

———. *Behind the Trail of Broken Treaties*. New York: Dell Publishing Company, 1974.

———. *Custer Died for Your Sins: An Indian Manifesto*. New York: The Macmillan Company, 1969.

———. *God is Red*. New York: Grosset and Dunlap, 1973.

Deloria, Vine, Jr., and Clifford M. Lytle. *American Indians, American Justice*. Austin: University of Texas Press, 1983.

———. *The Nations Within: The Past and Future of American Indian Sovereignty*. New York: Pantheon Press, 1984.

Ole E. Rolvaag and Frederick Manfred

By and about Ole E. Rolvaag:

Haugen, Einar. *Ole Edvart Rolvaag*. Twayne's United States Authors Series No. 455; Boston: Twayne Publishers, 1983.

Huseboe, Arthur R. "Rolvaag and Krause: Two Novelists of the Northwest Prairie Frontier," *A Literary History of the American West*. Ed. J. Golden Taylor, et. al.; Fort Worth: Texas Christian University Press, 1987, pp. 716–738.

Jorgenson, Theodore, and Nora O. Solum. *Ole Edvart Rolvaag: A Biography*. New York: Harper, 1939.

Moseley, Ann. *Ole Edvart Rolvaag*. Western Writers Series No. 80; Boise, Idaho: Boise State University, 1987.

Paulson, Kristoffer F. "Berdahl Family History and Rolvaag's Immigrant Trilogy." *Norwegian-American Studies*. Northfield, Minnesota: The Norwegian-American Historical Association, XXVII (1977), pp. 55–76.

Reigstad, Paul. *Rolvaag: His Life and Art*. Lincoln: University of Nebraska Press, 1972.

Rolvaag, Ole E. *The Boat of Longing*. Trans. Nora Solum; New York: Harper, 1933.

———. *Giants in the Earth*. Intro. by Lincoln Colcord; New York: Harper, 1927.

———. *Peder Victorious*. Trans. O. E. Rolvaag and Nora Solum; New York: Harper, 1929.

———. *Pure Gold*. Trans. Sivert Erdahl and O. E. Rolvaag; New York: Harper, 1930.

———. *The Boat of Longing*. Trans. Nora Solum; New York: Harper, 1933.

————. *The Third Life of Per Smevik.* Trans. Ella Valborg Tweet and Solveig Tweet Zempel, Intro. by Ella Valborg Tweet; Minneapolis: Dillon, 1971.

————. *Their Fathers' God.* Trans. Trygve M. Ager; New York: Harper, 1931.

————. *When the Wind is in the South and Other Stories.* Trans. Solveig Zempel; Sioux Falls: Center for Western Studies, 1984.

Thorson, Gerald, ed. *Ole Rolvaag: Artist and Cultural Leader.* Northfield, Minnesota: St. Olaf College Press, 1975.

By and about Frederick Manfred:

Flora, Joseph. *Frederick Manfred.* Boise, ID: Boise State University, 1974, Western Writers Series No. 13.

Manfred, Frederick. *Conquering Horse.* Foreword Delbert E. Wylder; Lincoln: University of Nebraska Press, 1983.

————. *Conversations with Frederick Manfred.* Moderator John R. Milton; Salt Lake City: University of Utah Press, 1974.

————. *The Golden Bowl.* St. Paul: Webb Press, 1944.

————. *King of Spades.* Foreword Max Westbrook; Lincoln: University of Nebraska Press, 1982.

————. *Lord Grizzly.* Foreword John R. Milton; Lincoln: University of Nebraska Press, 1983.

————. *Riders of Judgment.* Lincoln: University of Nebraska Press, 1982.

————. *Scarlet Plume.* Foreword Arthur R. Huseboe; Lincoln: University of Nebraska Press, 1983.

Mulder, Rodney J., and John H. Timmerman. *Frederick Manfred: A Bibliography and Publishing History.* Sioux Falls, S.D.: Center for Western Studies, 1981.

Smith, Robert W. "Frederick Manfred, Outsize Man and Writer." *North Dakota Quarterly*, LV (Spring 1987), pp. 139–150.

Wright, Robert C. "Frederick Manfred." *A Literary History of the American West.* Ed. J. Golden Taylor et al; Fort Worth: Texas Christian University Press, 1987, pp. 792–805.

————. *Frederick Manfred.* Boston: Twayne Publishers, 1979.

Laura Ingalls Wilder and Rose Wilder Lane

Anderson, William. "Laura Ingalls Wilder and Rose Wilder Lane: The Continuing Collaboration," *South Dakota History*. XVI, no. 2 (Summer 1986), pp. 89–143.

———. *Laura Ingalls Wilder, Pioneer and Author*. New York: Kipling Press, 1987.

———. *Laura's Rose: The Story of Rose Wilder Lane*. De Smet, SD: Laura Ingalls Wilder Memorial Society, 1976.

———. *Laura Wilder of Mansfield*. De Smet, SD: Laura Ingalls Wilder Memorial Society, 1974.

———. "The Literary Apprenticeship of Laura Ingalls Wilder," *South Dakota History*. XIII (Winter 1983), pp. 281–331.

———. *The Little House Sampler*. Lincoln, Nebraska: The University of Nebraska Press, 1988.

———. *The Story of the Ingalls*. De Smet, SD: Laura Ingalls Wilder Memorial Society, 1971.

———. *The Story of the Wilders*. De Smet, SD: Laura Ingalls Wilder Memorial Society, 1971.

———. *A Wilder in the West*. De Smet, SD: Laura Ingalls Wilder Memorial Society, 1985.

Lane, Rose Wilder. *Free Land*. Lincoln: University of Nebraska Press, 1984. Original edition published in 1938 by Longmans, Green.

———. *Let the Hurricane Roar*. New York: Harper and Row, 1985. Original edition published in 1935 by Longmans, Green.

———. *Old Home Town*. Lincoln: University of Nebraska Press, 1985. Original edition published in 1935 by Longmans, Green.

Wilder, Laura Ingalls. *By the Shores of Silver Lake*. New York: Harper & Row, Publishers, 1939.

———. *The First Four Years*. New York: Harper and Row, 1971.

———. *Little Town on the Prairie*. New York: Harper and Row, Publishers, 1941.

———. *The Long Winter*. New York: Harper and Row, Publishers, 1940.

———. Rose Wilder Lane, ed; *On the Way Home*. New York: Harper and Row, 1962.

———. *These Happy Golden Years*. New York: Harper and Row, 1943.

Oscar Howe

100 Years of Native American Painting. Oklahoma City: The Oklahoma Museum of Art, 1978.

Dockstader, Frederick J., ed. *Oscar Howe*. Tulsa: The Thomas Gilcrease

Museum Association, 1982. The catalogue raisonne' for a retrospective exhibition of Howe's paintings.

Howe, Oscar. "Theories and Beliefs–Dakota." *South Dakota Review*, VII (Summer 1969), pp. 69–79.

———. *Oscar Howe: Artist*. Vermillion: The University of South Dakota, 1974. Seventeen color plates of Howe paintings, each with a commentary by the artist.

Milton, John R. *Oscar Howe: The Story of an American Indian*. Minneapolis: Dillon Press, 1972.

Pennington, Robert. *Oscar Howe: Artist of the Sioux*. Sioux Falls: Dakota Territory Centennial Commission, 1961.

Harvey Dunn

Dunn, Harvey. *An Evening in the Classroom*. Tenafly, NJ: Published Privately, 1934.

Howell, Edgar M. "An Artist Goes to War: Harvey Dunn and the A.E.F. War Art Program," *The Smithsonian Journal of History*, II (Winter 1967–68), pp. 45–56.

Karolevitz, Robert F. *Where Your Heart Is: The Story of Harvey Dunn, Artist*. Aberdeen, SD: North Plains Press, 1970.

———. "Harvey Dunn: Artist of the A.E.F.," *V.F.W. Magazine*, (November 1971).

———. "Harvey Dunn of South Dakota," *Persimmon Hill*, 1979 National Cowboy Hall of Fame and Heritage Center, Oklahoma City.

Pitz, Henry C. *Howard Pyle*. New York: Clarkson N. Potter, Inc., 1975.

Reed, Walt. *The Illustrator in America, 1900–1960s*. New York: Reinhold Publishing Corporation, 1966.

Watson, Ernest W. "Harvey Dunn: Milestone in the Tradition of American Illustration," *American Artist*, June 1942.

Doane Robinson, William Henry Over, and Herbert S. Schell

Helgevold, Mary K. *A History of South Dakota Archaeology*. Vermillion: South Dakota Archaeological Society, 1981.

Realf, James. "A Poet of the Northwest," *The Arena*, XII (May 1895), pp. 308–320.

Robinson, Doane. "Some Functions of a Historical Society," *South Dakota Historical Collections*, XXI, pp. 120–126.

————. "The Value of History," *South Dakota Historical Collections*, XII, pp. 131–137.

Schell, Herbert. *History of South Dakota*. 3rd ed.; Lincoln: University of Nebraska Press, 1975.

————. *The Profession Under Fire: The 1954 Version*. Vermillion: The University of South Dakota, 1954.

————. *South Dakota: A Student's Guide to Localized History*. New York: Teacher's College, Columbia University, 1971.

Sundling, Charles W. "W. H. Over: A Biography." Unpublished master of arts thesis, University of South Dakota, 1975.

The Leaders

Pierre Chouteau, Jr., b. 1789, d. 1865.

Newton Edmunds, b. 1819, d. 1908.

Spotted Tail, b. 1823 or 1824, d. 1881.

Sitting Bull, b. 1831 or 1832, d. 1890.

Crazy Horse, b. 1840, d. 1877.

Annie Tallent, b. 1827, d. 1901.

Thomas Williamson, b. 1800, d. 1879.

Stephen Return Riggs, b. 1812, d. 1883.

John P. Williamson, b. 1835, d. 1917.

Alfred Riggs, b. 1837, d. 1916.

Thomas Riggs, b. 1847, d. 1940.

Bishop William Hobart Hare, b. 1838, d. 1909.

Bishop Martin Marty, OSB, b. 1834, d. 1896.

Mother Joseph Butler, PBVM, b. 1859, d. 1935.

Mother Raphael McCarthy, PBVM, b. 1888, d. 1966.

Mother Jerome Schmitt, OSB, b. 1899, d. 1983.

Reverend Joseph Ward, b. 1838, d. 1889.

William Henry Harrison Beadle, b. 1838, d. 1915.

Arthur Calvin Mellette, b. 1842, d. 1896.

Richard Franklin Pettigrew, b. 1848, d. 1926.

Andrew E. Lee, b. 1847, d. 1934.

Coe I. Crawford, b. 1858, d. 1944.

Peter Norbeck, b. 1870, d. 1936.

William Henry McMaster, b. 1877, d. 1968.

John L. Pyle, b. 1860, d. 1902.

Mamie Pyle, b. 1866, d. 1949.

Gladys Pyle, b. 1890.

Seth Bullock, b. 1847, d. 1919.

James "Scotty" Philip, b. 1858, d. 1911.

Myron John Smiley, b. 1872, d. 1929.

Niels Hansen, b. 1866, d. 1950.

Emil Loriks, b. 1895, d. 1985.

Francis Higbee Case, b. 1896, d. 1962.

Karl Earl Mundt, b. 1900, d. 1974.

George McGovern, b. 1922.

Benjamin Reifel, b. 1906.

Elaine Goodale Eastman, b. 1863, d. 1953.

Charles Eastman, b. 1858, d. 1939.

Reverend Philip Joseph Deloria, b. 1854, d. 1931.

Ella Cara Deloria, b. 1890, d. 1972.

Reverend Vine Victor Deloria, b. 1901.

Vine Deloria, Jr., b. 1933.

Ole E. Rolvaag, b. 1876, d. 1931.

Frederick Manfred, b. 1912.

Laura Ingalls Wilder, b. 1867, d. 1957.

Rose Wilder Lane, b. 1886, d. 1968.

Oscar Howe, b. 1915, d. 1983.

Harvey Dunn, b. 1884, d. 1952.

Doane Robinson, b. 1856, d. 1946.

W. H. Over, b. 1866, d. 1956.

Herbert S. Schell, b. 1899.

The Contributors

Ruth Ann Alexander is Professor of English and Head of her department at South Dakota State University. Recent publications include "The Pioneer Heroine as Idea: South Dakota Women Writers, 1940–1970," *A Common Land, A Diverse People* (Sioux Falls: The Norland Heritage Foundation, 1987), pp. 50–70; and "Elaine Goodale Eastman and the Failure of the Feminist Protestant Ethic," *Great Plains Quarterly*, VIII, no. 2 (Spring 1988), pp. 89–101.

William T. Anderson teaches at Lapeer West High School in Michigan. From long dedication to Wilder lore and literature, he has published *Laura Ingalls Wilder, Pioneer and Author* (New York: Kipling Book Press, 1987); and *Little House Sampler* (Lincoln: University of Nebraska Press, 1988).

Leonard Rufus Bruguier, a Yankton Sioux, nears the completion of a Ph.D. in history at Oklahoma State University. With Herbert T. Hoover and John A. Rau he has co-authored a study of Missouri River environmental history entitled "Gorging Ice and Flooding Rivers: Springtime Devastation in South Dakota," *South Dakota History*, XVII, nos. 3 and 4 (Fall/Winter 1987), pp. 181–201; and has been collaborating author with Hoover for *The Yankton Sioux* (New York: Chelsea House Publishers, 1988).

Loren Carlson, a former Dean of Continuing Education for the University of South Dakota, is Professor of Political Science. Out of long personal experience in public administration as well as research, he has been a contributing author for *A Bibliography of South Dakota Government and Politics* (Vermillion: Governmental Research Bureau, University of South Dakota, 1965); and *Government of South Dakota* (Vermillion: Dakota Press, 1979).

Alan L. Clem is Professor of Political Science at the University of South Dakota. His numerous publications include *Prairie State Politics* (Washington, DC: Public Affairs Press, 1967); *Law Enforcement: The South Dakota Experience* (Sturgis: South Dakota Peace Officers' Association, 1982); *The Government We Deserve: Principles, Institutions, and Politics of American National Government* (Vermillion: Dakota Press, 1986); and *Congress: Powers, Processes, and Politics* (Monterey, CA: Books/Cole, 1988).

Richmond L. Clow is Associate Professor in Native American Studies at the University of Montana. He has written "The Indian Reorganization Act and the Loss of Tribal Sovereignty: Constitutions on the Rosebud and Pine Ridge Reservations," *Great Plains Quarterly*, VII, no. 2 (Spring 1987), pp. 125–134; and "Taxing the Omaha and Winnebago Trust Lands, 1910–1917," *American Indian Culture and Research Journal*, IX, no. 4 (1985), pp. 1–22.

William O. Farber, Professor Emeritus in Political Science at the University of South Dakota, is the primary author of *South Dakota: Politics and Government* (Vermillion: Dakota Press, 1979). Recently he has also published *The Impact of Reagan Federalism on South Dakota and South Dakota Government* (Vermillion: Governmental Research Bureau, University of South Dakota, 1984); and *Home Rule in South Dakota* (Vermillion: Governmental Research Bureau, University of South Dakota, 1986).

Thomas J. Gasque is Professor of English at the University of South Dakota. His growing interest in the importance of place names in South Dakota has been expressed in several articles, and he plans to publish on the subject in book form. He is editor of the journal *Names*.

Mary Keepers Helgevold, a housewife who remains active in professional archaeology, is known well across the state for *A History of South Dakota Archaeology* (Vermillion: University of South Dakota Archaeology Laboratory, 1981).

Kenneth E. Hendrickson, Jr., is Hardin Distinguished Professor of American History and departmental Chairman at Midwestern State University, Wichita Falls, TX. His recent publications include *The Waters of the Brazos: A History of the Brazos River Authority, 1929–1979* (Waco: Texian Press, 1981); *Hard Times in Oklahoma: The Depression Years* (Oklahoma City: The Oklahoma Historical Society, 1983); and "A Leak in the Dike: The Problem of Water Resource

Management and Conservation in Texas," *Agricultural Legacies* (Vermillion: University of South Dakota Press, 1986), pp. 191–205.

Herbert T. Hoover, Professor of History and Director of Oral History at the University of South Dakota, has served as Project Director for the development of this volume. His publications on Indian-White relations extend from *To Be An Indian* (New York: Holt, Rinehart and Winston, 1971) to *The Yankton Sioux* (New York: Chelsea House Publishers, 1988). His evaluation of regional history is introduced in "South Dakota: An Expression of Regional Heritage," *Heartland* (Bloomington: Indiana University Press, 1988), pp. 186–205.

Jami L. Huntsinger is a student of literature at the University of South Dakota with special interests in women and American Indians. Her interest in publication is introduced by "Books and Things," *South Dakota Review*, XXV (1987), p. 171. Her inspiration for writing a chapter in this volume came partly from her being a descendant of M. J. Smiley.

Arthur R. Huseboe is Professor of English and Chairman of the Humanities Division at Augustana College in Sioux Falls. His works include *Through Trials and Triumphs: A History of Augustana College* (Sioux Falls: Center for Western Studies, Augustana College, 1985); *Sir George Etherege* (Boston: G. K. Hall, 1987); and several anthologies on themes of South Dakota history.

Robert F. Karolevitz is known well across the northern Great Plains region as a professional writer. The most recent of his twenty-five book titles is *From Quill to Computer: A History of Community Newspapers in the U.S. From 1690* (Freeman: Pine Hill Press, 1985), and *Yesterday's Motorcycles* (Mission Hill: Homestead Publishers, 1986). Earlier works of greater influence include *Yankton: A Pioneer Past* (Aberdeen: North Plains Press, 1972) and *Bishop Martin Marty: The Black Robe Lean Chief* (Yankton: Published Privately, 1980).

Sister Ann Kessler, OSB, is Professor of History at Mount Marty College in Yankton. Her recent titles are "Benedictine Mission and Ministry," *Benedictines*, XL (1985), pp. 31–42; and *Benedictine Men and Women of Courage: A Fifteen Century History*, at press.

Jeannette E. Kinyon is English Professor Emeritus from the South Dakota School of Mines and Technology in Rapid City. With Jean Walz she coauthored *The Incredible Gladys Pyle* (Vermillion: Dakota Press, 1985).

Frederick Manfred is the leader among active authors of works on "Sioux Land." A description of his career in this book indicates that among the best known of more than twenty-five book titles are *The Golden Bowl* (Albuquerque: University of New Mexico Press, 1980); *Lord Grizzly* (Boston: Gregg Press, 1980); and *Conquering Horse* (New York: The New American Library, 1965).

David B. Miller is Professor of History at Black Hills State College in Spearfish. Recently he has written *Gateway to the Hills: An Illustrated History of Rapid City* (Woodland Hills, CA: Windsor Publications, 1985); and with Nancy Veglahn *The South Dakota Story* (Pierre: South Dakota Department of Education, 1985), a standard elementary school textbook.

John E. Miller is Professor of History at South Dakota State University. The diversity of his interests is evident in the recent articles "The Distance Between Gopher Prairie and Lake Wobegon: Sinclair Lewis and Garrison Keillor on the Small Town Experience," *The Centennial Review*, XXXI (Fall 1987), pp. 432–446; "Place and Community in 'The Little Town on the Prairie': DeSmet in 1883," *South Dakota History*, XVI (Winter 1986), pp. 351372; and "Restrained, Respectable Radicals: The South Dakota Farm Holiday," *Agricultural History*, LIX (July 1985), pp. 429–447.

John Milton is Professor of English at the University of South Dakota. Known best as the founder and editor of *South Dakota Review*, he has made substantial contributions in book form with *South Dakota: A Bicentennial History* (New York: Norton, 1977); and *The Literature of South Dakota* (Vermillion: Dakota Press, 1976).

John S. Painter is Associate Professor of History at Northern State College in Aberdeen. While doing biographical work on Benjamin Reifel, he has published such pieces from original sources as "An Historical and Cultural Perspective of Implementing the I.R.A.," *Indian Self-Rule* (Salt Lake City: Howe Brothers, 1986).

Susan Peterson is Professor of History at the University of North Dakota. Ample justification for her recognition as an authority on women in the West is obvious in her recent title, authored with Courtney Ann Vaugn-Roberson, *Women With Vision* (Urbana: University of Illinois Press, 1988), a history of the Presentation Sisters of Aberdeen. She has also published several articles and is now at work on a general history of nursing in North and South Dakota.

John A. Rau is the National Register Coordinator for the South Dakota Historical Preservation Center in Vermillion. He has published with Herbert T. Hoover and Leonard Rufus Bruguier "Gorging Ice and Flooding Rivers: Springtime Devastation in South Dakota," *South Dakota History*, XVII, no. 3 (Fall/Winter, 1987), pp. 181–201; and has written "Czech Houses in South Dakota," *Old House Journal*, XVI (January-February 1988), p. 81. He has also made a contribution with guides to historical preservation, such as his "South Dakota Historic Contexts, Architectural and Historical Resources," published by the Preservation Center.

Larry Remele earned enormous respect as the editor of *North Dakota History*, and increasing prominence as an author. The depth of his grasp of liberal politics in northern Great Plains history was evidenced by his careful study of the Nonpartisan League, expressed in "The North Farmers Union and the Nonpartisan League: Breakdown of a Coalition, 1917–1920." *North Dakota Quarterly*, XLV, no. 4 (Autumn 1978), pp. 40–50.

Robert J. Stahl is Associate Professor of Anthropology at Northern State College in Aberdeen. "Joe True: Convergent Needs and Assumed Identity" in *Being and Becoming Indian* (New York: Dorsey Press, 1988) demonstrates his knowledge of Indian-White relations. The work of increasing scope on the Native American Church represents his established place as a scholar of cultural anthropology for the northern Great Plains.

Lesta Van Der Wert Turchen is Vice President for Academic Affairs at Dakota Wesleyan University in Mitchell. Among her contributions on the history of the state are the works she coauthored with James D. McLaird: *The Black Hills Expedition of 1875* (Mitchell: Dakota Wesleyan University Press, 1975); and *County and Community: A Bibliography of South Dakota Local Histories* (Mitchell: Published Privately, 1979).

Elizabeth Evenson Williams is Reading Series Coordinator for the South Dakota Committee on the Humanities. Along with several articles on the subject of her essay she has published in book form *Emil Loriks: Builder of a New Economic Order* (Sioux Falls: Center for Western Studies, Augustana College, 1987).

Gerald Wolff is Professor of History at the University of South Dakota. The diversity of his interests is evident in "Mark Hanna's Goal:

American Harmony,'' *Ohio History*, LXXIX (Summer/Autumn 1970), pp. 138–151; *The Kansas-Nebraska Bill: Party, Section, and the Coming of the Civil War* (New York: The Revisionist Press, 1977); and ''Father Sylvester Eisenman and Marty Mission,'' *South Dakota History*, X, (1975), pp. 360–389.

Larry J. Zimmerman is Professor and Director of Anthropology at the University of South Dakota. The past Editor of *South Dakota Archaeology*, he now serves as editor for *Plains Anthropologist*. The seven publications in book form he has written or edited include *Peoples of Prehistoric South Dakota* (Lincoln: University of Nebraska Press, 1985).

Acknowledgments

Primary recognition belongs to the National Endowment for the Humanities for its support through the efforts of John Whalen, Executive Director of the South Dakota Committee on the Humanities. Some eight years before the state centennial year, 1989, Director Whalen called the writer to invite a proposal for the use of NEH funds by scholars recognized for their expertise regarding the history and cultures of the northern Great Plains region. In his opinion, their involvement would assure his Committee that the expenditure of its funds would accomplish more than the mere celebration of a century of statehood in 1989. They would be charged with responsibility to create a body of literature with abiding value about experiences of South Dakotans through their first century of statehood.

The initial phase was a retreat at Blue Cloud Abbey for a select committee: Herbert T. Hoover (Project Director), Agnes Picotte, Robert A. and Lynn M. Alex, Ruth Alexander, Dayton C. Cook, Knight E. Hoover, Robert J. Stahl, Duane Addison, and Peter J. McGovern. Deliberations lasting two days resulted in a plan for the production of two publications in book length: a bibliography of primary and secondary sources about the history of the state and its cultures, and a volume comprising either essays about themes or chapters about leaders in the history of the state. The volume containing sources appeared as *Planning for the South Dakota Centennial: A Bibliography* (Vermillion: University of South Dakota, 1984), which was printed in limited edition for distribution to libraries across the state. A contributing author was Jack W. Marken, who was spared additional responsibility because of his commitment to the role of general editor for the *Native American Bibliography Series*. To the planning bibliography was added, with funding from the National Endowment for the Humanities, *A Selected Annotated Bibliography: South Dakota, Changing,*

485

Changeless, 1889–1989 (Brookings: South Dakota Library Association, 1985). The editor Sue Laubersheimer and the authors Bob Carmack, Jack W. Marken, Ruth Alexander, and Herbert T. Hoover composed a volume of some 1,200 entries with annotations and index. To this Ms. Laubersheimer soon added *A Selected Annotated Bibliography: Supplement.*

Confident that professional humanists had for the time supplied enough guidance for readers with interests in South Dakota history and cultures, a second phase began at the assembly of a planning committee on the campus of Augustana College in Sioux Falls. Included in the group were Herbert T. Hoover (Project Director), Arthur R. Huseboe, David Miller, Skyland Hauser, Nancy Koupal, Sister Ann Kessler, Lesta Van Der Wert Turchen, Dayton Cook, Ruth Alexander, Larry J. Zimmerman, and Loren Carlson. Quickly they reached the decision to construct a tentative table of contents for *South Dakota Leaders*, leaving a work on historical themes to another time. This committee pared a list of leading persons and families comprising more than 100 names to approximately forty. Its members drew from a pool of some forty accomplished authors the names of twenty-nine.

With support from the South Dakota Committee on the Humanities, the authors began their work on biographies during the spring of 1986, and all of them delivered manuscripts by May of 1988. Herbert T. Hoover and Larry J. Zimmerman assumed editorial responsibility. Larry Remele provided editorial counsel. As the editors read and the authors revised their chapters, others made vital contributions. Christopher J. Hoover accepted responsibility for manuscript management on computer. In addition to typing and revising numerous drafts, he developed computer programs and supplied editorial assistance. Without his prompt response to every charge the volume could not have appeared in time for distribution during the state centennial year. Vital to production in final phases was Patricia Peterson, who replaced Larry Remele at his death as editorial consultant. Karen Zimmerman accepted responsibility for the search and management of photographs. Simon Spicer gave prompt and professional service in photographic reproduction at the Educational Media Center of the University of South Dakota. Maps were produced by Herbert T. Hoover. USD History Department Secretary Thelma Dykstra took charge of budgetary management. USD President Joseph M. McFadden and USD Office of Research Director Howard E. Coker, Jr., found funds to match those supplied by NEH through the South Dakota Committee on the Humanities to meet the expenses of composition and production.

From the suggestion of planning for a centennial publication with abiding value by John Whalen, the evolution of this volume has been a team effort that has drawn upon the intellectual resources of nearly every higher educational institution in the state as well as on the expertise of able scholars at work off-campus or at educational institutions outside the state. With manuscript of book length in hand, Larry J. Zimmerman has worked as Managing Editor of the University of South Dakota Press to assure the delivery of books for distribution by the autumn preceding the centennial year of South Dakota.

Herbert T. Hoover

Index